Functional Images
of the Religious Educator

Functional Images
of the Religious Educator

TIMOTHY ARTHUR LINES

Religious Education Press
Birmingham, Alabama

Library of Congress Cataloging-in-Publication Data

Lines, Timothy Arthur.
    Functional images of the religious educator / Timothy Arthur Lines.
    Includes bibliographical references and index.
    ISBN 0-89135-087-X
    1. Religious educators.   I. Title.
  BL42.L56   1992   92-26111
  291.7—dc20   CIP

Religious Education Press, Inc.
5316 Meadow Brook Road
Birmingham, Alabama 35242
10 9 8 7 6 5 4 3 2

Religious Education Press publishes books exclusively in religious education
and in areas closely related to religious education. It is committed to enhancing and professionalizing religious education through the publication of
serious, significant, and scholarly works.

PUBLISHER TO THE PROFESSION

FOR
EMILY LEANORA LINES
BORN FEBRUARY 2, 1988
PRECIOUS GIFT FROM THE EAST TO THE WEST
WHO IS TEACHING ME WHAT LIFE IS TRULY ALL ABOUT—
THE RICHEST BLESSING SHE COULD EVER BESTOW;

AND FOR ALL THOSE IN HER GENERATION
FROM EVERY LAND AND NATION
WHO ARE FREELY OFFERING THE SAME TO EACH OF US
IF WE WILL BUT LISTEN AND LEARN AND LOVE.

THEY ARE THE REASON FOR CARING SO PASSIONATELY ABOUT THE FUTURE OF
RELIGIOUS EDUCATION AND THE REASON WHY HOPE IS STILL POSSIBLE.

Contents

List of Figures

Preface

The functional images of the religious educator, when thoroughly under-stood and integrated into a clear and holistic identity, provide a comprehensive view of the religious educator. Because this book focuses on the identity of the religious educator through the use of these foundational images, two issues are immediately apparent. First, the book is about the *religious* educator: not the Baptist or Methodist religious educator, not the Protestant or Catholic religious educator, not the Christian or Jewish religious educator, but simply the reli-gious educator. An examination of the literature in the field reveals some books being written about religion, a few about religious education, but very little about the religious educator. Second, it is about the religious *educator*: not so much about the field or its procedures as about the identity of the professional, the images that describe him or her, and the individuals who populate it. Further research and examination of the literature reveals far too little being produced on the professional identity of the religious educator. This book seeks to address this dearth of material related directly to both of these emphases concerning the reli-gious educator.

There are some good reasons that explain the lack of attention to the identi-ty of the religious educator and to the functional images of the religious educa-tor. One of the more prominent reasons is that a book on the religious educator risks describing an identity that few if any will claim as their own. Most books ostensibly about the religious educator are actually about a particular brand of reli-gious educator, be it Baptist or Methodist, Protestant or Catholic, Christian or Jewish—or any of the other categories within the wide range of possibilities. These particular expressions of the religious educator end up getting so much attention that the general one—that of the religious educator—goes virtually unacknowledged. Such an approach not only obscures the general view of the reli-gious educator, but also distorts the understanding of the particular. The par-ticularistic religious educator who does not perceive how he or she fits into the larger picture of religious education is in danger of becoming egocentric, isola-tionist, and imperialistic, or has already become so.

1

Other good reasons for a lack of attending to the religious educator could signal either no interest in the subject, or no real understanding of the religious educator and what he or she has to offer. The latter of these two is more probable. John Westerhoff edited a book in 1978 with the haunting and disturbing title *Who Are We?: The Quest for a Religious Education.*[1] The book's subtitle indicated that the search was for the identity of the field of religious education, rather than for the identity of the religious educator. Most discouraging, though, was that the question of "who are we?" needed to be asked in the first place. A field, a profession, or a grouping of individuals with any degree of status or self-esteem does not go around asking such questions. It simply goes about its business—since it has both an identity and a purpose. The title of Westerhoff's book told religious educators, and the world, that such an identity and purpose did not yet exist in religious education—and may never.

Who Are We? was published in 1978. Has the situation improved since then? In spite of some efforts aimed at helping resolve the problem, the confusion continues, but now with the added burden of Westerhoff's omnipresent question. Being a part of a profession that does not know who it is or what it does holds little appeal or attraction, but it does produce a lot of irritation and frustration among its practitioners. After a while, the futility of hand-wringing must be translated into positive action. Because of this, the purpose of this book is not to ask once again, "who are we?" but is instead an attempt to declare *who we are* as religious educational professionals.[2]

To make such a claim or even to venture into such territory may be evidence of either pure folly or dangerous megalomania—and possibly both. The attempt to express "who we are," however, is not meant to be foolish or presumptive, but simply to hack a path out of the wilderness of despair. It is written out of an unwillingness and an inability to function any longer with such a nebulous and undifferentiated professional identity. This book is offered as a statement of who religious educators are through an explication and exposition of its foundational images. If it is not an adequate proposal of who religious educators are, and it probably is not, then at least it can be an impetus for deciding who we are and who we are not. The present ambiguity is intolerable.

This book has the dual purpose of being both descriptive and prescriptive. It is an effort to describe the images of the religious educator as they have appeared throughout history and as they are experienced in the present, in their various apparitions and forms. It is also intentionally prescriptive, in that it is an attempt to set the boundaries and the agenda for the future development of the religious educator. There is no sense in which the book can be received as dispassionate

---

1. John H. Westerhoff III, ed., *Who Are We?: The Quest for a Religious Education* (Birmingham, Ala.: Religious Education Press, 1978).

2. Use of the term "professional" does not limit the discussion to paid personnel or ordained clergy. A professional is someone prepared, able, and committed to the tasks assigned to the area. Charles Stewart has defined a profession as "a type of work performed in a social setting which requires particular education, entrance, and relationship to one's peers and to the public. Commitment to the education, entrance rights, and public one serves gives the profession its unique character." Charles William Stewart, *Person and Profession: Career Development and the Ministry* (Nashville: Abindgon, 1974), p. 24.

or unbiased. It is clearly both passionate and biased—it has a definite message and point of view. Clinical objectivity is neither the goal nor the result of the book.

Another word of admission is necessary related to objectivity. Every effort is made in the book to be nonparticularistic, but such a stance is difficult if not impossible to sustain. As later explained in the book,[3] particulars (faith traditions, or religions) are contained *within* the broader category of religion, and hence most people are able to view religion only from their own particularistic perspective. While this book attempts to reduce this egocentrism, the degree of success is debatable. I write as a Baptist, as a Protestant, and as a Christian,[4] and all this inevitably has its influence on the book. How or if this book would differ had it been written by a Methodist, or a Catholic, or a Jewish religious educator is unknown and impossible to determine—but fun to imagine. I cannot completely distance myself from my environment or my historical setting, and I have neither desire nor need to do so. I can make the effort to transcend them, however, and not to be completely blinded by them.

This book is in many ways a follow-up to *Systemic Religious Education*, published in 1987.[5] To those who have read that previous book, this one will be an actualization of the systemic theory presented there—this time applied to the religious educator rather than to the field itself. The present book is wholly consistent and consonant with the earlier one and is in many ways an illustration of it. To those who have not read the previous book, enough background is provided in the text to allow this book to stand on its own.[6] A prior understanding of systems theory is not necessary, and the technical language is deliberately muted in this book to reach the broadest possible audience. Those interested in the theory, philosophy, language, and resources behind this book are encouraged to consult *Systemic Religious Education*.

This book is composed of three parts. Part One, "Interpretive Taxonomies of the Religious Educator," is made up of three short chapters. One introduces the environmental contexts of the religious educator; one overviews some of the extant differentiative typologies of the religious educator; and one explains the diagnostic categories proposed for examining the religious educator. Part Two, "Multiple Roles of the Religious Educator," comprises the heart of the book. Here, in ten chapters, the ten roles of the religious educator are explored in some detail. Each of these ten central chapters follows the same pattern to allow for comparison and contrast of the images. Part Three, "Holistic Perspectives of the Religious Educator," has two brief chapters which work at uniting and har-

3. See this explained in Chapter One, "The Environment of the Religious Educator."
4. I can place myself in these categories, but not everyone in them would include me—particularly some of the Baptists. The Southern Baptist Convention, of which I have long been a part, has been overtaken administratively by a fundamentalist regime. The results of such a coup has left me, and other true Baptists like me who value religious freedom and personal integrity, at least temporarily without a home. How I describe myself in the future is still to be determined, but one thing is certain: Bowing the knee to the Baal of creedalism, rigidity, and subservience to tyrannical authoritarianism is not one of my viable options.
5. Timothy Arthur Lines, *Systemic Religious Education* (Birmingham, Ala.: Religious Education Press, 1987).
6. This kind of context is provided in Chapter One, "The Environment of the Religious Educator," and in Chapter Fourteen, "The Integration of the Religious Educator."

monizing the multivariate identity of the religious educator. One chapter introduces some of the ways that the ten roles combine and interrelate to form the integration of the religious educator. The final chapter is a "concluding personal conversation," written in dialogue format, which anticipates some questions the broad issues of the book may raise and provides some partial responses to them.

This book can be read a bit differently than *Systemic Religious Education*, where the stern instructions were that "the chapters should be read in consecutive order and not in piecemeal fashion."[7] Any author would prefer the book to be read in the order he or she presents it, but in the earlier work stepwise progress was essential. One perceptive student wrote that while reading *Systemic Religious Education* she had the sense of "drowning in a two hundred forty-three page sentence," and indeed that image is not misleading. Each successive paragraph depended upon the previous ones. The situation in this book is different. As desired, the ten chapters on the roles of the religious educator can be read in any order since each of them has an independent quality to it. The greatest danger, though, is that the reader would get the impression that the book is a cafeteria where one can pick the role that looks like the most satisfying and skip the others. The message of the book is that the genuine (systemic) religious educator is an integration and synthesis of *all* the ten roles. Picking and choosing destroys the wholeness.

This last sentence of the previous paragraph raises such a key issue that any misunderstanding of its importance cannot be permitted. Each of the ten roles, though given a separate chapter in the book, is ultimately both iterative and integrative with one another. They are *iterative*, meaning that some of each role is contained in the other roles, and so the ten roles should not be perceived as separate and totally distinct from one another. A more appropriate image is that of observing ten facets of one beautiful and precious diamond. They are also *integrative*, meaning that they make sense and have value only as elements of a systemic whole. One image by itself does not a religious educator make. The complete religious educator emerges in the attempt to synthesize all of the roles into one harmonic and dynamic entity.

Another word of caution is necessary, this time regarding the nature of the images themselves. Obviously there is nothing sacrosanct about the particular images that have been chosen. They simply represent the identity of the religious educator as I now conceptualize it. Any one image taken to its extreme will eventually break down in its ability to communicate, as will any analogy that is stretched too far. Any one role developed in isolation from the rest will result in the one image exacerbating the weaknesses of that particular role. The challenge is to keep all ten images in at least peripheral vision, with balance, synthesis, and harmony among all of them foremost on the agenda. Becoming the complete religious educator is a commitment to a lifelong task, and one that is never totally accomplished or finished. There is always more to being a religious educator than any one individual can master—but this does present a worthy goal to pursue.

For whom is this book written? Several audiences are in view. One is the

---

7. Lines, *Systemic Religious Education*, p. 3.

religious educator whose vocational calling is to provide religious instruction in the parish, in the synagogue, or in an academic environment. This book is a way of presenting the "big picture" of the religious educator so that each can improve his or her strengths and shore up his or her weaknesses. The book can function as a mirror to reveal "who we are," or at least who we can and should be. A second, much more vast, audience is the person who is doing effective religious education but may neither claim it as such nor choose to so identify his or her work. One of the prime goals of this book is to free the conception of religious education from the boundaries and limits some paid "hired hand" types tend to put upon it. A walk through the images discussed in this book should begin to sketch the broad dimensions of genuine religious education—and its vast multitude of resources. A third audience is represented by the person who is considering becoming a religious educator. This book is an effort to provide a panoramic view of what is involved. A religious educator—as presented in this book—is called upon to be one of the most knowledgeable, most mature, and most responsible members of society. The possibilities are endless, but so are the demands. Future religious educators must understand the needs and the potential and be prepared to give their very lives to bring about wholeness and health. Nothing less is worthy of the call, and such commitment is necessary from the start.

Two struggles are apparent throughout the book. One has to do with gender-specific language. I have employed inclusive language throughout the book in what I have written, but the difficulty came in using quotes from those who used exclusivist or particularistic language. In virtually every instance I decided to keep the integrity of the quote. While the language may offend the sensibilities of some readers, it seemed unfair to impose the present standards of writing upon the writers of the past. This makes for some awkwardness, but it was the only honest and academically acceptable solution I could find. The other struggle was how to distinguish the student from the teacher in a meaningful way. Occasionally I used terms such as student, client, or learner to separate out the teacher or the religious educator. The limits of language then make it appear that the teacher is not a learner, for example, or that the student does not teach the teacher. While none of that is true, for convenience and clarity the distinctions were often made and should not to be taken as some kind of denigration of either the "student" or the "teacher." In most cases I have used the term "learner" to denote the dimension of activity and involvement of the individual in the learning process, and the term "student" less frequently, when the situation described a more formal, structured educational environment. "Client" is used only in those rare contexts where one is a receptor or consumer of therapeutic treatment.

Words of appreciation are necessary to these friends for having read and reacted to portions of the manuscript: David Britt, Joey Clifton, Tom Leuze, Kathryn Chapman, Linda Givens, the long-suffering students of the summer of 1991, colloquium participants of 1990-1991, and Sunday school class members. Untold numbers of students have listened to me muse about these ideas and have for the most part been patient if not perplexed while I verbally wandered through my mental mazes in front of them. Faculty members of the School of

Christian Education at the Southern Baptist Theological Seminary have also been supportive and interested in what I have been doing—which of course is different than being convinced.

I need to say a special word about William Rogers, Dean of the School of Christian Education at Southern Seminary. He did his best to allow diversity and creativity in the midst of a seminary environment being overcome with intolerance, closed-mindedness, and fascist tactics. His experiment in allowing me to think for myself, and to speak for myself, was a short-term success but a long-term failure related to my future at Southern. It seems that developing or rewarding individuality, personhood, and integrity were not priorities or even much of an interest to others further up the seminary hierarchy, much to my surprise and disappointment; obedience, conformity, and capitulation were the true values that were upheld and modeled by those persons in positions of supposed authority. Teaching at Southern Seminary was a fun and eye-opening experience while it lasted, however, and sincere thanks are due to Bill Rogers for giving me the opportunity.

Deborah and Emily get the final thanks: To Deborah for helping me find both the freedom and the security I constantly seek, and to Emily for letting me experience once again what hope feels like. Without them, I would have given up long ago. With them, I am ready to create the future.

Part One

Interpretive Taxonomies
of the Religious Educator

Chapter One

The Environmental Context
of the Religious Educator

The first step in identifying the religious educator is knowing where to look for him or her. This brief introductory but indispensable chapter establishes that broad milieu for identifying the foundational images of the religious educator—the environmental context of the religious educator. The other two chapters of Part One are also introductory, indispensable, and contextual, but they are aids in further delineating the parameters sketched in this chapter. In fact, the entire book takes place within the complex environment described here, with more and more of the details regarding the identity of the religious educator being added with each successive chapter. Clarity concerning the basic environmental context of the religious educator is essential, because it determines the degree of success for all that follows.

The environmental context of the religious educator is religious education. This simple and seemingly tautological sentence actually marks the outermost boundaries for discussing the identity of the religious educator. Not everyone (by any means) agrees that this defining sentence is an accurate, adequate, or even a meaningful statement—and there resides the crux of the problem. Some would say the proper environment of the religious educator is first, foremost, and centrally that of theology,[1] while others would argue that the concrete specificity of

---

1. An example of this kind of religious educator would be Randolph Crump Miller, who understood theology to be the clue to religious education. See Randolph Crump Miller, *The Clue to Christian Education* (New York: Scribner's, 1950). The keys to Miller's approach are found in this sentence: "The clue to Christian education is the rediscovery of a relevant theology which will bridge the gap between content and method, providing the background and perspective of Christian truth by which the best methods and content will be used as tools to bring the learners into right relationship with the living God who is revealed in Jesus Christ, using the guidance of parents and the fellowship of life in the church as the environment in which Christian nurture will take place." Ibid., p. 15.

the faith traditions is the place to begin.[2] If there is no agreement on identifying the environmental context of the religious educator, then there can be no agreement on identifying the religious educator. The fundaments of the disagreement run much deeper than word games or logic chopping, which some believe when first introduced to the complexity of the issues. The way the environmental context of the religious educator is circumscribed in large measure predetermines how the identity, and hence the foundational images, of the religious educator will be developed.[3]

The purpose of this chapter, then, is to provide an overview of the environmental context of the religious educator as the initial step in identifying the religious educator. First, brief attention is given to some basic definitions, providing a general orientation of the territory from a variety of positions. Second, one set of these definitions is utilized for mapping out the primary relationships found within the environment of the religious educator. This chapter prepares the way for the more detailed exploration of other interpretive taxonomies[4] of the religious educator pursued in the following two chapters.

Definitional Contexts

A few representative samples of how some contemporary religious education theorists have depicted the environmental context of the religious educator, as seen through their definitions of the field, help to explain the position taken in this book. The types of definitions surveyed are political definitions, historical definitions, social-science definitions, and systemic definitions. The systemic definitions are the ones used as the foundation for this book. The overall purpose of this section is to indicate some of the other contemporary religious education theorists who have recognized that the proper environment of the religious edu-

---

2. This would be the position of Christian religious educators such as James D. Smart. For an example, see his classic statement on what he regarded as the proper starting point for the field in James D. Smart, *The Teaching Ministry of the Church: An Examination of the Basic Principles of Christian Education* (Philadelphia: Westminster, 1964). For example, Smart gave this as the goal of Christian religious education (as distinct from religious education): "That what is done in the educational program of the church today should be a valid continuation of what was done by Jesus and his disciples, then by those disciples with the people to whom they ministered, and by the Early Church with Jews and Gentiles who found their way into it." Ibid., p. 84. All this is not to say that Smart denied the theological issue as fundamental. He did indeed see theology as foundational, as he stated in the conclusion to his analysis of the problem of the church: "At every point it has become evident that it is a theological problem." Ibid., p. 205.

3. This issue concerning the environmental context of the religious educator could well be all-consuming, and indeed it has consumed many a book—and writer. In fact, this present work is a follow-up to a book that did deal primarily with this issue, entitled *Systemic Religious Education*. See Timothy Arthur Lines, *Systemic Religious Education* (Birmingham, Ala.: Religious Education Press, 1987). It is not necessary to be familiar with that book for this one to make sense, as this introductory chapter provides sufficient background, but the point is that the topic is vital, complicated, and still being hotly contested. The position taken in this book is not different from the one in *Systemic Religious Education*, only stated more briefly and shown more graphically here.

4. Taxonomy is the systematic study of classifications and groupings within a particular field. The three chapters of Part One all contribute to different levels of the taxonomies that help to identify the religious educator and to distinguish the field of religious education.

cator is religious education, even though these positions toward and definitions of the field vary quite widely from one another.

Political Definitions

Thomas Groome, in his book *Christian Religious Education*,[5] began his study by defining the basic terms in the field and built them one upon another. He started by defining *education* as "a political activity with pilgrims in time that deliberately and intentionally attends with people to our present, to the past heritage it embodies, and to the future possibilities it holds for the total person and community."[6] His definition is labeled "political" here because he stated his position initially in terms of political activity and built the rest of his definitions on that basis.[7] Such a designation should not necessarily be seen as negative or harmful, but it is important to understand from the first where a person begins the construction process, and for Groome the beginning point is politics, with the rest of his definitions then evolving from that type of perspective.

Groome next proposed his definition of *religion* as "the human quest for the transcendent in which one's relationship with an ultimate ground of being is brought to consciousness and somehow given expression."[8] Combining the definitions of education and religion, he defined *religious education* as "a deliberate attending to the transcendent dimension of life by which a conscious relationship to an ultimate ground of being is being promoted and enabled to come to expression."[9] The title of Groome's book made clear that religious education itself was not the subject of his book. The focus was instead on *Christian religious education*, which he portrayed by weaving the strands of the previous definitions together: "A political activity with pilgrims in time that deliberately and intentionally attends with them to the activity of God in our present, to the Story of the Christian faith community, and to the Vision of God's Kingdom, the seeds of which are already present."[10] After establishing this basic definitional environment, Groome went on to develop Christian religious education throughout the rest of the book, preferring that focus to the more broadly based religious education.[11] Significant, however, is the fact that Groome did identify religious education as the broader politico-environmental context from which he continued his more particularistic discussion of Christian religious education.

---

5. Thomas H. Groome, *Christian Religious Education: Sharing Our Story and Vision* (San Francisco: Harper & Row, 1980).

6. Ibid., p. 21.

7. In Groome's later work, he reiterated his stance on politics: "I contend that the essential characteristic of all education is that it is a *political activity*." Thomas H. Groome, *Sharing Faith: A Comprehensive Approach to Religious Education and Pastoral Ministry—The Way of Shared Praxis* (San Francisco: HarperSanFrancisco, 1991), p. 12. See Groome's fuller discussion in ibid., pp. 12-14. Further discussion of politics and religious education is given in the present book in Chapter Eleven, "The Religious Educator as Revolutionary."

8. Groome, *Christian Religious Education*, p. 22.

9. Ibid.

10. Ibid., p. 25.

11. For example, when Groome did discuss the role of the teacher (he always included students in the discussion of teachers, and called them "copartners"), it was in terms of the *Christian* religious educator rather than the religious educator. See ibid., pp. 261-274.

Historical Definitions

Mary Boys took a different tack than did Groome in structuring her book *Educating in Faith*.[12] Instead of beginning with her own definition of religious education, Boys first took her readers on a tour of twentieth-century religious education.[13] In Part One, called "Mapmaking," she showed how others had used the term "religious education" and its variants, such as Christian education. In Part Two, called "Visions," Boys drew from these earlier sources and developed her own definition of religious education: "Religious education is the making accessible of the traditions of the religious community and the making manifest of the intrinsic connection between traditions and transformation."[14] Although Boys did not present her definitions of education and religion as fully or as explicitly as Groome did, her understandings of both are embedded in this definition of religious education and were given exposition in her discussion of the definition.[15] Boys chose to leave the definition open and applicable to a variety of particularistic expressions, indicative of the term "religious education," and did not in this book apply her definition to a specific religion, such as Christianity. Most important for the moment, however, is noticing that she, like Groome, identified the proper environment of the religious educator as religious education albeit from a historical rather than an overtly political perspective.[16]

Social Science Definitions

The prime figure in contemporary religious education that has advanced the use of social science as the basis for defining and theorizing about religious education is James Michael Lee.[17] Although the primary focus of his writings has been on religious instruction, he has made it abundantly clear that religious instruction is but one element of the larger environmental context of religious education. Lee defined *education* simply as "the broad process whereby a person learns something."[18] *Instruction*, then, he defined as "the process by and through which learning is caused in an individual in one way or another."[19] For Lee, the two have an intimate but clear relationship: "Instruction is to education as part is to the whole."[20] As he has said in a number of places, the broader field of

---

12. Mary C. Boys, *Educating in Faith: Maps and Visions* (San Francisco: Harper & Row, 1989).

13. "My construct evolved from two thoughts that permeated my attempts to teach the literature of twentieth-century religious education. The first was the importance of history as the crucial context for interpretation. . . . The second persistent notion revolved around certain questions." Ibid., p. 5.

14. Ibid., p. 193.

15. See ibid., Chapter 8, pp. 192-215.

16. It would be inaccurate to say that Boys' work was indifferent to or unaware of the political dimension, however. For example, one of the guiding and foundational questions of her study on the historical development of twentieth century religious education was this one: "In what way is education a political activity?" Ibid., p. 7. Also see the discussion in ibid, pp. 175-188.

17. Lee's work is covered in more detail in Chapter Five, "The Religious Educator as Coach."

18. James Michael Lee, *The Shape of Religious Instruction: A Social Science Approach* (Birmingham, Ala.: Religious Education Press, 1971), p. 6.

19. Ibid., p. 8.

20. James Michael Lee, "The Authentic Source of Religious Instruction," in *Religious Education and Theology*, ed. Norma H. Thompson (Birmingham, Ala.: Religious Education Press, 1982), p. 110.

religious education is made up of instruction, guidance, and administration.[21] His own particular scholarly and missional interest is in one of those—religious instruction.[22] The crux of the matter remains, however, that from his social science perspective, Lee understands that the widest environmental context of the religious educator is indeed religious education.[23] Indeed, more than virtually any other religious educator, Lee attaches great importance to the power of the environment.

Systemic Definitions

Functional Images of the Religious Educator holds much in common with the approaches taken by Groome, Boys, and Lee, but uses a different—although related—set of definitions. It builds upon the three foundational definitions of religion, education, and religious education developed in the 1987 book *Systemic Religious Education.* The definition of *religion* was given there as "holistic (health-full) nexus: the existential 'binding together' of the heritage of the past with a guiding vision of the idealized future."[24] This definition stays away from any particularistic means for the accomplishment of holistic nexus, but instead points to the connectedness and the integration characteristic of true religion. It also promotes health as the functional criterion for the evaluation of religion, rather than some external, artificial standard such as tradition or orthodoxy. *Education* was defined as "the existential learning-adaptive process of leading out from past heritage into an idealized future."[25] The emphasis here is on movement and transformation. Without some kind of actual or potential change aimed at positively affecting the future, there is no true education. The definition of *religious education* flowed naturally and logically from the two previous definitions, becoming "the search for, attempt at, and creation of holistic nexus through the existential learning-adaptive process of transforming the heritage of the past into an actualized vision of the ideal future."[26] Systemically, religious education is chiefly identified by the terms "searching," "attempting," and "creating." Religious education is not just a body of information, a set of procedures, or a method of instruction, but it is more inclusively a process of promoting wholeness, unity, and synthesis. The effort is to find means of integration that are "health-full," and not segregative, divisive, reductionistic, simplistic, or stereotypical. The means of such a systemic process are multitudinous, and can never

---

21. One of these places is ibid., p. 111.

22. It is important to note, however, what Lee said about the relationship of religion and instruction: "It will be noted that 'religious' is the adjective and 'instruction' is the noun. In other words, the term 'religious' specified the kind of instruction that is done. Religious instruction, then, is situated within the total context of instruction, whether instruction is viewed vertically . . . or horizontally." James Michael Lee, *The Shape of Religious Instruction*, p. 183.

23. For an introductory discussion on Lee's view of how the structural and substantive contents relate in the religious instruction act, see James Michael Lee, *The Content of Religious Instruction: A Social Science Approach* (Birmingham, Ala.: Religious Education Press, 1985), pp. 8-13. Briefly stated, it is this: "Religion is thus the substantive content; instructional practice is the structural content. The substantive content plus the structural content as they are existentially formed and fused in the religious instruction act itself comprise the proper content of religious instruction." Ibid., p. 8.

24. Lines, *Systemic Religious Education*, pp. 143-144.

25. Ibid., p. 185.

26. Ibid., p. 216.

be totally systematized or categorized. True religious education is ceaselessly dynamic, innovative, and evolutionary.

The set of interlocking definitions in the paragraph above serves as the basis for this book, laying the foundation for the effort to identify the religious educator. Further explanation of the concepts and definitions themselves can be gained by consulting *Systemic Religious Education* as necessity or curiosity leads. The issue here is simply that the proper environmental context of religious education is the broad, generic, and nonparticularistic field of religious education.

What remains to be done in this chapter to clarify the importance of understanding this environmental context of the religious educator is to show the relationships among the various elements in that environmental context. Most often the disagreements arise not so much over *what* elements are in the environment, but rather *how* these elements are defined and how they relate and connect. For example, probably most would agree that religious education is intimately related in some fashion with both religion and education. It is the definitions of them and the relationships among them that cause the difficulties and the disagreements. Now that the working definitions for the book have been presented, it is appropriate to demonstrate how the definitions function in their relational contexts.

Relational Contexts

This section presents four portraits of the religious educator's environment, helping to put the systemic definitions given above in relationship to one another. In addition, other elements in the environment of the religious educator are also identified and put in perspective. The first three figures of the chapter move from a broad view through finer degrees of resolution, as if adjusting the lens of a telescope from its widest angle to more focused ones. The final figure of the chapter shifts to an even wider angle, showing the potential for destruction as well as for construction that is ever-present in the environment of the religious educator.

Religious Education

A sweep of the eye across the horizon first brings into view the three key elements of the environment of the religious educator—religion, education, and religious education. The relationship of these elements is portrayed in Figure 1. The importance of the interdependent definitions given in the previous section should be obvious now, since the graphic shows how the definitions, and the realities which they describe, are fundamentally related and connected.

Although it is always dangerous to translate abstract concepts into the concrete, since much of the subtlety of ideas can be so easily lost in the process, in this case the risk seems worth taking. Note how Figure 1 reveals that there is more to religion than education, and more to education than religion, but that religious education is a result of their union. In turn, religious education does not consume the whole of either religion or education but is created by the effort to integrate the two. Religious education combines religion and education into a totally new entity, which is not simply a *mixture* of religion and education but a *compound*—

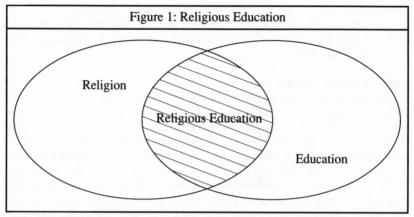

Figure 1: Religious Education

a new kind of whole with its own properties, identity—and images. Religious education needs to be understood *systemically*, since in a true system the parts are not simply joined together to make a whole.[27] The whole (religious education) is more than a mere summation of the parts (religion and education).[28] At the same time, without religion and education, the term "religious education" and the reality to which it points has no meaning. This explains the statement made earlier in the chapter that the proper environment of the religious educator is religious education. This confluence of the streams of religion and education into the river of religious education provides the environmental context for accurately identifying the religious educator.

One of the distortions of this graphic, and of the later ones that evolve from it, is the appearance that there are no other influences on religious education other than those of religion and education. Other spheres[29] could be included—representing especially other social sciences—but religion and education are the primary foci. Religious education, then, can be suitably described as the integration of religion and education only if it is recognized that religion and education are not absolute or isolated entities in and of themselves.

Another distortion of the graphic is that the boundaries of religion, education, and religious education may appear to be stark, well-defined, and precise. In reality, the boundaries should be seen as interfaces that connect and integrate

27. This is a description of an *aggregate*, which is a collection of parts without interrelationship among the parts. Instead, the system is a *whole*, where there is integration and interaction among the elements. See the fundamental property of an open system—holism—discussed and contrasted with that of the aggregate in Lines, *Systemic Religious Education*, p. 49.

28. James Michael Lee has termed this process the mediator stage: "Religious instruction is not an arbitrator between religion and theology or between pedagogy and theology. Nor does religious instruction serve as theology's intercessor, or vice versa. The mediatorship to which I refer is mediatorship in its highest, most authentic, and most effective form, namely mediatorship in which two or more realities become united in a new reality. This new reality is of such a nature that it not only unites its components, but unites them in such a fashion that the components are no longer separate entities but rather are subsumed into a new reality." James Michael Lee, "The Authentic Source of Religious Instruction," in *Religious Education and Theology*, pp. 165-166.

29. The figure should be viewed as portraying spheres (three-dimensions) rather than circles (two dimensions).

rather than divide or dissect. In addition, the boundaries should be viewed as permeable membranes, allowing flow-through and interchange among the areas rather than as hindrances or barriers that interrupt or check the dynamic processes that unite them.

Faith Tradition Education

The next level of resolution is shown in Figure 2. It brings into view another set of entities—faith traditions and faith tradition education. These new appearances are totally submerged within their larger environmental contexts of religion and religious education, respectively. The environmental context of the faith tradition is religion, and when placed in relationship to education the environmental context of faith tradition education is religious education. The specifics (faith traditions, faith tradition education) do not comprise the entirety of the general (religion, religious education), but only contribute to it and illustrate it. The mistake of confusing the environmental context of the religious educator (religious education) with faith tradition education (or with a specific faith tradition education, such as Christian education) is made obvious by this relational graphic.

A *faith tradition* is a community of believers bonded together in the practice

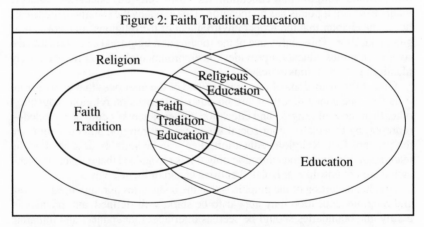

Figure 2: Faith Tradition Education

and belief of a specific, particular, historical religion.[30] Examples of faith traditions are Christianity, Judaism, and Buddhism. These particular kinds of religions are actual, concrete expressions of religion. These are the religions in which people find their identity and their community. Not any one of them makes up the whole of religion, and all of them together do not equal the sum total of religion. They all, instead, exist and function within the larger environmental context of religion. Faith traditions should not be perceived as isolated pockets of segre-

---

30. In *Systemic Religious Education*, these two were discussed in terms of religion and religions. See Lines, *Systemic Religious Education*, pp. 164-166. This followed a similar pattern to that of James Michael Lee, who spoke of religion and a religion. See Lee, *Content of Religious Instruction*, p. 3. "Faith tradition" and "faith tradition education" are attempts to expand the concepts and to show the relationships more distinctly.

gation, totally separate and distinct from one another, just as one particular faith tradition cannot be held as normative for all the others. True faith traditions are open to one another and work to integrate adherents into the larger spheres of reality.

The same kind of distinction applies to *faith tradition education*. It is fully a subset of religious education, dealing with the educational processes related to the practices, traditions, and lifestyle (faith traditions) of a *specific* religion. This is the area of Christian religious education, Jewish religious education, and Buddhist religious education. Again, no one of these is the totality of religious education, and simply summing them all up does not total religious education. There is still more to religious education than what faith tradition education contributes, yet all of faith tradition education is within the environment of religious education. It is simply a case of keeping the specific manifestations of the faith traditions within the broader context of the more general field of religious education.

Doctrinal Education

Figure 3 offers yet finer degrees of resolution, showing other possible sets of elements within the environment of religious education.[31] Within the province of faith traditions one may find the spelling out of that particular faith tradition's doctrine, and within the province of faith tradition education one would then find what would logically be termed doctrinal education. *Doctrine* is that set of cognitive and propositional beliefs or principles held by adherents of a particular faith tradition which are considered by those adherents to be true and necessary statements about their faith tradition.[32] As the distinction between faith traditions and doctrine shows, there is more—much more—to faith traditions than cognitive, rational, and codified doctrine. *Doctrinal education* is a subset of faith tradition which is responsible for communicating the cognitive doctrines to members, or potential members, or the particular faith tradition.[33] In like manner, faith tradition education covers much more area than the subset of beliefs and propositions related to doctrinal education.

Further degrees of resolution are shown as possibilities in Figure 3. Doctrine includes within its purview what Christianity, for example, terms *theology*— its belief statements about God.[34] Theology, then, is a subset of doctrine. A conceivable subset of doctrinal education would be known as *theological education*— the study, communication, and application of what a particular faith tradition

---

31. "Possible" because not every faith tradition deals with explicit doctrinal statements or with theology. This is the reason for the question marks after the terms "theology" and "theological education" in the figure.

32. There are a variety of names for doctrine that have been used or suggested. One that has gotten renewed attention is "catechesis" because of the writings of John Westerhoff. Westerhoff has tried to resurrect a term normally associated exclusively with Catholic religious education. See one such proposal in John H. Westerhoff III, "Risking an Answer: A Conclusion," in *Who Are We?: The Quest for a Religious Education*, ed. John H. Westerhoff III (Birmingham, Ala.: Religious Education Press, 1978), pp. 264-277, especially pp. 268-277.

33. It would probably not be overstating the case to say that this is the realm of indoctrination—the place where doctrine is "put into" the faith community members by any variety of transmissive measures or procedures.

34. Even from an etymological basis, theology is literally the study of θεός—God.

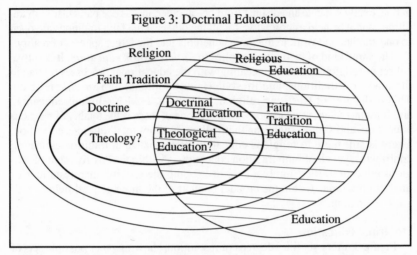

Figure 3: Doctrinal Education

community believes cognitively about its theological system. It makes sense in this limited and specialized context that a specific formulation of theology would influence or determine to at least some degree the means or processes of theological education. In this case, theological education would naturally follow and be derived from the propositions of its particularistic theological presuppositions or beliefs. These statements and the accompanying figure should make clear that theology may certainly be an element within the broad context of religious education but that theology is by no means determinative for all of religious education and is not even necessarily essential to some expressions of it. A faith tradition that has no concept of divinity, for example, would not even include theology or theological education within its doctrinal spheres.[35] Surely this is clear evidence that theology, and theological education, are not *the* prime issues for the much wider and more inclusive fields of religion and religious education as various forms of theological imperialism would assert.[36]

Figure 3, then, illustrates what has been one of the most contentious issues in recent religious education—the proper placement of theology within the environment of religious education.[37] Theology is the formulation by a particular faith tradition community about what it believes concerning divinity.[38] As this fig-

---

35. Some forms of Buddhism, for example, do not discuss theology since they do not have a theistic stance. If the theological macrotheory would be the operative theory at work here, then these forms of Buddhism could not legitimately be conceived as religions or to have religious education!

36. James Michael Lee defined theological imperialism as "the attempt to bring under direct theological jurisdiction and control all areas of reality, especially those which in one way or another may be related to theology. Contemporary theological imperialism represents a modern elaboration and hardening of the old 'theology is the queen of the sciences' position taken by many theologians during the Middle Ages." Lee, "The Authentic Source of Religious Instruction," in *Religious Education and Theology*, p. 146. See the fuller discussion in ibid., pp. 146-165.

37. This issue received extensive discussion in Lines, Systemic Religious Education, especially in pp. 11-28. Probably a more accurate rendering of the situation would be to say that this has been one of the most contentious issues in twentieth-century Christian religious education within the United States. For a good overview of the issues and the wide variety of positions taken by con-

ure shows graphically, theology is doctrine, which is wholly a product of its own particular faith tradition. Within the faith tradition of Christianity, for example, there can be the working out of a Christian theology because Christianity can be understood and interpreted theistically; however, there is no universally accepted, or acceptable, theology for *all* faith traditions, and obviously none that is serviceable to all of religion. Each faith tradition has its own particular version or rendition of theology, just as each may have its own formulation of doctrine. Theology, in this schema, cannot possibly be the deciding issue for religious education, just as the part does not identify the whole. Theology may provide a "clue,"[39] but only to the faith tradition education and to its doctrinal education in which that particular theology operates—not for the whole of religious education.[40] Indeed, theology need not even be a factor at all. It depends upon the faith tradition in which one is operating and upon its doctrinal propositions.

One of the ways to interpret Figure 3 is that all faith traditions are subsets of religion, and all faith tradition education is a subset of religious education. Faith traditions may have subsets of doctrine, and of ways to teach that doctrine whose subsets are called doctrinal education. Not all faith traditions, however, will have the additional subset of theology, and not all faith tradition education will have a subset of theological education. By no means are the spheres of theology and theological education subsuming or controlling of the larger, more general spheres.

An additional factor hopefully made clear in Figure 3 is the place of theological education within the larger environmental context. Theological education is a term that is thrown about without much precision, but generally within much of Christianity it is used to denote the professional education of those entering the vocational ministry (clergy).[41] The web gets tangled beyond comprehension when many institutions of theological education (seminaries and divinity schools in the Christian tradition) categorize Christian religious education as a *subset* of theological education![42] In this confused and confusing view, the two get completely reversed where theological education becomes the broader term and religious education is subsumed by it—which then reduces the term "religious education" literally to nonsense. What may be more helpful and descriptive,

temporary religious educators, see Religious Education and Theology. In addition, the issue receives attention in virtually every chapter of Part Two of this book under the discussion of the contemporary examples of religious educators.

38. If the particular faith tradition has no beliefs or conceptions of God or divinity, then obviously theology is superfluous.

39. This is a reference to the way Randolph Crump Miller saw the situation in *The Clue to Christian Education*. The thing to be noted here is that Miller identified the "clue" as relating specifically to Christian religious education rather than to religious education in general.

40. Of course, not everyone (by any means) agrees on this point. For example, Mary Boys said flatly: "Theology is without doubt elemental to religious education." Boys, *Educating in Faith*, p. 200.

41. For one example among the many alternative views, see the work of Edward Farley, such as *Theologia: The Fragmentation and Unity of Theological Education* (Philadelphia: Fortress, 1983).

42. The situation gets even more complex and complicated when one realizes that even within Christianity there are very different institutions of theological education for Protestants and Catholics; within Protestantism, there are different institutions for, say, Methodists and Baptists; and even different institutions for different kinds of Baptists! No wonder the systemic nature of religious education is hard to discern when the faith traditions have succeeded in chopping it up into so many isolated segments.

rather than the misused term of theological education in seminaries and divinity schools, would be to substitute a term (descriptive but linguistically awkward) such as "professional doctrinal faith tradition education"[43] to indicate that some of the persons in the faith tradition are specially trained, educated, indoctrinated, and possibly employed in the specific faith traditions.[44]

One of the illusions created by Figure 3 is that theology depicted in this way may appear to be central to, indeed at the very core of, religious education.[45] In some manifestations of religious education, this could very well be true, but it is not symptomatic of all of religious education. Such an appearance is only an illustration of the problem of portraying abstracts concretely. Sometimes the exact opposite of what is intended is expressed—in some round about fashion. In the quest for clarity, sometimes as much is lost as is gained!

Healthy Religious Education

One additional figure is left to examine in this introductory "atlas of maps" for the book. The discussion thus far may have led one to assume that any kind of religion, or education, or religious education (and subsets thereof) is acceptable. As various sections of the chapters in Part Two will indicate, such is certainly not the case.[46] Figure 4 is a depiction of healthy—and correspondingly, of unhealthy—religious education.

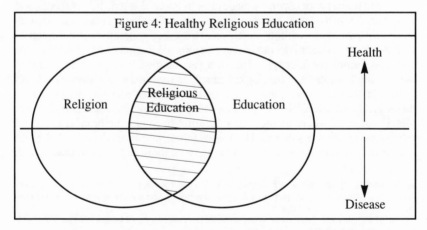

Figure 4: Healthy Religious Education

Seeing this figure takes a bit of imagination. Go back to Figures 1-3 and envision the circles as cross sections of spheres, cut by a plane. Each figure

---

43. Or more simply, cleric education.

44. See Chapter Two, "Differentiative Typologies of the Religious Educator," for a discussion of professional typologies of religious educators, referring to those who have specific administrative responsibilities (as clergy) rather than to the larger, more general category of religious educators.

45. Such a misreading of the figure would lead one to the theological macrotheory rather than the social science macrotheory being espoused. See these macrotheories explained and contrasted in Lee, "The Authentic Source of Religious Instruction," in *Religious Education and Theology*, p. 146. See the fuller discussion in ibid., pp. 121-146.

46. Each of the chapters on the roles of the religious educator includes a section of the shadow role, which points to the abuse and misuse of authentic religious education.

then represents one-half of the spheres. Now, instead of looking at the cross section, tilt the plane ninety degrees and look at the spheres holistically as depicted in Figure 4. The top half of the figure represents the part of the spheres of religion, education, and religious education that promote healthy, life-giving virtues. These are the areas of this book which make up the proper environmental context of the genuine religious educator. The bottom half of the figure represents the unhealthy dimensions of religion, education, and religious education that lead toward disease and death. These areas are but rarely addressed directly in the book (except in the sections on the "shadow roles"), but they are ominous reminders of the power of religious education.

Religion, education, and religious education, in and of themselves, are not necessarily good, and can do as much or more damage as good.[47] What Alfred North Whitehead said of religion is conceivably just as true for education and religious education: "The uncritical association of religion with goodness is directly negatived by plain facts. Religion can be, and has been, the main instrument of progress. But if we survey the whole race, we must pronounce that generally it has not been so."[48] The religious educator has the same dual-pronged potential for good and evil. It is the task of the true religious educator to promote health, and to defeat or replace (heal?) sickness and disease. Demonstrating how (if) he or she can do this in a nonparticularistic sense—*religious* education—is the purpose of this book.

Summary

This introductory chapter has been an initial survey of the most fundamental interpretive taxonomies regarding the religious educator, and its primary message has been simple: The environmental context of the religious educator is religious education. Basic definitions were provided which underlie the discussion in the remainder of the book, and then the relationships among the elements of the definitions were graphed in four figures. The four figures offered in the chapter should be kept in mind throughout the book since they provide the canvas upon which the portraits of the genuine and systemic religious educator are sketched. Two additional introductory aspects of the context of the religious educator are yet to be explored—some differentiative typologies of the religious educator and the diagnostic categories of the religious educator. The first of these is the subject of the following chapter.

---

47. This issue of health as the basis for evaluating religious education was given extensive discussion throughout *Systemic Religious Education*. The notion of health is a prime reason for using the systemic (open systems) language and metaphor. It is a way of leaving behind the divisive and ultimately useless arguments about right or wrong religious education, as well as debate over orthodox or heretical religious education. Open (living) systems grow and evolve, and can be diagnosed in terms of health, while categories like "good" and "bad" contribute nothing to understanding or to moving toward "holistic nexus."

48. Alfred North Whitehead, *Religion in the Making* (New York: Macmillan, 1923; reprint edition; New York: The American Library, 1974), p. 13.

Chapter Two

Differentiative Typologies
of the Religious Educator

The subject of this book is the *religious* educator, rather than such particularistic versions of the religious educator as the Christian religious educator or the Jewish religious educator. Because the literature on the identity of the religious educator is quite limited, a chapter on current differentiative typologies[1] of the religious educator could turn out to be a very short one indeed. The purpose of this chapter, however, is to establish a context for identifying the generic (nonparticularistic) religious educator. This can be accomplished by selecting a few extant typologies of the Christian and Jewish religious educator and then showing how the religious educator as identified in this book compares and contrasts with those typologies.

What follows is first a brief overview of two kinds of typologies related to the particularistic (primarily Christian) religious educator—the historical and the professional. The religious educator can then be portrayed against this backdrop, which is the third kind of typologies explored in the chapter—metaphorical typologies of the religious educator. The totality of the true religious educator is neither defined nor limited by the first two typologies but rather is informed and contextualized by them. Since particularistic educators are embedded in the broader sweep of religious education (as explained in the previous chapter), traces of their historical and the professional typologies will naturally appear in the typologies of the religious educator.

---

1. Typologies are the result of comparative and analytical study of historical or structural classifications within a specific field or subject area.

22

Historical Typologies

The first groupings of typologies considered are historical ones, drawn from the work of two religious educators who dealt with the history of the Christian church—one from the past generation (Lewis Joseph Sherrill) and one from the efforts of a later scholar (Marianne Sawicki). The particular historical typologies of the religious educator have by necessity been "constructed" from their writings, since neither Sherrill nor Sawicki wrote specifically on the topic of the religious educator (as defined in this book). Both were more concerned with the general flow of church history within Christian religious education. The resultant typologies therefore have a certain amount of contrivance, but their existence is clearly revealed by an examination of the evidence.

Lewis Joseph Sherrill

The classic exposition of the historical identity of the religious educator was produced by Lewis Joseph Sherrill in the 1944 book *The Rise of Christian Education*.[2] Sherrill's book presented two predictable problems in the quest for typologies of the religious educator. First, Sherrill wrote about the rise of *Christian* religious education (in which he included foundations from Judaism)— a focus on a particular version of religious education. It is no criticism of Sherrill or of his work to acknowledge that he was addressing a particular faith tradition's education—in this case, Christian religious education. It is simply to acknowledge that he did not address the primary and more generic focus of this book, religious education, and fortunately he was perceptive enough to identify his work properly. The attention Sherrill gave to Christian religious education serves as an example or a paradigm of how the same analysis could be done with religious education. Second, Sherrill wrote about the rise of Christian religious *education*, which differs from a discussion of the rise of the Christian religious *educator*. The Christian religious educator can be found within Sherrill's book, to be sure, but a focus on that personage exclusively was not Sherrill's intent. The comments that follow need to be understood in that light.

In the face of these difficulties (which, incidentally, point out the need for a book on the identity and on the images of the religious educator), historical typologies of the "religious" (Christian) educator can be distilled from Sherrill. Since Sherrill traced the "rise of Christian [religious] education" from Hebrew origins through the beginning of the fifteenth century, a study of his entire book would produce a comprehensive but massive set of typologies. What follows here is only a sample from three of his divisions of history, which illustrates the process of identifying the religious educator within the flow of Judeo-Christian heritage.

Hebrew Education. Sherrill described the period of Hebrew education as reaching "from the earliest days to about the time of the destruction of Jerusalem in 586 B.C.[E.]," when "the teachers of first importance were parents, prophets, priests, sages, and poets."[3] These five teaching roles form the earliest of Sherrill's

---

2. Lewis Joseph Sherrill, *The Rise of Christian Education* (New York: Macmillan, 1944).
3. Ibid., p. 6.

typologies concerning the religious educator. He described the parent as having three basic methods of teaching.[4] First was to facilitate the informed participation of the children in the activities expected of all family members, or what we would now recognize as vocational education. Second was to control the conduct of the children—behavioral and moral education. Third was to pass on the oral traditions of the Hebrew faith as well as to instruct in the meaning of the communal religious rites. The *priest* performed the role of teacher by mediating between the people and God, which was accomplished through the means of codifying and interpreting the law, of offering the sacrifices, and occasionally through the exercise of divination.[5] The *prophet* had the task of "speaking forth for God, whether regarding the immediate present or the distant future," when he or she had "to act as mouthpiece and messenger for some utterance with which he felt overpowered."[6] The *sage* was an aged person in the community who distilled wisdom from a long life into a "single drop, summing up a view of life's values in one pithy saying—a 'proverb'" which "became the heritage of each succeeding generation."[7] The *poet* taught primarily by singing, and the Psalms are evidence of the type of curriculum created by the poet.[8]

Jewish Education. Sherrill marked the move from Hebrew education to Jewish education by the fall of Jerusalem to Babylon, since the effects of the exile "guided the development of the religion into the orthodox form known as Judaism."[9] Sherrill identified the *scribe* (also known as "Rabbi") as the primary teacher of religion during this era, described as "a person who devoted himself to professional acquaintance with the law, scientific study of it, and interpretation of it to the laity."[10] Sherrill depicted the scribe as fulfilling four duties[11] (which could be labeled as roles using the language of the present book). The first duty was that of the *jurist*, "elaborating the Law, pronouncing legal decisions." The second was the *student of scripture*, who "examined the meaning of the Law, the history, and the didactic portions." Third was the *teacher*, teaching the Law (Torah) to pupils and delivering addresses in the synagogue. Fourth was the *custodian of scripture*, preserving the sacred texts against corruption.

Education in the Primitive Church. Skipping to distinctively Christian religious education, Sherrill identified the "primitive church" era as existing from the time of Jesus up to approximately 125 C.E.[12] At least three forms of ministry existed in this very early stage—*apostles, prophets,* and *teachers*, which eventually stabilized into the more familiar offices of *bishops, presbyters,* and *deacons.*[13] Rather than discussing clearly demarcated roles or personages, Sherrill told of five different kinds of teaching that various persons performed within the prim-

---

4. Ibid., pp. 17-18.
5. Ibid., pp. 8-10.
6. Ibid., p. 11.
7. Ibid., p. 16.
8. Ibid., p. 17.
9. Ibid., p. 31.
10. Ibid., p. 41.
11. Ibid., p. 42.
12. Ibid., p. 137.
13. Ibid., p. 143.

itive church. These five were: Christian interpretation of Hebrew scriptures; the teaching of the gospel (the tradition); the Christian confession of faith (public profession); the life and "sayings" of Jesus; and the teachings of the "Two Ways" (moral and ethical conduct).[14] These later evolved into the basis for catechumenal instruction, which provided the means for including converts into the life of the church. Sherrill skillfully traced this path of teaching to show how it became the foundation for authority in the church, where "teachers" became less concerned with passing on the traditions and the attitudes of the church than they were admitting into the church those who had acquired—accepted— the right, and the authoritative, information.

Summary. The above paragraphs have only been the briefest of looks at Sherrill's extensive research and are not meant to be comprehensive. They are but illustrations of how one can find typologies of the religious educator through Judeo-Christian history if the search is so defined. Further reading of Sherrill reveals many more discernible roles, but the ones mentioned serve to provide a historical context for the examination and search for the identity of the religious educator.

Marianne Sawicki

Marianne Sawicki has written a much more recent historical treatment of Christian religious education than the one by Sherrill,[15] but both used the broad sweep of history to discuss the evolution of Christian religious education, and both included some attention to the roles of individual educators in their study. Sherrill's inclusion of the religious/Christian educator was rather incidental, but Sawicki intentionally highlighted what she called the "personnel" of Christian religious education in her work. Where Sherrill used divisions of history ("primitive Christianity," "The ancient Church"), Sawicki used selected representative centuries to illustrate her view of history. A few samples of the way Sawicki identified Christian religious educators throughout history provide alternatives to the typology constructed from Sherrill's work.

Apostolic Age. Sawicki designated the years following the death of Jesus (c. 30 C.E.) as the "Apostolic Age," and she focused on several outstanding New Testament figures ("apostles") who illustrated the early teaching and preaching of the church, primarily Peter and Paul.[16] She named some of the categories found within the historic Christian community which evolved into the offices of the later institutional church. One was the *wandering prophet,* who traveled among the various forming Christian communities, preaching and teaching in the manner of Jesus: "Those whom Jesus called to follow him in that wandering life continued after his death to work in the manner in which he had worked and to teach what he had taught."[17] There were the *apostles,* like Peter and Paul, who were trying to establish doctrine and authority. Later, the appellation of "apostle" was generalized into "someone who is sent out and who founds a

---

14. Ibid., pp. 142-153.
15. Marianne Sawicki, *The Gospel in History: Portrait of a Teaching Church—The Origins of Christian Education* (New York: Paulist, 1988).
16. See Chapter Four, "First Century: Apostolic Age," ibid., pp. 69-109.
17. Ibid., p. 77.

Christian community."[18] A *teacher*, by contrast, generally followed the apostle into the infant Christian community and established some basic and foundational understandings of the new faith. *Presbyters* and *deacons* were more involved with the organizational life of the early church than with the actual teaching of the gospel. They were resident members of the individual assemblages who were charged with overseeing the various activities of the congregation.[19]

Classical Age. Sawicki's narrative jumped from the first century to the fourth, which supported her interest in the relating the movement of "the gospel in history." The fourth century[20] was what Sawicki called a watershed period, for here the church crystallized its doctrine, liturgy, and rituals.[21] The role of the Christian religious educator, of course, was formalized as well. The attention and authority now centered on the *bishop*. As Sawicki said: "Teaching, like all ministry in the fourth-century church, is the responsibility of the bishop."[22] The bishop at least oversaw the instruction of the catechumenates, and probably performed such ceremonies as the ritual initiation into the church. Most of the instruction process he left to the appointed clergy—*deacons* or *presbyters*—to accomplish. To supplement the work of the clergy was a *sponsor*—parents or godparents—who gave example, advice, and companionship through the instructional period and who accompanied the initiate through the rite of baptism.

Feudal Age. Sawicki termed the period of the sixth through the eighth centuries the feudal age, where the movement was from a classical culture to a medieval one.[23] During this time of increasing isolation, it was still the *bishop* who had primary responsibility for seeing that the gospel was preached and taught.[24] The great difference was that now the bishop no longer had direct contact with the people in his charge. Sawicki explained: "The bishop's role became privatized: he was father and teacher primarily of the group of town clergy, the cathedral canons, who lived the common life under his direction. He taught them; it was they who preached to and instructed the people of the town."[25] As far as the people were concerned, the prime religious educator of the period, then, was the *priest*, who at best had a minimal education of any kind and virtually no preparation in what could be termed today as religious education.

Summary. In the same way that Sherrill's historical typologies of the Christian religious educator had to be constructed from a historical narrative, so they must be garnered from Sawicki's work. Sawicki's intentional focus was to reveal how the church taught the gospel through its history, thus forming the origins of Christian religious education. Neither the figure of the religious educator nor of the Christian religious educator was her primary interest. What she did reveal for

---

18. Ibid., p. 91.
19. Ibid., pp. 96-97.
20. See Chapter Five, "Fourth Century: The Eclipse of Antiquity," ibid., pp. 110-144.
21. Ibid., p. 110.
22. Ibid., p. 128. Sawicki went on to say: "When authority is 'institutionalized' in the church, it is placed in the hands of the bishop—largely so that he might ensure the integrity of Christian teaching." Ibid., p. 129.
23. See Chapter Six, "Seventh Century: Feudal Bondings," ibid., pp. 145-173.
24. Ibid., p. 163.
25. Ibid., p. 164.
26. The term "professional" here relates to career specialty.

purposes here was how the roles and the identity of the Christian religious educator evolved through the centuries, just as the role and the identity of the Christian church did. Sawicki, together with Sherrill, provide a base of historical (albeit particularly Christian) insights from which to begin discerning the identity of the religious educator.

Professional Typologies

In contrast to the historical typologies of the religious/Christian educator are the professional[26] typologies. Some history is of course involved, since to trace the development of the profession is to be aware of the passage of time, but the parameters of history shrink drastically here. The prime focus is on the Christian religious educator as a distinct professional and vocational entity, and this is a twentieth-century phenomenon. Two examples of typologies produced from this specialist approach are taken from the work of Dorothy Jean Furnish and of Donald Emler.

Dorothy Jean Furnish

Dorothy Jean Furnish followed the development of the professional religious educator with the title of Director of Religious Education (DRE) or Director of Christian Education (DCE) in *DRE/DCE—The History of a Profession.*[27] Furnish described the profession as evolving through five distinguishable periods from approximately 1906 through the mid-seventies, and located the activity of this new profession as taking place primarily within the boundaries of the local church. These five periods are summarized below to provide another typology for contextualizing the identity of the religious educator.[28]

Birth. Furnish saw the profession of the DRE/DCE as being born in the United States during 1906-1910,[29] but she was careful to note earlier foundational influences. The primary factor was the Sunday school movement, which up to this time had been under the supervision of two groups—laity and clergy. As Furnish put it: "Now a third groups was coming on the scene, neither lay nor clergy, but people who would call themselves 'professionals.' They had different concerns, different methodologies, and different standards."[30] The profession itself arose during this period not only because of the Sunday school, however, but "from a combination of concern for the young, the hope presented by a new educational psychology and an enlightened biblical scholarship, and the desire to match the public school in the quality of education provided."[31] The impetus

---

27. Dorothy Jean Furnish, *DRE/DCE—The History of a Profession* (Nashville: Christian Educators Fellowship of the United Methodist Church, 1976).

28. Furnish focused her attention exclusively on the Protestant manifestations of the professional religious educator and did so at quite a different level of scholarship then the previous examples of Sherrill and Sawicki. Furnish wrote more of a popular history for a non-academic audience, so that the evidence and information she provided was more on the order of narrative and anecdotes rather than on hard empirical data.

29. Furnish, *DRE/DCE*, pp. 15-24.

30. Ibid., p. 16.

31. Ibid., pp. 16-17.

for formal organization Furnish attributed to the establishment of the Religious Education Association in 1903.

Optimism. The period of 1910-1930 Furnish reported as one of great optimism—within the new profession certainly, but also throughout the United States generally. The profession grew in numbers, as did the various Christian denominations. New educational facilities were built by the churches, new curriculum materials were produced, and the general mood was one of expansion and excitement. Furnish quoted Harrison Elliott remembering these days: "Unless one participated in the events of this time, it is difficult to realize the sense of mission and the feeling of confidence which characterized this period in religious education."[32] The opportunities for the future of the profession appeared to be limitless.

Disillusionment. The halcyon days of the 1920s were soon replaced by the period of "disillusionment and despair," 1930-1945.[33] Furnish summed up the changes this way: "And so a new period began, marked at the outset by the economic crash of 1929 and at the end by V-J Day. In between, there was a new orthodoxy in religion, a realization that religious education was not the cure for all the world's ills, and the grim consequences of a Great Depression and World War II."[34] Churches were forced to cut budgets, and often the newly created position of the DRE/DCE was one of the first places cuts were made. In the light of these changing economic realities, the question the profession faced now was: "Is the director of religious education a fad?"[35]

Recovery. 1945-1965 marked yet another period of great growth and expansion of religious fervor, and the profession of the DRE/DCE accordingly reaped some of these benefits.[36] The cycle repeated itself: "With the end of World War II, Directors of Religious Education picked up the pieces of their profession that had begun to disintegrate as a result of the Depression. An increase of church school attendance, new education buildings, new curriculum materials, and money enough to pay for all of it encouraged churches to employ directors, and the shortage of trained persons encouraged young people to choose the profession."[37] Once again, all appeared to be upbeat and promising: The profession was back in vogue.

Challenge. Furnish characterized the last ten years of her study (1965-1975) as "a period of transition in the history of the profession."[38] She cited the "societal revolution and economic instability" of the era[39] as being similar to the previous period of disillusionment (1930-1945). As before, the nation was faced with a depression and a war, while the churches had to deal with declining attendance and income. The profession was threatened and vulnerable once again. Furnish ended her work by counseling both "urgency and enthusiasm [tem-

---

32. Ibid., p. 26.
33. Ibid., pp. 37-42.
34. Ibid., pp. 37-38.
35. Ibid., p. 42.
36. Ibid., pp. 43-47.
37. Ibid., p. 47.
38. Ibid., p. 97.
39. Ibid., p. 103.

pered] with a patience that is rooted in an optimistic confidence about the future."[40]

Summary. One of the problems in using Furnish's work as a basis for a typology of the religious educator (as used in this book) is her emphasis on the local church environment. Whether the term DRE or DCE is used, the focus remains on one faith tradition—Christianity, and on one segment of it—Protestantism. Another problem is the portrayal of the Christian religious educator as an administrative parish professional, so that the boundaries are necessarily drawn much more narrowly. Using the typology from Furnish's work produces a Christian religious educator that definitely has a more distinct identity but at the cost of isolating him or her within one faith tradition and one local community. The larger tasks of "binding together" cannot be even glimpsed, much less accomplished, from such a confining definition of the role. An additional difficulty in identifying the religious educator with the DRE/DCE is that the fate of religious education then rides with the vicissitudes of the profession. As Furnish revealed, the development of the administrative professional has been a checkered one at best. Such a small, although important, part of religious education cannot be allowed to represent the whole; so while the professional administrative type of religious educator described by Furnish is certainly included within the audience of this book, he or she is by no means the entire focus. A broader identity is sought, and the following section helps in this search.

Donald Emler

A later book on the DRE as an administrative parish professional was written by Donald Emler, entitled *Revisioning the DRE*.[41] In that book, Emler had two foci: One, to "revision" the framework in which the DRE operates; and two, to "revision" the administrative profession and its functions. The first part of the book, dealing with the framework, gave an alternative version of the profession's evolution to the one provided by Furnish. In addition, Emler discussed the differences between a theological and a social-science approach to the profession.[42] It is the second part of the book that best informs the topic at hand, however. There, while revisioning the administrative profession, Emler discussed five "functional roles" of the DRE. A brief review of these roles will help to compare and contrast the DRE with roles of the religious educator explored in Part Two of this book.

Administrator and Program Developer. Emler started his review of the DRE's functions with the ones most expected and most maligned—administration and programing. As administrator, the DRE defines and interprets goals and policies, determines budget needs, oversees equipment purchase and maintenance, supervises personnel, and conducts research.[43] As program developer, the DRE diagnoses needs, plans for curriculum, and then designs, implements, and evaluates

40. Ibid., p. 119.

41. Donald G. Emler, *Revisioning the DRE* (Birmingham, Ala.: Religious Education Press, 1989).

42. Emler's discussion is consonant in many ways to the environmental context of the religious educator covered in the previous chapter of this book.

43. Emler, *Revisioning the DRE*, pp. 96-101.

the religious education programs for the local church.[44] As Emler pointed out, these are important and essential responsibilities of the DRE, but they are not the only ones. Emler went on to give a fuller description of the DRE's tasks.

Educational Consultant. Emler described the educational consultant as a resource person and as a facilitator who operates in at least four ways. First was the *advocate*, who speaks on behalf of others and seeks to allow all to have access to necessary information. Second was the *teaching-learning expert*, where the DRE is expected to be the resident authority on matters related to the entire teaching-learning process. Third was the *stimulator*, whose task is "to help others to ask the right questions, to explore the possible avenues, and to help them consider alternatives."[45] Fourth was the *change agent*, who innovates, communicates, and evaluates the necessary changes.

Learning Specialist. The third function Emler discussed was accurately described as the most important and yet most neglected facet of the DRE, that of being the learning specialist. Emler said: "The DRE is the virtuoso teacher of the church, modeling the best teaching behavior in each class taught. The DRE must be skilled in the art of teaching."[46] Among the topics covered in this chapter was a detailing of the components in the teaching act—the subject-matter content, the teaching strategies, and the classroom dynamics. Such a discussion reinforced Emler's argument that this function lies at the very heart of the work of the DRE.

Information Specialist. In this section, Emler focused on the DRE as an information specialist from three perspectives: the DRE as researcher, as diagnostician, and as evaluator. Emler summarized these functions this way: "Religious education requires . . . *research* into the learner and improved ways for communication of ideas and feelings. . . . Through *diagnosis* the DRE must be able to discover the real religious education needs of persons and groups so that a variety of educational opportunities can be created for the benefit of the whole congregation. . . . Through ongoing *evaluation*, experiences can be redesigned and created to match the learner's needs as well as institutional needs and societal goals."[47]

Faith Interpreter. The final function Emler discussed was faith interpreter, which focused on the spirituality of both the DRE and of individuals in the congregation. Emler cited the DRE as a *mentor*, who facilitates the faith pilgrimage of another, and as a *counselor*, who is available to help in times of crisis or emergency.

Summary. Emler provided a broad range of functions and roles for the practicing DRE, which was both a help and a hindrance to the purposes of this book. On the "help" side, Emler prepared the way for opening up the roles and functions of the religious educator to be inclusive and expansive. Many of the ones discussed in the chapters to follow in this book appear to be very close to the ones offered by Emler. On the "hindrance" side, Emler addressed (as Furnish did) only

44. Ibid., pp. 102-110.
45. Ibid., pp. 122.
46. Ibid., p. 131.
47. Ibid., p. 209. Emphasis added.

the DRE as specialist.[48] This is no criticism of Emler's work, since the book addressed an audience of, and the topic of, DREs.[49] Further, there is little doubt that Emler was targeting not only the professional specialist but also the Christian specialist. This makes it impossible to generalize what Emler wrote about the professional administrative DRE to the more generic and broadly defined religious educator. What Emler did for the DRE with his discussion of roles, however, is what this book hopes to do for the religious educator. This necessitates an introductory look at the ten roles—the metaphorical typologies—proposed in this book, and which are more fully explored in Part Two.

Metaphorical Typologies

The ten chapters that compose Part Two provide views of the religious educator by means of ten different images, or metaphors. These ten roles are not absolutes, as if they were Platonic discoveries of long-hidden truth waiting to be uncovered. They are images selected to help illustrate the complexity of the tasks and functions undertaken by the religious educator. The exact titles and the exact descriptions are neither designed nor intended as a kind of bible for the religious educator, since they do not dispense revealed truth. They are heuristic offerings, intending to shed light on a dimly understood activity, but drawing heavily from the historical and professional typologies described earlier in the chapter.

Although each chapter, and hence each role, is treated individually, this should *not* be taken as evidence that the ten roles are separate and distinct from one another. The ten are best seen as different facets of the same reality, but seen from different viewpoints. The total reality only comes into view when *all ten are integrated and synthesized* into the vision of one whole and complete identity. Although it may be true that individuals may tend to use one or more of the roles predominantly, and hence some of the others sparingly, the goal is to provide a vision of wholeness, allowing the religious educator not only to enhance strengths but even more importantly to recognize and improve weaknesses in the never-ending quest to become a more complete religious educator.

Each of the roles is vitally important to the effective and genuine religious educator. As will become apparent in the unfolding of the images, there should be elements and degrees of each image within the identity and performance of every religious educator. Although each of the roles is treated separately in a chapter of its own, in actuality the roles need to combine and integrate into a larger whole in true systemic fashion. Just because a particular religious educator has a natural tendency toward one or two of the roles does not mean that he or she can ignore or eliminate any of the others that are not so naturally within his or her

---

48. Emler stated this in the Preface of his book: "Central to the book is the assumption that the DRE is a professional religious educator who offers a specific body of knowledge to the church. In that professional competence, the DRE is a specialist in contrast to clergy who are trained to be generalists." Ibid., p. x.

49. Emler stated this clearly as well: "This book is about roles of the professional educator who is employed by a local church." Ibid., p. 4.

repertoire. The goal is for each to become the systemic religious educator—able to function fully within all ten of the images as the specific situation and understanding of needs call them forth. Any objective less than full functioning is a dishonoring of the call to be a religious educator, which is a call to a lifetime of discipline and growth where each individual builds upon his or her strengths while also working on his or her unique weaknesses.

The following roles are meant to form a comprehensive description of the religious educator. While the actual ten images themselves may not be described in terms that will bring universal agreement, these ten are an attempt to encompass the entire field. It is just as important to recognize what is excluded, then, as what is included. The ten roles are an attempt to describe the genuine, effective, healthy—systemic—religious educator. Just as many (if not more) other roles and activities were deemed inappropriate for identifying the true religious educator.[50]

The following roles are an experiment in metaphorical religious education—the roles presented are metaphors of the identity of the genuine religious educator. The worst that could happen is that the metaphors would be concretized into some harsh reality or job description. Let the roles and the metaphors speak, but do not squeeze them so tightly that no life remains in them. Any metaphor and its applications have limits, after which all meaning and value is lost. Let the metaphor dance, but when it is finished, let another take its place.

A brief introduction to the ten proposed images—the metaphorical typologies—of the religious educator is included below. Since each image is given a chapter of its own in Part Two, nothing more than initial identification of the images is attempted in this chapter. An attempt to show the integration and synthesis of the roles is provided in Part Three of this book.

Parent

The first role discussed in Part Two of this book (in Chapter Four) is that of the religious educator as parent. This image was seen in the historical typologies supplied by Sherrill and is probably one of the roles most expected and universally acknowledged. The parent is the nurturing figure, giving the appropriate care and attention to the individual, while also judging when to hold back and allow the individual to try it alone. The image of the parent is one that encourages the learner toward maturity, providing support while realizing that eventually the learner will move on to greater independence and individuality—in which the true parent rejoices. The traditional linkage of family and religion teaching is at work here, although care must be exercised not to mix role and concrete reality. The "parent" in this chapter is but a metaphor for the religious educator, so the chapter should not read as merely a description of the parental tasks. The focus is on the religious educator as parent, which is a somewhat different focus than the parent as religious educator. This type of emphasis is true for each of the following roles as well.

---

50. Samples of these inappropriate identities are provided in each of the ten chapters of Part Two under the heading of "shadow role."

Coach

A somewhat more modern term, but not concept, is that of the coach, and Chapter Five explores the role of the religious educator as coach. A person who stands alongside and teaches participants both the fundamentals and the permutations of "playing the game" is hardly a twentieth-century phenomenon since the sports analogy reaches back to at least early Grecian days. Indeed, this role is at the heart of the religious educator—the performance of instruction. Since the role of coach does not end with teaching fundamentals, the larger identity is that of the person who insists on practice, practice, and more practice. Even after the preparation is complete, the coach then orchestrates the performance of the players during the actual playing of the game. The coach is involved in the art and science of coaching—the science is the teaching of the principles and basics requisite for good performance, and the art is the ability to motivate the players while also adapting the plays to the specific environment. The role of the coach is intimately related to that of the parent, but it has its own distinct sense of identity and interdependence. It is one role that no religious educator can be allowed to undervalue, and one that must be exercised constantly.

Scientist

Logic, evidence, analysis, and evaluation are not often enough linked to the identity of the religious educator, but these are terms and activities affirmed by imaging the religious educator as scientist. The true scientist is motivated by insatiable curiosity into the nature of things and backs up that curiosity with careful and precise experimentation. The scientist creates a firm operational base by doing basic research, collecting empirical data, and then building theory that is based upon that evidence. An imbalance of this role to the exclusion of the others could result in a cold, harsh empiricism with no soul. Religious education without this role, however, would result in soft, fuzzy, devotional platitudes. If there is an absence of the former, there is no dearth of the latter. Religious education as a whole appears to need a rather strong infusion of persons committed to this role and its fulfillment to counteract so much of the fluff that is being dispensed under the label of religious education.

Critic

If the role of the scientist is scarce in the annals of religious education, then that of the critic is virtually invisible. Far too often religious educators have mindlessly handed on information without critically examining the content and form of that information. The critic calls a halt to such subservience and demands that the religious educator be circumspect in what he or she promotes and teaches. Tradition or antiquity are not valid reasons for the veneration of ideas, and the critic rigorously evaluates both concepts and activities for their merit and message. The effective critic establishes a sound basis for the evaluation and critique, and submits the evidence to the harsh light of objectivity—following it wherever it may lead. Performance of the role of critic in religious education is somewhat risky, since a critic who is constantly criticizing becomes like the little boy crying "wolf!"—after a while no one listens. Without the occasional warnings of the critic, however, the wolves would soon devour the flock. The genuine critic, though, is not some nay-sayer, or just a prophet of gloom. He or she is someone who analyzes the evidence from all the possible angles and shows why the issues demand both attention and alteration.

Storyteller

Identity and community result from shared stories. The religious educator plays a major part in developing identity and in binding the community together through the artful telling of these shared stories. The ancient role of the storyteller is not as easy to perform as it may initially appear, however. While the role does involve telling the basics of the story, as one would expect, it also carries responsibility for helping in the search for an interpretation and application of the story—all the while making the activity interesting and enjoyable. The storyteller is responsible for finding the deeper meanings in the panoply of facts and data and for communicating in a way that a mere presentation of data bits could never accomplish. The storyteller invites listeners to participate through the sharing of stories but at the same time teaches them to mold their identity by evaluating, modifying, and then applying these stories to the present. This may involve revising the stories themselves. The deceptively simple role of storyteller quickly reveals itself to be a complex but absolutely vital role for the religious educator to master.

Artist

The artist brings freshness, fun, and creativity to the work of religious education. Although some pedants seem to do their best to quash the life out of religious education, the artist rescues it from such a dire fate. Artists introduce their own kind of magic into religious education: They can take the boring and mundane and suddenly transform it into life itself with the flick of a brush or the stroke of a pen. Artists help people discover who they are—and who they are not—through their gifts of art, but in a very different fashion than that of the storyteller. They use, for example, music, painting, and sculpture to reveal dimensions of reality not discernible by the more earth-bound methods. The artist strives not only to portray reality; he or she helps to create and even invent it. Even more, it is not just that the artist sees the world differently; the artist enables each individual to see the world differently as well—and what amazing things suddenly appear!

Visionary

Some of these amazing sights also come from the unique viewpoint of the visionary. The visionary's watchword is: "The grass is always greener on the other side of the fence." The future is always beckoning, and the visionary brings people the hope, the imagination, and the courage to stretch toward the "not yet." The visionary generates energy, animation, and motivation that will not allow complacency or blissful acceptance of the status quo. The visionary offers insight into the farther reaches, and inspiration that more—always more—is possible. The visionary teaches followers to see with more than their eyes; he or she helps them to see the future with their hearts and their minds. The present is never adequate and is never quite satisfying to the religious educator in the role of visionary. There is always something beckoning just around the next bend in the road. The visionary refuses to let religious education ever become satisfied and sedentary but pulls it into tomorrow with a vision of what can be.

Revolutionary

Visions of the future that the visionaries give are necessary and important, but sometimes the mechanisms and technicalities of the current system seem to block the way to fundamental and permanent change. The revolutionary is an expert at analyzing the system, as well as in working to change its character—not just working within its strictures and structures but working to revolutionize the system itself to meet the current needs. The revolutionary prods the people into action, making them realize that at times the process of deconstruction must take place before any construction can take place. The religious educator as revolutionary does not sit back and wait for events to transpire or unfold but causes them to happen. The religious educator is no political animal or terrorist who manipulates people for his or her own power needs but instead works for the equality and autonomy of all peoples. The genuine revolutionary does not use force or power but acts to give all individuals the opportunities they require to become whole persons. The revolutionary is easy to identify—there is an unquenchable fire burning in the eyes and in the soul that demands transformation for the good of all, not just the powerful few.

Therapist

Comfort, support, healing, and companionship are the offerings of the religious educator as therapist. It is no accident that the role of therapist follows that of the revolutionary, since the upheaval of revolutionary change often requires a sympathetic ear and the healing touch. After the revolution, the issue is how to find integration and synthesis—how to make order out of the chaos. The therapist teaches each person to be present in as full a way as possible—emotionally, cognitively, and behaviorally. The therapist works to allow the true inner identity of each individual to be revealed, prized, and a honored—by the individual, by the therapist, and by the community. The therapist nurtures the fundamental courage to *be*.

The religious educator as therapist encourages the person to confront and to accept his or her true self and to bring it to wholeness. The therapist's role is an ironic one: It fades from view the closer it is studied, because the client is the true focus and intent of the process.

Minister

The task of the minister is simply put: The minister gives himself or herself away to any and to all that are needy, regardless of class, status, or creed. The call to ministry is the call to sacrifice and servanthood, and the genuine minister finds fulfillment in self-giving. The minister is not a gray eminence, sober and sour, but a celebrative and joyful person because he or she has tapped the vast wells of humanity—and found them to be truly satisfying. The minister pours out his or her life without regret, without fear, and without reserve. The minister does not give in order to gain identity. The minister already knows who he or she is and therefore offers all of himself or herself freely to others. The minister does not give to receive fame, fortune, or even thanks, but simply gives out of a deep source of humility and compassion. The risks are enormous, but the minister has discovered what is worth more than life itself—and is both ready and willing to give it away so that others may also find and experience true life.

Conclusion

These ten roles comprise the differentiative typologies that are offered to help define the true identity of the genuine religious educator. Each of the images receive fuller development—a chapter each—in Part Two, but even there the treatment is not complete. Rather than to try to be exhaustive, the attempt in Part Two is to be introductory, suggesting the rich potential which can be found within the ten integrative and systemic roles of the religious educator. To complete the survey of the identifying taxonomies of the religious educator, the task of Part One, it remains to describe the diagnostic categories used to describe these ten images. This is the subject of the next chapter.

Chapter Three

Diagnostic Categories
of the Religious Educator

Finding examples of categories for analyzing the religious educator is not nearly as difficult as searching for examples of differentiative typologies. The same two problems—particularism and a focus on the field rather than the educator—are still present, but they are familiar enough by now that they can be taken in stride. A recital of two of the standard ways of categorizing the field serves to introduce the primary agenda of this chapter—a presentation and brief explanation of the diagnostic categories of the religious educator employed throughout Part Two of this book.

What is now generally regarded as one of the classic statements of religious education categories was proposed by Harold William Burgess in 1975.[1] In his analytic work, *An Invitation to Religious Education*, Burgess employed these six categories: aim, content, teacher, student, environment, and evaluation. As Burgess admitted at the time: "No claim is made that this category system is exhaustive of the possibilities."[2] The categories served him well in his book and they have been employed by others in the field.[3]

More recently, Mary Boys created another set of categories in the work *Educating in Faith*.[4] Boys used what she called "foundational questions" as a means of analyzing the history of twentieth-century Christian religious educa-

---

1. Harold William Burgess, *An Invitation to Religious Education* (Birmingham, Ala.: Religious Education Press, 1975), especially p. 11.
2. Ibid.
3. Most notably by Ian P. Knox in *Above or Within?: The Supernatural in Religious Education* (Birmingham, Ala.: Religious Education Press, 1976).
4. Mary C. Boys, *Educating in Faith: Maps and Visions* (San Francisco: Harper & Row, 1989).

tion.[5] Under the guiding question of "What does it mean to be religious?" she asked further questions related to revelation, conversion, faith and belief, theology, and faith and culture. The basic question of "What does it mean to educate in faith?" prompted more questions about the goal of education, knowledge, social sciences, curriculum and teaching, and education as a political term.[6]

The categories used in this book to describe the roles of the religious educator have much in common with those of both Burgess and Boys, although at first glance may appear unconnected to either of them. The categories proposed here refer directly to the religious educator, rather than to the field, and this fact alone would make them distinctive. In addition, the categories offered are an effort to be both nonparticularistic and inclusive of more than the religious education of the twentieth century, and this has also changed the way the categories were selected and constructed.[7] What Burgess said about his categories is just as applicable here: "The . . . categories here employed do embody several notions evident in the category frameworks previously reviewed. However, the responsibility for the selection of these particular units rests with the present writer."[8]

Each of the following ten chapters of Part Two detailing the ten roles of the religious educator use the same categories. This allows for easy comparison of the images and for fitting the ten together into an integrated whole (addressed in Part Three). In introductory fashion, the elements of the outline used in Chapters Four through Thirteen are presented below along with a few explanatory remarks. A skeletal chart is provided at the end as Figure 5, and this paradigmatic chart reappears to sum up each of the chapters of Part Two.

Dimensions of the Role

Following a few short introductory paragraphs, each of the chapters on the roles of the religious educator begins with a section on the dimensions of the particular role being examined. In every case, four dimensions are given. Nothing magical or mystical should be attached to the number four. It is simply a matter of being uniform throughout the chapters when surveying the role in question. The four dimensions are never meant to be comprehensive descriptions of the role, nor are they designed to be definitive treatments of the role. The only purpose for the four dimensions is to provide a brief overview of the role where some commonality can be established for relating the role to the religious educator. Every effort has been made to use dimensions that both explicate the role and that connect the role to the religious educator. With this dual foci, some of the dimensions chosen will necessarily leave some areas of the image untouched, and other areas may receive undue attention in light of other aspects of the image. The

---

5. Boys struggled with the terminology of religious and Christian education too. See ibid., pp. 8-10, for her attempt at a solution.

6. See the discussion of these categorical questions in ibid, pp. 5-8, and the skeleton chart in ibid., pp. 9-10.

7. The categories of both Burgess and Boys make a good effort at nonparticularism. In addition, the books by Burgess and Boys are excellent resources for typologies of the religious educator discussed in the previous chapter.

8. Burgess, *An Invitation to Religious Education*, p. 11.

attempt is not so much to tell everything possible about the role, however, as it is to establish some common ground for the discussion of the religious educator when viewed from the perspective of the role. The intent is to concentrate on the relationship of the role with the religious educator, so some of the roles and their dimensions may look a bit skewed in their descriptions.

One of the most important considerations related to the images and to their dimensions is the matter of connectedness and integration. This topic receives specific attention in Chapter Fourteen, but it is vital to acknowledge here that the roles and the dimensions are all intimately connected and related and creating sharp divisions between any of them is neither possible nor desirable. Each of the roles and each of the dimensions are treated separately, out of necessity, but this should *not* be taken as a sign that they are totally distinct from one another. There is by design some degree of overlap, for example, between the roles, between the aims, and between the individuals chosen to represent the various roles. Because one person may illustrate a religious educator in the role of parent by no means disqualifies a person from participating in another role or in a dimension of another role. This book is not trying either to create or to enforce a rigid system of categories or stereotypes into which all religious educators must fit themselves exclusively. Such a reading would negate the systemic design, purpose, and intent of the book.

The truth is that the complete and genuine religious educator emerges through the composite of all these images and through an integration of all the dimensions presented. While various religious educators will display natural tendencies and inclinations toward one or more of the roles, the goal of the book is to encourage each religious educator to become ever more holistic and mature by expanding his or her repertoire of behaviors and approaches. The book affirms each person's strengths and abilities, while it encourages each to examine his or her weaknesses in order to become the more complete religious educator.

The parallel is found in leadership studies.[9] There is no one best way to lead, just as there is no one best way to be a leader. The challenge of being a leader is to be skilled in the practice of a wide variety of leadership styles, to be expert in diagnosing the environment and the specific situation, and then to perform the most suitable and productive form of leadership. Each person enters the study and practice of leadership with a preferred style of leadership, but becoming a better leader means matching styles of leadership with the needs of the particular situation. What is an effective leadership style in one situation is a failure in another—and just so with religious education. No one image is appropriate or helpful in every situation. The religious educator must first learn a variety of teaching styles and approaches, then develop the ability to diagnose the environment and the needs, and then finally employ the applicable role. The religious educator needs to be a master of all the roles and dimensions. Admittedly, no one enters the field with such diverse abilities or ever becomes totally adept at performing each and every role. The challenge and the commitment is to spend a lifetime

---

9. See, for example, the discussion on "situational leadership" in Paul Hersey and Ken Blanchard, *Management of Organizational Behavior: Utilizing Human Resources*, 4th ed. (Englewood Cliffs, N.J.: Prentice-Hall, 1982), pp. 149-175.

learning, diagnosing, and practicing, all to become an effective and complete religious educator.

Aim

Each chapter has a separate discussion on the aim of the religious educator from the perspective of the particular role being considered. In every case, the aim is derived first from the individual image itself and then applied to religious education. The image in its own right must be taken seriously, with the aim accurately portraying the purpose of someone functioning in the role; only then can it legitimately express the aim of the religious educator in that role. The goal is to let the role—the metaphor—speak for and of itself, thereby allowing it to illuminate the work of the religious educator. Every effort is made to keep from doing unnecessary violence to the role so that it can reveal itself freely.

The reason for the section on aim is to give clarity and focus to the work of the religious educator. After the discussion of the dimensions of the role, which provides context, the exposition of the role moves immediately to the aim. This is intentional and essential, because all that the religious educator does must have a clearly understood purpose and reason. The aim related to the specific role is stated early, and everything said about the religious educator in that role needs to contribute toward attaining that aim. The aim, discerned through analyzing the role, marks out the boundaries for what is appropriate to the role, as well as for what is inappropriate. This kind of specificity and clarity should help define the identity and the tasks of the religious educator, as well as make obvious who and what is not to be included in the assignments of the religious educator.

The depth of the religious educator becomes recognizable when all ten aims are disclosed. Religious education is not simple to accomplish, not easy to conceptualize, and not minor in its potential contribution. The sections on the aims of the religious educator are meant both to simplify and to complicate. Simplicity comes through understanding clearly the aims of the religious educator. Complexity arises when all ten aims are revealed and the enormity of the full task of the religious educator is realized.

Function

Immediately following the section on aims is a section on function. The first addresses the issue of purpose, the second the means of attaining that purpose. These two are not totally separate entities but are intimately related one to another. Just as the aim is clarified and molded through understanding function, so function affects and modifies the aim. Function is not simply that which "works." It is that which helps attain the stated aim. If the identified aim is not being achieved, then either the function is inappropriately chosen or the aim must be reevaluated. One of the criteria for deciding the propriety of functions depends on the successful attainment of aims.

The obvious question is, does the end (aim) justify the means? The answer is, no, of course not. Attainment of the end is only *one* criteria for evaluating the effectiveness of the means and for selecting appropriate means. The end no more dictates the means than the end is unaffected by the means. Again, the two are not mutually exclusive items but are two elements of the decision-making process religious educators employ to accomplish their tasks. A consideration of one necessitates a companion consideration of the other, and a modification of one calls for the modification of the other.

One danger is believing that the end justifies the means, but the opposite pitfall is believing that no overarching purpose or end is necessary for there to be a function. This is the source of random behavior which is so prevalent in much of religious education. Religious educators may have an hour to fill up every Sunday morning (euphemistically called Sunday school), for example, so whatever keeps the students quiet and orderly must be useful and effective. No intentional purpose—other than quietness and obedience—is ever stated, so virtually any function that is quiet and time-consuming (glorified baby-sitting) is acceptable. This is a case of the means justifying the end, which is just as ridiculous as its reverse and perhaps worse. Function without aim is damnable irresponsibility.

Primary Virtues

Each of the roles discussed is credited with responsibility for inculcating two primary virtues, which are then appropriated into the work of religious education. As in the dimensions of the roles, there is nothing magical or cosmic about the number of them. Two is the number selected for the discussion on virtues both to give adequate insight into the value-laden activity of religious education as well as to draw attention to the issue of virtues, thereby making it an overt part of the discussion on the religious educator.

It should be clear by now that this book is not addressing the religious educator from an exclusively or strictly Christian (or any other particular faith tradition) viewpoint, so for some the issue of values as expressed in naming the virtues of the religious educator is already out of bounds. These people would say that only faith traditions legitimately promote values, and probably would also believe (at least surreptitiously) that only their own particular faith tradition (or portion of it) promotes the proper values. It is the contention here that virtually any activity is a reflection of values, whether or not done intentionally or consciously, and that the religious educator can and does constantly promote values which are not the sole possession of any one faith tradition. This discussion of values is broader than any one faith tradition can call its own.

If this book were written from a particularistic position exclusively, then it would discuss and promote the specific values and practices identified with that faith tradition, such as Christianity or Buddhism. As detailed in Part One, this book is written from a more inclusive perspective, that of religion, and it specifically addresses religious education—as distinct from, say, Christian religious education. Religious education transcends or subsumes the particular faith traditions, so the values discussed are not those of any one faith tradition but are those of religion. The discussion of values is an effort to turn away from a particularistic argument about values and behavior, such as what happens in a theological argument. There the discussion is about beliefs or doctrines promoted by the specific faith tradition, and one ends up arguing that one set of beliefs is better than another because it rests on the particular faith tradition. The result is a round-robin argument that has no solution or resolution other than more argument that "my theology/faith tradition/creed is better than yours." The effort here, by contrast, is to try to identify values that transcend such petty divisions and arguments and that address a broader view of reality than any one faith tradition can hope to express. Whether or not it is successful is a legitimate question, but the issue of nonparticularistic values is important enough to qualify it for taking the risk.

The term "virtues" was chosen as a way to signal the intentional effort to highlight the healthy values of the genuine religious educator.[10] In the first chapter of this book, mention was made of the distinction between healthy and unhealthy religious education (see Figure 4). The religious educator who promotes values that lead toward health, integration, and harmony will display the virtues developed throughout each of the following ten chapters. The discussion on the overt designation of positive virtues may sound out of place in a book that espouses a social-science perspective, but in fact it is this very social-science approach which allows it. The social-science approach is value-free in the sense that no theologically driven system dictates the particular values or virtues.[11] The social-science approach is value-laden, however, in the sense that it *can* take on the positive values of science and of the improvement of health—exploration, data collection, objective evaluation, and so on—just as easily as it can underline the negative abuses of science—manipulation, objectification, reductionism, and so on. The sections on the virtues of the religious educator are only an attempt to highlight the "health-full" values that identify the genuine elements of the image under examination. Acknowledgement of the negative aspects of the images is made in a section of its own.[12]

Activity

An identifiable and distinctive activity flows naturally from each of the considered roles. These activities are expressed in the chapters as gerunds—verbal nouns—to denote the emphasis on action, on involvement, on doing. These sections stress that religious education is so much more than mere cognition or language. Religious education entails these but requires that the full range of human capacities be turned to the task as well. To shut off other capacities for religious education is to impoverish both the field and those that come to it for help. Fitting all of the ten identified activities together should give a sense of the

---

10. The term follows the use by Erik Erikson in his work on psychosocial development. In *Insight and Responsibility*, Erikson described virtues as "certain human qualities of strength." See Erik H. Erikson, *Insight and Responsibility: Lectures on the Ethical Implications of Psychoanalytical Insight* (New York: Norton, 1964), p. 113. For more, see the entirety of Chapter Four, "Human Strength and the Cycle of Generations," in ibid., pp. 109-157. Later Erikson used the phrase "basic strengths" in place of virtues. See Erik H. Erikson, *The Life Cycle Completed: A Review* (New York: Norton, 1982), pp. 32-33, in Chart One.

11. See this discussed, for example, in James Michael Lee, *The Content of Religious Instruction: A Social Science Approach* (Birmingham, Ala.: Religious Education Press, 1985), pp. 23-26.

12. This is the section discussed below concerning the shadow role.

diversity of religious education and of the variety of tasks both the religious educator and the learner are called upon to perform.

Shadow Role

In order that the religious educator not be seen as all sweetness and light, each role is turned around so that the shadow side of the role appears. The shadow role is the dark side, the dangerous part, the unfortunate result of any role when it is pressed too far. This section is a warning that not all religious education has to offer under its banner is healthy, regardless of its guise or garb. Every aspect of the religious educator must be examined and evaluated before it is integrated into the whole.

The concept of the "shadow role" is derived from the work of Carl Jung, where he referred to the shadow archetype.[13] The concept of this archetype has been described this way: "The shadow contains more of man's basic animal nature than any other archetype does. Because of its extremely deep roots in evolutionary history, it is probably the most powerful and potentially the most dangerous of all the archetypes. It is the source of all that is best and worse in man, especially in his relations with others of the same sex."[14] The shadow archetype in and of itself is not evil. It certainly has potential for evil if left unattended and uncontrolled, but the shadow also has great potential to offer to the positive side if it is acknowledged and integrated into the personality. The fuller description also contains this warning, however: "The person who suppresses the animal side of his nature may be civilized, but he does so at the expense of decreasing the motive power for spontaneity, creativity, strong emotions, and deep insights. He cuts himself off from the wisdom of his instinctual nature, a wisdom that may be more profound than any learning or culture can provide. A shadowless life tends to become shallow and spiritless."[15]

The use of the shadow role in this book springs from this basic idea but generally treats the shadow role as that which is left unattended, untamed, uncivilized, and unintegrated. In virtually every instance, the shadow roles of the religious educator are threats to the field, a result of taking potential in the direction of self-service and selfishness of the religious educator, rather than using the potential for the good of the learner.[16] The shadow roles are meant as warning sig-

---

13. As Jung wrote of the shadow: "This confrontation is the first test of courage on the inner way, a test sufficient to frighten off most people, for the meeting with ourselves belongs to the more unpleasant thing that can be avoided so long as we can project everything negative into the environment. But if we are able to see our own shadow and can bear knowing about it, then a small part of the problem has already been solved: We have at least brought up the personal unconscious. The shadow is a living part of the personality and therefore wants to live with it in some form. It cannot be argued out of existence or rationalized into harmlessness." Carl G. Jung, "Archetypes of the Collective Unconscious," in Vol. 9, Part 1, *The Archetypes and the Collective Unconscious,* trans. R.F.C. Hull, in *The Collected Works of C.G. Jung* (New York: Pantheon, 1959), p. 20.

14. Calvin S. Hall and Vernon J. Nordby, *A Primer of Jungian Psychology* (New York: Penguin Books, 1973), p. 48.

15. Ibid., p. 49.

16. The term "learner" is used here to designate the recipient of religious education. This is not an attempt to make a strict division between the educator and the recipient but is only a convenience of language.

nals as to what can result when the religious educator loses sight of the needs of the learner and instead uses the learner for his or her own needs. It is important to remember that the shadow role is omnipresent, always tracking what the religious educator does. The genuine religious educator acknowledges the presence and the temptations of the shadow but keeps the focus upon the learner and off himself or herself.

Faith Tradition Resource

It should be clear by now what this book means by faith tradition, since the discussion in Chapter One was an effort at definition and contextualization which included this concept. It is a term which signifies one specific expression of religion within the great sea of religion. Christianity provides one faith tradition, for example, and Buddhism provides another. Religion is the wider category that subsumes them both. "Faith tradition" recognizes that the total life of faith of an individual in a community is important and that the particular expression of faith is expressed and interpreted through an inherited set of traditions. Faith—active and present—is actualized within a set of traditions that are transmitted from one generation to the next. A faith tradition links together past and present within a specific context and within a particular environment.

"Faith tradition resource" is a way of saying that the various faith traditions stand as a vast array of potentiality for understanding and interpreting reality. Stepping into a faith tradition other than one's own provides a different perspective from which to view the same broad horizon. All the faith traditions are available to the religious educator as resources to deepen and widen the teaching and interpreting of religion. The use of the word "resource" is important because, regardless of one's own faith tradition, the other faith traditions stand as a deep repository of information, insight, and wisdom from which each person can draw. To utilize the resources other faith traditions offer does not mean one must join or commit his or her life to those faith traditions. The only commitment is to be open to learn from others and to respect their ways.

To be a genuine religious educator means to be aware and open to the resources available and not to be limited to the small pieces or fragments of truth each individual's faith tradition may have to offer. The partaking of a variety of faith tradition resources is an exercise in breaking down the old barriers of threat and exclusivism and meeting other faith traditions on their own terms—without fear or bigotry. Religious educators of the various faith traditions must welcome one another into the treasury of resources each has to offer the other, each learning and growing from intimate contact and sharing with the other. A religious educator who knows only his or her own faith tradition, and who works to keep it that way, is a sham and a fraud, unable and unworthy of accepting either the role or the responsibility of the effective and genuine religious educator.

Each of the roles is assigned a different faith tradition that serves as a resource for expanding the vision of the religious educator and for understanding more profoundly the particular role in question. There is no organic connection between the image and the faith tradition resource. It just provides another set of lenses through which to view and interpret the role.

Only enough of the various faith traditions is provided to introduce it and to show its possible contribution to the understanding of the role. Such a partial treatment of the faith traditions is not meant as a slight to any or all of the faith traditions, just as the exclusion of a particular faith tradition should not be taken as an indication that the specific faith tradition is somehow unworthy as a resource. These sections are meant to stimulate interest and to reveal the great value the wide assortment of faith traditions have for the work of religious education. Religious education is immeasurably disvalued and undernourished if it is forced to draw from only one or two faith tradition resources. This particular section of each chapter is designed to open up the panoramic vistas made visible by gazing through the perspectives of the different faith traditions.

The social-science approach allows for this kind of resourcing, while a strictly theological approach would need to rule it out. Social science is free to examine both the frameworks and the contents of the faith traditions and to learn from both activities. The theological approach is forced to design and determine one way, the right or orthodox theological way of its faith tradition, and stay within those specified boundaries. Social science is open to the variety of faith tradition resources, and is able to do evaluation, comparison, and integration, while the theological approach, if followed exclusively, most often separates and divides itself from other faith traditions in order to give its self its own identity. It seems that the theological approach decides which of the ways are right, and which are wrong, and never the twain shall meet. The social-science approach as espoused in this book suggests determining what is healthy and unhealthy based upon examination of the evidence, rather than on right belief or proper orthodoxy, and then learning from the encounter with truth and health wherever it may be discovered.

Historical Personage

Modern religious education is often assumed to have begun in the United States with the appearance of *Christian Nurture*, by Horace Bushnell, in the middle of the nineteenth century.[17] Another possible way to identify the dawn of the modern era is the establishment of the Religious Education Association (R.E.A.) in 1903. However helpful these historical designations may be to those locked in the confines of their own little slice of history and civilization, they do not adequately circumscribe the existence or the power of true religious education within the flow of human history. Religious education, in its broadest definition, ranges far beyond the categories of any one century, any one faith tradition, or any one culture.

The sections on historical personages are attempts to identify figures from history that can be identified as representatives of religious education activity, whether or not they were so understood or regarded either by themselves or by their contemporaries. This is a way of breaking free from rigid and stiff per-

---

17. The basic ideas of Horace Bushnell's *Christian Nurture* originated in some essays he published in 1838 but came to its final form when published in 1861. This is discussed in more detail in Chapter Four, "The Religious Educator as Parent."

ceptions of the religious educator that artificial boundaries like the publication of *Christian Nurture* or the establishment of the Religious Education Association tend to create. Religious educators have been active in a wide variety of contexts through the centuries, and these sections are an effort to help them appear in this new and different light. The historical personages sections of the book illustrate the respective roles, which is the individuals' more normal designation, as well as portrays them as religious educators, which will strike some as being a bit of an abnormal representation. Any cognitive dissonance that arises from such a viewpoint in the short term hopefully will serve to elucidate in the longer term.

Contemporary Example

Where the purpose for the sections on historical religious education personages is an attempt to be somewhat nontraditional in the selection of religious educators, the purpose of the sections on contemporary examples of religious educators is generally to provide some treatment of the traditional and expected representatives from present-day religious educators. Cognitive dissonance is not so much the goal here as analysis and evaluation of current activity in the field related to the various roles of the religious educator. These sections that identify religious educators of today present them in the light of the various roles and demonstrate that the roles selected are not totally new ideas or concepts unrelated to religious education but rather are different means of surveying and perceiving the field.

Admittedly, these religious educators did not write or perform consciously to fit into the images described here, so care and attention to fairness is absolutely essential. Failure of any of the writers to fulfill their assigned roles cannot be their fault, since the roles are being laid over work already completed. It may also be that, given the option, individual writers would choose not to be identified in the roles assigned here. This again was not their choice, but a result of my consequent effort to illustrate and explain the various roles.

Two additional caveats related to the use of contemporary examples are quite important. First, all of the writings of the persons chosen as examples could not be included here, for the obvious reasons of space and focus. This necessarily gives a biased and partial view of the theorists' work. Though the vast majority of the representatives' work has been examined, only a tiny portion is offered as illustration of the fulfillment of the roles. Hopefully the small slices offered here will be faithful representations of the whole, while stimulating readers to do their own reading of the primary sources in more depth. Nothing more than introduction and categorization is attempted here. Second, the classifications employed in the book are not intended to be straitjackets from which there is no escape. Because a theorist is presented as representing one particular role does not exclude him or her from participating in another. The boundaries between the roles are not rigid, but flexible and permeable. Some overlap of the roles and their illustrators is expected and natural. The desire here is not to isolate or fragment, but to identify and distinguish positions and approaches. The *dominant* role for each contemporary example is the one examined, with awareness that other images may, and probably do, complement it.

Each contemporary example is treated in two ways. The first section overviews the religious educator's approach as related to the assigned role. The second section evaluates the theorist's contributions, both in relation to the field of religious education and to the understanding and fulfillment of the specific role. In every case, the focus remains on the *role*, which is the subject of the chapter, while the theorist is only one possible manifestation of that role. The role is the standard and the theorist is being compared to it—not the other way around. This allows the primary attention and evaluation to fall upon the standard and not the individual theorist. This is important because of the limited amount of space given to each theorist in the midst of the much larger volume of writings each of them has produced.

Representative Teaching Procedure

Further illustration of the roles of the religious educator is provided through the suggestion of a teaching procedure that relates specifically to the image under scrutiny. This emphasizes that at bottom the religious educator is always doing some kind of teaching and that as a teacher he or she must possess a variety of procedures, skills, and approaches to attain his or her aim.[18] The panoply of roles for the religious educator suggests at least as many teaching styles that correlate to the various roles.

For ease of reference for the reader, and for some sense of continuity, many of the basic teaching procedures have been drawn from or at least make reference to the book *Models of Teaching* by Bruce Joyce and Marsha Weil.[19] Books on teaching procedures abound, but this particular one is used in a wide variety of contexts of teacher training. Hopefully it is available readily enough to readers so that it can be consulted for pursuing the necessary details. In addition, in virtually every case primary resources related to the teaching procedures have been referenced so that the reader can do some exploration beyond the limits of what is contained in any one resource.

No one should have the idea that the only way to perform the role in question is to use the representative teaching procedure. The procedure is only a suggestion. It is a way of saying that different roles require different teaching approaches. In religious education, there is no one best way to do anything—especially when it comes to teaching procedures.

The sections on teaching procedures are acknowledgment that the religious educator is essentially a teacher and that variety is integral to the performance of the roles. It is also only one aspect of the religious educator and one to be pur-

---

18. "Teaching is that orchestrated process whereby one person deliberately, purposively, and efficaciously structures the learning situation in such a manner that specified learning outcomes are thereby acquired by another person." James Michael Lee, *The Flow of Religious Instruction: A Social Science Approach* (Birmingham, Ala.: Religious Education Press, 1973), p. 206. For a fuller explanation of this definition, see all of Chapter Eight, "The Nature of Teaching," in ibid., pp. 206-229.

19. Bruce Joyce and Marsha Weil, *Models of Teaching*, 3rd ed. (Englewood Cliffs, N.J.: Prentice-Hall, 1986).

sued in light of other issues such as aims, functions, and virtues. Teaching procedures are selected and performed for reasons other than the sake of variety, which is to say that the teaching procedures themselves must never be allowed to take primacy over what they are to teach. The religious educator must know why he or she employs the various teaching procedures; otherwise, the cart begins pulling the horse.

Experiential Simulation

In *Systemic Religious Education*, the term "simulation" was defined as "an actual, concrete demonstration of a theoretical model."[20] Simulations move from the purely abstract toward the realm of experience. In each chapter of Part Two, suggestions for translating the words about the role into an activity or experience provide a way of actualizing the concepts. Simulations are also a signal to put the book down and go do something, rather than just to think about doing it.

Simulations are still one step away from full participation in the role. Simulations are for practicing the role. They prepare as closely as possible for real-life experience without actually performing the role in a religious education activity. The next step from simulations is religious education "in the flesh." As described in *Systemic Religious Education*, simulations are an integral part of the systemic perspective, along with paradigms, worldview, and models.[21] Simulations are the confirmation and the working out of the systemic process, much like experiments verify and demonstrate the value of a particular theory.

The term "experiential" emphasizes that religious education is more than either theory or practice but is a dynamic synthesis of both that creates a whole and radically different entity. Experiential simulations are means for accomplishing and for demonstrating this integrative activity in some concrete and substantive manner.

Summary

Each chapter of Part Two closes with a brief attempt to summarize the particular role. The chief feature of the summary section is the chart, which provides a reference point for each role. Each of the sections and its specific manifestation in the chapter is mapped for purposes of review and comparison (see the example, Figure 5, below). So that the roles and their component categories may be viewed together, a comprehensive chart of all ten roles is provided in Chapter Fourteen.

---

20. Timothy Arthur Lines, *Systemic Religious Education* (Birmingham, Ala.: Religious Education Press, 1987), p. 38.

21. See, for example, ibid., pp. 34-39. Further discussion of the systemic perspective and its influence on the development of the ten roles of the religious educator is provided in Chapter Fourteen, "Systemic Integration of the Religious Educator."

Figure 5: Diagnostic Categories of the Religious Educator	
Dimensions of the Role	
Aim	
Function	
Primary Virtues	
Activity	
Shadow Role	
Faith Tradition Resource	
Historical Personage	
Contemporary Example	
Representative Teaching Procedure	
Experiential Simulation	

Part Two

Multiple Roles
of the Religious Educator

Chapter Four

The Religious Educator as Parent

The religious educator in the role of parent is by no means a new or novel invention. From a historical and developmental perspective, the role of parent may very well be the earliest and most fundamental role of all.[1] The goal of this chapter is therefore not so much to suggest anything particularly new or revolutionary about the role of parent as to compile and integrate a variety of thoughts and perspectives on the role as it relates specifically to the religious educator. In so doing, the field of religious education should be stimulated by viewing itself from this standpoint. This chapter, then, is part of an overview of the religious educator's professional identity rather than a complete and comprehensive description of the individual role of parent itself.

One of the thickets from which there seems to be no exit is the search for an adequate and inclusive definition of family. A discussion of the role of parent inevitably becomes closely tied to that of family, but this chapter does not focus on the family per se. It accents the parent, which represents an integral part of the larger family system while remaining a valid system in and of itself. For

---

1. The helplessness of the newborn and the time it takes to mature was described years ago by the pioneering developmentalists Arnold Gesell and Frances Ilg: "Man, of all creatures, has the longest period of relative immaturity. He is so complex that it takes him over twenty years to grow up, physically and mentally." Arnold Gesell and Francis L. Ilg, *Child Development: An Introduction to the Study of Human Growth* (New York: Harper & Row, 1949), p. 10 of Book II, "The Child from Five to Ten." In Book I, "Infant and Child in the Culture of Today," these authors wrote: "It is man's distinction that he has the longest infancy. . . . The more complex and advanced the mature organism, the longer the period of infancy." Ibid., p. 13. This period of increasing maturity and development is the period that requires the care and nurture of the parent. The roles of the parent and of the religious educator have also been linked for centuries. Jewish scripture, for example, instructs parents to "keep these words that I am commanding you today in your heart. Recite them to your children and talk about them when you are at home and when you are away, when you lie down and when you rise." Deuteronomy 6:5-6, NRSV.

example, William Nichols and Craig Everett defined the family as "a multi-generational system characterized by several internally functioning subsystems and influenced by a variety of external, adjunctive systems."[2] While this definition stays away from the kind of definition of family that describes a father, a mother, two children, and a dog, if this definition were the operational one for this chapter a lot of time would be spent looking at other internal systems as well as external ones. The focus on the parent would be lost in the welter of environmental concerns. This chapter targets only specific "internally functioning subsystems" while recognizing the value and influence of the myriad of environmental forces.[3]

The preferred term in this chapter is "parent," but others have proposed different or alternative phrases. One term that has some popularity is "primary care giver," but that sounds rather cold and impersonal for describing the fullness of the role under discussion in this chapter. To try to be generic, Erik Erikson used the term "maternal person" to refer to the female parental role, and then "parental persons" to refer to the mother and father figures.[4] These too seem to be unnecessary substitutions for the purposes of this effort. The term used in this chapter is simply "parent," denoting a person of an earlier generation who is responsible for giving care and nurture to a member of a later generation.[5]

While the attention in this chapter is primarily upon the member of the "earlier generation" (the parent), there must be members of a later generation who need that care and nurture[6] (the children) in order for the role to have meaning. The dynamism inherent in the role of the parent thus immediately becomes apparent. Heraclitus, a philosopher of ancient Greece, said that you can never step in the same river twice.[7] The same can be said of parenting: You can never par-

---

2. William C. Nichols and Craig A. Everett, *Systemic Family Therapy: An Integrative Approach* (New York: Guilford Press, 1986), p. 91.

3. The difficulties of trying to find acceptable terminology was illustrated by Gabriel Moran. He proposed defining families as "patterns of life in which . . . people find inclusion, care, and a sense of personhood." See Gabriel Moran, *Religious Education as a Second Language* (Birmingham, Ala.: Religious Education Press, 1989), p. 42. Moran then ran into the problem of homosexual relationships and whether or not they could constitute a family in his definition. He ended up calling these a "nonfamilial but personalizing form of life," which certainly has a hollow ring to it at best. Ibid. Also see a related discussion in Gabriel Moran, *Education Toward Adulthood* (New York: Paulist, 1979), pp. 96-100.

4. Erik H. Erikson, *The Life Cycle Completed: A Review* (New York: Norton, 1982), p. 32 (listed on the chart under the category of "Radius of Significant Relations").

5. In this definition, I am hesitant to call the parent the primary care giver, not just because it sounds so sterile, but because of the systemic nature of the care and nurture of a child. Although in one sense it is of course true that the parent or parents are primarily responsible for giving the care needed by the infant, in a broader view there are hosts of familial and societal persons who play a highly influential part in the development of a child's personality and environment. The message and the metaphor of this chapter is not limited only to those biological or legal individuals normally assumed to be parents within the nuclear family. One caveat must be added to the definition above: When parents age, then their children often have to provide the care and nurture, thus reversing the generational formula. The issue, in other words, is not really one of chronological age.

6. This is what Erik Erikson called living in a "community of life cycles." See Erik H. Erikson, *Identity and the Life Cycle* (New York: Norton, 1980; first published in 1959), p. 130.

7. "You cannot step twice into the same river, for fresh waters are ever flowing in upon you." Heraclitus, as quoted by Frederick Copleston, *A History of Philosophy*: Vol. I, "Greece and Rome," Part One, rev. ed. (Garden City, N.Y.: Image Books, 1962), p. 55.

ent the same child twice. Even more sobering: You are called upon to parent a different child each day! The ceaseless processes of development manifested in each child each day require that we must constantly learn to parent differently. No one tried-and-true pattern is effective for each day and for each child. Being a good parent means growing, developing, and responding appropriately to the perpetually changing needs of the individual child.

Another disquieting but crucial facet of the parental role was expressed by Nichols and Everett: "In a very real sense, parents are putting themselves out of a job from the beginning of their days as parents. Childrearing involves a continual and sometimes tenuous balancing of the dependency scales, providing the youngster with adequate amounts of support and dependency while at the same time encouraging autonomous and independent functioning."[8] The parent has the long-range task of enabling the child eventually to become independent of—or more accurately, interdependent with—the parent.[9] From the very first, the goal is to prepare the little one to begin functioning effectively without the parent. It is imperative (if not also threatening) to keep this view of "unemployment" within at least peripheral vision during the exploration of the role of parent[10] and its applicability to the religious educator. One of the keys to the role of parent is understanding that the children of today are the parents of tomorrow and that the parents of today will be gone tomorrow.

Dimensions of the Role

Four dimensions of the role of parent are examined below to see what they have to teach the religious educator: provider, protector, model, and theologian. These dimensions, and the discussions of them, are not intended to be fully descriptive of the parent's task. They are the dimensions most instructive to the formation of the religious educator. The role of the parent is proposed as an illustrative metaphor, and after a point any metaphor becomes strained. In other words, what follows is not a parenting manual but a look at parenting for the edification of the religious educator. Just enough is provided to get a feel for the various dimensions of the role of parent so that points of application can be found for the religious educator.

Provider

The first and foremost responsibility of a parent is to provide the child with proper and necessary provisions that permit healthy development. Food, clothing, and shelter are basic elements needed for all human growth and health. While every culture and every era has its own types of resources to give, the basic necessities remain the same. The responsibility of the parent is to provide what is needed at the appropriate time and in sufficient quantities. Whatever else

---

8. Nichols and Everett, *Systemic Family Therapy*, p. 167.

9. This is evidence of how the roles of the parent and the child change and evolve as the relationship and the needs change and evolve.

10. "The repeated rejection and recovery of the parents is historic, adaptive, and inevitable, if painful for the parents." Jerome Kegan, *The Evolving Self: Problems and Process in Human Development* (Cambridge: Harvard University Press, 1982), p. 217.

societies demand, the meeting of these fundamental needs is always required.

Part of the difficulty of being a parent is trying to decide what is truly necessary and appropriate, as opposed to simply what is desirable. Clothing, for example, is a requirement for all parents to satisfy, but what kind? Is a child being deprived if he or she is made to wear "plain pocket" jeans and not designer jeans? Shelter is another necessity, but does this mean a house with a roof that does not leak or one with a swimming pool in the backyard? These trivial examples illustrate the kinds of decisions the parent must make to provide the "basic elements" a child needs for proper development.[11]

Similarly, what are the basic requirements for being "religiously educated"? If the religious educator in the role of parent is to provide the basic necessities, what are they, and who decides? What is necessary, and what is merely desirable? The precise answers to these questions are culture specific, but raising the questions identifies a fundamental responsibility of the religious educator. Religious educators, in the role of parent, must help determine what the basic necessities of the field should be for the development and health of those in their care and then find effective means of making them available.

Another aspect of the dimension of provider is that the parent makes certain resources available but is not finally responsible for how they are consumed, Prospective parents, for example, are often worried about how they are going to make the newborn baby eat. That problem normally turns out to be the least of many when the baby does indeed arrive. Parents find that they do not "make the baby eat." They simply see that proper food is available to the child at the appropriate times (appropriate for the child, that is) and in appropriate forms. The actual consumption of the food is beyond the responsibility of the role of the parent and illustrates what the child must and will learn to do for himself or herself. What parents are able to do, instead, is to structure the situation and the environment properly so that the eating does take place in a proper and timely fashion.[12]

These issues are parallel to those confronted by the religious educator performing in the role of parent. The responsibility of the religious educator is to prepare and to provide appropriate kinds of resources for his or her charges, at appropriate times, in appropriate amounts, and in appropriate forms. The religious educator is not responsible for consuming and utilizing those resources for the students, since religious education is not so totally under the control of the religious educator that the engagement of the learner is excluded. Religious education is an interaction, an interface of relationships that posits just as much responsibility and respect onto the learner as it does on the provider. If the religious educator is providing some kind of "food" that is not being consumed, then the

---

11. The issue of what is essential and what is indulgent received popular discussion in David Elkind, *Miseducation: Preschoolers at Risk* (New York: Knopf, 1988), especially in pp. 29-51.

12. This illustration demonstrates that in some ways the parent is like a social scientist in his or her educational activities, since the effective educator does not force learners to learn but so structures the environment that the conditions for learning are greatly enhanced. For example, see James Michael Lee, who wrote: "Indeed the extent of an individual's learning is typically dependent on the power of his environment." James Michael Lee, *The Flow of Religious Instruction: A Social Science Approach* (Birmingham, Ala.: Religious Education Press, 1973), p. 65.

problem is a mutual one for both the provider and the "consumer."

One challenge of the religious educator is matching the level of complexity of the subject matter or experience with the development level of the person needing it. Just as formula and cereal are good and nourishing for an infant but quite inadequate for a teenager, so the religious educator must learn what form of "nourishment" is appropriate for those particular individuals he or she is teaching. In terms of curriculum development, the concept that attempts to describe this need is the "spiral" curriculum discussed by the educational psychologist Jerome Bruner. Bruner was convinced that virtually any topic or subject could be taught to nearly any child of any age if the instructor is adequately skilled. He said: "Any idea or problem or body of knowledge can be presented in a form simple enough so that any particular learner can understand it in a recognizable form."[13] The "spiral" part of the curriculum relates to ensuring that what is learned at a younger age and level of complexity is wholly consonant with what is being done by those more advanced in both age and complexity. Bruner believed it essential for there to be "a continuity between what a scholar does on the forefront of his discipline and what a child does in approaching it for the first time."[14] This need for continuity is essential so that eventually the learner does not have to "unlearn" some of the information or procedures learned earlier.

The idea of a spiral curriculum presents the religious educator as provider with some difficult practical realities. Take an obvious but still troublesome example, as when Christians try to explain Easter to a preschooler. The challenge is to be honest, factual, and orthodox while also paying attention to the child's intellectual development, sensitivity level, and emotional well-being. The religious educator is forced to make decisions carefully about exactly where on the "spiral" he or she begins to tell the story. While the gruesome details of crucifixion and burial are obviously unnecessary and inappropriate for younger children, these tender and sensitive learners can still be helped to celebrate and appreciate Easter without nightmares haunting them. The religious educator carries the dual responsibility for teaching the children in such a way that they do not have to "unlearn" at a later date what was taught and for taking care of the children developmentally.

The above paragraph illustrates only one type of provision, in this instance a conceptual one. The parent and the religious educator in the role of parent are responsible for providing much more than just stories or basic cognitive information. More sweepingly, the parent is responsible for providing a rich, experiential environment where child and parent engage in deep relationship with one another on a wide variety of levels. The parent and the child experience life together, learn about each other, and reflect on their experiences together, thereby forging a bond much stronger than a superficial exchange of words could ever allow. Provision relates fundamentally to an entire lifestyle, never limited to the material or to the mental aspects of life.

---

13. Jerome S. Bruner, *Toward a Theory of Instruction* (Cambridge: Harvard University Press, 1966), p. 44.

14 . Jerome S. Bruner, *The Process of Education* (New York: Vintage Books, 1960), p. 28.

The dimension of provider also helps to determine what the religious educator does *not* provide. A large part of the role of parent is gradually allowing the child to become interdependent (not necessarily independent—none of us ever becomes totally self-sufficient). Where early in life the infant has virtually every need and desire met immediately by the parent, over time the child is expected to do more and more for himself or herself. Demanding too much responsibility too soon for taking care of oneself can of course be damaging, but so can too little too late. The fine art of being a parent is learning when and how to let the child do things on his or her own. The religious educator must learn the same lesson as the parent: At times the only way for a person to learn something is to try it on his or her own. The caring religious educator is constantly evaluating when it is better to hold back and let the individual do his or her own searching alone. This often proves to be as difficult for the religious educator as it is for the searcher, but it is the path to personal growth and interdependence.

Protector

Closely related to the dimension of provider is that of protector—so closely related, in fact, that in some respects they need to be taken together. While it is the responsibility of the parent to provide the basic resources for a child such as food and clothing, it is just as essential for the parent to provide a safe and protective environment. This dimension of protector is so important, however, both to the parent and to the religious educator, that it is addressed in this separate section.

A time-honored, if not somewhat romantic, notion of the parent is that of the gardener. Jean-Jacques Rousseau (1712-1778) used the idea with far-reaching influence, portraying the parent[15] (or more properly, the tutor) as primarily charged with the responsibility of keeping evil society away from the guileless child, allowing that child to grow and develop "naturally."[16] Rousseau took the approach that the child would unfold like a blossoming flower in its natural habitat, so the tutor or care-giver was charged with the task of keeping external "unnatural" forces away from the child. The tutor did not protect the child from the effects of the natural environment. If the child learned about fire from burning himself, then this was proper and expected. It was the foreign influences of society that Rousseau believed would inhibit and deform the fresh and innocent new "plant" and which posed the real danger to the child. The opening words of Rousseau's *Emile* heralded in many ways the coming age of developmentalism: "Everything is good as it leaves the hands of the Author of things; everything degenerates in the hands of man."[17]

Not far removed from Rousseau's naturalistic gardening ideas were the humanistic psychology propositions of Abraham Maslow (1908-1970). As he

---

15. There is some risk in citing Rousseau in a discussion on the role of parent, since his own well-known failings in this area certainly do not set him up as the paragon of fatherhood. I also distance myself from Rousseau's views on the education of Sophia!

16. "Plants are shaped by cultivation, and men by education." See Jean-Jacques Rousseau, *Emile, or On Education*, trans. Allan Bloom (New York: Basic Books, 1979), p. 38.

17. Ibid., p. 37. Note the male language in this quote. The sexism of Rousseau was intentional, since he was writing primarily on male education.

tried to position his approach alongside behaviorism and psychoanalysis—now referred to, logically, as "Third Force" psychology—Maslow mused about what he called the "inner nature" of the human.[18] He warned: "This inner core . . . is weak in certain senses rather than strong. It is easily overcome, suppressed or repressed. It may even be killed off permanently."[19] Therefore, the parent (actually Maslow was writing as a psychologist) must take special pains to ensure that this "inner core" be adequately protected and nourished,[20] thereby nurturing the "self-actualization" of the child's personality. Maslow was saying that the task of the psychologist/parent/religious educator is to provide a sheltered environment for the young, allowing their "inner natures" to develop and grow—to bloom like the blossoming flowers Rousseau imagined.

A religious educator who has focused on providing a proper environment for growth and development has been John Westerhoff. In his book *Will Our Children Have Faith?* Westerhoff proposed that religious educators move from the "schooling-instructional paradigm"[21] to what he called a "community of faith-enculturation paradigm."[22] Within this community of faith, the individual would be given the needed support and nurture for healthy and natural development. The community that Westerhoff envisioned would help the person move through various "styles" of faith,[23] one of which would be "searching" faith, where the individual would be allowed and expected to experiment with different faith communities before deciding which faith community to join as an adult.[24] Westerhoff was suggesting that if a faith community takes its task seriously then it will provide a safe environment for as long as the individual needs it. At the appropriate time, prepared with adequate development and identity, the person ventures out of that protective environment and seeks his or her own way. Such "leaving the nest" is evidence of the success of the nurture the environment provided. Interestingly enough, Westerhoff believed that if the nurture was properly given, in most instances the person, when fully grown, would later return to the original faith community and commit his or her life to it through an "owned faith."[25]

---

18. See Abraham H. Maslow, *Toward a Psychology of Being*, 2nd ed. (New York: Van Nostrand Reinhold, 1968), especially pp. 189-214.

19. Ibid., p. 191.

20. "This inner nature is not strong and overpowering and unmistakable like the instincts of animals. It is weak and delicate and subtle and easily overcome by habit, cultural pressure, and wrong attitudes toward it." Ibid., p. 4. For a summary of Maslow's description of the "inner nature," see ibid. pp. 3-4.

21. John H. Westerhoff III, *Will Our Children Have Faith?* (New York: Seabury, 1976), p. 6. Weterhoff was rejecting the notion that religious education must take its procedures and methods from the secular or public school educational processes.

22. Ibid., p. 50. This basic idea of faith enculturation was advanced by C. Ellis Nelson in his writings and is discussed in greater detail later in this chapter.

23. Ibid., pp. 89-103. These "styles" are distinct from but related to James Fowler's stages of faith. Fowler's work is discussed in Chapter Six, "The Religious Educator as Scientist."

24. Ibid., pp. 96-97.

25. Ibid., pp. 98-99. It is important to note that Westerhoff was not basing his "styles" of faith on empirical evidence or developing them from a theory base. It was purely his speculation that such styles may exist. The approach of Westerhoff differs greatly from that of Fowler, who did employ the gathering of supporting data for his propositions.

Rousseau, Maslow, and Westerhoff depict the dimension of the protector within the role of parent. An image descriptive of each is the gardener: one who provides the essential protection of a safe environment so that each individual "plant" can develop to its fullest potential.

Model

A model is "a pattern of behavior that can be copied by someone else,"[26] and modeling is the type of "learning process in which individuals copy the behavior of others."[27] The dimension of model in the role of parent, therefore, surprises no one who has spent much time caring for children. Modeling, or imitation, means that the actions, moves, and expressions parents see in their children are often mirror images of their own actions, moves, and expressions. Much of the teaching that happens is accomplished through modeling, which means that humans do a lot of this kind of teaching—virtually constantly—and that most of this teaching remains unintentional and unevaluated. Modeling is one of the most potent and prevalent forms of teaching, although admittedly one difficult to evaluate in its total effect.

The need for the religious educator to plumb the depths of this manner of teaching is crucial. Too often it is assumed that teaching is done primarily through an identified subject matter or curriculum, or in formal environments.[28] While certainly this kind of subject matter is vitally important, the religious educator as a person, the conduct of the religious educator in community, and his or her priorities in life provide the primary content regardless of the assigned, formalized curriculum. Modeling leads inexorably to the topic of identification, which is defined as "incorporating within oneself the behavior and qualities of a person one respects and wants to emulate."[29] The personal example set by the religious educator as parent is thus a potent influence on the ensuing identity of the learners under his or her care. The result of all this is that the personhood and the lifestyle of the religious educator are just as powerful teaching agents as the chosen subject matter—if not more so.

Albert Bandura's social learning theory has begun to fathom the awesome power of modeling. Other than inborn reflexes, Bandura believed that all other behavior "repertoires" must be learned. These new behaviors can be learned in one of two ways: through direct experience or through observation.[30] Direct experience, in and of itself and without an intervening matrix of theory and research, is an effective but relatively inefficient way of learning, since everything must be performed in order to learn it, as in the trial and error method.[31]

26. Guy R. Lefrancois, *The Lifespan,* 2nd ed. (Belmont, Calif.: Wadsworth, 1987), p. 587.

27. Riva Specht and Grace J. Craig, *Human Development: A Social Work Perspective*, 2nd ed. (Englewood Cliffs, N.J.: Prentice-Hall, 1987), p. 270.

28. This is the point Westerhoff and others, such as C. Ellis Nelson (discussed in the contemporary example section of this chapter), were making about the power of the community to teach. It is a recognition of the influence informal environments have on personal development.

29. Specht and Craig, *Human Development*, p. 269.

30. Albert Bandura, *Social Learning Theory* (Englewood Cliffs, N.J.: Prentice-Hall, 1977), p. 16.

31. "The more rudimentary mode of learning, rooted in direct experience, results from the positive and negative effects that actions produce." Ibid., p. 17.

While something learned in this manner often does stay with a person, to have to do everything in order to learn it is not only time-consuming but redundant. A great many things can be learned much more quickly and efficiently through the second method of learning, that of observation, or modeling. As Bandura put it: "Learning would be exceedingly laborious, not to mention hazardous, if people had to rely solely on the effects of their own actions to inform them what to do. Fortunately, most human behavior is learned observationally through modeling: From observing others one forms an idea of how new behaviors are performed, and on later occasions this coded information serves as a guide for action. Because people can learn from example what to do, at least in approximate form, before performing any behavior, they are spared needless errors."[32] Bandura went on to detail how this "social learning" takes place,[33] providing a useful guide for the religious educator as he or she becomes aware of how he or she serves as an observational model of behavior.[34]

The rule here is the old adage that "actions speak louder than words." Teach a child the Ten Commandments while smoking a cigarette, and probably the most predominant and memorable lesson you have taught the child is how to smoke a cigarette.[35] The same holds true for every act the religious educator performs, whether he or she is conscious of it or not.

Theologian

The fourth dimension of the religious educator as parent makes a special case of the previous dimension. Though modeling is still in focus, now the discussion turns to how one's image of God is reformed through modeling, or more specifically, how the religious educator plays a part in the development of the God representation. In more common parlance, this is the dimension and the activity of the theologian.[36]

---

32. Ibid., p. 22.

33. Ibid., especially pp. 22-29. Here Bandura explained the processes of observational learning. More on this crucial teaching processes is discussed later in the chapter under the heading of "representative teaching procedure."

34. "Social learning theory" covers broad territory, and I do not wish to imply that either the discussion above or the one book by Bandura is an adequate treatment of it. Additional study on Bandura should include his *Principles of Behavior Modification* (New York: Holt, Rinehart and Winston, 1969) and *Aggression: A Social Learning Analysis* (Englewood Cliffs, N.J.: Prentice-Hall, 1973). For early work in the area, see Julian B. Rotter, *Social Learning and Clinical Psychology* (Englewood Cliffs, N.J.: Prentice-Hall, 1954), and O. Hobart Mowrer, *Learning Theory and Behavior* (New York: Wiley, 1960). For later developments see Robert R. Sears, Lucy Rau, and Richard Alpert, *Identification and Child Rearing* (London: Tavistock Publications, 1965); Arthur W. Staats, *Social Behaviorism* (Homewood, Ill.: Dorsey, 1975); and Ted L. Rosenthall and Barry J. Zimmerman, *Social Learning and Cognition* (New York: Academic Press, 1978). For an overview of the area, a good place to start is "Social Learning Theories of Child Development," which comprises Chapter 18 of Alfred L. Baldwin, *Theories of Child Development*, 2nd ed. (New York: Wiley, 1980), pp. 439-480.

35. An interesting parallel point was made by James Michael Lee in "Facilitating Growth in Faith Through Religious Instruction," in *Handbook of Faith*, ed. James Michael Lee (Birmingham, Ala.: Religious Education Press, 1990), p. 266.

36. Most parents, and probably many religious educators, may feel a bit uncomfortable with the designation of theologian. I am not suggesting here that the term be understood in its academic or scholarly sense but that parents and religious educators in the role of parent be "functional theolo-

The concept of God representation stems from object relations and transitional object relations theory, based in large part on psychoanalytic presuppositions.[37] One of the more fruitful discussions has been the one led by Ana-Maria Rizzuto in the ground-breaking work, *The Birth of the Living God*.[38] Rizzuto built her work upon a psychoanalytic foundation, which meant a necessarily heavy reliance on the writings of Sigmund Freud, but she did not accept the theories of Freud uncritically; indeed, she brought some highly important criticisms and revisions to bear on his approach.[39] Rizzuto, incidentally, did not address whether or not there is a God.[40] She only investigated *how* an individual develops a personal *image* of God. The question of whether or not there is a "God above God," to use Paul Tillich's phrase,[41] did not concern Rizzuto in her study. She stated the limits of her position clearly: "My area of competence is the formation of the God representation during childhood and its modifications and uses during the entire course of life. It is the process that I call the 'birth of the living God.'"[42]

Where Sigmund Freud was convinced that any belief in a supernatural being was evidence of illusion and delusion,[43] Rizzuto made no such claim. In fact, Rizzuto claimed that all persons, healthy or disturbed, carry within themselves an image of God (this was also Freud's contention), but that this image is not evidence of delusion (contra Freud). The internalized image of God is simply one of the "givens" of being human. Images of God will never be eliminated from human experience,[44] because it is forged from the relationship between child and parent(s). Rizzuto explained: "It is out of this matrix of facts and fantasies, wishes, hopes, and fears in the exchanges with those incredible beings called parents, that the image of God is concocted."[45] Humans in the future are sure to have God images as long as children have parents, because "every human child

---

gians"—teaching and influencing the development of the image of God in the midst of communal and personal lifestyles.

37. Although the development of object relations theory cannot be traced here, an excellent place to start reading on this topic is the work of D. W. Winnicott. For a primary work that presents the concept succinctly, see D. W. Winnicott, *Playing and Reality* (New York: Basic Books, 1971). For a secondary source, see Madeleine Davis and David Wallbridge, *Boundary and Space: An Introduction to the Work of D. W. Winnicott* (New York: Bruner/Mazel, 1981).

38. Ana-Maria Rizzuto, *The Birth of the Living God: A Psychoanalytic Study* (Chicago: University of Chicago Press, 1979).

39. It is still true, however, that those convinced Freud had nothing useful to say to religion and to its educators will probably not appreciate Rizzuto either.

40. She began her book with these important words: "This is not a book on religion. It is a clinical study of the possible origins of the individual's private representation of God and its subsequent elaborations. It is also a study of the relation existing in the secret chambers of the human heart between that God and the person who believes in him during the vicissitudes of the life cycle." Rizzuto, *Birth of the Living God*, p. 3.

41. See Paul Tillich, *Courage to Be* (New Haven: Yale University Press, 1952), pp. 181-190.

42. Rizzuto, *Birth of the Living God*, p. 41.

43. This discussion presupposes some familiarity with the classic work by Sigmund Freud, *The Future of an Illusion*, trans James Strachey (New York: Norton, 1961; first published in 1927).

44. Which, of course, was what Freud was hoping for. He believed that the introduction of psychoanalysis would eradicate both the need for and the image of God. See Freud, *Future of an Illusion*, especially pp. 40-45.

45. Rizzuto, *Birth of the Living God*, p. 15.

will have some precarious God representation made out of his [or her] parental representations," with the result that "as long as the capacity to symbolize, fantasize, and create superhuman beings remains in men . . . God will remain, at least in the unconscious."[46]

If the family were the subject of this chapter, then we would need additional space for this crucial issue, for as Rizzuto said: "God is found in the family."[47] Instead, the subject of this chapter is the role of the religious educator as parent. In this regard both Rizzuto and Freud agreed that the *origin* of the God representation, the "birth of the living God," is not the responsibility of religious education. Rizzuto pointed out: "The transformations produced in the image by formal religious education can only be added to a representation of God that has already been formed. Religious education will not contribute essentially to the creation of the image."[48]

What, then, is the role of the religious educator in God representation? The religious educator, in the role of parent, helps *transform* and *revise* the primitive and infantile images of God the individual carries. While the religious educator does not form the original image, he or she can play a significant part in the re-formation of the image—which explains the dimension of theologian. This revision can be facilitated at least in partial form through the cognitive approach of theological discussions, but it can be done much more effectively and pervasively through the same manner that the original image was produced: through modeling. One of the major conclusions of Rizzuto's study was that "the psychic process of creating and finding God—this personalized representational transitional object—never ceases in the course of human life. It is a developmental process that covers the entire life cycle from birth to death."[49]

Here is a task religious educators never complete or finalize. Religious educators carry responsibility for facilitating (primarily through modeling but also through various cognitive means) the recreation of the God image that resides in those they teach throughout the learners' lifespans. Unlike the belief of Freud that religious educators were simply contributing to the continued delusion of the human race through their teaching about God,[50] Rizzuto suggested that religious educators were performing a service for humanity, since (in at least some cases!) "religion is not an illusion. It is an integral part of being human, truly human in our capacity to create nonvisible but meaningful realities capable of containing our potential for imaginative expansion beyond the boundaries of the senses."[51] That sounds like an activity worthy of a lifelong investment for the genuine religious educator—that of performing as a functional theologian.[52]

46. Ibid., p. 52.
47. Ibid., p. 8.
48. Ibid., p. 10.
49. Ibid., p. 179.
50. See Freud, *Future of an Illusion*, especially pp. 34-39.
51. Ibid., p. 47.
52. Rizzuto is by no means the only source for such types of research. For example, see André Godin, *The Psychological Dynamics of Religious Experience* (Birmingham, Ala.: Religious Education Press, 1985); John McDargh, *Psychoanalytic Object Relations Theory and the Study of Religion* (Lanham, Md.: University Press of America, 1983); John W. Bowker, *The Sense of God: Sociological, Anthropological, and Psychological Approaches to the Origin of the Sense of God* (Oxford: Clarendon

Summary

This section has been a selective look at some of the possible dimensions of the role of the religious educator as parent: provider, protector, model, and theologian. Only enough information was introduced to provide a basic understanding of the role. These dimensions have revealed that some common ground does exist between the parent and the religious educator. Next, to give further insight into the role of the religious educator as parent, the discussion moves to the aim of the religious educator in the parental role.

Aim: Maturity

The religious educator in the role of parent works constantly to help the learner achieve the everbroadening aim of maturity.[53] Maturity is most faithfully treated as a developmental issue, which means that each age has its own particular manifestations of maturity: being appropriately equilibrated[54] chronologically, intellectually, affectively, socially, and spiritually while never reaching a static state of total completion or perfection.[55] The religious educator alone

---

Press, 1973); and David Elkind, "The Development of Religious Understanding in Children and Adolescents," in *Research on Religious Development: A Comprehensive Handbook,* ed. Merton P. Strommen (New York: Hawthorn, 1971), pp. 655-685. Rather well-known books that were written directly to religious educators include Ronald Goldman, *Religious Thinking from Childhood to Adolescents* (New York: Seabury, 1964); Ronald Goldman, *Readiness for Religion: A Basis for Developmental Religious Education* (New York: Seabury, 1965); and Edward Robinson, *The Original Vision: A Study of the Religious Experience of Childhood* (New York: Free Press, 1983). Two popular books that provide little in the way of scholarly contributions are David Heller's books: *The Children's God* (Chicago: University of Chicago Press, 1986) and *Talking to Your Child about God* (New York: Bantam books, 1988). Between Heller's work and scholarly efforts is Robert Coles, *The Spiritual Life of Children* (Boston: Houghton Mifflin, 1990). A good overview of the entire topic was provided by Kenneth E. Hyde in *Religion in Childhood and Adolescence: A Comprehensive Review of the Research* (Birmingham, Ala.: Religious Education Press, 1990), especially Chapter Four, "Children's Ideas of God," pp. 64-82, and Chapter Five, "Parental Images and the Idea of God," pp. 83-97.

53. The term I am using here is *maturity,* which is somewhat different from the meaning of "maturation." The two should not be confused. Maturation has been defined as the "successive, active unfoldment of various innate bodily and mental functions and capacities." Morris L. Bigge and Maurice P. Hunt, *Psychological Foundations of Education: An Introduction to Human Motivation, Development, and Learning,* 3rd ed. (New York: Harper & Row, 1980), p. 203. Maturation has also been explained as "a term used to describe changes in human development that are relatively independent of the environment." Lefrancois, *The Lifespan,* p. 586. Maturation is closer to what Deanna Kuhn discussed as "nativism," contrasted with empiricism, in her article "Cognitive Development," in *Developmental Psychology: An Advanced Textbook,* ed. Marc H. Bornstein and Michael E. Lamb, 2nd ed. (Hillsdale, N.J.: Lawrence Erlbaum, 1988), pp. 206-212.

54. This is a Piagetian term that helps elucidate the concept of maturity. Equilibration has been described by John Phillips as "a process of attaining equilibrium between external intrusions and the activities of organism. . . . Equilibration is 'coming into equilibrium.' . . . In Piaget's theory, equilibrium is dynamic; it is a system of compensating actions that maintain a steady state. That steady state is a condition of the system in which the internal activities of the organism completely compensate for intrusions from without." John L. Phillips, Jr., *The Origins of Intellect: Piaget's Theory,* 2nd ed. (San Francisco: Freeman, 1975), pp. 13-15. Equilibration, incidentally, is incorporated in maturation (see preceding footnote) within Piaget's framework. This is explained in ibid., pp. 17-29.

55. Excellent resources that provide a fuller discussion of maturity include a historical study by Christie W. Kiefer, *The Mantle of Maturity: A History of Ideas about Character Development* (New

does not accept anything like total responsibility for this aim, but the religious educator does everything conceivable to facilitate and to contribute to the continual development of maturity in his or her charges. One of the prime factors about maturity, however, is that each person must ultimately accept responsibility for his or her own life. Obviously this is not something that can be done *for* a person, so that the best a religious educator can aim for is nurturing the person toward increased interdependence and individuality.

A brief look at what maturity is *not* may help explain the concept of maturity. First, maturity is not a gift or an inborn quality received genetically. Mature parents have no guarantee of producing mature children. Living in an environment where maturity is modeled may certainly be an advantage, but maturity is not something inherited from or given away by the family to its constitutive members.

Second, maturity is not a state that is fully and finally achieved. None of us can ever sit back and congratulate ourselves that we have finally become the wholly mature people we have always wanted to be. In fact, the very act of such self-congratulation probably signals missing the mark. In this regard, maturity is like humility: If you are sure you have it, then you probably do not.

Third, maturity does not result from merely having a lot of experiences. "Having experiences" may mean that you have been through a large number of life's activities and maybe even have suffered in the midst of those experiences. Merely enduring or muddling through events, though, does not automatically produce maturity. Learning, adapting, and changing are aspects of maturity that do not necessarily result from simply living through a particular set of trying circumstances.

Fourth, and finally, maturity is not just growing old. While it is true that maturity does involve the passage of time, maturity does not come magically or naturally because of advanced age. A story makes this point. A newspaper reporter was preparing an article on the small-town wonder—a man who was about to turn one hundred years old. The reporter began interviewing people who knew the old gentleman and asked one of those persons if she were proud of the soon-to-be centenarian. The response was frank and honest: "Well, I wouldn't say proud. The only thing he has done all his life is grow old, and it took him a hundred years to do that!"

A kernel of truth exists in each of the inadequate versions of maturity, so they can help define the general contours of maturity. Maturity is influenced and strengthened through family modeling. Maturity is a process, a way of life that is never completely fulfilled and never achieved finally in every area of life. Maturity is linked to experiencing what life has to offer, both in good times and bad, but it also involves learning from the experiences and becoming adaptable and flexible in the face of the vicissitudes of life. Finally, the older we become the more opportunity we have to evaluate our experiences and to seek

York: State University of New York Press, 1988); a psychological treatment by Lorene A. Stringer, *The Sense of Self: A Guide to How We Mature* (Philadelphia: Temple University Press, 1971); and an existential view of the subject by Bernard J. Boelen, *Personal Maturity: The Existential Dimension* (New York: Seabury, 1978).

a way of integrating them into a coherent and meaningful view of human life.[56]

William Bridges described maturity as "that difficult process of letting go of an old situation, suffering the confusing nowhere of in-betweenness, and launching forth again into a new situation."[57] Specifically, Bridges was addressing the issues of transition and change. The ability we find at the very core of what it means to be mature is coping with and being open to change. One outstanding mark of a mature person is his or her ability to accept and incorporate change while retaining some basic and fundamental identity and personality. Each individual demonstrates how and to what degree this is done uniquely in his or her own life.

Charles Kao made a somewhat broader and more comprehensive effort to encompass the boundaries of maturity. Kao identified three principles of maturation: differentiation, integration, and transcendence.[58] *Differentiation*, Kao wrote, "creates diversity and plurality and at the same time threatens unity and harmony."[59] Differentiation denotes the process of separation, whether it is a physical act—as in the birth of an infant who "differentiates" from the mother—or psychological—as when the toddler yells the first defiant "no!" at the surprised mother. *Integration* is pulling together the disparate elements to make a fully functional whole, or as Kao put it, creating "unity, harmony, balance, and homeostasis."[60] This can be the coordination of physical behaviors to learn to walk and talk, or the task of learning to be a functional part of a human family, where each individual is allowed and expected to be a unique but also an inseparable and contributing member of the family system. *Transcendence*, Kao explained, "intermingles with the processes of differentiation and integration in making particular highlights of growth at certain parts and times."[61] This is often designated as stage theory, where different tasks and abilities have their own special periods of ascendancy.[62]

Maturity as the aim of the religious educator as parent is dual-pronged. It focuses on both the religious educator and on the learner. By all accounts the religious educator needs to be a mature person or, more accurately, a maturing person. He or she must be continually dealing positively with the issues of change in his or her life and seeking to embody the principles of differentiation, integration, and transcendence. In the midst of this personal ongoing process of maturity, the religious educator encourages and facilitates maturity in each of

---

56. This is similar to what Erik Erikson meant when he spoke of "ego integrity." See Erik H. Erikson, *Childhood and Society*, 2nd ed. (New York: Norton, 1963), pp. 268-269.

57. William Bridges, *Transitions: Making Sense of Life's Changes* (Reading, Mass.: Addison-Wesley, 1980), p.5.

58. Charles C. K. Kao, *Psychological and Religious Development: Maturity and Maturation* (Washington, D. C.: University Press of America, 1981), pp. 58-59.

59. Ibid., p. 58.

60. Ibid., p. 59.

61. Ibid.

62. Psychological stage theories have been developed for all types of human dimensions, such as moral development, cognitive development, and faith development. Two of the most well-known are Sigmund Freud's psycho-sexual stages, and the correlative psycho-social stages of Erik Erikson. See especially Chapter Seven, "The Eight Ages of Man," in Erikson, *Childhood and Society*, pp. 247-274 for an example of this approach to human development.

those under his or her care. It is not the responsibility of the religious educator to determine the specific nature or outcome of the learner's maturity. It is, however, the undeniable and inescapable responsibility of the religious educator to see that each one of the learners is given the time and attention appropriate to help develop his or her own unique form of maturity. Such a formidable task requires turning to the function a religious educator uses to meet the aim of maturity.

Function: Nurture

If the aim of the religious educator as parent is maturity, then the means for achieving that aim—the function of the religious educator as parent—is nurture. The literal meaning of "nurture" stems from the Latin roots of the word. The base word is "*nutrix*," which means to suckle and breast-feed. This term originally referred to a child's wet nurse and now is used to designate the more modern vocation of nurse. In more general usage, nurture means to nourish, as in promoting growth and well-being. While understanding that "promoting the growth and well-being" does require the imposition of limits, boundaries, discipline, and basic guidance, nurture in religious education primarily refers to the more positive aspects of providing nourishment and promoting the well-being of persons.

This function of nurture played a prominent part in the birth and growth of the modern religious education movement in the United States. Horace Bushnell is generally credited with major responsibility for the reemphasis on nurture through the influence of his monumental book *Christian Nurture*.[63] The foundation laid by Bushnell was developed by the great champion of nurture and one of the chief powerhouses in the establishment of the modern religious education movement (and of the Religious Education Association[64]), George Albert Coe. The necessity for Christian nurture and its need to be tended by a field of professional religious educators were prime motivators for Coe, for example, in producing his highly influential book *A Social Theory of Religious Education*.[65] When neo-orthodox theology began to make its presence known and to challenge the liberal theologies of the established religious educators such as Harrison Elliott[66] (Coe's protégé), once again nurture was the key topic, as evidenced by

---

63. Horace Bushnell and his book *Christian Nurture* receive focused attention in the historical personage section of the present chapter.

64. See Stephen A. Schmidt, *A History of the Religious Education Association* (Birmingham, Ala.: Religious Education Press, 1983), p. 22.

65. George Albert Coe, *A Social Theory of Religious Education* (New York: Scribner's, 1917). In many ways, this book can be seen as one of the quintessential, defining books of the modern religious education movement in the United States. To appreciate the continued relevance and power of Coe's book, see the call for a revised social theory of religious education grounded in Coe's work and other progressive theorists by Allen J. Moore in "A Social Theory of Religious Education," in *Religious Education as Social Transformation*, ed. Allen J. Moore (Birmingham, Ala.: Religious Education Press, 1989), pp. 9-36.

66. See the pivotal book by Harrison S. Elliott, *Can Religious Education Be Christian?* (New York: Macmillan, 1940). This book is often now regarded as the symbolic highwater mark of the liberal theologians' dominance of the new field of religious education, who were soon to be replaced by the neo-orthodox theologians. See this discussed, for example, by Kendig Brubaker Cully in

the title of the pivotal book *Faith and Nurture*[67] by H. Shelton Smith. When neo-orthodox theology became established as the theological position of choice, nurture continued to be given attention—albeit in quite different formulations than the earlier theologically liberal theologians had used.[68] Two examples are Randolph Crump Miller in the classic work *The Clue to Christian Education*[69] and Harry Munro in *Protestant Nurture*.[70] The continued importance of nurture in the field is evidenced by the appearance of such books as *On Nurturing Christians* by Wayne Rood,[71] and *The Salvation and Nurture of the Child of God* by G. Temp Sparkman.[72]

A parent carries the responsibility for meeting a variety of nurture needs, not the least of which is providing for such physical needs as food and shelter. The religious educator as parent is generally less involved in the physical type of nourishment and more concerned with the emotional and psychological kind. Ruth Greenberg-Edelstein proposed the term "nurturance" to denote this supportive type of activity: "Nurturance is the caring and helping that are fundamental to human relationships and groups. It includes any interactions that build unity and support. It may run the gamut from exploratory nurturing remarks to intense personal exchanges. Nurturance includes aiding, comforting, confiding, nursing, exchanging, fondling, establishing solidarity, and promoting development and growth. It always moves in at least two directions and includes positive reactions by the person being aided, comforted, or confided in. It may occur any place: the nursery, school, home, workplace, hospital, political organization, legislature, or court room. . . . Strong peer relationships . . . are based on egalitarian exchanges of nurturance."[73] Greenberg-Edelstein, as a psychotherapist, was writing specifically about the processes of group therapy, yet her words quoted above still help describe accurately the activity of the religious educator in the role of parent.

The aim of the parent as the religious educator is maturity, and the means toward that end is the provision of an environment that provides adequate and

---

The Search for a Christian Education—Since 1940 (Philadelphia: Westminster, 1965), pp. 13-25; by Robert W. Lynn in Chapter Two, "Continuity and Change," of *Protestant Strategies in Education* (New York: Association Press, 1964), pp. 27-50; and by Timothy Arthur Lines, *Systemic Religious Education* (Birmingham, Ala.: Religious Education Press, 1987), pp. 11-16.

67. H. Shelton Smith, *Faith and Nurture* (New York: Scribner's, 1941).

68. For an overview of how these theological terms are being used here, see Lines, *Systemic Religious Education*, pp. 11-15.

69. Randolph Crump Miller, *The Clue to Christian Education* (New York: Scribner's, 1950). Of particular relevance is this key sentence: "The clue to Christian education is the rediscovery of a relevant theology which will bridge the gap between content and method . . . using *the guidance of parents* and the fellowship of life in the church as *the environment in which Christian nurture will take place.*" Ibid., p. 15. Emphasis added.

70. Harry C. Munro, *Protestant Nurture: An Introduction to Christian Education* (Englewood Cliffs, N.J.: Prentice-Hall, 1956).

71. Wayne R. Rood, *On Nurturing Christians: Perhaps a Manifesto for Education* (Nashville: Abingdon, 1972).

72. G. Temp Sparkman, *The Salvation and Nurture of the Child of God: The Story of Emma* (Valley Forge, Pa.: Judson Press, 1983).

73. Ruth R. Greenberg-Edelstein, *The Nurturance Phenomenon: Roots of Group Psychotherapy* (Norwalk, Conn.: Appleton-Century-Crofts, 1986), p. 1.

appropriate experiences of nurture—one that allows those we teach to grow and develop into unique individuals. It is the task of the religious educator to nourish and promote the well-being of those he or she teaches, thereby allowing maturity to manifest itself. If maturity is not "handed out," then it is nurtured, encouraged, and permitted to develop in a safe and healthy environment. Maturity is the result of nurturing environments and of nurturing relationships within those environments, identifying a major area of concern for every conscientious religious educator.

Primary Virtues: Morality and Faith

Covering the vast topics of morality and faith in just a few paragraphs is more than a bit daunting. These are indeed enormous areas with no possibility of a complete discussion in this present context, but they are introduced at this point as highlighting the primary virtues that are demonstrated and inculcated by the religious educator as parent. Any full and complete analysis of the topics themselves needs attention in some other forum than in this brief overview.

Morality and faith are both at the very heart of the task of the parent, and of the religious educator in the role of parent. Whatever the specific substantive contents of morality and faith that are eventually inculcated and adopted, the parent and the religious educator in the role of parent spend a great deal of time and effort teaching and shaping the structural content.[74] Quite often, morality and faith are also the issues used to evaluate the effectiveness of the parenting activity, as in: How did the child "turn out" in terms of morality and faith? The implication, and the reality, is that morality and faith have more to do with lifestyle than with mere intellectual assent or mental reasoning.[75] The parent may indeed be sensitive to the question of "how the child turned out" because the morality and the faith the child displays can be perceived at least in some degree to reflect the parent's own true morality and faith.[76] Because of the intimate systemic nature of families, and because of the varieties of formal and informal environments for teaching that parenting provides, it is often difficult to separate the identity and the actions of the child from that of the parent. Much is at stake at the juncture of morality and faith, for both the parent and the child.

Peter Lifton has given a helpful and relatively simple functional definition of morality. He said morality "reflects behavior which is based on principles of right and wrong, where right and wrong are determined both by the individual

---

74. "Substantive" content is more related to specific subject matter or information, while "structural" content relates more to the processes and procedures used to communicate or teach the selected substantive content.

75. See the chapters "Cognitive Processes in Moral Development," by Lawrence J. Walker, pp. 109-145; "Affective Processes," by Norman A. Sprinthall, pp. 146-166; and "Moral Development in Adulthood: Lifestyle Processes," by Tod Sloan and Robert Hogan, pp. 167-181 in *Handbook of Moral Development: Models, Processes, Techniques, and Research*, ed. Gary L. Sapp (Birmingham, Ala.: Religious Education Press, 1986) for the breadth of the domain of moral education.

76. This sentence refers to the power and influence of modeling, which was discussed initially in the dimension of the parent as model and in more detail in the section below on the representative teaching procedure.

person and the societal group within which the person resides."[77] These salient points about morality in Lifton's definition need emphasis. First, morality "reflects *behavior*." Behavior surely is influenced by what a person thinks, but Lifton was stressing that morality is more than thinking the right or proper thoughts; ultimately, the performance of behavior is the proper focus of morality. Second, morality is taught by way of "*principles* of right and wrong." The principle approach is polar to the indoctrinational approach, which is either "the inculcation of any set of beliefs when the foundations of, or evidence for, those beliefs is not open to public scrutiny" (the "content" only view) or where the parent/religious educator "demands acceptance of the beliefs he is attempting to inculcate while refusing to permit those beliefs to be criticized" (the "intention" or methodological view).[78] The "principle approach," by contrast, does not dictate what a person must do in every situation or circumstance but instead aids in the process of moral decision making.[79] Third, "rights and wrongs" are determined by the individual person *and* by his or her societal group. This dual emphasis of the individual and societal group allows the person the freedom and responsibility for deciding but also holds that the parent and the religious educator (among others in the individual's societal environment) play a momentous role in helping determine the foundations of morality—the functional "rights and wrongs."[80]

Peter Scharf identified three models of moral education that help the parent and religious educator decide on adequate procedures for teaching morality.[81] Scharf first mentioned the *indoctrination* model (discussed briefly in the above paragraph), which "seeks to teach values defined by society as societally valid and correct by rewarding 'good' values and punishing 'bad' ones."[82] Second

---

77. Peter D. Lifton, "Personological and Psychodynamic Explanations of Moral Development," in *Handbook of Moral Development*, p. 56.

78. Robert T. Hall and John U. Davis, *Moral Education: Theory and Practice* (Buffalo: Prometheus Books, 1975), pp. 31-32. Either of these indoctrinational views are inadequate for effective teaching. The authors then gave the alternatives to these two points: "Indoctrination can be avoided in either of two ways: (1) by assuring oneself of universal mutual consent on the doctrines taught, or (2) by giving equal consideration to existing alternatives where mutual agreement does not exist." Ibid., p. 40.

79. This is indeed how Hall and Davis defined moral education: "Moral education, therefore, is not education simply in the right things to do (taking the term in its evaluative sense) but rather education in the nature of moral thinking and in the skills and abilities of decision-making." Ibid., p. 15. For a classic example of a book that made the effort to discuss the basis for moral decision making, see Joseph Fletcher, *Situation Ethics: The New Morality* (Philadelphia: Westminster, 1966). In the book, Fletcher stated that there are three alternative routes to making moral decisions: legalism, antinomianism, and situational. Obviously, he espoused the third—situational. The parallels to the discussion by Peter Scharf below, however, are striking, although Fletcher was writing as an ethicist and as a minister, not as a moral educator per se.

80. These themes are picked up later in the chapter in the section on Horace Bushnell's embrace of Christian nurture and in the section on C. Ellis Nelson's emphasis on community.

81. Peter Scharf, "Indoctrination, Values Clarification, and Developmental Moral Education as Educational Responses to Conflict and Change in Contemporary Society," in *Readings in Moral Development*, ed. Peter Scharf (Minneapolis: Winston, 1978), pp. 18-35. The quotes in this paragraph are taken from p. 19.

82. Some may cite behaviorism here, although to do so would require misusing the terminology of the behaviorists. For example, an operant behaviorist like B. F. Skinner did not advocate punishment. See B. F. Skinner discuss this in *On Behaviorism*, (New York: Vintage Books, 1974), p. 69.

came *values clarification*, "which through self observation and analysis, seeks to help the child find values which only he or she can judge valid or invalid."[83] Third was *developmental moral education*, which "offers the hypothesis that there are stages of moral values which might be taught through moral conflict and dialogue," and this was the one Scharf himself seemed to prefer in the article.

Scharf was by no means alone in his preference for the cognitive-developmental approach to moral education, and much of the interest in it springs from the work of Lawrence Kohlberg (1927-1987) who proposed a stage theory for diagnosing and then facilitating the development of moral reasoning.[84] In reality, Kohlberg proposed not so much a theory of moral development as a theory of moral reasoning which relied heavily on the cognitive stage theory of Jean Piaget.[85] Piaget had postulated a two-stage theory (following a "premoral" stage) of moral reasoning: an earlier stage of "heteronomy," based on a morality where the prime consideration was the observance of rules and laws, and a later stage of "autonomy," based on a morality where decisions hinged more on the intentions of the person.[86] Kohlberg followed Piaget's lead and eventually developed a model where the Piagetian stages became six stages (divided into three levels) while still using much of the same methodology and procedure utilized by Piaget.[87]

---

83. Some representative sources for this position include: Maury Smith, *A Practical Guide to Value Clarification* (La Jolla, Calif.: University Associates, 1977); Roland S. Larson and Doris E. Larson, *Values and Faith Value-Clarifying Exercises for Family and Church Groups* (Minneapolis: Winston, 1976); Sidney B. Simon, Leland W. Howe, and Howard Kirschenbaum, *Values Clarification: A Handbook of Practical Strategies for Teachers and Students* (New York: Hart, 1972); Brian P. Hall with Michael Kenney and Maury Smith, *Values Clarification as a Learning Process: A Sourcebook* (New York: Paulist, 1973); and Robert Meyners and Claire Wooster, *Solomon's Sword: Clarifying Values in the Church* (Nashville: Abingdon, 1977).

84. Kohlberg's theory can be found in a variety of places and in a variety of forms. For primary works written some years after the initial introduction of his schema, see Lawrence Kohlberg, *Essays on Moral Development: Volume I: The Philosophy of Moral Development* (New York: Harper & Row, 1981), and Lawrence Kohlberg, *Essays on Moral Development: Volume II: The Psychology of Moral Development* (San Francisco: Harper & Row, 1984). A good overview of Kohlberg's work was provided in *The Kohlberg Legacy for the Helping Professions*, ed. Lisa Kuhmerker with Uwe Gielen and Richard L. Hayes (Birmingham, Ala.: Religious Education Press, 1991).

85. See Jean Piaget, *The Moral Development of the Child*, trans. Marjorie Gabain (New York: Free Press, 1965; originally published in 1932).

86. See this summarized in ibid., pp. 100-108.

87. See the birth of this in Kohlberg's PhD dissertation. See Lawrence Kohlberg, "The Development of Modes of Thinking and Choices in the Years from 10-16," PhD dissertation (Chicago: University of Chicago, 1958). Kohlberg later made these comments about the evolution of his work from that of Piaget: "The stages that Piaget talked about were a premoral stage, a stage of heteronomous or unilateral respect for adult authorities or rules, and a morality of reciprocity and mutual respect and cooperation, especially among peers. Piaget's observations began with children around age three and ended at around age eleven. In my own thesis work I proposed to follow the development of moral judgment and reasoning through adolescence. Using dilemmas created by philosophers or novelists, I was struck by the fact that the adolescents had distinctive patters of thinking which were coherent and were their own, just as Piaget had seen distinctive patterns of thinking in younger children. In my dissertation I tentatively characterized these patterns as qualitative stages and added three stages to those formulated by Piaget." Lawrence Kohlberg, "My Personal Search for Universal Morality," in *The Kohlberg Legacy for the Helping Professions*, p. 15.

In the subsequent years after the initial euphoria over Kohlberg's proposals, increasing criticism has swirled around the topic of not only moral development but of developmental theory itself. The resulting controversy has not so much been because of Kohlberg's reliance on Piaget, or even that Kohlberg said moral development is a matter of stage development.[88] The largest amount of criticism of Kohlberg's theory has come at the point of gender bias. The argument has been made that Kohlberg used primarily male perspectives, subjects, and interviewees to determine the standards of moral development, thereby leaving females to appear either as morally underdeveloped or as aberrations.[89] Female researchers, using different perspectives, subjects, and interviewees have produced differing stages and understandings of development.[90] The result has been tumult in the field of developmentalism, with female researchers and theorists presenting evidence that brings into question all of the older, stereotypical stage theories. Where all of this will lead, and even whether stage theory itself will survive, is presently unknown.[91] The point of this illustrative paragraph has been to show that a subject as important and as vital to parenting and to religious education as moral development has as yet no final answers to it, and none is in sight.[92] Doubtless the quest will continue, as will both the need and the desire. The parent/religious educator must be aware of current ideas and approaches but just as importantly must evaluate and analyze those theories to see what is useful and what is not. Simply put, no foolproof manual for teaching morality exists.[93]

---

88. An excellent evaluation of Kohlberg and suggestions for alternatives in religious education can be found in Craig Dykstra, *Vision and Character: A Christian Educator's Alternative to Kohlberg* (New York: Paulist, 1981).

89. See Carol Gilligan, *In a Different Voice: Psychological Theory and Women's Development* (Cambridge: Harvard University Press, 1982). Also see *Mapping the Moral Domain: A Contribution of Women's Thinking to Psychological Theory and Education*, eds., Carol Gilligan, Jane Victoria Ward, and Jill McLean Taylor, with Betty Bardige (Cambridge: Harvard University Press, 1988); and *Women and Moral Theory*, eds. Eva Feder Kittay and Diana Meyers (Totowa, N.J.: Rowmans and Littlefield, 1987).

90. One representative book that took Gilligan's criticism farther and confronted the bias back of the cognitive theories of Piaget is Mary Field Belenky, Blyth McVicker Clinchy, Nancy Rule Goldberger, and Jill Mattuck Tarule, *Women's Ways of Knowing: The Development of Self, Voice, and Mind* (New York: Basic Books, 1986). These authors propose "ways of knowing" that were drawn from women and their experiences.

91. A stage theory by definition is universal for all humans. If stage theory is truly fundamentally different for males and females, then the whole idea of a universal human development theory has been dealt a heavy blow.

92. A good overview of the range and complexity of the issues in historical perspective is John L. Elias, *Moral Education: Secular and Religious* (Malabar, Fla.: Krieger, 1989).

93. There is a multitude of resources available on the topic of moral development in addition to the ones cited. Some others include: *Moral Development, Moral Education and Kohlberg: Basic Issues in Philosophy, Psychology, Religion, and Education*, ed. Brenda Munsey (Birmingham, Ala.: Religious Education Press, 1980); *Lawrence Kohlberg: Consensus and Controversy*, ed. Sohan Modgil and Celia Modgil (Philadelphia: Falmer Press, 1986); John Martin Rich and Joseph L. DeVitis, *Theories of Moral Development* (Springfield, Ill.: Charles C. Thomas, 1985); *The Emergence of Morality in Young Children*, ed. Jerome Kegan and Sharon Lamb (Chicago: University of Chicago Press, 1987); James R. Rest, in collaboration with others, *Moral Development: Advances in Research and Theory* (New York: Praeger, 1986); F. Clark Power, Ann Higgins, and Lawrence Kohlberg, *Lawrence Kohlberg's Approach to Moral Education* (New York: Columbia University

Just as morality includes much more than intellectual knowledge, so too must faith be understood as covering much broader territory than cognition alone. Wilfred Cantwell Smith, a historian of comparative religions, discussed faith in terms of being "a quality of human *living*."[94] He said: "At its best it [faith] has taken the form of serenity and courage and loyalty and service: quiet confidence and joy which enable one to feel at home in the universe and to find meaning in the world and one's own life, a meaning that is profound and ultimate, and is stable no matter what may happen to oneself at the level of immediate event."[95] To provide a contrast, Smith said: "Belief, on the other hand, is holding of certain ideas."[96] Smith made it a point to clarify faith as a uniquely human virtue[97] when he wrote: "We human beings differ in the depth and richness and vitality, as well as in the contours, of faith. By being human, we all share in common both the capacity for it and also a potentiality always for growth in it."[98] He then went on to make this recommendation: "Faith can be understood better, I am suggesting—and more importantly, man can be understood better—if faith be recognized as an essential human quality, a normal if priceless component of what it means to be a human person."[99] What Smith was saying about faith to the parent and to the religious educator in the role of parent is this: As they facilitate the growth of faith in their learners, they are actually helping the learners to become more fully human. Can there be any more important or pressing task?

Theologian Paul Tillich defined faith similarly to Smith, emphasizing its dynamic nature: "Faith is the state of being ultimately concerned: the dynamics of faith are the dynamics of man's ultimate concern."[100] Tillich, like Smith, was unwilling to see faith as a separate or isolated part of human existence. Instead, he understood faith to be found at the very center of human experience: "Faith as ultimate concern is an act of the total personality. It happens in the center of the personal life and includes all its elements."[101] The contrast of faith with belief was also stressed by Tillich, when he called belief the "intellectualistic distortion of the meaning of faith."[102] Tillich was one whose voice can be added to the

---

Press, 1989); *Moral Development and Character Education: A Dialogue*, ed. Larry P. Nucci (Berkeley: McCutchan, 1989); Kenneth Stokes, *Faith Is a Verb: Dynamics of Adult Faith Development* (Mystic, Conn.: Twenty-Third Publications, 1989); Carolyn Pope Edwards with Patricia G. Ramsey, *Promoting Social and Moral Development in Young Children* (New York: Teachers College Press, 1986); and Richard W. Kropf, *Faith—Security and Risk: The Dynamics of Spiritual Growth* (New York: Paulist, 1990).

94. Wilfred Cantwell Smith, *Faith and Belief* (Princeton: Princeton University Press, 1979), p. 12. Emphasis added.

95. Ibid., p. 12.

96. Ibid.

97. "Faith is a virtue. Believing is not." Ibid., p. 142.

98. Ibid., p. 141.

99. Ibid. Also note in this quote how Smith emphasized both the differentiation and the sameness of faith in humans. He was making the distinction between the substantive contents and the structural contents of faith, which of course are still other than belief.

100. Paul Tillich, *Dynamics of Faith* (New York: Harper & Row, 1957), p.1.

101. Ibid., p. 4.

102. Ibid., p. 30. See the entire second chapter, "What Faith Is Not," of *Dynamics of Faith* for a broader understanding of his discussion of faith. Ibid., pp. 30-40.

chorus[103] that faith is fundamental to human existence and therefore demands the proper care and nurture from the parent—and from the religious educator in the role of parent.

Two key points have pervaded this discussion of morality and faith. One is the awareness that both morality and faith are constantly being taught by the total environment. Too often tunnel vision allows one to make the assumption that moral and faith education are done only intentionally and expertly, as in a class-room by the teacher or in the home by the parent in a relatively formal circum-stance. In reality, this is much less often the case than the informal opportunities and circumstances that arise. The vast majority of morality and faith is learned and processed in the ebb and flow of life, probably without most people paying any particular attention. What a child observes and interprets from riding in the car with the parent, or on the playground with peers, or sitting on the couch in the living room watching television are also true and determinative sources of learn-ing morality and faith. Though in no way denigrating the intentional environments we use to educate formally, the effective religious educator must realize the power and the extent of the informal and the unintentional environments. He or she will never have an adequate or realistic view of moral or faith education if one only thinks of them in terms of a Sunday school/synagogue type of set-ting.[104] The cumulative effect of the other multitudinous aspects of life is too easily missed because of its continual presence.

The second fundamental issue within the present section was that while each individual ultimately becomes responsible for his or her own morality and faith decisions, the parent and the religious educator must utilize every resource and structure every environment as carefully as possible to facilitate the growth of morality and faith. In short, the issue becomes one of boundaries. The parent/reli-gious educator has the awesome responsibility of teaching morality and faith with all the power and influence he or she can muster. This responsibility carries full expectation that the parent/religious educator will leave no energy unspared in trying to shape and influence. The responsibility, though, ends where the skin of the person being taught begins. What the person finally does *with* the instruction remains outside the boundary of the parent/religious educator. However painful or however joyful the results of the instruction, the outcome must be performed by the individual. The parent/religious educator does not seek absolute dictation of the learner's morality and faith but to facilitate his or her responsible decision making. He or she may encourage, argue, shape, model, nurture, threaten, and pray, but the decisions of the individual are eventually out of the parent's and the

---

103. Other "voices of the chorus" that should be included in the study of faith and its place in the role of the religious educator as parent are V. Bailey Gillespie, *The Experience of Faith* (Birmingham, Ala.: Religious Education Press, 1988); *Handbook of Faith*, ed. James Michael Lee; and James W. Fowler, *Stages of Faith: The Psychology of Human Development and the Quest for Meaning* (San Francisco: Harper & Row, 1981). Fowler especially wrote in agreement with the ideas of Wilfred Cantwell Smith and Paul Tillich. Fowler receives extended treatment in this book in Chapter Six, "The Religious Educator as Scientist."

104. This kind of problem and awareness is precisely the reason that people like C. Ellis Nelson talk of the power of the community and of the environment to educate. A discussion of Nelson and the communal nature of religious education comes later in this chapter. Also closely related is the dis-cussion later in the chapter on modeling and observational learning.

religious educator's hands. The abiding hope is that those he or she teaches will continue to grow and develop in their own understanding and exercise of the virtues of morality and faith, aided in their journey by the parent's or religious educator's participation in it.[105]

Lest we lapse into thinking that morality and faith are new topics for parents and religious educators, harken back to one of the older views of moral and faith education. Johann Heinrich Pestalozzi (1746-1827) suggested three basic types of education: the education of the head (the intellect), of the heart (morality), and of the hand ("practical" education).[106] Pestalozzi suggested that the means for teaching all of these aspects of education were love, encouragement, and affection as opposed to fear, harsh discipline, and obedience.[107] As John Elias put it, Pestalozzi "dedicated his life to developing practices for humanizing the processes of educating children."[108] Whatever else may be learned in the future about teaching the virtues of morality and faith, the advice of Pestalozzi to teach through love, encouragement, and genuine affection will never be surpassed. In fact, it may be that there is no other effective way to teach morality and faith than through these gentle means. The greatest educational insights and the finest theoretical advances of the future will never remove the responsibility of the parent/religious educator to teach out of an attitude of care and concern. Even if no others are gained, these ample means of teaching the virtues of morality and faith to coming generations remain.

Activity: Trusting

So much of what the parent does, and hence of what the religious educator in the role of parent does, is so basic and foundational to the health and well-being of the young that the responsibilities are awesome and at times overwhelming. Considering the most fundamental activity of the parent makes this even more true: the activity of trusting. The parent/religious educator engages in the activity of trusting at three levels. One is the constant struggle to trust yourself and to have confidence that you are doing the best possible for those in your charge. Another level is working to trust those with whom you live and serve, such as learners and colleagues. The third level is helping others to learn to trust. This third task is impossible, incidentally, if the first two are not given proper attention. The activity of trusting, then, is the absolute foundation of parenting, of religious education, and of human relationships. Nothing is more essential to the health and development of humans than learning and deciding when it is safe to trust. Nothing is more essential to the fulfillment of the role of the parent/religious educator than demonstrating our own trustworthiness, which in turn allows others to learn to trust us.

---

105. This is the message of the proverb that comforts many a parent and religious educator: "Train children in the right way, and when old, they will not stray." Proverbs 22:6, NRSV.

106. All three were important to Pestalozzi, but he specifically worked to overcome the rationalism of his own Kantian age.

107. See Johann Heinrich Pestalozzi, *How Gertrude Teaches Her Children* (Syracuse: Bardeen Press, 1894).

108. Elias, *Moral Education*, p. 15.

The previous paragraph depends heavily on the work of Erik Erikson (b. 1902). Erikson called this foundational sense of trust the "ontological source of faith and hope," the "first and basic wholeness" where the "inside and the outside can be experienced as an interrelated goodness."[109] On the other side of trust resides the sense of basic mistrust, which is the "sum of all those diffuse experiences which are not somehow successfully balanced by the experience of integration."[110] Erikson described the "infant's first social achievement" as that time when the infant allows "the mother out of sight without undue anxiety or rage, because she has become an inner certainty as well as an outer predictability."[111] Erikson used all of this to say that the "parental faith which supports the trust emerging in the newborn, has throughout history sought its institutional safeguard . . . in organized religion."[112] The establishment of trust, according to Erikson, forms the basis of religion and religious education, which in turn is based upon the parental task of creating a relationship of trust.[113] Without trust there can be no healthy religion. Without proper activity within the role of the parent there is no establishment of trust. Erikson wrote: "Trust, then, becomes the capacity for faith."[114]

Simply put, the parent/religious educator allows and encourages the development of trust as his or her fundamental activity. Although an environment of complete trust is never achieved (Erikson was careful to speak of trying to tip the balance toward trust over mistrust), the goal is for each individual to have a basic orientation toward life built upon trust. Erikson believed that a sense of trust permitted a "primal hope" to permeate life, where a basic sense of mistrust created an attitude of doom throughout life.[115] The overarching activity of the parent/religious educator, then, is to develop and nurture an environment of trust, opening the way for a healthy orientation to life and to a fundamental sense of hope and faith.

Shadow Role: Child Abuser

In the midst of all the optimistic and positive talk about the role of the religious educator as parent, it seems almost sacrilegious to bring up such a frightening and painful subject as child abuse.[116] No one enjoys looking at the darker side of any role,[117] but there is something so special and privileged about the role of parent

---

109. Erik H. Erikson, *Identity: Youth and Crisis* (New York: Norton, 1968), p. 82.
110. Ibid.
111. Erikson, *Childhood and Society*, p. 247.
112. Ibid., p. 250.
113. Erikson said that trust comes from the quality of the parental relationship. Ibid., p. 249.
114. Erikson, *Identity*, p. 106.
115. Erikson, *Childhood and Society*, p. 80.
116. It may be that child abuse is too limiting a term. This is the term normally employed and relates directly to the following discussion, but in a sense the more appropriate term may be person abuse—abuse knows no limits of age or stages.
117. In all likelihood, it is this reluctance to talk about it and the ensuing silence that only serves to exacerbate the problem. See Peter DeCourcy and Judith DeCourcy, *A Silent Tragedy: Child Abuse in the Community* (Port Washington, N.Y.: Alfred, 1973); Renitta L. Goldman and Virginia R. Wheeler, *Silent Shame: The Sexual Abuse of Children and Youth* (Danville, Ill.: Interstate Printers and Publishers, 1986); and John Crewdson, *By Silence Betrayed: Sexual Abuse of Children in America* (Boston: Little, Brown, 1988).

that to give the dark side attention, or even to acknowledge that it exists, may appear to damage or denigrate the role. The unfortunate truth is that child abuse not only exists but appears to be rampant throughout the general population.[118] To ignore it or deny it only further exacerbates the problem. Idealized notions of parenting need to be cleared away for the health of the children in all environments, because abuse is not limited to the traditional family or home environment. Religious education has its own participation in the cycle of abuse to examine.

Alice Miller, in a disturbing but revealing book entitled *For Your Own Good*,[119] traced the roots of violence in society to our practices of child-rearing. In her view, the "former practice of physically maiming, exploiting, and abusing children seems to have been gradually replaced in modern times by a form of mental cruelty that is masked by the honorific term *child-rearing*."[120] Simply because current society appears to be more sensitive to the needs of children, Miller said, is no evidence that the abuse has abated. Only its form has changed. She stated her understanding of the abuse this way: "The greatest cruelty that can be inflicted on children is to refuse to let them express their anger and suffering except at the risk of losing their parents' love and affection."[121] This was important to Miller because of the reciprocal and continuing effect the quashing of emotion has on future generations: "The reason why parents mistreat their children has less to do with character and temperament than with the fact that they were mistreated themselves and were not permitted to defend themselves."[122] Miller warned: "If it was never possible for us to relive on a conscious level the rejection we experienced in our own childhood and to work it through, then we in turn will pass this rejection on to our children."[123] The circumstances are set for a cyclical, generational repetition of violence, whether physical or mental, through what Miller called our "poisonous pedagogy" of child-rearing: that we (primarily unknowingly and unconsciously) pass on to our children our own unresolved needs we experienced as abused children, which they in turn pass on to their children.[124]

Miller's conclusion was that child abuse comes primarily when children are used to meet the needs of adults, rather than adults appropriately meeting the needs of the children. Until that imbalance is corrected, abuse and violence will necessarily continue, and in fact be perpetuated by the very role and activity of the parent.

---

118. For evidence of its extent, see such sources as Chapter One, "Prevalence," by Stephanie Doyle Peters, Gail Elizabeth Wyatt, and David Finkelhor, in *A Sourcebook on Child Sexual Abuse*, ed. David Finkelhor and Associates (Beverly Hills: Sage Publications, 1986), pp. 15-59; Section One, "Seeking Parameters: An Overview," in *Out of Harm's Way: Readings on Child Sexual Abuse, Its Prevention and Its Treatment*, ed. Dawn C. Haden (Phoenix: The Oryx Press, 1986), pp. 1-17; and Chapter One, "Establishing the Dimensions of Child Maltreatment," in David A. Wolfe, *Child Abuse: Implications for Child Development and Psychopathology*, (Beverly Hills: Sage Publications, 1987), pp. 12-23.

119. Alice Miller, *For Your Own Good: Hidden Cruelty in Child-Rearing and the Roots of Violence*, 2nd ed. (New York: Farrar, Straus, Giroux, 1984).

120. Ibid., p. 4.

121. Ibid., p. 106.

122. Ibid., p. 105.

123. Ibid., pp. 3-4.

124. Ibid., pp. 58-63.

Miller proposed a twofold solution. First, the adults—those in the role of parent—must become aware of their own needs and their own "wounded child" within themselves and work to find their own healing. This process begins by simply seeing the issues clearly: "Once a child's eyes are opened to the power game of child-rearing, there is hope that he or she will be freed from the chains of 'poisonous pedagogy,' for this child will be able to *remember* what happened to him or her" and consequently may be able to resolve his or her problems appropriately.[125] The second part of the solution includes careful listening to and for the needs of the children once the adults have reduced the noise level of their own needs. As Miller said: "We need to hear what the child has to say in order to give our understanding, support, and love. The child, on the other hand, needs free space if he or she is to find adequate self-expression."[126] Miller insisted that we focus on the child instead of merely passing along what we experienced as children, repeating whatever our parents did. This approach, as logical as it sounds, is not universally accepted: "The idea that we as parents can learn more about the laws of life from a newborn child than we can from our parents will strike many as absurd and ridiculous."[127]

This last point, when considered from the perspective of the religious educator, is particularly crucial. Does the impetus and direction for the religious education of children arise from the children and their needs, or from the adults and their repetition of what they experienced as children? Perhaps some further words from Miller will be revealing: "Learning is a result of listening, which in turn leads to even better listening and attentiveness to the other person. In other words, to learn from the child we must have empathy, and empathy grows as we learn. It is a different matter for parents or educators who would like the child to be a certain way or think they must expect him to be that way. To reach their sacred ends, they try to mold the child in their image, suppressing self-expression in the child and at the same time missing out on an opportunity to learn something. Certainly, abuse of this sort is often unintentional; it is not only directed against children but—if we look more closely—pervades most human relationships, because the partners frequently were abused children and now are showing unconsciously what happened to them in childhood."[128] In this quote, the seriousness and the extent of the abuse Miller had in mind becomes clearer. Through lack of listening to and learning from others, and through imposing the standards and expectations of the past onto future generations, the abuse is perpetuated and institutionalized to where it becomes for some the very definition of what it means to be a parent—and a religious educator.

The shadow role of child abuser, as expressed by Alice Miller, is by no means absent from the larger picture of the religious educator as parent. If child abuse means using children to meet the needs of adults, intentionally or not, then the call is for a close and objective evaluation of current religious education activ-

125. Ibid., p. 76.
126. Ibid., p. 101. Lest Miller be understood as naive, see ibid., pages 96-97, where she clearly distinguished her position from what she called a "Rousseauistic optimism."
127. Ibid., p. 101.
128. Ibid.

ity *from the perspective of the child.* This is not to advocate an abdication of the responsibility carried by the adults for nurture and care of the young. It is to realize that what adults want to give and what children need to receive may not always match up. Alice Miller's advice was to focus on the needs of the child and to solve the adults' issues by other means than through the use and abuse of children.

Faith Tradition Resource: Judaism

Probably no injunction to educate is as well-known or as inclusive as the one in Jewish scripture that follows the Shema: "Keep these words that I am commanding you today in your heart. Recite them to your children and talk about them when you are at home and when you are away."[129] With this type of approach and attitude, Judaism has much to say to the religious educator about the role of parent. Time and space prevent taking a comprehensive look at the educational resources of Judaism, so only enough is mentioned to encourage further investigation of the resources available.

The verses quoted above encapsulate the genius of the early Jewish approach to education. In reality, it is probably not even entirely accurate to speak of "Jewish religious education" because all Jewish education formed an integral whole in which "religious education" was inseparable from vocational or literacy education. Education was primarily the responsibility of the family, and especially of the father to teach his sons.[130] It was to be done night and day, at work and at rest, in the house and outside. Education was envisioned as part of the natural family activity, and education in religion was integral to the whole of life. Realizing that the parent/religious educator constantly educates, the Jews sought to make their educational efforts intentional and constructive.

To speak of Jewish education, and to speak of Judaism at all, is to speak of Torah. Common usage refers to Torah as the first five books of the Jewish scriptures, or the Pentateuch, but Torah is not limited to the Five Books of Moses. Torah is "the general name for revelation of the divine will," as Bernard Bamberger wrote. "'Law' is not an incorrect translation, but it is inadequate. Torah includes law, but its basic meaning is guidance, direction, instruction. Torah is divine guidance for human living."[131] Samuel Blumenfield wrote that Torah "in the broad sense . . . connotes the sum of Jewish spiritual and cultural heritage," although literally it means "to cast," "to direct," "to teach."[132] These authors were saying that the responsibility of the Jewish parent/religious educator is not limited to teaching the scripture itself but covers the entire lifestyle and culture of being a Jew that follows directly from living with the Torah. Blumenfield summed up the connection succinctly by saying: "A deep concern for education

---

129. Deuteronomy 6:6-7, NRSV. The Shema is found in the two previous verses.

130. Judaism has "little mention, either in the Bible or Talmud, of the education of daughters or the educational role of mothers." See Samuel M. Blumenfield, "Thou Shalt Teach," in *God, Torah, Israel: Concepts that Distinguish Judaism*, ed. Abraham Ezra Millgram (Washington, D. C.: B'nai B'rith Books, 1985), pp. 138-139.

131. Bernard J. Bamberger, "Torah as God's Revelation to Israel," in *God, Torah, Israel*, p. 63.

132. Blumenfield, "Thou Shalt Teach," in *God, Torah, Israel*, p. 134.

is inherent in the conception of Torah as an integral part of Judaism."[133]

Another key factor in Jewish education found in the verses quoted at the head of this section was the priority put on the parent knowing the information, and then passing it on to the children. The emphasis, then, was upon adult education. Hayyim Schauss said that the appearance of the synagogue (probably during the Babylonian exile, sixth century B.C.E.) was not so much for worship as for "religious instruction, to hear the Torah and the Prophets read and expounded," and that the ones who came to the synagogue for the instruction were adults.[134] The children were taught in the home. Only later were the synagogues redesigned to provide teaching for the children. Religious instruction of children in ancient Judaism was nearly exclusively a familial responsibility, with only occasional references in early Jewish scripture to "schools of prophets" and the like.[135] The initial educational plan was to teach the adults publicly and to have the parents do the instruction of children privately in the family context.

The synagogue schools that were eventually developed[136] served to supplement the somewhat informal home education with a more formal type of education. The schools did much to ensure that Judaism survived, not only during the exile but to the present day. The current Jewish schools are products of the ancient synagogue schools originally created during the exile and were intended to complement but not to replace the continued need and importance of the family teaching. William Boyd noted the irony of the Jews using the Hellenistic concept of an institutional school during the exile to "save themselves from being overborne by the Greek culture" in which they found themselves immersed.[137] He went on to note that such a result "is striking testimony to the tremendous power of that [Hellenistic] culture that the one Oriental people who succeeded in freeing themselves from its influence did so by making use of its educational methods."[138] It is also striking testimony to the power of the Jewish culture that its education could be so grounded in family and religion that it preserved its heritage in the face of adapting to such challenges.

Further clarification of the role of the parent and its relation to the religious educator was given by Gerald Blidstein in his comments on Deuteronomy 6:6-7. Blidstein gave evidence that "the command to teach Torah to one's own children [was] broadened to include a responsibility toward all the children of the peo-

133. Ibid., p. 141.

134. Hayyim Schauss, *The Lifetime of a Jew: Throughout the Ages of Jewish History* (Cincinnati: Union of American Hebrew Congregations, 1950), p. 96.

135. See such biblical references as II Kings 4:38; 6:1; and II Chronicles 17:7-9.

136. The date for the establishment of formal schools for children is uncertain. Marvin Taylor stated that the *Beth Hassepher* (House of the Book) for younger children (beginning at age six or seven) probably originated between 75 B.C.E. and 64 C.E. See Marvin J. Taylor, "A Historical Introduction to Religious Education," in *Religious Education: A Comprehensive Survey*, ed. Marvin J. Taylor (New York: Abingdon, 1960), p. 12. Lewis Joseph Sherrill arrived at the same general date for the establishment of formal schooling for children, but gave more historical evidence for these dates. See Lewis Joseph Sherrill, *The Rise of Christian Education* (New York: Macmillan, 1944), pp. 52-55. Sherrill's treatment of both the *Beth Hassepher* and the *Beth Hammidrash* (what we would today call secondary education) is discussed in ibid., pp. 52-64.

137. William Boyd, *The History of Western Education*, 5th ed. (London: Adam and Charles Black, 1950), p. 61.

138. Ibid.

ple: since they can all become your pupils, they are all potentially your sons; indeed it is precisely through this teaching and receiving that they do become your sons."[139] The Jewish teacher ("master") "learns that his sons are not his biological offspring alone, but those in whom he has fathered wisdom and the love of God."[140] Blidstein went on to remark that in the laws of the Jewish common court (*eruv*) there were only two pairs of individuals which the Talmud fused into a single legal identity: father-son and teacher-student.[141]

Much of the Jewish scripture's commentary on the parent-child relationship is directed toward filial responsibility rather than parental. For example, the commandment to "honor thy father and thy mother" (Exodus 20:12) is spoken to the children about the proper treatment of their parents. What if that commandment had been directed to the parents, saying something to the effect: "Honor thy sons and thy daughters in the years that they are with you, that they may so honor you in your old age"? This would have put the emphasis on the responsibility of the parent, and by extension on the parental religious educator, to teach and instruct in a loving and caring manner. As the commandment came to us, less emphasis was placed on the duty of the parent/religious educator to demonstrate love than on the responsibility of the son or daughter to give respect.[142].

The importance of the rituals in family life is a final addition to the list of contributions of Judaism. As the book of Exodus (Chapter 12) tells the story of the first Passover, for example, Moses is heard teaching the Hebrews to observe the memorial yearly so that every generation will remember and understand the meaning of it: "And when your children ask you, 'What do you mean by this observance?' you shall say . . . "(Exodus 12:26-27, NRSV). The practice continues to this day with much of the meaning seemingly intact. The importance Jewish parents place on their responsibility to educate, such as through observation of these yearly rituals of the faith, is a powerful and abiding reminder of the impact of the parent in teaching the essentials of the faith.

In the same vein, the fragility of the faith is a matter for each generation to consider. Just as the strength of Judaism has remained because of the family and education, a weakening of either or both threatens the very existence of Judaism. This was the message of the book by Jack Spiro, *To Learn and To Teach*.[143] Spiro cited the statistic that "only 40 percent of Jewish children in the United States receive any kind of Jewish education," and of these, most obtain a "minimal 'Sunday School' education" where their Jewish education is completed by "the ripe age of thirteen in time to parrot the Torah blessings."[144] He said that the statistics

---

139. Gerald Blidstein, *Honor Thy Father and Mother: Filial Responsibility in Jewish Law and Ethics* (New York: KATV Publishing House, 1975), p. 138.

140. Ibid., p. 140.

141. Ibid.

142. For further consideration of this thought, see Chapter Five of Blidstein. Also see a discussion of parental responsibilities in Abraham P. Bloch, *A Book of Jewish Ethical Concepts: Biblical and Postbiblical* (New York: KATV Publishing House, 1984), pp. 236-240. Compare the comments of Hayim Halevy Donin in *To Be a Jew: A Guide to Jewish Observance in Contemporary Life* (New York: Basic Books, 1972), pp. 128-132.

143. Jack Spiro, *To Learn and to Teach: A Philosophy of Jewish Education* (New York: Philosophical Library, 1983).

"spell disaster for the future of American Judaism" because of the threat of Jewish illiteracy regarding their historic language: "Education must be the first priority of the American Jewish community if we are to cope with this crisis of survival. The 'now' generation must be educated if there is to be a new generation."[145] No amount of heritage or history can overcome the power and the threat of weak links in the chain of generations. Each generation must work to see that the next generation has the faith tradition to pass along. Spiro told an old Hasidic story to make his point:

> The Baal Shem Tov, having a difficult task before him, would go to a certain place in the woods, light a fire and meditate in prayer. One generation later, faced with the same task, a Jew would go to that place in the woods and say, "I can no longer light a fire, but I can still utter a prayer."
>
> A generation after that, facing a similar task, a Jew went into the woods and said, "I can no longer light a fire nor do I know the meaning of prayer, but I know the place in the woods to which it belongs and that should be enough."
>
> When still another generation had passed, and confronted with a similar task, a Jew remained where he was and said, "I cannot light the fire, I cannot speak the prayer, I don't know the place, but I can tell the story about how it was done."
>
> This Hasidic allegory points to the dismal possibility that the subsequent generation will not even be able to tell the story.[146]

Historical Personage: Horace Bushnell

A chapter on the religious educator as parent, especially one that has emphasized the function of nurture, is virtually required to mention Horace Bushnell (1802-1876). Bushnell's impact on the field is difficult to overstate. Luther Weigle said: "The modern movement for the better religious education of children owes more to Horace Bushnell, doubtless, than to any other one man."[147] Randolph Crump Miller referred to Bushnell as "the father of the religious education movement"[148] and as "the great emancipator of children."[149] William Adamson called Bushnell "a genius, a sensitive and much loved pastor, a man of profound insights and controversial ideas, and one of the great historical figures of the Christian church in America."[150] The primary reason for including Bushnell here, however, is that Bushnell penned his classic *Christian Nurture*[151] as a parent to parents on how to nurture their children.[152]

---

144. Ibid., p. 9.
145. Ibid., p. 10.
146. Ibid., p. 11.
147. Luther A. Weigle, "The Christian Ideal of Family Life as Expounded in Horace Bushnell's 'Christian Nurture,'" *Religious Education* 19:1 (February, 1924), p. 47.
148. Randolph Crump Miller, *Education for Christian Living*, 2nd ed. (Englewood Cliffs, N.J.: Prentice-Hall, 1963). p. 30.
149. Ibid., p. 29.
150. William R. Adamson, *Bushnell Rediscovered* (Philadelphia: United Church Press, 1966), p. 7.

Christian Nurture went through a series of revisions and modifications before its final form was reached in 1861. In 1838 Bushnell published an essay on "Spiritual Economy of Revivals of Religion" and in 1844 one on "Growth, not Conquest, the True Method of Christian Progress,"[153] where the seeds of his position which came to fruition in *Christian Nurture* were already planted. He then wrote two articles entitled "Discourses on Christian Nurture" in 1846 for the Massachusetts Sabbath School Society, but they were withdrawn from publication within a few months because of the controversy which resulted. Bushnell took it upon himself to republish the "Discourses" along with an additional argument chapter, the earlier two essays, and two related sermons, in book form in 1847.[154] By 1861 the book took its final form that we know today, with the first two chapters remaining as the two original "Discourses." This final edition included eight chapters (designated as Part Two) specifically addressed to parents as to the "mode" of parental nurture. In this section he was not writing to scholars or to theologians, but directly to parents on how to do the work of Christian nurture. The stance Bushnell took in the book, then, was not accidental or impulsive but representative of a lifelong position developed while serving as pastor, learning from his parishioners about how to deal effectively with children.

At the same time as serving as pastor Bushnell was experiencing the role of parent himself, and his life experiences indelibly enriched and shaped his writings. One example was reported by his daughter. In 1842, Bushnell's only son died barely four years old, an event which Mary Bushnell Cheney said was "a heavy blow, never to be forgotten—one which influenced his whole future life and character."[155] Not long after this event, Bushnell said: "I have learned more of experiential religion since my little boy died than in all my life before."[156]

Bushnell was caught in the crosscurrents of controversy, and different sides of the argument have frequently both used and abused his writings. As William Adamson put it: "For the most part, Horace Bushnell has either been bypassed or misinterpreted,"[157] meaning that the entire argument of Bushnell has generally not been fully appreciated. On their first appearance, the "Discourses" (retained in the current *Christian Nurture*) were withdrawn from publication because some charged that they were "full of dangerous tendencies."[158] These charges were not unfounded. Bushnell proposed a means of Christian teaching and parenting definitely at odds with the harsh views of the "ostrich nurture"[159]

---

151. Horace Bushnell, *Christian Nurture* (Grand Rapids, Mich.: Baker, 1979; reprint of 1861 edition).

152. Although Bushnell dealt exclusively with Christian nurture, and not with the more non-particularistic religious nurture (education) that is the focus of the present book, what Bushnell had to say is easily generalized and transferred to the larger realm of religious education.

153. Weigle, "The Christian Ideal," p. 47.

154. Ibid.

155. Mary Bushnell Cheney, *Life and Letters of Horace Bushnell* (New York: Scribner's, 1903; reprint of 1880 edition), p. 105.

156. Ibid.

157. Adamson, *Bushnell Rediscovered*, p. 128.

158. Cheney, *Life and Letters of Horace Bushnell*, p. 179.

attitudes of the revivalists and therefore addressed and challenged some of the fundamental theological positions of the day.[160] However, his critics from the conservative side never appeared to appreciate that Bushnell did not oppose conversion.[161] Bushnell was envisioning the day when conversion, of the type generated by the revivalists,[162] would be largely unnecessary: "That the child is to grow up a Christian, and never know himself as being otherwise."[163] His theologically conservative critics failed to read the next paragraph, however, which stated in part: "I do not affirm that every child may, in fact and without exception, be so trained that he certainly will grow up to be a Christian."[164] Bushnell was writing to *parents* about their rightful responsibility, which was to give the child Christian *nurture*. His belief in human *nature* can be understood in the following passage: "The growth of Christian virtue is no vegetable process, no mere onward development. It involves a struggle with evil, a fall and a rescue."[165]

If Bushnell's detractors from the theological right have not read all of Bushnell's argument, then neither have his "disciples" from the theological left. As William Adamson aptly stated: "Certain educators have appropriated him as their kin, but in the process they have actually twisted his doctrines of growth and the immanence of God to their own liking."[166] One of these was George Albert Coe. His famous article, "Religious Education as a Part of General Education," closed with a paraphrase of the thesis statement of Bushnell's book.[167] It is difficult, if not impossible, to reconcile Coe's positions on the nature of persons as well as the task of religious education squarely with those of Bushnell's. For example, Bushnell wrote: "There are many who assume the radical goodness of human nature, and the work of Christian education is, in their view, only to educate or educe the good that is in us. Let no one be disturbed by the suspicion of a coincidence between what I have here said and such a theory."[168] It is difficult to imagine Coe giving such a disavowal his blessing. What Coe and his

---

159. See Chapter Three of *Christian Nurture* for a fuller understanding of Bushnell's use of this term.

160. Bushnell insisted, and rightly so, that his proposal was by no means new but was indeed "as old as the Christian church." He believed he was calling the church back to its historic position. See Bushnell, *Christian Nurture*, p. 11.

161. Bushnell, *Christian Nurture*, pp. 195-223. Bushnell described two "principal modes by which the kingdom of God among men may be, and is to be extended": conversion and "family propagation," the latter of which is the province of Christian nurture. Ibid., pp. 195-196. Bushnell saw himself as trying to bring balance back into the means of populating the kingdom, since he believed the "conversion" approach had held nearly exclusive sway far too long.

162. It is important to keep in mind, however, that Bushnell was in the main quite opposed to the methods and tactics of the revivalists. For one example among many, see Bushnell, *Christian Nurture*, pp. 77-79.

163. Ibid., p. 10.

164. Ibid.

165. Ibid., p. 23.

166. Adamson, *Bushnell Rediscovered*, p. 128.

167. George Albert Coe, "Religious Education as a Part of General Education," in *Who Are We?: The Quest for a Religious Education*, ed. John H. Westerhoff III (Birmingham, Ala.: Religious Education Press, 1978), p. 22. This article originally was presented as an address by Coe to the first convention of the Religious Education Association in 1903.

168. Bushnell, *Christian Nurture*, p. 22.

followers did with the concept of nurture and with the whole of religious education can be said to have its roots in Bushnell's writings, but it would be misleading to say that they were always faithful to Bushnell's positions. The danger of reading history "backwards," of seeing Coe in Bushnell, is damaging to the legacy of Bushnell. It is certainly appropriate, however, to see the traces of Bushnell in Coe and company.[169]

The key to understanding Bushnell is his concept of the "organic unity of the family."[170] Bushnell tried to overcome what he believed was a "bent toward individualism"[171] that destroyed the family bonds and the family responsibilities, and therefore stressed the "organic unity of the family" instead. By this phrase Bushnell meant the natural "power exerted by parents over children," an influence and a "bond which is so intimate that they [parents] do it [teach and nurture] unconsciously and undesignedly—they must do it."[172] Bushnell once explained this "organic unity" in terms of biology: "We are parts or members of a common body, as truly as the limbs of a tree."[173] In another passage, he used a different analogy: "Your character is a stream, a river, flowing down upon your children, hour by hour."[174]

Bushnell, then, spoke directly to the parents about their responsibilities. How were parents to teach their children? The answer was simple to give, but difficult to do: "I beseech you turn yourselves to the true life of religion. Have it first in yourselves, then teach it as you live it; teach it by living it; for you can do it in no other manner. Be Christians yourselves, and then it will not be difficult for you to do your true duties to your children. Until then it is really impossible."[175] A final summary statement of Bushnell's directions to parents, and to religious educators in the role of parent, reveals the difficulty and the challenge of parenthood: "To be Christians ourselves—ah! there is the difficulty."[176]

Contemporary Example: C. Ellis Nelson

Moving from Horace Bushnell to C. Ellis Nelson (b. 1916) not only requires jumping over a century but changing the focus of the source of Christian nurture just a bit. In Chapter IV of *Christian Nurture,* Bushnell noted the various systems in society that were being ravaged by the "bent toward individualism," and among them were the state, the church, and the family.[177] Instead of trying to address all of these societal systems, however, Bushnell narrowed his focus: "My design, at the present time, is to restore, if possible, the conception of one of these organic forms, viz: the family."[178] He then went on to discuss the "organic unity of the family." Bushnell did have some things to say to the church in rela-

169. See the insightful comments of Adamson in *Bushnell Rediscovered*, pp. 124-126.
170. See Chapter Four of *Christian Nurture*.
171. Ibid., p. 91.
172. Ibid., p. 93.
173. Ibid., p. 95.
174. Ibid., p. 119.
175. Ibid., p. 87.
176. Ibid., p. 89
177. Ibid., pp. 91-92
178. Ibid., p. 92.

tion to nurture, but the primary audience he addressed was the family—or more specifically, the parents in the church.

With C. Ellis Nelson, the situation reverses itself. Nelson did address the family and the parents, but his primary audience was the church or, in his words, the congregation as the "community of believers."[179] Where Bushnell spoke expressly to the parents, on the whole Nelson did not. He addressed instead the entire congregation as parental religious educators. Nelson rejected the notion that the religious educator is only a lone individual, or a group of self-identified professionals. The "religious educator," especially in the role of parent, is far more than a single entity. From Nelson's perspective we see that the local faith community is the primary focus of religious nurture.

Following is a brief overview of relevant material written by Nelson and an evaluation of that material for the subject of the religious educator as parent. What follows, then, is a very narrow and specialized use of the work of C. Ellis Nelson. The overview does not cover the entire corpus of Nelson's writings, or even the ultimate and lasting significance of them. Nelson's work is used instead to illustrate a view of the religious educator as parent. For Nelson's message to be heard on its own terms, the primary sources themselves must be consulted in their entirety.[180]

Overview

This overview deals primarily with two of Nelson's books: *Where Faith Begins*[181] and *How Faith Matures*. Though separated by publication dates more than two decades apart, these two books hold as much in common as the similarity of titles implies. The books are nearly perfect companions, complementing each other in style, message, and audience. It is difficult to imagine two representative works which better summarize and encapsulate a person's career.

The similarity and consistency of these books makes them easy to overview. The books were written clearly and simply with precise, step-wise logic. Nelson

---

179. Nelson explained: "For ordinary Christians the agency for blending and communicating a proper social self-image is *the community of believers*. I use this term because it is broader than the term "church." It includes residential religious communities, the kind of people who are dissaffected with their denomination but are seriously seeking a congenial group of believers in retreat centers or elsewhere, and stable groups that gather in homes for Bible study and a simple celebration of the sacraments." C. Ellis Nelson, *How Faith Matures* (Louisville: Westminster/John Knox, 1989), p. 51. Emphasis added.

180. To get the flavor of Nelson's writings, the following sources should be consulted in addition to those discussed below: C. Ellis Nelson, *Love and the Law: The Place of the Ten Commandments in the Christian Faith Today* (Richmond: John Knox, 1963); *Conscience: Theological and Psychological Perspectives*, comp. C. Ellis Nelson (New York: Newman, 1973); C. Ellis Nelson, *Using Evaluation in Theological Education* (Nashville: Abingdon, 1975); C. Ellis Nelson, *Don't Let Conscience Be Your Guide* (New York: Paulist, 1978); C. Ellis Nelson, "Our Oldest Problem," in *Tradition and Transformation*, ed. Padraic O'Hare (Birmingham, Ala.: Religious Education Press, 1979), pp. 58-72; *Value Conflicts in Health Care Delivery*, ed. Bart Gruzalski and C. Ellis Nelson (Cambridge, Mass.: Ballinger, 1982); C. Ellis Nelson and Daniel Aleshire, "Research in Faith Development," in *Faith Development and Fowler*, ed. Craig Dykstra and Sharon Parks (Birmingham, Ala.: Religious Education Press, 1986), pp. 180-201; *Congregations: Their Power to Form and Transform*, comp. C. Ellis Nelson (Atlanta: John Knox, 1988).

181. C. Ellis Nelson, *Where Faith Begins* (Atlanta: John Knox, 1967).

carefully developed his arguments point by point, leading the reader to conclusions which appear to be inevitable because of the tight logic Nelson employed. Both books had their genesis as lecture series: *Where Faith Begins*, as the James Sprunt Foundation Lecture Series at Union Theological Seminary in Virginia (1965), and *How Faith Matures*, as the Caldwell Lectures at Louisville Presbyterian Seminary in Kentucky (1983). Extensive rewriting followed, but the resultant books still have the readability and accessibility intended for a broadbased audience of "ministers, Christian educators, lay leaders, church school teachers, administrators, and parents."[182] These books by Nelson are on the serious and scholarly side of religious education and not "preachy" or sermonic like Bushnell's *Christian Nurture*.

A casual glance at the titles of Nelson's two books may lead one to assume that Nelson was writing from a psychological or a developmental perspective, but such an assumption would be incorrect. Although Nelson did come at the task from what he identified as an overall social-science type of perspective,[183] he drew more from the fields of cultural anthropology and sociology than from developmental psychology.[184] In fact, Nelson began his 1989 book with a critique of "secular individualism"[185] within a discussion of the topic of the "social construction of beliefs."[186] For Nelson, the current emphases on the individual and on the secular to the exclusion of the communal influences are contributing factors to the confusion and the disarray apparent within Christian religious education. Nelson focused on the congregation as the community of believers, rather than on the development of isolated individuals, and such a focus was much better served by a discipline like sociology (the influences of social interaction) than psychology (the development of the individual).[187]

Both books are examples of what Nelson called "practical theology," as distinguished from theology.[188] Theology he defined as "a careful, systematic, critical examination of biblical, historical, philosophical, and often psychological data concerning beliefs about and ideas about God," which "although based on human experience, is several steps removed from human experience."[189] Practical theology, or as Nelson suggested, "operational theology," is theology which "arises out of and attends to practical situations about which decisions must be

---

182. Nelson, *How Faith Matures*, p. 18.

183. Nelson, *Where Faith Begins*, pp. 16-18.

184. See, for example, his comments in *Where Faith Begins*, p. 10.

185. See Chapter One, "Our Age of Secular Individualism," in Nelson, *How Faith Matures*, pp. 21-41.

186. Ibid., "Part One," pp. 19-59.

187. "From my study of cultural anthropology and sociology, I discerned that what these social scientists were describing as the socializing process (or acculturation process) was the process by which faith and its meaning was transmitted by a community of believers." Nelson, *Where Faith Begins*, pp. 10-11.

188. Interestingly enough, Nelson used the tools of social science, and many of its procedures, but continued to champion the term "practical theology." It may be that Nelson can be interpreted as something of a precursor of the social science approach, especially in light of his comments in his earlier book. See, for example, Nelson, *Where Faith Begins*, pp. 16-18.

189. Nelson, *How Faith Matures*, p. 11.

190. Ibid. Compare Nelson, *Where Faith Begins*, pp. 10-13.

191. Nelson, *How Faith Matures*, p. 15.

made."[190] In addition, Nelson stressed that "practical theology always starts with present life situations—that is what makes it practical."[191] His point of distinction was that practical theology would deal with what people do, rather than simply with what they think, and what causes these actions. Nelson observed how "the situation of the people influences the theological message addressed to them."[192] Nelson did not provide any simple and universal solutions for the church but instead gave principles[193] by which congregations could utilize their own experience and life situations to address their own unique problems.

The methodology used in both books was similar, what Nelson called a "historical critical method" in the earlier book,[194] and a "critical social method" in the later one.[195] In each Nelson took special pains to take the Bible seriously by looking at the cultural situations in which biblical characters had religious experiences and then applying that same sensitivity to modern cultural situations and experiences. This is also to say that Nelson based his books on biblical study, but from a critical rather than a devotional perspective.

Nelson's chief offering to religious educators functioning in parental roles can be found in the themes of the books. In *Where Faith Begins*, Nelson asked the question: "How does a person develop trust in the God of the Bible . . . and what does that faith mean in his life?"[196] The thesis statement provided the answer: "My thesis is that faith is communicated by a community of believers and that the meaning of faith is developed by its members out of their history, by their interaction with each other, and in relation to the events that take place in their lives."[197] Nelson saw that what the "social scientists were describing as the socializing process (or acculturation process) was the process by which faith and its meaning was transmitted by a community of believers."[198] His message of "where faith begins," then, was that it begins in the community of believers, which not only creates meaning but infuses that meaning through its environmental atmosphere: "I believe that the local church is the community that can develop a contemporary meaning of faith before it is passed on to the rising generation."[199] This faith is not to be communicated casually or infrequently. It must be done determinedly, constantly, and intentionally through interpersonal relationship: "What a community of believers must have is face-to-face personal relationships of enough permanence for the group to worship, work, and study together under a common commitment to the God of the Bible."[200]

Nelson stated his case just as clearly in *How Faith Matures*: "The question [the book] attempts to answer is: How does faith in God become mature? The answer is 'through religious experience.'"[201] It is really not fair to stop the quote there,

---

192. Ibid., p. 12.
193. Ibid., pp. 16-18.
194. Nelson, *Where Faith Begins*, pp. 10-13.
195. Nelson, *How Faith Matures*, p. 13.
196. Nelson, *Where Faith Begins*, p. 9.
197. Ibid., p. 10.
198. Ibid, pp. 10-11.
199. Ibid., p. 12.
200. Ibid., p. 34.
201. Nelson, *How Faith Matures*, p. 11.

because he admitted that such a broad response is not ultimately helpful, but it does illustrate the simplicity and directness of Nelson's style, with the message of the book stated on the first page and in the first paragraph where no one can miss it. The complexity surrounding the simple answer was also acknowledged, as he continued by saying that "to be helpful the answer must explore the meaning of religious experience, must provide ways of judging the authenticity of such experience, and must suggest some practical means of relating personal religious experiences to the needs of the people."[202] These were the issues that made up the bulk of the book, but Nelson was careful to keep the perspective in focus: "The book is about these matters, with special reference to the way a congregation in its educational activity may focus attention on experience as the arena in which faith matures."[203] Later in the book, Nelson restated the thesis in this concise and summary form: "The way a congregation worships and works and the way members relate to each other form a dynamic teaching and learning situation."[204]

Evaluation

As much as any one person, C. Ellis Nelson is responsible for the emphasis in the 1970s and 1980s on socialization in religious education.[205] It was primarily his 1967 book that gave impetus to the trend, with others like John Westerhoff and Thomas Groome following sometime afterward. Just as Horace Bushnell focused attention on the family and the home as the primary agency of religious education in the middle of the nineteenth century, C. Ellis Nelson has aroused increased interest in the congregation as the "community of believers" where "faith can be incubated and nurtured"[206] during the latter part of the twentieth century. Such an influence signals the high value of Nelson to the field of religious education, as well as to the role of parent. Keeping the topic of parent as the boundary, the works of C. Ellis Nelson are given some evaluative remarks. Some positive contributions are mentioned first, and then a few possible areas of concern are noted second.

The first positive contribution to observe is that Nelson attempted to refocus the educational strategy of the church to make the congregation the agency of education rather than to relegate education to some isolated and fragmentary part of the congregation. A reconsideration of the relationship between Sunday school and overall religious education serves as an example of his approach.[207] Nelson neither advocated demolishing the Sunday school, nor did he see it as the one last

202. Ibid.
203. Ibid.
204. Ibid., p. 181.
205. This is not to imply that socialization has been ignored or displaced since then, but that it has been recognized as such a foundational issue that it is now an assumption regularly taken into consideration.
206. Nelson, *Where Faith Begins*, p. 101.
207. For those who see Sunday school as virtually if not entirely the sum total of religious education, this sentence will appear nonsensical. Nelson was pointing out that there is so much more to religious education than one organization could possibly be responsible for. For an excellent article on this topic, see C. Ellis Nelson, "Is Church Education Something Particular?" in *Who Are We?: The Quest for a Religious Education*, ed. John H. Westerhoff III (Birmingham, Ala.: Religious Education Press, 1978), pp. 193-217.

hope for religious education. If the congregation as a whole takes greater responsibility for the totality of the nurture, then the Sunday school becomes one element of the larger educational plan.[208] As Nelson expressed it: "Rather than being *the* place where children are supposed to learn the Christian faith, it will become *a* place where they learn something about the faith, to *supplement* what they get in the home and through participation in other aspects of the congregational life and work."[209]

A second contribution has been Nelson's reminder that religious education often takes place in "an unplanned, unpretentious way."[210] This is not to say that religious education is always unintentional or accidental. It is to say that religious education which takes place in an informal atmosphere of care and nurture provides teaching and allows learning that is easily overlooked and undervalued: "We tend to forget that congregations can be helpful just by being a 'fellowship of kindred minds.'"[211]

A third contribution is that Nelson, like Bushnell, wrote to adults about their task of being Christians, so that the children could thereby learn to be Christians. Expressed in less particularistic language, both men highlighted the influence of modeling. For example, Nelson wrote: "We must give first attention to the continual training of adults who are parents, so that they may grow 'in grace and knowledge' and then, as part of their training, help them better to perform their roles as parents and teachers in the home."[212] Even more pointedly, he said: "We must help the adults learn how they can function as Christian parents in the home."[213]

A fourth contribution is the practicality of Nelson's writings. In both books, Nelson devoted significant space and effort to specific and practical suggestions as to how to implement his ideas. In *Where Faith Begins*, the final chapter ("Guidelines for Communicating Faith") gave nine ways to concretize and utilize the more theoretical work found earlier in the book. In *How Faith Matures*, the "how" was addressed in Part Three ("Experiential Religion"), composed of three chapters. Nelson cannot be accused of theorizing without attending to how those theories can be put into practice.

A final contribution is the simplicity, clarity, and completeness that these associated volumes provide. Even the titles give a sense of wholeness. First considered was the issue of where faith begins, and second was a discussion of how that faith matures. Just as remarkable as the completeness is the continuity of the books. In virtually every respect, the two provide a kind of "stereo" effect: Both are a bit different, yet both are amazingly similar—especially in light of the twenty-two years that separate their publication dates. Taken together, these books seem to provide as complete an overview of Nelson's position as one can imagine.

---

208. See Nelson, *How Faith Matures*, pp. 199-202.
209. Ibid., p. 200.
210. Ibid., p. 158.
211. Ibid.
212. Nelson, *Where Faith Begins*, p. 209.
213. Ibid., p. 211. For additional comments by Nelson on the duty of the family, see *How Faith Matures*, pp. 193-202.

A few concerns about Nelson's contributions can be raised. Two of them are related specifically to his works, and three of them relate to the way that they have been utilized here.

The first concern addresses the use of the terms faith and trust, particularly as employed in *Where Faith Begins*. In this earlier book, Nelson appeared to use the words interchangeably, as in the question he used to open the book: "How does a person develop trust in the God revealed to us in the Bible . . . and what does that faith mean in his life?"[214] In *How Faith Matures*, Nelson went to some lengths distinguishing between faith and trust.[215] One way to resolve this concern is to assume the later work clarifies the earlier.

A second potential problem relates to the perennial discussion of "What is Christian/religious education?" Some may argue that Nelson was certainly addressing practical theology but that practical theology is different than Christian or religious education. In other words, some may say that Nelson has not addressed the field in strict terms. One must take a narrow view of either Christian or religious education for this to be a major concern. Nelson tended to take a broader view of the field than do some others,[216] and was therefore providing some alternative language for this expanded view.

This concern leads to another set of issues that relates more specifically to the design and intention of this chapter. One of these is that Nelson's work is so integrally Christian that it is difficult to generalize his views into the broader scope of nonparticularistic religious education.[217] Again, this is an issue only within the context of this specific chapter. A slight misreading of this point accuses Nelson of being too Christian! A clearer articulation is that Nelson is too particularistic for universal application, since he wrote specifically for and intentionally to Christian congregations.

An even more finely-tuned difficulty for this chapter is that Nelson was expressly writing "for mainline Protestant denominations in America."[218] The same thin line of discomfort exists here as in the paragraph above. Nelson had the privilege of addressing whomever he chose. A problem arises only in trying to generalize from his intended audience.

The final point is similar to the previous two. Nelson did not write, of his own admission, as a religious educator addressing the role of the parent. He

---

214. Nelson, *Where Faith Begins*, p. 9

215. Nelson, *How Faith Matures*, pp. 127-130.

216. An excellent overview of this entire issue was given by D. Campbell Wyckoff in "Religious Education as a Discipline," in *Who Are We?: The Quest for a Religious Education*, pp. 165-180. For an example of a strict use of the term "Christian education," see Lawrence O. Richards, "Experiencing the Dream Together: Toward the Impossible Dream," in *Religious Education and Theology*, ed. Norma H. Thompson (Birmingham, Ala.: Religious Education Press, 1982), pp. 198-217.

217. This difficulty in generalizing reveals one of the great differences in a theological macrotheory and a social science macrotheory. Since theology is always particularistic, it is impossible to change theological (substantive) content without altering the entire structural content. In the social science approach, the substantive content does not dictate or determine the structural content. See this discussed, for example, in James Michael Lee, "The Authentic Source of Religious Instruction," in *Religious Education and Theology*, pp. 100-197; and in James Michael Lee, *The Shape of Religious Instruction: A Social Science Approach* (Birmingham, Ala.: Religious Education Press, 1971), especially Chapter Eight, "The Place of Theology," pp. 225-257.

218. Nelson, *How Faith Matures*, p. 153.

was writing as a practical theologian to Christian congregations. The adaptations to the role of the parent are external ones. Although it appears that the selection of Nelson for this role has been adequately presented, perceived failure at this should be no reflection on him. If the view of the congregation as a nurturing community of believers which functions in a parental fashion is an aberration or perversion of Nelson's writings, then the blame is not justifiably fixed upon him.

Representative Teaching Procedure: Observational Learning

The role of the parent for the religious educator demands displaying an attitude of constant teaching, whether the educator is in a formal environment, such as a classroom, or an informal one, such as the playground. The teaching that goes on is pervasive and effective, whether or not the educator is unintentional about his or her activity.[219] Indeed, the living out of the role is so difficult, and so essential, precisely because of these incessant educational stances and expectations. The representative teaching procedure that facilitates this kind of teaching must enable the educator to be as intentional and as focused as possible in the teaching that is performed. The skillful employment of the teaching procedure known as observational learning has this kind of potential.

Observational learning was the formal term used by Albert Bandura for facilitating social learning.[220] This teaching procedure, and its foundational theory of learning, is based solely on neither a cognitive-developmental approach nor an environmental, behaviorist approach[221] but is an attempt to find some consensus between these two that combines the strengths of both. Bandura expressed it this way: "In the social learning view, people are neither driven by inner forces nor buffeted by environmental stimuli. Rather, psychological functioning is explained in terms of a continuous reciprocal interaction of personal and environmental determinants."[222] Bandura made it clear that such observational learning is of no little consequence: "The abbreviation of the acquisition process through observational learning is vital for both development and survival,"[223] and "the more costly and hazardous the mistakes, the heavier is the reliance on

---

219. This issue was initially considered earlier in this chapter under the dimension of model.

220. Bandura, *Social Learning Theory*, p. 22.

221. Bruce Joyce and Marsha Weil include such terms as individually prescribed instruction, direct instruction, and mastery learning within the same teaching family as social learning. See Bruce Joyce and Marsha Weil, *Models of Teaching*, 3rd ed. (Englewood Cliffs, N.J.: Prentice-Hall, 1986), pp. 317-330. These previous terms are more reflective of the operant conditioning paradigm than of social learning theory, which is the focus of observational learning. Social learning theory may legitimately be called a neo-behavioristic approach, because it adapts many of the operant conditioning procedures while still being open to other means. In Bandura's case, the openness is particularly oriented toward cognitive-developmental theory and information processing.

222. Ibid., pp. 11-12. Bandura placed this kind of integrative theory in context: "Psychological theories have traditionally assumed that learning can occur only by performing responses and experiencing their effects. In actuality, virtually all learning phenomena resulting from direct experience occur on a vicarious basis by observing other people's behavior and its consequences for them. The capacity to learn by observation enables people to acquire large, integrated patterns of behavior without having to form them gradually by tedious trial and error." Ibid., p. 12.

223. Ibid.

observational learning from competent examples."[224] When the focus is religious education, by all accounts an essential and integrated element of the total lifestyle of persons, then the value of observational learning becomes all the more obvious, since "some complex behaviors can be produced only through the aid of modeling."[225]

Observational learning is governed by four component processes, according to Bandura. First are the *attentional* processes: "People cannot learn much by observation unless they attend to, and perceive accurately, the significant features of the modeled behavior."[226] The models "who possess engaging qualities are sought out, while those lacking pleasing characteristics are generally ignored or rejected."[227] Of extreme importance, especially to the religious educator who may still be somewhat unconvinced about the value and influence of community, is what Bandura called the associative patterns: "The people with whom one regularly associates, either through preference or imposition, delimit the types of behavior that will be repeatedly observed and hence learned most thoroughly."[228] The obvious and virtually inescapable result is that we tend to imitate the people with whom we associate. The responsibility for the religious educator performing in the omnipresent role of parent is unmistakable.

Second are the *retention* processes. Bandura remarked, reasonably enough: "People cannot be influenced by observation of modeled behavior if they do not remember it."[229] Retention is accomplished by representing the behavior in permanent memory through the medium of symbols, which are primarily represented by imaginal and verbal systems. In addition, the value of rehearsal—mental and/or physical—is an important aid to retention. Bandura stated: "The highest level of observational learning is achieved by first organizing and rehearsing the modeled behavior symbolically and then enacting it overtly."[230]

Third are *motor reproduction* processes, or "converting symbolic representations into appropriate actions."[231] The key point here is that observational learning is not limited to cognitive process. Physical activity—reproducing the modeled behavior—is an integral and inextricable part of modeling. This is the level of skill achievement, as Bandura explained: "In most everyday learning, people usually achieve a close approximation of the new behavior by modeling, and they refine it through self-corrective adjustments on the basis of informative feedback from performance and from focused demonstrations of segments that have been only partially learned."[232] Surely this is an indictment of any reli-

---

224. Ibid.
225. Ibid. Bandura added: "A comprehensive theory of behavior must explain how patterns of behavior are acquired and how their expression is continuously regulated by the interplay of self-generated and external sources of influence. From a social learning perspective, human nature is characterized as a vast potentiality that can be fashioned by direct and vicarious experience into a variety of forms within biological limits." Ibid., p. 13.
226. Ibid., p. 24.
227. Ibid.
228. Ibid.
229. Ibid., p. 25.
230. Ibid., p. 27.
231. Ibid.
232. Ibid., p. 28

gious educator who believes that thinking alone determines action! The religious educator in the role of parent is required to aid in the performance of modeled behavior.

Fourth is *motivational* processes. People do not enact everything they observe and learn. Significantly, Bandura observed that people "are more likely to adopt behavior if it results in outcomes they value than if it has unrewarding or punishing effects."[233] Bandura did stress the role of reinforcement as a motivational aspect of observational learning but differed from more traditional reinforcement-oriented theories, such as operant conditioning. Bandura found that reinforcement was most powerful as an antecedent rather than as a consequent influence.[234] This means that "observational learning can be achieved more effectively by informing observers in advance about the benefits of adopting modeled behavior than by waiting until they happen to imitate a model and then reward them for it."[235]

Bruce Joyce and Marsha Weil took these processes of observational learning and adapted them into a teaching procedure appropriate for a formal, structured environment. They called it the "basic practice model" containing five phases.[236] Phase one is orientation, where the educator establishes the content, objectives, and procedures of the lesson to be taught. Phase two is presentation, where the educator explains and demonstrates the new concept or skill for the learners—which in Bandura's terms is modeling. Phase three is structured practice, where the learners are led through practice examples and given corrective feedback. Phase four is guided practice, where learners do their own practice semi-independently of the educator, with the educator serving primarily as a monitor and resource person. Phase five is independent practice, where learners practice totally on their own in the environment of their choice and the feedback of the educator is indefinitely delayed until returning to the formal (classroom) environment. The goal through this teaching procedure is to wean the learner away from the educator gradually, so that the learner can hone the desired skills in a variety of environments and circumstances.

While observational learning as described in the paragraph above is valuable and effective, there is no need for the environment to be a formal one for its implementation. As this chapter on the role of the religious educator as parent has stressed, most of the environments employed for teaching turn out to be informal ones. They key issue for the parent role is lifestyle. Anything and everything that the parent does, and that the religious educator in the role of parent does, is a potential instructional act that may be observed and modeled. This is a role, therefore, that demands constant attention and care.

Experiential Simulation: Parent Training

It is certainly not true that the only way to experience the role of the religious educator as parent is to become a parent. First, such would be an unrea-

---

233. Ibid.
234. Ibid., pp. 36-37.
235. Ibid., p. 37.
236. Joyce and Weil, *Models of Teaching*, p. 136.

sonable expectation, shutting out a great number of persons from the role. Second, such a stance would contradict what has been expressed about the role of the religious educator throughout the chapter. The parent is but a metaphor to be used to better understand the various facets and responsibilities of the religious educator. The role and the functions of the religious educator are not limited to flesh-and-blood parents. Third, just being a parent does not ensure a person of becoming a better religious educator. Poor parenting only makes for poor religious education.

The most basic need of religious educators is to become aware of how each of us parents himself or herself.[237] If it is at all true that poor parenting makes for poor religious education, then each of us needs to examine our own internal parenting patterns and skills.[238] The suggestion for a simulation moves from the assumed interpersonal activity to an intrapersonal one. Because this book deals specifically with the religious educator, rather than the more impersonal topic of religious education, such introspection seems not only appropriate but necessary.

One resource for working on intrapersonal parenting is a book by Hugh Missildine entitled *Your Inner Child of the Past*.[239] Missildine wrote that we parent ourselves as we were parented, regardless of the quality of the initial parenting. Missildine began his explanation of this with two sentences, the first of which was: "One essential difference between adults and children in an emotional sense is that children have parents who provide in many ways an inner sense of direction and guidance, reassurance, esteem and worthiness—while adults act as parents to themselves, giving themselves the guidance and direction, the reassurance or the scolding that parents give to children."[240] The second sentence, then, was: "Adults (as parents to themselves) continue the parental attitudes that were imposed on them in childhood, perpetuating these attitudes toward themselves in adult life."[241]

Missildine then went on to help adults become aware of how they have learned to treat themselves and to make decisions about changing the inherited parental attitudes toward themselves that no longer are needed or fit. The healthy and nurturing attitudes are not the ones that cause problems and need changing. It is the destructive and painful ones that need revision. Missildine's approach was given in capsule form as follows: "The *first* step is to recognize these disturbing feelings and their childhood origin. The *second* is to accept and respect these feelings as part of oneself—as unavoidable as childhood itself. The *third* step is to establish limits so that these old childhood feelings do not control or dominate one's actions and abilities to function. All this takes hard, patient, repetitious work."[242]

This approach can be helpful for several reasons. First, it focuses on the

---

237. This was the point of the earlier discussion on the shadow role of the child abuser.

238. This is an issue of adult education, a point made throughout the chapter in such places as the discussion on Jewish religious education as well as on the contributions of Horace Bushnell and C. Ellis Nelson.

239. W. Hugh Missildine, *Your Inner Child of the Past* (New York: Simon & Schuster, 1963).

240. Ibid., p. 11.

241. Ibid.

242. Ibid., pp. 21-22.

adult, much in the same way that both Bushnell and Nelson did. Healthy, nurturing adults can then provide children with a safe and caring environment. The place to start, in other words, is with adults. Second, it helps make the adults more self-aware and self-guided. They need not be driven by unconscious and unhealthy motivations instilled in the past. Third, producing healthy religious educators requires producing psychologically healthy humans. This approach is one way of encouraging and promoting emotional health. Fourth, and finally, this kind of personal work must be undertaken for the sake of those we teach.[243] Since at least some of our teaching is done (as Nelson said) in the midst of "being a fellowship of kindred minds," then we need to be sure that what we are communicating is as healthy and as intentional as possible. Since all we say and do teaches, let us be sure that what we teach does no harm while preparing the way for health and wholeness.

Summary

The role of the religious educator as parent is a complex and difficult one to describe and prescribe. In the midst of all this verbiage, however, it is reassuring to note that humans have been parenting for quite a long while with apparently some measure of success! The avenues of learning for the religious educator concerning this role abound and are certainly not limited to any one model or process. The concern for the health and security of the next generation, and the next, drives us to find ever better and more effective ways to fulfill the role of parent.

---

243. This is the same point emphasized so strongly by Alice Miller, discussed in the section of this chapter on child abuse.

Figure 6: The Religious Educator as Parent	
Dimensions of the Role	Provider
	Protector
	Model
	Theologian
Aim	Maturity
Function	Nurture
Primary Virtues	Morality
	Faith
Activity	Trusting
Shadow Role	Child Abuser
Faith Tradition Resource	Judaism
Historical Personage	Horace Bushnell
Contemporary Example	C. Ellis Nelson
Representative Teaching Procedure	Observational Learning
Experiential Simulation	Parent Training

Chapter Five

The Religious Educator as Coach

To follow the role of the religious educator as parent with that of the religious educator as coach seems altogether appropriate, since in many ways a coach can be understood and experienced as something like "another parent." So much of what a coach does is parental in nature, and it may be that the coach is also a parent in real life. There are some very real parallels and similarities between the roles of parent and coach, especially as portrayed in the life of the religious educator.

At the same time, the roles are divergent. The coach, for example, may be quite interested in the care and nurture of the player, but the coach is not charged with the responsibility for seeing that the player has all the personal necessities of life. The coach has primary responsibility for the player only as long as he or she is a player for the coach. The parent is a parent continuously, twenty-four hours a day, seven days a week. If the player does not perform acceptably, or if the player is no longer needed, the coach can kick a player off the team and the coach's responsibility ends at that point.[1] The parent does not have those options, or even that attitude. The appropriate levels of commitment, responsibility, and love are necessarily different for the parent and coach.

While acknowledging that there are some similarities with that of the parent, then, the role of the coach does go on to expand and broaden the scope and work of the religious educator. The role of the parent need not be left behind and forgotten in turning to the role of coach. The ideas and concepts are transformed and reformed to portray the image of the coach, thereby giving an even more

---

1. The other side of this issue is that the player normally has the option of whether or not to play the game and can choose as well whether or not to continue playing under the particular coach's direction. The son or daughter does not have this kind of volitional choice in deciding on his or her parents.

extended view of the identity and tasks of the religious educator addressed thus far in the book. This evolution, accumulation, and eventual integration of the roles is important to the overall perspective of this book. While each of the roles, and chapters, in Part Two can be taken individually and separately, in the larger perspective they all need to be seen as integral elements of the whole. Ultimately, the entire identity of the ideal religious educator should become visible, with all ten roles becoming to one degree or another complementary and contributory to each other. One role may indeed describe the way an individual primarily approaches the work of religious education, but the further goal is to see how all of the ten roles can be incorporated and utilized as every religious educator strives to help accomplish the larger, corporate mission of religious education.

The role of the religious educator as coach has some inherent difficulties attached to it that could become barriers to its full implementation if left unattended. One of the most prominent is that the image of the coach may inaccurately portray the coach as someone who relies only on the trial and error method and who lacks scholarly preparation for the responsibility of coaching.[2] While discussing coaching as a teaching metaphor, Bill Lovin and Emery Casstevens made these comments that do indeed seem to reinforce this faulty view of the coach: "A reason that coaching is generally not good is that the coaches have simply not thought enough about it. They feel the need to coach more and better, but many have not worked out how to do it. The principles, *if there are any*, have not been identified and widely studied. Yet there is hardly anything that a coach could do that would yield more results than identify and study the *principles* of coaching."[3] These authors appear either unaware of the principles related to coaching or doubt that any really exist, making the enactment of the coach's role sound like an undisciplined, untaught, and random activity. Such a view is certainly not the one advanced in this chapter. The effort here is to determine some of the principles that govern the effective fulfillment of the role of the coach so that they can be applied to the work of the religious educator.

A second potential difficulty with the role of coach is the wide variety of facilitational styles that are practiced. Is it helpful or even valid to speak of coaching when, even if the discussion were limited to, say, football coaches, coaching styles vary in successful coaches from those of a Lou Holtz to those of a Joe Paterno? Is there any common ground?[4] This question is one that will provide a challenge throughout the chapter, yet it need not discourage the examination of the role of the coach. In fact, this perceived difficulty is an example of the depth and richness the role of coach has to offer the religious educator. There is not one style or manner of coaching that must be adopted, just as there is not one type of teaching procedure that must always be performed for one to be an effective

---

2. The same danger applies to seeing the learner in the role of "player," if he or she is prejudged as just being a "stupid jock," who is "all brawn and no brains." These pervasive stereotypes are difficult to root out.

3. Bill C. Lovin and Emery Reber Casstevens, *Coaching, Learning, and Action* (New York: American Management Association, 1971), p. 2. The first emphasis is mine; the second is from the authors.

4. This is probably what the comments by Lovin and Casstevens quoted above actually referred to.

religious educator. The objective is to pinpoint some principles and some research that point in the direction of good coaching and then for each person to contribute his or her own uniqueness and individuality to religious education through the employment of those principles.[5]

To address these erroneous views of the coach, and to accent the necessity of a principled approach to the role of coach, nine "keys," or principles, of the effective coach are suggested in the following few paragraphs. Each of these keys receives some degree of development or explication within the discussions of the chapter, but setting them out here in a stark, clear fashion underlines their importance and presents them in such a way that they can be easily recognized as the chapter progresses.

Key #1. The effective coach keeps his or her attention and energy focused on the players, rather than on himself or herself. The coach's responsibility is to facilitate and improve the performance of the players. Whatever glory or honor is bestowed on the coach comes as a result of the players being aided in their efforts by the teachings of the coach.

Key #2. The effective coach consciously and constantly operates from a base of theory and research that guides his or her instructional activity. This kind of coach uses theory to explain, predict, and evaluate and uses research to determine which procedures are effectual and which are not. Coaching in this manner is far removed from random activity or trial and error. Such a coach operates according to the *science* of coaching.

Key #3. The effective coach insists on practice, practice, practice—but only when the practice is performed for specific reasons founded on the principles. This type of preparation instituted by the coach represents the *art* of coaching.

Key #4. The effective coach fulfills his or her coaching responsibilities alongside of and in personal relationship with the players. This coach is not distant or removed from the action and is not isolated or separated from the players but is deeply and personally involved in all aspects of the game.

Key #5. The effective coach is concerned for and engages in addressing the totality of the players' being. Cognitive, affective, and lifestyle dimensions of the players are all important to the true coach. This coach does not see the players as pawns in a life-size game of chess but as complete human beings who need care and nurture on and off the field.

Key #6. The effective coach sets high standards for the team, for individual players, and for himself or herself. While it may not be possible to win every time the game is played, the effort to improve is constantly at the heart of the coach's work. The coach teaches competence, and the evaluation of that competence is measured through the implementation of performance objectives so that each person's achievement level can be effectively monitored.

Key #7. The effective coach carefully structures the learning environment

---

5. One of the values of the social-science approach to religious education is that a variety of procedures and techniques are possible when the theory and the research provide the basis for decision making. This process is quite different and distinct from trial and error, hit or miss guesswork. In reality, then, this chapter is viewing the coach from a social-science perspective, just as every other role in the book is similarly viewed. This important theme and point is woven throughout the chapter and the book.

so that the best possible results are achieved. The coach does not teach just through "telling" the players things but through utilizing the entire experience of preparing, practicing, and playing the game, all of which presents useful teaching opportunities.

Key #8. The effective coach empowers players to play the game. The coach of this type is not the only one on the team who is expected to think or to have ideas. The players are taught the basics of the game, are trained in the requisite skills, and they are also taught and expected to make decisions. The good coach does not constantly dictate every play or move but prepares the players before the game as completely as possible and then goes with them into the game situation to aid them in the strategizing that necessarily develops during the game.

Key #9. The effective coach develops a game plan in advance of the game and then constantly revises it and perfects it during the unfolding of the game itself. This coach is the clinical problem-solver, who evaluates and makes decisions in the midst of the action. The successful coach is never stuck on one way to play, or dependent on one procedure, but makes appropriate adaptations as the situation and as the environment changes.

The rest of this chapter is an exposition and development of these keys to the effective coach. The purpose of this chapter is to introduce and overview the role of the coach for the religious educator, setting the role in perspective and context so that both its merits and its dangers are adequately highlighted. As in the previous chapter, this is pursued through brief discussions of such topics as aim, function, and virtues. The first of these discussions takes up the task of overviewing a few of the various dimensions within the coach's role.

Dimensions of the Role

Among the many dimensions and facets of the role of the coach, these four should give a sufficient feel for the role: supervisor, trainer, motivator, and strategist. Given the fact that there are so many philosophies and methods of coaching, these selections are inevitably open to criticism. Some would want to select other dimensions they consider more important or descriptive because of a preferred style of coaching. Whatever the differences of opinion, the particular dimensions that follow at least reveal the multivariate role of the coach and open up the role to utilization by the religious educator.

Supervisor

The supervisor is the person who delegates, guides, directs, and "watches over"[6] those who are performing the work—or in the case of the coach, the players who are playing the game. The supervisor, as a dimension of the role of the coach, does not actually suit up and play the game, although he or she is a full participant in the flow of activity and is engaged in every aspect of it. The supervisor is the one who teaches the fundamental knowledge and the basic skills

---

6. This is literally what "super-vision" means—watching over. Watching over, in this case, does not mean disinterested looking but instead refers to careful, analytic, and evaluative observation.

necessary to play the game, who prepares others to play the game, and who leads the players in practice to help them increase the level of their performance. When the game is underway the coach as supervisor remains on the field, observing the players and the unfolding of events, evaluating the players' performance, and helping with strategies to achieve the desired results.

Implied in the preceding paragraph is the fact that although the supervisor is not the one playing the game, normally he or she has at one time or another performed the task (played the game) with a certain degree of skill and competence. One of the qualifications of a supervisor is to possess the fundamental knowledge and the basic expertise necessary in order to do an adequate job of delegating, directing, guiding, and observing.[7] The skills of playing, of course, are not precisely the same ones that are required of the coach or of the supervisor.[8] The point is that the coach is expected to have some prior experience in the game and not to be a novice or an ingénue at it. As one text on supervision stated it: "Supervisors usually have technical training and experience in the functions they oversee. Most first-line supervisors, in fact, are promoted from the working ranks, often supervising people who were once co-workers."[9] Taken from the point of view of the coach, the coach is expected to have experience in the game, to understand the basics as well as the nuances of the game, and so to have played the game at one time; just as "first-line supervisors" are normally chosen from the workers, so a coach is frequently one selected from among those who have played the game—at whatever level of ability they performed as players.[10]

Along with being knowledgeable about the technical dimensions of the task, the supervisor must be adept at helping others accomplish the task through what Clark Lambert called "applied coaching techniques."[11] This addresses both facilitative competence and personnel skills. Finding effective ways to match and combine individual achievement with group or team goals allows the supervisor to be interested and concerned about individuals and their needs, as well as to pay

---

7. These terms recall the variously identified functions of management. For example, one management text listed them this way: planning, organizing, staffing, directing, and controlling. See John R. Schermerhorn Jr., James E. Hunt, and Richard N. Osborn, *Managing Organizational Behavior* (New York: Wiley, 1982), pp. 19-20. A similar categorization of these functions is planning, controlling, organizing, staffing, and leading. See these discussed by Leslie W. Rue and Lloyd L. Byars, *Management: Theory and Application*, 4th ed. (Homewood, Ill.: Richard D. Irwin, 1986), pp. 10-11.

8. The skills of the supervisor include analytic skills, control skills, and facilitative skills. For a teacher improvement model that incorporates these skills, see James Michael Lee, *The Flow of Religious Instruction: A Social Science Approach* (Birmingham, Ala.: Religious Education Press, 1973), pp. 279-284.

9. Jan P. Muczyk, Eleanor Brantley Schwartz, and Ephraim Smith, *Principles of Supervision: First-and Second-Level Management* (Columbus, Ohio: Merrill, 1984), p. 13.

10. The best players, incidentally, do not necessarily make the best coaches. In fact, it is often the case that a mediocre player becomes a good coach. Concomitantly, just because someone is a good worker on the line does not mean that he or she has the potential to be a supervisor; by extension, because someone has been a great player does not suggest that this person automatically has the potential to be a great coach. For a good discussion on the move from line work to supervising, see "Role Transition: Moving Completely into Supervision," in Paul O. Radde, *Supervising: A Guide for All Levels* (San Diego: University Associates, 1981), pp. 27-41.

11. See Clark Lambert, *The Complete Book of Supervisory Training* (New York: Wiley, 1984), pp. 88-106.

attention to corporate (team) objectives. The supervisor works to find ways to sacrifice neither the person's rights nor the team's progress but instead attempts to forge the energies and the needs of the two into a synergistic whole. As the supervisor "coaches" the worker/learner to higher degrees of competence, the supervisor is also helping to improve the productivity and effectiveness of the larger group or team.

The supervisor is frequently called upon to coach both individuals and a team simultaneously. The procedures and needs of these two are ordinarily quite different. The supervisor as coach always strives to balance appropriately the time and attention given to individuals with the time and attention devoted to the larger entity. Too much energy focused on an individual harms the cohesiveness of the team. Too much interest concentrated on the team to the exclusion of individuals destroys the possibility for relationships and for understanding the separate needs of those who make up the team.[12]

The supervisor must remember that the position calls for continuous analytic observation, being ever vigilant to the growth and development of the team toward the attainment of its goals. The supervisor does not attend only to those persons or areas that appear to be performing below expectations or wait to give assistance until a difficulty arises. It is as much the job of the supervisor to anticipate needs and skills and to see that these are in place and ready for use, as it is to be available in the event of crises. The experienced supervisor works to prevent and to prepare for emergencies with the preparation of adequate contingency plans, as well as actually to help with the emergencies when or if they do arise.

Finally, the supervisor has to realize that success does not equal perfection. When supervising others, which means delegating and letting others do the work, things will occasionally go wrong or get confused. Clark Lambert spoke to this issue this way: "A supervisor can be roughly compared to a head coach of a professional sports team. While hoping to win *every* game, the coach does expect to lose a few along the way but fully expects to learn from mistakes that are made and to end the season with a winning record! In the world of supervisory management, coaching failures will occur. It's a basic reality that one has to live with, but at the same time one that should never be allowed to detract from the overall effort."[13] In supervising, a key aspect of coaching, one defeat need not be a final defeat, and defeat may actually prove to be a prime learning experience. For the coach, winning is not the only motivation or objective. Learning and improving the performance of the players, as well as contributing to the overall personal development of the players, speaks to the deeper, root issue of true

---

12. This need for balance is representative of a systemic approach to management, where proper attention is given to the system along with its interconnected subsystems and suprasystems. For a good introduction to this structure of systems and its relationship to management, see Kenneth E. Boulding, "General Systems Theory—The Skeleton of Science," in *Classics of Organizational Theory*, ed. Jay M. Shafritz and Philip H. Whitbeck (Oak Park, Ill.: Moore, 1978), pp. 121-131, and Fremont E. Kast and James E. Rosenzweig, "General Systems Theory: Applications for Organizations and Management," in *Management Classics*, ed. Michael T. Matteson and John M. Ivancevich, 2nd ed. (Santa Monica, Calif.: Goodyear, 1981), pp. 371-389.

13. Ibid., p. 91.

coaching. Whatever else happens, the effective coach uses every opportunity and situation to teach, and "losing" presents an opportune moment for just such learning.[14]

In summary, the religious educator in the role of coach needs the skills and the approaches of the supervisor in his or her facilitative repertoire.[15] The supervisor is not the one who plays the game but is the one who observes ("watches over") the players analytically and evaluatively in order to facilitate increased performance. The religious educator is required to have a base of technical information in order to serve as a resource person. The religious educator as supervisor must possess facilitative and personnel skills, always monitoring both individual and team performance. Supervision is continual, preventive as well as remedial, and is willing to accept some degree of failure for the good of overall learning.

Trainer

The coach from the dimension of the trainer focuses his or her attention specifically on the conduct of the player. What the player actually does on the playing field is of crucial importance, and quality performance is not something that can be accomplished only by thinking about it, by reading about it, by doing research on it, or by watching others. These are all very useful and requisite processes in preparation for the activity, or for reflection on it, but there is absolutely no substitute for rigorous training through practice. The coach as trainer emphasizes practice, practice, and more practice. This dimension of trainer is vital to the totality of the role, since here the particular and fundamental skills are learned and honed that are so essential to playing the game.

In real life, people are not divisible into the dualities of body and mind, as if these are distinct entities that somehow exist separately from one another. At the same time, however, the trainer is particularly interested in the behavioral abilities of the player/student. One definition of training is "the systematic development of the attitude/knowledge/skill behavior pattern required by the individual to perform adequately a given task or job."[16] This definition gives proper consideration to the holistic nature of the human, in that psychological (attitude), cognitive (knowledge), and physical (skill) aspects are all necessarily integrated so that the assigned task can be completed. Until these activities are performed behaviorally, the player cannot be of use to the team and cannot

---

14. For an interesting philosophical development of this idea, and for a rather surprising twist to the old trial and error argument as learning, see William Berkson and John Wettersten, *Learning from Error: Karl Popper's Psychology of Learning* (LaSalle, Ill.: Open Court, 1984), especially pp. 2-8, where learning is described as primarily the correction of expectations that have been upset or disturbed.

15. Some additional helpful resources on supervision include: Lawrence L. Steinmetz and H. Ralph Todd Jr., *First-Line Management: Approaching Supervision Effectively*, 3rd ed. (Plano, Tex.: Business Publications, 1983), especially Chapter Two, "The Supervisor's Role and Functions," pp. 24-50; Jane Whitney Gibson, *The Supervisory Challenge: Principles and Practices* (Columbus, Ohio: Merrill, 1990); and Claude S. George, *Supervising in Action: The Art of Managing Others* (Reston, Va.: Reston, 1979).

16. Robert Stammers and John Patrick, *The Psychology of Training* (London: Methuen, 1975), p. 10.

improve his or her performance. The trainer, then, is certainly not just interested in the physical, but unless and until the behavior is manifested physically there is no way to evaluate the integration of the player's abilities.

This issue cuts two ways in application to religious education. On the one hand, all too frequently some religious educators have been so cognitive and so "belief" oriented that the importance of people's actions have too often been ignored. The implication is that if people think the right thoughts, then they will automatically perform the proper or at least acceptable behavior.[17] Only a few moments of reflection reveal the fallacy of implementing the cognitive approach exclusively. Excluding the performance aspects of religious education cuts it off from real life. On the other hand, the scale could be tipped too far toward only being interested in what people do, treating humans as automatons without minds, personality, or individuality: Do these things because these are the right things to do, becomes the perceived message; Do not do these things, because these are the wrong things to do. The truth more probably lies somewhere between these two extremes, but they illustrate the difficulty of integrating the entire human into the totality of religious education. Good performance depends on the religious educator providing adequate preparation before and constant integration during the teaching/learning act.

Motivator

The dimension of coach as trainer aligns closely with that of the coach as motivator. Again, the need for integration emphasized above is crucial. The coach does not train players one day, and then motivate them the next. These processes are dynamic and interactive elements of the whole, so that motivating and training are continuous and co-existent, yet distinguishable from one another for purposes of analysis and discussion. In actuality, the processes need not, indeed should not, be separated. Where the trainer focuses primarily on the physical aspects of the player, though, the coach as motivator emphasizes the affective dimension.

The key issue for the motivator is deciding on the source of motivation. Is motivation an external reward system that is manipulated by the authority who has the ability and the resources to provide the desired reward? Is motivation an internal need satisfaction that can be directed toward individual attainment while also achieving group goals? Both of these starting points are valid ones, and both have been proven effective.[18] It has become apparent, thanks in part to the

17. For example, it is precisely for this reason that James Michael Lee has criticized Thomas Groome's "shared praxis" procedure. Lee sees shared praxis as a "reflection-reflection" teaching procedure which is exclusively cognitive and void of empirical validation. See this discussed, among other places, in James Michael Lee, "How to Teach: Foundations, Processes, Procedures," in *Handbook of Preschool Religious Education*, ed. Donald Ratcliff (Birmingham, Ala.: Religious Education Press, 1988), p. 161, and *The Content of Religious Instruction: A Social Science Approach* (Birmingham, Ala.: Religious Education Press, 1985), pp. 76-77, n. 98.

18. Additional insight into the topic of motivation beyond limits of the discussion here can be found in sources such as the following: Edward L. Deci and Richard M. Ryan, *Intrinsic Motivation and Self-Determination* (New York: Plenum, 1985); Douglass G. Mook, *Motivation: The Organization of Action* (New York: Norton, 1986); Russell G. Geen, William W. Beatty, and Robert M. Arkin, *Human Motivation: Physiological, Behavioral, and Social Approaches* (Boston: Allyn and Bacon,

insightful work of Douglas McGregor (1906-1964), that one's view of motivation is primarily fueled by one's view of human nature.[19] McGregor pointed
out: "Behind every managerial decision or action are assumptions about human
nature and human behavior."[20]

The first view mentioned above, where motivation is external to the person,
was described by McGregor as resulting in a management style he characterized
as "Theory X." The assumptions behind the "traditional view" of the direction
and control of humans—Theory X—were crystalized as follows:

1. The average human being has an inherent dislike of work and will avoid it
   if he can.
2. Because of this human characteristic of dislike of work, most people must
   be coerced, controlled, directed, threatened with punishment to get them to
   put forth adequate effort toward the achievement of organizational objectives.
3. The average human being prefers to be directed, wishes to avoid responsibility, wants security above all.[21]

Since coaching engages people in that gray area somewhere between work and
play,[22] the above presuppositions of a Theory X manager are entirely applicable
to the assumptions of a coach who relies on external motivational procedures.

The alternative approach, Theory Y, is also based on a set of assumptions about
human nature, although quite different than those given above. The "Theory
Y" type of manager—or coach—has these kinds of beliefs about people:

1. The expenditure of physical and mental effort in work is as natural as play
   or rest. The average human being does not inherently dislike work.
2. External control and threat of punishment are not the only means for bringing about effort toward organizational objectives. Humans will exercise self-
   direction and self-control in the service of objectives to which they are
   committed.
3. Commitment to objectives is a function of the rewards associated with
   their achievement.
4. The average human being learns, under proper conditions, not only to
   accept but to seek responsibility.
5. The capacity to exercise a relatively high degree of imagination, ingenu-

1984); David C. McClelland, *Human Motivation* (Glenview, Ill.: Scott Foresman, 1985); Robert C.
Beck, *Motivation: Theories and Principles,* 3rd ed. (Englewood Cliffs, N.J.: Prentice-Hall, 1990);
Deborah J. Stipeck, *Motivation to Learn: From Theory to Practice* (Englewood Cliffs, N.J.: Prentice-
Hall, 1988); and of course the classic, Abraham H. Maslow, *Motivation and Personality*, 3rd ed., rev.
Robert Frager, James Fadiman, Cynthia McReynolds, and Ruth Cox (New York: Harper & Row,
1987).

19. For a good introduction to the different approaches to understanding human nature, see
Leslie Stevenson, *Seven Theories of Human Nature*, 2nd ed. (Oxford: Oxford University Press,
1987).

20. Douglas McGregor, *The Human Side of Enterprise* (New York: McGraw-Hill, 1960), p. 33.

21. Ibid., pp. 33-34.

ity, and creativity in the solution of organizational problems is widely, not narrowly, distributed in the population.

6. Under the conditions of modern industrial life, the intellectual potentialities of the average human being are only partially utilized.[23]

This set of assumptions differs radically from the earlier one and, if taken seriously, fundamentally alters the way of the performance of managing and coaching.

Of supreme importance to this discussion is the acknowledgement that McGregor was simply referring to *assumptions* about the nature of humans and was not basing his suggestions for management on empirical research.[24] He was trying to show that what a manager/coach sees in, and what he or she expects from people, depends to a great extent on which anthropological perspective is employed.

When the religious educator as coach gives his or her concern to the topic of motivation, the first issue to be consciously addressed is the set of assumptions held as to what and who the human is. The religious educator must attend to his or her unconscious and unexamined set of presuppositions that he or she carries to the coaching/teaching task, and attempt to have some degree of integrity and coherence in his or her view of humans as it relates to a coaching/teaching style. Since surely one of the goals of effective religious educators is to create some kind of congruence between theory and our practice, the dimension of the coach as motivator provides the opportunity, if not the requirement, to be intentional about this relationship.

Strategist

The fourth dimension of the coach to be discussed here is that of the strategist. While it is not the coach who plays the game—that performance must ultimately be left to the players—the coach is constantly and intimately a part of the dynamics of the game. Many of the primary tasks of the coach are performed prior to the game, as was discussed in the dimensions of the trainer and motivator above. When the game begins, the players must then utilize what the coach has prepared, taught, and trained them to do. Even during the game, however, the

---

22. See the section on playing and working as the primary activity of the coach later in this chapter.

23. Ibid., pp. 47-48. To add to Theory X and Theory Y, see Chapter Twenty Two, "Theory Z," in Abraham H. Maslow, *The Farther Reaches of Human Nature* (New York: Viking, 1971), pp. 280-295. See also William G. Ouchi, *Theory Z: How American Business Can Meet the Japanese Challenge* (Reading, Ma.: Addison-Wesley, 1981), and John J. Morse and Jay W. Lorsch, "Beyond Theory Y," in *Management Classics*, pp. 396-407.

24. Douglas McGregor's wife Carolyn wrote of her husband's familial background that seemed to influence his own point of view: "As I look back on my first contacts with Doug's family, I am impressed with the deep concern for mankind, which Doug shared, and an equally deep pessimism in respect to man's potential goodness and strength, which Doug continued to challenge in his work and writings. It is significant that he chose to work with leaders in our society rather than failures." Quoted by Warren G. Bennis in "Introduction," *Leadership and Motivation: Essays of Douglas McGregor,* ed. Warren G. Bennis and Edgar H. Shein, with Carolyn McGregor (Cambridge: The M.I.T. Press, 1966), p. xi.

players are not left on their own. The other aspect of preparation and performance that falls to the coach is the strategy—the game plan and its implementation. What should the players do, and what should their objectives be in the game? This strategy can, and should be, drawn out before the game in a manner that is based on empirical research and developed from the principles of coaching and from the past/present performance of the players. The specific strategy devised for the particular game is thoroughly explained and discussed with the players. The strategy is not ironclad or rigid, but it supplies the players with a basic plan and a procedure, which admittedly will probably change during the progress of the game. By all accounts, the coach is fully present and active during the game, observing the action and reacting with new strategies that reflect the realities and the activities at the moment. Regardless of how the actual game turns out, though, the coach is still responsible for being the chief strategist.

The original Greek word "strategy" (στρατηγός, literally, "a general") was a military term, meaning the view of a general.[25] The concept was that the general—the leader of the military battle—had a vantage point above the battle and could see the overall needs and dangers more clearly than could those actually doing the fighting. The general could issue orders and make troop movements that made sense from a longer view, even if the directions seemed like nonsense to those fighting on the battlefield. This same image is relevant to the coach as strategist. He or she can see the entirety of the team, its strengths and weaknesses, as well as the objective to be attained. The coach can devise strategy appropriate to the team and its members that will achieve the goals.

The coach as strategist returns full circle to the coach as supervisor. The coach as supervisor is one who analytically and evaluatively observes ("watches over") and who sees the progress of the team, or the lack of progress. The coach as strategist may be watching from the sidelines but is constantly devising ways to achieve greater progress and to limit the damage. The strategist is at bottom involved in planning,[26] which Russell Ackoff defined as "the design of a desired future and of effective ways of bringing it about."[27] Planning starts with ideas, relevant research, and goals as to what needs to be accomplished and then moves to the means by which the ends can be accomplished. In the normal course of events, the ends probably will not change, while the means will almost inevitably change continually. The coach draws up the best strategy possible before the game that utilizes the strengths of the players, deemphasizes their weaknesses, and that hopefully will win them the game. During the game itself, the coach must be able to react to the realities of what is transpiring and to alter the game plan sufficiently, abandoning when necessary ineffective means in order to achieve the desired ends. These decisions are based on the empirical evidence presented during the game, rather than random selection

---

25. George Steiner, *Strategic Planning: What Every Manager Must Know* (New York: Free Press, 1979), p. 348, n. 4.

26. For more on the dimension of the planner, see Chapter Eleven, "The Religious Educator as Revolutionary."

27. Russell L. Ackoff, *A Concept of Corporate Planning* (New York: Wiley-Interscience, 1970), p.1.

or panic born of threat.[28] The coach as strategist and as supervisor work in concert.

The coach as trainer focuses primarily on the physical; the coach as motivator focuses mainly on the affective. The coach as strategist relies principally on the intellect. George Terry spoke of strategic planning as being "intellectual in nature; it is mental work. Reflective thinking is required; imagination and foresight are extremely helpful."[29] These comments reveal that coaching, and winning, is more than the result of brute force or dumb luck. Long-term success as a coach requires deep and creative thinking and planning.

The religious educator is deeply immersed in the dimension of strategist every time he or she puts together a teaching plan.[30] The goals and objectives are determined, and then means and procedures for achieving them are devised. The teaching plan is not rigid or inflexible and may be abandoned at any time the "teachable moment"[31] appears to lead in a different direction. The "players" (learners) are still the focus and purpose of teaching, not the teaching plan itself. Whenever the plan is not meeting the needs of the learners, it is immediately revised and amended, followed by the practice, performance, and evaluation of the teaching act. All of this, though, never excuses the careful and intentional "strategic planning" of teaching. Just as a good coach would never send players into the big game without designing a detailed game plan, so a responsible religious educator would never begin a formal teaching opportunity without a lesson plan that has clearly stated and achievable learning objectives, as well as flexible means by which to reach those objectives.

Summary

The dimensions of the role of coach have been sketched by way of four descriptive terms: supervisor, trainer, motivator, and strategist. These dimensions do not necessarily exhaust the role but should provide an adequate background of the role to allow for further exploration. While it may have seemed initially that the religious educator has little in common with a coach, by now some of the

---

28. This kind of dynamic, effective, and interactive teacher/coach James Michael Lee has called the "researcher-on-the hoof": "She [the teacher] is always encountering learners not only through the prism of what they are actually learning at any given moment but also what the empirical research says about this learning. In this way, the teacher may be able to instantly alter her pedagogical procedures to better facilitate desired learning outcomes. Furthermore, the teacher as researcher-on-the hoof is also gathering impressionistic and objective data about these particular learners as they are here-and-now concretely engaged in the learning task so that she can sharpen her pedagogical procedures for these learners." James Michael Lee, "How to Teach," in *Handbook of Preschool Religious Education*, pp. 156-157.

29. George R. Terry, *Principles of Management*, 3rd ed. (Homewood, Ill.: Irwin Press, 1960), p. 123, as quoted in Steiner, *Corporate Planning*, p. 346, n. 1.

30. This sentence illustrates the reason why each of the chapters of Part Two includes a section on representative teaching procedures. The principles of teaching provided there can then be adapted as needed to any particular situation, content, or environment.

31. "When the body is ripe, and society requires, and the self is ready to achieve a certain task, the teachable moment has come. Efforts at teaching, which would have been largely wasted if they had come earlier, give gratifying results when they came at the *teachable moment*, when the task should be learned." Robert J. Havighurst, *Developmental Tasks and Education*, 3rd ed. (New York: David McKay, 1972). p. 7.

parallels have started to appear. A continued look at the role will bring even more similarities to the fore, and the reality may be that this role may indeed prove to be one of the most common to the work and identity of the religious educator.

Aim: Performance

The coach is never able to forget that game day is approaching, which is to say that the coach must always be interested in and concerned with performance. The effectiveness and the efficiency of the practice and of the preparation—the prime contributions of the coach—are evaluated when the players step onto the field or the court and begin to play. The coach's responsibility is to be sure that the players are as ready to perform as humanly possible, but the results are ultimately out of the coach's hands. Performance is not only the aim of the coach, but it is also the means of evaluating the coach.

One definition of performance is "those outcomes that are produced or behaviors that are exhibited in order to perform certain job activities over a specific period of time."[32] Three relevant points can be extracted from this simple definition. First, successful performance is determined by the learning outcomes or demonstrated behaviors, be they cognitive, affective, or lifestyle dimensions of performance. These are external, measurable, empirical, and testable results. Whatever may be involved in coaching and playing must eventually be evaluated in terms of solid and demonstrable results. Second, performance demands that the person be able to handle and carry out acceptably "certain job activities." Specific, clearly identified, and known needs must be met in order for the person to be able to do the tasks expected. On a team, all of these tasks, though different, must come together in an integrated fashion so that they lead toward an overall objective. If each person adequately fulfills his or her responsibility, then the team is more likely to achieve its overall objective. Third, time is a essential factor. In performance, the activity must be displayed in a timely as well as an effective manner. On a team, all of the individuals are expected to perform individual roles and responsibilities in a unified and coordinated manner. A "good play" contributed after the whistle is of no use whatsoever to the team, or for that matter to the individual. A truly "good play" is one performed at the right time and in the right place, for the good of the team.

The previous paragraph reveals the difficulty and the complexity of the coach's task. The coach not only has to train and prepare each individual on the team to perform, but just as importantly he or she must teach the players how to perform together. Individual and team performance are both essential, and one does not necessarily follow the other. Great individual performances do not guarantee a good team effort, and a team that may function well together may still not have the competence to win. All of this is compounded by the fact that the coach does not play the game. The coach coaches, on the sidelines, while the players play. In the ultimate analysis, coaching means enabling others to perform their best.

---

32. H. John Bernadin and Richard W. Beatty, *Performance Appraisal: Assessing Human Behavior at Work* (Boston: Kent, 1984), p. 12.

All of this is difficult for the religious educator to accept and to do. Many religious educators are so performance-oriented that they tend to want to do all of the performing themselves. The point of being a religious educator in the role of coach, however, is to facilitate the performance of *others*. The religious educator trains, practices, instructs, prepares, and then turns the players loose to play the game. The training, the practicing, the instructing, and the preparing are for playing the game. While for the religious educator this largely unseen and unheralded activity is descriptive of the life and the calling of the religious educator as coach, it is not the end in itself. The end, or the aim, is quality performance by the "players" (learners).[33]

Function: Instruction

Aims and functions are easily confused, as evidenced in the previous section. Religious educators may become so wrapped up in their activity of religious instruction that they tend to lose sight of the goal of performance.[34] At the same time, they can be so involved in watching the "game" that they may forget that one of their primary responsibilities as religious educators is to be experts in instruction. This balance is difficult to strike, but it is an essential and an ongoing effort. Coaches and religious educators instruct for the purpose of helping others perform, while what coaches and religious educators are "performing" is the instructional activity. There is no way to be an effective religious educator and not in some form or another be a skillful instructor.

In a very real sense, this entire book focuses on the importance of the multivariate dimensions of instruction and teaching. As James Michael Lee has said: "Instruction is the process by and through which learning is caused in an individual in one way or another. Instruction, then, is identical with teaching."[35] The entire purpose of a religious educator is to instruct or teach, albeit performed through a variety of forms, contexts, and images. The ten chapters of the book (comprising Part Two) that deal with the various roles of the religious educator are ways of identifying and explaining the multifaceted and wide-ranging perspectives and procedures available to the religious educator. This particular chapter, though it addresses instruction as the function of the religious educator in the role of coach, should not be taken to imply that the other roles do not

---

33. This stance was emphasized by Findley Edge in an article he wrote specifically directed toward the Christian church entitled "A Search for Authenticity," in *Modern Masters of Religious Education*, ed. Marlene Mayr (Birmingham, Ala.: Religious Education Press, 1983), pp. 33-64. In this article Edge stated: "Thus we get from organized sports two basic principles for the church: Inherent in joining the team is a commitment to play the game! Inherent in the commitment to play the game is a commitment to practice!" Ibid., p. 64.

34. For example, this is where James Michael Lee has said that "the ultracognitivist emphasis in religious instruction ignores and neglects the body, and thus in effect disvalues the body's central place in an holistic Christian lifestyle." Lee, *Content of Religious Instruction*, p. 612. He then gave the examples of Thomas Groome, Gerard Sloyan, and Gabriel Moran as representatives of the ultracognitivist approach to religious instruction. Ibid., note 11, p. 702.

35. James Michael Lee, *The Shape of Religious Instruction: A Social Science Approach* (Birmingham, Ala.: Religious Education Press, 1971), p. 8. Instruction relates to an individual, as in the quote, as well as to groups of learners, or players, as on a team.

instruct or teach. "Instruction" in this chapter is indeed a part of teaching, but more finely focuses the term as Lee did when the quote above was continued. Lee went on to say that "instruction can be seen as the arrangement of those situations and conditions which will most effectively facilitate desired learning outcomes in an individual. . . . It is a technical term used in pedagogical parlance to indicate a specific type of educational activity."[36] Instruction is the intentional teaching that leads to desired outcomes and behaviors. Instruction, in other words, is the term for what the coach does to and for the team in order to enable the team to achieve the aim of performance.

Performance determines whether or not the coach has really taught or not. If the desired and expected performance of the learners is not achieved, the coach cannot be said to have done his or her job, which is to facilitate the performance of the players. He or she must instruct in such a way that the desired performance is achieved. If the performance desired is not being achieved, then the coach has but one choice: to change the procedure of instruction. One of the dangers of coaching is that a coach will get stuck in one way of instructing and will use it regardless of the circumstances, the environment, or the needs of the players. A capable coach does not hone only one style of coaching to perfection but instead develops a wide repertoire of styles from which he or she can select as appropriate. Performance serves as the source of feedback that tells the coach whether or not the instruction is effective. If performance is lacking, then the coach must change how he or she instructs. This means that the coach, to be an expert in instruction, must also be an expert in the diagnosis of needs and an expert in the utilization of instructional procedures. For the coach, the performance of the players reveals the effectiveness of the instruction.

The obvious implication of this function of instruction to the religious educator is the requirement to be competent in the employment of a variety of teaching styles. Diagnosis of the needs of the learners and of the situation, selection of the appropriate teaching procedure and successful use of it, and evaluation of the entire process are all absolutely essential to the functioning of the religious educator. If learners are not learning, and if performance is not being achieved, then it is incumbent upon the religious educator to examine his or her own level of performance in the instructional act.[37] Although the success of the learners is always dependent on more than what the religious educator provides, able instruction is the minimum that the religious educator as coach can be expected to give.

Primary Virtues: Competence and Discipline

Talk of competence and discipline may initially sound hopelessly archaic, but in reality these two virtues remain foundational to the role of the coach and to the entire process of religious education. They play a crucial role in filling the larg-

---

36. Ibid.
37. This relates to the issue of summative evaluation. For a definitive treatment of this important topic, see Benjamin S. Bloom, J. Thomas Hastings, and George F. Madaus, *Handbook on Formative and Summative Evaluation of Student Learning* (New York: McGraw-Hill, 1971), especially Chapter Four, "Summative Evaluation," pp. 61-85.

er identity of the religious educator as coach.

Without competence, there is no attainment of adequate performance. Without this kind of desire for performance, there is no aim for the role of the coach to fulfill. While it is obviously essential for the coach to be competent, the discussion here is not on competency-based educational techniques or approaches performed by the coach. That is more a matter of teaching style demanded of the religious educator.[38] The spotlight here is focused on the learner, where he or she is the one who gains the virtue of competence as a way of life and practice. The coach is charged with the responsibility of helping the players desire to be—and to become—competent, not just in the particular sport or game of the moment, but in every phase of their experience.

One could be easily repulsed by such a focus on competence if it is not clearly delineated. Followers of John Gardner, for instance, would cite his comments in *Excellence* where he agreed that competence was basic to a democratic way of life: "Free men must be competent men. In a society of free men, competence is an elementary duty. . . . Men and women doing competently whatever job is theirs to do to tone up the whole society."[39] He went on to say, though, that competence is an inadequate virtue and that excellence is necessary: "But excellence implies more than competence. It implies a striving for the highest standards in every phase of life. We need individual excellence in all its forms—in every kind of creative endeavor, in political life, in education, in industry—in short, universally."[40]

The problem with Gardner's position is his seeming call for universal excellence, which is purely and simply unachievable—and in many ways nonsensical and unhealthy. While of course all of us want some areas of excellence in our lives, to strive for excellence every moment in every circumstance is both compulsive and obsessive. To suggest the virtue of competence in its place is to call, not for unreasonable expectations and pressure upon already over-stressed learners, but to encourage them to make decisions about what should be done competently and what is worthy of attempts at excellence. This virtue of competence, then, is a moderating effort at making each individual responsible and productive as well as intentional and reasonable.

It is a distortion to claim that competence as a virtue places an inordinate amount of emphasis on skills and ignores the theoretical and the cognitive. In both general terms and in specific terms as competence relates to religious education, such a splitting of skill and cognition misses the point. True competence requires ability to perform a skill, certainly, but it also demands the reflective and meaningful performance of that skill. Skills have to be grounded in reality where

---

38. I am referring here to the well-known move toward competency-based teacher education (CBTE). In CBTE, the essential issue of accountability is faced squarely and effectively. For more on this approach, see, for example, *On Competence: A Critical Analysis of Competence-Based Reforms in Higher Education*, ed. Gerald Grant et al. (San Francisco: Jossey-Bass, 1979); *Defining and Measuring Competence*, ed. Paul S. Pottinger and Joan Goldsmith (San Francisco: Jossey-Bass, 1979); and *Competence: Inquiries Into Its Meaning and Acquisition in Educational Settings,* ed. Edmund C. Short (Lanham, Md.: University Press of America, 1984).

39. John W. Gardner, *Excellence: Can We Be Equal and Excellent Too?* (New York: Harper & Row, 1961), p. 193.

40. Ibid.

things are worked out and achieved. Skills facilitate the acquisition of competence. The mere repetition or reproduction of a skill is not competence; it is mimicry. Competence includes not only possessing the ability to do something but also knowing when and why it is to be done.[41] True competence requires education, not robotics.

Companion and complement to competence is the virtue of discipline. Just as misunderstood as competence, discipline is seemingly even more misused as a virtue. The greatest danger arises when discipline comes to be defined as punishment and when punishment is seen as a major component of learning. Punishment is not the primary or the original meaning of the word discipline, and it has very little if anything to do with facilitating learning.[42] Discipline has a positive and affirming meaning that need not have any of the threatening overtones it takes on when disguised as punishment.[43]

Discipline has its etymological roots in the Latin word *disciplina*: teaching, instruction, or training. The word for disciple, *discipulus*, derives from the same Latin root, and means one who is a pupil, a learner, or a trainee.[44] At base, the Latin root *capio* (with the prefix *dis*, "separation") meant to grasp, to seize from, to take possession of, so that "discipline" literally means training or experience that is separated out and taken for oneself. Discipline is a word that describes learning from the viewpoint of the learner, since it is his or her experience and not something given or imposed externally. To understand discipline as that which an authority figure demands of an underling removes the word from its

---

41. This issue received some illumination by Selma J. Mushkin in "Performance Toward What Result? An Examination of Some Problems in Outcome Measurement," in *Performance Contracting in Education—What Is It?: Toward a Balanced Perspective*, ed. Donald M. Levine (Englewood Cliffs, N.J.: Educational Technology Publications, 1972), pp. 95-117. The difficulty is finding ways to match up results with objectives. Just because a skill can be performed, in other words, does not necessarily imply that full competence has been gained in the larger sense.

42. Some persons take one verse of the Bible and assume it to give them license to punish, such as the paraphrase of Proverbs 13:24, "Spare the rod and spoil the child." Such a use of scripture, and of children, has no place in the role of coach or in the work of the religious educator. For more on this abusive approach to discipline, see Philip J. Greven, *Spare the Child: The Religious Roots of Punishment and the Psychological Impact of Physical Abuse* (New York: Knopf, 1991), and Phil E. Quinn, *Spare the Rod: Breaking the Cycle of Child Abuse* (Nashville: Abingdon, 1988). Also see the works of Alice Miller, such as *Thou Shalt Not Be Aware: Society's Betrayal of the Child* (New York: New American Library, 1986), and *For Your Own Good: Hidden Cruelty in Child-Rearing and the Roots of Violence* (New York: Farrar, Straus & Giroux, 1984).

43. Indeed, the behaviorists say that punishment does not really extinguish the undesired behavior. For example, B.F. Skinner wrote: "If the effect [of punishment] were simply the reverse of reinforcement, a great deal of behavior could be easily explained; but when behavior is punished, various stimuli generated by the behavior or the occasion are conditioned in the respondent pattern, and the punished behavior is then displaced by incompatible behavior conditioned as escape or avoidance. A punished person remains 'inclined' to behave in a punishable way, but he avoids punishment by doing something else instead, possibly nothing more than stubbornly doing nothing." B.F. Skinner, *About Behaviorism* (New York: Vintage, 1974), p. 69.

44. The Latin terms carries overtones of cognitive aspects, such as knowing and learning information; of affective aspects, such as being closely related emotionally and psychologically to the teacher or mentor; and also of lifestyle aspects, since the disciple lived with the teacher, being constantly in the learning environment. Those familiar with the gospels of the Christian New Testament will see elements of all these aspects demonstrated in the relationship of the "twelve" (the disciples) with their rabbi Jesus.

roots of disciple, follower, and learner. Discipline, as a virtue taught by the coach, is learning that allows the player to "seize for oneself" the experiential moments of life (*carpe diem!*).

James Michael Lee made a similar point about true discipline in an article entitled "Discipline in a Moral and Religious Key." He wrote: "Discipline is not something prior to the learning process or outside the learning process. Discipline is the learning process itself, or more precisely, a manner in which the learning process occurs. In a word, discipline is purposeful, goal-directed, channeled learning. Discipline is learning at its highest, most effective form."[45] Discipline, when perceived in this light, is not something to be feared or endured but to be enjoyed and experienced to the fullest—indeed, celebrated.[46] One further distinction is important here. The issue is not simply self-control, which is the ability to *control* what you have or who you are. More significantly, discipline is that which puts self-control to *use*, a harnessing of all the energies of the person in order to achieve a certain task.

The connections between the virtues of competence and discipline are obvious. Where competence deals with the performance and understanding of particular skills, discipline describes the way in which these skills are acquired and perfected. Both virtues point toward the achievement of performance and are communicated by the coach through instruction. As any good coach would verify, the primary asset a player gains from participation in sports is not only the specific skills learned or even the thrill of winning; it is also and possibly more importantly the experience of learning competence through discipline, and this kind of experience and ability is transferable to all phases of life.

The religious educator in the role of coach is just as dedicated to the virtues of competence and discipline as the coach of a sports team, but for slightly different reasons. These virtues are not taught for the purpose of winning, or even competing. Rivalry is not the issue in religious development. The religious educator is seeking to facilitate competence and discipline so that each learner can become mature, independent (actually the word is interdependent), and self-directed in his or her own journey of faith. At the same time, the individual is engaged in a faith community, where others are also on a similar journeys—individuals, with personal goals and objectives, linked with others in a corporate experience to seek larger and more universal ends. One does not sacrifice individuality to become a member but instead discovers resources to become an even stronger individual as a result of walking with others on a shared path. One does not give up personal efforts toward competence and discipline simply because he or she is joined with others on the path—indeed, such an experience demands that each be highly committed to his or her own levels of competence and discipline. Individuals seeking personal growth and fulfillment while also seeking communal strength and achievements share the common

---

45. James Michael Lee, "Discipline in a Moral and Religious Key," in *Developmental Discipline*, ed. Kevin Walsh and Milly Cowles (Birmingham, Ala.: Religious Education Press, 1982), p. 149. Also in this article, Lee gave some additional information on the etymology of the term discipline.

46. It is in this sense that the title for Richard J. Foster's devotional classic, *Celebration of Discipline: The Path to Spiritual Growth*, rev. ed. (San Francisco: Harper & Row, 1988) can be understood.

virtues of competence and discipline. They actualize these virtues in the activity of playing/working, the subject of the next section.

Activity: Playing/Working

The activity highlighted for the role of the coach is a compound one, playing/working, with one aspect related and interconnected to the other. Essentially, the coach's approach to religious education is through "doing," through activity itself—not random or frantic activity, but through that which is concrete and meaningful. From this perspective, religious education is not divisible into theory and practice,[47] or into mental and physical realities. Religious education is that which is performed, experienced, and encountered through the existential activity of playing/working. The coach is thus committed to engagement: involving the players in solving real problems in the real world through concentrated effort.

A word about the use of the compound term, playing/working, is necessary. The two are not identical or synonymous,[48] since discussions of the differences can be found in a variety of sources.[49] Erik Erikson, for example, said adult play is recreation and that this differs from the play of children: "The playing adult steps sideward into another reality; the playing child advances forward into new stages of mastery."[50] Play for a child in Erikson's definition appears very close to what adults would call work![51] Rather than spending time and effort distinguishing between the two, it is more profitable in the present context to take them together as a whole. Combining playing and working stresses the effort, interest, and energy inherent in both and says that both are essential to religious education.

---

47. To avoid making theory and practice dichotomies, Thomas Groome uses the term "praxis" so that theory and practice can be understood as "twin moments of the same activity that are united dialectically. Instead of theory leading into practice, theory becomes or is seen as the reflective moment in praxis, and articulated theory arises from the praxis to yield further praxis." Thomas H. Groome, *Christian Religious Education: Sharing Our Story and Vision* (San Francisco: Harper & Row, 1980), p. 152. This Groome view is not new, and has been discussed by virtually every scholar in every field who dealt with theory as contrasted to speculation.

48. John Dewey had an interesting discussion of play and work, declaring that they "are by no means antithetical to one another." See the discussion in John Dewey, *Democracy and Education: An Introduction to the Philosophy of Education* (New York: Macmillan, 1916), pp. 237-242.

49. For some introduction into the study of play, the following sources should be consulted: Jerome W. Berryman, *Godly Play: A Way of Religious Education* (San Francisco: HarperSanFrancisco, 1991); Frank Caplan and Theresa Caplan, *The Power of Play* (Garden City, N.Y.: Anchor Press, 1973); *Child's Play: Developmental and Applied*, ed. Thomas D. Yawkey and Anthony D. Pellegrini (Hillsdale, N.Y.: Erlbaum, 1984); *Play in Animals and Humans*, ed. Peter K. Smith (Oxford, England: B. Blackwell, 1984); Cosby S. Rogers and Janet K. Sawyers, *Play in the Lives of Children* (Washington, D.C.: National Association for the Education of Children, 1988); Helen B. Schwartzman, *Transformations: The Anthropology of Children's Play* (New York: Plenum Press, 1978); *Play: Its Role in Development and Evolution*, ed. Jerome S. Bruner, Allison Jolly, and Kathy Silva (New York: Basic Books, 1976); and *The Psychology of Play*, ed. Brian Sutton-Smith (New York: Arno Press, 1976).

50. Erik H. Erikson, *Childhood and Society,* 2nd ed. (New York: Norton, 1963), p. 222. See also Erik H. Erikson, *Toys and Reasons: Stages in the Ritualization of Experience* (New York: Norton, 1977).

Playing and working demand the previously identified virtues of competence and discipline. Whether the subject is a twelve-year-old taking batting practice or a thirty-year-old laboring over a computer keyboard, the virtues demanded are the same. At the same time who is to say which of the previous subjects is working and which is playing? One may assume that batting practice is more like playing than is typing, but not necessarily. What if the thirty-year-old is a professional athlete, who "works" at batting practice in the afternoons but enjoys "playing" by writing an autobiography during free time in the mornings? Working and playing hold both competence and discipline as prized virtues.

This raises the question, Is religious education play or work? The answer, of course, is yes! From the perspective of the role of the coach, religious education is both playing and working.[52] It is activity facilitated by instruction and accomplished through the virtues of competence and discipline. It is activity performed in the "real world," with results that can be identified, evaluated, and measured. It is activity that can be demonstrated, practiced, and perfected at the same time that it can be enjoyable, fulfilling, and meaningful. It is activity that can be guided, coordinated, and appreciated, carried out individually or in corporate entities.

Religious education, to the coach, is performed in the mainstream of life. It is play, and it is work, but most of all it makes a difference in real and identifiable ways. If it is not making a difference, then the coach is not really coaching, and the players are not really performing.

Shadow Role: Procrastinator

One of the marks of a good coach, as we have seen, is that he or she insists on focused and intensive practice—but only if that practice has a specific purpose

---

51. This exact point was made by Adam Blatner and Allee Blatner: "Play differs from work in being an activity done for its own sake, for fun. Play is also the major activity of the child; it is engaged seriously by children." Adam Blatner and Allee Blatner, *The Art of Play: An Adult's Guide to Reclaiming Imagination and Spontaneity* (New York: Human Sciences Press, 1988). p. 28. These authors made an additional comment about play that has special significance to religious educators: "In play, children and adults experience a holistic integration of many components of learning: Spontaneous originality, emotional reactions, unconscious motivations, personal temperament and style, social and cultural context, as well as the more researched intellectual processes. Play, therefore, is a primal form of learning by doing, and this complex co-creative process is becoming recognized as one of the most effective forms of education." Ibid., p. 34. See this idea of "learning by doing" expanded in the representative teaching procedure section later in this chapter.

52. For an example of a sharply different view, see David Elkind, "The Role of Play in Religious Education," *Religious Education* 75:3 (May-June, 1980), pp. 282-293. Early in the article, Elkind wrote: "In some respects the conjoining of play and religious education might seem to be generous, whimsical. Religious education is, almost by definition, serious business—the antithesis of play." Ibid., p. 282. Later in the same article he continued this theme, even further maligning or completely misunderstanding true religious education: "Secular education, by definition, prepares young people primarily for adaptation to the larger society, to its economic, political, and social demands. Religious education, in contrast, prepares the child primarily for adaptation to the spiritual world, to the demands of conscience, goodwill, and love." Ibid., p. 291. Where Elkind came upon these definitions of secular and religious education, which he seems to assume as universally accepted, is unknown.

to achieve. The coach who drills the players in endless practice sessions but never lets them play a real game is really fulfilling the shadow role of the coach—that of the procrastinator. A procrastinator is a person who habitually postpones doing the tasks he or she knows are necessary and that need to be done in a timely fashion.[53] The procrastinating coach, for example, may do a fine job of fulfilling most of the expectations of a coach, such as leading the players in practice regularly, helping them develop the requisite skills and abilities, and teaching them the rudiments of the game, but yet never allowing the players to test and evaluate their prowess in an actual arena of play. The role of the coach is to prepare the players as well as humanly possible, but they must eventually play the game or all the preparation is meaningless. Preparing continually but never actually playing is only performing the shadow role of the coach.

A humorous and probably apocryphal story from Civil War days makes this point. Early in the war, the Army of the Potomac was being led by General George B. McClellan. McClellan drilled the massive army mercilessly, but he always seemed to avoid engaging his men in combat. The president, Abraham Lincoln, was anxious for action and sent the following message:

My Dear McClellan:
If you don't want to use the Army I should like to borrow it for a while.
Yours respectfully, A. Lincoln.

Lincoln's point to the general was made rather clearly: An army eventually is supposed to fight, not practice. The same is true for the coach: A team eventually is supposed to play, not merely practice. While at first glance this shadow role may not seem too great a threat, upon closer examination it becomes obvious that procrastination has the potential to eviscerate the role. The coach has the aim of performance, and the procrastinator continually delays, postpones, and avoids that very aim.

There are several possible reasons why a coach constantly procrastinates and makes the team practice instead of play. One may be that he or she is afraid to lose,[54] or is afraid to engage in action, thus showing the inadequacies of the coach's abilities. This is the cowardly coach. Another may be that the coach has no confidence in the players and does not believe that they can account for themselves, so the coach "protects" them from themselves. This is the paternalistic or maternalistic coach. The shadow role may exhibit itself in the endless quest for perfection, where every detail is planned and worried over to

---

53. A similar definition was given by Loren Broadus in *How to Stop Procrastinating and Start Living* (Minneapolis: Augsburg, 1983), p. 15. James B. Burka and Lenora M. Yuen say procrastination is "the behavior of postponing" in *Procrastination: Why You Do It, What to Do About It* (Reading, Mass.: Addison-Wesley, 1983), p. 5. For a scholarly treatment of the deeper issues behind those discussed in this section, see *Self-Defeating Behaviors: Experimental Research, Clinical Impressions, and Practical Implications*, ed. Rebecca C. Curtis (New York: Plenum Press, 1989).

54. This fear of failure and a parallel fear of success is discussed in Burka and Yuen, *Procrastination*, pp. 19-42; in David D. Burns, *Feeling Good: The New Mood Therapy* (New York: New American Library, 1980), pp. 83-85; and in *Self-Defeating Behaviors*, pp. 159-187. The issue here is a fear of risk-taking, which playing the game demands.

such a degree that effective functioning is actually inhibited. This is the perfectionistic coach.[55] It could be that the coach does not think that playing is necessary but that extended, strenuous practice is what is really important. This is the taskmaster coach, who sees himself or herself as the drill sergeant, roughly and harshly whipping the players into shape. Finally, the coach may be unaware that there are real games to be played. He or she sees coaching as relatively insignificant, as a pleasant pastime but not as a pressing need, and the players as powerless to make any kind of ultimate difference by just "playing around." This is the myopic coach, who believes the practice field is the only place playing can be done.

Surely religious education has its share of procrastinators in the shadow role of coach. Some religious educators are cowards. They are so afraid of taking any kind of risk in the event their own inadequacies will show up in their students that they refuse to give the "players" anything substantive to perform. These shadow coaches thereby condemn religious education to triviality and marginalia. There are paternalistic/maternalistic religious educators who "protect" their players from harm, such as keeping women or minority races in their "places," off the true playing field. These coaches degrade religious education into encouraging prejudice and bigotry. A few religious educators are perfectionists, which may sound great at first. The problem is that perfectionists spend so much time fiddling and tinkering that their productivity and quality of work actually tend to decrease and performance may never get truly accomplished.[56] These coaches reduce vibrant religious education to nothing more than the minutia of calendaring and programing.[57] There are religious educators who consider themselves as drill sergeants, rigorously training their charges in the mechanics of religious education but failing to show the learners how to translate these mechanics into useful, mature behavior. These taskmasters replace religious education with the husks of rules, laws, and obedience training. Finally, religious educators can be found who appear to be virtually blind to the deeper issues involved in true religious education, who seem unaware that religious education is performed by real people in real life and that it is a vital and essential force for the good of the human race. Genuine religious education does not cloister or harbor the person, separating them in an artificial or antiseptic environment. These shadow coaches, with their severe myopia, mistake the practice field for the playing field and see the church, temple, synagogue, or classroom as the only recognizable arenas for playing and miss the better arenas for making an impact—a true "difference"—in the world at large. These are the coaches who smile happily when their charges continue to come to their formal religious education activities but who never seem to grasp the need for leading the players outside into vastly larger playing fields. This kind of coaching eventually dilutes religious education into banal irrelevance.

One of the most damaging shadow roles of the religious educator is that of the

---

55. See Joseph W. Critelli, *Personal Growth and Effective Behavior: The Challenge of Everyday Life* (New York: Holt, Rinehart and Winston, 1987), pp. 161-164, for an overview of perfectionism.

56. Ibid., p. 161.

57. Yes, these kinds of things must be done, but they cannot be allowed to completely devour the religious educator as coach.

procrastinator—performed by those "holding to the outward form of godliness but denying its power. Avoid them!"[58]

Faith Tradition Resource: Islam

A chapter that deals with a subject as playful and as recreational as that of the coach can be may appear to be a highly inappropriate place to discuss Islam, which is not known for its frivolity. In a chapter that has emphasized discipline, competence, and performance, however, Islam would be quite appropriate. It is in the latter context that Islam is addressed here.

The word "Islam" is a verbal noun that means "surrender" and "submission." The term "Muslim" means "one who submits" or "one who commits to Islam."[59] From the outset, Islam clearly focuses on the serious side of the coaching role. To be a Muslim is to take the game seriously and to commit to play the game. A deeper look at the faith tradition resource of Islam, though, brings out an issue not yet considered in this discussion, that of submission and obedience. For the Muslim, this submission and obedience is rendered unto God. For the religious educator in the role of coach, he or she must have some degree of control over the team in order to be effective in supervisory and leadership capacities; this leads naturally enough to the concept of the player's willingness to be submissive to the needs of the team and obedient to the directions of the coach. The submissiveness and obedience to God's will that is so essential to understanding the Muslim lifestyle must always be counter-balanced to some degree by the individual's rights and opinions when considered from the point of view of the coach. The resource of Islam teaches more about submission and obedience to God than it does about individual rights and opinions and as such is the source of much confusion and misunderstanding to those in the Western world who begin with a mind-set that assumes democracy and individual freedom as fundamental values.

When Westerners turn their attention to Islam, another problem is that too often the only focus is the violence and the fanaticism that has resulted from political upheavals in some Muslim countries, but a Muslim could easily say the same about how some so-called Christian (for example) countries spawn their own kinds of violence. To identify Islam or any other religion with these worst-case excesses does little to help understand what they have to offer. Charles Le Gai Eaton addressed this difficult barrier for the Western world's understanding of Islam, offering this advice: "Beneath the surface, however, and invisible to the casual observer, there exist a vast number of simple men and women who remain

---

58. 2 Timothy 3:5 (NRSV).

59. See David S. Noss and John B. Noss, *A History of the World's Religions*, 8th ed. (New York: Macmillan, 1990), p. 532. An Islamic source makes the same point even more forcefully: "The meaning of Islam is: Obedience and dutifulness to God. To give over oneself to God is Islam. To relinquish one's freedom and independence in favor of God is Islam. To surrender oneself before the authority and sovereignty of God is Islam. One who entrusts all his affairs to God is a Muslim, and one who keeps his own affairs in his own hands or entrusts them to someone else than God is not a Muslim." S. Abdul A'La Maududi, *The Fundamentals of Islam*, 5th ed. (Lahore, Pakistan: Islamic Publications, 1980), p. 21.

exemplary Muslims and who redeem Islam today as they did in the past . . .
whose selfless thirst for God reduces the sins of the mighty to little more than rude
irrelevance. Islam is not always discoverable in the hands or the hearts of its
leaders or of its official spokesmen, but those who seek it will find it."[60] Probably
many Christians (and indeed the adherents of virtually any other faith tradition)
would also plead for the same sort of search for sincerity among those who are
not often the most visible examples! In the context of this chapter, Eaton was saying in his own way that the players need to be the central focus while the coaches are simply their facilitators.

Another key issue raised by Eaton was the unity of the Muslim perspective.[61]
Where earlier in this chapter it was stressed that playing and working have a
harmony and a unity that is in many ways indivisible, so in Muslim life such divisions as the "sublime" and the "mundane" are not discernible dualities. Islam is
a lifestyle religion, and to be a part of it is to be fully integrated in its demands,
expectations, and rituals. Eaton expressed the holism of Islam this way: "For the
Muslim, his worship and his manner of dealing with his bodily functions, his
search for holiness and his bartering in the market, his work and his play are elements in an indivisible whole which, like creation itself, admits no fissures. A single key unlocks the single door opening to the integrated and tight-knit world of
the Muslim."[62] Later, Eaton said: "Islam itself is an organic whole, a *gestalt*, in
which everything is interconnected and in which no single part can be considered
in isolation from the rest."[63] While this sounds rather ecumenical or even systemic,[64] it is important to note that Islam does not seek the permeable and open
boundaries requisite for a truly open system. As the statements by Eaton above
imply, Islam tends to see itself as a faith community that is self-sufficient and is
not particularly interested in how other faith traditions can be included in the
gestalt. Eaton had the courage to admit this: "The battle for tolerance and the
broad definition [of Islamic orthodoxy] has never been finally won, and this is
particularly clear at the present time when for various reasons, including what may
be called an 'identity crisis,' many Muslims have taken refuge in narrowness and
literalism."[65] Sadly, Muslims are not alone in seeking this comforting but dead-

---

60. Charles Le Gai Eaton, *Islam and the Destiny of Man* (Albany: State University of New
York Press, 1985), p. 5.

61. True Muslims were described as "those who completely merge into Islam their full personality and entire existence. All the positions they hold get submerged into the position of a
Muslim. Their roles as fathers, sons, husbands or wives, businessmen, zamindars, labourers, employ-
ees, or professionals should signify the characteristics of a Muslim. Their sentiments, their desires,
their ideologies, their thoughts and opinions, their hatreds and inclinations, their likes and dislikes,
everything is subservient to Islam. There is a complete sway of Islam on their heart and mind, on their
eyes and ears, on their stomach and private parts, on their hands and feet, on their body and soul."
A'La Maududi, *The Fundamentals of Islam*, p. 69.

62. Eaton, *Islam and the Destiny of Man*, p. 1.

63. Ibid., p. 12.

64. See Timothy Arthur Lines, *Systemic Religious Education* (Birmingham, Ala.: Religious
Education Press, 1987), especially pp. 143-146 and pp. 149-160 for a discussion of what I mean by
a systemic view of religion. While Islam in the above quote is described as integrated ("an organic whole") in and of itself, it actually tends toward being more of a closed system than in being
integrated with other religions.

65. Eaton, *Islam and the Destiny of Man*, p. 4.

ening type of refuge. All religions have those followers who are closed-minded, but these should not be allowed to define completely the larger whole of the believers.[66]

The community plays a vastly important role in Islam. To understand how Islam can serve as a faith community resource for the role of coach it is crucial to see that in Islam the larger faith community determines belief and practice rather than do particular individuals. This Muslim community is known as the *Umma*, described by Frederick Denny this way: "The Muslim *Umma* is the totality of Muslims in the world at a given time, as well as the sense of shared history of the Islamic venture inherited from the past."[67] While in simplest terms becoming a Muslim requires only saying with sincerity before witnesses the Arabic words *La Illaha Illallah Muhammadur Rasullullah*—"There is no god but God: Muhammed is the prophet of God"—in practice and in reality becoming a Muslim is coming into submission and obedience not only to God but also to the *Umma*. There is no room for a "lone ranger" who decides for himself or herself what is to be believed or practiced in Islam. These decisions are prescribed by the *Umma*, which in turn follows the teachings of the Qur'an. This understanding of community, with its expectations of individuals to surrender to the will of the corporate body, can be instructive to the religious educator as coach as he or she strives to communicate the concept of a team to the players. The struggle, of course, is to find a way to stress this team concept without squelching the individual's unique and essential contributions to the team.

This section has only opened the door to Islam as a potential faith community resource to those approaching the role of coach. Certainly no one should mistake these few paragraphs as anything like an overview or even an introduction of this major world religion but should instead see them as an invitation to do more exploration into the richness and complexity that resides in Islam. The religious educator as coach will find there much to learn about discipline, practice, submission, lifestyle, and the power of community.

Historical Personage: Ignatius Loyola

As odd as it may seem, moving from Islam to the Catholicism of Ignatius Loyola (Iñigo López de Loyola, 1491-1556) is not as difficult a journey or as an abrupt a change as one might expect. The person of Ignatius stands as a paragon of the coach in the history of the church, even though to designate him thusly entails a conscious "misuse" of terms. In a similar way, the faith tradition of Islam represents the discipline and obedience necessary to the role of the coach, although probably no Muslim would express it in quite that manner. The point is that the role of the coach and the function of coaching can be found throughout the history of religions and of religious education, while admittedly the terms "coach" and "coaching" are more modern neologisms.

---

66. To emphasize this, for example, one Muslim said of Islam (while discussing the necessity of *Zakat*, almsgiving): "There is no place for narrow-minded people in this party. Only those can enter this party who are large-hearted." A'La Maududi, *Fundamentals of Islam*, p. 168.

67. Frederick M. Denny, *Islam and the Muslim Community* (San Francisco: Harper & Row, 1987), p. 10.

Ignatius is by no means the only or the most prominent model of the coach to be found even in Christian church history. For example, Jean-Baptiste de La Salle (1651-1719)—founder of the Brothers of the Christian Schools; Cornelis Jansen (1585-1638)—inspiration for the Little Schools of Port Royal; and François de Fénelon, Archbishop of Cambrai (1651-1715)—pioneer in women's education, could all be cited as valid representatives of coaching during the same general time period. Ignatius was chosen as the model for four reasons.

The first reason for spotlighting Ignatius is his entrance into the educational role through unconventional means. Ignatius did not come to the educational task through the priesthood and through formal training. He came from a life as a soldier and learned of the deeper life during recovery from a serious war injury.[68] As Robert McNally noted, such a practical and experiential form of preparation made Ignatius, his writings, and his teachings suspect to the church leaders: "For in the eyes of many Ignatius, the former soldier, the uneducated layman, was ineligible to preach and teach Catholic faith and morals. His doctrine was suspiciously regarded as a novelty. His apostolic activity was resented, especially since by force of personality and method his appeal was popular."[69] In the true manner of a coach, Ignatius came to his calling with experience "from the field," and not from a purely cognitive perspective.[70] He was a man of the people serving the people, keeping human need foremost in view over structures or ritual.[71] While this approach threatened many of the traditionalists, his results made him a force to be recognized.

A second reason for looking at Ignatius is his part in establishing the "Company of Jesus," a name soon changed to the Society of Jesus, and more popularly called the Jesuits. This Society sprang up as a reform movement from within the church, and focused its attention on personal and corporate piety. Michael Mullett has written: "The Society of Jesus ('Jesuits') was the most important new religious order of the Catholic Church to be founded in the Counter-Reformation period."[72] The reason for this importance was not only

---

68. For an interesting account of Ignatius' entrance into religious life, see Chapter One, "The Converted and Penitent Knight," in Henri Joly, *Saint Ignatius of Loyola*, trans. Mildred Partridge (London: Duckworth, 1899; reprint ed., New York: Benziger Brothers, 1976), pp. 1-36.

69. Robert E. McNally, *The Council of Trent, the Spiritual Exercises, and the Catholic Reform* (Philadelphia: Fortress, 1970), p. 12.

70. This base of practice and of experience marked the life and contributions of Ignatius and later continued to distinguish the Jesuits themselves. As George Ganss observed: "He [Ignatius] was an innovator in the form of religious life; and in his *Constitutions* he manifested his practical wisdom by devising new measures to meet the needs of his era and by constantly stressing the need of adaptation to circumstances of persons, places, and time. Inevitably his single constitutions were culturally conditioned by concepts and customs characteristic of religious life in the sixteenth century. But through his genius he provided for their adaptation to new conditions. This flexibility is one more reason why his *Constitutions* still retain their inspirational vitality today." *The Constitutions of the Society of Jesus*, by Saint Ignatius of Loyola, translated, with an introduction and commentary by George E. Ganss (St. Louis Institute of Jesuit Resources, 1970), p. 32.

71. "If one considers the activity of Ignatius of Loyola, General of the Society in its entirety, one can affirm that he was more concerned with people than with structures." Andre Ravier, *Ignatius of Loyola and the Founding of the Society of Jesus*, trans. Maura Daly, Joan Daly, and Carson Daly (San Francisco: Ignatius Press, 1987; first published in 1973), p. 342.

72. Michael Mullett, *The Counter-Reformation and the Catholic Revolution in Early Modern Europe* (London: Methuen, 1984), pp. 22-23. The term "Counter-Reformation" is more construc-

because of the Society's stress on spiritual discipline, however, but because of the educational process it spawned. The need for spiritual "directors" (coaches) to facilitate the spiritual growth brought about a renewal in the call for more responsible and serious education.[73] The so-called Jesuits, even to this day, are known for their emphasis on intellectual as well as spiritual discipline.[74]

A third reason closely follows the second. Ignatius established an order that was neither to retreat from society nor to spend its time continually engrossed in unnecessary or purely narcissistic self-examination.[75] The Society of Jesus was to be found in the midst of society, serving and working. McNally stated Ignatius' intentions this way: "In terms of this apostolate of service, Ignatius broke ruthlessly with the monastic and mendicant tradition of the medieval church. His society would be unique for its mobility and agility, for its freedom from the ascetical presuppositions of the past. It would be ordered to work, concretely to do the work of the church throughout the world."[76] This emphasis on work and performance by Ignatius and the Jesuits illustrates the role of the coach discussed throughout the present chapter.

A fourth and final reason for highlighting Ignatius has to do with his venerated "coaching manual," *The Spiritual Exercises.*[77] This writing actually gave birth to the Society of Jesus as a book of instructions for spiritual growth through the learning (*didache*) of discipline.[78] Remaining a classic in spiritual literature

---

tively phrased "Catholic Reformation." This removes the argument about whether the Catholic Reformation was only a reaction to the Protestant Reformation or a legitimate movement in and of itself. In the case of Ignatius, his motives appear to have stemmed from within the church rather than as a reaction to the Protestants. As Mullett said: "Ignatius seems to have thought very little about the Protestant Reformation." Ibid.

73. "The aim which the Society of Jesus directly seeks is to aid its own members and their fellowmen to attain the ultimate end for which they were created. To achieve this purpose, in addition to the example of one's own life, learning and a method of expounding it are also necessary. Therefore . . . it will be necessary to provide for the edifice of their learning and the manner of employing it, that these may be aids toward better knowledge and service of God, our Creator and Lord." Saint Ignatius of Loyola, *The Constitutions of the Society of Jesus*, pp. 171-172.

74. An excellent resource for a history of the Society of Jesus is Joseph de Guibert, *The Jesuits: Their Spiritual Doctrine and Practice—A Historical Study*, trans. William J. Young (Chicago: Loyola University Press, 1964; first published in 1953).

75. Jesuits have always been known for their personal and corporate spiritual discipline, of course, which was the purpose behind the writing of the *Exercises*. Joseph de Guibert wrote: "The acquisition of solid virtues against self have been the themes to which the generals [of the Society] have ceaselessly reverted in their letters. The place given to daily examens, especially the particular examen as the preeminent means of correcting faults and acquiring virtues, has always remained equally large. When the custom of periodic retreats and triduums preparatory to the renewal of vows developed, in them the reformation of life remained one of their essential aims." De Guibert, *The Jesuits: Their Spiritual Doctrine and Practice*, p. 568. The regular examination and efforts for improvement described by de Guibert are clearly in the lineage of the role of coach. Ignatius thus can be said to have stressed "behavioral analysis" and lifestyle performance to his "players."

76. McNally, *The Council of Trent*, p. 15.

77. See *The Spiritual Exercises of St. Ignatius Loyola*, trans. Elisabeth Meier Tetlow (Lanham, Md.: University Press of America, 1987). This translation uses gender inclusive language and makes the *Exercises* more accessible to a new generation of readers.

78. One of the marks of the Society is the freedom of the Jesuits to disagree with one another in lively discussions and debates. This has its roots in the personality and approach of Ignatius himself: "By character and temperament he [Ignatius] was a born leader. He loved people and was ever

today, it served as an early guide for spiritual directors—coaches—to follow as they led others on the path. The experiential nature of the book was made clear by Elisabeth Tetlow when she remarked: *"The Spiritual Exercises* was designed to be a school of love. The book was intended, not to be read through, but to be lived through."[79] Daniel Fitzpatrick made a similar comment: *"The Spiritual Exercises* is not just a book for reading; it is rather a manual to be translated into personal experience and purposeful activity."[80] Although the coach himself (Ignatius) is long gone, his "coaching style" and expectations live on through his writings. It is interesting indeed to read this coaching manual, and after all the centuries still to be able to receive supervision and motivation from Ignatius, an exemplary "coach" from religious history.

Contemporary Example: James Michael Lee

Let's take a break from this serious discussion for a moment and take a quick quiz. There are only four questions, and the answers to them should not be difficult to determine.

Question #1: What contemporary religious educator is well-known in the field for his scholarly writings, in spite of the fact that he rarely uses the term "religious education"?

Question #2: What contemporary religious educator has constructed "for the first time in the history of the field a truly comprehensive and systematic macrotheory" for explaining the "religious instruction act"?

Question #3: What contemporary religious educator has written a trilogy covering this "macrotheory" which he says is "a work for beginners in the field," but which would need to be expanded to thirty volumes to do in proper depth?

Question #4: What contemporary religious educator is quite possibly the most published, most quoted, and least understood?

---

eager to converse with them, assuredly in the hope of drawing spiritual fruit. He won the affections of the followers whom he inspired and whose opinions he constantly sought before he issued commands. Thus he made them feel that they were persons as well as a part of an organization in which their opinions were valued. He made much of discussion between a superior and subjects, whom he expected to be respectfully but completely frank and open." Commentary by Ganss in *The Constitutions of the Society of Jesus, by Saint Ignatius of Loyola*, pp. 26-27.

79. *The Spiritual Exercises of St. Ignatius Loyola*, trans. Elisabeth Meier Tetlow, Translator's Preface, p. xiv. The phrase "service in love" is found often in Ignatius' writings, stressing that the performance of service be done in love, through love, and resulting in love. As Ganss put it: "The founder [Ignatius] expected the members of his society to love their Lord in contemplation and to manifest their love in deeds." Commentary by Ganss in *The Constitutions of the Society of Jesus, by Saint Ignatius of Loyola*, p. 22.

80. Daniel J. Fitzpatrick, *Confusion, Call, Commitment: The Spiritual Exercises and Religious Education* (New York: Alba House, 1976), p. xv.

If your answer to each of the above questions was James Michael Lee, you may proceed. If not, please reread the heading of this section!

The subject of this section is indeed James Michael Lee (b. 1931), and the previous questions will be used to introduce him as the contemporary example for the role of coach. Be reminded that this effort is not to be an overview and evaluation of all of Lee's contributions; instead, the intent is to suggest that the role of coach is a predominant one within Lee's writings and that it can be used to characterize his approach. The term "coach" is not one used by Lee for his position and is my own designation. The success or failure of the term related to his work should not be a reflection on it, since obviously his work can stand on its own.

Overview

The four questions at the head of this section are easily enough answered, certainly, but they also provide some opportunity to gain a more thorough understanding of Lee's purposes in writing. Taking them in seriatim allows for some introductory comments to Lee's work.

Question #1: What contemporary religious educator is well-known in the field for his scholarly writings, in spite of the fact that he rarely uses the term "religious education"?

Whatever else may be said of James Michael Lee and his contributions to religious education, he has played the role of scholar to near perfection. Indeed, his writings are probably more scholarly than nearly anyone who has ever published in religious education. To call him a "coach" is in no way meant to denigrate his academic achievements. In a field not generally known for its scholarly writings, Lee has published with the desire and purpose of increasing the field's respectability. One does not need to look very hard for his opinion of some of the things being produced in the area: "Unfortunately, mature scholarship has been a relatively rare commodity in the field of religious instruction. With only a touch of facetiousness one can remark with some legitimacy that not a few religious educators (and educationists?) appear to derive their basic principles of religious instruction from bumper stickers and banners than from high-class scientific books and research treatises in the field."[81]

This quote exposes the real point of the first "test" question, and it was something of a trick question. Lee is indeed a scholar in religious education, but his writings typically center on religious *instruction* rather than the broader field of religious education. He focuses on religious instruction which, he emphasizes, is but one portion of the larger field of religious education. Here is what he says when describing the scope of his three volume theoretical work (the "trilogy"): "The trilogy in both its sum and its parts does not deal with the entire range of intentional religious education. It deliberately excludes from its purview two of the three basic constituents of intentional religious education, namely religious counseling and the administration of religious education activ-

---

81. Lee, *Content of Religious Instruction*, p. 750.

ities. The focus of the trilogy is squarely on the third of these fundamental components of intentional religious education, namely religious instruction."[82] It cannot be stated strongly enough that Lee generally has written not about religious education but about that part of religious education which focuses on the learning-instructional act, religious instruction. This is critically important for understanding Lee for three reasons. First, he contends that religious educators incorrectly describe the field because they equate only one part (instruction) with the whole (education). These religious educators rarely discuss administration of religious education activities or religious counseling, which are almost universally recognized as two of the three major forms of intentional education. Second, by unambiguously delineating his focus as religious instruction Lee stresses the centrality of the purposeful, scientifically based teaching act. Lee contends that one deleterious side effect of the use of the undifferentiated term "religious education" is to lessen the unremitting focus on the teaching/learning act. In Lee's view, what makes religious instruction a separate and distinct field is not its philosophical or theological or social foundations but rather the ongoing dynamics which take place in the teaching/learning act itself. A third reason why Lee's use of the term religious instruction is crucial to understanding Lee is his place in this chapter. It is because of Lee's emphasis on religious instruction, on the dynamics of the teaching/learning act, that he represents the role of coach. The prime function of the coach is instruction; hence Lee is a natural and appropriate section for this role. More than virtually any other religious educator in the history of the field, Lee has highlighted the central role of the religious educator as quintessentially the facilitator who makes things happen by constantly focusing on those dynamics which bring learning to pass.

> Question #2: What contemporary religious educator has constructed "for the first time in the history of the field a truly comprehensive and systematic macrotheory" for explaining the "religious instruction act"?

This question was constructed from the following quote from Lee: "The purpose of the trilogy is to provide for the first time in the history of the field a truly comprehensive and systematic macrotheory which produces the power to adequately explain, predict, and verify the religious instruction act."[83] More about the trilogy is found in the discussion of the next question, but for now the importance of this quote relates to what this "macrotheory" represents.

First, Lee is trying to place religious instruction on an empirical, theoretical, and research basis rather than on an ideological, or a merely presupposi-

---

82. Ibid., p. 747. This quote is from the third and final book of the trilogy. Lest one think Lee changed his position from the first book of the trilogy, see Chapter One, "Prolegomenon," in *The Shape of Religious Instruction*, pp. 6-8. You will find exactly the same position spelled out. The second book of the trilogy was Lee, *Flow of Religious Instruction*. More about the trilogy is found in the discussion of Question #3 below.

83. Lee, *Content of Religious Instruction*, p. xii.

tional basis.[84] The key words "explain, predict, and verify" point to the use of theory, which Lee defined as "a set of interrelated facts and laws which present a systematic view of phenomena by specifying relations among variables in order to explain and predict the phenomena."[85] This type of language and procedure should reveal the reason why each of the books of the trilogy has the same subtitle: "A Social Science Approach." His attempt in the trilogy was to find and articulate a firm, empirical footing for carrying on the "religious instruction act" that would not be dependent on some prior philosophical, theological, or ideological position. This stance has allowed Lee to make statements such as the following: "The social-science approach to religious instruction is value-free in terms of any and all specific theological positions."[86] It is not that the social-science approach is absolutely "value-free," since it is obviously based on scientific values; however, it is value-free, as Lee said, "in the sense that in the religious instruction act itself the relatively neutral facilitation dynamic can and does take on the coloration of any one or other of theological systems of thought."[87]

Second, the quote emphasizes that theory alone was not the fundamental framework, but rather it was macrotheory which served as the prime focus. Lee defined macrotheory as "an overall and global form of theory into which are inserted theories and subtheories of lesser scope,"[88] and Lee's attempt was to provide a comprehensive "theoretical and scientific foundation for religious instruction."[89] In Lee's view, previously no one had done that for the field, and that failure explained the "identity crisis" which has continually plagued the field.[90] His hope was that by setting the field on the macrotheoretical basis of the social-science approach it would finally "mature" and take its place as a respected and useful contributor to academia. Here we find a "coach" who does not advocate random trial-and-error methods but one who develops careful and extensive strategy for the game founded on a reliable and firm macrotheory. This macrotheory, in all of its complexity, is the reason for the composition of a trilogy, which is now considered more directly.

Question #3: What contemporary religious educator has written a trilogy covering this "macrotheory" which he says is "a work for beginners in the field" but which would need thirty volumes to do in proper depth?

---

84. Lee advocates and proposes a social-science approach to religious education (in his specific area of focus, religious instruction) rather than a theological approach for the very reason that social science tends to be free from ideological or presuppositional bias. This has received extensive treatment in Lee's writings. Some representative ones are James Michael Lee, "The Authentic Source of Religious Instruction," in *Religious Education and Theology*, ed. Norma H. Thompson (Birmingham, Ala.: Religious Education Press, 1982), pp. 100-197; Lee, *Shape of Religious Instruction*, pp. 225-229; Lee, *Flow of Religious Instruction*, pp. 14-22; and Lee, *Content of Religious Instruction*, pp. 23-26.

85. Lee, *Shape of Religious Instruction*, p. 156.

86. Lee, *Flow of Religious Instruction*, p. 292.

87. Lee, *Content of Religious Instruction*, p. 24.

88. Ibid., p. 752.

89. Ibid., p. 750.

90. For his view on this "identity crisis," see Chapter Four, "Religious Instruction as a Discipline," in Lee, *Shape of Religious Instruction*, pp. 94-100.

In the process of trying to put the field on a "solid scientific and theoretical foundation" of macrotheory, Lee found sufficient material to fill three books which from his perspective still only scratched the surface of what is needed. Lee wrote in the conclusion ("Epilogue") to this trilogy these words from which the above question was developed: "Therefore the trilogy should not be considered as an advanced work, a work which explores topics with requisite depth and subtlety. Rather, the trilogy is a work for beginners in the field of religious instruction. It provides nothing more than a broad introduction to the field, namely, the bases and the primary components of religious instruction activity. As an introductory work, the trilogy necessarily covers a vast amount of territory; hence its intent and strength lie in its breadth and not in its depth. In order for the trilogy to be as deep as I would have liked, it would have had to be expanded to at least thirty volumes."[91]

The first book in the trilogy was *The Shape of Religious Instruction*, which provided "the rock-bottom foundation and rationale for the existence of religious instruction as a distinct enterprise in its own right."[92] There Lee gave the most extensive exposition and argument for religious instruction being a "mode of religious instruction and not a branch of theology."[93] As such, it is the most general and foundational of the three books and is essential reading for understanding the two that followed.

The Flow of Religious Instruction was the second volume of the trilogy, which constituted a contemporary "coaching manual" for the religious instructor. In this volume the "structural content" of the teaching-learning act was explained, by which Lee meant the "actual pedagogical dynamic in and of itself."[94] He wrote: "Structural content is the teaching process. Structural content is not simply how a religious educator teaches, but how the religious instruction act qua pedagogical act is itself something which is learned by learners."[95] For those religious educators looking to improve their teaching skills a la the coaching style, this book is quintessential.

The third volume of the trilogy was *The Content of Religious Instruction*, which dealt with the other type of content—what Lee called "substantive content," or more commonly, subject matter. The substantive content is "lived religion in all its rich dimensionalities,"[96] or as Lee further stated it: "The substantive content of religious instruction is religion as religion exists in the religious instruction act."[97] In this book, Lee discussed the "nine types of fundamental molar forms of substantive content" which he believed he had uncovered: product content, process content, cognitive content, affective content, verbal content, nonverbal content, conscious content, unconscious content, and lifestyle content.[98] As one would

---

91. Lee, *Content of Religious Instruction*, p. 750.
92. Ibid.
93. Ibid.
94. Ibid., p. xii.
95. Ibid., p. 751.
96. Ibid., p. 752.
97. Ibid., p. xii.
98. Ibid., p. xii. Each of these types of content is given a chapter of its own in the book with the exception of conscious content.

imagine, this made for a book of "substantive content" virtually unparalleled in the field.[99]

The trilogy, ironically, opens the door to the fourth and final question on our "test."

Question #4: What contemporary religious educator is quite possibly the most published, most quoted, and least understood?

Admittedly, the above statement is not one that can be proved, or empirically justified. It does, however, have a ring of truth: James Michael Lee is quoted— or at least referenced—quite often from his many works by other authors but seemingly almost as often with misunderstanding or confusion. Too much on this point would move into the section on evaluation, which follows, so only two comments are provided for clarification.

The first comment is that even though Lee may say his works are for beginners,[100] these texts are substantial enough and detailed enough to invite misunderstanding and confusion to those who do not read carefully and thoughtfully. Almost invariably, this misunderstanding and confusion arises from sloppy and inattentive reading—or just skimming over the surface ever so lightly. After all, even his most severe critics agree that Lee is crystal clear, even if his writings are not of the bedside-reading genre. The all too common misunderstanding of Lee might well be more of a reflection of the current state of the field and its inhabitants than of Lee's writing. Yet Lee does make heavy demands on his readers. Lee is not unaware of this. He strongly believes that any profession, especially a religious profession dealing directly with God's own work of facilitating religious outcomes in others, must necessarily put heavy demands on persons who choose to enter and remain in that profession.

The second comment is that Lee was calling for a radical change in the way religious education/instruction is perceived and performed. Rather than advocating that the religious educator be treated as a "messenger boy" [or girl] or even as a translator, of theology, Lee insisted that the religious educator/instructor is actually a mediator: "This new reality of mediator is of such a nature that it unites not only its components (substantive contents and structural contents) but unites them in such a fashion that the components are no longer separate entities but rather are subsumed into a new reality, the reality called religious

---

99. By this I refer to the book's length, which is 814 pages, as well as to its comprehensive nature.

100. When Lee writes that his trilogy is intended for beginners in the field, he was influenced by Thomas Aquinas who stated that his *Summa Theologica* was written for beginners. Both the *Summa* and Lee's trilogy are massive, thorough, comprehensive, and, for the novice, even daunting books. What Lee and Aquinas seem to have meant by calling their works "books for beginners" is that these books are intended to provide a comprehensive overview of the field, something which beginners should know. Other previous and subsequent books are to be regarded as more focused, in-depth treatments of topics covered less intensively in the "work for beginners." Actually in the case of both Lee and Aquinas, their trilogy and *Summa* respectively also constitute the beginning of a new field, or at least a very different way of construing the field.

instruction."[101] This is so disconcerting to some religious educators who see themselves either as "pure" or applied theologians that they are unwilling to take Lee seriously. Lee was saying neither that theology is unimportant nor that theology should be dismissed as a factor in religious instruction, only that theology does not supply the fundamental framework and is not the determinative issue in religious education/instruction.[102] It appears that this commonsense insistence on a theologically "neutral" approach is enough to outlaw Lee's "coaching" in many theologically-imperialistic camps. As Lee expressed early in his trilogy: "The social-science approach to religious instruction is so obvious that one wonders why it is regarded by some religious educators as new or innovational."[103] Is the thought of being a mediator, which means not only knowing and communicating theology but having to do something useful with it, too much to expect? Lee was claiming that as coaches, religious educators must not only be involved in transforming others, but that they must be transformed by and through the teaching/learning process.

This overview of Lee was designed to give just enough information to justify categorizing him as a contemporary example of the role of coach. Obviously, a full treatment of Lee's position is beyond the limits of this section. Some words concerning evaluation, other than what have already given, continue the discussion on Lee.

Evaluation

There is no denying the scholarly contributions to the field of religious education by James Michael Lee. No one else comes to mind who has written a trilogy to put the field on a macrotheoretical footing. The fact remains, however, that "Coach" Lee has not totally won the day with his social-science approach. Some possible reasons for its struggle for acceptance are considered in this section.

The first one was alluded to earlier, and it is probably more of an indictment of Lee's readers than a criticism of Lee himself. It appears too few religious educators have read Lee carefully enough or fully enough to see all or even most of what he was trying to say. His trilogy is intimidating to the nonprofessional or semi-professional in its length, breadth, and style, and the temptation is either to read only brief portions of it or turn to easier or less-troublesome resources for help. This is no mark of pride for the field and no complaint against Lee but rather an observation of the status quo. The result of this haphazard reading is either a misunderstanding of some of Lee's comments when taken out of context or a by-passing of his work altogether. In terms of evaluation, this point

---

101. Lee, *Content of Religious Instruction*, p. 25. This has received attention from Lee in many places. See, for example, *Shape of Religious Instruction*, pp. 246-248, and *Flow of Religious Instruction*, pp. 17-19.

102. Lee makes the distinction between substantive and structural content, as when he wrote: "Religion is thus the substantive content; instructional practice is the structural content." Lee, *Content of Religious Instruction*, p. 8. Theology may be included in the substantive content, but substantive content is not limited to theology. Lee wrote: "Religious content is not only distinct from theological content but is also far wider than theological content." Ibid., p. 9.

103. Lee, *Shape of Religious Instruction*, p. 25.

is a rather back-handed compliment to Lee and a note of concern about the depth and comprehensional abilities of some religious educators.

Second, Lee has primarily addressed religious instruction[104] rather than devoting the bulk of his attention to religious counseling, the administration of religious education activities, or to the foundations of religious education.[105] Such a steady focus appears to constitute a strong threat to the legitimacy and competence of most religious education writers, many of whom seem to be inadequately versed in the research, theory, or concrete enactment of the teaching/learning act. Faced broadside with such a serious threat, it is quite understandable that quite a few religious education writers criticize Lee. After all, the overwhelming majority of religious education writers do not address the teaching/learning act but rather deal almost exclusively with the theological, philosophical, ecclesiastical, or psychological foundations of religious education, or with religious education as politics and ideology. Thus they fail to understand the basic thrust and content of Lee's writings. (Interestingly enough, Lee does treat at considerable length the foundations of religious education but in a manner suggested by the term *foundations*, namely, that constellation of disciplines which externally support and interpret the religious instruction act but which are not the act itself. And it is ironic that Lee seems to have read and cited more top-flight theologians than almost all those religious education writers who equate the theological foundations of religious education with all of religious education, including the act of teaching religion.)

Third, Lee has been criticized because he has proposed and detailed a revolutionary approach[106] to religious instruction/education. As Howard Grimes noted as early as 1973: "What Lee says about the nature of teaching [in this case, in *The Flow of Religious Instruction*] challenges much that has been written in the field of religious education during the past twenty-five years."[107] In a

---

104. Lee has occasionally written on religious education per se. For example, see James Michael Lee, "Toward a New Era: A Blueprint for Positive Action," in T*he Religious Education We Need: Toward the Renewal of Christian Education,* ed. James Michael Lee (Birmingham, Ala.: Religious Education Press, 1977), pp. 112-155. Here he identified, as he has other places, that religious education has three basic services: religious instruction, religious guidance, and the administration of religious education. Ibid. p. 114. Lee does in this chapter give an account of all three, but he also wrote, characteristically: "Because instruction is the heart and the *raison d'etre* of religious education, the bulk of this chapter will be devoted to religion teaching." Ibid., p. 114.

105. This problem presents a related difficulty in terms of the status and legitimacy of the field. If it takes three large, meticulously wrought volumes to set forth just the basics of the field, then religious educators wishing to advance beyond the basics to become truly proficient must read much more. Unfortunately — and this is a reflection on the status and legitimacy of the field — there comes a point when beginners often give up and turn to popularized, watered-down, and otherwise less professional resources, a genre of religious education writing of which there is no shortage.

106. For more on the religious educator as revolutionary, see Chapter Eleven. Lee is an example of a revolutionary who is not a political type, and this type of nonpolitical revolutionary is the focus of Chapter Eleven. This point about Lee also illustrates that the contemporary examples examined in this book can be understood from more than the one role in which they are analyzed and evaluated.

107. Howard Grimes' review of *The Flow of Religious Instruction* in *Religious Education* 68:6 (November-December, 1973), p. 758. Placing Lee's challenge to the traditional approaches in an historical context is covered in such works as Didier-Jacques Priveteau and J. T. Dillon, *Resurgence of Religious Instruction: Conception and Practice in a World of Change* (Birmingham, Ala.: Religious

classic, understated, and probably unintentionally humorous way, François Darcy-Bérubé once wrote: "But I think it is honest to say that many educators react to [Lee's] work with a certain defensiveness."[108] There certainly are legitimate reasons for religious educators to be threatened, challenged, or defensive, because Lee is calling for religious education to become "thoroughly professionalized" in every dimension and procedure.[109] His quest is not mere reform, but "to basically change fundamental theory and practice"[110] of religious instruction/education.

Fourth, "social science" may at least initially (and inaccurately) sound cold, inhuman, nontheological, and just not very "churchy." For religious educators used to nice, warm "fuzzy" words and concepts, the harsh light of performance, competence, and discipline appear much too impersonal—or threatening.[111] The image of the relaxed, friendly, if slightly irrelevant, religious educator with a cup of coffee in hand is challenged by Lee's image of a competent, intentional, pro-

Education Press, 1977); in Harold William Burgess, *An Invitation to Religious Education* (Birmingham, Ala.: Religious Education Press, 1975); and in Lines, *Systemic Religious Education,* pp. 11-26.

108. Françoise Darcy-Bérubé, "The Challenge Ahead of Us," in *Foundations of Religious Education,* ed. Padraic O'Hare (New York: Paulist, 1978), p. 112. One of the more critical reviews of Lee's work can be found in this chapter by Darcy-Bérubé (pp. 112-120). She was technically commenting on an earlier chapter by Lee (pp. 40-63) in this edited book, but she actually covers more than this one chapter. Many of her comments are the result of an inadequate study and understanding of Lee's position, which is further illustration of the difficulties cited in the previous paragraph. But even more than this, Darcy-Bérubé's comments (for which she offers no scholarly support) seem to display that kind of seemingly intense feat that some religious education writers have about exposing their untested assumptions and emotional "fuzzies" to the harsh light of both logical and empirical investigation. Also, Darcy-Bérubé is basically a writer of religious curriculum materials, and so Lee's insistence on basing teaching on proven facts rather than on pious hunches is dangerous not only intellectually but also economically. If Lee were political, he might win over persons like Darcy-Bérubé to his side. But Lee believes, rather passionately, that a field must be based on tested theories, laws, and facts rather than on political activity or ideology, however skillful or suave such activity might be. Such a view makes Lee controversial in some religious education quarters, as would be expected.

109. "If there is any one basic guideline which is the most important and the most necessary for the successful future of religious education, it is this: Religious education should become thoroughly professionalized." James Michael Lee, "Toward a New Era: A Blueprint for Positive Action," in *The Religious Education We Need,* p. 121. See the rest of the paragraph from which this quote was taken to get an idea of the extent to which Lee is talking about professionalizing the field. Also see such specific proposals as those offered in James Michael Lee, "Catechesis Sometimes, Religious Instruction Always," in *Does the Church Really Want Religious Education?: An Ecumenical Inquiry,* ed. Marlene Mayr (Birmingham, Ala.: Religious Education Press, 1988), pp. 32-66, and James Michael Lee, "CCD Renewal," in *Renewing the Sunday School and the CCD,* ed. D. Campbell Wyckoff (Birmingham, Ala.: Religious Education Press, 1986), pp. 211-244.

110. See James Michael Lee, "To Basically Change Fundamental Theory and Practice," an autobiographical chapter in *Modern Masters of Religious Education,* pp. 254-323. This idea of fundamental change is a constant theme in Lee's writings. For example, see the Preface to *The Content of Religious Instruction,* especially pp. xiii-xiv.

111. Jeff Astley, a British religious educator trained as a theologian, makes a similar point in his review of Lee's *The Content of Religious Instruction*: "But at the end of the day the social-science research that Lee does commend to us may provide a contribution of more lasting and practical use than many of the contributions of either the philosophers or the theologians. This will be a hard claim by someone who finds himself most at home among these more philosophical and theological disciplines. The present reviewer is one such (rather reluctant) convert. There will be many others." See Jeff Astley's review in *Religious Education* 81:1 (Winter, 1986), p. 146.

fessional facilitator who has a carefully wrought and empirically verified game plan in hand. Even worse, social science has the means of evaluation to show that the religious educator may be missing the mark. Who needs this kind of trouble?

Fifth, Lee's forthright use of language is always precise—but it is too forthright and too revelatory for some religious educators. To a field like religious education which more often than not tends to cloak itself in pious nostrums and overly simplistic feel-good treatises, Lee's direct and incisive use of language can be cutting and even at times painful. For example, *The Flow of Religious Instruction*[112] includes a masterful and comprehensive analysis of eight pseudo "theories"[113] of religious instruction currently in use. When Lee gets to the fourth pseudo "theory," he labels it the "blow theory" which "holds that the invisible and incomprehensible action of the Holy Spirit represents the basic and at bottom the sole causal variable involved in the modification of the learner's behavior along religious lines."[114] (The term "blow theory" comes from John 3:8 which states that the Spirit blows where it wills and no person can contain or direct it.) While the label "blow theory" is accurate, descriptive, and certainly memorable, it is also possibly offensive either to someone who holds such a position or to someone who sees such a label as disrespectful to divine activity. A similar issue arises when Lee speaks of the "despookification" of religious instruction, which is the stance that "effective religion teaching ought not to be explained of any amorphous, spooky conception of the mysterious workings of God in the religious instruction act."[115] While these and other examples[116] make Lee's position perfectly clear, it is also true that Lee's forthright unmasking of empty cliches, pious rhetoric, and untested assumptions can be for some religious educators a cutting scalpel, or even a sword. For his part, Lee sees his own scholarship, and indeed all genuine scholarship, as prophetic in that it can hasten the future by putting the field on a firm, solid, and empirically verified basis, something sorely lacking in today's religious education. Like all prophets, Lee firmly believes that it is necessary to call attention to those foundational and practical elements of a field which hinder or choke the effective flowering of that field. And like all prophets, Lee's use of language cuts to the heart of the matter, and so his work represents a reprimand and a threat to those religious educators who prefer to sail on smooth, unexamined seas.

Sixth, Lee's wholehearted support of the social science macrotheoretical

---

112. Lee, Chapter Seven, "Theoretical Approaches to Teaching Religion," in *The Flow of Religious Instruction*, pp. 149-205.

113. "Theories" is in quotes here because of Lee's comments about the use of the term in this regard in ibid., p. 151.

114. Ibid., p. 174.

115. Ibid., p. 293. Also see this same idea expressed in James Michael Lee, "Lifework Spirituality and the Religious Educator," in *The Spirituality of the Religious Educator,* ed. James Michael Lee (Birmingham, Ala.: Religious Education Press, 1985), pp. 29 and 39.

116. See Lee describe "pill mentality," "recipe mentality," and "Mr. Fix-It mentality" in *The Flow of Religious Instruction*, pp. 35-36; "bogeymen" of the social-science approach in "Key Issues in the Development of a Workable Foundation of Religious Instruction," in *Foundations of Religious Education,* pp. 57-62; and the religious educator as "messenger boy" for theology in James Michael Lee, "The Authentic Source of Religious Instruction," in *Religious Education and Theology*, pp. 156-165.

approach[117] and his subsequent dismissal of the theological macrotheoretical as being an inadequate foundation for religious education necessarily makes people divide up and take sides.[118] It is not possible to start and continue with both fundamental approaches—one must be adopted and the other rejected, so there is no middle ground. Using both ontic and empirical evidence, Lee believes that the way to define the field and build it up is through the social-science approach and that a part of this requires that theology assume its authentic supportive role rather than be imperialistic.[119] This places his understanding of theology at special risk, notably with those religious educators who are not well-versed in theology or have not immersed themselves in the writings of major theologians. Citing world-recognized theologians from Catholic, mainline Protestant, and evangelical Protestant traditions, Lee views theology as "the speculative science investigating the nature and workings of God,"[120] basically an "intellectual endeavor."[121] Quite a few religious educators conceptualize theology as representing more than a purely cognitive activity. Even though such an understanding of theology on the part of quite a few religious educators is not supported by major contemporary or deceased theologians from various faith traditions, nonetheless that is the way many religious educators view theology. For those who disagree with his definition or conceptualization of theology, there is little other choice but to reject Lee and his social-science approach to religious instruction/education. The battle over theology—its definition and its role as foundational or as supportive—permeates much of the discussion pro and con of the social-science approach. For Lee, it does not matter at all which *brand* of theology is used as one content in the entire religious instruction act, since the social-science approach is inherently "relatively value free"[122] and so "can and does take on the coloration of any of one or other theological systems of thought."[123] For Lee, what *does* matter is whether theology or social science is capable of adequately explaining, predicting, and verifying the religious instruction act, and indeed all of religious education. It is precisely this issue which makes Lee so threatening to many religious educators, especially the "old guard."

In summary, James Michael Lee stands as an example of the coach par excel-

---

117. In an otherwise favorable review of *The Shape of Religious Instruction*, Charles Melchert took exception to what he saw as Lee's overly trusting acceptance of social-science research, especially the research done in relation to religion. Melchert's review was written in the days when social science, not just as data but as a macrotheory, had just begun to impact religious education — and religious education felt uneasy and uncomfortable as a result. Since those early days, many religious educators have come to appreciate and even to rely on social science, while many others reject it out of fear or out of intellectual conviction. See Charles Melchert, "Review," in *Religious Education* 57:4 (July-August, 1972), p. 306.

118. All of this was really the focus of the first book of the trilogy. See Lee, *Shape of Religious Instruction*.

119. For example, see ibid., Chapter Eight, "The Place of Theology," pp. 225-257.

120. Lee, *Content of Religious Instruction*, p. 6.

121. Ibid., p. 5. Lee has discussed the definition of theology in depth in a number of places besides *Content Of Religious Instruction*. For example, see *Shape of Religious Instruction*, pp. 103-106; and *Flow of Religious Instruction*, pp. 14-22.

122. This is how Lee spoke of it in *The Content of Religious Instruction*, p. 24. Note the careful use of the term "relatively."

123. Ibid.

lence. His work in religious instruction has emphasized the need for performance through competence and discipline. He has stressed the importance of both preparation and evaluation. There are traceable elements in his work of the supervisor, the trainer, the motivator, and the strategist. Finally, he has brought the passion and the commitment of his point of view to the field, which he will not allow to be ignored. Whatever the final results of his efforts to influence and shape religious education/instruction, he has forever changed the way the game is played because of his participation and contribution.

Representative Teaching Procedure: The Project

If the role in question is that of the coach, then the logical representative teaching procedure for that role is learning by doing, which is best facilitated by utilizing what has come to be known as the project.[124] Some other names that have been attached to this procedure have been the purposeful act,[125] the activity movement[126] or process,[127] practicums,[128] and the experimental method,[129] but all of these terms point to the need to *perform* in order to learn. The idea is by no means a new one. It may be that what we now call "the project" may be our oldest teaching procedure.[130] The role of the coach, who teaches how to perform and how to improve that performance, is a time-honored and absolutely essential role for anyone involved in educational activity, and the religious educator can certainly be no exception.

A fully satisfying definition of "the project" is difficult to find, since it can mean so much and be used in so many ways.[131] A helpful one was provided by

---

124. The classic formulation of the "project method" was given by William Heard Kilpatrick in *The Project Method: The Use of the Purposeful Act in the Educative Process* (New York: Teachers College, Columbia University, 1925); first printed as an article by the same title in *Teachers College Bulletin*, Tenth Series, No. 3 (October 12, 1918).

125. Ibid., p. 3.

126. For a full account of the activity movement, including a historical sketch of "activism" and critical evaluations of it, see *The Twenty-third Yearbook of the National Society for the Study of Education, Part II—The Activity Movement*, ed. Guy Montrose Whipple (Bloomington, Ill.: Public School Publishing Company, 1934).

127. See Lois Coffey Mossman, *The Activity Concept: An Interpretation* (New York: Macmillan, 1938).

128. See Mason Crum, *The Project Method in Religious Education* (Nashville: Cokesbury Press, 1924), p. 2.

129. This was the way John Dewey spoke of it most often. See, for example, John Dewey, *Democracy and Education: An Introduction to the Philosophy of Education* (New York: Macmillan, 1916), pp. 228-242. The project is most often today associated with the progressive education movement, of which Dewey and Kilpatrick were the leaders. The force behind this movement was "that education be considered as life itself and not as a mere preparation for living." Kilpatrick, *The Project Method*, p. 6. Because of this emphasis on living and doing in education, the "project method" was ideal for furthering these ends. For an update and an endorsement of the project procedure, see Lee, *The Content of Religious Instruction*, pp. 699-701.

130. "Is activism a principle just discovered by modern educators? It is as old as man's earliest education." Thomas Woody, "Historical Sketch of Activism," in *The Twenty-Third Yearbook of the National Society for the Study of Education, Part II—The Activity Movement*, p. 9.

131. See the in-depth treatment by William Heard Kilpatrick, "Definition of the Activity Movement To-day," in ibid., pp. 45-64. An example of the frustration many have with the definitional problem was provided by Boyd H. Bode: "The Activity Movement, in brief, appears to include

Erwin Shaver: "A project may be tentatively defined as a single unified experience, utilized because of its social values, which can be entered into with a whole-hearted purpose, which is representative of real life situations, and which makes for control of new experiences as they are met."[132] The key issues, then, emphasized by Shaver and other educators involved with the project procedure are experience, purposefulness, real-life situations, and application of past learning to new situations. These are all issues of prime importance to the religious educator in the role of coach.

William Heard Kilpatrick discussed four types or classifications of projects.[133] First was the occasion "to embody some idea or plan in external form, as building a boat, writing a letter, presenting a play." Second was an aesthetic experience, such as "listening to a story, hearing a symphony, appreciating a picture." Third was the opportunity to "straighten out some intellectual difficulty, to solve some problem, as to find out whether or not dew falls, to ascertain how New York outgrew Philadelphia." Fourth was the effort to "obtain some skill or knowledge, as learning to write . . . [or] learning the irregular verbs in French." For at least types one and four, Kilpatrick proposed four steps for implementation: purposing, planning, executing, and judging.[134]

Expanding on the four basic steps of the "project method" suggested by Kilpatrick, Bruce Joyce and Marsha Weil devised six phases in the learning cycle under the heading of the group investigation model.[135] Their first phase called for learners to encounter a puzzling or interesting situation—either by intentional planning or by unplanned circumstance—that stimulates the imagination and involvement of the learners. Second, the learners identify their reactions to the problem and their depth of interest in it. Third, the educator aids the learners in formulating the problem and in devising ways it can be explored and investigated. Fourth, the learners do the necessary activity, research, or analysis, report their findings, and settle on a possible solution to the problem. Fifth, the group evaluates the solution and sees if it indeed solves the problem, answers their questions, or clarifies the phenomenon. Sixth, based upon the previous results of the evaluation step, the activity is recycled, either to further investigate the problem or to work on another that has arisen as a result of the earlier evaluative activity.[136]

Examples of how the project procedure can be implemented in religious edu-

---

everything from 'incidental learning' to any kind of learning that involves purposefulness and interest. . . . A reader who expects to gain a simple and workable notion of the Activity Movement . . . is likely, before long, to find himself coming up for air." Ibid., p. 79.

132. Erwin L. Shaver, *The Project Principle in Religious Education: A Manual of Theory and Practice for Church-School Leaders* (Chicago: University of Chicago Press, 1924), p. 10.

133. The four types and the following quotes in this paragraph are from Kilpatrick in *The Project Method*, pp. 16-17.

134. Ibid., p. 17. Kilpatrick referred the reader to John Dewey, *How We Think: A Restatement of the Relation of Reflective Thinking to the Educative Process* (Boston: Heath, 1933), Chapter Six, "Examples of Inference and Testing," pp. 91-101 for steps in facilitating the third type, and offered no procedures for the second type. Kilpatrick, *The Project Method*, pp. 16-17.

135. Bruce Joyce and Marsha Weil, *Models of Teaching*, 3rd ed. (Englewood Cliffs, N.J.: Prentice-Hall, 1986), pp. 219-238.

136. Ibid., pp. 233-234.

cation are legion.[137] The point is that learners are having an experience that is purposeful and meaningful to them, making the appropriate and necessary preparations, acquiring the requisite skills to do the work, and evaluating their progress toward the goal. All of this is led and facilitated by the religious educator as coach, who teaches the players to play the game—by playing the game.

Experiential Simulation: Coaching Styles

The progression from teaching procedure to simulation, in this chapter at least, is not too far to move, since the discussion has gone from discussing the teaching procedure which employs simulations to suggesting that a simulation actually be experienced by a religious educator who chooses to be a coach. It is time to apply this "learning from simulations" procedure specifically and directly to religious education—in other words, to show how the religious educator can experience the role of coach. The prime issue here is not so much whether or not one will be a coach, but what kind of coach one will decide to be.

Two coaching manuals have already been suggested within the chapter—one classic if not a bit archaic, and one modern if not complex. The two are radically different in terms of goals, in subject matter, in writing style, and in historical context, but still they are both excellent examples of coaching manuals. The first was *The Spiritual Exercises* by Ignatius Loyola. This manual can still be—and is—used for exercise of spiritual discipline, either alone or with a group. The second was *The Flow of Religious Instruction* by James Michael Lee. This is a very different kind of manual, one which teaches the reader how to *perform* in the role of a coach. Separately these volumes of course lead in very different directions. Taken together, they can be used as a pair of coaching manuals—one for training in spiritual exercise, the other for education in a teaching approach. The common factor is that both teach how to coach.

Ignatius' book is primarily a book of "substantive content," to use Lee's phrase. It has been used for centuries to learn about discipline and spiritual formation. The interesting thing about working through this manual is seeing how the content determines the process. There are no options about how or when to go about the exercises. The whole philosophy of the book is to learn obedience and submission, and the teaching style adopted reflects such a goal. The educator/coach in this book is no friend or companion, but is a disciplinarian who leads down the narrow path. It is difficult if not impossible to separate the authoritarian teaching style from the authoritarian content. This produces no surprise when it is recalled that this was—and is—the primary manual for

---

137. Older books from the progressive era are a treasure-trove of ideas for the religious educator, and in many cases only the terminology needs to be updated. The projects themselves are often quite relevant. For example, see Shaver, T*he Project Principle in Religious Education*, Part Two: "Descriptions of Church-School Projects," pp. 181-352; Gertrude Hartley, *The Use of Projects in Religious Education* (Philadelphia: Judson, 1921); and practically the entirety of Crum's *The Project Method in Religious Education*. Interestingly enough, a book originally distributed in 1943 that heavily employed the project method was only slightly revised and re-issued in 1973 as a shining example of current educational teaching procedures for Southern Baptists! See Gaines S. Dobbins, *The Improvement of the Sunday School*, rev. ed. (Nashville: Convention Press, 1973).

becoming a Jesuit, known since their founding by Ignatius for their obedience and discipline in both behavior and intellectual pursuits. Indeed, they were formed as part of the Catholic Reformation, and their founder would tolerate little deviation from his high expectations of them. If this is the view of coach one desires to emulate, then this is an exemplary manual for such an exercise.

Lee's book, *The Flow of Religious Instruction*,[138] is a coaching manual radically different from the one produced by Ignatius, and working through Lee's manual provides a very different kind of learning experience than what Ignatius offered. Lee's book does not specify *what* to teach, in terms of substantive content—substantive content was the subject of his massive third volume of the trilogy was entitled *The Content of Religious Instruction*—but rather *how* to teach, the structural content.[139] He provided "a set of generalized, effective pedagogical guidelines"[140] to be used in performing the best and most appropriate teaching style according to the four major clusters of independent variables: the teacher, the learner, the subject matter content, and the environment.[141] Lee, as a coach who specializes in religious instruction, helps to put the person on the road toward becoming an expert and professional religious educator.

The suggestion for a simulation is to read and work through these two coaching manuals. Experience coaching from two masters vastly separated in time and procedure. Decide for yourself which is the more personally helpful coach, and which you choose to follow. There is no one way to coach. There are, however, better and worse ways. Reading and experiencing Ignatius and Lee should help clarify the differences in goals and in procedures.

Summary

This chapter has been an introduction to the role of coach for the religious educator. The stance has been that the coaching role is one of the more accepted and historic roles used by religious educators over the centuries, albeit called by different names. It has also been stated that there are nearly as many ways to coach as there are coaches. The attempt was to focus and to outline the role of coach without saying precisely how it must be done. The decision on how each individual religious educator coaches is a personal decision to be made carefully, seriously, and intentionally. A summary of the various facets of the coach discussed in the chapter follows in Figure 7.

---

138. I am selecting this particular book from the trilogy because it is the one that specifically addressed giving "attention to and control of the teaching act." See Lee, *Flow of Religious Instruction*, p. 2.

139. A good overview of the differences between substantive and structural content can be found in Lee, *Content of Religious Instruction*, pp. 106-110.

140. Lee, *Flow of Religious Instruction*, p. 2.

141. All of these are given detailed treatment in the key chapters of ibid., Chapter Eight, "The Nature of Teaching," pp. 206-229, and Chapter Nine, "The Structure of Teaching," pp. 230-268.

Figure 7: The Religious Educator as Coach	
Dimensions of the Role	Supervisor
	Trainer
	Motivator
	Strategist
Aim	Performance
Function	Instruction
Primary Virtues	Competence
	Discipline
Activity	Playing/Working
Shadow Role	Procrastinator
Faith Tradition Resource	Islam
Historical Personage	Ignatius Loyola
Contemporary Example	James Michael Lee
Representative Teaching Procedure	The Project
Experiential Simulation	Coaching Styles

Chapter Six

The Religious Educator as Scientist

One of the abiding riddles for Western civilization has been how to perceive properly the relationship between science and religion, and coincidentally but not accidentally how to perceive properly the relationship between scientists and religionists—or more commonly, "people of the faith."[1] That the riddle exists tells more about the structure and history of Western civilization than it does about science and religion. Too often science and religion have been allowed to become dichotomies: two different and at times incompatible ways of seeing and interpreting reality. The danger of the riddle is that Westerners have created and utilized this duality for so long that they now tend to believe that the two really *are* dichotomies—separate and distinct pieces of reality—and that either they must learn to live with the division as best they can or find a way to wrestle the two into some kind of workable configuration.[2] It rarely seems to occur to them that it may be their own self-created categories that are causing the problems.

This appetite for discrete compartmentalization pervades Western civilization and contemporary society, so deeply rooted that it sounds virtually heretical to

---

1. Occasionally books or magazine articles are written about a scientist—who (gasp) has a religious faith! It is as if such occurrences are anomalies which must be cataloged, remembered, and savored. See such examples as Henry M. Morris, *Men of Science, Men of God: Great Scientists of the Past Who Believed the Bible*, rev. ed. (El Cajon, Calif.: Master Books, 1988), and *Scientists Who Believe*, ed. Eric C. Barrett and David Fisher (Chicago: Moody Press, 1984). In a rather nice twist of fate, Hanbury Brown reported that it was a minister—William Whewell—who coined the term "scientist" in 1840 with this quote: "We need very much a name to describe a cultivator of science in general. I should incline to call him a Scientist. Thus we might say that an Artist is a Musician, Painter or Poet, a Scientist is a Mathematician, Physicist, or Naturalist." William Whewell, *The Philosophy of the Inductive Sciences*, as quoted by Hanbury Brown, *The Wisdom of Science: Its Relevance to Culture and Religion* (Cambridge: Cambridge University Press, 1986), p. 31. Note the natural science cast to the term from its invention.

question it. The range of dualisms that have been created goes beyond religion and science. For instance, humans have divided up the way they think of themselves. If their bodies get sick, for example, they go to a medical doctor. If they have some emotional trauma, they go to a psychologist. If they have a spiritual problem, they go to a minister or priest. The only difficulty is deciding what the exact problem is. Once that is determined, then they can go to the appropriate specialist, get the proper solution, and live happily ever after.

All of which, if accepted, leads to the enigmatic subject of the present chapter: the religious educator as—scientist? Surely this cannot be a useful image! If these two persons operate in separate and distinct worlds, then one has nothing to say to the other.

Perhaps the case has been overstated a bit, but not to the extent that the problem is unrecognizable. Years ago, C. P. Snow addressed this problem of polarization, but his opposing camps were characterized as humanists and scientists.[3] He saw, and experienced, a gulf between these two groups "of mutual incomprehension—and sometimes (particularly among the young) hostility and dislike, but most of all lack of understanding."[4] Snow noted that "this polarization is sheer loss to us all. To us as people, and to our society. It is at the same time practical and intellectual and creative loss. . . . The degree of incomprehension on both sides is the kind of joke which has gone sour."[5] In short, Snow insisted that the solution would come through education: "There is only one way out of all this: It is, of course, by rethinking our education."[6] Snow was referring to the British educational system specifically, but what he said has merit if taken seriously on a larger scale: The entirety of Western civilization needs to rethink and reformulate the way it goes about education and to find ways of designing out the false divisions that have been created—such as those between humanists and scientists and between religious educators and scientists. Though it may be just a bit beyond the capacities of one chapter to reformulate education, or even to integrate science and religion, to visualize the religious educator in the role of scientist may in some small way contribute to both of these idealistic dreams.

Three assumptions undergird this chapter, and they need to be made explicit at the outset. First, the social sciences seem to offer the most direct connection to the work of the religious educator, so most often this chapter focuses on the

---

2. "When we consider what religion is for mankind, and what science is, it is no exaggeration to say that the future course of history depends upon the decision of this generation as to the relations between them." Alfred North Whitehead, *Science and the Modern World* (New York: Macmillan, 1925; reprint edition, New York: Free Press, 1967), p. 181.

3. C. P. Snow, *The Two Cultures: And a Second Look* (New York: Cambridge University Press, 1963). Actually Snow used the term "literary intellectuals" instead of humanists. He was describing the age-old conflict in academic environments between the humanities and the sciences. Snow was advocating that scientists learn from humanists, and that humanists learn from scientists—with no artificial academic barriers to separate them. A scientist needs to be, and is expected to be, a well-rounded scholar, just as is the humanist. They each need the other to achieve such wholeness.

4. Ibid., p. 12. In a similar vein, Jacob Bronowski commented: "It has been one of the most destructive modern prejudices that art [the humanities] and science are different and somehow incompatible interests." Jacob Bronowski, *The Common Sense of Science* (New York: Random House, 1951), p. 5.

5. Snow, *The Two Cultures: And a Second Look*, pp. 17-18.

6. Ibid., p. 23.

social scientist rather than on the natural or physical scientist. There is of course much to be gained by the religious educator who studies virtually any branch of science. The chief difference between the social and the natural sciences, however, is not so much in procedure or methodology but in subject matter.[7] Social scientists study humans, their relationships, and their activities,[8] while the natural scientists study such phenomena as matter and energy and their interrelation and transformations.[9] When examples from the natural sciences are used in this chapter they will be identified as such and applied to the social-science approach. Second, religious educators have nothing to fear from scientists (social or natural), just as scientists should have nothing to fear from religious educators. In a very real sense religious educators themselves are (or can be) social scientists. The whole point of building a social-science approach to religious education allows religious educators to join the ranks of the social scientists and to put religious education on a firm empirical, research-based, and theory-guided foundation.[10] Persons in the fields of religion and religious education and those in the various fields and types of science need to cooperate with one another for their work to be more complete and to have deeper meaning, rather than to compete as if one were trying to overcome the other.[11] Third, there are limits to what sci-

---

7. The same basic idea stated in reverse: "Science is not unified by its subject matter but rather by its methodology." David Nachimus and Chava Nachimus, *Research Methods in the Social Sciences,* 3rd ed. (New York: St. Martin's Press, 1987), p. 14.

8. "Social science is the systematic attempt to discover and explain behavior patterns of people and groups of people." Manuel G. Mendoza and Vince Napoli, *Systems of Society: An Introduction to Social Science,* 4th ed. (Lexington, Mass.: Heath, 1986), p. 2. Science, then, was more generically defined as "the systematic attempt to discover and explain relationships among phenomena." Ibid., p. 12. For more on the overall discussion of what science is, see such resources as Frederick Aicken, *The Nature of Science* (London: Heinemann Educational Books, 1984), and Steve Woolgar, *Science: The Very Idea* (London: Tavistock Publications, 1988), especially Chapter One, "What Is Science?," pp. 15-29.

9. The noted social scientist George C. Homans had this to say about the validity of social science: "There are scholars who argue that, if social science is a science at all, it is a radically different kind of science from the others and that it makes a mistake pretending to be the same sort of thing. I do not believe this in the least. The content of the propositions and explanations is naturally different in social science, because the subject matter is different from what it is in the others, but the requirements for a proposition and an explanation are the same for both. . . . I believe that the social sciences should become more like the others rather than less." George C. Homans, *The Nature of Social Science* (New York: Harcourt, Brace, and World, 1967), p. 28. Homans did discuss the differences that distinguish the social sciences, as when he said: "It is certainly less easy for the social sciences than in some physical and biological sciences to manipulate variables experimentally and to control the other variables entering into the concrete phenomenon. . . . It is less easy to control the variables because it is less easy to control men than things. Indeed, it is often immoral to try to control them." Ibid., p. 21. For a related discussion, see *The Nature and Scope of Social Science: A Critical Anthology,* ed. Leonard I. Krimerman (New York: Appleton-Century-Crofts, 1969), especially Fritz Machlup, "On The Alleged Inferiority of the Social Sciences," pp. 168-180, and H. A. Hodges, "The Separatist Case: Basic Contrasts Between the Social and Natural Sciences," pp. 146-152.

10. The social-science approach to religious instruction/education has been discussed in detail in the previous chapter under the examination of the works by James Michael Lee. Also see Timothy Arthur Lines, *Systemic Religious Education* (Birmingham, Ala.: Religious Education Press, 1987) for another view of religious education and its relation to social science.

11. For some good discussions on this historic conflict, see such works as Charles E. Garrison, *Two Different Worlds: Christian Absolutes and the Relativism of Social Science* (Cranbury, N.J.: Associated University Presses, 1988); Robert A. Segal, *Religion and the Social Sciences: Essays on*

ence can do and teach.[12] This chapter does not promote "scientism," defined by D. C. Phillips as "a term used in a mildly abusive way to indicate slavish adherence to the methods of science in a context where they are inappropriate . . . or to indicate a false or mistaken claim to be scientific."[13] This chapter only attempts to allow religious educators to look at themselves from the perspective and role of the scientist and to see what can be learned. It is not intended as a panacea for all of the ills of religious education.

This chapter proceeds as the previous ones have done, examining first the dimensions of the role and then moving on to discuss aim, function, and so on. The religious educator as scientist is a fertile and exciting role and one that holds tremendous potential. What follows at best can only whet the appetite for what can be done with the role and encourage each religious educator to explore the possibilities opened by this introductory excursion.

Dimensions of the Role

Although the various particular vocational roles of the scientist are diverse and broad and depend heavily upon the type of science being pursued, enough generalization is possible to determine four generic dimensions that every scientist embodies to some degree. The four chosen to illustrate how the religious educator can learn from the overall role of scientist are discoverer, theoretician, experimenter, and cyberneticist.

These four dimensions are outgrowths of the one thing that is constant throughout science—the scientific method. The steps of the scientific method are well-known and have been expressed in a number of ways. For example, John Dewey gave them classic exposition in *How We Think*,[14] and his five step formulation has been repeated and rephrased often. For the sake of common agreement on science and its basic approach, those steps are recited here. First is the

---

the Confrontation (Atlanta: Scholar's Press, 1989), especially Chapter Four, "Have the Social Sciences Been Converted?," pp. 57-62; Ted S. Clements, *Science vs. Religion* (Buffalo: Prometheus Books, 1990); and Eric L. Gans, *Science and Faith: The Anthropology of Revelation* (Savage, Md.: Rowman and Littlefield, 1990). Of course, the point of my earlier book, *Systemic Religious Education*, was to demonstrate that there need to be no conflict or duality between the fields of religion and religious education and the fields of science through employment of General Systems Theory.

12. See this discussed in such places as *The Use and Abuse of Social Science*, ed. Frank Heller (London: Sage Publications, 1986), especially the contributions by H. Igor Ansoff, "The Pathology of Applied Research in Social Science," pp. 19-23, and by Frank Heller, "Use and Abuse of Science," pp. 123-142; *Ethical Issues in Social Science Research*, ed. Tom L. Beauchamp, Ruth R. Faden, R. Jay Wallace Jr., and LeRoy Watkins (Baltimore: Johns Hopkins University Press, 1982), especially the writings by Dorothy Nelkin, "Forbidden Research: Limits to Inquiry in the Social Sciences," pp. 163-174; and Chapter 36, "The Nature, Powers, and Limits of Social Science," in Julian L. Simon and Paul Burstein, *Basic Research Methods in Social Science*, 3rd ed. (New York: Random House, 1985), pp. 445-456.

13. D. C. Phillips, *Philosophy, Science, and Social Inquiry: Contemporary Methodological Controversies in Social Science and Related Applied Fields of Research* (Oxford: Pergamon Press, 1987), p. 206. Also see Roger E. Cavallo, *The Role of Systems Methodology in Social Science Research* (Boston: Martinus Nijhoff, 1979), especially Chapter One, "Science and Scientism," pp. 5-26.

14. John Dewey, *How We Think: A Restatement of the Relation of Reflective Thinking to the Educative Process* (Boston: Heath, 1933), pp. 106-118.

encountering of an obstacle or an idea in real life as a felt difficulty. The scientist somehow must become personally engaged with an issue—to find a problem to overcover, or an idea to investigate. Second comes the development of a hypothesis, a "conjectural statement, a tentative proposition about the relation between two or more phenomena or variables"[15] that attempts to unravel or to explain the problem that has been encountered. Third is deductive reasoning, which decides on the best way to proceed with investigating the problem. Fourth is the activity of conducting the experiment itself, where the hypothesized relationship between the variables is tested empirically. Fifth is the evaluation of the data generated by the experiment. Either the hypothesis has been supported by the data and deserves more testing, or the hypothesis has been shown to be faulty and the process must be recycled to reformulate a new hypothesis.

The dimensions of the role of scientist that follow, as well as to some degree the rest of the chapter, stem from some aspect or corollary of this foundational scientific method.

Discoverer

One of the more interesting and paradigmatic stories about the dimension of the scientist as discoverer has been told by natural scientist James Watson in *The Double Helix*.[16] In this book, he described the discovery process he and his partner followed in tracking down the structure of DNA, the so-called "heredity molecule." Watson told of the competition and rivalry, the despair and exhilaration, and the twists and turns the investigation took. These researchers were so involved and obsessed with the quest that with but a little imagination one could believe these researchers were trying to solve the murder of the century, or to find the fountain of youth. Too often the excitement and the drivenness of the discoverer is lost when science is cut and pasted into the pages of the high-school textbook. This personal investment was included in Watson's account, and the difference in the view is dramatic.

A scientist is more often the discoverer than the creator[17] or inventor. Although at times the scientist may indeed engage in producing new products or substances, these normally come about as a result of a solution to the problem being studied rather than forming the original intention. The scientist is primarily involved in trying to understand phenomena and a particular relationship of variables, which is the process of discovery.[18] The scientist does not so much try to create a relationship between variables as he or she tries to uncover a relationship that is already there. Creativity is an aspect of the scientist's repertoire, but the creativity is most often directed at finding new or different ways of discovering or understanding what already exists. The story Watson told of dis-

15. Fred N. Kerlinger, *Foundations of Behavioral Research*, 2nd ed. (New York: Holt, Rinehart and Winston, 1973), p. 12.

16. James D. Watson, *The Double Helix: A Personal Account of the Discovery of the Structure of DNA* (New York: New American Library, 1968).

17. The religious educator's use of creativity is further explored in Chapter Nine, "The Religious Educator as Artist."

18. "Discovery is the job of stating and testing more or less general relationships between properties of nature." Homans, *Nature of Social Science*, p. 7.

covering the structure of DNA is of this sort. He and Francis Crick certainly did not create the structure, but they needed a great amount of creativity and understanding to replicate it in model form and to explain it.

Thomas Kuhn, himself a philosopher of science, spoke about this dimension of the scientist as explorer and discoverer in the context of scientific revolutions. He described how scientists make truly exciting discoveries as a result of the paradigm shifts that come during a scientific revolution. These discoveries happen when the researchers begin "seeing" differently, although what they are looking at is usually the same phenomenon they have been examining for years. Kuhn wrote: "During revolutions scientists see new and different things when looking with familiar instruments in places they have looked before. It is rather as if the professional community had been suddenly transported to another planet where familiar objects are seen in a different light and are joined by unfamiliar ones as well. Of course, nothing of quite that sort does occur: There is no geographical transplantation; outside the laboratory everyday affairs usually continue as before. Nevertheless, paradigm changes do cause scientists to see the world of their research-engagement differently."[19] So, while scientists may not primarily be creators, inventors, or even travelers who do explorations in strange and exotic localities, still they are involved in very real acts of discovery. Scientists quite often make discoveries in the midst of what most persons take for granted. These discoverers see things that actually are available for all to observe. The difference is their ability to "see" and to understand what they see.[20]

Religious educators can learn to be discoverers just as scientists are. The trick is developing the ability to see, and learning to appreciate, understand, and interpret what is seen.[21] In other words, the greatest discoveries that one can make may very well be staring them in the face—now—if they could only learn truly to see them. Perhaps each religious educator needs to keep this in mind each time he or she rises to teach the same group of people day after day and week after week!

Theoretician

Not often is a religious educator accused of being a theoretician. The terms more usually associated with a religious educator are ones such as practical the-

19. Thomas S. Kuhn, *The Structure of Scientific Revolutions*, 2nd ed. (Chicago: University of Chicago Press, 1970), p. 111. While Kuhn had natural science primarily in view here, the relevance and applicability to the social sciences is just as strong.

20. These scientists/discoverers realize that what they now see is truly revolutionary. What Kuhn called "normal" science represents assimilative learning—the rules do not change, and the basic structure is the same, only additional and cumulative information or data is gathered and compiled to the known theory. The paradigm shifts, what Kuhn called the scientific revolutions, represent accommodative learning, where everything is different—new rules, new theory, and new worldviews: "The extraordinary episodes in which that shift of professional commitments occurs are the ones known . . . as scientific revolutions. They are the tradition-shattering complements to the tradition-bound activities of normal science." Kuhn, *Structure of Scientific Revolutions*, p. 6. Kuhn continued this discussion of scientific revolutions by saying: "That is why a new theory . . . is seldom or never just an increment to what is already known. Its assimilation requires the reconstruction of prior theory and the re-evaluation of prior fact, and intrinsically revolutionary process." Ibid., p. 7.

21. For a parallel and related discussion of "learning to see," refer to Chapter Nine, "The Religious Educator as Artist," especially the section on a representative teaching procedure.

ologian, program administrator, or personnel manager—terms that imply a fear, an ignorance, or an outright disavowal of the need for theory-based religious education. To suggest that a part of being a religious educator is being a theoretician would amaze some and repulse others. A religious educator true to his or her calling, however, must have some competency in the area of theory construction in order to build up the field of religious education and to have a guiding purpose and reason for performing each particular instructional act. Without theory to direct it, religious education becomes nothing other than guesswork, impulse, or random behavior. The use of theory helps the religious educator plan, implement, and evaluate the activity of purposeful religious education. Some guidance on this topic rather foreign to the religious educator can be gained from understanding the scientist as theoretician.

To whatever degree, the scientist has no choice but to be a theoretician, since theory lies at the heart of the scientific method. Fred Kerlinger has defined theory as "a set of interrelated constructs (concepts), definitions, and propositions that present a systematic view of phenomena by specifying relations among variables, with the purpose of explaining and predicting the phenomena."[22] Kerlinger made at least three points in that definition that need further exegesis. First, theory has to do with interrelating thoughts and data into a systematic view of the phenomena. Theory is simply a way of clarifying and articulating in a comprehensive manner what reality is, or at least what one believes reality to be, based on the best information possessed at the moment. Second, theory provides the opportunity for testing out present notions about reality and not being forced to live forever with it as if it were gospel truth. Theory is a means for stating a belief that a relationship exists between two or more variables, put in such a way that it is possible through testing to find whether or not the relationship does exist in the way that has been hypothesized. Third, and all-important, theory explains and predicts. It explains what has happened in the past and predicts what will happen in the future as a result of the relationship of the variables that have specified and described. If a theory does not reliably explain and predict, it is useless and is no longer a viable candidate as a theory. Something other than the relationship of the specified variables is causing the result, and therefore the theory must be revised in light of the data.

This issue of explaining and predicting is probably one of the prime reasons why many religious educators shy away from theory. Some say that their work is not subject to explanation or prediction, since the true credit or glory belongs to God, or the Spirit, or to something other than themselves, and that such otherworldly influences cannot be tested. Such objections to theory have been addressed elsewhere, most notably in the work of James Michael Lee.[23] This kind of objection can be either an excuse for the hard work of being a responsible religious educator who does his or her work with requisite care and attention, or

---

22. Kerlinger, *Foundations of Behavioral Research*, p. 9.

23. See, for example, James Michael Lee, "The Lifework of the Religious Educator," in *The Spirituality of the Religious Educator*, ed. James Michael Lee (Birmingham, Ala.: Religious Education Press, 1985), p. 29 n. 16. Also see James Michael Lee, *The Flow of Religious Instruction: A Social Science Approach* (Birmingham, Ala.: Religious Education Press, 1982), pp. 202-204 and 174-180.

simple ignorance about theory and its place in the task of the religious educator. Although religious education is never completely under the direct control of the religious educator—there is a multitude of variables that may be uncontrollable or unmeasurable—the religious educator is bound to and responsible for the utilization of theory for achieving the best results possible. Just because the full and final theory of learning has not yet been devised is no reason to be a sloppy religious educator who refuses to give theory proper attention.

One other characteristic of theory important for understanding the work and environment of the theoretician has been expressed by Stephen Hawking. Hawking is a professor of mathematics and a theoretical physicist confined to a wheelchair and forced to communicate through a computerized voice synthesizer because of motor neuron disease. He is by all accounts a brilliant and contributing theoretician, since his theorizing (performed primarily in the area of higher mathematics, which by definition is pure abstraction) takes place inside his brain. Hawking wrote that "a theory is just a model of the universe, or a restricted part of it, and a set of rules that relate quantities in the model to observations that we make. It exists only in our minds and does not have any other reality (whatever that may mean)."[24] To be a theoretician requires that one be able to think—to understand, explain and predict the relationships that exist among variables. Hawking can do his work as a mathematical theoretician from his wheelchair just as well as a fully ambulatory mathematical scientist because the environment in which theory is born and formulated is primarily within the mind.[25] The theoretician is always required to acknowledge and interrelate with the relevant data, however, which is why Hawking spoke of the relationship of the "quantities in the model to the observations that we make." Data in and of themselves are meaningless. It is theory that gives the data its meaning,[26] while data is additionally that which confirms or disconfirms the effectiveness of the theory. Theory interprets the data, and data revises and improves theory.

The above paragraph recalls all those religious educators, and a multitude of learners in religious education, who may insist that theory has no place or value for them in the kind of work they do because religious education is only a practical field—which of course misses the point of what religious education is and what theory is. There is nothing more practical than true theory, since true theory is always being evaluated by research. Refusal to be a theoretician either puts religious educators at the mercy of some outmoded, unevaluated shell of a theory, or condemns them to ceaseless and mindless random activity.

---

24. Stephen W. Hawking, *A Brief History of Time: From the Big Bang to Black Holes* (New York: Bantam Books, 1988), p. 9.

25. Hawking the theoretical mathematician gives a nice illustration of the essential place cognition has in all theory building, although in most fields of science, and certainly in social science (the real focus here), theory must constantly be kept in constant interplay with the research data. As two social scientists wrote: "Theory and research may be said to be in a reciprocal relationship to one another. That is, research is used to evaluate theory, and theory is used to guide and direct research." John M. Neale and Robert M. Liebert, *Science and Behavior: An Introduction to Methods of Research*, 3rd ed. (Englewood Cliffs, N.J.: Prentice-Hall, 1986), p. 13.

26. Richard Morris wrote: "It is theory that makes observations meaningful. It imposes order over them, and makes it possible for experimental data to be interpreted." Richard Morris, *Dismantling the Universe: The Nature of Scientific Discovery* (New York: Simon & Schuster, 1983), p. 121.

Both results are currently observable in contemporary religious education. At least a partial solution to this dilemma can be found through the implementation of theory: careful, deeply considered, and serious thinking about what religious educators do and why, in tandem with continuous data-gathering from the field. No amount of frantic commotion or pointless busywork will ever take the place of the construction of theory and the hard work of cognitive activity, all of which is to say that religious education could do with a few more theoreticians who operate with the comparable mental abilities of Stephen Hawking.

Experimenter

At the same time that theory-building must receive adequate attention, the same measure of insistence must also accompany the companion process of experimentation. Although one needs to guard against doing without thinking, just as importantly one must not allow himself or herself just to think but never really accomplish anything. Neither thinking nor doing is complete without the other. Religious educators may feel better about themselves in the current section of the chapter than the previous one, because many of them are so activity-oriented. To be an experimenter, however, is still different from merely being a "doer." The experimenter carries out activity along the lines and intentions prescribed by the theory. Just because religious educators are busy does not imply that they are experimenters. Theory and experiment are partners that cannot be divorced.[27]

The primary distinction between the theoretician and the experimenter is that whereas the theoretician uses the fruits of empirical research to formulate better and better hypotheses, the experimenter goes about the business of actually confirming or disconfirming those hypotheses with data collection. The experimenter is the empiricist, who does the research and the investigations, makes considered inferences from the data, and then reports the findings.[28] The experimenter carries on what Thomas Kuhn called "normal" science, which is "research firmly based upon one or more past scientific achievements, achievements that some particular scientific community acknowledges for a time as supplying the foundation for its further practice."[29] Kuhn contrasted "normal" science with periods of scientific revolutions, where new paradigms are introduced which

---

27. The comments above should not be taken as saying that the order is always theory to experiment. The whole concept of praxis is about the interrelationship of theory and practice, and that each influences the other. I am certainly not denying the value of the concept of praxis but am instead highlighting the value of theory and experiment. A fuller examination of the concept of praxis is provided in Chapter Eleven of this book, "The Religious Educator as Revolutionary." For a good introduction to the systematic connections between theory and research, and the order in which they can be pursued, see Nachimus and Nachimus, *Research Methods in the Social Sciences*, pp. 49-52.

28. The experimenter keeps science from being mere speculation or guesswork by doing the requisite empirical research. Neale and Liebert described empirical research as "any activity that systematically attempts to gather evidence through observations and procedures that can be repeated and verified by others." Neal and Liebert, *Science and Behavior*, p. 7. They went on to say that "the purpose of research in science is to bring a higher level of confidence and certainty to our understanding than is possible by belief, faith, or reason alone." Ibid., p. 9. Speculation, or speculative thinking, is "the mental exploration of possible relationships among data." Mendoza and Napoli, *Systems of Society*, p. 14.

29. Kuhn, *Structure of Scientific Revolutions*, p. 10.

radically change the way this normal science proceeds. In other words, scientific revolutions are usually instigated by theoreticians, but the longer-term success of the revolutions depends upon the experimenter. Kuhn extended his use of a military analogy by identifying the primary task of the normal scientists to be that of a "mopping up operation": "Few people who are not actually practitioners of a mature science realize how much mop-up work of this sort a paradigm [shift as a result of a scientific revolution] leaves to be done or quite how fascinating such work can prove in the execution. . . . Mopping-up operations are what engage most scientists throughout their career. They constitute what I am here calling normal science."[30]

Kuhn then went on to discuss the important role these practitioners of normal science play: "No part of the aim of normal science is to call forth new sorts of phenomena. . . . Nor do scientists normally aim to invent new theories. . . . Instead, normal-scientific research is directed to the articulation of those phenomena and theories that the paradigm already supplies. . . . [These procedures] turn out to be essential to the development of science. By focusing attention upon a small range of relatively esoteric problems, the paradigm forces scientists to investigate some part of nature in a detail and depth that would otherwise be unimaginable."[31]

The quotes above should not imply that either the theoretician or the experimenter is superior to the other, or more valued than the other. Neither should they be taken to say that these roles or activities are somehow totally separate and distinct. Without doubt, the work of the theoretician influences that of the experimenter just as the work of the experimenter has great impact on that of the theoretician. Indeed, the same person may very well be engaged in both types of activity. Theory and experiment are inextricably linked. The environment of the theoretician is mainly mental and cognitive, while that of the experimenter is related more to the physical and empirical. One dimension without the other inevitably leads to meaninglessness.

Cyberneticist

The fourth dimension of the scientist's role is that of the cyberneticist. This aspect attends specifically to evaluation, regulation, and control. The issue of control can be misused and distorted so that it becomes a very threatening and sinister one, or it can be a natural and essential topic in any discussion of the work of the scientist.[32] The darker side of the issue is addressed later;[33] for now, the helpful elements related to control in science are the focus.

The term "cybernetics" is a transliteration of the Greek word κυβέρνησις, which originally referred to guiding and directing—controlling—a ship. The

---

30. Ibid., p. 24.

31. Ibid.

32. It is true that social science manipulates variables and the environment to study the interactions among them, but this is very different from the coercive or surreptitious manipulation of persons. True social scientists are not out to control people, but to control the variables in experimental environments.

33. More on this critical issue is to be found below in the section on the shadow role of the scientist-king.

steering of a ship (or any other example of goal-directed activity) is rightly accomplished through cybernetics, the study and use of feedback.[34] If the ship is on the desired course, determined by comparing the current position with the final destination, then the feedback is positive and no adjustments are required. If the ship is found to be off course, again revealed by citing the final goal, then the feedback received is negative and changes in the steering are necessary. Feedback, both positive and negative, is the means of evaluation, regulation, and control. Accurate feedback is so valuable precisely because it can be used to change the source or the originator of the data, which means that feedback is the primary way change becomes incorporated into the entire process.[35] Cybernetics, then, is the study of control through the examination and interpretation of information gained by feedback.[36]

Scientists determine the effectiveness of their work by employing feedback. Theories are created, experiments are performed, and the results are evaluated through feedback. If data received from the experiment are interpreted as giving positive feedback, then the theory is in the process of being confirmed. If data received from the experiment are interpreted as providing negative feedback, then the theory is deemed inadequate and in need of revision.

Feedback is possible only when activity is directed toward some kind of goal, as when the activity is purposeful.[37] An endpoint, destination, or purpose must exist in one form or another in order for the feedback to be interpreted as positive or negative. Only when people have some idea of where they are going can they evaluate, regulate, and control their progress toward getting there. Steering a ship according to feedback, for example, requires that the helmsman know where the ship is supposed to be headed so that the proper adjustments and course corrections can be made to arrive there. The same is true for the scientist. The performance of random "experiments" is of no value unless there are explicit guides as to what is to be tested and criteria that are to be achieved.[38] This is the

34. For a more complete discussion of feedback and cybernetics, especially on how these relate to religious education, see Lines, *Systemic Religious Education*, pp. 52-53 and elsewhere throughout that book.

35. "Feedback operates as the guidance process within an open system. A system monitors its output and is able to evaluate the information from the output to regulate both its rate of intake from the environment and its transformational activity." Ibid., p. 52.

36. A thorough discussion of feedback and cybernetics as related to communication theory can be found in Ludwig von Bertalanffy, *General System Theory: Foundations, Development, Applications*, rev. ed. (New York: Braziller, 1968), pp. 41-44; also refer to pp. 149-150. Also see Norbert Wiener, *The Human Use of Human Beings: Cybernetics and Society* (New York: Avon Books, 1967), and W. Ross Ashby, *An Introduction to Cybernetics* (London: Methuen and Company, 1956).

37. The more technical term for purposeful, goal-directed activity is "teleology." This is discussed throughout my earlier book *Systemic Religious Education*. See especially pp. 113-114.

38. Many different kinds of evaluation criteria are necessary, and they need to be given attention constantly—not just at the end of the journey, or at the end of the instructional activity. The concepts of formative and summative evaluation are pertinent and helpful here. Formative evaluation is primarily used "to determine the degree of mastery of a given learning task and to pinpoint the part of the task not mastered." Summative evaluation, by contrast, "is directed toward a much more general assessment of the degree to which the larger outcomes have been attained over the entire course or some substantial part of it." Benjamin S. Bloom, J. Thomas Hastings, and George F. Madaus, *Handbook on Formative and Summative Evaluation of Student Learning* (New York: McGraw Hill, 1971), p. 61. As the authors explained further: "This distinction [of the two kinds of evaluation]

purpose of hypotheses and theories: They establish the criteria to be met, which in turn determine the success or failure of the experiments. This dimension of cyberneticist is crucial to science, and it permeates all of science. Evaluation, regulation, and control are found in the warp and the woof of science—and of effective religious education.

Goals need not and should not be understood as static and inert, as if they were fixed points in the future, encased in concrete. Goals are as dynamic, flexible, and transformable as the people that create them. The achievement of one goal may change the design of the next, or the failure to reach one particular goal may change the nature of many others. The goal may be indistinct at first, the result of intuition and the scientist's best guess, and it continues to be refined and honed and developed as research informs the process. Such heuristic activity[39] is descriptive of the excitement and fun of being a scientist: They are convinced they are headed someplace important and know the general direction to travel but exactly where and how to get there is still in the process of being determined.

The religious educator, then, stands to gain much from observing the cyberneticist. The religious educator must accept at least some responsibility for regulating, evaluating, and controlling goal-directed activity; the religious educator must learn to be open and responsive to both positive and negative feedback; and the religious educator must develop the ability to adjust and change goals as appropriate by evaluating this constant inflow of different kinds of feedback. The dimension of cyberneticist is so critical that it must permeate all that the religious educator does.

Summary

Four dimensions of the role of scientist are discoverer, theoretician, experimenter, and cyberneticist. These four are not meant to be comprehensive terms, inclusive of everything about the role. They simply give some background and feel for the complexity and depth of the role. The result of this introductory discussion demonstrates that the role of scientist is not as divergent or as foreign to the identity of the religious educator as might be imagined from the first impulse. Indeed, there is much more to the role of scientist that can inform and improve the work of the religious educator. The sections that follow attempt to make this relationship even more pronounced.

Aim: Problem Solving

The aim of the scientist, and hence of the religious educator as scientist, is to solve problems. The scientist devises hypotheses, performs experiments, and

---

has been introduced primarily in hopes of bringing the evaluation process closer to the teaching and learning processes. Too often in the past, evaluation has been entirely summative in nature, taking place only at the end of the unit, chapter, course, or semester, when it is too late, at least for that particular group of students to modify either process. . . . Formative evaluation, as the name implies, intervenes during the formulation of the student, not when the process is thought to be completed." Ibid., p. 20. In other words, the ability to respond to specific content questions at the end of the Sunday school hour does not qualify as effective evaluation criteria for religious education!

39. See heuristics, cybernetic teleology, and open-ended goals discussed in Lines, *Systemic Religious Education*, pp. 113-115.

interprets data, all for the purpose of better understanding the phenomena that are causing problems. So also the religious educator conducts research into the content related to religious education, into the specific learners who are involved in the instructional activity, and into adequately structuring the learning environment, all for the purpose of solving problems. The scientist, and the religious educator in the role of scientist, do not conduct research just for fun, or as an excuse for performing activity. The attempt is always to be purposeful—to identify problems and to find the best possible solutions to them.

One of the chief contributions of science in recent decades has been its increasingly integrative approach to problem solving.[40] The first step in this direction has been a movement from perceiving problems and the relationships that cause them deterministically and mechanistically to perceiving them organismically and systemically.[41] Ervin Laszlo stated the change this way: "The systems view is the emerging contemporary view of organized complexity, one step beyond the Newtonian view of organized simplicity, and two steps beyond the classical worldviews of divinely ordered or imaginatively envisaged complexity."[42] Though the shift in perception is much more pervasive than any one field or discipline can contain, scientists have been leaders in providing solid ground that supports this more inclusive and integrative view.[43] Science has found that the exclusive use of the piecemeal approach of dissection and reductionism hides and distorts information as much as it helps reveal and that more than tunnel vision is required to see and understand the larger realities.

This change in perception and understanding, then, considers problems and ways to go about solving them quite differently when viewed from this larger perspective. Russell Ackoff put it simply: "The Systems Age is more interested in putting things together than in taking them apart. . . . A problem is not solved by taking it apart but by viewing it as a part of a larger problem."[44] Laszlo made a similar statement: "The age of analysis has done its work; the age of synthesis has begun."[45] It is not that the process of analysis has become any less important or necessary; it is acknowledgment that useful analysis can only be done in the context of sensitivity to and awareness of the environment which is surrounding and influencing the phenomena. This scientific study of the interconnectedness of phenomena is identified as systems theory, as Fritjof Capra explained: "Systems theory looks at the world in terms of the interrelatedness and interdependence of all phenomena, and in this framework an integrated whole whose

---

40. This approach is the systemic one discussed at length in Lines, *Systemic Religious Education*, but especially on pp. 39-65.

41. The predominant image of the previous approach was the machine (ibid., pp. 89-98), while that of the latter is the organism (ibid., pp. 104-115).

42. Ervin Laszlo, *The Systems View of the World: The Natural Philosophy of the New Developments in the Sciences* (New York: Braziller, 1972), p. 15.

43. A superb example of this kind of person was Ludwig von Bertalanffy, who is often referred to as the father of General Systems Theory. The range of his interests and abilities can be glimpsed by reading his major work *General System Theory*, particularly Chapter Two, "The Meaning of General Systems Theory," pp. 30-53.

44. Russell L. Ackoff, *Redesigning the Future: A Systems Approach to Societal Problems* (New York: Wiley, 1974), p. 14.

45. Ervin Laszlo, *Evolution: The Grand Synthesis* (Boston: New Science Library, 1987), p. 6.

properties cannot be reduced to those of its parts is called a system."[46]

Attention to interrelatedness and interdependence in problem solving necessitates that the basic understanding of reality be dynamic rather than static. If the focus is on the relationship of the parts, instead of on the isolated parts themselves, then the situation demands that perception give awareness and appreciation to the connections that are only perceivable in process. One of the places this has become clear is in the recent investigations of chaos. James Gleick has written a good introductory book on this fascinating topic, and he said: "Where chaos begins, classical science stops. . . . The irregular side of nature, the discontinuous and erratic side—these have been puzzles to [classical] science, or worse, monstrosities."[47] One of the results of studying chaos is this demand for the inclusion of dynamism: "To some physicists chaos is a science of process rather than state, of becoming rather than being."[48] In addition, chaos research has begun to erase some of the strict boundaries that had previously kept the various disciplines distinct: "Chaos breaks across the lines that separate scientific disciplines."[49] The point is that scientists studying chaos are making the trip from mechanism to organicism: "They feel they are turning back a trend in science toward reductionism, the analysis of systems in terms of their constituent parts. . . . They believe that they are looking for the whole."[50]

What contemporary science has to offer first, then, is a perspective of understanding: A perspective that is inclusive, integrative, dynamic, and systemic. This perspective, second, allows for effective and integrated problem solving. Rather than perceiving problems individually and in isolation, such an approach understands that problems are intertwined and interrelated. The problems revealed in this systemic view demand integrated solutions where scientist and religious educator work together—along with a great host of others—to find solutions.[51] The days of isolation for the religious educator are over, *if* the religious educator is ready and willing to contribute to studying real problems and to creating real solutions.

Function: Experimentation

The aim of problem solving is achieved through the function of experimentation. However mental or esoteric some of the aspects of science may be, in order for these conjectures, ideas, or hypotheses to be taken seriously, some testing must

---

46. Fritjof Capra, *The Turning Point: Science, Society, and the Rising Culture* (New York: Simon & Schuster, 1982), p. 43.
47. James Gleick, *Chaos: Making a New Science* (New York: Penguin Books, 1987), p. 3.
48. Ibid., p. 5.
49. Ibid.
50. Ibid.
51. This point—that the religious educator must integrate his or her work with the larger environment—is absolutely essential to the thesis of this book. Each chapter, for example, offers a different faith tradition that can contribute to a larger understanding of the whole. Each of the ten chapters of Part Two offers a role or image that broadens the understanding of the work of the religious educator. The theoretical underpinnings of this has been presented, of course, in *Systemic Religious Education*. This present book shows how the theory developed in the earlier book is put into practice.

be done to confirm or disconfirm the ideas. Furthermore, theory does not always mark the beginning of the scientific process. Theory often results from long periods of prior effort in gaining initial information and background on the situation.[52] These kinds of activity are all within the domain of experimentation.

Earlier in the chapter, it was stated that if theory and experiment are split apart then both are rendered meaningless. To this it can now be added that to a large extent experimentation continues and furthers the job started by theory. One may have an idea, a hunch, or a hypothesis, but until it is tested out in the "real" world, it will never be anything but an idea, hunch, or hypothesis. James Gleick, discussing a natural science model, commented on the differences between theorists and experimenters: "Theorists conduct experiments with their brains. Experimenters have to use their hands, too. Theorists are thinkers, experimenters are craftsmen. The theorist needs no accomplice. The experimenter has to muster graduate students, cajole machinists, flatter lab assistants. The theorist operates in a pristine place free of noise, of vibration, of dirt. The experimenter develops an intimacy with matter as a sculptor does with clay, battling it, shaping it, and engaging it."[53] Although Gleick probably overstated the case since in actuality theorists must always be in constant contact with the research data, the distinctions he made help illustrate some of the differences between theory and experiment. Experimentation takes place in the midst of real life and real problems. Experimentation may at times be dependent on theory, confirming or disconfirming it. It may work independently, searching for new ideas or procedures in the trial and error mode. Experimentation represents the core functioning of science, and without this "hands-on" process science could not progress.

Continually, and quite appropriately, the religious educator functions as the experimenter. He or she does the "dirty work" of religious education in the midst of life, where actual, live people are found, and it is the religious educator who must develop the intimacy that Gleick spoke of—battling, shaping, and engaging others in order to teach and educate. None of these "real life" dimensions of genuine religious education is to be denied, and none of them is ever to be disparaged. Religious education separate and distinct from the welter of humanity is unthinkable, as is any other manifestation of social science.

At the same time, it would be misleading to characterize the religious educator as one who simply carries out experiments on someone else's theories or who uses someone else's research data. Because the religious educator is often found in the "laboratory"[54] doing experimentation means that likewise the religious educator

---

52. These statements are meant to underline the reality that the scientific process is not so "cut and dried" or mechanical as it may appear. The scientific process is certainly not some slavish devotion to the five steps mentioned at the head of the chapter in that precise order. The scientific process is evolutionary, changing and developing the perspectives of its adherents as evidence builds up over time.

53. Gleick, *Chaos,* p. 125.

54. The Latin word from which the English word "laboratory" derived is *laboratorium* (the Latin *labor* means "to work"), signifying a place to do work. In truth, then, a laboratory is the place to do the work of experimentation, certainly, but also the place to build, evaluate, and revise theory. Of course, when I use the term "laboratory" in this way, I am not restricting it to formal or clinical environments, or to the "ivory towers" of academe, but rather to all those everyday, normal environments where activity is naturally performed.

should be just as deeply engaged in the development, evaluation, and revision of theory. Again, there can be no divorce between theory and experiment. Each gives the other meaning. The religious educator is just as responsible for developing theory as he or she is for carrying out the experiments that connect with, and give life to, the theory.[55]

Primary Virtues: Curiosity and Analysis

In the introduction to this chapter, the reductionistic but historical conflict between science[56] and religion was mentioned. By all accounts, each area has its own procedures and interests, but these alone do not seem to explain the reason for the viciousness of the conflict that has raged for so long. The two virtues of the scientist that are the subject of this section are prime reasons for the disagreements: curiosity and analysis. These virtues get at the roots of all science and reveal some of the paranoia that has ruled some conceptions of religion and religious education in the past, if not to the current day. Genuine religion and religious education must foster and encourage these two virtues just as actively as science does and must not assign them to someone else outside the boundaries of religious education, or even worse, work to inhibit them. Curiosity and analysis are part and parcel of the attitude that the true religious educator both embodies and inculcates.

Curiosity is pervasive of all of science, and it is responsible for initially motivating the scientist. Recall that the scientific process normally starts with the scientist encountering a problem or a hindrance that does not readily explain itself.[57] If the scientist were not curious, wondering why or how certain variables interact to cause or result in a specific phenomenon, then likely no research would ever be conducted. If the sense of curiosity were not strong enough to sustain the scientist through the times when trial brings more error than success, then the scientist would soon quit. Genuine curiosity instills a type of doggedness that does not give up in the face of difficult odds. The curious scientist keeps after it, trying different ideas and approaches until something in the knotty problem starts to unravel. A true scientist, in other words, does not easily accept "no" as an answer. Neither, incidentally, does he or she accept such simplistic solutions as the "god of the gaps" approach tries to offer.[58]

---

55. "The challenge of the research process is to relate theory and research in such a way that questions are answered. Both theory and data are required. When we are faced with a question we formulate a theory about its answer and test it by collecting data, that is, evidence, to see if our theoretical answer works. Data cannot be collected without some idea (theory) about the answer to the question. Theories alone are unsatisfactory because they are unproven, untested. To answer our questions we need both theory and data." Beverly R. Dixon, Gary D. Bouma, and G. B. J. Atkinson, *A Handbook of Social Science Research: A Comprehensive and Practical Guide for Students* (Oxford: Oxford University Press, 1987), p. 24.

56. This conflict is normally expressed as coming between natural science and religion, but social science has in more recent times also waded into the battle.

57. Fred Kerlinger described the beginning of the scientific process this way: "The scientist will usually experience an obstacle to understanding, a vague unrest about observed and unobserved phenomenon, a curiosity as to why something is as it is." See Kerlinger, *Foundations of Behavioral Research*, p. 11.

58. See this discussed by Ian G. Barbour in *Issues in Science and Religion* (New York: Harper & Row, 1966), pp. 1-3.

This stubbornness and unwillingness to let good enough alone—otherwise known as curiosity—tends to get some scientists and some religionists crosswise. The closed-minded and authoritarian type of religionists insist that there must be limits to curiosity. They are convinced that there are some things that cannot and must not be questioned, whether the reasons stem from expecting acceptance of official dogma, divine revelation, or approved standards of morality. Scientists refuse to accept any such inhibiting boundaries: A better explanation or solution is always possible.[59] Nothing is unquestionable. A religious educator in the role of scientist must reflect the same indomitable curiosity.

Whether it is profitable or acceptable to question need not and should not divide science and religion. One of the primary tasks of the religious educator is to ask progressively better and better questions.[60] Indeed, if nothing is unquestionable, then it is the duty of the religious educator to ask those progressively better and better questions constantly and without restriction. The questions may be just as important as the answers—if not more so. Our task is to ask questions first, and then to seek out, search for, or create whatever answers may follow. At this point in particular, the scientist and the religious educator stand as one: Curiosity, whatever it asks and wherever it leads, need have no limits.[61] Curiosity may have killed the cat, but the lack of curiosity would undoubtedly kill science, religion, and religious education.

Inextricably intertwined with curiosity is the virtue of analysis. If curiosity is to be prized, then so must analysis, since analysis is carried out in order to satisfy curiosity. Analysis is critical reflection on a phenomenon, problem, situation, or experience. Fred Kerlinger defined analysis for the behavioral scientist as "the categorizing, ordering, manipulation, and summarizing of data to obtain answers to research questions" and said the purpose of analysis "is to reduce data to intelligible and interpretable form so that the relations of research problems can be studied and tested."[62] While Kerlinger was speaking directly to the scientific use of the term, what he had to say is useful in conceptualizing a more general meaning of analysis. Analysis is the activity of seeking answers from data,

---

59. "Scientists never achieve complete understanding. One reason is that every answer leads to new questions, every new fact, law, or theory presents new problems, so that no matter what the present state of scientific knowledge, there is always more to know." Royce Singleton Jr., Bruce C. Straits, Margaret M. Straits, and Ronald McAllister, *Approaches to Social Research* (New York: Oxford University Press, 1988), p. 27.

60. See this pursued in Timothy Arthur Lines, "A Plea for Authentic Religious Education," in *Does the Church Really Want Religious Education?* ed. Marlene Mayr (Birmingham, Ala.: Religious Education Press, 1988), p. 138.

61. I am adamant about this refusal to accept limitations on my thinking. If there are limits on what I can think and investigate, then those limits have been imposed upon me externally. This means allowing someone else to determine what and how I think, limiting my access to available information on which I can base my own decisions. I personally repudiate such attempts to restrict thinking and curiosity, and I refuse to participate in attempting to restrict the thinking and curiosity of others. The religious educator, among others, is charged with the responsibility for nurturing curiosity as a safeguard against the thought-control and fascism which are virtually omnipresent in modern society.

62. Kerlinger, *Foundations of Behavioral Research*, p. 134. Kerlinger went on to say that interpretation of the data follows from the analysis. This is indeed a key and indispensable element, and interpretation is given fuller consideration in Chapter Eight, "The Religious Educator as Storyteller."

provided in clear and understandable form. As such, analysis is distinguished from pure speculation, guess, or deduction. Analysis deals with data available and does so critically and judiciously.

The glaring contradiction that seems to present itself is an emphasis on analysis at the same time implying that the "age of analysis" has past.[63] The contradiction is apparent rather than real, however, The quote earlier from Laszlo about the "age of analysis" actually said that the age of analysis has done its work in that it has prepared the way for the age of synthesis. This should not be understood as implying that the work and the value of analysis has past. In the systems perspective, analysis is still important and necessary; in fact, it is now more functional and effective because of the possibility of an overarching kind of theory that the systems perspective offers. Analysis can now be done with much greater sensitivity and appreciation for both the environmental context of the system and for the interrelationships that exist between the elements of the system. Systems analysis is not performed as if the relationships among the parts either do not exist or are unimportant, as so often was the case in a mechanistic or reductionistic approach.[64] Analysis is broadened in the systemic approach to take the interconnections and the environmental factors into account and to take them seriously. All of this is possible because of the key role that theory plays in aiding the efforts toward integration and synthesis.

Analysis requires that one be critical: to be evaluative and to make hard choices based on the available data.[65] This may be relatively easy and acceptable in science, but less so in the areas of religion and religious education. Religion and religious education tend too often to be seen more as speculative than empirical, more supported by belief than data, and with a higher value placed on tradition than on demonstrable effectiveness. These are certainly obstacles in the effort to be critical and evaluative about one's religious practices, but they are not insurmountable. These inadequate ideas about religion and religious education do not by any means exhaust the possibilities of what religion and religious education actually represent, and it is crucial to be aware of the stakes involved. If, on the one hand, religion and religious education are bound and determined by what has been accepted or done in the past, regardless of critique or evaluation, then there is no room or need for analysis.[66] The present is therefore doomed

---

63. See the quote used above, taken from Laszlo, *Evolution*, p. 6.

64. An excellent discussion of this evolution in the procedures and in the worldviews of science and technology is found in Ackoff, *Redesigning the Future*, pp. 8-17.

65. The scientific approach is designed to allow questions to be answered on bases other than authority, tradition, or mere opinion. They key term is that science seeks to be *empirical*: "If science is to help us understand the real world it must be empirical; that is, it must rely on perceptions, experience, and observations." Nachimus and Nachimus, *Research Methods in the Social Sciences*, p. 8. This is necessary to achieve a clearer and more objective view of the relationship between variables, rather than simply reinforcing some long-held presuppositions or assumptions about humans: "The research practitioners in these [social-science] disciplines have undertaken the arduous task of applying the scientific approach to their investigations. Endeavoring to disentangle their efforts and results from the preconceptions and prejudices of earlier times, these workers have made remarkable strides . . . toward understanding human nature and the various ways it can be brought under scientific scrutiny." Neale and Liebert, *Science and Behavior*, p. 5.

66. Lois LeBar is an example of a Christian religious educator who prefers to base her teaching procedures on the ways of the "revealed past" instead of the insights of today. See Chapter Three,

to the endless repetition of the beliefs, traditions, and practices handed down to it. If, on the other hand, religion and religious education are alive, dynamic, and adaptable to the needs and hopes of persons, then analysis is indispensable for charting the course of the future.

In summary, these two virtues of curiosity and analysis have the same kind of bond as theory and experiment. Neither one can exist or make sense without the other. Each one sparks and motivates the other. A change in one has an impact on the other. Both are important and essential to the continued development and evolution of science, religion, religious education—and ultimately to all of humankind.

Activity: Exploring

Scientists are never fully satisfied with their work, and that work is never totally complete.[67] Scientists are always seeking something or someplace else to explore, in order to explain more and to further refine theory. By virtue of the scientific method, their explorations lead them to encounter new or different problems, to question old and accepted assumptions and traditions, to reformulate disproven hypotheses and theories into new possibilities and explanations, and to verify or revise theory by repeated evaluation of the data and replication of experiments.[68] As a result of following the scientific method, scientists are therefore obliged to change their minds, their theories, and their paradigms when the data and their interpretation so indicate that a change is necessary. Scientists are committed to letting their explorations shape, influence, and even determine what they think, even if—or, especially if—they do not discover in their explorations what they expected to find.

The boundaries of what and where science has explored, to say nothing of what and where it will venture in the future, are virtually impossible to discern. Science, with its ceaseless investigative activity, seems to have permeated every

---

"The Teacher Come From God," in Lois E. LeBar, *Education That Is Christian*, rev. ed. (Old Tappan, N.J.: Revell), pp. 47-88. LeBar gave further evidence in such comments as this one: "A chief reason for the lack of life and power and reality in our evangelical teaching is that we have been content to borrow man-made systems of education instead of discovering God's system." Ibid., p. 19. Also, she wrote: "Why waste our precious energy and limited time on mysteries that have already been explained? How discouraging to spend one's life formulating systems that will soon be discarded by the next generation! How encouraging to know that we can build structures that will endure! In His revelation God has given us all the insights that we need to know, all we cannot find out for ourselves." Ibid., p. 183. Compare this attitude and approach to that of scientific research, exemplified by the words of Kenneth Bailey: "Research is a never-ending cycle. We always accept each finding tentatively, aware that it may be proved wrong in further investigations." Kenneth D. Bailey, *Methods of Social Research*, 2nd ed. (New York: Free Press, 1982), p. 11.

67. "In science, change is built into the process. The product itself—knowledge—is never 'finished,' but is constantly remodeled to fit the facts. . . . The most characteristic feature of science is its cyclical nature." Singleton et al., *Approaches to Social Research*, p. 28.

68. A sense of the enormity and the range of the task is indicated by this quote: "The ultimate goal of the social sciences is to produce an accumulating body of reliable knowledge. Such knowledge would enable us to *explain, predict,* and *understand* empirical phenomena that interest us. Furthermore, a reliable body of knowledge could be used to improve the human condition." Nachimus and Nachimus, *Research Methods in the Social Sciences*, p. 9.

aspect of nature. It has driven into outer space, where exploring humans have left their human imprint (and, characteristically, their trash) on the moon, and where they have spun a Viking satellite into the sky so far that it has long ago left the solar system, spinning and beeping continuously—presumably to itself—to this day. Science has probed inner space, delving into the depths of the human by means of surgery, X-rays, and Rorschach ink blots. Science has peered into the atom, finding quarks and photons that resemble more phantom than phenomenon. Where or what else is left for scientists to explore?

Scientists have not only been content to investigate the natural world. They have explored the supernatural world. The logical result of such work, of course, is that scientists have necessarily turned what was assumed to be the supernatural into the natural by doing their routine scientific testing. The work of James Fowler related to faith development, examined later in this chapter, is an example. Some theologians have assumed that faith (if not all of their theological explanations) is beyond the province of scientific inquiry.[69] Fowler, in the role of the social scientist, defined faith as a "human universal," decided that it could be understood scientifically and empirically through the lens of psychological developmental theory, and proceeded to quantify faith development into stages through what he called "a theory of growth in faith."[70] No longer is faith the sole province of imperialistic theologians or the gift from a divine visitation that is beyond the investigatory efforts of the scientist.[71] Now it can indeed be explored (more or less) scientifically. Even the "supernatural," then, is fair game for the explorations of science, as long as the terms or phenomena are properly operationalized for investigation.

Turnabout is fair play, to coin a phrase. If science can pervade all of life, then so can religion and religious education; or, more accurately, since science is pervasive of all of life, then so is religion and religious education.[72] Since science knows no boundaries for exploration, then neither do religion or religious education. True religion and religious education are just as curious, just as inquisitive, and just as restless as science has proven to be. In a systemic approach, science, religion, and religious education are not antithetical or competitors with one another. They are co-explorers, seeking truths and data wherever and however they may be found.[73] The religious educator is a prime explorer in this joint search for truth.

69. Philip Clayton did a good job of describing Karl Barth as an example of this kind of theologian and also showed how he himself disagreed strongly with the Barthian stance. See Philip Clayton, *Explanation from Physics to Theology: An Essay in Rationality and Religion* (New Haven: Yale University Press, 1989), especially pp. 9-14.

70. James Fowler, *Stages of Faith: The Psychology of Human Development and the Quest for Meaning* (San Francisco: Harper & Row, 1981), p. xiii. See the section below on "Contemporary Example."

71. One could argue that the entire field of the psychology of religion, for example, is an effort to demystify (desacralize?) human religious activity and understand it scientifically.

72. As the great religious educator of a past generation put it: "Religion is pervasive of all life." Ernest J. Chave, *A Functional Approach to Religious Education* (Chicago: University of Chicago Press, 1947), p. v.

73. This is what I have called systemic religious education. See this explained in detail in Lines, *Systemic Religious Education*, Chapter Six, pp. 211-240.

To recall some previous statements made at the head of this section, it is only requisite to add a few words to be descriptive of both the scientist and the religious educator: Scientists and religious educators are never fully satisfied with their work, and that work is never totally complete. Scientists and religious educators are always seeking something or someplace else to explore in order to explain more and to further refine theory. By virtue of the scientific method, their explorations lead them to encounter new or different problems, to question old and accepted assumptions and traditions, to reformulate disproven hypotheses and theories into new possibilities and explanations, and to verify or revise theory by repeated evaluation of the data and replication of experiments. Both are willing and obliged to change their minds, their theories, and their paradigms when the data and their interpretation so indicate that a change is necessary. Scientists and religious educators are committed to let their explorations shape, influence, and even determine what they think, even if—or, especially if—they do not discover in their explorations what they expected to find.

Shadow Role: Scientist-King

C. P. Snow observed that "the scientific process has two motives: one is to understand the natural world, the other is to control it."[74] The focus of this chapter thus far has been on the first motive—understanding. This section deals more specifically with the second motive—that of controlling, or as some would phrase it, of ruling.[75]

Because the focus thus far has been the efforts of science to understand, predict, and evaluate, science has taken on a rather benign appearance. What is to be feared simply from knowing more about our world? The more malignant tendency of science becomes visible when understanding, predicting, and evaluation logically and inevitably moves to dangerous applications and misuse of that knowledge—which leads to the aforementioned concept of scientism.[76] What is to be feared from those who "seek to understand the natural world," and from those who desire to control and rule? The first part of the question can be answered simply: Nothing is to be feared from the legitimate scientist who is conducting research by the control of environmental variables. The latter part of the question can be answered just as simply, although differently: Plenty is to be feared, not from the genuine scientist, but from the follower of scientism who seeks to control and rule *people* instead of variables.

The relationship of knowledge and the use of it to control and rule is hardly a new one. In fact, it stretches back to the time of the ancient Greek philoso-

---

74. Snow, *The Two Cultures: And a Second Look,* p. 64.

75. As has been stressed repeatedly throughout this chapter, the scientist is indeed committed to control, but to the legitimate control of variables in an experimental environment. Those who move the discussion to that of science ruling, however, are talking about the manipulation of people, such as in political control.

76. Recall that scientism was defined by D. C. Phillips as "a term used in a mildly abusive way to indicate slavish adherence to the methods of science in a context where they are inappropriate . . . or to indicate a false or mistaken claim to be scientific." Phillips, *Philosophy, Science, and Social Inquiry,* p. 206.

phers,[77] for whom philosophy and science were intimately connected rather than dichotomized as sharply as is too often assumed today. For example, this connection was a central part of Plato's teachings on the hierarchy of society. He taught that the human "faculties" could be divided into three parts: base instincts, noble instincts, and reason or intellect. Corresponding classes of humankind identified with a dominant faculty could then be found in society: the common workers, or artisans (with base instincts); the warriors (with noble instincts); and the lawmakers or rulers (with reason). Because the rulers were those most possessed by reason and intellect, they would be instrumental in bringing in a Utopia. Plato predicted this Utopia would come when "philosophers are kings, or the kings of this world have the spirit and power of philosophy."[78] By pure coincidence, Plato himself would be positioned rather comfortably in his role as philosopher. The concept of philosopher-king, at any rate, is as least as old as the writings of the ancient Greeks. Those that have the knowledge seem to be the logical ones to determine how to use it, especially as it serves this intelligentsia who have devised the structure.

The shift from philosopher-king to scientist-king was illustrated in extreme form within the work of the pioneer social scientist Auguste Comte (1798-1857). Comte described the evolution of human intellect as following a "great fundamental law," which he said has a "solid foundation of proof, both in the facts of our organization and in our historical experience."[79] He explained: "The law is this: that each of our leading conceptions—each branch of our knowledge—passes successively through three different theoretical conditions: the Theological, or fictitious; the Metaphysical, or abstract; and the Scientific, or positive."[80] Such was the birth of the philosophy of positivism.

A brief introduction to these successive stages from Comte explicates the potential threat of the scientist-king, especially to those in religious education. Comte described the evolution of the stages as follows:

> In the theological state, the human mind, seeking the essential nature of things, the first and final causes (the origin and purpose) of all effects—in short, Absolute knowledge—supposes all phenomena to be produced by the immediate action of supernatural beings.
>
> In the metaphysical state, which is only a modification of the first, the mind supposes, instead of supernatural forces, veritable entities (that is, personified abstractions) inherent in all beings and capable of producing all phenomena.
>
> In the final, the positive state, the mind has given over the vain search

---

77. Reading and studying such ancients as Plato and Aristotle is as much an exercise in mathematics and science as it is in literature. Philosophy served as the bridge between the disciplines for the Greeks, much in the way that C. P. Snow was calling for some degree of synthesis between the "two cultures" of humanists and scientists noted earlier in the chapter.

78. Plato, *The Dialogues of Plato*, ed. Justine D. Kaplan (New York: Washington Square Press, 1950), p. 237.

79. Auguste Comte, *The Positive Philosophy*, trans. Harriet Martineau (New York: AMS Press, 1974; reprint of 1855 publication), p. 25.

80. Ibid.

after Absolute notions . . . and applies itself to the study of their laws. . . . Reasoning and observation, duly combined, are the means of this knowledge.[81]

Such a conception of the evolution of human intelligence and knowledge, while extreme in its language, is certainly not completely foreign to contemporary thought patterns.[82] Neither is it unrelated to the ancient Platonic notions. The difference of Comte from Plato was that instead of philosophers bringing in Utopia and serving as rulers, now scientists were seen as the ones with the means of access to true knowledge and were heirs to the role of becoming the rightful rulers. The specter of the scientist-king had arrived.[83]

Modern-day apparitions of this scientist-king who will control and rule have been occasionally cited and identified. B. F. Skinner (1905-1990), probably the most renowned social scientist of the twentieth century, came under fire as this sort of manipulator when he spoke of the need and necessity for humans to take control of their own environment. His novel *Walden Two* did little but fan the flame of fear (but also the fascination) of the scientist-king who would take people's babies and make them slaves to a scientific Utopia.[84] His reduction of freedom and dignity to conditioned "bit[s] of behavior . . . followed by a certain kind of consequence"[85] that could be easily explained and controlled was likewise met with less than the adoration of a messiah. More recently, Robert Lilienfeld has warned of the scientist-king who is coming in the garb of the systems theorist, variously and breathlessly described as "idealistic, utopian, and impractical."[86] Lilienfeld said of the work of systems theorists: "The world as a gigantic laboratory is their world, and their conception of systems is a world they can manipulate in order to make science. In manipulating that world they are not simply making science, they are ruling the world."[87] Of the theorists themselves he said: "They are not monsters out of science fiction or an immediate threat. So far as we know, they suffer the relatively innocent delusions of men who do not know their limits."[88] These and other infrequent warnings of a perceived threat to the future of civilization from supposed scientist-kings sound less frightening than do the writers of the warnings themselves.

Rather than seeing any of these candidates for scientist-king as being a real

---

81. Ibid., p. 26.

82. For example, recall the quote by Laszlo earlier in this chapter. Laszlo used the same succession of stages as Comte outlined, whether intentionally or not.

83. The rule of the theologian-king (or theologian-queen, if theology is perceived as the "queen of the sciences") is still the dream of some religious authoritarians, as if the example of such a figure as the Ayatolla Ruholla Khomeini were not vivid enough to reveal the dangers. Religious leaders in the garb of the ruler are probably even more of a threat than scientist-kings because there are no limits on the religionists like the ones science and its (at least ideally) disciplined approach demands. When religious leaders are convinced they are right, and God is on their side, there is no boundary they are unwilling to smash to ensure that "God's will" (as they define it) be done.

84. B. F. Skinner, *Walden Two* (New York: Macmillan, 1948).

85. B. F. Skinner, *Beyond Freedom and Dignity* (New York: Bantam Books, 1971), p. 25.

86. Robert Lilienfeld, *The Rise of Systems Theory: An Ideological Analysis* (New York: Wiley, 1978), p. 279.

87. Ibid., p. 280.

88. Ibid.

threat to society, the more generic attitude of scientism has the potential for posing such a threat. As defined earlier in this chapter, scientism is the slavish adherence to the procedures of science to the exclusion of any other means of understanding. This type of control or limit to the imagination or curiosity of humankind can only stunt progress. As the inclusion of the other chapters in this book reveal, there are parallel ways of viewing and interpreting reality. The chapter on the religious educator as artist, for example, provides a very different perspective on reality than the religious educator as scientist, but art does not seek to replace science—just as science does not seek to replace art.[89] The various and diverse views can be complementary and mutually informative. To use and insist only on the means and procedures of science (or on *any* one, exclusivist way of interpreting reality) is to miss the richness and the variety in the human experience.

In summary, while understanding the scientific method as one valid means for finding truth, it is still but one window into the panorama of existence. To allow science to provide the only perspective misses the fullness and the wholeness available from complementary views. The shadow role of the scientist-king is symptomatic of the dangers of assuming that there is only one path which leads to truth.

Faith Tradition Resource: The Enlightenment

Referring to the Enlightenment as a faith tradition resource requires a rather strong sense of irony. Whatever else the designation "Enlightenment" may imply, surely it points to a time when reason was believed to be the great and final arbiter of truth.[90] To suggest that such devotion to reason is like unto faith then seems contradictory, but it is also a revealing combination of often assumed opposites. The leaders of the Enlightenment[91] did put their faith in reason, as distinct from tradition, external authority, or divine mandate. This reason was not just a cognitive or a philosophical activity but a reason based on observation and empirical data. The Enlightenment, in short, was grounded upon faith in the scientific approach. The effects and the influence of this "faith tradition resource" are still very much alive and present in contemporary thought.

There is some risk in trying to identify exactly what or who the Enlightenment did include. As historian Peter Gay said, looking for synthesis in the movement "demands regard for complexity: the men of the Enlightenment were divided by

---

89. For an interesting and revealing account of how artists and scientists worked together on common problems and interests for their mutual benefit as professionals in fifteenth century Italy, see Joseph Ben-David, *The Scientist's Role in Society: A Comparative Study* (Englewood Cliffs, N.J.: Prentice-Hall, 1971), pp. 55-59.

90. The general time frame for identifying the Enlightenment was the seventeenth and eighteenth centuries C. E. Recognized leaders were such philosophers as René Descartes (1596-1650), Gottfried Wilhelm von Leibnitz (1646-1716), François Voltaire (1694-1778), and Denis Diderot (1713-1784).

91. These leaders, often designated as the *illuminati*, were primarily literary figures and not actually scientists. They relied on the rationalism of the scientific approach but did not carry through with the necessary experimentation themselves to really be classified as scientists. "Rationalists" seems to be the proper designation for these *illuminati*. A scientist, by contrast, may also deal in rationalism but not merely in speculation, moving into experimentation to prove or disprove hypotheses.

doctrine, temperament, environment, and generations."[92] After acknowledging the various types of differences among those in the movement, Gay decided to use the term Enlightenment "to refer to what I shall call a family, a family of intellectuals united by a single style of thinking."[93] This "style of thinking" he identified as paganism: not a paganism of sensuality, but an affinity for classical Greco-Roman modes of thought while still holding an appreciation for independence and discovery.[94] Gay wrote: "Theirs was a paganism directed against their Christian inheritance and dependent upon the paganism of classical antiquity, but it was also a modern paganism, emancipated from classical thought as much as from Christian dogma."[95] Gay pointed to the reliance on reason and its power to liberate people from superstition and tradition as those prominent things which held together this diverse and multifaceted movement.

Ernst Cassirer, a philosopher of science, discussed the Enlightenment within the historical context of the eighteenth century and showed much similarity to Gay's description: "When the eighteenth century wants to characterize [its formative] power in a single word, it calls it 'Reason.' 'Reason' becomes the unifying and central point of this century, expressing all that it longs and strives for, and all that it achieves."[96] Cassirer hastened to clarify what "reason" meant: "The Enlightenment does not take the ideal of this mode of thinking from the philosophical doctrines of the past; on the contrary, it constructs its ideal according to the model and pattern of contemporary natural science."[97] The approach of the Enlightenment was to start with data and analyze them to find principles, rather than to start with certain concepts and axioms and then search for evidence to support the presuppositions. Cassirer put it this way: "The procedure is thus not from concepts and axioms to phenomena, but vice versa. Observation produces the datum of science: the principle and law are the object of the investigation. This new methodological order characterizes all eighteenth century thought."[98] The Enlightenment appealed to reason: Not to a reason of Platonic Ideas, but to a reason born and bred of the scientific process.

Even if Plato's fundamental philosophical method was rejected by the leaders of the Enlightenment, however, a thread of connection to Plato's view of a hierarchical society was not far-fetched. Some type of hierarchical arrangement for society was still assumed to be proper. It was just that the structure of the hierarchy needed to be slightly reconfigured, with philosophers continuing to be seen as the appropriate rulers of society. The leaders of the Enlightenment, the so-called *illuminati*, were certainly not interested in building a democracy but rather a different type of aristocracy, what Elmer Wilds and Kenneth Lottich called "a new aristocracy of intelligence to replace the old aristocracy of fami-

92. Peter Gay, *The Enlightenment: An Interpretation—The Rise of Modern Paganism* (New York: Knopf, 1966), p. x.

93. Ibid.

94. Ibid., p. 9

95. Ibid., p. xi.

96. Ernst Cassirer, *The Philosophy of the Enlightenment*, trans. Fritz C. A. Koelln and James P. Pettegrove (Princeton: Princeton University Press, 1951), p. 5.

97. Ibid., p. 7.

98. Ibid., p. 8.

ly, position, and the church, a new aristocracy of talent to replace the old aristocracy of blood."[99] The arrogance of elitism dies hard, whether in the form of Plato's philosopher-king, or as it lived on in the Enlightenment as the somewhat more refined concept of the scientist-king. The issue of knowledge, its use, and who should control it continued as a dominant theme of discussion.

This faith tradition resource had no traditional temples or churches of worship; rather, the libraries, salons, and parlors became the centers of interaction. No sacred or inherited scriptures were treasured, since the *illuminati* were still in the process of discovering the deeper truths. No prayers were offered, only obeisance to the god Reason.[100]

As with any faith tradition resource (or ideology), however, the Enlightenment left behind some ideals to emulate and some demons to fear. Its positive values included a deep curiosity, a love for natural science, a high regard for reason, and a stubbornness against accepting anything that could not be verified objectively and empirically. Probably the chief attribute was its combative relationship with tradition. Gerald Cragg summed this up well: "Thus all forms of traditional authority were suspect. . . . Nothing was taken on trust. Men were to be taught to rely on the evidence provided by nature or reason, not on the arguments supplied by tradition."[101] These same strengths fed the weaknesses. The figures in the Enlightenment were so ready to reject tradition that they were in danger of throwing out whatever was of value in tradition. They tended toward a harsh rationalism, even scientism, which produced a tradition and a rigidity that became just as harmful and as stifling as the authoritarian religious systems they were trying to circumvent. Their appreciation for reason eventually led them into a cold and lifeless rationalism that became as barren and as useless as the philosophical and theological structures they had set out to destroy. By setting the limits as accepting only what could be verified by the senses, these thinkers effectively cut themselves off from the multiple sources of human experience.

The Enlightenment, standing in the age-old legacy of rationalism,[102] provid-

---

99. Elmer Harrison Wilds and Kenneth V. Lottich, *The Foundations of Modern Education*, 4th ed. (New York: Holt, Rinehart and Winston, 1970), p. 295.

100. The approach of the *illuminati* was in some ways a reappearance of gnosticism. Gnosticism, especially in Christian history, has proven to be a recurrent movement that emphasizes esoteric insights and special, private knowledge over against religious faith and traditional orthodoxy. For an introduction to gnosticism, see Geddes MacGregor, *Gnosis: A Renaissance in Christian Thought* (Wheaton, Ill.: Theosophical Publishing House, 1979); Robert M. Grant, *Gnosticism: A Source Book of Heretical Writings from the Early Church Period* (New York: Harper and Brothers, 1961); and Benjamin Walker, *Gnosticism: Its History and Influence* (San Bernadino, Calif.: Borgo Press, 1983). It seems each generation devises its own form of gnosticism. One current example is the mishmash of ideas, rituals, and secret information known as "scientology," based on the writings of L. Ron Hubbard. For a representative effort, see L. Ron Hubbard, *The Creation of Human Ability: A Handbook for Scientologists* (Los Angeles: Bridge Press, 1989).

101. Gerald R. Cragg, *Reason and Authority in the Eighteenth Century* (Cambridge: Cambridge University Press, 1964), p. 2.

102. One of the forms of this legacy is theological rationalism, where the primary issue becomes belief—or more precisely, cognitive assent to dogma. As has been thematic throughout this chapter, if not the entire book, thinking without action is as meaningless as theory without research data. The two simply cannot be divided up and separated and still retain any meaning or value. For one of the more thorough and helpful expositions of these issues, see Wilfred Cantwell Smith, *Faith and Belief* (Princeton: Princeton University Press, 1979).

ed many discoveries and many opportunities to escape the bonds of tradition. It has also left many slow-healing wounds, not the least of which is the continuing duality of science and religion. While the religious educator can learn much from a study of the Enlightenment as a type of faith tradition resource, and can appreciate its strike for independence and rationality, he or she can also find much that was ruined and still in need of repair. This duality of potential for good and for evil resides in all faith tradition resources, just as it did within the Enlightenment.

Historical Personage: Galileo

Galileo Galilei (1564-1642) was a man of contrasts and contradictions.[103] Referred to today as the "father of modern science,"[104] in the days following his death he was accused by Pope Urban VIII of giving rise to the "greatest scandal in Christendom."[105] Although a friend and political ally of this pope (Maffeo Cardinal Barberini, who became Urban VIII in 1623) for years, Galileo found himself condemned by him and his regime. Convicted of heresy and forced to recant his writings twice,[106] Galileo remained a devout Catholic and personally saw no conflict between his science and his faith.[107] If ever a man were caught in the cross-fire of science and religion, Galileo would qualify. A brief look at the achievements and predicaments of Galileo are instructive to any religious educator who deigns to perform in the role of the scientist.

The achievements of Galileo were many, but the procedure by which he achieved them was singular. He simply refused to bow to well-meant but unconfirmed hunches, philosophies, or theologies that ultimately proved to be inadequate for solving the problems at hand and instead used experimental data as the basis for his reasoning. Looking back with admiration for Galileo's work, the great twentieth-century physicists Albert Einstein and Leopold Infeld said: "The discovery and use of scientific reasoning by Galileo was one of the most important achievements in the history of human thought and marks the real beginning of physics. This discovery taught us that intuitive conclusions based on immediate observation are not always to be trusted, for they sometimes lead to the wrong clews."[108] They continued their tribute to Galileo by saying: "Galileo's contribution was to destroy the intuitive view and replace it by a new one. This was the significance of Galileo's discovery."[109] In a related vein, Stillman Drake also spoke of Galileo's method of reasoning and its continuing influence: "It is prob-

---

103. Galileo was a natural scientist, but his experience is both paradigmatic and highly relevant for social scientists.

104. See, for example, Capra, *The Turning Point*, p. 55.

105. See Jerome J. Langford, *Galileo, Science and the Church* (Ann Arbor, Mich.: University of Michigan Press, 1971), p. 158.

106. For an enlightening but different treatment of Galileo and his "heresy," see Pietro Redondi, *Galileo: Heretic,* trans. Raymond Rosenthal (Princeton, Princeton University Press, 1987). Also see Giorgio De Santillana, *The Crime of Galileo* (Chicago: University of Chicago Press, 1955).

107. Barbour, *Issues in Science and Religion*, p. 29.

108. Albert Einstein and Leopold Infeld, *The Evolution of Physics: From Early Concepts to Relativity and Quanta* (New York: Simon & Schuster, 1938), pp. 6-7.

109. Ibid., p. 9

ably to Galileo's inherent capacity to *observe* that modern science owes its inception; for despite his extraordinary capacity for reasoning, he turned away from excessive speculation about the causes of things in the tradition of the philosophers. His desire was to see precisely what things happen and how they happen, rather than to explain why they happen so."[110] Philosopher Alfred North Whitehead had a similar high regard for Galileo and his contributions but typically expressed it from a different perspective. In discussing Galileo's role in the beginnings of the scientific movement, and in describing the resultant difficulties encountered by Galileo, Whitehead wrote: "The way in which the persecution of Galileo has been remembered is a tribute to the quiet commencement of the most intimate change in outlook which the human race had yet encountered. Since a babe was born in a manger, it may be doubted whether so great a thing has happened with so little stir."[111]

As noble as all this sounds, one could wonder what all the noise was about. Galileo's achievement was relatively innocuous, in one sense. As Fritjof Capra stated it: "Galileo was the first to combine scientific experimentation with the use of mathematical language to formulate the laws of nature he discovered."[112] Einstein and Infeld said: "Science connecting theory and experiment really began with the work of Galileo."[113] The reason that Galileo has been called "the father of modern science" is precisely because of the point Einstein and Infeld made: Galileo, by following the scientific approach, implemented controls and performed repeatable experiments to verify and confirm his theories. These statements are by all accounts true and revealing, however, but they still do not explain the explosive and violent reaction of the church to Galileo's activity.

The following words of Ernst Cassirer, the philosopher of science, get at the real issue. Cassirer recounted the attempt of Galileo to prove Copernican cosmology and to discredit the old Ptolemaic one, illustrating in this specific example a general problem that Galileo had uncovered for the church: "In reality it was not the new cosmology which church authorities so vehemently opposed; for as a mere mathematical 'hypothesis' they could just as well accept the Copernican as the Ptolemaic system. But what was not to be tolerated, what threatened the very foundations of the church, was *the new concept of truth proclaimed by Galileo*. Alongside the truth of revelation comes now an independent and original truth of nature. This truth is revealed not in God's word but in his work; it is not based on the testimony of scripture or tradition but is visible to us at all times. But it is understandable only to those who know nature's handwriting and can decipher her text. The truth of nature cannot be expressed in mere words; the only suitable expression lies in mathematical constructions, figures and numbers. And in these symbols nature presents itself in perfect form and clarity. Revelation by means of the sacred word can never achieve such brightness and transparency, such precision, for words as such are always varicolored and

110. Stillman Drake, "Galileo: A Biographical Sketch," in *Galileo: Man of Science*, ed. Ernan McMullin (New York: Basic Books, 1967), p. 66.

111. Alfred North Whitehead, *Science and the Modern World* (New York: Macmillan, 1925), p. 2.

112. Capra, *The Turning Point*, pp. 54-55.

113. Einstein and Infeld, *Evolution of Physics*, p. 52

ambiguous admitting a variety of interpretations. Their meaning must always be given them by man and must therefore be fragmentary. In nature, on the other hand, the whole plan of the universe lies before us in its undivided and inviolable unity, evidently waiting for the human mind to recognize and express it."[114] Put in these terms, the work of Galileo and all those that followed him in this "new" kind of science did indeed bring cause for the church to feel threatened. In some very real ways, Western religion and the Christian church have still not totally reconciled themselves with Galileo and his approach to truth.

Personally, Galileo was evidently able to remain a man of faith while also being a man of science. One of the ways he accomplished this was to accept different starting points in order to answer different questions. This was illustrated in his correspondence with the grandduchess of Toscany, which included the line: "This therefore being granted [that scripture was written for the salvation of souls and not for secular knowledge], methinks that in the Discussion of the Natural Problemes, we ought not to begin at the authority of places of Scripture; but at Sensible Experiments and Necessary Demonstrations."[115] Ian Barbour's commentary on this letter was that "natural theology had for centuries been looked upon as a preamble to revealed theology; Galileo put nature and scripture on the same level as avenues to God."[116] Galileo was striking a blow against imperialism of any sort—theological, philosophical, or scientific. He chose to try a variety of ways to gain insight into the larger picture of reality. For Galileo, this multifaceted learning process removed any assumed conflicts and opened the doors to many different kinds of understanding. He willingly followed both avenues of theology and science, for example, and found truth and revelation wherever and however they could be found.

Is this "different path" method the best method for resolving the potential conflict between science and religion?[117] Is there any hope for a true integration of the two, where truth could be discovered or created without needing to travel two (or more) different paths and hope that they eventually integrate?

---

114. Cassirer, *Philosophy of the Enlightenment*, pp. 42-43. Emphasis added.

115. Galileo Galilei, "Letter to the Grandduchess of Toscany," as quoted in *Three Thousand Years of Educational Wisdom*, ed. Robert Ulich (Cambridge: Harvard University Press, 1957), p. 329; also see p. 305.

116. Barbour, *Issues in Science and Religion*, p. 30.

117. There are many paths or methods for arriving at truth, rather than only one that must be followed exclusively. This former position promotes the argument for pluralism. Pluralism is a term that indicates no one description of anything is entirely adequate. Many avenues are sought and perspectives gathered in order to get a larger, integrated picture of reality. Science employs a different method from that of theology, for example, but that does not necessarily make one wrong and the other right. The two working together can give a clearer understanding of human experience. Just so, Christianity does not have to be wrong for Buddhism to be right. The two of them can be studied to gain a broader understanding of reality through religious pluralism. This book does not give one role of the religious educator that every religious educator must perform in lockstep but provides a full range of roles that can come together to create an integrated whole. For some helpful introductory resources on religious pluralism, see the classic work by William James, *The Varieties of Religious Experience: A Study in Human Nature* (New York: Macmillan, 1961), first published in 1902; *Religious Pluralism and Religious Education*, ed. Norma H. Thompson (Birmingham, Ala.: Religious Education Press, 1988); and Wilfred Cantwell Smith, *The Faith of Other Men* (New York: Harper & Row, 1962).

Galileo's way has worked with varying degrees of success for generations. If there is another way, it would appear that religious education—situated as it is in relationship with both science and religion—may be in a position to bring it about. The work of "scientific" religious education, which makes the effort to integrate both good science and good religion, is the topic taken up in the next section.

Contemporary Example: James Fowler

Can the religious educator not only play the role of the scientist, but truly be a social scientist? Can the religious educator use the tools, the procedures, and even the worldview of the scientist and still be a religious educator? To many, these questions are ridiculous. Some would shrug and say—of course! Others would shudder and say—of course not! One representative religious educator[118] who has answered in the affirmative and who has recently been receiving the lion's share of attention for "scientific" religious education is James Fowler (b. 1940), whose primary work *Stages of Faith* is overviewed below.[119] Whether

---

118. James Fowler is identified here as a religious educator, but he could be identified by a number of other titles as well — psychologist, social scientist, and so on. Some have called him a theologian. But although Fowler's work does intersect theology, he is not just a theologian, since his investigative procedures are social-scientific rather than theological. Justification for considering him within the ranks of religious educators includes the fact that he does teach courses in religious education at Emory University, where he is a professor and director of the Center for Faith Development. He has occasionally addressed religious education directly, as in his chapter "Faith and the Structure of Meaning," in *Faith Development and Fowler*, ed. Craig Dykstra and Sharon Parks (Birmingham, Ala.: Religious Education Press, 1986), pp. 15-42. (Incidentally, this compilation by Dykstra and Parks, both religious educators, is further evidence of the intrinsic connection between Fowler's work and religious education.) In addition, he has reported on the progress of his work on faith development periodically in the professional journal *Religious Education*, starting with the first tentative statements in the article "Toward a Developmental Perspective on Faith," *Religious Education* 69:2 (March/April, 1974), pp. 207-219. Also see James W. Fowler, "Stage Six and the Kingdom of God," *Religious Education* 75:3 (May/June, 1980), pp. 231-248; and James E. Loder and James W. Fowler, "Conversations on Fowler's *Stages of Faith* and Loder's *The Transforming Moment*," *Religious Education* 77:2 (March/April, 1982), pp. 133-148. If for no other reason, Fowler is appropriately designated as a religious educator because his research on faith development addresses the essence of so much of what religious education regularly does. It would be hard *not* to see him and his work as being squarely positioned within the heart of the field. The difficulty of identifying or of classifying Fowler's work, however, was apparent early on, as when Henry Simmons reviewed *Stages of Faith* for *Religious Education*. Simmons wrote: "It needs to be asked, of course, just how directly applicable this work is to the field of religious education. As it stands, it is a serious work in the psychology of religion." Simmons concluded: "Out of it, indeed, may emerge solid insights for the practice of religious education." See the review of *Stages of Faith* by Henry Simmons in *Religious Education* 77:1 (January/February, 1982), pp. 112-113.

119. A religious educator who preceded Fowler in making some attempt at letting his work be guided and shaped by scientific research was Ronald Goldman. His first book in this regard was *Religious Thinking from Childhood to Adolescence* (New York: Seabury, 1964), and the companion book that followed was *Readiness for Religion: A Basis for Developmental Religious Education* (New York: Seabury, 1965). These two books attempted to form diagnosis and solution to the problem of inadequate and improper religious education, as revealed through the lens of developmental theory. Another religious educator, Edward Robinson, also took a scientific approach to his work, but it went in a divergent direction from that of Goldman's. Robinson, as detailed in the fascinating book *The Original Vision: A Study of the Religious Experience of Childhood* (New York: Seabury, 1983; first published in 1977), used cultural anthropology to inform religious education.

or not he deserves such attention and identification can only be considered after a brief overview of his approach. Any evidence that may suggest a negative response will be found in the section that evaluates Fowler, which follows the overview.

Overview

James Fowler exemplifies the religious educator as social scientist. The issues discussed here relate primarily to the social-science approach and procedures Fowler used in his research, and his stance on faith development—the content of his research—is considered only to the extent that it reveals that scientific approach and methodology. This is not the place for a full debate and evaluation of the appropriateness of faith development as an issue in religious education.[120] It is the place to debate and evaluate the role of the scientist in religious education, inclusive of how successfully Fowler fulfilled that role. Consideration of faith development is a means to that end.

The primary source for this overview, and subsequent evaluation, is Fowler's main exposition of his proposal as presented in *Stages of Faith*. Various other sources are important and revelatory,[121] but the bulk of the ideas and the research findings that support his theory are given in detail in this comprehensive book; therefore, this discussion limits itself to a consideration of Fowler's position as provided in this one book. It is true that research and data collection on faith development continues, but Fowler's basic stance toward faith development itself has remained essentially unchanged from its portrayal in *Stages of Faith*.[122]

In the introduction to this book, Fowler made some of his most fundamental statements, such as his declaration in broad terms of what he considered to be faith: "I believe faith to be a human universal. We are endowed at birth with

120. There are those who believe that faith development is the central issue for the religious educator to promote. For example: "Our conviction is that the process of faith development ought to be the actual primary task of the church." James D. Anderson and Ezra Earl Jones, *The Management of Ministry: Leadership, Purpose, Structure, Community* (San Francisco: Harper & Row, 1978), p. 125.

121. A fuller consideration of Fowler and his work would necessarily include consulting the following primary sources: James W. Fowler, *To See the Kingdom: The Theological Vision of H. Richard Niebuhr* (Nashville: Abingdon, 1977); Jim Fowler and Sam Keen, *Life Maps: Conversations on the Journey of Faith*, ed. Jerome Berryman (Waco, Texas: Word, 1978); James W. Fowler, Robin Lovin, with Katherine Ann Herzog, Brian Mahan, Linell Cady, and Jonathan P. Gosser, *Trajectories of Faith: Five Life Stories* (Nashville: Abingdon, 1980); James W. Fowler, *Becoming Adult, Becoming Christian: Adult Development and Christian Faith* (San Francisco: Harper & Row, 1984); James W. Fowler, "Faith and the Structure of Meaning," in *Faith Development and Fowler*; James W. Fowler, *Faith Development and Pastoral Care* (Philadelphia: Fortress, 1987); *Caring for the Commonweal: Education for Religious and Public Life,* ed. Parker J. Palmer, Barbara J. Wheeler, and James W. Fowler (Macon, Ga.: Mercer University Press, 1990); and James W. Fowler, *Weaving the New Creation: Stages of Faith and the Public Church* (San Francisco: Harper San Francisco, 1991). These would serve as good introductory reading to the larger corpus of Fowler's work.

122. This overview and evaluation deals primarily with Fowler's theoretical and empirical work rather than the applied efforts. Other books and articles by Fowler spell out more clearly how the facilitation of faith development can be done, while *Stages of Faith* presents the foundation of his approach. Only this foundation is explored here, but a fuller understanding of Fowler's contributions would include an examination of the applied work.

nascent capacities for faith. How these capacities are activated and grow depends
... on how we are welcomed into the world and what kinds of environments we
grow in. Faith is interactive and social; it requires community, language, ritual,
and nurture. Faith is also shaped by initiatives from beyond us and other people.
... How these latter initiatives are recognized and imaged, or unperceived and
ignored, powerfully affects the shape of faith in our lives."[123]

Fowler, then, immediately had set out the difficult task for himself of discovering and studying the *structural* content of faith. His activities were not so
much to describe the substantive contents of any one specific faith tradition and
how that substantive content is taught or learned. Fowler was interested in the
basic, underlying structure of faith that is represented and detectable in all the faith
traditions. He therefore stated explicitly what he believes faith to be, albeit in terms
that appear to defy quantification or experimental investigation, as the prerequisite
to finding stages of faith. Clarity concerning what *Fowler* meant by faith is central to understanding Fowler's work. How any one reader may wish to define faith
cannot be used as a substitute for Fowler's definition—and then try to use
Fowler's research to correlate with one's personalized definition of faith.[124]
Fowler's own definition must remain the operative one throughout.

In the paragraph following the above quote, Fowler expressed more fully
the essence of his work: "In these pages I am offering a theory of growth in
faith. At the heart of the book you will find an account of a theory of seven
stage-like, developmentally related styles of faith that we have identified."[125]
Since he twice used the term "theory" to describe what his work would cover, it
was necessary for Fowler to give his own definition of theory: "A theory means
an elaborate, dynamic model of very complex patterns in our lives."[126] It should
be obvious that what Fowler identified as theory differs somewhat from how the
term has been used thus far in the current chapter and differs from the more
precise and empirical way that many social scientists would choose to characterize
their work. Already one can get the sense from Fowler, by his definitions of
faith and theory, that he is going to lead the reader through an introductory journey of discovery and exploration, rather than a strictly statistical or empirical study
of faith development.[127]

Part I ("Human Faith"[128]) of Fowler's book, then, set the tone for what was to
follow. In Chapter 1 (also entitled "Human Faith"[129]) he discussed the concept of
faith from the perspective of theology, drawing heavily from such theologians
as Paul Tillich and H. Richard Niebuhr. Fowler did not produce here (or elsewhere) a quantifiable definition of faith and so did not produce an empirically
testable definition. Neither did he specify certain variables that he believed

---

123. Fowler, *Stages of Faith*, p. xiii.
124. See Chapter Twelve, "The Dynamic Triad of Faith," ibid., pp. 90-97 for Fowler's discussion of this necessity.
125. Ibid., p. xiii.
126. Ibid.
127. For a discussion of the difficulties of doing research on a topic such as faith development,
see C. Ellis Nelson and Daniel Aleshire, "Research in Faith Development," in *Faith Development
and Fowler*, pp. 180-201.
128. Fowler, *Stages of Faith*, pp. 1-34.

would or do interact to produce and expected result. Instead, he raised what he called "questions of faith" which "aim to help us get in touch with the dynamic, patterned process by which we find life meaningful."[130] These kinds of questions conform to Fowler's earlier definition of theory and lead in a different direction than toward experimentation, which would have required the manipulation and control of variables. Fowler was doing more foundational and philosophical work, and the questions he used allowed him to get at the issues involved in an introductory and exploratory way.

Another version of a definition—actually, a description—of faith given by Fowler was this one: "Faith . . . is the most fundamental category in the human quest for relation to transcendence. Faith, it appears, is generic, a universal feature of human living, recognizably similar everywhere despite the remarkable variety of forms and contents."[131] This last definition of faith has embedded within it many unprovable assumptions, such as faith being generic, universal, and dealing with the transcendent, and it would have been curious indeed if the research carried out would in any way contradict the inherent assumptions. This means that such a concept as faith that is by definition universal and generic would be virtually impossible *not* to find! As one would guess, the consequent research did not contradict but rather supported or extended these assumptions about the universality of human faith. Also of interest is that Fowler identified faith as "the most fundamental category of human existence," which would appear to make Fowler primarily interested in the intellectual or rational part of the human being. Fowler's research was not conducted in the laboratory or even in an experimental environment but rather through recollections and the taking of life histories. Such a procedure determines that the emphasis was placed on meaning, memory, and cognition rather than the actual physical behavior or lifestyle of the persons being examined.

Another definitional issue then appeared in these two sentences: "In the main we have—as we will throughout this book—avoided doing theology, systematic inquiry into and reflection on the transcendent to whom (or which) persons are related. Our concern here is with the human side of faith."[132] Fowler was attempting in his work to produce a "value-free" kind of theology, which in his personalistic configuration was consideration of the nature of the transcendent. Such an attempt further identifies Fowler as conducting social science, which always makes the effort to be value-free in the sense of describing and explaining rather than prescribing or dictating what should be.[133] It was not that Fowler avoided doing theology, but rather that he tried to avoid any particularistic form of theology. Nonetheless, it is difficult to base a book on faith, and to use such

129. Ibid., pp. 3-8.
130. Ibid., p. 3.
131. Ibid., p. 14.
132. Ibid., p. 33.
133. Earl Babbie made these points clearly in his introductory writings on social science research: "Social scientific theory has to do with what *is*, not with what *should be*. . . . It is important to realize that social *science* has to do with how things are and why. This means that scientific theory—and more broadly, science itself—cannot settle debates on value." Earl Babbie, *The Practice of Social Research*, 5th ed. (Belmont, Calif.: Wadsworth, 1989), p. 17.

theologians as Paul Tillich and H. Richard Niebuhr to explain it, and then to avoid completely doing some type of theology.[134]

A key to understanding Fowler's work is the dependence he had on other structural-developmental theories. As a cursory examination of Part II ("Windows on Human Development: A Fictional Conversation"[135]) shows, Fowler directs the reader through the theories of Erik Erikson, Jean Piaget, and Lawrence Kohlberg in the form of an imaginary round table discussion. This part laid the foundation for all the work on faith development that was to come throughout the rest of the book.[136] While Fowler's theory rode upon the strengths of the aforementioned figures, it also inherited all the weaknesses of them. Fowler took note of some of these strengths and weaknesses in Part III ("Dynamics of Faith and Human Development"[137]), particularly in Chapters 13[138] and 14.[139]

The above paragraph used the term "theory" out of regard for how Fowler and the other structural-developmental writers have used the term. Fowler made a perceptive comment in his analysis of the type of theorists he was building upon when he wrote: "A final important influence from the structural developmentalists on our research has to do with the *normative* directions and implications of their work. Without sacrificing commitment to empirical rigor in the testing of their claims, Piaget and Kohlberg have offered what we may call philosophical psychologies."[140] Here is a perfectly appropriate term to replace "theory" in the work of the structural developmentalists, inclusive of Fowler: "Philosophical psychologies." This term solves the problem of Fowler and others who are obviously doing research and collecting data but not in what could be considered a theoretical or strictly scientific manner. Instead, they are collecting and selecting evidence, seen through the lenses of such areas as philosophy and psychology (and in Fowler's specific case, also from theology), that supports their initial presuppositions. One can applaud Fowler for his creation of the term and only wish that it were employed more widely to distinguish this activity from the type of theory that specifies variables and the relations among them.

Part IV ("Stages of Faith"[141]) formed the heart of the book, where the narra-

---

134. Romney Moseley expressed similar perceptions of Fowler's theological foundations. He said, for example: "Fowler's theory of faith development stands out as one of the most significant contributions to the discourse on theological perspectives on Christian education." Romney Moseley, "Education and Human Development in the Likeness of Christ," in *Theological Approaches to Christian Education*, ed. Jack L. Seymour and Donald E. Miller (Nashville: Abingdon, 1990), p. 148. Moseley went on to say, however: "While Fowler does not specify the transcendent center of value as the Judeo-Christian God, it is evident that, following H. Richard Niebuhr, all other centers of value—henotheistic and polytheistic—do not sustain an ethic of living in a covenantal relationship with God the Creator, Redeemer, and Judge." Ibid., p. 149.

135. Fowler, *Stages of Faith*, pp. 37-88.

136. Compare the discussion of Erik Erikson, Daniel Levinson, and Carol Gilligan in Chapter Two, "Developmentalists as Philosophers and Gossips," in Fowler, *Becoming Adult, Becoming Christian*, pp. 20-47.

137. Fowler, *Stages of Faith*, pp. 89-116.

138. "Structural-Developmental Theories and Faith," ibid., pp. 98-105.

139. "Psychosocial Development and Faith," ibid., pp. 106-116.

140. Ibid., p. 101.

141. Ibid., pp. 117-213.

tive descriptions of the stages were provided.[142] At the beginning of life there is a pre-stage called Undifferentiated faith,[143] of which Fowler said: "Though really a pre-stage and largely inaccessible to empirical research of the kind we pursue, the quality of mutuality and the strength of trust, autonomy, hope, and courage (or their opposites) developed in this phase underlie (or threaten to undermine) all that comes later in faith development."[144] The first true faith stage in Fowler's structure is Intuitive-Projective faith,[145] described as "the fantasy-filled, imitative phase in which the child can be powerfully and permanently influenced by examples, moods, actions, and stories of the visible faith of primally related adults."[146] The second stage is Mythic-Literal faith,[147] the stage where "the person begins to take on for him- or herself the stories, beliefs, and observances that symbolize belonging to his or her community. Beliefs are appropriated with literal interpretations, as are moral rules and attitudes."[148] Stage Three is identified as encompassing Synthetic-Conventional faith,[149] where the task of faith is to "synthesize values and information; it must provide a basis for identity and outlook."[150] Fowler called this the "conformist" stage, "in the sense that it is acutely tuned to the expectations and judgments of significant others and as yet does not have a sure enough grasp on its own identity and autonomous judgment to construct and maintain an independent perspective."[151] Stage Four is Individuative-Reflective faith,[152] where the individual begins to break free of the restrictions and dependencies of the previous stage and struggles with the "double development" of self and worldview: "Self (identity) and outlook (worldview) are differentiated from those of others and become acknowledged factors in the reactions, interpretations, and judgments one makes on the actions of self and others."[153] The fifth stage was labeled by Fowler as Conjunctive faith,[154] which "involves the integration into self and outlook of much that was suppressed and unrecognized in the interest of Stage 4's self-certainty and conscious cognitive and affective adaptation to reality. This stage develops a 'second naiveté' (Ricoeur) in which symbolic power is reunited with conceptual

---

142. The following paragraph is a necessarily brief and incomplete description of the stages. The chapters indicated must be read and studied to get the fuller picture of what Fowler was trying to communicate, as well as to appreciate the effort he has made to describe the transitions between the stages. Incidentally, Fowler has stated or summarized these stages of faith in a number of other places as well. For some examples, see James W. Fowler, Chapter Four, "Stages in Selfhood and Faith," in *Faith Development and Pastoral Care* (Philadelphia: Fortress, 1987), pp. 53-77; Chapter Two, "Life/Faith Patterns: Structures of Trust and Loyalty," in Fowler and Keen, *Life Maps*, pp 14-101; and James W. Fowler, "Faith and the Structure of Meaning," in *Faith Development and Fowler*, pp. 28-31.
143. See Chapter 15, "Infancy and Undifferentiated Faith," Fowler, *Stages of Faith*, pp. 119-121.
144. Ibid., p. 121.
145. See Chapter 16, "Stage 1. Intuitive-Projective Faith," ibid., pp. 122-134.
146. Ibid., p. 133.
147. See Chapter 17, "Stage 2. Mythic-Literal Faith," ibid., pp. 135-150.
148. Ibid., p. 149.
149. See Chapter 18, "Stage 3. Synthetic-Conventional Faith," ibid., pp. 151-173.
150. Ibid., p. 173.
151. Ibid., pp. 172-173.
152. See Chapter 19, "Stage 4. Individuative-Reflective Faith," ibid., pp. 174-183.
153. Ibid., p. 182.
154. See Chapter 20, "Stage 5. Conjunctive Faith," ibid., pp. 184-198.

meanings."[155] In the final stage, Stage Six, Fowler found Universalizing faith.[156] Of all the stages, this one was the most nebulous and difficult for Fowler to describe. He said in part, however: "Stage 6 is exceedingly rare. The persons best described by it have generated faith compositions in which their felt sense of an ultimate environment is inclusive of all being. They have become incarnators and actualizers of the spirit of an inclusive and fulfilled human community."[157]

Part V ("Formation and Transformation in Faith"[158]) concluded the book by giving an extended case study in Chapter 22[159] and final reflections in Chapters 23[160] and 24.[161] From a scientific standpoint, these last two chapters were of less significance because the actual research and quantitative information was provided primarily in the appendices. Appendix A[162] gave an explanation of the research methodology and the format of the research interview. Appendix B[163] provided the "empirical foundations of the theory of faith development" based upon three hundred fifty-nine interviews conducted from 1972-1981.[164] Statistical information and resultant charts were given, with such distributions as age, sex, and race among the "stages of faith" found by Fowler and the other researchers that helped him interview. As Fowler noted, the sample given here was not designed to be a random sample, but was "overwhelmingly white, largely Christian, evenly divided by sex and distributed throughout the age categories."[165] Fowler closed the book with this modest appraisal: "This description of the data collected to this point is provided not to confirm or refute the theory developed herein. The data are in rough form. . . . It has been encouraging to find that the preliminary evidence does reveal the predicted pattern for this sample. . . . These findings are offered to provoke thought and comment from the readers and to provide a glimpse at the evidence that does now exist."[166]

Evaluation

It is always difficult to separate evaluation from an overview, and the two have not been kept entirely distinct here. In a few places above some critical attitudes and comments toward the work of Fowler may have already been noted. It should be repeated that there is no attempt here to evaluate the potential or the influence that Fowler's faith development theory has had for the field of religious education.[167]

---

155. Ibid., p. 197.
156. See Chapter 21, "Stage 6. Universalizing Faith," ibid., pp. 199-213.
157. Ibid., p. 200.
158. Ibid., pp. 215-305.
159. "Mary's Pilgrimage: The Theory at Work," ibid., pp. 217-268.
160. "Form and Content: Stages of Faith and Conversion," ibid., pp. 269-291.
161. "Faith on Earth," ibid., pp. 292-305.
162. "The Research Interview," ibid., pp. 307-312.
163. "Interview Analysis and Characteristics of Our Sample," ibid., pp. 313-323.
164. Ibid., p. 313.
165. Ibid., p. 317.
166. Ibid., p. 323.
167. An excellent example of this kind of necessary and valuable effort can be found throughout the various chapters of *Faith Development and Fowler*. Also see the applications made to religious education in Gary L. Chamberlain, *Fostering Faith: A Minister's Guide to Faith Development* (New York: Paulist, 1988), especially Chapter Three, "Religious Education and the Growth of Faith," pp. 42-62, and Chapter Four, "Religious Education for Maturing Faith," pp. 63-81.

The primary focus is to examine Fowler as a representative religious educator fulfilling the role and activity of the scientist. In other words, the general activity of Fowler as a religious educator in the role of scientist is much more at issue here than the specific content of Fowler's contribution to religious education.

The easiest and most logical way to evaluate Fowler as a scientist and his work as scientific is to employ the standard of the scientific method and to see if "scientific" is the proper term to use.

The first step of the scientific method is to encounter an idea or a problem that does not seem to have an adequate or at least a readily apparent answer or solution. Fowler has high marks here. His interests centered on the growth and development of faith: How does it happen, and why? By any account, this issue has had no adequate solution or explanation, leaving the area wide open for Fowler's research.

The second step is to create a hypothesis that explains the phenomena encountered in the first step. A hypothesis was defined earlier in this chapter as "a conjectural statement, a tentative proposition, about the relation between two or more phenomena or variables."[168] As has been noted, Fowler did not engage in this kind of strict scientific research. He did not propose or fashion a hypothesis, clearly stated, that posited a relationship between two or more variables that could be seen as causative or explanatory. Fowler's contribution was primarily in the area of exploration, probing the issues to find out about what he called the "human side of faith." This was no small accomplishment and has provided no end of research projects. The possibility of studying faith from a social-scientific, value-free perspective was a great emancipation from the narrow limits of specific theologies.

The third step in the scientific process is the deductive reasoning that finds a way to proceed from merely holding a hypothesis to confirming or disconfirming it. Fowler had a good measure of success here. Since he wanted to know about the development of human faith, he decided to interview humans about their faith. The data he collected does give evidence of the stages he proposed.[169] The crucial problem, of course, was that without an experimental hypothesis, and without a control group, there was no way to confirm or disconfirm the actual development of faith, or to show what caused or nurtured the development. Fowler was in the position of starting with a theological, philosophical, and psychological definition of faith and then trying to find evidence that it existed in some stage-like form. In one sense, there was little chance that he would not find such evidence since he already posited its existence even before he did empirical research.[170] In scientific nomenclature, Fowler's research efforts tended to be nonfalsifiable: There was no way to *disprove* the existence of faith, and its predicted stage development, so by definition there could be no way to prove its exis-

---

168. Kerlinger, *Foundations of Behavioral Research*, p. 12.

169. See Appendix B, "Interview Analysis and Characteristics of Our Sample," Fowler, *Stages of Faith*, pp. 313-323.

170. This was made starkly evident when Fowler began by saying (on page xiii of *Stages of Faith*): "I believe faith to be a human universal." To be human is to have faith, so there must be no humans who do not have faith. Such a self-defining statement, then, is in danger of becoming a tautology.

tence.[171] Fowler was not alone in this dilemma, as many social scientists have had the same difficulty,[172] but it is a definite hindrance to the construction of true and verifiable theory.

Fourth in the process is experimentation. Again, Fowler had no testable hypothesis and did no experimentation. Experimentation is performed by manipulating the variables to determine their cause and effect, and ultimately to explain and predict the behavior of those variables. What Fowler did instead was to conduct interviews[173] and assemble data related to these interviews that conformed to his understandings of faith and its presumed growth and development. This effort was heuristic, interesting, and suggestive, but significantly different from and on a decidedly lower acceptance level than scientific experimentation and controls.[174] It may be best to say that what Fowler conducted was "quasi-empirical" research. He conducted interviews that relied on the memory, emotional investment, and honesty of the interviewees as well as the rating and interpretive abilities of the interviewers.[175] This of course puts the actual results in some doubt as to their veracity and reliability but prepares the way in the future for further study and research.[176]

Fifth is the evaluation of the data and its effect on the hypothesis. Fowler did work (and continues to work) on evaluating his data. Since there was no testable hypothesis, however, the data cannot be used to improve the hypothesis. More and more data will continue to be collected which relates to the initial

---

171. For a good though brief discussion on falsifiable and nonfalsifiable hypotheses and theories, see R. Murray Thomas, *Comparing Theories of Child Development*, 2nd ed. (Belmont, Calif.: Wadsworth, 1985), pp. 21-22.

172. Particularly is this true of psychological stage theorists. One of the chief criticisms against Freud's work, for example, has been that he did this type of unjustifiable generalizing.

173. As was mentioned in the overview section above, such a research process of conducting interviews for an understanding of how people interpret their lives emphasizes the rational, cognitive aspects of the human, virtually to the exclusion of the affective and lifestyle dimensions. For an example of a study of faith from an experiential perspective, and for an interesting contrast to the treatment of the subject by Fowler, see V. Bailey Gillespie, *The Experience of Faith* (Birmingham, Ala.: Religious Education Press, 1988).

174. There are many good examples of how to conduct social-science research that produce real empirical evidence. One can be found in the work of Milton Rokeach who studied how beliefs "become somehow organized into architectural systems having describable and measurable properties, which, in turn, have observable consequences." See Milton Rokeach, *Beliefs, Attitudes, and Values: A Theory of Organization and Change* (San Francisco: Jossey-Bass, 1968). The quote is from pg. 1. For further evidence of Rokeach's empirical and experimental work, also see Milton Rokeach, *The Nature of Human Values* (New York: Free Press, 1973); and Milton Rokeach, *The Open and Closed Mind: Investigations Into the Nature of Belief Systems and Personality Systems* (New York: Basic Books, 1960). Another good model of how to conduct social scientific experimentation, especially as it relates to the psychology of religion, is the work of C. Daniel Batson. One representative source is C. Daniel Batson and W. Larry Ventis, *The Religious Experience: A Social-Psychological Perspective* (New York: Oxford University Press, 1982).

175. See Fowler, *Stages of Faith*, p. 315, for an explanation of the scoring and analyzing processes employed in evaluating the faith development interviews.

176. Natalie Sproull, for example, listed seven reasons to avoid questioning people through the interview method if at all possible: lying, omission, inaccurate recall, insufficient information, interviewer bias, interviewer-respondent interaction, and item bias, all of which greatly influence the validity of the data gathered. Natalie L. Sproull, *Handbook of Research Methods: A Guide for Practitioners and Students in the Social Sciences* (Metuchen, N.J.: Scarecrow Press, 1988), p. 164.

presuppositions. It may be the case that as more information and perspectives on the issue of faith development are gathered, more scientifically reliable work can be carried out which will feed into an eventual restatement of the theory. The ultimate worth of this kind of data collection and analysis is left for each individual religious educator to evaluate, but surely all will agree that Fowler has made invaluable contributions—not only to the emancipation of the concept and analysis of faith from theology, but to the continued injection of religious education into the world of social science.

In summary, how well did Fowler fulfill the role of scientist? Kerlinger defined scientific research as the "systematic, controlled, empirical, and critical investigation of hypothetical propositions about the presumed relations among natural phenomena."[177] If this deductive definition of scientific research[178] is scrupulously followed, then Fowler did not conduct it in any strict sense. Fowler can be said to have followed instead the inductive method—"the drawing of conclusions that exceed the information contained in the premises."[179] If it is sufficient to say that since Fowler did use a form of inductive scientific reasoning and process, then he adequately performed in the role of the scientist. To be fair, though, Fowler should probably be seen as casting about for an explanation of the possible relationship between faith and human development, creating an environment and an atmosphere where in the future more scientifically reliable research could be performed. Fowler was thus following his curiosity and his interests—the initial act of engagement for any scientist—and for this he is to be commended.

The examination of James Fowler as a contemporary example causes religious educators to ask these key questions: What are the appropriate boundaries of the role of social scientist for the religious educator?[180] Is it enough to use some of the ideas and procedures of social science and call ourselves scientific? Or is it incumbent upon us to learn deeply from social science, to understand its true methods and processes, and then to conform to its highest standards before we call ourselves scientific? Is this second option truly possible? The answers we provide to these questions will dictate the degree of seriousness with which we religious educators take the role of social scientist.

---

177. Kerlinger, *Foundations of Behavioral Research*, p. 11.

178. A review of the differences between deduction and induction may be helpful: "The two types of reasoning are deduction and induction. The primary distinction between deduction and induction rests with the strength or certainty of the claim that is made about the conclusion on the basis of the premises. When a person uses deductive reasoning, or presents a deductive argument, he or she is claiming that the conclusion absolutely must be true if all the premises are true. When a person argues inductively, he or she is claiming that the conclusion is probably true but not necessarily true if all the premises are true." Royce Singleton et al., *Approaches to Social Research*, p. 44. For the fuller discussion, see ibid., pp. 44-61.

179. Ibid., p. 44.

180. The difficulties confronted here are not present only for the religious educator but in a real sense are problems for all social scientists. Kenneth Bailey's comments are relevant here: "Throughout its history, practitioners of social science have sought the proper position of their discipline with respect to physical science and, to a lesser extent, with respect to the humanities. To this day you will find within social science both those who think of themselves as scientists in the strictest sense of the word and those with a more subjective approach to the study of society, who see themselves more as humanists than as scientists." Bailey, *Methods of Social Research*, p. 5.

Representative Teaching Procedure: Inquiry Training

The issue regarding the extent to which the religious educator chooses to play the role of scientist is determinative in the choice of an appropriate representative teaching procedure. In this section, the assumption is that the religious educator is able and does desire to function with the seriousness and within the structures of the genuine scientist.

The inquiry training procedure[181] is a direct outgrowth and application of the scientific method. Its design allows learners to experience the activity of scientific investigation firsthand, with all its inherent excitement and frustration. Like the scientific method itself, the inquiry training procedure is composed of five phases. First comes a problem or an interesting and unusual situation that does not seem to have a readily apparent explanation. This encounter can be one created or presented by the religious educator, but it is even more engaging if the learners themselves are allowed to decide upon an appropriate issue or problem to explore. This ensures that the learners have a vested interest in the experiment and its results. Second is the gathering of sufficient information to have an initial and fundamental understanding of the identified problem or situation and then stating the problem as clearly and as precisely as possible. Such preliminary work then permits the development of a testable hypothesis. Third is the actual testing of the hypothesis, where experiments are performed by testing the relationship of the variables isolated and identified in the hypothesis. Fourth is the analysis and comprehension of the data collected in the experiment. Do the data support the relationship described in the hypothesis, or do they tend to lead toward a different and revised statement of the hypothesis? This fourth phase is the place where the learners must make a decision about the veracity of their hypothesis. If the data do not confirm it, then they must be ready to test again because of suspected failure of the execution of the experiment itself, or to change the hypothesis to conform more closely with the collected evidence. Fifth, and finally, the learners evaluate and discuss the scientific process in which they have just participated. The overall scientific process, as distinct from the specific hypothesis and experiment, is examined and analyzed for continued application in other relevant realms of activity.

The religious educator could have each individual learner investigate a problem or situation on his or her own, or ask several learners to cooperate in a group investigation. The scientific process of inquiry is just as well-performed individually as jointly. Two or more learners investigating a problem simulta-

---

181. See Chapter 4, "Inquiry Training: From Facts to Theories," in *Models of Teaching* by Bruce Joyce and Marsha Weil, 3rd ed. (Englewood Cliffs, N.J.: Prentice-Hall, 1986), pp. 55-69. Two people should be credited with much of the initial work for developing the inquiry training procedure. One is Hilda Taba, in such works as *The Dynamics of Education: A Methodology of Progressive Educational Thought* (New York: Harcourt, Brace and Company, 1932); "Teaching Strategies and Cognitive Functioning in Elementary School Children," Cooperative Research Project 2404 (San Francisco: San Francisco State College, 1966), and *Teacher's Handbook for Elementary Social Studies* (Reading, Mass.: Addison-Wesley, 1967). The other person is J. Richard Suchman, represented by such work as "Inquiry Training: Building Skills for Autonomous Discovery," in *Merrill-Palmer Quarterly of Behavior and Development* 7 (March, 1963), pp. 147-169, and Richard Suchman, *Idea Book for Geological Inquiry* (Monroe, N.Y.: Trillium Press, 1981).

neously but independently can compare research methodology and research results, giving them some external insight into the credibility of their work.[182]

As with any teaching procedure, the religious educator needs to be highly attuned to the cognitive ability of the learners involved. Younger learners will need much more supervision and relatively simple problems to investigate. Yet with proper preparation and guidance, there are few limits on the ages appropriate for the inquiry training procedure. With varying degrees of supervision and sophistication, virtually any person can be led to understand, appreciate, and experience the scientific process. This procedure is quite useful for adults, for example, to test out some of their presuppositions and to find some evidence as to why they may need to change their minds about a particular issue.

A difficulty for religious educators new to the role of scientist in utilizing the inquiry training procedure is finding, or helping learners to find, a problem in the purview of religious education that is amenable to hypothesizing and testing. It is precisely at this point that the integration and complementarity of science and religion becomes the focus for the religious educator. The religious educator must understand the substantive content of religion to be of such a nature that it can be hypothesized and tested, and only then can the scientific process and the role of scientist become of value to the religious educator.[183] A scientific process that has no variables to test and no hypothesis to confirm of disconfirm is an empty shell appropriated for use in a foreign environment. For some religious educators, then, the initial task is to rethink what religion and religious education are all about in order that the variables within them can be operationalized and tested. Another difficulty is the religious educator who does not have the skill or the interest it takes to develop clear and precise hypotheses that posit testable relations between variables in order for experiments to be conducted. The depth of commitment and the degree of applicability of the role of the scientist to the religious educator is the determinative issue at this crucial juncture.

Experiential Simulation: Scientific Experimentation

Guiding learners effectively through the process of scientific inquiry is virtually impossible if the religious educator himself or herself is not both convinced of its worth and experienced in its procedures. As with all the other experiential simulations offered in this book, what follows demands that the reader leave the world of these pages and enter the world of real live people and activity. Two kinds of suggestions are made for religious educators that have two different levels of commitment and interest in the scientific approach and its applications.

---

182. While the discussion above has been primarily concerned with a formal educational environment, this need not be the case. An informal environment can be just as effective and productive.

183. The point here is that if the religious educator sees the content of religious education to be only information-based, then experimentation seems out of place. The problem, then, becomes a misunderstanding of what religion and religious education truly are. Cognition is a part of them, but ultimately the *whole* person—cognitively, affectively, and experientially—is the responsibility of the effective religious educator. For some evidence of this, see the discussion of the work of Rodney Stark and Charles Glock in James Michael Lee, *The Shape of Religious Instruction: A Social Science Approach* (Birmingham, Ala.: Religious Education Press, 1971, pp. 265-268.

For those religious educators with a somewhat lower level of scientific appreciation or appetite, a return to the work of James Fowler on faith development provides a safe and worthwhile introductory foray into this new environment. The earlier criticisms of Fowler's procedures could be construed as saying that Fowler's work holds little of value to religious educators. This is not true. Religious educators have much to learn from him and his type of research, and tremendous amounts of investigation remain to be done along the lines Fowler has proposed. This first suggestion for an experiential simulation is a simple one: to encourage each religious educator to conduct a faith development interview as outlined in Appendix A of *Stages of Faith*.[184] As Fowler explained in his book, the interview may take up to three hours, but with that kind of investment of time and energy you can begin to recognize the significance of what Fowler was (and still is) trying to explore. Fowler and his associates described the interview as often concluding in this way: "If you are typical of the vast majority of our adult interviewees . . . although you feel tired, you appreciate the experience of the interview. Many of our respondents follow words of appreciation with the remark, 'I never get to talk about these kinds of things.' "[185] The scientific process of interviewing and collecting data—experiencing the structure and architecture of science—is a valuable experience in and of itself, but an additional reward in this kind of interview is the chance to help someone evaluate and talk about life and faith experiences.

A second and somewhat more involved suggestion for an experiential simulation is directed at religious educators already convinced of the social-science approach to religious education and who are ready to do some independent research. For those religious educators who desire to conduct their own experiments and who want to submit to the strict standards of the scientists, the suggestion is to follow the five steps of the scientific process by finding and solving a problem of your own.[186] Rather than replicating a part of someone else's research, conduct an experiment with an original design and with different subject matter. Especially in the beginning, do not be overly concerned about the degree of sophistication of your research design. The important thing initially is for you as a religious educator to experience the role of the scientist and to think in terms of hypotheses and relationships of variables. Not only would this type of activity increase the knowledge in the field, but it would better prepare you to teach the inquiry training procedure. If you expect your learners to be able to perform scientific research, then you should be able to do the same.

Summary

This discussion of the role of the religious educator as scientist makes no claim to be either complete or exhaustive, only introductory. Hopefully, the

---

184. Fowler, *Stages of Faith*, pp. 310-312.
185. Ibid., p. 310.
186. Using an introductory text can make the process much easier and more enjoyable. For example, one that leads you step by step through the social science research process is by Dixon, Bouma, and Atkinson, *A Handbook of Social Science Research*; of a similar nature is the one by Sproull, *Handbook of Research Methods*.

subjects raised and the perspective offered have sparked sufficient interest to encourage further reading, thought, and experimentation. The role of the scientist is one of the least developed roles for religious educators, and for some religious educators is the most foreign area to explore, but it holds vast potential for significant contribution. If religious educators are to speak to the larger scientific community, and to work with it to create a more integrated and holistic worldview, then there is no other viable option than to commit to the difficult task of submitting the work of religious education to the same high standards that scientists do. The alternative is to remain isolated, to risk becoming totally irrelevant, and to support at least tacitly the dualism of science and religion.

A summary chart of the characteristics regarding the religious educator in the role of scientist follows in Figure 8.

Figure 8: The Religious Educator as Scientist	
Dimensions of the Role	Discoverer
	Theoretician
	Experimenter
	Cyberneticist
Aim	Problem Solving
Function	Experimentation
Primary Virtues	Curiosity
	Analysis
Activity	Exploring
Shadow Role	Scientist-King
Faith Tradition Resource	The Enlightenment
Historical Personage	Galileo
Contemporary Example	James Fowler
Representative Teaching Procedure	Inquiry Training
Experiential Simulation	Scientific Experimentation

Chapter Seven

The Religious Educator as Critic

The religious educator as critic initially probes the most basic and foundational issues of humanity by contemplating and analyzing them deeply and consequently makes suggestions for improvement based on this meticulous process of examination and inquiry. Two of the most important and descriptive qualities of the effective religious educator, then, must be careful listening and incisive critiquing. Personal experience with and observation of religious educators reveals these same two qualities to be largely underdeveloped and undervalued by too many practitioners in the field. Far too often the presuppositions about what religious education is, and about what the religious educator does, lead in different directions than toward this kind of careful listening or incisive critiquing related to the entire teaching/learning act. Most religious educators seem always to be so busy telling that serious and careful listening is denied the attention it deserves and to be so busy giving answers that honest and fundamental critiquing is left undone. This chapter on the religious educator as critic changes the priorities around so that foremost the religious educator is one who listens and questions. Only when religious educators are adept and practiced at listening and questioning are they ready for telling and working toward providing answers.

There are good reasons why the religious educator as critic—one who probes, contemplates, analyzes, listens, and critiques—is too rare a commodity. First, the religious educator may be perceived as an employee (a "hired hand") who is engaged primarily to impart information and to answer questions. If he or she is honest enough to admit occasionally that he or she does not know something, does not believe something, or even that a certain issue may be open to interpretation, after a while those paying the bills begin to wonder if this person is worthy of retention. The last thing most employers want to do, especially those in the church, is to pay some maverick who continually listens to the "other side" and seriously considers the questions of the "enemy." Many expect the religious educator to be the one who quiets the disorder or the disagreements rather than to be the one who stirs it up.

Second, the religious educators are like any other persons: They just want to be liked. The polite, the popular, or the prudent person steers away from controversial or unsettling topics, and the religious educator is certainly not immune to this pressure or mind-set. If people come to religion for comfort and affirmation, then confrontation or controversy is regarded as indiscreet activity, improper in the church or synagogue and deadly to the career of the religious educator.

Third, the religious educator is not often enough taught, encouraged, or expected to listen with a distinguishing ear and to question the most fundamental values. The preparation of the religious educator may indeed include training in a type of listening that leads to obedience or submission but not often enough to the kind of aggressive and involved participation that nurtures critical reflection and frank questions. More often the educational system generally, and the educational preparation of the religious educator specifically, is a listening process of hearing, receiving, memorizing, and accepting the orthodox theology, the right philosophy, and the proper methodology. The assignment is then to go and spread this "good news," which is actually little more than spreading someone else's thoughts and prejudices. It may be that a misrepresented and a distorted view of the honorable profession of the religious educator attracts those obedient souls who are satisfied with the mindless activity of dispensing approved answers, and that authoritarian educational institutions which produce this subservient kind of religious educator only exacerbate the problem.

These illustrative observations of a critic are of a sort not always deeply appreciated—especially by those members of the status quo toward whom they are usually directed. Is it any wonder that the role of the critic remains too little-known and severely undernourished in the larger realm of religious education? This chapter aims at reconsidering critical, evaluative listening and at relearning the value of serious and fundamental critiquing. It is safe to say at the beginning that the role of the critic probably differs from what many people expect of the "normal" religious educator and probably differs from what many religious educators themselves would identify as their usually practiced role. The hope is that after this examination of listening and critiquing, these activities and the role will be accepted and claimed as natural, essential, and endemic to the full identity of the religious educator.

In this chapter, the term "critic" is not used in the specialized sense of art critic, literary critic, or music critic. These are all valid types or examples of the role of critic, but a careful analysis of any or all of them would require more expertise than necessary for having a working knowledge of the general role of the critic. In discussing the complexity of modern criticism, Helen Gardner observed: "The amateur is being squeezed out in every field by the immense extensions of knowledge and of the technical means for acquiring it."[1] She upheld the place of the "amateur" in criticism and swam against the tide of increased specialities and professions. Such is the approach of this present chap-

---

1. Helen Gardner, *The Business of Criticism* (Oxford: At the Clarendon Press, 1959), p. 4.

ter. The need is not for a certain few religious educators to be full-time critics but for each one of them to become regular, functional critics—those who listen and critique—as they go about their variously assigned tasks in the field of religious education.

The requirements for the role of the religious educator as critic are simple ones, albeit qualities too rarely found: Honesty, clarity, courage, openness—and a flat refusal to be bullied. If these words are not sufficiently descriptive, then perhaps a story can explain. In this story, the role of the critic is not performed by the best educated person in the group, not the most sophisticated, and not even the most professional. In "The Emperor's New Clothes," by Hans Christian Andersen, the role of critic is played by a child. Recall how the Emperor has surrounded himself with swindlers and sycophants who have convinced the monarch that he is wearing a beautiful new suit of clothes when in reality he is totally naked. As the Emperor was parading his supposedly new finery, the story drew to a close:

> Then the Emperor walked along in the procession under the gorgeous canopy, and everybody in the streets and at the windows exclaimed, "How beautiful the Emperor's new clothes are! What a beautiful train! And they fit to perfection!" Nobody would let it appear that he could see nothing, for then he would not be fit for his post, or else he was a fool.
>
> None of the Emperor's clothes had been so successful before.
>
> "But he has got nothing on," said a little child.
>
> "Oh, listen to the innocent," said its father. And one person whispered to the other what the child had said. "He has nothing on—a child says he has nothing on!"
>
> "But he has nothing on!" at last cried all of the people.[2]

Behold! Here is the essence of the critic's role for the religious educator: To discover and to proclaim the truth to all the people if, and when, the Emperor has got nothing on!

Dimensions of the Role

How can such truth be discovered and declared? The search starts by examining four dimensions of the role of critic to gain some perspective on the role and to perceive its depth. These dimensions are not meant to be fully comprehensive but to be illustrations of the various configurations the role can assume. The four dimensions selected to introduce the role of the religious educator as critic are analyst, philosopher, debunker, and infidel. While others may prefer slightly different terminology, these seem sufficient to connect the critic's role with the work of the religious educator. Keep in mind that the plan and purpose of this chapter is to reaffirm listening and critiquing without fear of where these activities may lead, or of what results they may eventually produce.

---

2. Hans Christian Andersen, "The Emperor's New Clothes," in *Fairy Tales of Hans Christian Andersen* (New York: Orion, 1985), pp. 63-64.

Analyst

An analyst is one who makes a detailed examination of a complex problem, phenomenon, or issue by the taking into consideration as much of the relevant and available (or accessible) information as possible and seeing how the evidence fits together, with the purpose of determining the essential features and understanding them more fully. The analyst looks for meaning in the midst of data bits that may at first seem to have no relationship among them until they are combined or interpreted in a particular fashion. For example, the stories of Arthur Conan Doyle about the great fictional detective Sherlock Holmes are primarily narratives relating the steps of analysis Holmes used to reach the solutions to the crimes. By themselves, the "clues" that are offered seem to make no sense and to provide no solution whatsoever. It is not until Doyle through Holmes puts the pieces together into the proper relationship that the mystery is dispelled. Solutions arise as a result of painstaking and thorough analysis—which holds true both for detectives and for religious educators in the role of critic.

A good paradigm for the critic as analyst is found in the work of Lewis Mumford (1895-1990). Mumford himself virtually defies categorization or designation, coming close to achieving the "Renaissance man" ideal of knowing a lot about a tremendous number of subjects, as even a quick survey of his voluminous writings will reveal.[3] Probably the best label for him, though, is that of the social critic, which he exemplified by being the careful and scholarly analyst. The perusal of one of his many works, *The City in History*,[4] supplies the model for the conduct of effective analysis and for the critique which is then made possible. Such a model is instructive to the religious educator who also wishes or needs to engage in analysis and the resultant critique.

A chief value in studying Mumford's book and his method of critique is realizing that he simply did not rail against the modern city, complain about its problems, and moan about its future destructive influence on human civilization; instead, he first provided a sweeping history of the development of the city and its role and influence on human life based on serious and careful analysis. Only then did he venture into criticisms of the modern city—which were then based upon a solid historical and contextual understanding. He explained in the first one of his books on the city: "If we would lay a new foundation for urban life, we must understand the historic nature of the city, and distinguish between its original functions, those that have emerged from it, and those that may still be called forth.

---

3. For example, see this sampling of other books by Lewis Mumford: *Faith for Living* (Harcourt, Brace, 1940); *Values for Survival: Essays, Addresses and Letters on Politics and Education* (Harcourt, Brace, 1946); *The Conduct of Life* (Harcourt, Brace, 1951); *Art and Technics* (New York: Columbia University Press, 1952); *Sticks and Stones: A Study of American Architecture and Civilization*, 2nd rev. ed. (New York: Dover, 1955); and *Interpretations and Forecasts: 1922-1972, Studies in Literature, History, Biography, Technics, and Contemporary Society* (New York: Harcourt Brace Jovanovich, 1973).

4. Lewis Mumford, *The City in History: Its Origins, Its Transformations, and Its Prospects* (New York: Harcourt, Brace and World, 1961). A closely related earlier work, which Mumford expanded greatly to develop his 1961 book, is Lewis Mumford, *The Culture of Cities* (New York: Harcourt, Brace, 1938). Also see his *City Development: Studies in Disintegration and Renewal* (New York: Harcourt, Brace, 1945), and *The Urban Prospect* (New York: Harcourt, Brace and World, 1968).

Without a running start in history, we shall not have the momentum needed, in our consciousness, to take a sufficiently bold leap into the future; for a large part of our present plans, not least many that pride themselves on being 'advanced' or 'progressive,' are dreary mechanical caricatures of the urban and regional forms that are now potentially within our grasp."[5] Mumford was saying that to criticize the present without doing the requisite analysis of the past is not to perform as helpful critics but merely to be chronic complainers. The critic as analyst must first do the serious, hard work of analysis which permits valid and constructive critique.[6]

Mumford's *The City in History* is a representative work that takes the reader through a narrated development of the human social communities, from the archaeological findings of primitive civilizations to the present day. As Mumford said: "This book opens with a city that was, symbolically, a world: it closes with a world that has become, in many practical aspects, a city."[7] It is no narrow path that the book takes: subjects as diverse as religion, politics, agriculture, art, fashion, architecture, and economics are analyzed and then woven together in a unique and readable fashion to explain how the "megalopolis" of today has come into being. Mumford provided a purposeful, clear, scholarly, and thorough exposition of over five hundred pages before he arrived at the present, which then provided the proper context for his attempts at application, interpretation, and critique of the modern city.[8] The point is that Mumford performed the necessary historical and analytical work before he could legitimately offer criticisms and evaluation that had validity and relevance.

One other aspect of Mumford as analyst and critic is particularly important to note. He did his careful work as an analyst, and then his work of critiquing followed,[9] but he still was not finished with the book. In the final brief chapter,[10] Mumford gave his vision and hope of what the city could yet become, what he called "a fresh analysis of the role of the city as magnet, container, and transformer, in modern culture."[11] Mumford was teaching by example that the true critic does not have to be only a naysayer or a prophet of doom. The critic analyzes and then is able to offer solutions based on that information. It is not enough to be perpetually negative. It is incumbent upon the critic as analyst to utilize the data collected and occasionally at least to offer some possible solutions to the mess he or she has uncovered.

The religious educator as analyst and then as critic has much to glean from a

---

5. Mumford, *City in History*, p. 3.

6. Mumford continued: "In our attempt to achieve a better insight into the present state of the city, we must peer over the edge of the historic horizon, to detect the dim traces of still earlier structures and more primitive functions. That is our first task. But we shall not leave this trail till we have followed it forward . . . through five thousand years of recorded history, into the emerging future." Ibid., p. 4.

7. Ibid., p. xi.

8. Chapter Seventeen, "The Myth of Megalopolis," ibid., pp. 525-567, is the place where Mumford the critic—following the work of Mumford the analyst—is revealed.

9. Thus Chapter Seventeen contained these words:"In the present chapter, I propose to look more closely at some of the formidable negative aspects of metropolitan civilization." Ibid., p. 528.

10. "Retrospect and Prospect," ibid., pp. 568-576.

11. Ibid., p. 528.

skilled social critic like Lewis Mumford. The religious educator is required to do the hard work of historical research and to get a firm grasp on the problem or phenomenon being analyzed; to interpret and apply the analysis to the current situation; and to let the analysis lead into the development of alternative solutions and understandings. The religious educator need not always be negative about the future but must always be honest, clear, disciplined, and eventually constructive on the basis of solid and thoughtful analysis.

Philosopher

A role somewhat more familiar and integrated into religious education than that of the analyst, although closely related, is that of the philosopher. Like the analyst, the philosopher tries to understand as much as possible about the inner workings of human processes. More than the analyst, however, the philosopher tries to create an even larger and more integrated conceptual framework into which the analysis fits. The philosopher uses analysis in constructing a cognitive perspective that explains or refutes different truth claims.

A simple but useful working definition of philosophy is the attempt to think rationally and critically about the most fundamental questions of human existence.[12] One value of this definition is that it points to the prominence of thinking in philosophy. Philosophy can be described in no other way than as pure cognitive activity, what has been called "thought thinking upon itself." This disturbs superficial persons who are interested *only* in visible and immediate displays of behavior, but a philosopher warns that acting without deep and careful forethought can be foolish and dangerous. The second value recognizes the kind of thinking done by the philosopher. Philosophical thinking is both rational and critical, meaning that reason, logic, and evaluation are given high priorities in order to "eradicate from our perspectives every taint and vestige of ignorance, superstition, prejudice, blind acceptance of ideas, and any other form of irrationality."[13] A third value of the definition is that philosophy seeks to address "the most fundamental questions." The final form of these questions is by no means ever certain, but generally philosophers work with the following types of questions: What is the basic structure of existence (ontology)? What is the validity of what we know (epistemology)? What is beauty (aesthetics)? What is right (ethics)? What is the basis of value (axiology)? This is to say that philosophers do indeed ask the most fundamental, if not the most difficult, questions.

On the whole, religious educators are not generally opposed to philosophical inquiry. They just tend not to see the necessary relationships between the fundamental questions and what they actually do,[14] therefore preferring to leave such philosophizing to someone else who has the time, the interest, and the

---

12. A similar definition of philosophy that I have modified to be more inclusive and accurate is "the attempt to think rationally and critically about the most important questions." See Ed. L. Miller, *Questions That Matter: An Invitation to Philosophy*, 2nd ed. (New York: McGraw-Hill, 1987), p. 14.

13. Ibid., p. 8.

14. For examples of this kind of religious education, see the two companion volumes by Howard Hancher, *Creative Christian Education: Teaching the Bible Through the Church Year* (Wilton, Conn.: Morehouse-Barlow, 1986), and *Christian Education Made Easy: Strategies and Teaching Aids to Building a Strong Program in Any Size Church* (Harrisburg, Pa.: Morehouse, 1989).

ability. Religious educators are infamous for needing and demanding activity—and not necessarily the cognitive kind. Rather than to ask the type of philosophical questions posed in the above paragraph, the religious educator is more inclined to ask: "How do I do it?" "How will this help me teach three-year-olds?" "Does this really work in the classroom?" These religious educators have not been taught or encouraged to link up their methodology with the fundamental questions and as a result have a false sense of philosophy and of practicality. Such religious educators tend to emphasize what they call the "practical" side of life, apparently devaluing the philosophical side, captured by the old adage: "*Philosophia panem non torrit*" ("philosophy bakes no bread"). Philosophers could retort with another well-known saying of their own: ὁ δὲ ἀνεξέταστος βίος οὐ βιωτὸς ἀνθρώπῳ("For man, the unexamined life is not worth living").

The primary objection against making philosophical inquiry into religion and religious education is that, aside from taking away too much valuable time from activity, it seems only to disturb and confuse the "thinker." This implies that after hard consideration, some if not all of the truth claims of religion are first questioned and then thrown out. In other words, the presumption is that if people think too much and too hard, they will lose their faith.[15] That people discard some beliefs and practices after careful critiquing does sometimes happen. Listen to the words of one philosopher—and critic—who did think deeply about the claims of Christianity (and of religion in general) and to his conclusions about what humans should do: "We want to stand upon our own feet and look fair and square at the world—its good facts, its bad facts, its beauties, and its ugliness; see the world as it is and not be afraid of it. Conquer the world by intelligence and not merely by being slavishly subdued by the terror that comes from it. The whole conception of God is a conception derived from the ancient Oriental despotisms. It is a conception quite unworthy of free men. When you hear people in church debasing themselves and saying that they are miserable sinners, and all the rest of it, it seems contemptible and not worthy of self-respecting human beings. We ought to stand up and look the world frankly in the face. We ought to make the best we can of the world. . . . A good world needs knowledge, kindliness, and courage; it does not need a regretful hankering after the past or a fettering of the free intelligence by the words uttered long ago by ignorant men. It needs a fearless outlook and a free intelligence."[16]

Is such a refusal of Christianity a fatal or devastating blow to either Christianity or to the whole of religion? Certainly not. It is simply the result of one person's critical analysis. It is the price that must be paid for encouraging philosophical inquiry, which means that in the end not everyone will come to share one particular point of view and therefore not everyone will agree.

In summary, what is to be feared from the critical and rational thought of the philosopher? If the fear is that the truth claims of religion are too tenuous to survive scrutiny, then there is all the more reason for close examination of them.

---

15. In this context, "to lose one's faith" really only means "to change one's mind."

16. Bertrand Russell, "Why I Am Not a Christian," in *Why I Am Not a Christian and Other Essays*, ed. Paul Edwards (New York: Simon & Schuster, 1957), p. 23.

If the fear is that people will "think too much," the fear is groundless. Thinking too much—at least too deeply—cannot be done.[17] If the fear is that people may disagree, change their minds, and come up with a new configuration of their faith, then this possibility is well-grounded but nothing to be feared. This is to be welcomed, encouraged, and celebrated: It is the difference between authoritarian religious training and genuine religious education! Religious educators need to hear from the philosophers; they themselves need to be philosophers; and they need to produce other philosophers. There is always room in religious education for more rational and critical thought—especially in view of the following dimension of the role of critic.

Debunker

One of the great tragedies of religion is the existence if not the omnipresence of the charlatans who corrupt the good news to humankind into good news only for themselves, whether for personal, financial, or ideological gain. Christianity has had no lock on such manipulators, but it has dealt with it in some form of it or another from the very beginning. The temptations of Jesus recorded in the gospels were opportunities for exchanging integrity for material or personal gain.[18] The early church confronted the problem, as related in the strange story of Ananias and Sapphira in the Book of Acts which related the misuse of funds and false pretense of piety.[19] The Apostle Paul got himself and Silas thrown into prison for silencing a slave-girl who had a "spirit of divination," and who when freed of the "spirit" was no longer able to make money for her masters.[20] Even the Protestant Reformation inaugurated by Martin Luther was influenced by the financially profiteering monk John Tetzel, who disgusted Luther[21] with his searing jingle:

As soon as the coin in the coffer rings,
The soul from purgatory springs.[22]

These random illustrations from the history of the Christian church only acknowledge the inevitability of the intrusion of the shyster and the huckster into all of religion.

The demand for the religious educator is not only to be an analyst and a philosopher but to combine these dimensions into the further dimension of the

---

17. One potential problem here is a person who only thinks and never puts any action to those thoughts. This is the shadow role of the daydreamer, discussed in Chapter Ten, "The Religious Educator as Visionary."

18. See, for example, Matthew 4:1-11.

19. Acts 5:1-11.

20. Acts 16:16-24.

21. Luther called Tetzel "impudent" and "ranting," giving some idea of his distaste for the monk. See "Recollection of the Conflict with Tetzel," No. 4446, March 25, 1539, in *Table Talk*, Vol. 54 of *Luther's Works*, ed. and trans. Theodore G. Tappert (Philadelphia: Fortress, 1967), pp. 341-342.

22. Roland Bainton, *Here I Stand: A Life of Martin Luther* (Nashville: Abingdon, 1950), p. 78.

debunker.[23] A debunker is an iconoclast who exposes the shams, the exaggerations, the pretensions, and the fakeries of those supposed authorities who are only out to fool the public. The little boy in the story of the Emperor's new clothes was not only a critic, but was also a debunker—someone who revealed the foolishness of the Emperor's parading for what it was. The true religious educator must occasionally accept the difficult and distasteful task of exposing the outright impostor. There is a difference between fostering free and creative thinking and allowing the wolves to capture and devour the sheep. The religious educator must at times help the vulnerable see through the ploys of the predators.

Some would object that such a dimension limits the freedom of the individual to choose. The goal of the debunker is not to deny the right of persons to follow whomever or whatever they choose. The religious educator in this role does not seek to think for the learners, or to make learners' thought patterns conform exactly to his or her own. The religious educator does, however, have responsibility for demonstrating and modeling the skills of discernment and careful decision making. The simple analogy of learning to write makes the point. The educator teaches the skills of making the letters properly and legibly, so that the learner can begin the written communication process. The educator insists on continued practice until the skills of writing are natural and free-flowing. The educator does not, however, dictate the content that must be written for the rest of the learner's life. The person is finally left to do his or her compositions and creations. The religious educator is in a similar position. The religious educator teaches decision making, and is present while it is initially experienced to ensure that the skill has been adequately acquired. Eventually, however, individuals must make their own decisions and live with the consequences—independent of religious educators and their particular values or opinions.

Modern society has such people as James Randi ("The Amazing Randi") who keep alive the activity of debunking the religious fakers.[24] James Randi is an entertainer and "conjurer," which he defined as "one who gives the impression of performing acts of magic by using deception.[25] Randi, in other words, is a magician, who does tricks (feats of magic) by diverting attention and by sleight of hand—not by invocation of the supernatural. Certainly not a man with a need to convince people of the veracity of religion (Randi has called himself an agnostic[26]), he instead exposes the psychics, mentalists, and faith-healers for the "conjurers" they are. Randi and a team of compatriots regularly disguise themselves and attend the various shows or services, disrupting the performances by revealing the underlying trickery involved.[27] Randi, incidentally, has

---

23. My apologies for the use of a colloquialism like the term "debunker," but no other word seems to impart the emotional impact of this one.

24. James Randi is, among other things, a professional magician, so he is not in the business of debunking, or giving away the secrets, of his fellow magicians. He is a debunker of those who use the same tricks but say that they are calling on the power of the divine—the religious fakers.

25. James Randi, *The Truth About Uri Geller* (Buffalo: Prometheus Books, 1982), p. 11.

26. Ibid., p. 303.

27. For a full explanation of his exploits, see James Randi, *The Faith-Healers* (Buffalo: Prometheus Books, 1987).

learned to perform the same tricks as the so-called "faith healers" but without depending on "supernatural" powers derived from heaven, hell, or outer space.

Religious educators need not become professional debunkers like James Randi, but each one does need to foster the same healthy skepticism: They must be prepared to speak out when "the Emperor has got nothing on." Each one needs to be able to sort out the genuine and the honest from the false and the dishonest and to foster that same ability in those they teach. The obvious problem is where and how to draw the line. If I draw the line to include those you accept as genuine, then there is no difficulty. If I draw the line so that those you accept are excluded, then you will put me in the category which is the subject of the next section.

Infidel

Technically, an infidel is one who does not accept, and denies the fundamental basis of, a generally held belief, doctrine, or faith tradition. An infidel, in fact, actually holds another fundamental position that is an outright challenge to the one predominantly held by the majority or the orthodox and uses his or her position to critique the status quo. The infidel may indeed be an "unbeliever" who denies holding any particular religious faith, but more likely an infidel is someone who does not hold a specific religious tenet that another party deems necessary and essential. "Infidel," then, is normally a pejorative term used to describe a person with whom one disagrees and who is believed to hold inadequate, unorthodox, or false beliefs. Rarely do individuals call themselves infidels, since the beliefs they hold are perfectly acceptable—to them.

There are times, admittedly rare, that religious educators need to so fulfill the role of critic that they will be labeled as infidels. This is not a request for anyone to "deny the faith," or to reject any particular doctrine but an observation that each religious educator doing his or her own, independent, rational, critical thinking will inevitably lead one to wander into areas of disagreement with those who will then think them to be infidels. If religious educators faithfully fulfill the dimensions of the analyst, the philosopher, and the debunker, then there may well be instances when certain dogmas or practices are no longer acceptable. Each must be prepared to go his or her own way in these situations and live with the label others will use. The basic issue is one of integrity and courage, where religious educators are committed to standing by what they come to see as truth—or more dangerously what is seen as untruth—as a result of the critical endeavors. If others brand such a stance as that of an infidel, then so be it.

In the larger scheme of things, hopefully there will be relatively few times in a person's life when he or she is put in such a precarious position. Particularly for paid professional religionists, only a limited amount of "coloring outside the lines" is possible before one tends to lose credibility—and employment. Each individual has to decide when and for what the risks are worth taking. Beyond how those specific decisions work themselves out, though, is the deep and unshakable commitment to remain true to oneself in full recognition of the consequences.

One person who lived life this way was Clarence Darrow, certainly not an oft-referenced figure in regard to religious education. While it would be misleading to claim him as a religious educator, at least he illustrates one who was willing to accept the label of "infidel" in cases where he thought the cause justified the abuse. Lincoln Steffens called Darrow "the attorney for the damned" because he took so many seemingly hopeless—and highly unpopular—cases.[28] Whether against vengeance, against prejudice, against privilege, or for (at least his own version of) justice,[29] Darrow always seemed able to summon the necessary courage to take the position of the "infidel" and plead the cause with passion and power. Even when he lost the decision, he had given the alternative view an open hearing.

The most famous "loss" of Darrow's was the Scopes evolution trial held in Dayton, Tennessee, in the summer of 1925. Darrow came to be known nationwide as an "infidel" for his support and defense of Thomas Scopes, who was accused of teaching evolution illegally (according to Tennessee state law). The loss came about as the result of a request by Darrow himself, so that he could appeal to a higher court the constitutionality of the anti-evolution law.[30] Indeed, the famous examination of William Jennings Bryan by Darrow was eventually stricken from the court records, but it continues to live in an assortment of transcripts.[31] On the face of it, Darrow lost his most important case. The actuality was that few took the fundamentalist views of Bryan—which had a huge following at the time—seriously after Darrow's "surgery" of the fallacious logic upon which it was built.[32] Oddly enough, such foolishness has reappeared in our time, now thinly disguised under such pseudoscientific terminology as "creationism." Current society desperately needs those persons today who will fulfill Darrow's role!

At times it is appropriate if not essential that religious educators take up the unpopular cause or side and make it their own. Each one must decide when those times are and what the issues involve. If the cause is right, it is worth the risk of being called an infidel. Anything less is a surrender of integrity, and ultimately of personhood.

Summary

The dimensions of the role of critic have been purviewed in an introductory fashion as analyst, philosopher, debunker, and infidel. In most instances, these are not dimensions often associated with the religious educator. Because these dimensions are descriptive of the role of the critic, this role itself is not one frequently seen as normative for the religious educator. One of the goals of this chapter is to make the role of critic for the religious educator more visible. Although such a role may never dominate the identity of the religious educator, it should

---

28. See *Attorney for the Damned*, ed. Arthur Weinberg (New York: Simon and Schuster, 1957), p. xv.

29. These are the divisions used to present the transcripts of the various court actions Darrow was involved in, as given in *Attorney for the Damned*.

30. On appeal, the Tennessee Supreme Court did overturn the lower court's decision on a technical point.

31. One source is in *Attorney for the Damned*, pp. 174-228.

32. Tragically, but as some would say, symbolically, Bryan died a few days after the close of the Scopes trial.

permeate and influence to some degree every act that the religious educator is called upon to perform.

Aim: Awareness

The aim of the religious educator as critic is to increase awareness of the basic, fundamental issues. As simple as this is to state, it is not so simple to accomplish for at least two reasons. First the critic must gain the requisite awareness, and second, the critic must try to help others become aware. Neither of these is easy or automatic, and quite often those that are unaware remain blissfully so. Anger, disbelief, and outrage can result when the critic announces the unwelcome news that "the Emperor has got nothing on." Not everyone welcomes the burden and responsibility brought on by the arrival of awareness.

The honesty and the simplicity of the child in "The Emperor's New Clothes" was an outgrowth of the child's awareness to the real world. In adulthood, this tends to be called naiveté or a lack of social grace. It may be that adults need to cultivate the openness and the sincerity that is so natural in childhood. Rachel Carson, in a book published posthumously, wrote the following reflections on children: "A child's world is fresh and new and beautiful, full of wonder and excitement. It is our misfortune that for most of us that clear-eyed vision, that true instinct for what is beautiful and awe-inspiring, is dimmed and even lost before we reach adulthood. If I had influence with the good fairy who is supposed to preside over the christening of all children I should ask that her gift to each child in the world be *a sense of wonder* so indestructible that it would last throughout life, as *an unfailing antidote against boredom and disenchantments of later years*, the sterile preoccupation with things that are artificial, the alienation from the sources of our strength."[33] Here was Rachel Carson's description of awareness: An inborn but fragile sense of wonder that serves as an antidote for the blight of unawareness.

In what was probably her best-known book, *Silent Spring*, Carson began with a "fable for tomorrow" in which she described "a town in the heart of America where all of life seemed to live in harmony with all its surroundings."[34] Then one spring, things were different: "There was a strange stillness. The birds, for instance—where had they gone?"[35] No chickens were hatched, no streams had fish, no trees had leaves. The reason: "No witchcraft, no enemy action had silenced the rebirth of new life in this stricken world. The people had done it themselves."[36] With this dramatic story, Carson introduced the issue of the dangers of pesticides specifically, but more generally the threatened state of the environment as well. Much of the current ecological awareness probably stems from this popular book, and Carson caught the attention of the nation. Carson sensitized her readers by being a critic, but in an unusual fashion. She made them aware through silence: Of what did not, or may not, exist. The critic need not always

---

33. Rachel Carson, *The Sense of Wonder* (New York: Harper & Row, 1965). The emphases are added.

34. Rachel Carson, *Silent Spring* (Boston: Houghton Mifflin, 1962), p. 1.

35. Ibid., p. 2.

36. Ibid., p. 3.

be the obnoxious evangelist who forces knowledge into the public arena. The critic may create awareness by paying attention to such subtleties as "what has already silenced the voices of spring in countless towns in America."[37]

Alice Miller took a similar path to creating awareness, in that she too emphasized silence, but a very different kind of silence from that described by Carson. This silence is just as destructive as the ecological silence, but what it destroys is the core of humanness—the silence imposed on children by adults through the pedagogical commandment of "thou shalt not be aware."[38] In a book by that title, Miller illustrated how children are "taught" to be unaware of their feelings and personal desires and to accept the answers of adults without question. A silence created for the convenience and protection of adults, it is a silence destructive to the development of children, and a threat to the generations that follow. In Miller's view: "Our whole system of raising and educating children provides the power-hungry with a ready-made network they can use to reach the destination of their choice. They need only to push the buttons that parents and educators have already installed."[39] Miller called this conspiracy of silence a form of child abuse, all the more damaging because it is ignored—and thereby tacitly endorsed—by society at large, to the eternal harm of children. Miller's aim was to bring the "unawareness" into awareness and the unspoken into words so that this "realization [would] force us to revise the pedagogical ideology handed down to us, even though it has been venerated for thousands of years."[40] Here was a critic who demonstrated that the essence of her task was to create awareness, accomplished by both noting the silence and working to overcome it.

The religious educators seem especially susceptible to subscribing to the mind-numbing commandment of "thou shalt not be aware," because of the temptation to think that the religious education they perform and propagate is impeccable and infallible. Such a delusion is dangerous for all concerned. Some form of authority[41] continually seems to state or imply "thus far and no farther" concerning certain questions and answers. Believe this, and not that, because this is orthodoxy, and that is heresy. Religious educators often get caught in a double-bind. Not only are many religious educators initially instructed as to what is orthodox and what is heretical, but then they are expected to see that this kind of "right thinking" is instilled and reproduced in the next generation in approved fashion. Religious educators are too often taught *not* to be aware (not to question) and then they return the favor by teaching others not to be aware. The critic, who listens carefully and questions incessantly, is obviously not a welcome figure in a world where "unawareness" is considered normal, expected, and prized. The cry of "But the Emperor has got nothing on!" shatters the silence.

---

37. Ibid.
38. This is the title of Miller's book. See Alice Miller, *Thou Shalt Not Be Aware: Society's Betrayal of the Child* (New York: New American Library, 1984).
39. Ibid., p. 20.
40. Ibid., p. 35.
41. These authorities (authoritarians) can be on the theological far right or the theological far left, just as easily as they can be on the political far right or the political far left. By being somewhere in the middle, one can get squashed from either direction—or both—and it can be just as painful and as damaging.

The religious educator in the role of the critic, then, is one who creates and nourishes awareness, which means that first the religious educator must be aware. How is this awareness born? While there may not be a full answer to the somewhat mysterious "dawning of awareness," this "how" is at least the subject of the next section.

Function: Investigation

The direct means for achieving awareness of the fundamental issues is through investigation—the detailed, exhaustive, and probing examination of the evidence or of the available data for the purpose of gaining a fuller and more complete understanding of the issues or phenomena. Awareness need not only come indirectly, in a brief flash of insight, since that kind of experience is serendipitous and beyond human control. Most of the time people do not have the luxury of waiting for a revelation to hit like a bolt of lightning, so they need to pursue the demanding, meticulous, and sometimes tedious work of investigation, which will eventually provide them with the desired sense of awareness that is so important and central to the work of the critic. Investigating is much like what Thomas Edison is supposed to have said about inventing—it is 1 percent inspiration and 99 percent perspiration. The investigatory process involves two interacting components: observation and inquiry.

One aspect of investigation is observation. Observation may seem an odd thing to point out as important, since one may assume that it is seeing—a natural activity that is done without training. Observation, though, is more than just "seeing." It is taking notice and paying careful attention to all that one sees and then giving it critical thought and consideration.[42] A person who has raised observation to an art form as well as a career is Alvin Toffler. Ostensibly called by some as a "futurist," Toffler is in reality someone who is describing changes that are going on today,[43] which he determines as a result of careful observation. He is interested in the future and makes predictions about it, but these predictions are not based on astrological charts or tarot cards. They are based on what trends and currents he notes in the present. Toffler does not have a crystal ball that permits him to know any more about the future than anyone else does, but what he does have is keen observational powers.[44]

---

42. See a similar definition in Millie Almy and Celia Genishi, *Ways of Studying Children: An Observational Manual for Early Childhood Teachers*, rev. ed. (New York: Teachers College Press, 1979), p. 21.

43. For example, Toffler began the immensely popular book *Future Shock* this way: "This book is about what happens to people when they are overwhelmed by change. It is about the ways in which we adapt—or fail to adapt—to the future." Alvin Toffler, *Future Shock* (New York: Bantam Books, 1970), p. 1.

44. Toffler has a trilogy of books, beginning with the aforementioned *Future Shock*, and then including his *The Third Wave* (New York: William Morrow, 1980) as well as *Powershift: Knowledge, Wealth, and Violence at the Edge of the 21st Century* (New York: Bantam Books, 1990). Toffler gave this brief summary of the trilogy: "Thus *Future Shock* looks at the process of change—how change affects people and organizations. *The Third Wave* focuses on the directions of change—where today's changes are taking us. *Powershift* deals with the control of changes still to come—who will shape them and how." Toffler, *Powershift*, p. xix.

Religious educators must develop and learn to trust their own observational abilities to ensure that they are not seeing only what appears to be true, or what they have been instructed or taught to see by some expert or authority. To become aware is to learn the discipline of sharp and alert observation. To teach awareness is to encourage "critical seeing," since it may be that no one can truly "teach" anyone else to see or observe. Therefore, if religious educators observe in the role of critic that "the Emperor has got nothing on," then they must not be intimidated into believing that he does, and they must not be so dishonest as to teach that he does. Observing is not blindly believing, but truly seeing.

Observation alone, though, is insufficient to explain investigation. Another of the elements inseparably linked to investigation is rigorous and systematic inquiry. It is this activity that keeps the critic from being someone who only speaks off the cuff, with no substantial grounding or backing to what he or she is saying. Investigation through hard-nosed research and examination provides that essential foundation the critic needs in order to be taken seriously. An example of a critic who first does the requisite probing inquiries before going public with his complaints is the consumer advocate Ralph Nader and his group of researchers ("Nader's raiders"). Probably few people in the United States in the latter part of the twentieth century have been more vocal, more effective, and more productive in getting their criticisms noticed than Ralph Nader,[45] and the primary reason is that he and his associates are at least perceived as having done their homework thoroughly, presenting the results of their investigative inquiries to the public in the form of narrative reports with documentation and accumulated evidence.[46] It is much harder to ignore or refute a critic who has the evidence in hand and who makes it widely available for further scrutiny and testing.

Religious educators have no excuse for bypassing the tough effort involved in inquiry. Research, study, experimentation, and data gathering are as essential to the religious educator in the role of critic as to the consumer advocate. The critic cannot simply stand and say whatever comes to mind without proper support, for there is no need to heed the cry of one who shouts "Wolf!" if no wolf has indeed been verifiably spotted. The religious educator has hours, days, and years of hard work to do before the role of critic can be fulfilled adequately.

The function of investigation is fulfilled through the complementary efforts of attentive observation and probing inquiry.[47] This kind of work will produce the

---

45. For a review of this activity, see Robert F. Buckhorn, *Nader: The People's Lawyer* (Englewood Cliffs, N.J.: Prentice-Hall, 1972).

46. The reports from Nader are many, covering a diverse range of subjects. Three representative examples are Ralph Nader's Study Group Report on Nursing Homes, *Old Age: The Last Segregation*, Claire Townsend, project director (New York: Grossman Publishers, 1971); Ralph Nader's Study Group Report on the National Institute of Mental Health, *The Madness Establishment*, Franklin D. Chu, project director and co-author and Sharland Trotter, co-author (New York: Grossman Publishers, 1974); and The Ralph Nader Report on the Educational Testing Service, by Allan Nairn and Associates, *The Reign of ETS: The Corporation That Makes Up Minds*, private printing by Ralph Nader, 1980.

47. To connect observation with inquiry, this quote from the third volume of Alvin Toffler's trilogy is instructive: "While each of the works in the trilogy is built on a model different from, but compatible with, the others, all the books draw on documentation, research, and reportage from many disparate fields and many different countries." Toffler, *Powershift*, p. xxi.

desired goal of awareness. If religious educators expend the required 99 percent of perspiration through aggressive and tangible investigation, the 1 percent of inspiration will take care of itself—as will the valued dawning of awareness that eventually results from the investment of energy and devotion to the task.

Primary Virtues: Skepticism and Evaluation

Each role in this book on the religious educator is examined in part by highlighting two primary virtues that the particular role exemplifies. Generally, the primary virtues sections of each chapter are the least controversial and the least threatening topics considered within the chapter. As could be expected from the role of the critic, the virtues proposed in this chapter are both potentially controversial and threatening to at least some religious educators who are not comfortable with the role of critic. Of course, raising such controversy and threat in this context is the whole point. Any discussion of the role of critic that did not include the possibility of controversy or threat would be unworthy of the critic!

The first virtue is skepticism, which means a fairly pervasive attitude of doubt, or a disposition of incredulity, toward virtually any sort of imputed authority or a dogma that expects acceptance without inquiry or evaluation. Skepticism involves taking an initial inclination toward agnosticism (not necessarily of rejection) of a particular belief—until or unless it can be proven worthy of adoption. Simply put, it is the stance of being open-minded, and tough-minded, enough to tolerate some ambiguity until a degree of reliability can be ascertained. Such a virtue needs to be handled with some care, but not for reasons of controversy or threat. It needs circumspection because it can mean much more, and demand much more attention, than what is intended in this discussion. Skepticism as a philosophical system is not what is being proposed. There is a long and honored tradition of philosophical skepticism that runs from the ancient Greeks to modern-day existentialists.[48] In addition is the danger of pressing skepticism too far, toward absoluteness. Here, if you accept the position of skepticism absolutely (say, if you are absolutely certain that there is nothing absolutely certain), then you can no longer be a skeptic. Ed Miller stated the dilemma this way: "If absolute skepticism is *true*, then it must be *false*!"[49]

The virtue of skepticism can be perceived in a more commonsense way, as the balancing end of a continuum with faith on the other end. In this approach, skepticism and faith are not to be taken as antithetical, but as complementary and contributory to each other. As pointed out in the paragraph above, it is very difficult to deny believing *everything*, since such a statement reveals a degree of faith itself. Skepticism in this section simply means an attitude of doubting and inquir-

---

48. I am not without sympathy for this philosophical axis, but the technical use of the term is not what I wish to explore presently. For some introduction to this philosophical position, see Miller, *Questions That Matter*, pp. 185-200; Franklin L. Baumer, *Religion and the Rise of Skepticism* (New York: Harcourt, Brace, 1960); Richard H. Popkin, T*he History of Skepticism from Erasmus to Descartes* (Assen, Netherlands: Koninklijke Van Gorcum, 1960); and E.D. Klemke, A. David Kline, and Robert Hollinger, eds., *Philosophy: The Basic Issues*, 2nd ed (New York: St. Martin's Press, 1986), pp. 30-45.

49. Miller, *Questions That Matter*, p. 193.

ing in the midst of trusting and believing. It is meant to be an antidote to mindlessness or gullibility, as an intentional effort to suspend full and final judgment. How can this be seen as opposed to faith? Without some measure of doubt or uncertainty, faith has no meaning.

In his discussion of the terms skepticism and skeptic, Franklin Baumer noted the following: "The doubting of the skeptic is in many cases accompanied by some form of believing. Doubting, that is to say, is often only the negative side of the skeptic's mental outlook; the skeptic, paradoxical as this may sound, may be and often is a person who believes very strongly in something."[50] To embolden and expand Baumer's statement even more: A person who doubts strongly is also one who can believe strongly. In fact, to doubt may be to believe, since doubt and belief are arguably all part of the same process.[51] Faith without the possibility or chance for doubt is not faith; it may be naiveté, compliance, laziness, or stupidity, but it is not true faith. This is to say that the religious educator who wants to be a believer, or a person of faith, must be prepared to be a skeptic, as well as a nurturer of skepticism (doubting and inquiring) in those being taught. Anything less is the acceptance and the teaching of something other than genuine faith.

Suddenly, when the opportunities to doubt are presented, threatening and troublesome questions arise in the mind of the person who has never been encouraged to doubt—or possibly to believe—strongly: "Yes, but how much skepticism can I have? How much and what is proper to doubt? What are the limits? How much can I doubt and still be a member of my faith tradition?" These are not questions that anyone can answer for someone else. These are the questions of faith—and of doubt. These questions can lead, however, to another virtue also encouraged by the critic, that of evaluation.

The balancing virtue of evaluation tempers but never squelches skepticism. Evaluation permits, and actually expects, questions to arise but does not leave them hanging unattended, as skepticism alone can too often do. Evaluation can be defined as sorting out the differences between doubt and faith and then moving toward decision making. Evaluation considers, judges, compares, contrasts, and weighs truth claims, and works to be fair, honest, and objective with the information available. Evaluation suspends judgment until the larger picture comes into view, and until some determination about how all the pieces of the puzzle fit together—if they do. Evaluation does not limit skepticism, or stop it. Evaluation ensures not only that doubt will be taken seriously but also that doubt will not be an excuse to avoid doing deep thinking and making hard choices.

Evaluation combined with skepticism finds illustration in the work of Peter Abélard (Pierre du Palets, yclept Abailard, 1079-1142). Abélard is probably most remembered for his relationship with Heloise, and for the "*historia calami-*

---

50. Baumer, *Religion and the Rise of Scepticism*, p. 31.

51. Paul Tillich spoke of doubt this way: "Where there is daring and courage there is the possibility of failure. And in every act of faith this possibility is present. The risk must be taken." Paul Tillich, *The Dynamics of Faith* (New York: Harper & Row, 1957), p. 17. He also said of this kind of courageous doubt, which he called "existential doubt": "Existential doubt and faith are poles of the same reality, the state of ultimate concern." Ibid., p. 22.

tatum" that followed,[52] but the approach Abélard took in his book *Sic et Non*[53] is what demonstrates the combination of the virtues of skepticism and evaluation. *Sic et Non* was essentially one hundred fifty-eight questions or propositions regarding theology or Christian practice in which Abélard presented both pro and con arguments. He gathered the opposing positions, and their buttressing arguments, and then presented them in juxtaposition, allowing the reader to make his or her own judgments on the end result. Take the first question posed by Abélard as an example: *"Quod fides humanis rationibus non sit adstreunda et contra"* ("That faith must be supported by human reason and the contrary").[54] Not only did Abélard have the temerity to formulate both a positive and a negative argument on this topic, but merely considering the proposition that there were historic arguments for the support of faith by reason was itself explosive. Of course, it was not long before Abélard and his arguments were acceptable church doctrine (e.g., Thomas Aquinas' approach in the *Summa*), which reveals the impact a critic can have just by raising certain "touchy" issues.

The other one hundred fifty-seven questions addressed in Abélard's book were just as irritating, or just as interesting, depending on the reader's level of open-mindedness. Roger Lloyd said this of Abélard and *Sic et Non*: "In this book he stated the difficulties of biblical and doctrinal interpretation with embarrassing frankness by setting on opposite sides of the same page contradictory texts and sentences from the Bible and the Fathers. Then he stated the principles by which such apparent contradictions and difficulties might be reconciled . . . .Having given heed to all this counsel, and applied it so far as he was able, the reader must balance in his own mind the difficulties of interpretation still remaining, and take his stand with what seems to him to be the better side."[55] Here is an excellent description of how evaluation is accomplished. Two positions are laid side by side, and the reader is left to make up his or her own mind. There was a price to pay for such brashness, as Lloyd said of Abélard's work: "It was not heresy: but it was most inflammable."[56] Abélard, while famous in his day, was also a feared if not a reviled figure: "In the *Sic et Non* Abélard had, in a most devastating manner, brought the principles of dialectics to bear upon the interpretation of Scriptures. It filled all good Churchmen with horror."[57]

Although Abélard was quite circumspect in giving both sides of each argument, it does not take a lot of imagination to suppose that someone who doubted the original doctrine would be likely to go to the trouble of finding an alter-

---

52. For an interesting "inside" view of these events, see Peter Abélard, *The Story of My Misfortunes: The Autobiography of Peter Abélard*, trans. Henry Adams Bellows (Glencoe, Ill.: Free Press, 1958). This book also gives fascinating insight into Abélard's personality. There is irony in using the example of Abélard, in light of the mutilation he received, but the focus here is on his writings only. I can only hope that Abélard's misfortunes were not paradigmatic for all critics of religion!

53. See Peter Abailard, *Sic et Non: A Critical Edition*, Blanche B. Boyer and Richard McKeon, eds. (Chicago: University of Chicago Press, 1977).

54. Ibid., p. 113.

55. Roger Lloyd, *Peter Abélard: The Orthodox Rebel* (London: Latimer House Limited, 1947), p. 99.

56. Ibid., p. 100.

57. Ibid., p. 218.

native view of it. The following words from J. Ramsay McCallum spoke to this underlying issue: "Throughout the *Sic et Non* the tone of the writing is that of a thinker who is balancing divergent points of view and subtly suggesting that a further reconstruction of the matter under scrutiny is desirable. . . . No vote is cast either for one belief or the other. But the discerning reader rises from perusal, here as elsewhere, in the volume with an awakened alertness, with a sense of mind aware, like a water-diviner, of new springs beneath the contemporary surface of things."[58] Abélard is a worthy example of the demonstration of the virtues of skepticism and evaluation because of his careful, if not crafty, balancing of positions and then allowing this critical ability to awaken further possibilities.

The religious educator as critic must embody the virtues of both skepticism and evaluation, as the two virtues are part and parcel of one another. One without the other gives a distorted and inaccurate picture of the critic, and does damage to these primary virtues as well. The example of Abélard is a good reference point for the blending of both virtues, because his spirit of inquiry, questioning, curiosity, and dialectic permitted if not forced each person to make up his or her own mind. The religious educator today could not instill better virtues or hope for a better result.

Activity: Reflecting

Can you imagine a world without mirrors? Without mirrors, one would not know what he or she looks like: is my hair mussed, is my face clean, is my tie straight, is my slip showing? Admittedly, there are times when what is seen in the mirror is not what one wants to see. A true mirror reflects back the plain truth. If one does not like what is learned from this mirror, it can be accepted and the information used to improve the appearance, or one can take down the offensive mirror and buy a new one. If you look hard enough, you may be able to find a mirror that will show you what you want to see. Distorted and dishonest mirrors are available for a price.

The critic acts as a true mirror for society. The critic provides a clarifying view of persons and of what they do, reflecting back what they really look like. Without the reflections of the critic, humankind would go blindly through life, never knowing what they look like and never realizing the consequences of their actions. In other words, the critic can be a valuable source of feedback.[59]

One of the problems with this analogy is that a mirror is always objective, with no agenda and no stake in the outcome of the reflection. While the critic is by definition objective in the sense of evaluation and balance, there is no reason to believe that in reality the critic is always, if ever, driven with pure motives and a pure heart. Criticism is always going to include an element of subjectivity

---

58. J. Ramsey McCallum, *Abélard's Christian Theology* (Merrick, N.Y.: Richwood, 1976; reprint of 1948 edition), p. 106, n.1.

59. Feedback is the guidance mechanism of an open system that monitors and evaluates output and then regulates the input from the environment as well as the system's transformational activity based on that output. See Timothy Arthur Lines, *Systemic Religious Education* (Birmingham, Ala.: Religious Education Press, 1987), p. 52. A more extensive discussion of feedback and cybernetics is contained in Chapter Six, "The Religious Educator as Scientist."

and personal agenda.[60] This implies that just because someone offers criticism, and suggests or demands change, there need be no automatic acceptance of the advice without deep consideration. Critics reflect, but the reflection must itself be evaluated. The commitment to hear the critic must be genuine. The decision on whether to act upon the advice of the critic must be made carefully and judiciously. Hearing and considering the critic does not necessitate following the directions of the critic.

How does the critic act as a mirror? How does the critic produce the reflection for society? Here is the opportunity to peer into the personal activity of the critic. Ironically, the critic's prime activity is also that of reflecting. The reflection of the critic is primarily cognitive work. The critic takes an issue or an idea or a problem, turns it over and over mentally, and thinks about it from every possible perspective and angle. Based upon what is found by this personal and mental reflection, the critic is ready to show society the results of his or her reflective activity. The critic moves from personal and cognitive reflection to public and societal reflection. Neither aspect can be undervalued. The critic must do sufficient cognitive work to have authenticated and valuable criticism. When the criticism is formulated, the critic must see that it is communicated effectively. The critic, then, is responsible for both internal and external reflection.

As the critic does his or her reflecting, what are the characteristics that are requisite? At least three must be addressed. First, the critic must be skilled in the use of logic. The arguments presented must be clearly posed and artfully defended. Second, the honest critic must commit to examining the totality of the evidence available.[61] Simply giving biased and prejudiced information that only supports one predetermined position is not worthy of the true critic. All positions need to be perused, and their points given careful consideration as objectively as possible.[62] Third, the genuine critic needs to buttress his or her position with complementary sources that support him or her. The critic need not mislead people into believing that the position the critic advocates is totally new or just created. The critic should identify those resources that have been helpful to him or her in reaching conclusions, so that others can pursue and examine them as well for

---

60. The crucial issue of the grounding, or the evaluation base of the critic arises here. The person listening to the critic needs to find the basis of the critic's information. Is it simply a personal bias, a philosophical axis, an ideological attack, an empirical investigation, or a rational, logical argument? The examples of the critic given in the investigation section made their basis of evaluation known. In the case of Ralph Nader, the information is compiled and published in both statistical and in narrative form. Alvin Toffler identified his perspective of "futurism" and also documented his sources of information. The kind of critic I am trying to elevate here is one who uses a firm basis of evaluation, rather than the "arm-chair" type of yarn-spinner who speaks with no solid data to back up his or her opinions.

61. The following notes from an old-style guide on the work of the researcher elucidates this aspect of the critic's responsibility: "The researchers seek to find out about all aspects and backgrounds of his subject. He gets access to all available knowledge about it. . . . He looks for all that has been contributed. . . . Thus the researcher, when he has done his task properly, is not ignorant . . . of various little points which might invalidate the conclusions reached." George Shelton Hubbell, *Writing Documented Papers*, rev. ed. (New York: Barnes and Noble, 1946), pp. vii-viii.

62. This was the reason Abélard was used as the example in the previous section. He examined the opposing positions and presented the information so that the reader could determine the best estimate of the truth.

themselves.[63] This responsibility to document and support a position is well-known and expected in academic circles, and without it the critic is regarded as nothing more than a plagiarist or an ignoramus, unaware of the larger fields of scholarship. The critic has the same kind of incumbent responsibility to research the positions and to mark the way for others who may want to follow the journey of his or her decision making.

At the heart of the role of the critic for the religious educator is this all-important activity of reflecting. The religious educator must do some internal processing concerning the content and the practice of religious education and see the various strengths and weaknesses. It is then incumbent upon the religious educator to voice these reflections, addressing his or her particular environment in order to effect and encourage change.

All the while, the religious educator must keep in mind that some do not care for and appreciate mirrors. Some would prefer not to view themselves from different perspectives. The critic is bound to reflect, both internally and externally, but the acceptance of the criticism is beyond his or her control. The actual result may be that the old mirror is taken down and replaced by a new mirror that reflects back a prettier, albeit a distorted, picture of reality. The responsibility of the effective religious educator is to provide clear and honest reflections. Let those who choose to gaze into distorted mirrors bear the burden, and pay the price.

Shadow Role: Cynic

The greatest danger inherent to the role of the critic is that of evolving into the shadow role of the cynic. A cynic, as defined in this section,[64] is someone who at bottom expects nothing but the worst from humans, suspecting every act of kindness or generosity to be but a cover for some darker, self-promoting motive. The cynic begins to disbelieve and mistrust every attempt at sincerity, seeking the "real" reason for the person's concern or conduct. The critic spends so much time and effort in reflection and evaluation that it is quite easy to get stuck in the process of tearing down to the exclusion of building up. The critic who is locked into seeing the dark side of the issues can become convinced that either the lighter side will never appear, or that the light side does not

---

63. Neal Doubleday made this same point, again in a style guide: "The documentation allows the reader, if he wishes, to go back to the sources for himself, to see quotations in their context, to judge whether the sources have been understood and properly represented, and perhaps to follow a newly acquired interest of his own." Neal Frank Doubleday, *Writing the Research Paper*, rev. ed. (Lexington, Mass.: Heath, 1971), p. 41.

64. I am not directly referring to the philosophical Cynics of ancient Greece, of whom Donald Dudley had this to say: "The Cynics are the most characteristically Greek expression of that view of the World as Vanity Fair, and the consequent rejection of all current values, and the desire to revert to a life based on the minimum of demands." Donald Dudley, *A History of Cynicism: From Diogenes to the 6th Century A.D.* (London: Methuen, 1937), p. ix. He continued: "The conclusion of this study is that cynicism was really a phenomenon which presented itself in three not inseparable aspects—a vagrant ascetic life, an assault on all established values, and a body of literary genres particularly well-adapted to satire and popular philosophical propaganda." Ibid., pp. xi-xii. There is at least an indirect link from these Cynics to the ones I refer to above, as well as an interesting and illuminating one.

exist. The result is cynicism, which is ultimately destructive to the critic as well as to the potential contributions of the critic.

The cynic is a critic turned bitter, hopeless that the criticisms being offered will actually have any impact or will really make any difference. The tendency is to shift from giving thoughtful analysis to belittlement. A critic turned cynic becomes isolated, pessimistic, and harsh. Whatever humor arises from the cynic is twinged with anger and pain. The smile may appear, but it is a sardonic, twisted smile that displays no warmth or pleasure. In the final analysis, the cynic capitulates, asking: "Does it really matter?"

An illustrative personality for the critic turned cynic is Voltaire (François-Marie Arouet, 1694-1778). There is no doubt that Voltaire was a scathing but able critic. His powers of analysis and observation were well-developed, and his literary abilities gave him ample opportunity to be heard by the common person. The seemingly inevitable result, though, was as Kenneth Applegate put it, that "he sometimes got carried away with himself, he is *l'infant terrible*, making witticisms that have a *double entendre* or are of questionable propriety or exceed what many would consider to be the bounds of normal restraint."[65] Voltaire had a flair for making bold and outrageous statements that served a dual purpose in that they "were undoubtedly calculated to infuriate 'good' Christians while conditioning sympathetic readers to use their reason and common sense in examining Christianity and Judaism."[66]

Two examples will suffice to show both the cynicism and the style of Voltaire. They are taken from "Zapata's Questions," which Voltaire composed as an imaginary author (Zapata, professor of theology) writing to the religious authorities. In fact, these "questions" are a means of pointing to the inconsistencies and lapses of logic Voltaire believed to reside in scripture. In one, Voltaire (as Zapata) asked: "How shall I explain the law that forbids the eating of hare because 'they chew the cud, but divide not the hoof' [Deut. 14:7], whereas hares have a split hoof and are not ruminant? We have already seen that this good book has made of God a bad geographer, a bad chronologist, a bad physicist; it makes him no better a naturalist."[67] In another, Voltaire inquired about the story of Samson: "Pray tell me by what cunning did Samson capture three hundred foxes, tie them together by their tails, and attach torches to their rumps in order to set fire to the crops of the Philistines. Foxes inhabit only wooded country. There was no forest in that area, and it seems difficult enough to take three hundred live foxes and attach them by their tails. Finally it is said that he slew a thousand Philistines with a large jawbone of an ass, and that from one of the teeth of this jawbone a fountain came forth. When it comes to asses' jawbones, you owe me an explanation."[68]

It is not difficult to see how Voltaire would ruffle some feathers in his day. To so address the church authorities today would be bad enough, and the Inquisition has long since passed as a threat for us. It goes without saying that Voltaire's crit-

---

65. Kenneth W. Applegate, *Voltaire on Religion: Selected Writings* (New York: Frederick Ungar, 1974), p. 9.

66. Ibid., pp. 10-11.

67. Ibid., p. 25.

68. Ibid., p. 28.

icism had a definite bite, while his satire and sardonic wit fit rather comfortably under the characteristics of a cynic.[69]

Faith Tradition Resource: Classical Buddhism

This section on classical Buddhism is only an invitation to study Buddhism in all its complexity and nuances, and more precisely it is the recognition of one faith tradition supportive and helpful to the understanding and development of the role of critic. Buddhism certainly cannot be summarized in a few paragraphs, and these words only function as a motivator to encourage a deeper encounter with it, especially as it relates to the role of critic.

The study of Buddhism is a very real boon to understanding the role of the critic, because in many ways the Buddha himself personified the role in his own unique way. The story of the early life of the Buddha reveals that he was brought up in a sheltered and protective environment, but upon venturing outside the home he discovered the harsh realities of birth, sickness, old age, and death.[70] When he finally received his enlightenment, he remained (rather than going immediately to nirvana) to teach others both about the realities of this suffering and of how to be freed from them.[71] The Buddha did not teach followers to ignore the difficulties, nor did he explain them away.[72] In the true manner of the critic he made the problems even plainer and allowed them to be central in his teachings. He did not leave the disciples without hope or alternatives, however. He taught them, as Einosuke Akiya wrote, "in order to emancipate all mankind from the fetters of 'birth, old age, sickness, and death,' or in other words to make them happy in the truest sense of the word."[73]

The term employed here as a section heading, "classical Buddhism," refers to the birth of Buddhism from the teachings and life of this Buddha, Siddhartha Gautama (c. 563-483 B.C.E.).[74] The focus is on the founder of the faith and

---

69. While Voltaire at times certainly exemplified the cynic, it would be unfair and dishonest to leave the impression that he was nothing but a cynic. Three months before he died, Voltaire wrote a friend: "I die revering God, helping my friends, forgiving my enemies, and detesting superstition." As quoted in Lawrence F. Abbott, *Twelve Great Modernists* (New York: Doubleday, Page, 1927), p. 73.

70. See this story told, among other places, in Chapter One, "The Origin of Buddhism," by J. Barthelemy Saint-Hilaire, *Life and Legend of Buddha*, trans. Laura Ensor (Calcutta, India: Susil Gupta, 1957), pp. 1-29.

71. "It is obvious then that the objective of [the Buddha's] renouncing the secular life or his purpose of teaching as the Buddha lay in relieving people of their miseries and enabling them to attain true happiness." Einosuke Akiya, *Guide to Buddhism* (Tokyo: Seikyo Press, 1968), p. 3.

72. Alexandra David-Neal explained "four possible attitudes toward suffering: 1) the denial, in the face of all the evidence, of its existence; 2) passive resignation, the acceptance of a state of things which one considers inevitable; 3) the 'camouflage' of suffering by the help of pompous sophistries, or by gratuitously attaching to it such virtues and transcendent aims as one thinks may ennoble it or diminish its bitterness; 4) the war against suffering, accomplished by faith in the possibility of overcoming it. The fourth attitude is that adopted by Buddhism." Alexandra David-Neal, *Buddhism: Its Doctrines and Its Methods*, trans. H.N.M. Hardt and Bernard Miall (London: Bodley Head, 1977), p. 27.

73. Akiya, *Guide to Buddhism*, p. 4.

74. One book, for example, referred to this period as "Buddhism in its first phase." See David S. Noss and John B. Noss, *A History of the World's Religions*, 8th ed. (New York: Macmillan, 1990), pp. 157-166.

by-passes as much as possible the later traditions and schools that grew up around the figure of Gautama. That this could be done totally is highly doubtful, since the various traditions have deeply and indelibly influenced the known portraits of the Buddha. The difficulty encountered in trying to identify the historical Gautama is exactly the same as trying to identify the "true" historical Jesus by using the documents developed by believers to portray the figure of their belief.[75] Objectivity and "true" history concerning religious leaders like Jesus and the Buddha are not easy to find.

The title (rather than a name) of Buddha is itself a revelatory designation. It is derived from the root meaning "to awaken," so the Buddha is the "Awakened One," explained by J. Evola as "applied to one who attains the spiritual realization, likened to an 'arousing' or to an 'awakening'."[76] This reference to the founder of Buddhism has a close connection to the activity and aim of the critic, in that the critic also acts to awaken, to bring to awareness, and to reflect for the purpose of evaluation. Indeed, it was through an intense mental process of concentration that Gautama became the "Enlightened One."[77]

Parallel to the Buddha as the Enlightened One, Young Bong Oh and Sun Young Park identified the current primary goal of Buddhist education as "spiritual awakening and ultimate enlightenment."[78] The enlightenment of the Buddha was not the only enlightenment possible. The Buddha left his teachings to permit others to find their enlightenment as well, to become what Mahayana Buddhism[79] calls a Boddhisatva:[80] A "fellow-traveler-cum-guide on the road to enlightenment."[81] Oh and Park explained: "A Boddhisatva is one who explores the truth by himself and then teaches it to others while trying himself to be independent and helping others to be independent. In other words, Buddha is the ideal man in the ultimate sense, while the Boddhisatva is the ideal man in the real sense."[82]

---

75. This issue of the historical Jesus is taken up further in Chapter Thirteen, "The Religious Educator as Minister."

76. J. Evola, *The Doctrine of Awakening: A Study on the Buddhist Ascesis*, trans. H.E. Musson (London: Luzac, 1951), p. 5.

77. The Buddha is reported to have achieved Enlightenment (*bodhi*) while mediating under a fig tree.

78. Young Bong Oh and Sun Young Park, "Buddhist Education and Religious Pluralism," in *Religious Pluralism and Religious Education*, ed. Norma H. Thompson (Birmingham, Ala.: Religious Education Press, 1988), p. 250.

79. For an excellent overview of the schools and divisions that have developed in Buddhism, see H. Wolfgang Schumann, *Buddhism: An Outline of it Teachings and Schools*, trans. Georg Fenerstein (London: Rider, 1973).

80. A Boddhisatva is roughly equivalent to a saint in Christian understandings.

81. Young Bong Oh and Sun Young Park, "Buddhist Education and Religious Pluralism," in *Religious Pluralism and Religious Education*, p. 257.

82. Ibid. The term "real sense" needs a bit of explanation. As one author expressed it: "According to Buddhists, the only thing that can be regarded as real is that which is self-engendered and homogeneous, that which is a 'self' whose existence does not depend on any external cause, which nothing has begotten, and which is not constituted by the grouping of various parts of different kinds." Alexandra David-Neal, *Buddhism*, p. 137. For a helpful discussion of how insight and intuition in Buddhism are distinguished from Western concepts of insight and intuition, and for a chart on how they interrelate with the different divisions of Buddhism, see Junjiro Takakusu, *The Essentials of Buddhist Philosophy*, ed. W. T. Chan and Charles A Moore (Honolulu: University of Hawaii Press, 1947), pp. 17-19.

Revealingly, Young and Park also said: "The ideal man in Buddhism should be independent, free from every dogma and authority, even the authority of Buddha."[83] In a very real sense, these are aims and intentions familiar to every religious educator who takes the role of critic seriously, whatever the faith tradition.

In the sermon of the Four Noble Truths, Gautama taught his followers to find what he called the Middle Path. This was explained in the first few sentences of that sermon (as we have it today): "Two extremes, monks, are not to be approached by him who has withdrawn from the world. Which two? One is that which is linked and connected with lust, through sensuous pleasures. . . . The other is that which is connected with mortification and asceticism. . . . Avoiding both these extremes, monks, take the Middle Path . . . which brings insight, brings knowledge, and leads to tranquility, to full knowledge, to full enlightenment, to *Nirvana*."[84] The Buddha taught that enlightenment comes neither as a result of materialism nor of asceticism, but rather in pursuit of this Middle Path, which he went on to describe in the next paragraph of the sermon as the Noble Eightfold Path. The lesson for the critic is that the way to experience awakening is to keep the virtues of skepticism and evaluation in balance—a middle path of moderation. Neither extreme is the course of the critic. In fact, the critic is one who observes and warns when an extreme position is being perverted into a dangerous distortion.

The further dimension of the sermon instructive to the critic is that of the four noble truths themselves: Human sorrow is universal; the cause of this sorrow is greedy desire; the relief from sorrow is cessation of desire; and liberation from desire is attained by following the Eightfold Path.[85] As simple as these four truths sound, the actualization of them and the paths in which they lead are anything but simple. Gautama offered an outright challenge to much if not all of what most religious traditions consider to be sacred and untouchable. Nowhere does the Buddha talk of loving or honoring divinity. Truth is within the person, waiting to be awakened by the individual. No one else, be it Buddha, the gods, or the Boddhisatvas, can accomplish this for the person. In words and attitudes reminiscent of other critics seen throughout this chapter, the Buddha taught that each person must find his or her own way. Any other path is a delusion and only adds to human sorrow.

Gautama's final words, shrouded as they are in the mists of history, portray a critic to the end: realistic, reflective, devoid of sentimentality or romance. He is reported to have said to his disciples: "Life is transient. Strive ahead with attentiveness."[86] Could there be a more appropriate watchword spoken to the religious educator fulfilling the role of the critic?

83. Oh and Park, "Buddhist Education and Religious Pluralism," in *Religious Pluralism and Religious Education*, p. 257.

84. As quoted in Antony Fernando with Leonard Swidler, *Buddhism Made Plain: An Introduction for Christians and Jews*, rev. ed. (Maryknoll, N.Y.: Orbis, 1985), p. 18.

85. These paths are: right understanding; right thought; right speech; right action; right livelihood; right effort; right mindfulness; right concentration.

86. As quoted in Fernando, *Buddhism Made Plain*, p. 17.

Historical Personage: Socrates

Another historical figure just as enigmatic as Siddhartha Gautama, and possibly even more paradigmatic for the role of the critic, was Socrates (c. 470-399 B.C.E.). Although probably no person in the Western world is more identified with the role of the critic than Socrates, all that is actually known for certain about the historical Socrates, as Alfred Taylor noted, is that "he was put to death at Athens on a charge of impiety in the 'year of Laches' (399 B.C.[E.]). Any account . . . which goes beyond such a statement is inevitably a personal construction."[87] Socrates, for all we know, never wrote a word. All that remains of him is what others, contemporaries among them, have written about him and these accounts do not corroborate one another. Taylor suggested that the only valid sources are those who had direct knowledge of Socrates and who left a written record of him, namely Aristophanes, Plato, and Xenophon, and he himself opted for Plato's picture of Socrates.[88]

Using Plato's description of Socrates, then, is one way of focusing on this rather mythic figure. Kenneth Richmond called Socrates "the very archetype of the Wise Old Man,"[89] and Luis Navia called him "the very embodiment and personification of philosophy itself."[90] Such appellations may point more toward the *idea* of a person rather than to a real one, but Plato's Socrates can be used as the archetype, embodiment, and personification of the critic. Socrates is portrayed by Plato as constantly engaging the men and youth of Athens in dialogue, probing them with questions about the fundamental issues.[91] Socrates referred to himself as the gadfly of society and as a midwife of true knowledge. All this can be gained simply by limiting the perusal to Plato's *Apology*,[92] written with Socrates as the main character. Here Socrates was giving his self-defense at his trial where he was charged ostensibly with impiety toward the gods, with misleading and corrupting the youth, and with generally being a menace to the Athenian democracy[93]—but primarily because of his effective fulfillment of the role of critic. Socrates dug through the superficial and the

---

87. Alfred E. Taylor, *Socrates* (New York: D. Appleton, 1933), p. 1.

88. For this discussion of the "Socratic problem," see Taylor, *Socrates*, pp. 6-24. Also see the discussion of the issue in Frederick Copleston, *A History of Philosophy: Vol. 1, Greece and Rome, Part 1*, rev. ed. (Garden City, N.Y.: Image Books, 1962), pp. 120-124. Copleston added Aristotle to the list of valid commentators on Socrates.

89. W. Kenneth Richmond, *Socrates and the Western World: An Essay in the Philosophy of Education* (London: Alvin Redman, 1954), p. 7.

90. Luis E. Navia, *Socrates: The Man and His Philosophy* (Lanham, Md.: University Press of America, 1985), p. 1.

91. Michael Despland put it this way: "He [Socrates] spends his time in the public places of the city with the elite young men, discussing and questioning apparently accepted premises." Michael Despland, *The Education of Desire: Plato and the Philosophy of Religion* (Toronto: University of Toronto Press, 1985), p. 21.

92. The translation I will use in this section is the one by Benjamin Jowett in Plato, *Apology*, in *The Dialogues of Plato*, ed. Justin D. Kaplan (New York: Washington Square Press, 1950). Many other translations and editions are available, but Jowett's translation is probably the most familiar.

93. "Socrates was accused of introducing new religious observance (rather than new gods), corrupting the youth, and not accepting the gods of the city (or not giving them the customary worship)." Despland, *Education of Desire*, p. 15.

artificial, searching for the deeper and ultimate realities. Plato used Socrates as a mouthpiece in many other works,[94] but Socrates in the role of critic is sufficiently described in this one.

Early in the dialogue, Socrates dealt with the question of his own wisdom. In doing so, he told the story of his friend Chaerephon who went to the oracle at Delphi: "He asked the oracle to tell him whether any one was wiser than I [Socrates] was, and the Pythian prophetess answered, that there was no man wiser."[95] Such a response set Socrates to thinking, and his conclusion was this: "And I am called wise, for my hearers always imagine that I myself possess the wisdom which I find wanting in others: but the truth is, O men of Athens, that God only is wise; and by his answer he intends to show that the wisdom of men is worth little or nothing; he is not speaking of Socrates, he is only using my name by way of illustration, as if he said, He, O men, is the wisest, who, like Socrates, knows that his wisdom is in truth worth nothing."[96] Then Socrates gave the quintessential description of the critic's occupation: "And so I go about the world obedient to the god, and search and make enquiry into the wisdom of any one, whether citizen or stranger, who appears to be wise; and if he is not wise, then in vindication of the oracle I show him that he is not wise; and my occupation quite absorbs me, and I have no time to give either to any public matter or interest or to any concern of my own, but am in utter poverty by reason of my devotion to the god."[97]

The ideal critic believes his or her first task is to show the other that he or she is not really wise. Questions that push back the insignificant and the trivial, revealing the depths of the unknown and the unfathomed, begin to put the conversation—and the realities of life—in an entirely different context. When this change in perspective is accomplished, the rest of the critic's task comes much more easily!

Another passage from the *Apology* gave the most famous and apt description of Socrates the archetypal critic, that of the societal gadfly. In this passage, Socrates was arguing with the Athenians not to condemn him, since he was God's gift to them: "For if you kill me you will not easily find a successor to me, who, if I may use such a ludicrous figure of speech, am a sort of gadfly, given to the State by God; and the State is a great and noble steed who is tardy in his motions owing to his very size, and requires to be stirred to life. I am that gadfly which God has attached to the State, and all day long and in all places am always fastening upon you, arousing and persuading and reproaching you. You will not easily find another like me, and therefore I would advise you to spare me."[98] It is interesting that the critic here thought of himself as the gift of God, but those he was afflicting did not seem so reverential about the gift. "The

---

94. For a helpful resource that combines several of the Platonic Dialogues related to the trial and death of Socrates, as well as gives a running commentary, see Romano Guardini, *The Death of Socrates: An Interpretation of the Platonic Dialogues: Euthyphro, Apology, Crito and Phaedo,* trans. Basil Worthington (New York: Sheed and Ward, 1948).

95. Plato, *Apology,* p. 10.

96. Ibid., p. 13.

97. Ibid. Socrates was defending himself against the charge that he was teaching for profit.

98. Ibid., p. 25.

State," or any other authoritative body, is not often appreciative of the gadfly's sting.

Speciously, the stated charges against Socrates were these: "It says that Socrates is a doer of evil, who corrupts the youth; and who does not believe in the gods of the State, but has other new divinities of his own."[99] It was in reply to these charges that Socrates uttered what would become the shibboleth of educators, philosophers, and critics alike for generations to come: "The unexamined life is not worth living."[100] Yet the words immediately following that now-famous declaration explained Socrates' true difficulty with his examiners. It was (in Socrates' mind) his attitude and his recalcitrance toward compromise of the truth that was the crime: "But I had not the boldness or impudence or inclination to address you as you would have liked me to do, weeping and wailing and lamenting, and saying and doing many things which you have been accustomed to hear from others, and which, as I maintain, are unworthy of me. I thought at the time that I ought not to do anything common or mean when in danger: nor do I now repent of the style of my defence: I would rather die having spoken after my manner, than speak in your manner and live."[101] Socrates remained true to his own style—true to his own death. The one undeniable truth this critic taught was that to be a critic is dangerous and largely unappreciated work. There are easier ways to make friends and influence people.

Before leaving the personage of Socrates, it seems only fitting for Socrates to come once again under the gaze of another, more modern, critic. I.F. Stone, in his classic study of Socrates, *The Trial of Socrates*,[102] did not accept the prevalent mythology of Socrates as the paragon of virtue. His questions initially were: "How could the trial of Socrates have happened in so free a society? How could Athens have been so untrue to itself?"[103] Stone's conclusion was that the Athenians were essentially correct in their condemnation of Socrates. Socrates was so much of a troublemaker and enemy of the free state that he was expendable. The mistake they made was executing him and hence turning him into a martyr at the hands of the dramatist Plato. Stone concluded: "His [Socrates'] martyrdom, and the genius of Plato, made him a secular saint, the superior man confronting the ignorant mob with serenity and humor. This was Socrates' triumph and Plato's masterpiece. Socrates needed the hemlock, as Jesus needed the Crucifixion, to fulfill a mission. The mission left a stain forever on democracy. That remains Athens' tragic crime."[104] Here is a fascinating example of a critic examining a critic: The modern-day critic demythologizing the paradigmatic critic in a delicious turn of the critic's knife upon one of his own! This is also to say that the critic is never satisfied with the boundaries of criticism.

The religious educator as critic has much to learn form Socrates, through both positive role modeling and by warning about possible outcomes of the

---

99. Ibid., p. 15.
100. Ibid., p. 34.
101. Ibid., pp. 35-36.
102. I.F. Stone, *The Trial of Socrates* (New York: Anchor Books, 1989).
103. Ibid., p. xi.
104. Ibid., p. 230.

role. The contribution of I.F. Stone helps keep the proper perspective that the critic himself or herself is never beyond criticism.

Contemporary Example: Gabriel Moran

After looking at so many of these historical and mystical figures such as the Buddha and Socrates, it is time to consider a contemporary and very mortal religious educator: Gabriel Moran (b. 1935).[105] Moran is one of the leading figures in the field today and is considered here as one of the outstanding critics within religious education.

Moran has written so widely over such a long period of time that it is very difficult if not impossible to categorize his writings as being of any one sort.[106] He has written in such diverse areas as moral development,[107] psychological development,[108] adulthood,[109] catechesis,[110] and overall religious education concepts,[111] and this is certainly no comprehensive listing. Including all the articles he has written for journals and edited books, there has been a prodigious amount of work produced. Such an output does not bode well for the person who wants to give an encapsulated view of Moran's position, for a faithful summary of the content of Moran's work would surely demand a book of its own. The intention here focuses on his method and his approach, which have some greater common denominator throughout his writings, rather than on the content. Such an examination reveals Moran to be a contemporary example of the religious educator as critic.[112]

The plan for this section is simple. Three of Moran's more recent books[113] have been chosen to reveal his stance as a critic: *Religious Education Development,*

105. There are those would rather treat Moran more reverentially. For an example, see Padraic O'Hare, "The Concrete, the Communal and the Contribution of Gabriel Moran," *Religious Education* 70:1 (Winter, 1984), pp. 109-120. O'Hare does admit on p. 109 that the article was not intended to be a "hagiography" of Moran(!).

106. Mary Boys had a similar opinion. She wrote: "Gabriel Moran's prolific writings defy easy categorization." Mary C. Boys, *Educating in Faith: Maps and Visions* (San Francisco: Harper & Row, 1989), p. 126.

107. Gabriel Moran, *No Ladder to the Sky: Education and Morality* (San Francisco: Harper & Row, 1987).

108. Gabriel Moran, *Religious Education Development: Images of the Future* (Minneapolis: Winston, 1983).

109. Gabriel Moran, *Education Toward Adulthood* (New York: Paulist, 1979).

110. Gabriel Moran, *Catechesis of Revelation* (New York: Herder and Herder, 1966).

111. Gabriel Moran, *Interplay: A Theory of Religion and Education* (Winona, Minn.: Saint Mary's Press, 1981).

112. This designation of Moran as critic is my designation alone and does not represent some stated intention of Moran in his writings.

113. The later books of Moran have been chosen for study here, but it would be an interesting study in itself to see how Moran has changed and evolved in his positions over the years. Moran frequently has changed his mind, and the result is that his later writings occasionally contradict his earlier ones. Moran himself indicates this tendency to switch, for example, in his writings about the religious community. See Gabriel Moran, "Where Now, What Next," in *Foundations of Religious Education*, ed. Padraic O'Hare (New York: Paulist, 1978), pp. 99-102. For this reason, the present evaluation of Moran will deal primarily with his later period of writings rather than trying either to overview all of the various positions he has taken, or to indicate how and where he has changed positions over time.

No Ladder to the Sky, and *Religious Education as a Second Language.*[114]Proper understanding of Moran's message in terms of subject matter can only be achieved by reading the various books, but an appreciation for his role of critic can be attained by a brief look at a few passages from these three representative books.

Overview

The distinguishing marks of Gabriel Moran throughout his writings are first, tough and occasionally biting examples of skepticism and criticism; second, acute and detailed analysis and evaluation of language; and third, a serious and contemplative style of reflecting on the workings of religious education. These, of course, are also the necessary distinguishing marks of any religious educator performing in the role of critic. These traits can be found throughout Moran's writings, and it is not necessary to manipulate his work or to oversimplify it to see them. Virtually everything he wrote has these characteristics, but they do not produce a particularly offensive or overbearing attitude. They give the sense of a person thinking deeply, but thinking aloud.

It is important to understand this classification of Moran as a thinker, which indicates that he is neither an experimenter nor a true theoretician in any scientific sense. In none of his writings does he produce or show any real interest in empirical data or testable hypotheses. Moran is primarily a cognitivist and a rationalist—he prefers to do his work on religious education mentally and linguistically.[115] In James Michael Lee's distinctive categorizations, Moran follows a speculative approach: "The *speculative method* is that process of knowing in which phenomena are investigated and examined from a mental point of view, and are verified by the use of mentally derived and mentally validated principles. Speculation utilizes the manipulation of ideas as its virtually exclusive *modus operandi*. It relies heavily on the metaphysical rules of logic. Much of the speculation emanates from careful and systematic meditating and pondering on a problem, often in reflective awareness."[116] Such a description fits Moran's work quite satisfactorily, expressing not only what Moran does in his writings, but apparently describing how he arrives at his positions. Moran's investigations are mental ones, conducted from behind the study desk rather than in the field or in the laboratory.[117]

---

114. Gabriel Moran, *Religious Education as a Second Language* (Birmingham, Ala.: Religious Education Press, 1989).

115. It is highly appropriate and instructive, then, that probably the most comprehensive statement of his approach to religious education is *Religious Education as a Second Language.*

116. James Michael Lee, *The Shape of Religious Instruction: A Social Science Approach* (Birmingham, Ala.: Religious Education Press, 1971), p. 120. Lee went on in this passage to contrast the speculative method with the empirical method: "The *empirical method* is that process of knowing in which phenomena are investigated through procedures gained from and tested in experience. Empirical methodology is focused on the use of systematically observable, testable, and replicable procedures." Ibid., p. 121.

117. Moran has called his approach "political/aesthetic," distinguishing it from Lee's social-science approach by saying: "Theology and social sciences have definite contributions to make to Christian religious instruction. In my view, neither theology nor social science should have the right to define what constitutes the overall meaning of religious education." Gabriel Moran, "From

Moran began *Religious Education Development* with these words, giving insight into his type of approach to research: "In most of the educational world, developmental theory still seems to be a best seller. Nevertheless, I meet many colleagues these days who say they are skeptical about all theories of development. I share much of their skepticism, but I am also interested in specifying the problem as clearly as possible."[118] Here is a capsule of what Moran did best: To be skeptical, but not to stop there. He went on to try to clarify, analyze, and understand the issue from as many cognitive angles as possible. It was an interesting way to begin a book on developmental theory: To be skeptical of the idea of development from the start. It was this stance of initial skepticism, however, that gave Moran room to explore and analyze. While he was always critical, he also made the effort to escape the shadow role of the cynic—Moran was critical for the purpose of preparing the way for a possible solution.

Moran, as a representative critic, was able to ask the musing, unsettling type of questions. In *Religious Education Development*, for example, he was searching for some initial room to explore and asked: "Who assigned the course Human Development to the psychology department?"[119] A few sentences later he asked: "Why bother? Why put forth a theory of development when no one can possibly devise a theory that describes everyone's life?"[120] It seems that Moran's penchant for asking penetrating (withering?) questions such as these qualifies him for exemplifying the role of the critic, even if there were no other evidence.

Another characteristic of Moran was his critical attitude toward the field of religious education itself. In his opinion, "religious education, both as an academic field and as a functioning profession, does not yet exist."[121] His reason for writing was to set the field on a more academic footing, and to give it some greater substance. He exemplified the classic attitude of a critic toward his or her own field of work. A critic may be loyal, involved, and committed to the task at hand while realizing that the task is not yet accomplished or even properly understood. Moran was not pessimistic about the future of the field of religious education, but he was honest enough to say that he did not yet see it as fully formed.

Probably the most prominent feature of Moran's later writings has been his emphasis on the analysis and evaluation of language. More specifically, he spent much of his time defining terms. He spent pages in *Religious Education Development* defining the term development, as distinguished from such related terms as growth, evolution, and progress.[122] More pointedly, the entire second part of that book was devoted to developing a "grammar" for religious education

---

Obstacle to Modest Contributor: Theology in Religious Education," in *Religious Education and Theology*, ed. Norma H. Thompson (Birmingham, Ala.: Religious Education Press, 1982), p. 58. See also Lee's comments in *The Content of Religious Instruction*, p. 162, note 3.

118. Moran, *Religious Education Development*, p. 1.

119. Ibid., p. 5. Indicative of a speculative approach, however, is the fact that Moran did not show why human development has been placed in the psychology department. He left this kind of research undone, which may have proved to support his position—or, more likely, have uncovered a good rationale for its placement.

120. Ibid.

121. Ibid., p. 11.

122. Ibid., pp. 15-27.

and how this grammar would facilitate a theory of religious education. This theme returned in his 1989 book to reach full flower.

The role of critic was underscored in *No Ladder to the Sky*.[123] Here, as the title reveals, Moran took on the whole concept or image of psychological stage development, albeit without careful research (at least visibly documented) or empirical evidence. He stated his criticisms of stage theory more on the basis of personal opinions or observations. His thesis was that "the modern Western world is tied to the image of a ladder to the sky" which "invites us to climb upward, and in business, government, sport, or war we continue trying to climb the ladder of success in search of the good life."[124] As an alternative, Moran challenged this monolithic image and tried to suggest ways to experience "the world without having recourse to the image of a ladder to the sky."[125] His solution was to invent a "new category of writing, what I [Moran] call 'educational morality.' "[126] Moran said later that "this book is a study of morality from the perspective of education."[127] He rejected the normal categories and took it upon himself to create a more appropriate one—to his thinking. He was unwilling to accept the prevalent image in the Western world of the "ladder" and proceeded to discuss the differences and the difficulties when images and metaphors are confused. Moran the critic did not limit his criticism to religious education but to the much broader sweep of education and morality.

A further glimpse of Moran as the genteel but loyal skeptic was provided in Chapter Eight of *No Ladder to the Sky*, "Three Moral Issues."[128] In this chapter, Moran addressed three moral issues of a highly controversial nature, especially in his own context of Catholicism: birth control, care of the dying, and homosexuality. What is important is not so much the particular positions he took but that he raised these issues for discussion at all. Indeed, here is probably the key contribution that Moran, or virtually other genuine critic, can provide—emphasizing certain important issues so that they will eventually receive the focused attention they deserve.[129] In the best tradition of a critic, Moran first was concerned to increase the awareness of his readers to the problems and to encourage them to be sensitive to the issues as well as to the persons involved. His efforts, linked with the work of others, will have the long-term effect of raising these troubling and troublesome issues to fuller awareness. Over time, these observations and "troubling of the waters" will inevitably change the environment of the church and force it to confront these issues more directly in the long term.

---

123. Charles F. Melchert said in his review of this book: "Gabriel Moran is at it again. He is seeking to make us think and change our praxis by renaming what we do." See Charles F. Melchert's review in *Religious Education* 83:1 (Winter, 1988), p. 312. This is a good description of Moran's writing as a whole, incidentally.

124. Moran, *No Ladder to the Sky*, p. 3.

125. Ibid.

126. Ibid., p. 9

127. Ibid., p. 10. These quotes should give an indication of how Moran toys with terminology and definitions. One must be careful to see how he uses or interprets the individual words.

128. Ibid., pp. 117-146.

129. This raising of issues is the specialty of the critic and of the speculationist. Hopefully, careful researchers and scholars will follow soon after to provide necessary solid evidence on which to base the future decisions, as opposed to pure conjecture or mere opinion.

Religious Education as a Second Language could not have a more appropriate title. Already noted was the characteristic of Moran to spend much of his time dealing with language and meaning of words, and this book dealt with such an approach throughout. As Moran said: "This book is an answer to the question: 'What is the meaning of religious education?' "[130] Chapter One was a discussion, logically enough, of the meaning of the term "meaning." Chapter Two then gave a discussion of what the term "education" means, and so on throughout the book. It truly was an attempt to have religious education become a second but meaningful language.

Moran the reflective critic was apparent from the first words of the 1989 book, *Religious Education as a Second Language*: "This book results from thirty years of reflection."[131] Moran the tireless critic was also visible from the first: "These reflections do not constitute a complete system. . . . I feel more like a beginner who is just starting to see how the pieces fit together. I need at least another thirty years to round off my thinking."[132] What better description of the religious educator as critic at work could be devised than this: "I am reflecting on what people do and how they might better describe their efforts so that a language of religious education might have more reality than it currently has."[133]

Religious Education as a Second Language was written to clarify and unify the positions Moran had taken in previous books. One can detect Moran the critic as either feeling a bit misunderstood or his approaches being regarded as irrelevant, since he tried to explain and correct some prevalent perceptions of his work: "During the past decade I have written on various aspects of what I conceive to be the whole of religious education. When a book does not address the big picture, it may seem to some people not on the topic at all. When religion is not dealt with in the most explicit form, the author may seem to have abandoned religious education. Although nearly everything I write is intended to be part of religious education, that may not be the category which is used in publishers' lists, review journals, and people's minds. . . . The present book is an attempt to relate the themes of those [earlier] books . . . to an overall meaning of religious education."[134] Moran, performing in the role of critic, was expressing the frustration of not being heard or understood. There is something endemic to the role that seems to guarantee that this frustration will never be totally excised.

Evaluation

This section on evaluation, just as did the section on the overview, deals primarily with how effectively Moran has fulfilled the role of critic, which is necessarily different from an exhaustive evaluation of his writings and his theories. The focus is on the strengths and weaknesses of Moran from the perspective of the critic's role.

The strengths are easily detected. Moran used his ability to ask the hard questions, not just of religious education, but of society and its structures. He has been

130. Moran, *Religious Education as a Second Language*, p. 9.
131. Ibid., p. 1.
132. Ibid.
133. Ibid., pp. 8-9.
134. Ibid., pp. 4-5.

contemplative and reflective, dwelling on issues of meaning and definition to an extreme. He has been appropriately skeptical of the fields in which he has performed and has not hesitated to challenge what appears to him to have been fallacious within them. One of the interesting things about Moran and his criticisms is that he was able to offer them civilly enough that he was able to remain within his faith tradition, while at the same time refusing to accept everything within it without some deep questioning.

Also of value has been Moran's use of a broad range of sources and input regarding the discussion of religious education. He did not limit himself to the traditional understandings of religious education, or strictly to use the writings normally associated with religious education.[135] He did not allow others to draw the boundaries for him, although the price for such free ranging made it difficult to understand how it all fits together. Near the end of *Religious Education as a Second Language*, Moran noted his attempt: "The contribution of books like this one is to call for a wider conversation and demonstrate some of the steps toward actualizing the conversation."[136] Moran was relentless in pushing at the boundaries or, maybe more accurately, in struggling to redraw them.

Along with the desire to widen the horizons of religious education, and to increase the breadth of the conversations, Moran was sensitive to the dangers of non-distinct boundaries. For example, the following quote demonstrates his awareness of the difficulties in producing a truly *religious* (as distinct from a specific faith tradition's) education perspective: "As soon as one moves out of the parochial limits of one's own religion, any full-blown theory of religious education seems absurdly inadequate to the task of addressing everyone's religion and education. I stake no claim to speak authoritatively on how Hindus should practice religious education. . . . My modest hope is to approach this area in such a way that if Hindus or any other religious group wish to join the conversation, they could find their way into it."[137] Moran cannot legitimately be criticized for denying or removing all boundaries. He was searching for ways to rethink and redefine the boundaries.

Moran and his work are not above criticism, however—which only seems appropriate for one serving as a representative critic. Five areas are raised that cause particular concern. First, and most seriously, is Moran's heavy dependence on cognition. He does intellectual reflection, to be sure, but there is the danger here of never getting involved in the flow of life, or of not permitting one's writings to be influenced by the tug and pull of experience. The prime example of this tendency is the way Moran has used the analogy of second language, grammar, and conversation. All of these are verbal and rational activities, often far removed from the larger experiences of life. As Moran himself acknowledged: "Like all analogies, this one eventually limps."[138] The problem is that so

135. A good indication of Moran's eclectic tendencies is found in an earlier example of Moran's work not examined in the overview section. Refer to Gabriel Moran, *Interplay: A Theory of Religion and Education* (Winona, Minn.: Saint Mary's Press, 1981). See especially Chapter Two, "The Limits of the Past," pp. 21-36.

136. Moran, *Religious Education as a Second Language*, pp. 216-217.

137. Ibid., p. 8.

138. Ibid., p. 23.

much focus on religious education in terms of language and conversation can easily make it become a verbal and cognitive activity to the exclusion of the affective and behavioral aspects. Admittedly, Moran did acknowledge that religious education is more than this, as when he said: "Religious education has to do with the religious life of the human race and with bringing people within the influence of that life."[139] Still the problem remains of using as the primary analogy one that is verbal and cognitive. Religious education in such a schema quickly becomes identified as just another academic discipline or set of theoretical exercises, having a content separate and distinct from its process and structure. Logic chopping in religious education is not a viable substitute for a religious education which flows from life experiences and flows back again to enrich life experiences.

The second concern is the lack of depth that Moran reflects in his documentation.[140] Oddly enough, one of the strengths mentioned earlier was Moran's broad range of interests, but the concomitant problem is that he does not delve into the sources or the issues deeply enough. Part of the issue here is that, as already discussed, Moran uses the speculative method as opposed to the empirical method. The speculative method is good for conjuring up new ideas and for integrating a great amount of territory, but the difficulties arise in failing to back up those ideas with documentation and solid research and in properly treating the vast areas covered. This concern relates directly to the discussion of the critic's responsibility to be exhaustive and thorough in his or her research (as discussed under the section of this chapter on reflecting). Moran's documentation indicates that he does not seem to be fully conversant with the field of linguistics —literary linguistics, psycholinguistics, sociolinguistics, and so on. This apparent lack of awareness is damaging to Moran since he places so much emphasis on the importance of language in religious education. Furthermore, Moran's documentation hints at the strong possibility that he might not have widely read other religious educators—thus his broadside criticisms of religious education might not be adequately situated within the actuality of the field. Moran has done some of the initial necessary work in alerting religious educators to some areas which might need attention. Now some hard-core, reality-related supportive work needs to be done so that a solid footing for his armchair speculations can be put into place, allowing Moran to have a long-term impact on religious education.

The third concern is connected to the previous one. Do all of the parts of Moran's writings fit together as nicely as he has intimated that they do? Are they truly synthetic, or are there some artificial connections? Looking at the

---

139. Ibid., p. 218.
140. A perusal of the endnotes of *No Ladder to the Sky* provides sufficient illustration (pp. 183-189). The notes give reference to quotes he has made in the chapters of the book, but there are no fuller content or research guidelines there. Another random example from the same book is found on page 173 when Moran made this statement: "The physical training of the young in play as well as in work is needed for moral development." What evidence is there for this kind of generalization, or on what basis does Moran make such a statement? The statement may very well be true, but who knows whether or not it is without the proper research, support and documentation? Moran is prone to making these kinds of global but unsupported statements repeatedly.

parts of (for example) *Religion as a Second Language*, the book with the stated intention of being the one to bring some integration to his work,[141] gives more a sense of separate chapters strung together without intimate correlation to each other. This was apparently not a central concern of Moran's, since he was not seeking to build a comprehensive or consistent approach to religious education. There is still the nagging desire—on my part, at least—to feel a sense of continuity that seems to be lacking among his various books, as well as within some of the books themselves. It is also something of a matter of individual judgment and taste. What looks a bit disjointed to one may look cohesive to another. Still, Moran's writings often contradict one another, as he himself has admitted on a number of occasions. Thus some of Moran's admirers speak of Moran's writings as the early Moran, the later Moran, and so on, because what is contained in the later Moran contradicts what is written in the early Moran. As a result, it is difficult to implement what Moran says because there is the danger that, in a future book, he will reverse what he wrote in an earlier volume.

The fourth concern relates to the need to not only be critical but to go beyond the negatives to offer positive proposals for improvement. In the previous chapter, for example, James Fowler's massive attempt to fathom the mysteries of faith development were overviewed and evaluated. Fowler not only disagreed with the status quo but took on the project of offering a clear alternative in its place. James Michael Lee is also very critical, but he always offers specific and general positive alternatives for the procedures, theories, and speculations he critiques. C. Ellis Nelson likewise offers a wide variety of positive alternatives. Moran is somewhat vulnerable as a helpful critic because of the relative absence of positive and substantiated alternatives. Without doubt he has given large amounts of criticism and trenchant opinions, but other than offering interesting terminology he has not as yet offered a full or comprehensive alternative to the problems he has raised—or in many cases, even to specific problems which he has raised.[142] This is not to say that Moran, as well as everyone else who aspires to the role of critic, must give just as much attention and effort—if not more—to the processes of construction as to those of deconstruction. The reason for the critic's critiques is to open the way for alternatives. Leaving the revisions incomplete or unattended eventually vitiates the credibility of the critic. Indeed, one wonders if Moran assumes the role of the critic just to criticize rather than to ameliorate—always a great temptation to those who criticize. Ironically, Moran is well known to be exceptionally sensitive to anyone who criticizes his own work.

---

141. "The present work is an attempt to relate the themes of those books [e.g., *Education Toward Adulthood, Religious Education Development*, and *No Ladder to the Sky*], as well as themes in others of my books and essays, to an overall meaning of religious education." Moran, *Religious Education as a Second Language*, p. 5.

142. Moran has occasionally made the attempt to provide constructive answers or solutions. For example, see Part Two, "A Proposed Theory for Religious Education," in *Religious Education Development*, pp. 127-207. Two of the three chapters of this part of the book provide the familiar linguistic suggestions. The last chapter ("A Theory of Religious Education Development," pp. 183-207) is labeled as theory, but nowhere can I find in the chapter anything that could qualify as a real theory (see the discussion of theory throughout the previous chapter, "The Religious Educator as Scientist"). Moran suggests some possible "stages" and "moments" in the chapter, but they are speculatively stated and have no empirical or experimental basis whatsoever.

Finally, the role of critic as performed by Moran is a tiring one—for this reader at least. Since Moran has primarily done an analysis of the language in religious education, to read Moran is to encounter an array of definitions, analyses, and searches for meaning. So much analysis and dissection is difficult to assimilate over a short period of time and space. The role of critic is one best taken in small, but regular, doses. Maybe the same applies to the analytical and evaluative work of Gabriel Moran, who in the final analysis does indeed exemplify the role of the religious educator as critic.

Representative Teaching Procedure: Maieutic Teaching

One important facet of Socrates' example not included in the earlier section as historical personage was that of Socrates' teaching method—if indeed those are the appropriate words to use.[143] Socrates himself did not claim to be a teacher per se but instead only claimed to possess the skill of enabling others to give birth to their thoughts. This activity he identified as that of a midwife, rather than a teacher.[144] His point was that he, Socrates, did not teach in the sense of causing the other person to learn something that Socrates knew, but rather asked questions which stimulated the other person to think and to develop his or her own thoughts. Socrates saw himself as helping the other person "give birth" to his or her own truth—or as Eduard Zeller put it, "the philosopher (Socrates) by his questions obliges others to unfold their inner self before him."[145]

In simplest terms, maieutic teaching—intellectual midwifery—focuses on dialogue between a questioner, such as Socrates, and others with whom the questioner engages. The start of the interchange has already been noted in the previous section on Socrates, where Socrates was described as helping these others to recognize first what it is that they do *not* know. As Francis Cornford said: "He [Socrates] begins by puzzling them in order that they may see how little they really understand, and be ready to seek the truth in his company."[146] Then Cornford made a revealing point about maieutic teaching: "Once the genuine search has begun, he always treats the other party to the conversation as a companion and ally, not as an opponent."[147] A distinctive about this method of teaching is that competition is out of bounds, because the issue is for each person to find his or her own truth. It is not a matter of who gets there first, or who does it best. The focus remains on truth, wherever and whenever it can be found.

Maieutic teaching as modeled by Socrates has a playful side and a serious

---

143. I do not wish to imply that there is some formal procedure with a strict outline that must be followed. See the quote by J.T. Forbes a few paragraphs below.

144. In "Theaetetus," Socrates revealed that he was the son of a midwife, and that he, too, now practiced midwifery, albeit of a somewhat different sort. See Plato, "Theaetetus," in Vol. 7, *The Dialogues of Plato*, in the *Great Books of the Western World*, ed. Robert Maynard Hutchins, trans. Benjamin Jowett (Chicago: Encyclopaedia Britannica, 1953), p. 515-517.

145. Eduard Zeller, *Socrates and the Socratic Schools*, trans. Oswald J. Reichel, 3rd rev. ed. (New York: Russell and Russell, 1962), p. 126.

146. Francis MacDonald Cornford, *Before and After Socrates* (Cambridge: At the University Press, 1958), p. 45.

147. Ibid.

side. Michael Despland helped elucidate both. On the one hand, Despland said: "The practice of philosophical conversation must be taken with a minimum of seriousness. There is, of course, an element of play."[148] The dialogues are full of lively interchange with a high degree of give and take. There is also another side to the Socratic method, as Despland went on to describe: "We must note, therefore, that in each dialogue Socrates demonstrates a certain firmness. He ferrets out any miscommunication. He sticks to the topic, persistently. He demands coherence. . . . He does not adhere to all the rules of polite discourse; he is too stubborn, always striving to bring the conversation back to the point."[149] Though there is play in the midwife's task, it is equally as arduous and as demanding. For good reason did Despland conclude about the Socratic method: "The road to philosophical discovery is long and rough, and most prefer a shorter, smoother one."[150]

In his discussion of Socratic teaching, J.T. Forbes wrote: "There has been much harm done by imposed systematisation. In their own anxiety to secure for the splendid work of Socrates its full measure of recognition, men have been led to attribute to it more of a scientific procedure in method than it can fairly claim. . . . The only way in which great systematisation can be secured for the loose and informal Socratic teaching is by calling in the imagination to do for us what the sources fail to do."[151] Indeed, there is no formalized structure that Socrates left to be followed. As A.E. Baker observed: "This was his method: he followed wherever the argument led him."[152] There is no desire to add to the confusion of excessive "systematisation" but a simple listing of the basic three processes involved in maieutic teaching as explained by Eduard Zeller seems appropriate. First is the attainment of "the Socratic knowledge of self. . . . Nothing is so necessary as self-examination to show what we really know and what we only think we know. Nothing, too, is more indispensable for practical relations than to become acquainted with the extent of our knowledge and capacities, with our defects and requirements."[153] Second, once humility has been established, the process moves one to where "it involves in itself a demand for enlightenment; the knowledge of ignorance leads to a search for true knowledge."[154] Third is "the attempt to create real knowledge. For real knowledge he could only allow that to pass which emanated from the conception of a thing . . . referring a particular case to this universal quality."[155] By this, Zeller was referring to Socrates' use of inductive arguments: "He begins with examples taken from daily life, with well-known and generally admitted truth. On every disputed point he goes back

148. Despland, *Education of Desire*, p. 43.
149. Ibid., p. 48.
150. Ibid., p. 45.
151. J.T. Forbes, *Socrates* (Edinburgh: T. and T. Clark, 1913), p. 134.
152. A.E. Baker, *Prophets For an Age of Doubt* (London: Centenary Press, 1934), p. 44.
153. Zeller, *Socrates and the Socratic Schools*, pp. 122-123.
154. Ibid., p. 125. Note that in accordance with the genuine tradition of the critic, this kind of teaching does not stop with the negative or deconstructive phase. It really only starts there, opening the way for the construction process that follows.
155. Ibid., p. 129.

to such instances and hopes in this way to attain a universal agreement."[156]

A formalized representative teaching procedure that builds upon this basic method of "Socratic dialogue" is the Jurisprudential Inquiry procedure.[157] Bruce Joyce and Marsha Weil said that this procedure was designed as a "high-level model for citizenship education" and that it is "especially useful in helping people rethink their positions on important legal, ethical, and social questions."[158] Such a procedure is faithful to the maieutic approach of Socrates and is valuable to the religious educator functioning in the role of critic. The purpose of the procedure is not to reinforce an orthodox position as dictated by some authority but to enable persons to formulate their own opinions and defend them in a public arena.[159]

For a religious educator who is ready to put the role of critic into practice, there is no better way to begin than to follow in the steps of the master teacher and critic, Socrates. The invitation is to engage others, but not for the purpose of giving them your information or insights. The effort is to help them give birth to their own truth through the activity of midwifery—maieutic teaching.

Experiential Simulation: Socratic Dialogue

These sections of each chapter on experiential simulations are designed to take the reader outside the pages of this book and to help him or her encounter a more "real" type of education. The idea is that an experiential activity will engage more than just the mind and will also produce some action. The line of least resistance, and of least interaction, would be to read some of Plato's Socratic dialogues, where the literary personalities created in whole or in part by Plato engage in the finest sort of discussion and debate. The struggle to follow the lines of argument and to see the answers to the probing questions stretch over the pages is an excellent exercise of the critical faculties and should be adequate motivation to attack a contemporary issue with similar vigor. One need not be an idealist and share the epistemology of Plato to gain insight into the value of dialogue. Of course, the problem here is the loss of a

---

156. Ibid. "The essence of the method is to start the argument . . . from what is granted or asserted by his opponents." Baker, *Prophets For an Age of Doubt*, p. 45.

157. See Bruce Joyce and Marsha Weil, *Models of Teaching*, 3rd ed. (Englewood Cliffs, N.J.: Prentice-Hall, 1986), pp. 258-274.

158. Ibid., p. 259.

159. This procedure has six phases. First is the overall introduction to a particular case, where basic materials and facts are provided by the leader. Second is the process of identifying the issues within the case: isolation of specific issues or policies and identification of the values that are in conflict. Third, at the heart of the exercise, each person determines and articulates a personal position on the case. The values inherent in the position are acknowledged, as are the consequences of the taking such a position. Fourth is where the actual "Socratic dialogue" takes place. Exploration of the positions is accomplished through questioning and analyzing the various values that are surfaced. The consequences of the positions are clarified in the cold light of the facts that are uncovered. This phase does not persuade others to adopt a particular position through eloquence (as in rhetoric) but clarifies, usually through analogies, the consequences of taking such a position and the values that are underlying (as in dialectic). Fifth is a restating and a qualifying of positions based on the dialogue. Sixth is the testing out of the positions in reality to determine if the consequences predicted are factual. Ibid., pp. 268-269.

personal interchange with another human experientially.

The major suggestion is to have a "Socratic dialogue" of your own with someone truly alive and present today. The assignment is to find someone who will engage you as a critic, who will probe your positions much like the historical Socrates would have done. Probably the most valuable encounter would be between you and someone with whom you know you can disagree. The task is to encounter a true critic: someone who knows you, and what you do, and who will confront you at the deepest levels—not about superficial or surface issues, but about the fundamental realities. Dialogue with a critic who will feel free to be critical to a high degree. Such an activity is necessary for the religious educator as critic, because to be a critic one must accept others who also are fulfilling the role. Experience the onslaught of a critic personally before you impose such an experience upon others. You will not only learn how it is done, but you will experience the pain and the liberation a true critic can bring. If you are not able to endure it, then you have no right to bring it to others.

As you prepare for a dialogue, do not forget that there are always two parties or sides. For a dialogue to be effective, each side must be intensely engaged. This means that you must be prepared to do some probing of others. There are many resources available to facilitate this "higher order" of questioning. One of the best and most relevant to the topic at hand is Kenneth Seeskin's book, *Dialogue and Discovery*,[160] but virtually any teaching resource that discusses the topic of interpretive, evaluative, or higher order questioning will be of help.[161] After reading, of course, there is no substitute for practice. Probing questions cannot be perfected without someone to probe. The religious educator in the role of the critic must be enacted to be of any real value, so make the commitment to engage in Socratic dialogue despite whatever the fears and whatever the threats that may initially hinder you. The result of helping to give birth to truth is well worth the investment.

Summary

This chapter began by saying that the most important tasks of the critic are careful listening and incisive critiquing and that the least exercised activities of the religious educator are often these same two. This conviction remains, but perhaps the problem has at least gotten an airing. If this chapter helps religious educators to listen more carefully, to allow more questions, and to raise a larger and more fundamental variety of issues, then it has served its purpose: To say that the role of the critic in religious education—though grossly undervalued—is absolutely vital for the continued health and development of the field,

---

160. Kenneth Seeskin, *Dialogue and Discovery: A Study in Socratic Method* (Albany: State University of New York Press, 1987).

161. See, for example, Chapter Four, "Questioning," by Thomas P. Kasulis in *The Art and Craft of Teaching*, ed. Margaret Morganrouth Gullette (Cambridge: Cambridge University Press, 1984), pp. 38-48; Carolyn Pope Edwards with Patricia G. Ramsey, *Promoting Social and Moral Development in Young Children: Creative Approaches for the Classroom* (New York: Teachers College of Columbia University, 1986), pp. 26-31; Philip Groisser, *How to Use the Fine Art of Questioning* (New York: Teacher's Practical Press, 1964), and Chapter Six, "The Art of Questioning," by Ray E. Sanders in *Adult Learning Methods: A Guide for Effective Instruction*, ed. Michael W. Galbraith (Malabar, Fla.: Krieger, 1990), pp. 119-129.

and of society. Such a role must be highlighted and encouraged in the education of those who will lead into tomorrow. The course of the future depends upon those few who will stand at the right time and shout the truth: "But the Emperor has got nothing on!"

Figure 9 summarizes the characteristics and resources related to the religious educator as critic as discussed throughout the chapter.

Figure 9: The Religious Educator as Critic	
Dimensions of the Role	Analyst
	Philosopher
	Debunker
	Infidel
Aim	Awareness
Function	Investigation
Primary Virtues	Skepticism
	Evaluation
Activity	Reflecting
Shadow Role	Cynic
Faith Tradition Resource	Classical Buddhism
Historical Personage	Socrates
Contemporary Example	Gabriel Moran
Representative Teaching Procedure	Maieutic Teaching
Experiential Simulation	Socratic Dialogue

Chapter Eight

The Religious Educator As Storyteller

Telling, by itself and isolated in procedure, does not totally describe teaching, and it certainly does not describe the entirety of religious education. Telling may be a part of the total task of the educator, but by no means does it represent the whole. Indeed, most contemporary religious education writers have denounced this simplistic and authoritarian methodology. As James Michael Lee once said: "Teaching is not just standing up in front of learners and telling them things."[1] Lee has gone to great lengths to distinguish the lesser "telling" roles of messenger boy and translator from the more desirable role of the religious educator as mediator.[2] John Westerhoff took special aim at the "schooling-instructional paradigm" with its attendant emphasis on lecture, cognition, memorization, and recitation in order to clear the way for the "community of faith-enculturation paradigm," with its focus on communal relationships and experiential learning.[3] These representative writers, along with a multitude of others, are appropriately committed to ensuring that the religious educator not be reduced to the image of a heartless or mindless pedagogue who simply transmits information

---

1. James Michael Lee, "How To Teach: Foundations, Processes, Procedures," in *Handbook of Preschool Religious Education*, ed. Donald Ratcliff (Birmingham, Ala.: Religious Education Press, 1988), p. 158.

2. Lee's stance is addressed more fully in Chapter Five, "The Religious Educator as Coach." See this discussed, among other places, in James Michael Lee, *The Flow of Religious Instruction: A Social Science Approach* (Birmingham, Ala.: Religious Education Press, 1973), pp. 17-18.

3. John H. Westerhoff III, *Will Our Children Have Faith?* (New York: Seabury, 1976), pp. 23-25 and 49-50. The problem here is that Westerhoff does not seem to realize the parameters of schooling/instructions, since both in theory and in practice lecture, cognition, and so on, form only a small portion of schooling and instruction.

to his or her charges.[4] The obvious question, then, in the face of all this opposition to the telling process is how and why should one aspire to the role of the
religious educator as storyteller? The answer, surely just as obvious, is that the
true storyteller includes so much more than being just a "teller." What greater possibilities can emerge from this rich and historical role is the topic of this chapter.

An initial glance at the role of the storyteller reveals a need to secure some
basic definition of story, a requirement that would seem to require little effort.
Thomas Leitch, though, started his scholarly work on stories this way: "Everyone
knows what stories are—fortunately; for it is excessively difficult to say just
what they are."[5] He concluded his opening paragraph with these rather fore-
boding words: "What is a story? This question remains the most fundamental in
narrative theory, and the most difficult to resolve."[6] A look at a few representative definitions will resolve the question satisfactorily for purposes here, at least.
A much-quoted definition of story from early in the century is still a quite serviceable one: "A story, then, may be said to be a narrative of true or imaginary
events which form a vitally related whole, so presented as to make its appeal
chiefly to the emotions rather than to the intellect."[7] Three issues were raised in
this definition which are vitally important and which will resonate throughout the
present chapter. First, when it comes to story, the focus is not so much on facts
and verifiable data ("true or imaginary events") as it is on the narrative—on the
meaning and the implications of the story. Stories deal in images, where the
data need not be purely objective or historical to be truthful.[8] Second, a story provides an integrated whole which needs to be kept intact and respected as a unit.
As Woutrina Bone said: "Stories show us life written small; we see it whole; we
see events worked out; we see *today* as the outcome of *yesterday*; we can see that
the present is making the future."[9] Third, a story is not aimed just at the intellect,

---

4. A helpful image here is what educator Paulo Freire referred to as the "banking" concept of education: "Education thus becomes an act of depositing, in which the students are the depositories
and the teacher is the depositor." Paulo Freire, *Pedagogy of the Oppressed*, trans. Myra Bergman
Ramos (New York: Seabury, 1968), p. 58. See more about Freire and his ideas on education in
Chapter Nine, "The Religious Educator as Revolutionary."

5. Thomas M. Leitch, *What Stories Are: Narrative Theory and Interpretation* (University Park,
Pa.: Pennsylvania State University Press, 1986), p. 3.

6. Ibid.

7. Edward Porter St. John, *Stories and Story-Telling in Moral and Religious Education*, rev. ed.
(Boston: Pilgrim Press, 1918), p. 9.

8. The definition of story by progressive educator H.H. Horne made this point crystal clear:
"We may agree to define story as a free narration, not necessarily factual but truthful in character." Herman Harrell Horne, *Story-Telling, Questioning and Studying: Three School Arts* (New
York: Macmillan, 1919), p. 23. Horne's additional comments are instructive: "The story is not history, though there may be historical stories, but it is an imaginative invention. The terms 'story' and
"history" are indeed derived from the same root, meaning inquiry and what is learned thereby, but
for us history tells us what happened at a definite place and time, while story tells us only what
might have happened at some indefinite place and time." Ibid. Even more forcefully, Horne said: "It
follows from the definition of story that its purpose is not primarily to give information, but to nurture the soul; that is, to expand the imagination, to widen the sympathies, to give pure pleasure." Ibid.,
pp. 27-28.

9. Woutrina A. Bone, *Children's Stories and How to Tell Them* (New York: Harcourt, Brace,
1924), p. 44.

or just at the emotions, but at the whole person. Margaret Eggleston put it well: "Of course you may teach facts by telling a story, you may amuse a crowd by giving them a tale . . . but you have failed if that is all you have done. A well-told story should stir the emotions, create a deep desire to be like the hero of the tale; it must speak to the soul life of the hearers."[10] Ruth Sawyer said it this way: "Not a clever sharing of the mind alone, but rather a sharing of heart and spirit: I think storytelling must do this if it is to endure."[11]

Anne Pellowski's comprehensive and generic definition of storytelling was "the art or craft of narration of stories in verse and/or prose, as performed by one person or led by one person before a live audience; the stories narrated may be spoken, chanted, or sung, with or without musical, pictorial, and/or other accompaniment, and may be learned from oral, printed, or mechanically recorded sources; one of its purposes must be that of entertainment."[12] She went on to distinguish six particular types of storytelling, past and present: bardic, folk, religious, theatrical, library or institutional, and camp, park or playground storytelling. Her definition of religious storytelling is most relevant here: "Religious storytelling is that storytelling used by official or semi-official functionaries and leaders of a religious group to explain or promulgate their religion through stories, rather than through laws."[13]

This last part of Pellowski's definition—"through stories, rather than through laws"—is a key to the current chapter, and deserves a further look because it stresses one of the deeper values of stories for the religious educator. As Joseph Wagner and Robert Smith observed of educators in general: "Storytelling, an art as ancient as oral communication, has often been neglected by educators. Unfortunately, it has been looked upon as a frill in recent years."[14] Just so has this too often been the case in the church and synagogue. William White said: "One of the major obstacles in the acceptance of storytelling in the church is that it is viewed as appropriate primarily for children. Many people believe that serious theology must be abstract. Storytelling, they say, is something to use in Sunday schools, libraries, and children's sermons."[15] To address this misconception of the power of stories, Beldon Lane has proposed that we return to rabbinical stories for perspective. As he said: "Ask a rabbi a deep theological question, and you'll likely not get an answer; you'll be told a story."[16] The difference, said

10. Margaret W. Eggleston, *The Use of Story in Religious Education* (Garden City, N.Y.: Doubleday, Doran, 1920), p. 17. In a related vein, Jeanette Brown wrote: "It is the element of feeling in the well-told story that makes all the difference. . . . The story is an invaluable tool in an educational area, in which the creation of attitudes and relationships is more important than facts." Jeanette Perkins Brown, *The Storyteller in Religious Education: How to Tell Stories to Children and Young People* (Boston: Pilgrim Press, 1951), p. 5.

11. Ruth Sawyer, *The Way of the Storyteller* (New York: Viking, 1953), p. 28.

12. Anne Pellowski, *The World of Storytelling* (New York: R.R. Bowker, 1971), p. 15.

13. Ibid., p. 63. She then described how different world religions used storytelling.

14. Joseph Anthony Wagner and Robert W. Smith, *Teacher's Guide to Storytelling* (Dubuque: William C. Brown, 1958), p. 3.

15. William R. White, *Stories for Telling: A Treasury for Christian Storytellers* (Minneapolis: Augsburg, 1986), pp. 16-17.

16. Beldon C. Lane, "Rabbinical Stories: A Primer on Theological Method," *The Christian Century* 98:41 (December 16, 1981), p. 1306.

Lane, is that between the Jewish traditions of *Halakah,* "the way of reasoned reflection on the law," and *Haggadah,* "the way of story."[17] The religious educator as storyteller walks the path of Haggadah—the way of metaphor, of images and pictures, and of story.

Storytelling requires a storyteller, who Woutrina Bone identified as the "middleman"—the connector of learner and story.[18] As she intimated, the storyteller is not just a mechanical reciter of lines (or as James Michael Lee would say, a "messenger boy") but an important and necessary part of the interactive process: "[The learners] look before all else for something which comes from the teller, an intimacy of relation between him and themselves, a *personableness* which reading from the page inevitably lacks."[19] G.R. Nash agreed, saying: "A storyteller is the medium through whom a good story comes to life. He is as important as the story itself."[20] Others have said that "the story-teller is an interpreter of life—he interprets the life embodied in his story to the common life which throbs through his audience."[21] Closely related was Walter Benjamin's definition: "The storyteller takes what he tells from experience—his own or that reported by others. And he in turn makes it the experience of those who are listening to his tale."[22] Maybe the best way of describing the storyteller is to remember the words of Ruth Sawyer: "To be a good storyteller one must be gloriously alive. It is not possible to kindle fresh fires from burned out embers."[23]

These opening paragraphs have overviewed the essential definitions and some of the distinctions among them, introducing such terms as story, storytelling, religious storytelling, and storyteller. These terms will reappear throughout the chapter, and they should be indicators of the importance of this role to the overall professional identity of the religious educator. The following words from Edward Porter St. John, written very early in the twentieth century, provide some good and valuable advice as well as perspective that leads to the heart of the storyteller's work: "The loss of love for stories may be the result of sophistication, but it is not an evidence of wisdom. To feel contempt for their use reveals an ignorance of the art of education. The conscientious teacher will hardly be content to say, 'I cannot tell a story.' He will make himself a teller of tales. This is his duty and his opportunity, and when he has mastered the simple art it will be his joy as well."[24]

---

17. Ibid.

18. Bone, *Children's Stories and How to Tell Them*, p. x.

19. Ibid.

20. G. R. Nash, "Preface," in Archa O. Dart, *Tips for Storytellers*, rev. ed. (Nashville: Southern Publishing Association, 1966), p. 5.

21. J. Berg Esenwein and Marietta Stockard, *Children's Stories and How to Tell Them* (Springfield, Mass.: Home Correspondence School, 1919), p. 1.

22. Walter Benjamin, *Illuminations* (New York: Schocken, 1969), p. 87.

23. Sawyer, *The Way of the Storyteller*, p. 28. Esenwein and Stockard pursued this point by saying: "Storytelling, then, rightly belongs to the arts, and the storyteller's preparation for his work as an artist must begin with the enrichment of his own personality." Esenwein and Stockard, *Children's Stories and How to Tell Them*, p. 2. This aspect was so important to Archa Dart that she suggested the term "story liver" in place of "storyteller." See Dart, *Tips for Storytellers*, pp. 54-55.

24. St. John, *Stories and Story-Telling in Moral and Religious Education*, p. 5.

Dimensions of the Role

The role of storyteller, however simple the art may sound, is in reality quite diverse and broad. One way to gain some clarity and definition for the role is to look at the various dimensions or manifestations of this role as they appear in society. Four of these dimensions illustrate the complexity of the role: the storyteller as evangelist, as historian, as mythologist, and as raconteur.

Evangelist

Mention the term or profession "evangelist" in conversation today and the response likely will be a sneer, a sigh, or an embarrassed silence. The ancient and previously honored role of evangelist has fallen on hard times, due primarily to unscrupulous hucksters and reprobates who have misused the role and its audience for personal gain. Although the term is currently in disrepute, it actually signals an important and necessary function in society. An evangelist is fundamentally a proclaimer of a story—a story that gets at the deeper meaning of good news.

"Evangelist" comes from the compound Greek word εὐαγγέλιον, which literally means good (εὐ) message (ἀγγελῖον). While the term originally had no inherently religious connotation, εὐαγγέλιον came to be used by and identified with early Christians who went about spreading what they considered to be the "good news" of the Christ event. The four "evangelists" confronted regularly by readers of the New Testament are identified as "the gospel according to Matthew," or Mark, Luke, or John.[25] These first four New Testament books, then, are clearly identified as four different versions, or interpretations, of the story of "good news" concerning the Christ event. In true educational—storyteller—fashion, each of these "proclaimers of good news" not only told the story through explicit, implicit, and null curricula,[26] but heralded the truth that each one had a particular manner and purpose for telling the story.[27] As it happened, the church canonized these four versions of the story. Other versions exist from the early church period, each with its own curriculum design, style, and purpose.[28]

An evangelist of today uses the same selective process to communicate his or her message of good news. Recall that a storyteller weaves diverse images into

---

25. The word "gospel" ("god's spell") is the old English for good news—εὐαγγέλιον.

26. Elliott Eisner discussed three types of curricula: the explicit curriculum, the implicit curriculum, and the null curriculum. The explicit curriculum is education done intentionally, consciously, and overtly. The implicit curriculum happens unintentionally, unconsciously, and covertly. The null curriculum stems naturally from the first two types of curricula: If some things are included, whether explicitly or implicitly, then other things have been excluded—which compose the null curriculum. See Chapter Three, "The Three Curricula," in Elliot W. Eisner, *The Educational Imagination: On the Design and Evaluation of School Programs*, 2nd ed. (New York: Macmillan, 1985), pp. 87-108.

27. "Between the story and the reader is the narrator, who controls what will be told and how it will be perceived." Wallace Martin, *Recent Theories of Narrative* (Ithaca, N.Y.: Cornell University Press, 1986), p. 9.

28. For an interesting and related discussion, see Elaine Pagels, *The Gnostic Gospels* (New York: Random House, 1979).

a unified whole,[29] rather than just imparting objective facts; therefore, an evangelist appropriately tells his or her own version of a story in order to present his or her own curricula of good news.[30] By common consent, every evangelist pursues some agenda by which the story is selected, shaped, and delivered. By necessity, the listener must accept some responsibility for identifying that agenda and for deciding whether or not the "good news" is indeed good for him or her. This simply acknowledges that no reputable evangelist pretends to present an unbiased and purely "true" story, but instead tells a tailored, selective, biased, and highly subjective version of a story to promulgate his or her point of view.

Perhaps the religious educator is reading the preceding paragraphs with a self-satisfied smirk, saying: "Thank God I am not like that sinner." The truth is that being an evangelist as described above is an integral part of being a religious educator. To tell the story of good news (or just one of news) inherently demands being selective and subjective. The evangelist is anyone who professes to teach and proclaim a particular version of good news. In a generalized sense, evangelists are omnipresent in modern society. Turn on a television set, and one will immediately be confronted with the "good news" of a particular deodorant, automobile, or brokerage firm. Open any newspaper, and read a particular version of interpreted world events. Evangelists always give their own version of events, filtered through explicit, implicit, and null curricula. The difference in evangelists is that some are more subtle, some are more dishonest, and some more effective than others in presenting their agendas. The purpose of convincing, however hidden or open, remains the same. What legitimate religious educators strive toward, however, is to be open, honest, ethical, and effective in their efforts to convince.

Historian

A historian is a scholar who synthesizes historical data and interpretations into an understandable narrative, always basing his or her decisions on the best available research and verifiable information.[31] Ironically, one task that never finds completion is the writing of history. At first blush, one would expect that once events have transpired, they would remain sealed and unchangeable in time. In reality, just the opposite is true. While the facts themselves may have a certain timelessness, what those facts (data bits) mean—how they fit together, what they reveal, and how they affect other aspects of reality—is open to continual reassessment. History, whether ancient or recent, is never free from continued research (the search for factual and verifiable information) and interpretation.[32]

---

29. As Woutrina Bone said: "For the good story teller . . . makes a harmony of parts in a whole clearly conceived." Bone, *Children's Stories and How to Tell Them*, p. 2.

30. For an excellent introduction to the use of narrative theory in analyzing the gospels, see R. Alan Culpepper, *Anatomy of the Fourth Gospel: A Study in Literary Design* (Philadelphia: Fortress, 1983).

31. This definition distinguishes the historian from the compiler, who collects data and puts it together into catalogue or list form without theory or documented rationale, and from a chronicler who assembles and arranges events in chronological order without benefit of interpretation or a search for meaning among the events.

32. See Jacques Barzun and Henry F. Graff, *The Modern Researcher*, rev. ed. (New York: Harcourt, Brace and World, 1970), pp. 8-9.

In fact, it may be that what is called history is simply the combined result of research and interpretation.

A historian, then, is a storyteller who arranges facts, with requisite selectivity, into a particular interpretation of events.[33] Although this may sound rather cavalier and serendipitous, in truth the historian deals in both science and art. The historian is bound as a social scientist to conduct proper research, to follow theoretical constructs, to consider the range of possibilities, and then to produce a version of history which best serves the facts and the context.[34] The historian as artist, on the other hand, is concerned with the flow and creativity within the facts and with how the facts could fit together to form a meaningful and revelatory gestalt. If the facts are considered from a different angle, or if a different combination of factors is tried, what new reality may appear?[35] What are the chief points of interest, and how does the inclusion of the historian's imagination help clarify or synthesize the objective data in hand?[36] A true historian is not merely an assembler of dates and places.[37] A historian creates a story with the known information by including this, excluding that, and finding a way to give meaning to the larger flow of events.[38]

Take as an example the activities that transpired in and around the city of Dallas on November 22, 1963. John F. Kennedy was riding in his presidential limousine with a motorcade through the streets of downtown Dallas during the noon hour. At approximately 12:29 p.m., while the motorcade was traveling

---

33. In this context, Steven Cohan and Linda Shires wrote: "The distinguishing feature of narrative is its linear organization of events into a story. But a story has to do with more than just the organization of events. . . . Story consists of events placed in a sequence to delineate a process of change, the transformation of one event into another." Steven Cohan and Linda M. Shires, *Telling Stories: A Theoretical Analysis of Narrative Fiction* (New York: Routledge, 1988), pp. 52-53.

34. For more on the role of the scientist, see Chapter Six, "The Religious Educator as Scientist." A related resource that is of help here is *Narrative in Culture: The Uses of Storytelling in the Sciences, Philosophy, and Literature*, ed. Cristopher Nash (London: Routledge, 1990).

35. For more on the role of the artist, see Chapter Nine, "The Religious Educator as Artist."

36. See Hayden White, Chapter Four, "Historicism, History, and the Figurative Imagination," in *Topics of Discourse: Essays in Cultural Criticism* (Baltimore: Johns Hopkins University Press, 1978), pp. 101-120.

37. An excellent example of the work of a chronologer, as distinct from that of the historian, is *The People's Chronology: A Year-by-Year Record of Human Events from Prehistory to the Present*, ed. James Trager (New York: Holt, Rinehart and Winston, 1979).

38. Oscar Handlin described the art and science—and the mixture of objectivity and subjectivity—of history this way: "Subtle links join subjective to objective in the practice of the historian's craft. While the world of the elapsed past has its own reality, independent of who attempts to view and describe it, and is thus objective, the scholar's vision is subjective, at least to the extent that his own point of observation and the complex lenses of prejudice, interest, and preconceptions shape what he discerns and therefore what he can portray. The historian consequently must know not only how to explore the sources and how to fit together the data garnered from them, but also the internal and external restraints which affect the performance of those tasks. As a result, he depends both on a command of techniques and on self-understanding. A manual of rules and procedures may ease the difficulties of research, analysis, and writing: application of the rules still requires self-understanding." Oscar Handlin, *Truth in History* (Cambridge: The Belknap Press of Harvard University Press, 1979), p. 1. For examples of other sources on this important topic, see Richard J. Bernstein, *Beyond Objectivism and Relativism: Science, Hermeneutics, and Praxis* (Philadelphia: University of Pennsylvania Press, 1988), and R.W. Newell, *Objectivity, Empiricism and Truth* (London: Routledge and Kegan Paul, 1986).

down Elm Street through Dealy Plaza, the president was shot in full view of the public. His wife was sitting beside him. Secret Service agents were all around him. The vice-president and many of the cabinet members were riding directly behind the presidential limousine. The entire press corps was present and in place, watching every move and taking notes. Hundreds of bystanders watched the murder happen before their eyes. Audio tapes of those chaotic seconds have been found, as have a multitude of still pictures. Even a movie of the murder was taken by the hapless amateur photographer Abraham Zapruder. From the accumulated evidence, facts, and witnesses, one would make the assumption that no mystery could possibly remain as to exactly what occurred. That assumption, of course, could not be more faulty. The more historians ponder the evidence of what occurred in those few seconds in question, the more the mystery grows as to what actually did happen. The controversy and the conjecture about the history of that day continues unabated.

A historian is by all accounts committed to gathering factual information, but just the uncovering of these data does not circumscribe the work of the historian.[39] Facts (if that is even the term to use) are but the raw data with which the historian starts. The fuller task of the historian is to so arrange, understand, interpret, and explain the facts so as to find the deeper meaning of them.[40] The historian, at base, is a scholarly and disciplined type of storyteller.

To the consternation of some and to the confounding of others, historians have not been at all hesitant in tackling religious story lines. Historians are a very different breed of storyteller than evangelists, though. Evangelists are witnesses to what they already believe. Their goal is to convince others of their version of the story. As has been seen, each of the four "evangelists" (gospels) in the New Testament told the story of the Christ event to a different audience, to a different time, and for a slightly different purpose, but each also was based on a fundamental belief in the subject of the story. Historians have a different perspective and goal in view, as well as a strict scientific methodology to follow,[41] and hence tell very different kinds of stories than evangelists. One need only to refer to the works of Flavius Josephus (37-c. 100 C.E.), the Jewish historian, for a historian's treatment of the "Christ event." At best there are a few fleeting references to a "wise man" who "was a doer of wonderful works,"[42] and even these references are usually regarded as later corruptions of the text. Extracting Jesus of Nazareth from Josephus' historical record of the Jews would not even be noticeable. Extracting Jesus the Christ from the gospel accounts would tear apart their very fabric. Historians and

39. For a fuller discussion of this point, see Chapter Seven, "History and Chronicle," in Arthur C. Danto, *Analytical Philosophy of History* (Cambridge: At the University Press, 1986), pp. 113-142.

40. See especially the essay by Fernand Braudel, "History and the Social Sciences: *The Longue Durée*," in Fernand Braudel, *On History*, trans. Sarah Matthews (Chicago: University of Chicago Press, 1980), pp. 25-54.

41. A good overview of the social-science approach to history is presented in Chapter Three, "The Impact of the Social Sciences," in Geoffrey Barraclough, *Main Trends in History* (New York: Holmes and Meier, 1978), pp. 45-94.

42. See, for example, Flavius Josephus, *The Antiquities of the Jews*, Book XVIII, Chapter 3, iii, in *Josephus: Complete Works*, trans. William Whiston (Grand Rapids, Mich.: Kregel Publications, 1960), p. 379.

evangelists, then, tell very different kinds of stories for very different purposes.

Mythologist

A mythologist, like the historian, must be a serious scholar, but this person is an expert in the study of myth[43] and of mythography[44]—its forms, structures, meanings, and interpretations. The mythologist is different yet from either the evangelist or the historian, although all three hold much in common under the aegis of storyteller.[45] The mythologist is just as interested in discerning basic and verifiable information as the previous two personages, but in the case of the mythologist the nature of the information is divergent. Where generally the evangelist and the historian choose to begin their investigations with facts they ascribe, at least initially, to hold some historical reality, the mythologist is not nearly as concerned with factual historicity. The mythologist researches and analyzes the interpretive story itself, searching for the meaning that it communicates in a manner that is too deep for bare facts or objective data to convey. In this instance, the mythologist does not try to convince others of his or her position in the manner of the evangelist and does not arrange, select, and interpret facts in the manner of the historian but instead focuses on a sacred story which is handed down because it contains a profound message for its hearers.[46] The emphasis shifts from facts to the structure and message of the story itself, while attention to interpretation remains common to all the tasks.

To some, classifying a story as myth implies that the story is false. If the facts are not true (verifiably accurate), then how can the story be true? Consideration of such a question gets at the very essence of myth, for as Alan Dundes wrote: "Myth may constitute the highest form of truth, albeit in metaphorical guise."[47] Dealing with a "true myth" is different from dealing with a "true

---

43. Myth has been defined by Alan Dundes as "a sacred narrative explaining how the world and men came to be in their present forms." Alan Dundes, "Introduction," in *Sacred Narrative: Readings in the Theory of Myth*, ed. Alan Dundes (Berkeley: University of California Press, 1984), p. 1. Myth was defined by James Michael Lee as "a narrative, story, or an exposition which portrays a phenomenon or a series of phenomena in an extrarational manner." James Michael Lee, *The Content of Religious Instruction: A Social Science Approach* (Birmingham, Ala.: Religious Education Press, 1985), p. 151.

44. Mythography has been defined as "the application of critical perspectives to mythological materials." See William G. Doty, *Mythography: The Study of Myths and Rituals* (University, Ala.: University of Alabama Press, 1986), p. xiii.

45. That these dimensions are by no means isolated from one another, see, for example, W. Taylor Stevenson, *History as Myth: The Import for Contemporary Theology* (New York: Seabury, 1969).

46. In his discussion of myth, James Michael Lee said: "A myth is an extrarational device used to supply information and interpretation of the most basic and ultimate questions about life and human existence, questions for which rational knowing can supply only inadequate answers or insights." Lee, *The Content of Religious Instruction*, p. 151. This allowed Lee to provide a good discussion of the kind of truth myth communicates, as when he said: "The factualness and truth of a myth do not reside in the objective reality or logic of the myth, but rather in its appropriateness to and congruence with its accuracy in portraying the religious or other profound reality which it is representing." Ibid., p. 152. See Lee's larger treatment of myth in ibid., pp. 151-154; 329-334; and 349-355.

47. Dundes, "Introduction," in *Sacred Narratives*, p. 1.

fact." The "truth" resides in the applicability and the appropriateness of the metaphor rather than in the verifiability of the historical event.[48] Myths are created to explain rather than to describe.

The term "mythologist," then, does describe someone who is seeking truth, but one who seeks it in a different way and in a different form than that sought by either the evangelist or historian. The mythologist takes the fabric of the story itself, as a whole and independent of its factual or objective historicity, as the primary subject of investigation.

Donna Rosenberg described myths as "serious stories that reflect a society's spiritual foundations. They are symbols of human experience that each culture values and preserves because they embody the worldview or important beliefs of that culture."[49] More simply, she said: "Myths were originally created as entertaining stories with a serious purpose."[50] While myths are indeed stories, and often quite entertaining ones at that, they are not mere flights of imagination with no deeper purpose. Myths are literary devices that cultures use to transmit and preserve their interpretation of the meaning of human existence. The manner or style of the transmission—the content of the myths—is distinctive to the particular culture, while the structure and function of myth is more universal. The mythologist, then, has the task of understanding and interpreting both myths and myth, coupled with the task of understanding and interpreting the culture out of which the myths arose.

One of the keys to unlocking the mystery of myths is through comparative study of them, and indeed similar story lines are often found among various cultures.[51] Thus the mythologist makes the "true believer"[52] somewhat uncomfortable (most critical thinking does) when the myths studied are ones currently in vogue. For example, take the various flood stories found in mythology. These were prevalent in a number of ancient Middle Eastern civilizations, and the similarities among them are striking. For example, to read portions of the Gilgamesh Epic[53] and then to compare it to the account of a flood recorded in the Jewish scriptures[54]

48. Joseph Campbell once said: "No, mythology is not a lie, mythology is poetry, it is metaphorical." See Joseph Campbell with Bill Moyers, *The Power of Myth*, ed. Betty Sue Flowers (New York: Doubleday, 1988), p. 163.

49. Donna Rosenberg, *World Mythology: An Anthology of the Great Myths and Epics* (Lincolnwood, Ill.: National Textbook Company, 1986), p. xiv.

50. Ibid., p. xv.

51. One of the better known comparative mythologists is Joseph Campbell. Campbell taught that myth serves basically four functions for humanity: mystical, cosmological, sociological, and pedagogical. The fourth one, he said, "is the one that I think everyone must try today to relate to . . . of how to live a human lifetime under any circumstances. Myths can teach you that." See Joseph Campbell with Bill Moyers, *The Power of Myth*, p. 31. Other good sources of his on comparative mythology include Joseph Campbell, *The Hero with a Thousand Faces*, 2nd ed. (Princeton, N.J.: Princeton University Press, 1968); and Joseph Campbell, *The Masks of God*, 4 vols. (New York: Viking, 1959-1969). The titles of the volumes are: *Primitive Mythology; Oriental Mythology; Occidental Mythology;* and *Creative Mythology.*

52. This is Erik Hoffer's term for the fanatic—an ideologue with a sealed mind and an irresolute point of view. See Erik Hoffer, *The True Believer: Thoughts on the Nature of Mass Movements* (New York: Harper & Row, 1951), especially Chapter Sixteen, pp. 130-133.

53. See Chapter 7 of the Gilgamesh Epic, pp. 202-212 in Rosenberg, *World Mythology.*

54. Genesis, Chapters 6 through 8.

reveals as much commonality as difference. This kind of comparative study,[55] while revelatory of Middle Eastern culture and society, represents to some an attack on and a denigration of the message found in the *biblical* record. One does not usually hear much concern for any possible harm done to the Gilgamesh Epic.[56]

For the mythologist, contextualizing helps explain the story and the culture. For others, like the "true believer," this tends to deemphasize the literalness of the specific "facts" themselves and does violence to the revealed and handed-down "truth" of the story itself (which is never described as a "myth" by this person in the first place). The comparatively detached and objective mythologist, with eyes focused on what the story meant (means) to the community from which it came, is not always the most welcome or revered figure in communities of believers. Where on the one hand the mythologist makes a concentrated effort to understand the story, on the other hand the procedures, intentions, and results often lead in a direction quite divergent from the "spiritual foundations" active at the time in the culture under scrutiny. The mythologist can be perceived as an interloper and as a violator of the sacred if encountered dabbling in the study of *present-day* myths. The committed mythologist, though, has no hesitancy in pursuing myth whenever and wherever it is found.

Raconteur

The fourth and final illustrative dimension of the religious educator as storyteller is the raconteur. A raconteur is the skilled "teller of tales," the person trained and practiced in the art of telling stories. In the midst of all the academic and intellectual reasoning attached to storytelling, it is easy to forget that people listen to stories because they enjoy them! Humans have an insatiable hunger for well-told stories. Evidence of this is obvious, from the nightly family ritual of "Daddy, tell me a story" to the lines which form in front of the theater entrance upon the arrival of a new box-office extravaganza. While the days of the tribal raconteur telling stories around the campfire are gone, the role of the raconteur is as healthy and as sought after as ever. Today the modern storyteller can be found writing fiction, producing films, or developing television shows. The art of the raconteur, and the public demand for it, has not been lost but transformed. The esteem the public holds for such diverse types of raconteurs as William Shakespeare, Charles Dickens, George Lucas, and Garrison Keillor

---

55. Some introductory work here can be explored in Foster R. McCurley, *Ancient Myths and Biblical Faith: Scriptural Transformations* (Philadelphia: Fortress, 1983), and Heinz Westman, *The Structure of Biblical Myths: The Ontogenesis of the Psyche* (Dallas, Tex.: Spring Publications, 1983). A very old study that is still in use is T.W. Doane, *Bible Myths and Their Parallels in Other Religions*, 7th ed. (New York: Truth Seeker Company, 1882).

56. Richard Ginn cogently observed: "To the detached observer, the practice of Christianity displays a rather unusual feature in the believer's awareness of the past. Believers can have an approach to the biblical narratives, particularly to the gospels, that is totally different from the approach that they would feel toward, for example, the biography of Julius Caesar. Furthermore, believers usually have a very different approach to the past described in the biblical narratives when compared with the approach of professed nonbelievers to the same material." Richard J. Ginn, *The Present and the Past: A Study of Anamnesis* (Allison Park, Pa.: Pickwick Publications, 1989), p. 1.

is testimony to society's love if not need for well-told stories.[57]

People enjoy stories, and want to hear stories, but only if the stories are told well. Stories do not tell themselves, and storytelling is not necessarily a gift with which one is born—for most it is an ability acquired with great effort.[58] It is a skill that needs and demands development and practice.[59] Just because one has information and knowledge of a particular subject does not say anything about whether or not the person can communicate it well, which means that being an effective educator requires more than the possession of knowledge. It is just as essential for an educator to be able to tell a story and create interest in a subject as it is for the educator to possess information about that subject. The two responsibilities go hand in hand, and an educator who has one without the other is doomed to failure.

If a raconteur is an expert in judging and diagnosing an audience, in selecting the right stories and sequence of stories, and in communicating both thought and emotion, then the religious educator and the raconteur are natural companions.[60] Religious educators already tell stories to inform, to nurture, and to educate. Why not do it well, and have fun in the process? The idea is as old as the stories we tell, since we inherited most of them from our ancestral raconteurs.[61]

Summary

The religious educator in the role of storyteller has at least these four dimensions: evangelist, historian, mythologist, and raconteur. While other dimensions to the role certainly could be cited, these are sufficient to introduce the role and to provide some common understandings. Indeed, the religious educator as storyteller has emerged as one of the most natural and expected of roles, since religious education and storytelling at times seem to be virtually inseparable. The sections that follow continue this examination of the role of storyteller, allowing religious educators to reclaim their heritage and birthright as storytellers.

---

57. William White noted the deep need people have for stories and their tellers: "We humans are storytelling creatures. Not only do we tell stories to entertain, but to learn from the past, to understand our world, and to grapple with the mysteries of life. Through stories we attempt to find patterns of significance in apparently meaningless events, as well as teach values to the next generation." White, *Stories for Telling*. p. 14.

58. Archa Dart had this way of making her point about adequate preparation: "The secret is out. One difference between the 'natural' storyteller and the one who appears to have no talent is that the first one builds his story well in advance and the other depends upon the inspiration of the moment. Of course, some have more talent than others for this art, but the main difference is in the planning, or the building, of the story." Dart, *Tips for Storytellers*, p. 20.

59. As Esenwein and Stockard put it years ago: "Happily for the storyteller, no intricate and confusing technique is needed for effective narration . . . notwithstanding the exacting demands of the art. . . . Intelligent study and much practice are necessary for him . . . if he would master his art." Esenwein and Stockard, *Children's Stories and How to Tell Them*, p. 42. More about teaching procedures related to storytelling is provided in the appropriate section later in this chapter.

60. "The story has been used as an instrument in religious education since time began. It is the oldest art in the world." Eggleston, *Use of Story in Religious Education*, p. 17.

61. It may be that very few different plot lines exist at all. Robert Hughes has concluded that there are basically eighteen plots, but reports other estimates of between three and thirty-six. See the discussion in Robert Don Hughes, *Talking to the World in the Days to Come* (Nashville: Broadman, 1991), pp. 49-51.

Aim: Interpretation

The primary aim of the religious educator within the role of the storyteller is to facilitate the interpretation of the deeper meanings of the story.[62] In doing this, the storyteller personalizes the story to relate to the hearer, contextualizing it within his or her purview of understanding and experience, and allowing the listener to grapple with the connotations, applications, and inferences contained within the story. The storyteller helps the entirety of the hearer interact with the story: not only with the mind through intellectual activity, but with the full range of the emotions, and with the vicarious experiential identification of the events or personalities being related. With the aim stated in this manner, the transmission of information—the data bits which combine to form the story—is subsumed within the larger activity.[63] The data bits are not inconsequential, and they are to be handled with care and respect. In storytelling, however, the data bits themselves do not dominate. The data bits serve only as the basic building blocks of the story, so that the message and its interpretation become preeminent. To focus only on the details of the story is ultimately to miss the story.

In the Judeo-Christian tradition, the Jewish scriptures provide both a rich resource of stories and a battleground concerning the accuracy of specific data bits. The story of Moses and his encounter with the burning bush is one case in point. Exodus Chapter Five relates the engaging story of Moses struggling with his call and mission in life. His experience with the divine powers was described in terms of a theophany,[64] where divinity appeared to Moses in the form of a fire that did not burn and a voice that had no body. The result of this encounter was a strengthening of Moses' resolve to become a leader of his people. As anyone who has taught this story knows, the challenge is to keep the eyes of the learners off the burning bush long enough to decipher the fuller meaning of the story. The questions that always seem to arise have to do with the more theatrical and dramatic elements of the story: What kind of bush did Moses see? Why didn't it burn? Did Moses feel heat? Whose voice did Moses hear and where did it come from? The theophany does catch interest and "spark" the imagination, and the questions are not inappropriate. In our current rationalistic and technological society, such an unusual and unique occurrence virtually begs for some

---

62. This section raises the more technical issue of *hermeneutic*, which James Michael Lee has defined as "a newer way of looking at the principles of textual interpretation" by focusing "its primary attention on the way which 1) verbal content was and particularly is 2) understood by the person." More traditional *hermeneutics* (plural) "is concerned with the theoretical aspects of the science of textual interpretation." Lee, *Content of Religious Instruction*, p. 338; see the fuller discussion on pp. 338-345.

63. Introducing hermeneutic into the teaching act undeniably complicates the teaching act, as well as removes a large degree of authoritarian control that the religious educator may have over what the learner does with the stories. E.D. Hirsch has said that hermeneutic is "a foundational and preliminary discipline for all literary interpretation." Quoted in Richard E. Palmer, *Hermeneutics: Interpretation Theory in Schleiermacher, Dilthey, Heidegger, and Gadamer* (Evanston, Ill.: Northwestern University Press, 1969), p. 4.

64. A "theophany" literally means the appearance of God. A definition of theophany is a "temporal manifestation of the deity to man, involving visible and audible elements that signal God's real presence." See C. Ellis Nelson, *How Faith Matures* (Louisville: Westminster/John Knox Press, 1989), p. 76. For Nelson's fuller discussion, see ibid., pp. 76-77.

scientific explanation or inquiry. The religious educator should neither be surprised nor distracted by the interest. The task, however, is to channel the curiosity from the details to the message the details reveal. The storyteller must be able to guide the discussion away from wondering how many degrees centigrade the fire was or whether the voice spoke in Egyptian or Arabic. The storyteller needs to be clear about why he or she is telling the story, what message or messages may be potentially hidden in the data bits, and how to help the learners see through the specifics of the story into its essence.[65]

The aim of the storyteller is simply stated but more complicated to accomplish: The storyteller does carry responsibility for legitimately using the data bits of information to communicate the message of a story but more foundationally and importantly for facilitating the interpretation and application of that message. The emphasis is on meaning and not on the data bits themselves. While this affirms the "telling" dimension within religious education, it also keeps it in its place and stresses that the transmission of information is by no means the primary aim of religious education. The broader aim is the interpretation of the selected, arranged, and connected bits of information. The broader aim is the interpretation of the selected, arranged, and connected bits of information. Interpretation is fostered, encouraged, and facilitated by the religious educator who tells stories in a skillful way.

The religious educator teaches how to interpret, but not what *the* interpretation is.[66] Transmission of interpretation can be just as corrupt as the transmission of information alone. The religious educator brings the heritage of the community to the task of interpretation and shows how various persons or groups in the community have made use of the stories. The religious educator also guards against the dangerous or irresponsible use of the stories. In telling the story of

---

65. Some may object to the hermeneutic approach because it appears not to give adequate dignity or respect to the literature of the faith traditions ("Holy Scripture"). Hermeneutical study has been employed to study both "secular" and "sacred" literature for some time, but this relatively recent use of secular procedures upon religious materials is still discomforting to some. Joseph Mazzeo said: "Although modern secular and skeptical temperaments have long transcended the distinction between the interpretation of a secular text and a sacred text, some distinction between *hermeneutica sacra* and *hermeneutica profana* was conserved in theory until the time of Schleiermacher." Joseph Anthony Mazzeo, *Varieties of Interpretation* (Notre Dame, Ind.: University of Notre Dame Press, 1978), p. 16. Beyond the borders of academia, however, not everyone is convinced that sacred and secular literature should be treated alike. Where one may have little or no interest or investment in how scholarship analyzes the *Aeneid*, that same person may very well have a definite opinion about how those same procedures are applied to something he or she holds dear (such as the New Testament). Religious educators need to be aware of the modern approaches to hermeneutical study but at the same time to be keenly sensitive to those they are trying to teach. Not all of them will have been disabused of the distinctions Mazzeo said were transcended. Religious educators must be initially circumspect in introducing teaching about hermeneutic, realizing that the process may be seen as destructive by some as it is seen to be constructive by others.

66. The issue of the "proper" hermeneutical method is a hotly debated topic, and even what the term "hermeneutic" itself means is predictably under extended discussion. Richard Palmer, for example, has given six "modern" definitions or approaches to hermeneutical study. These were: biblical exegesis; philological methodology; the science of linguistic understanding; as the methodological foundation for the *Geisteswissenschaften*; existential understandings; and as an overall system of interpretation. See Chapter Three, "Six Modern Definitions of Hermeneutics," in Palmer, *Hermeneutics*, pp. 33-45.

Moses, for example, the religious educator needs to help listeners understand that they should not set fire to bushes in order to hear voices but stops short of indoctrinating them in the one correct version of interpretation. The aim of the religious educator as storyteller in telling the stories is to facilitate interpretation of them and to allow listeners to find meaning and relevance for their own lives. Encroaching upon the freedom of the individual to search for personal meaning and relevance distorts the role of the effective religious educator and violates the personhood of the listener.

Function: Communication

In the barest of definitions, the storyteller is simply someone who communicates[67] a message by means of a story. The effective storyteller inserts the listener[68] into the story, making the listener a part of the action and personalizing it so that the listener truly experiences the story. Granted, the message may be cloaked in an entertaining story ("Let those who have ears, hear") and may need interpretation for the deeper message to be revealed, but the chief function of the storyteller remains that of relating stories from within his or her realm of experience to that of the listener.[69] If the storyteller has nothing to communicate and no message to pass on, then there is no purpose for telling the story.

Katherine Cather, a well-known storyteller of a past generation, had no hesitancy in claiming this function of communication, and she expected every storyteller to be quite purposeful in his or her use of story. She spoke directly to religious educators with this advice: "Success with storytelling in the religion field, as in any other, is possible only to the narrator who has a purpose in the use of the story, and who keeps that purpose clearly in mind. He must have a definite idea of what his tales are to accomplish both now and later or he will give them

---

67. I have chosen the broad and rather generic term "communication" here to signify the range of ways that the storyteller has to get the story across. I am not limiting the role to one person telling a story to another but am making it comprehensive enough to include dramatists, novelists, film makers, and the like. This term "communication" is intended to cover all of these, however imprecisely. Communication signifies interaction where there is feedback between the storyteller and the hearers. The storyteller gives away his or her stories (and in a very real sense, himself or herself) through an intimately personal, interconnected, and experiential process of relationships. "Telling" is a closely related word, but it may be taken as too one-sided: that the storyteller simply hands out the information to be passively received and accepted by the listeners without the necessary interaction between the parties. Similar is "imparting," which means to give away or grant to others by personal contact, association, or influence, but the word carries overtones of didactics and superiority that are inappropriate for the storyteller role. "Proclaiming" is also related, but it sounds too dictatorial, authoritarian, and impersonal.

68. Use of the term "listener" here should not imply that this person is passive or a mere receiver of information. It only refers to the audience of the storyteler.

69. Recall the quote used earlier from Walter Benjamin: "The storyteller takes what he tells from experience—his own or that reported by others. And he in turn makes it the experience of those who are listening to his tale." Benjamin, *Illuminations*, p. 87. The kind of involvement I am suggesting here is described in these instructions to the storyteller: "Think of the story. Know it well. Become personally acquainted with the characters. They are friends. The events have been lived through until they stand out vividly in the mind's eye. Let the room fade from the vision, and let the place where the story begins come into focus. Live the story again before the audience." Dart, *Tips for Storytellers*, p. 55.

to little purpose. He must understand what transpires in the minds and hearts of his auditors as they follow him and skillfully lead them along paths where he desires them to go."[70]

Cather's points deserve brief amplification. First, the religious educator uses stories in the same way that everyone else uses stories. The religious educator must be intentional and focused in the relating of the story, but there is no particular grace supplied or style demanded simply because the teaching is religious in nature. Second, the storyteller must be highly skilled in diagnosis. He or she must be able to detect how the listeners are receiving the story and what their reactions are.[71] Storytelling is an intensely interactive function. The storyteller must be prepared to adjust the tempo and flow of the story line in order to keep the listeners at least somewhere approximating the "desired path."

It is no accident that communication appears as the function rather than as the aim of the storyteller. Communication, the personal and interactive involvement in the story by both storyteller and listener, is the means to an end—one tells (actually, communicates) a story in order to achieve the aim of understanding, interpreting, and applying the message of the story. While it is true that many stories are told primarily for fun and enjoyment, or to stimulate interest, these are not the prime reasons for the religious educator to tell stories. The story serves as the vehicle, and the storyteller uses the story to attain a broader end. The aim, or purpose, of the storyteller is not just to tell the story, but to facilitate the interpretation and application of that story.

Identifying the religious educator as one who communicates a message via stories emphasizes the importance of the story itself. A storyteller must be circumspect in the choice of the story, since it serves as the teaching vehicle for the message. The end does not always justify the means: A poor story cannot suffice for the imposition of a prolonged and heavy-handed interpretation. The story itself must be a valid and legitimate teaching tool. An example of an "invalid" story—and interpretation—was inadvertently provided by Laura Emerson: "While teaching in a junior high in a resort community, I once used the story of little Peter Billhorn who, when drowning, had clasped his hands tightly in prayer as he came up for the last time. This act enabled the men to rescue him by putting a pole under his hands. I thought no more of the story until a few months later, when one of my junior girls drowned during a vacation period. Those who saw her come up the last time said her hands were clasped in prayer, though she was not rescued. The story had made a lasting impression and incited faith."[72] The story made a lasting impression indeed! The nonsense about the passivity of "little Peter Billhorn" was bad enough, but to be proud of sending a little girl to her death because of that sentimental, moralistic tale was unconscionable. Woe to the

70. Katherine D. Cather, *Religious Education Through Story-Telling* (New York: Abingdon, 1925), p. 35.

71. John Harrell made these useful comments on this point: "An essential and distinctive element of storytelling is the presence of a storyteller. There he is. One can touch him, and he responds. As his story unfolds it is obvious that he is aware of his audience, that his audience is supplying him with clues how best to tell his story this particular time to these particular persons." John Harrell, "Why Storytelling Now?" *The Living Light* 13:1 (Spring, 1976), p. 23.

72. Laura S. Emerson, *Storytelling: The Art and Purpose* (Grand Rapids, Mich.: Zondervan, 1959), p. 30.

religious educator who hangs the millstone of a corrupt and destructive story around the necks of those in his or her charge!

The value of recognizing communication as a function of the religious educator is twofold. First, such a designation gives the act of teaching significance and importance. Here is a valid means of telling—of transmitting vital information—within the larger context of storytelling. It is through storytelling that the religious educator has entrance into the world of the listener and has the opportunity to have an effect on the listener. The storyteller is bound to the disciplines of practice and diagnosis in order to become or remain an expert proclaimer.[73] Second, communication as function keeps the story and its details in proper perspective. Simply sharing the story is only the beginning of the educational process. The religious educator must also assist the listeners in dealing with the message of the story, helping assimilate or accommodate the interpretation into their lives through personalized application.[74]

Primary Virtues: Historicity and Contextuality

The two primary virtues the religious educator as storyteller inculcates are the personalistic dimensions of historicity and contextuality, which is to say that the storyteller helps the listener of the story step into the flow of life. Humans become connected to life and to others through telling and interpreting stories. Stories are a way of vicariously living the events of the story, and listeners are inserted into that world of fantasy through the efforts of the expert storyteller. As Shelly Rubin and Dennie Wolf put it: "As an inventor of imaginary worlds, the storyteller's task is to create and sustain narrative illusions. However illusory these worlds may be, their inhabitants, the characters of the story, must be infused with a richness and fullness that gives the story's world a reality apparently independent of the storyteller."[75] This reality is understood and experienced through the art and the craft of the storyteller.

Myth was defined earlier in the chapter as "a sacred narrative explaining how the world and men came to be in their present form."[76] Expanding this particularistic definition into a nonreligious context, the definition of story would then be "a human narrative explaining how to interpret and understand the world, the human, and their relationship." The storyteller is one who teaches us how to connect, both through personalistic history and current context.[77]

Historicity can be defined as the process of being placed into the stream of the

---

73. For help in doing and practicing this skill in a specifically Christian environment, see Donald E. Miller, *Story and Context: An Introduction to Christian Education* (Nashville: Abingdon, 1987).

74. The "Storyteller's Prayer" encapsulates the challenge of the storyteller: "O Lord, may I never tack a moral on to a story, and may I never tell a story without meaning." See Arthur Burrell, *A Guide to Storytelling* (Detroit: Gale, 1975; reprint of 1926 ed.), p. 6.

75. Shelly Rubin and Dennie Wolf, "The Development of Maybe: The Evolution of Social Roles into Narrative Roles," in *Fact, Fiction, and Fantasy in Childhood*, ed. Ellen Winner and Howard Gardner (San Francisco: Jossey-Bass, 1979), p. 15.

76. Dundes, "Introduction," in *Sacred Narrative*, p. 1.

77. For an interesting discussion on myth as a binding element of society, see David S. Noss and John B. Noss, *A History of the World's Religions*, 8th ed. (New York: Macmillan, 1990), pp. 13-14.

events and their historical development. Historicity is understanding the sense of flow in human history, and where individuals stand within the flow.[78] As useful and as instructive as the saying of George Santayana may be in some instances—"Those who cannot remember the past are condemned to fulfill it"[79]—historicity has a bit different focus. Historicity produces the sense of joining the ceaseless parade of humans through the ages who have had similar experiences and dilemmas. While hearers may learn from their predecessors' mistakes, more importantly they learn that they are not alone in their situation or in their decision making. Right or wrong, bright or stupid, brave or fearful, humans in the past and present have experienced kindred circumstances and made their way through them.[80] There is freedom if not wisdom in learners perceiving themselves as performing in a vast human drama. While never diminishing their individuality or their uniqueness, there is comfort and identity in finding themselves within the long line of the human race, with its collection of foibles and triumphs.[81] The religious educator reinforces this virtue of historicity through the use of storytelling.

Historicity helps explain why scriptures are so highly prized by societies. Scripture is the combination of story and instruction retold over the ages that keeps its followers in the flow of the events of human history. It becomes "holy scripture"[82] from the realization that here is human experience in clear, stark, and descriptive presentation. Take, as an example, a story from the Jewish scripture. The oft-repeated narrative recounting Adam and Eve in the Garden of Eden speaks to the human need and desire for historicity. An Adam and an Eve need not have actually existed in that particular paradise for the story to have its power, so historicity is not a form of literalism.[83] The mythic struggle of Adam

---

78. See Miller, *Story and Context*, pp. 116-117.

79. George Santayana, *The Life of Reason*, or *The Phases of Human Progress*, rev. ed. (New York: Scribner's, 1954), p. 82.

80. As John Harrell put it: "There is one way the storyteller can speak to the feeling of alienation, and it is uniquely in his power to do so. That is, to tell once again our story." Harrell, "Why Storytelling Now?" p. 27.

81. For further development of this line of thought, see Siegfried Kracauer, "Time and History," in *History and the Concept of Time*, ed. George H. Nadel (Middletown, Conn.: Wesleyan University Press, 1966), pp. 65-78.

82. By "scripture" I am including but not restricting the term to the Jewish scripture and to the Christian New Testament. Each faith tradition has its own body of literature which can be studied as a resource for the storyteller. One example of a compilation of creation stories from a variety of faiths and traditions in a form appropriate for teaching children is by Sophia Blanche Lyon Fahs and Dorothy T. Spoerl, *Beginnings: Earth, Sky, Life, Death—Stories, Ancient and Modern* (Boston: Starr King Press, 1958). Also see such works as Hamilton Wright Mabie, *Myths Every Child Should Know* (Garden City, N.Y.: Doubleday, Page, 1914); *The Book of Beginnings*, ed. Time-Life editors (Alexandria, Va.: Time-Life Books, 1986); and Virginia Hamilton, *In the Beginning: Creation Stories from Around the World* (San Diego: Harcourt Brace Jovanovich, 1988).

83. The special problem of literalism, which is teaching the basic elements of a story as if they were scientifically verifiable facts and the main focus of learning, can destroy any hope of the learners either stepping into history or learning anything about themselves vicariously through the story. What James Michael Lee had to say about the study of myth can be applied to the study of much of scripture: "It is cognitively erroneous to employ the canons of rational, logical historiography to judge mythical stories whose canons for veracity and verification are of a very dissimilar cognitive order. It is also erroneous to search in myths for rational truths which these myths are supposed to hide in

and Eve with wisdom and ignorance, desire and temptation, right and wrong, and with themselves, teaches contemporary hearers something important about themselves. From the standpoint of such a story, each listener is welcomed and affirmed as part of the human race. No one is better, or worse, than the humanity displayed in the first couple; instead, each individual is in the midst of the same eternal struggle. The story of Adam and Eve, then, does not need to reveal history that is literal, factual, and verifiable.[84] It provides historicity, where each person can find a sense of being a part of the larger human experience.[85]

Contextuality, as companion to historicity, helps place auditors in their own time and space within the flow of human history. Contextuality is learning to tell the differences over time that distinguish one era from another. Contextuality can be seen as that which helps individuals differentiate current experiences from previous experiences, in that it links together events into a whole which then becomes understandable and definable.[86] Historicity, on the other hand, is the virtue which identifies that flow of history. Contextuality formulates a particular point of coherence within the stream of historicity. Contextuality is the personalization of events.

The storyteller uses contextuality whenever the need for realism in the story arises. The storyteller has the liberty of going back into time and making the listener part of the "original context," or of bringing the event forward in time to make it contemporaneous.[87] Again the story of Adam and Eve can illustrate. The storyteller who chooses to move back into history uses the "once upon a time"

---

some 'mysterious' or 'enigmatically sacred' form." Lee, *Content of Religious Instruction*, pp. 152-153. A few sentences later, Lee then said: "Thus, for example, in teaching the Bible from the perspective of cognitive content, the religion teacher should treat its mythic elements, not just in terms of literary imagery or as culturally conditioned ways in which Neareasterners of those days communicated, but rather in a manner which will help the learner gain a deeper understanding of the structure and workings of that kind of reality which the mythic language portrays." Ibid., p. 153. More on this troublesome but important issue for the religious educator as storyteller is developed in the later section of this chapter on the shadow role.

84. The difficulties referred to here are not just related to Genesis 1-3, of course, but are key issues for the historian as a social scientist, and consequently for the storyteller. To get a sense of the problems, see such works as Handlin, *Truth in History*; Leon Golding, *Historical Knowing* (Austin, Tex.: University of Texas Press, 1976), especially Chapter One, "Reference and Verification," pp. 3-27, and Chapter Three, "Historical Facts," pp. 63-91; and Friederich Meinecke, "Historicism and Its Problems: Values and Causalities in History," in *The Varieties of History: From Voltaire to the Present*, ed. Fritz Stern (Cleveland: World, 1956), pp. 267-288.

85. For a scholarly treatment of this entire issue, see the essay by Frank Kermode, "New Ways with Bible Stories," in *Poetry, Narrative, History*, ed. Michael Payne and Harold Schweizer (Cambridge, Mass.: Basil Blackwell, 1990), pp. 29-48.

86. A helpful resource in dealing with history and storytelling, particularly within a religious context, is Richard Ginn's book, *The Present and the Past*. See especially Chapter Three, "An Appraisal of the Methodology and Philosophy of the Discipline of History," pp. 31-49.

87. "In trying to understand this ability of the storyteller to contextualize, we can turn to the study of narrative fiction. There, a *narrative* recounts a story, a series of events in a temporal sequence." Cohan and Shires, *Telling Stories*, p. 1. This consequently is an understanding of *anachronies*, meaning "specific points of disparity between the temporal order of the story sequence and that of the narration." Ibid., p. 84. There are two basic types of anachronies. One is an *analepsis*, which is "the textual point of retrospection," and a *prolepsis*, which "does just the reverse: it flashes ahead to events yet to occur in the story sequence." Ibid., p. 85. These two kinds of "time travel" are both possible for the storyteller to pursue, as discussed in the two paragraphs above.

device. Learners are transported back in time by means of imagination. They are able to see the tree of knowledge; they are able to hear the hiss of the serpent; they are able to taste of the fruit themselves—they are, that is, if the storyteller is an expert in the art. Their personal context is transformed and transcended, allowing the listeners to enter the fantasy garden created in their minds by the skilled storyteller, and from there they can experience the struggle of temptation and the loss of relationship which are the themes of the story line. A good storyteller can make hearers feel uncomfortable as if they, too, are found to be unclothed!

The storyteller can also create a modern-day Garden of Eden. Here the task is not to transport the listeners back in time, but to create the story with a contemporary set of circumstances. The storyteller uses the same dramatic events and themes but in effect bring Adam and Eve into the present. Instead of imagining the pristine beauty of Eden, the listener is now helped to envision the environment of Central Park in mid-town Manhattan. The serpent becomes the local drug pusher, and the naiveté of Adam and Eve relates to the ease of falling into the world of illegal drug use. Again, the figures of the story struggle with temptation, deal with questions of life and death, and the issue of healthy relationships, but this time the context is radically different from those presented in Genesis 1-3. The storyteller uses and develops the virtue of contextuality—of making the events real and applicable—so that the message of the story can be understood and used.[88]

The storyteller, then, exhibits the interwoven virtues of historicity and contextuality. One virtue invites the hearer into the stream of human history, while the other virtue helps the hearer find himself or herself within that stream. The storyteller is a kind of time-traveler, who uses the power of the story to transport his or her audience through time and enables them to learn and experience what it is to be part of the larger human family.

Activity: Participating

The role of the storyteller allows the religious educator to create a sense of at least vicarious participation in the events of the story being told, as well as a sense of belonging among those assembled to listen to the stories.[89] Participation implies more than just hearing data and facts; it means actively being a part of

---

88. Walter Wink has been instrumental in making biblical stories come alive through experiential teaching procedures. A good introduction to this kind of storytelling is Walter Wink, *Transforming Bible Study*, rev. ed. (Nashville: Abingdon, 1989). Also see his earlier book, *The Bible in Human Transformation: A New Paradigm for Bible Study* (Philadelphia: Fortress, 1973).

89. John Harrell expressed the power of storytelling in relation to participation and identity when he wrote: "A principal function of storytelling is the passing along of heritage. The heritage may be as inclusive as the whole human race, the stories told coming from the catholicity of myths and saga from ancient Greece or Iceland and Japan. The heritage may be as particular as the telling of one's family genealogy or the romance of one's town. Heritage gives us needed roots and helps us define who we are. By the way heritage is told, ideals are crystalized, modes of acceptable behavior are established, and one's responsible place in the order is made clear." Harrell, "Why Storytelling Now?" p. 26.

the events of the story.[90] Looking at the gathered community functionally, the ties that bind a community together are normally forged through some communal activity or experience.[91] One of the most powerful ways for community to be built is in sharing a common base of stories.

Stories are a way of bringing and linking people together, if only through imagination and illusion. Stories not only tell hearers who they are—give them their identity—stories create who listeners are and create identities.[92] The storyteller can bring forth a new creation by binding the listeners together through a common experience, one which all will share and hold in common. Listeners belong together because they know and enter into the shared story.[93]

One functional view of a family is that of individuals who participate together by means of their shared experiences and stories. Part of becoming a family is telling, learning, and enjoying these stories together. My daughter is coming to know who she is as a member of the Lines family by hearing and learning her story as a new Lines. One of my fundamental tasks as a parent is to be a storyteller and to help Emily know that she belongs to the family because she shares so intimately in the family stories. As she hears me tell the story of how she came to be a member of our family, and how she grew up among us, and of what we were like in the days of her infancy, she learns who she is as an individual and who we are now as a family. She is gaining her own identity from participating in the creation and the shaping of the family story—and it is the role of the storyteller that through the intimate involvement of participation facilitates these activities of belonging.

Joining and being a member of the extended family carries the same commitment to the learning and sharing of stories. When our threesome of the Lines family goes to visit the larger, extended family, our immediate task is to strengthen the ties of belonging. How do we accomplish that? We listen to and tell stories. Part of the effort is for everyone to share the events that have transpired since last we were all together, so that there is a continuing base of commonly-held sto-

---

90. Jeanette Brown addressed this same idea to religious educators: "We may know quite well what our duties are toward our fellow man, just as the lawyer probably did who invited the parable of the good Samaritan. But a story in which we can identify ourselves in a living way with the characters makes us see and feel the effects of certain types of behavior on persons like ourselves. It is the element of feeling in the well-told story that makes all the difference. There are no feelings in facts, in lists, in statistics." Brown, *The Storyteller in Religious Education*, p. 5.

91. This is given discussion from a religious context in S.D. Gaede, *Belonging: Our Need for Community in Church and Family* (Grand Rapids, Mich.: Zondervan, 1985).

92. An interesting and insightful work in this regard is *Stories Make People: Examples of Theological Work in Community*, comp. Sam Amirtham (Geneva, Switzerland: WCC Publications, 1989). In discussing the role of story in theological reflection, Amirtham said: "The theological task of the church cannot be left to the scholars alone; everybody needs to be a subject and participant in this enterprise. . . . When people become participants in doing theology, theology must take other shapes than that of systematic treatises. People will then create new and appropriate forms. . . . Among prevalent forms of people's theology are 'stories,' narratives, dramas, conversations, group discussions, personal musing, biblical reflections, and also songs, poems, drawings, paintings, etc. So, we say, people make stories." Amirtham, "Introduction," ibid., p. vi. Later, he went to say that in addition, "stories indeed make people." Ibid., p. vii.

93. "When they [the people] begin to tell their own stories of God acting in their daily lives and the lives of their communities, they do so from their own perspective and out of their own conviction. Then faith becomes a living faith, a lived-out faith." Ibid., p. vii.

ries. The familial task is by no means complete, however, when each family member begins to get "caught up" with the news of the various family members. Gradually, subtly, but surely, the conversations begin to include not only the addition of new stories, but the re-telling of the old, historical, family stories. Someone in the family, usually one of the older members, begins to recount the old stories of shared family experience. The "sacred history" of the family is recited for everyone's benefit and enjoyment. The stories of the grandparent's birthday celebrations, or of the weddings, or of funeral services are retold. The stories of the days when the children—now mothers and fathers—lived at "home" are remembered, as are times the family went on that big vacation, or when the children went off to camp. The point of all this activity is the family strengthening its ties of belonging. The younger members are hearing the stories maybe for the first time and are learning about the group of people to which they belong. The older members have heard and told the stories many times before, and they want to be sure that the stories are remembered, and valued. The older members want the fun and enjoyment of hearing and telling the stories, but they also have the responsibility of teaching the stories to the younger generation in order to keep the stories and the family alive.

The specific example of the family given above is easily generalized to a variety of cohesive groups. An obvious one is the joining and belonging to a faith tradition. This is done rather simply: We learn the stories and we become one with them. We are shaped by them, but we also shape the stories themselves. In my own heritage of Christianity, the stories of Jesus and his disciples were not told as irrelevant or isolated fables but as stories that gave me an identity and allowed me to belong to the people called Christians. I grew in my sense of belonging as I grew in my understanding of the stories. As I went off to church as a young boy, it was like going to visit the extended family. Certainly there were the current social relationships, where all of us at least weekly "caught up" on the news of the members of the church family, and this worked to bind us together. But the real reason we gathered together, and what bound us together indivisibly with the larger, historic church, was the old stories that were told and retold. The master storyteller—the "preacher"—told the ancient stories from the pulpit. Volunteer storytellers told the stories to me in Sunday school. I learned the same stories at home, heard them discussed and interpreted around the dinner table and then heard them again at the "church-house." At the church, we not only sat and listened to the stories, but we sang them,[94] memorized them, and acted them out in plays and dramas. The stories became as real and as alive as if I had actually had experienced them—since after a fashion I did.[95]

The dimension of belonging need not always be true of the activity of the storyteller, however, although participation—if only cognitively—certainly is. One

---

94. For a good discussion of this idea, see Linda J. Clark, "Hymn Singing: The Congregation Making Faith," in *Carriers of Faith: Lessons from Congregational Studies*, ed. Carl S. Dudley, Jackson W. Carroll, and James P. Wind (Louisville: Westminster/John Knox Press, 1991), pp. 49-64.

95. For a more formal treatment of this general idea of the church "family," see James F. Hopewell, *Congregation: Stories and Structures*, ed. Barbara G. Wheeler (Philadelphia: Fortress, 1978).

of the great values of storytelling is that one can vicariously experience any number of events or circumstances that in actuality one would never choose to do personally. Anything from skydiving to automobile racing to space travel can be experienced safely and easily by way of storytelling, although the individual may never move a muscle out of the story room. There are a multitude of stories outside of an individual's traditions that he or she will never experience directly, but from which one can still learn and participate by way of story.[96]

Storytelling helps people participate in a wide variety of activities and experiences through the sharing and teaching of stories. As listeners hear some stories, they may learn more of who they are and gain a stronger sense of identity. Some may be bonded into the extended family by the sharing in the old, old stories. Others learn at least something of what it is like to be a member of another culture, of another civilization, of another faith tradition. Stories are tickets to worlds unknown, opportunities to escape the tiny segments of individual life, or as one author put it: "Stories shift the center of interest from the self outwards; they often release use from the prison of our own thoughts, and in this way they illuminate."[97] The true storyteller invites hearers to the excitement and possibly to the liberation from the shackles of the present moment through the vicarious participation in stories.

Shadow Role: Dogmatist

In general terms, the shadow role of the storyteller is played by anyone who misuses stories. This misuse can take several forms. One of the most prevalent, if relatively benign, is demonstrated by the person who bores people with his or her stories. This violates the virtues the storyteller is supposed to be promoting: personalistic historicity and contextuality. The dull storyteller neither helps the hearers step into the flow of history nor adjusts the stories to fit the current context. The listeners have no sense of participation with the events of the story, and the storyteller ultimately fails at doing any effective teaching. In all likelihood, however, this storyteller does not intend to be boring. These flaws are not so much damaging to the listeners as they are anesthetizing. With skill, with commitment, and with another subject, there is at least hope that the soporific storyteller can improve.[98]

The shadow role of the dogmatist is of another type. The dogmatist does not misuse the story by accident or out of ignorance, but intentionally pursues an entirely different aim than the kind of storyteller that is being described through-

---

96. The experience of "living" through the stories of slavery as related by Alex Haley in *Roots* (Garden City, N.Y.: Doubleday, 1976) in book format and then in the television series is only one obvious example that captivated millions of readers and viewers during the 1970s and 1980s.

97. Bone, *Children's Stories and How to Tell Them*, p. 47.

98. Ruth Beam has this encouraging word: "Storytelling, like any art or sport, requires utmost dedication if the participators or spectators are to be kept interested. However, as Gladys Mary Talbot once observed, 'Unlike other arts, all of you may participate in this one, provided you are willing to pay the price—study, work, and practice.'" Ruth Beam, "Storytelling for Children," in *Childhood Education in the Church*, ed. Robert E. Clark, Joanne Brubaker, and Roy B. Zuck, rev. ed. (Chicago: Moody Press, 1986), p. 528. Beam was quoting from Gladys Mary Talbot, ed., *Stories I Love to Tell* (Chicago: Moody Press, 1949), p. 9.

out this chapter. This approach can indeed be damaging to those under the control of the dogmatist. Because the dogmatist is so intentional in his or her distortion of the role, there is much less hope for improvement. Working through the following four points taken from the paradigmatic story of Adam and Eve will give sufficient illustration of the scope of the problem.

First, the dogmatist perverts the story of Adam and Eve by missing its deeper values but focusing only on the "facts." The storyteller in the shadow role ceases to tell a story that engages and captures the imagination, what Katherine Cather called "truth through concrete example."[99] Instead, the dogmatist entombs the "truth" in concrete, concentrating on what he or she perceives as the all-important aspect of content.[100] Genesis 1-3 no longer is a story with universal mythic characteristics but is transformed into a documentary as sure and as complete as if recorded on videotape. The "storyteller" is now the on-the-scene reporter, citing dates (such as the well-known but ridiculous 4004 B.C.E.), time of day of the various acts of creation, and even making efforts to try to locate the exact geographic region of the Garden of Eden. Genesis 1-3 ceases to be a story in the hands and mouth of a dogmatist. It becomes full and factual truth without mixture of either error or imagination. This is the method of the literalist, who is unable to understand that the truth of stories can lie beyond the words or the specific events being related.[101]

Second, the aim of facilitating interpretational skills in the learner is nowhere in sight for the dogmatist. The aim instead is acceptance and acquiescence of the learner to the imposed interpretation of an authority.[102] The facts are known, and need to be received at face value. Interpretations undertaken by learners would only open the door to ambiguity and vagueness—idle speculation, if you

---

99. Cather, *Religious Education Through Story-Telling*, p. 44.

100. "Modern catechetics is characterized by the shift in emphasis from method to content of the message." Johannes Hofinger, *The Art of Teaching Christian Doctrine: The Good News and Its Proclamation*, rev. ed. (Notre Dame, Ind.: University of Notre Dame Press, 1962), p. 62. Interestingly enough, this is the opening sentence of Chapter Eight, entitled "Catechetical Method as Handmaid of the Message." Ibid., pp. 62-89.

101. For a sample of how ridiculous this position can become, see the unintentionally humorous tract, *Why I Preach that the Bible Is Literally True*, by W.A. Criswell (Nashville: Broadman, 1969). Some of the humor comes out when reading a passage such as the following: "The scriptures do not need to be supplemented from any other source, reason, or experience. The Bible is in itself a complete organism of truth and is sufficient for all our needs." Ibid., p. 88. If this statement is true, then why, pray tell, is Criswell writing a book supplementing these very same scriptures and receiving profit from it? Indeed, why does he preach at all if the Bible needs no corroboration? I think a closer reading of Criswell and his ilk reveals that he means his own interpretation and preaching needs no competition from those who may disagree with his own version of inspired truth. For a break from the current perspective of this book, incidentally, see Chapter Thirteen of Criswell's book, "Fact or Fable in Genesis," pp. 95-99.

102. This paragraph addresses the transmissive approach to education. Jim Wilhoit, in his often too-kind appraisal of the approach, did have this good point which has wider application than just to Christian religious educators: "Transmissive education fosters an unhealthy dependence on teachers. The students know that the teacher will give them the answers, and so they become more and more passive, expecting to be spoon-fed. Christian education must not support an educational consumerism in which students, being unable or unwilling to satisfy their own basic spiritual needs and those of others, simply consume the spiritual truths imparted by a teacher." Jim Wilhoit, *Christian Education and the Search for Meaning* (Grand Rapids, Mich.: Baker, 1986), pp. 75-76.

will. This approach says that since the ancient and revelatory scriptures give the essential facts in sufficient detail, further work on the story itself is unnecessary. The facts do not need a variety of interpretations, since the facts make up the story and those facts lead to one, proper interpretation. What the dogmatist demands, in actuality, is acceptance of his or her interpretation as the proper one, the correct one, the factual one, and the only acceptable one.[103] To "interpret" the story in another way, such as with the aid or insight of another literary form, is not only useless as far as the dogmatist is concerned, but wrong.

The third point, that of damage to the hearer, surely need hardly be mentioned. To teach that there is only one correct interpretation of any story, and that the interpretation given is the one that must be accepted, is destructive to the development of the person,[104] if not to the very nature of humanity. This places the story, in fact and interpretation, in the hands of one person or one profession. The seeds of manipulation and abusive control are planted when the role of the listener is reduced to hearing, accepting, and obeying.[105] Such behavior and thinking may be appropriate for training a pet, but it is of little merit in the effort to nurture humans toward increasing levels of maturity.

Fourth, virtually no hope survives that the dogmatist will become a genuine storyteller, since this would require relinquishing some control over the story and its hearers. It is hard to imagine why a dogmatist, in the position of power, would loosen the grip. To do so would be to "compromise the truth," and to permit the unlearned and ignorant to pervert the sacred narrative. For those who see themselves entrusted with preserving and reproducing the truth in pure and untainted form,[106] the prospects of throwing open the doors to ignorant and

---

103. See, for example, the words of the Catholic catecheticist Hubert Halbfas: "There is only one interpretation, and not a 'pious explanation of scriptures existing side by side with scientific exegesis,' since 'whenever understanding is involved, we must today be concerned with scientific and factual understanding.'" Hubert Halbfas, *Theory of Catechetics: Language and Experience in Religious Education* (New York: Herder and Herder, 1971), pp. 85-86. The linguistic and cognitive approach of Halbfas was made even clearer a few lines later when he stated: "I support the basic thesis that 'Christian religious education is fundamentally biblical teaching.'" Ibid., p. 86.

104. The issue addressed in this paragraph is authoritarianism. In a study of authoritarianism and its effect on the development of children's personalities, C.K. Shah said that in authoritarian environments "the responsibility for decisions is clearly placed in the hands of a given individual. He may delegate part of his authority to subordinates but his superiors would hold him accountable for the consequences. The authoritarian person would prefer not to delegate part of his authority. He would prefer to centralize all the powers of decision making with him." C.K. Shah, *Personality Development of Children: A Study of Personality Development of Children as a Function of Parental Authoritarianism* (Bombay, India: Multi-Tech Publishing Company, 1982), p. 7. For a broader understanding of this topic, see such works as Claire B. Ernhart and Jane Loevinger, *Authoritarian Family Ideology: A Measure, Its Correlates, and Its Robustness* (Society of Multivariate Experimental Psychology, 1969); T.W.Adorno, Else Frenkel-Brunswick, Daniel J. Levinson, and R. Nevitt Sanford in collaboration with Betty Aron, Maria Hertz Levinson, and William Morrow, *The Authoritarian Personality* (New York: Harper and Brothers, 1950); and *Studies in the Scope and Method of "The Authoritarian Personality": Continuities in Social Research*, ed. Richard Christie and Marie Johada (Glencoe, Ill.: Free Press, 1954).

105. This point is given more discussion in the shadow role section of Chapter Four, "The Religious Educator as Parent."

106. See Joseph Andreas Jungmann, *Handing on the Faith: A Manual of Catechetics* (New York: Herder and Herder, 1959), especially Chapter Two, "The Catechist," pp. 65-78.

dangerous rabble are to be avoided at all costs.

The dogmatists are the religious storytellers who have grasped the sacred stories by the neck, mistakenly thinking they can extract the truth from them. In reality they are squeezing not only the truth but the very breath of life from the stories, consequently depriving their hearers of the desperately needed stories that could help them all to know how and why to live.

Faith Tradition Resource: Greek Mythology

Greek mythology is a rich faith tradition resource for developing the role of the religious educator as storyteller. Dipping into the resources of a faith tradition outside the one in which an individual has been nurtured is valuable for understanding other peoples, for comparing one's own faith, and for broadening knowledge of the expressions of religion. These reasons hold true for the study of virtually any faith tradition other than one's own, but the mythology of the ancient Greeks opens yet another dimension. A serious study of Greek mythology provides enough emotional distance and perspective to hear and understand more clearly the myths endemic to one's own particular faith tradition. Sometimes it is difficult to grasp the extent and the power of myth in our own present faith tradition since it is held it so closely to the person. A look at Greek mythology may provide the degree of objectivity that allows for a more detached understanding of the traditions and stories in which each individual dwells and from which each one draws his or her identity. Reading or hearing myths, in turn, can help contemporary persons appreciate and learn of the storytellers and the interpreters of the Greek mythologies. Whatever else may be said of the myths and their meanings, the power and the skill of their storytellers receive the highest affirmation simply because the stories have endured for so many generations.

There are a number of reasons for turning to a study of Greek mythology as a paradigm for a faith tradition. First, Greek mythology is easily and immediately accessible. The stories are available in various translations, editions, and anthologies limited only by the scholar's time and financial or academic resources.[107] Libraries, schools, and bookstores have these ready for anyone's perusal.

Second, mythology is by no means a scholarly dead end. Classical and liter-

---

107. A few representative resources of an introductory nature to Greek mythology are as follows: Michael Grant, *Myths of the Greeks and Romans* (New York: Mentor Books, 1962); Edith Hamilton, *Mythology: Timeless Tales of Gods and Heroes* (New York: Mentor Books, 1942); W.H.D. Rouse, *Gods, Heroes and Men of Ancient Greece* (New York: The New American Library, 1957); Mark P.O. Morford and Robert J. Lenardon, *Classical Mythology*, 3rd ed. (New York: Longman, 1985); Robert Graves, *The Greek Myths*, Vol. One and Vol. Two, rev. ed. (New York: Penguin Books, 1960); H.J.A. Rose, *A Handbook of Greek Mythology: Including Its Extension to Rome*, 6th ed. (New York: Dutton, 1959); and Donald Richardson, *Great Zeus and All His Children: Greek Mythology for Adults* (Englewood Cliffs, N.J.: Prentice-Hall, 1984). This last book, by Richardson, is an excellent place for the adult who has little or no background in mythology to start reading. He made his case this way: "This is a first book in Greek mythology. Its concern is not so much with the representation of authentic folklore as it is with the lively depiction of characters and actions that have become so much the topics of art and the stuff of allusions and metaphor in our own tradition that an ignorance of them is an ignorance of our language itself." Ibid., p. xi.

ature study continues to dig deeply into the world of ancient mythology,[108] and all kinds of educational courses are available for such an enterprise. This is one type of religious study that public schools are not afraid of, so middle and high schools students are quite often introduced to these ancient stories.

Third, and most importantly, the myths and legends of the Greeks are captivating stories in and of themselves. An "assignment" to read the *Illiad,* for example, takes nowhere the motivational effort as a trigonometry lesson, since the world of gods and heroes is so engaging and absorbing. There are no intricate formulas to learn or bizarre rituals to attend. One simply reads the stories as narrated by some of history's greatest storytellers.

Some negatives are also involved in such a study. First, although ancient mythology is not an academic dead-end, and although interest in it remains high, lifestyle or personal commitment has nothing to do with the study. At best learners can turn their cognitive, scholarly interests toward the myths, but they cannot enter the experiential world of the ancient Greeks and see how the myths affected people's everyday living. There are no active churches or temples or synagogues for people to gather and worship Zeus, or Hera, or Triton. Greek mythology is not a "living world religion" on the scene today, so that persons of today cannot get a taste of the beliefs of adherents first-hand. There is no "community of faith" to visit that can interpret the stories in context.[109]

Second, since no practicing faith community exists, learners of myths today are left to depend on the necessarily dispassionate and relatively objective classical scholars for the historical information. It is no secret that a study of religion is very different from the practice of religion. Moderns have no way of knowing the power of the stories and their gods over the "common" people of the day. Were the myths seen as entertaining stories, or were they accepted as factual events? As far as the original hearers were concerned, were they hearing what are now called "myths" or learning sacred theology?[110] For all the erudition of pre-

---

108. A few representative sources in Greek mythology of a more scholarly nature are as follows: Walter Burket, *Structure and History in Greek Mythology and Ritual* (Berkeley: University of California Press, 1979); Marcel Detienne, *The Creation of Mythology*, trans. Margaret Cook (Chicago: University of Chicago Press, 1986); Lowell Edmunds, ed., *Approaches to Greek Myth* (Baltimore: Johns Hopkins University Press, 1990); W.K.C. Guthrie, *The Greeks and Their Gods* (Boston: Beacon Press, 1955); Michael Grant and John Hazel, *Gods and Mortals in Classical Mythology* (Springfield, Mass., Merriam, 1973); and Martin P.A. Nilsson, *A History of Greek Religion*, 2nd ed. (New York: Norton, 1963).

109. Other than experiencing the myths through storytelling, we are forced to depend on researchers such as archaeologists to help us understand the Greeks and their world. For a good introduction to this aspect of study, see E.O. James, *Myth and Ritual in the Ancient Near East: An Archaeological and Documentary Study* (New York: Praeger, 1958), and John Ferguson, *Among the Gods: An Archaeological Exploration of Ancient Greek Religion* (London: Routlege, 1989).

110. A fascinating book on this topic is by Paul Veyne, *Did the Greeks Believe in Their Myths?: An Essay on the Constitutive Imagination*, trans. Paula Wissing (Chicago: University of Chicago Press, 1988). Veyne helps us not only understand the Greeks, but ourselves through the study of the Greeks and their beliefs. In the last chapter of the book, he said: "Therefore, people believed in myths for a long time, according to programs that, to be sure, varied enormously from one era to another. It is normal for people to believe in the works of the imagination. People believe in religions, in *Madame Bovary* while they read, in Einstein, in Fustel de Coulanges, in the Trojan origins of the Franks. However, in certain societies some of these works are deemed fictions." Ibid., p. 117.

sent scholarship, no one can speak authoritatively or experientially about a lost religion and a lost civilization. As J.W. Rogerson said: "In the present state of our knowledge—and I would add, probably even in our future state—there is no such thing as the *real* meaning or purpose of myth."[111]

Third, building upon the two preceding points, there exists no genuine context for taking the myths, legends, and stories seriously in terms of faith. Apparently no one today prays to Zeus, but many pray to the God(s) of Jesus, Muhammad, or Moses. How are these people different, or just as appropriately, how are they alike?[112] Any answer someone today could give would do injustice to, say, a believer in Zeus, since there is no one to speak for him or her. Present-day learners run the risk of treating ancient peoples as sub-human and pre-modern beings who may have believed in a primitive religion that does not meet the standards of the present living religions. The egocentrism of the modern age is difficult to combat without living representatives of mythology goading the present examiners into proper respect.

Why look back at a "dead" religion or faith resource? One value is the possibility of approaching such a faith tradition precisely because of its lack of threat. There is no group or cult that will threaten or entice a person to join the worship of Zeus, for example. It may be that mythology can allow individuals to walk into the museum of a past religion and see somewhat objectively the dynamics of religion without the threat of being pulled into heresy or out of one's own present faith tradition resource. Hearers can simply let the stories speak to them, and study of the Greek myth—its form, structure, and interpretation—can then proceed without personal issues getting in the way and clouding judgment.

The critical step, however, is moving from Greek mythology back to a current faith tradition. When the analysis for form, structure, and interpretation learned in the objectivity of Greek mythology is then applied to the stories of the individual's faith community, storytellers can expect reaction from those disturbed by such activity.[113] Religious educators and storytellers in any age or faith tradition are never far from criticism when their stories, applications, or interpretations touch home—especially when these differ from the listeners' expectations. Since stories are so much a part of establishing identity, to change or challenge a story and its interpretation is a very personal and threatening activity.

---

111. J. W. Rogerson, "Slippery Words: Myth," in *Sacred Narrative*, p. 71.

112. This was precisely the point of Veyne's essay, as he concluded: "The theme of this book was very simple. Merely by reading the title, anyone with the slightest historical background would immediately have answered, 'But of course they believed in their myths!' We have simply wanted also to make it clear that what is true of 'them' is also true of ourselves and to [bring] out the implications of this primary truth." Veyne, *Did the Greeks Believe in Their Myths?* p. 129.

113. Even the revered Homer and Hesiod—paragons of Greek storytelling—were so attacked. Plato (speaking through Socrates) accused these two of being mere imitators of truth and not true teachers. See, for example, Plato, *The Republic*, Book V in *The Dialogues of Plato*, ed. Justin D. Kaplan (New York: Washington Square Press, 1950), pp. 335-336. Joseph Mazzeo reported Plato saying that these poets were telling "immoral and unworthy stories of the gods. They do not give a true picture of the divine nature and appeal to our base passions rather than that which is highest in us." Joseph Anthony Mazzeo, *Varieties of Interpretation* (Notre Dame, Ind.: University of Notre Dame Press, 1978), p. 71.

Historical Personage: Homer

The Greek poet, minstrel, and storyteller Homer can serve as a valuable role model for the contemporary religious educator, but he does so in a remarkable manner. One obvious difficulty in citing Homer is that there is no absolute assurance as to who he was, and whether or not he really existed. In his discussion on the topic, Gilbert Highet said: "The *Illiad* and the *Odyssey* are the oldest complete books in the Western world. No one knows for certain who wrote them, or where, or when. Suddenly they gush out of the earth like living water from a subterranean source, far back beyond the beginning of our recorded history, and like strong rivers they have continued to flow with incomparable force and vitality through nearly three thousand years and over half a planet."[114] Highet spent little time in his work exploring who Homer was and instead focused on the stories attributed to Homer—the *results* of the storyteller. The fog of history has effectively obscured the identity of the historical Homer: "Who, then, wrote the poems? We know little directly. We have only the name, Homer, and a few traditions placing his birthplace on the Greek coast of Asia Minor. The tale that he was blind comes from a little hymn written by one of his imitators. . . . The classical Greeks knew nothing certain about him, even the century when he lived. All we can say of him is inference."[115]

Highet's is not the only point of view on the identity of Homer, of course.[116] A more personal treatment of Homer was provided in the minor classic *The Singer of Tales* by Albert Lord.[117] This book, in stark contrast to Highet's view, was essentially a work on the person of Homer himself, describing Homer as a minstrel and a "singer of tales" who "represents all singers of tales from time immemorial and unrecorded to the present. . . . Among the singers of modern times there is none equal to Homer."[118] Lord had no hesitancy in speaking specifically about the historical Homer as a verifiable personage. How such a shadowy figure as Homer can be demonstrated to have no contemporary peer requires an interesting leap of logic, incidentally.

It is for the very reason that the human, and historical, face of Homer appears so inscrutable that Homer is presented as a model storyteller. It seems instructive that while the stories of Homer have remained alive through the ages, the identity of Homer himself has faded away.[119] To find the value and the person of

---

114. Gilbert Highet, "Introduction," in *The Complete Works of Homer* (New York: Modern Library, 1950), p. v.

115. Ibid., p. x.

116. For a classic and fascinating study of Homer's work as a "divine sage" and for the history of its allegorical interpretation, see Robert Lamberton, *Homer the Theologian: Neoplatonist Allegorical Reading and The Growth of the Epic Tradition* (Berkeley: University of California Press, 1986).

117. Albert Bates Lord, *The Singer of Tales* (Cambridge: Harvard University Press, 1960).

118. Ibid., p. vii.

119. Here as elsewhere in the discussion of historical(?) figures, parallels to the quest for the historical Jesus come to mind. The relationship of Jesus with Homer is apparent. The Christian church has many stories in scripture attributed to the historical Jesus, and indeed volumes of doctrine have derived from them, but virtually nothing about the historical personage of Jesus is known. As with Homer, the stories Jesus told have survived seemingly more intact than the personal information. For more on this, see Chapter Thirteen of this book, " 'The Religious Educator as Minister."

Homer, one must turn and listen to his stories. The importance of the stories does not rest upon the personhood of Homer but transcends him. This lesson in creativity, delivery, interpretation, and ultimate humility and submission to story is one that the "historical Homer" teaches from virtual anonymity.[120]

Religious educators must keep in mind that they, too, tell stories, and that the stories will endure, while the identities of the religious educators are subservient to them. Religious educators as storytellers need to sharpen their skills and develop their abilities to the fullest, since no one questions that stories are dependent on their tellers for force and interpretation. The fact remains, however, that storytellers are in service of the stories and that it is the stories that will and should survive over time.

Contemporary Example: Robert Béla Wilhelm

When the attention of the storyteller is turned directly toward religious education, a contemporary example who provides a good model of this ancient art is Robert Béla Wilhelm (b. 1943). Though possibly not as widely known in ecumenical circles as some of the other representatives of religious education examined in this book, or as widely published as most, Wilhelm is eminently qualified to teach his craft for one primary reason: He is an expert storyteller. When he is not engaged in the telling of stories, he is involved in training others to become storytellers—particularly as the telling of stories can relate to the improvement of religious education.[121] A brief overview of some of Wilhelm's suggestions and ideas on the art of storytelling will serve to bring together many of the themes and topics already discussed throughout the present chapter.

Because Wilhelm is a storyteller at heart, he has chosen not to produce a great quantity of written material that is available for examination. The unexpected but logical benefit of his decision is that this overview and evaluation of his work can be relatively brief and simple, but deeper reflection confirms this to be entirely appropriate. A storyteller needs to be about his or her work, which is different than scholarly analysis or erudite pronouncements. A storyteller needs to tell stories and to leave the more pedantic processes to those with more prosaic abilities.[122] The chief resource examined here is Wilhelm's doctoral dissertation,[123] which dealt specifically with the need for storytelling in religious education, as well as with some ways in which the religious educator can become more accomplished and skilled in the rich teaching style of the storyteller.

---

120. John Horgan quoted archaeologist Sarantis Symeonoglou: "'There is one faction of scholars who say that Homer's stories are myths and have no relation to reality,' he remarks, 'Others say there was a historical presence. It is really a matter of faith.'" See John Horgan, "Odyssey: Dig on Ithica Seeks the Dwelling of Homer's Famed Wanderer," *Scientific American* 257:5 (November, 1987), p. 18.

121. Wilhelm directs Storyfest Journeys, an organization that sponsors frequent training seminars around the United States (primarily) on the topic of storytelling. The base of operations is in Washington, D.C.

122. This is reminiscent of the earlier discussion of Homer, of whom so little is actually known other than the vibrancy of his legacy of stories.

123. Robert Béla Wilhelm, "Storytelling as a Religious Art Form for Contemporary Christianity," ThD. dissertation (Berkeley: Graduate Theological Union, 1976).

Overview

Probably the first reaction many people would have toward reading about someone's dissertation is at least trepidation if not outright refusal, since dissertations are not generally known either for their readability or for their exciting plot lines. In the hands of a storyteller, however, a dissertation becomes yet another avenue or opportunity to tell stories and to talk about their meaning, and such is the case with the effort by Wilhelm. Not the scholarly tome one would normally expect,[124] it is actually a combined description and transcription of a workshop Wilhelm led to train storytellers. He identified the workshop procedure this way: "This three-hour program uses a variety of storytelling techniques to help adults gain storytelling skills through a rediscovery of their storytelling childhood worlds. The written materials included in this part of the dissertation include descriptions of the workshop, as well as reflections upon it."[125] While the whole of the dissertation employed a range of media such as pictures, audio tapes, and guided fantasies to illustrate the use of stories in religious education, this overview focuses only on the sections that directly dealt with the art of verbally telling stories.[126]

As one would anticipate coming from a dissertation, Wilhelm's thesis was clearly stated: "The thesis proposed here is that storytelling is one artform that is especially useful for mythmaking in church communities today. Storytelling is more than a specific artform, however: it is a language that can be spoken through many artforms. Part of [this] thesis project, then, is to explore the effectiveness of using a number of artforms for storytelling in an attempt to lead the person to the rediscovery of mythic experience (in general) and the gospel myth (in particular)."[127] What must be clarified, though, is Wilhelm's use of the term "myth." He explained his reason for using this term: "The link between the mystery of the primal religious experience and its expression in theology is myth. Myth says enough of the experience to let it develop and grow, but it does not say so much as to become a substitute for it. . . . Myth is a threshold experience, linking together the realm of theology and the realm of faith."[128] In Wilhelm's writing, then, the terms "myth" and "story" are often used interchangeably. This adds a bit of threat for many people, as he acknowledged: "Today, myth is equated with falsehood, and the Christian is reluctant to accept the gospel as his personal and communal

---

124. For example, in the concluding section of his dissertation Wilhelm wrote: "This last section will not try to reduce my conclusions to a linear dimension. This will not even be an attempt at summary, and the format will certainly not be the familiar scholarly essay. Instead, I will try to express the conclusions of this study in the form most appropriate to the topic, and will attempt to express my conclusions in a series of poetic probes." Ibid., p. 199.

125. Ibid., p. ii.

126. This information is contained primarily in Part One: "Educator's Workshop on Storytelling," pp. 1-82. Part Two ("Illustrated Story," pp. 83-165) was an extensive discussion on an illustrated story, and Part Three ("Guided Mythmaking," pp. 167-198) was an exercise in a guided fantasy. These parts were written in an experiential format, not conducive to summary or narrative discussion.

127. Ibid., p. 3. These other artforms are the ones referred to in the previous footnote and are not explored in this overview.

128. Ibid., p. 2.

myth."[129] His point, though, was that religious educators need to recover the use of "fables and fantasies" so that faith is not totally reduced to "strict logical expression."[130] Myth, or in the present context, story, "gives tangible shape to our encounter with God on the levels of imagination, challenge, and commitment. Our encounter with God, person-to-person, is an experience that cannot be contained within the parameters of reason and history. The meeting is always an epiphany, and the sacred becomes present to us in the forms of images, rituals, and myths."[131]

For Wilhelm, myth and story are essential factors in human existence, because "all reality is a story. From the beginning—from the time of creation—there has been storytelling. Indeed, Creation happens because God himself begins to tell His Story."[132] This storytelling is not a set or predetermined monologue, however, because "there is a continual dialogue between God and ourselves."[133] God and humans reveal themselves to one another, and "in the flux of all human activity there is a process going on, a story being told. The story is our story, but it is also a response to His story."[134] It is impossible to read Wilhelm and separate out his understanding of God from the need of humans for stories. All are intimately intertwined, which is the reason why Wilhelm is so concerned that the art of storytelling should be revived. He pursued this line of thinking as he uncovered the core of the dissertation: "In order that we may more fully understand how storytelling is a dialogue between God and humans, we must discover some of the religious characteristics of storytelling."[135] Wilhelm found four of these basic characteristics, which are presented below.

Storytelling as a Special Language. Wilhelm determined that humans use three different kinds of language, only one of which is the special language appropriate for storytelling. The first kind of language was what he called "day-talk": "From the time we arise in the morning, until the time we go to sleep at night, we use a language to get us through the day . . . what can be called ordinary wake-a-day consciousness—or 'Day-Talk.'"[136] The purpose of this ordinary, conventional type of language is "to communicate with one another concerning all the aspects of conscious life"; it is a "tool for creating a cosmos out of chaos: language holds families, societies—and seemingly the whole world—together as it explains, describes, shares, identifies, shapes, limits, and nurtures all of life." As he said in summary: "Above all, the purpose of day-talk is that it 'makes sense.'"[137]

The second type of language Wilhelm treated was that which occurs during sleep, the language of dreams, or as he termed it, "night-talk": "Dream lan-

---

129. Ibid. This recalls the Joseph Campbell statement quoted earlier: "No, mythology is not a lie, mythology is poetry, it is metaphorical." See Campbell with Moyers, *The Power of Myth*, p. 163.

130. Wilhelm, "Storytelling as a Religious Art Form," p. 2. Wilhelm here echoes what was said earlier in the chapter about myth being an "extra-rational form of knowing."

131. Ibid.

132. Ibid., p. 6.

133. Ibid., p. 7.

134. Ibid.

135. Ibid.

136. Ibid., pp. 7-8.

137. Ibid., p. 8.

guage, or 'Night-Talk', however, is a language . . . in which the sleeper is both the teller and the listener. Night-talk is our own private language with ourselves."[138] This second language is used to "talk about all the myriad aspects of life: about that which gives joy or sorrow, about our hopes and fears, about the problems that need to be 'talked out.' We need to reconsider and re-evaluate that which has happened in the last day, and we need to look forward to tomorrow."[139] The key aspect of night-talk is that "it is rich in images, and the whole substance of night-talk is that it is a language of the imagination."[140] The result is two languages that are very different: "It is almost impossible to integrate day-consciousness with night-consciousness for each values reality in a different way. Dreams lack in clarity while wakefulness lacks in imagination. Yet, dreams are rich in images, and day-talk is clear and meaningful."[141]

The third language combines, integrates, and transcends the other two into what Wilhelm called "twilight talk": talk that transpires in the dusk and the dawn, where neither are actually "day nor night, yet have elements of both day and night within them."[142] This third tongue is the language of storytelling, described here by Wilhelm as he extended the twilight metaphor: "The magic of storytelling can be found in the way that it blends the best of day-talk and night-talk. For example, stories can take the rich images of dream-talk and express it in a structure that makes sense. Through storytelling we become consciously aware of a different kind of reality. Yet, at the same time, stories hold fast to the rules of day-talk. Stories make sense. They have beginnings, unfold through a plot, and come to a conclusion. We don't rub our eyes at the end of a tale and wonder what it was all about—like we do with dreams. Instead, we have a clear and definite experience that stays with us in our wake-a-day life."[143] Then Wilhelm made the application: "Storytelling, then, is always a bridge between the two parts of ourselves that are normally estranged: our reason and our dreams. It is a language that makes us whole again; it is a transition rite. Dawn and dusk are traditional times of prayer, meditation, and relaxation. The rituals that we perform at these times are crucial to our experience of wholeness in our lives."[144]

Storytelling as Escape and Recreation. One of the oft-forgotten but important aspects of storytelling is that it can allow the listeners to escape from the mundane and the routines of life, if only for a short respite. Wilhelm listed six basic types of escapes[145] people find in storytelling: escapes from reality, from boredom, from limitations, from loneliness, from hurt, and from fear.[146] Wilhelm hurried on to say that "any storytelling, however, is more than mere escape,

---

138. Ibid., p. 9.
139. Ibid.
140. Ibid.
141. Ibid., p. 10.
142. Ibid.
143. Ibid., pp. 10-11.
144. Ibid., p. 11.
145. An article Wilhelm wrote in 1972 addresses three of these fears—fear of the unknown, fear of limitations, and fear of death—from the perspective of rituals and celebrations that help us overcome these fears. See Robert Béla Wilhelm, "Community, Celebration, and Freedom," *The Living Light* 9:4 (Winter, 1972), pp. 58-67.
146. Wilhelm, "Storytelling as a Religious Art Form," pp. 11-13.

and should not be equated with 'escapism.' We do not enter into stories because life is too harsh and too much for us. Stories are not used to replace the wake-a-day world, and we do not remain in the bounds of the story (psychotic-fashion) once the tale comes to an end."[147] Instead of being a retreat from facing reality, stories are a way of making sense of those realities and of finding some sense of unity, as Wilhelm explained: "Yet, besides being an escape, storytelling is also a recovery of a wholesome view of life. It is a process of re-creating the world by relaxation and recreation in ourselves. In storytelling we are provided with a glimpse of life as it can be, and in the experience of hearing a story that glimpse begins to become real in the life of the hearer."[148]

Storytelling as a Joyous Ending. While Wilhelm admitted that not all stories truly have a happy ending, his point was that "the end of a story is also— simultaneously—a new beginning. Though the story objectively ends when the teller falls into silence, there is a subjective element that turns the tale into an opportunity for new beginning in the heart of the listener."[149] Wilhelm then described the underlying structure of many traditional stories as following these four steps: The hope and anticipation of the beginning; the difficulty and the struggle of the middle; the joyous resolution of the end; and the hope and anticipation of a new beginning.[150]

Wilhelm related the storytelling cycle to the life cycle of humans: Birth, with its beginnings; growth and its changes; death and its endings; and rebirth, with its new beginnings. He said that a primary function of good storytelling is the communication of this knowledge—indeed, the experience—of the ebb and flow of life that is given by the old to the young,[151] and that the communication is achieved in the rhythms of the story.[152] This deeper value of storytelling was made clear by Wilhelm this way: "Storytelling, then, is a process of affirming life. It is a basic way of saying that—despite all the difficulties of living—life is good. The elders in a community who tell stories over and over again come to the 'happy ending' which communicates the value to their listeners that life is worth living. And as the tale comes to an end, and the audience leaves that enchanted space with feelings of hope, joy, contentment, assurance, etc., there is renewal in the heart. The 'and they lived happily ever after' becomes a promise—and a pledge—that the listener will experience the same as he goes back into the everyday world refreshed, renewed, and re-Created."[153]

Storytelling as Entry into a Special and Sacred Time and Place. This fourth

---

147. Ibid., p. 13.
148. Ibid., p. 14.
149. Ibid., p. 19.
150. Ibid.
151. Wilhelm wrote an article in 1970 that expanded on this point. He said, in part: "But storytelling is the art of the old (as play is the art of the young), and storytelling has traditionally been reserved for the village elders, the grandmothers, and the poets and sages. Children themselves do not learn storytelling spontaneously—as they do learn play. Instead, they must learn a language from their elders and become story-*listeners*. The religious educator must do the same: he must first learn to listen." Robert Béla Wilhelm, "Catechists as Players and Story-Tellers," *The Living Light* 7:4 (Winter, 1970), p. 99.
152. Wilhelm, "Storytelling as a Religious Art Form," p. 21.
153. Ibid., pp. 22-23.

and final characteristic of religious storytelling is what Wilhelm said needs to be recovered from childhood: "These places are what gave significance to our childhood worlds, for we did not enter them in a disinterested adult manner. As adults, space is quantitative rather than qualitative. They are spaces to be filled by profane functions. For children, places are more frequently charged with 'Power'. . . . To enter into one of these spaces is, for the child, to step out of the ordinary world."[154] To illustrate, Wilhelm discussed briefly five kinds of "child-hood space": a secret place, a private place, a forbidden place, a boundary space, and a far-away space.[155] As Wilhelm explained: "[These spaces] indicate that children live in a far different world, a world where space has a qualitative, magical dimension missing in adult experience. This experience of space is almost 'sacred' for it is involved with the child's experience of Power."[156] He went on then to note: "Because the child lives in a world of enchantment, he or she finds it very easy to enter into the world of stories. Stories are always in some sense familiar, even if they take place in the safety of another realm—and don't threaten life in this ordinary world."[157]

These images from Wilhelm bring to mind those of the Galilean storyteller who instructed his followers not to disparage the interests of children: "Truly I tell you, whoever does not receive the kingdom of God as a little child will never enter it."[158] Perhaps adults have yet a bit more to learn about the magical world of stories—or to remember. Wilhelm said of this possibility: "Storytelling is still a taboo area for adults and for Christians. As adults, we assume that stories are an inferior form of entertainment for children. As Christians, we worry that stories and myths are somehow fanciful and untruthful. What that means is that religious educators have not enthusiastically become storytellers as part of their ministry. Yet, there are always a few people who are profoundly touched by the relevance of stories for their own lives and the lives of their children."[159] He then commented: "These are the people I am trying to reach."[160]

Evaluation

Although religious education has never totally been without its storytellers, and surely never will be, it seems that the role of the storyteller has come to be regarded as less important to the religious educator than some of the other roles in recent days. Robert Béla Wilhelm, for one, has struggled to overcome this unfortunate devaluation of the storyteller, not only pointing out the need for the role but providing excellent instruction in how to enflesh it. He has done his teaching in an interesting style appropriate to the storyteller, mixing stories,

---

154. Ibid., p. 67. To Wilhelm, one of the values of a story is to find oneself in the larger frames of human reference. In a journal article, Wilhelm said it this way: "To the extent that we live exclusively in the present, to the extent that what is new is important merely because of its newness and immediacy, then to that extent we have no sense of storyhood in our lives. We become trapped by the immediacy of the present." Wilhelm, "Catechists as Players and Story-Tellers," p. 100.
155. Wilhelm, "Storytelling as a Religious Art Form," pp. 67-73.
156. Ibid., p. 73.
157. Ibid.
158. Luke 18:17, NRSV.
159. Wilhelm, "Storytelling as a Religious Art Form," p. 82.
160. Ibid.

myths, guided fantasies, and pictures together into a workshop and dissertation that should be a delight for learners to experience. In fact, he is devoting his career to the training of others as storytellers, to ensure that the legacy of stories is included in the overall work of the religious educator. Nothing other than appreciation for this kind of devotion and contribution to the role can be directed toward Wilhelm, with the hope that his band of storytellers will continue to increase.

This is not to say that Wilhelm and his work are without spheres that need critique, however. Several problem areas discovered in his work are addressed in this evaluative section, and not only as they relate specifically to Wilhelm himself but particularly as they speak to any contemporary religious educator serving in the role of the storyteller. The first problem is the lack of scholarly apparatus in Wilhelm's work. He did not provide the reader with the resources he has obviously used to gain his information, leaving the reader without any guide as to how to retrace Wilhelm's steps. Granted, the format Wilhelm followed in the writing that has been overviewed here was a description of a representative workshop experience,[161] which is not an academic exercise by definition. However, anyone wanting and needing to go beyond the experiential is left unaided. Such a dismissal of the basics of research is not only a problem for Wilhelm in particular but is an occupational hazard for the storyteller in general. Wilhelm himself complained that stories and storytellers are not taken seriously enough by contemporary religious education,[162] but he compounded and exacerbated the problem by omitting the evidence of any solid backing for virtually all of his statements. He did such a good job of telling stories that he has left the serious, scholarly side of the activity unattended. This glaring lacuna will never convince true scholars of the value of the approach, regardless of how well the storyteller spins his or her craft.

A second difficulty with Wilhelm's work is the failure to distinguish between the various types of stories. He talks about such diverse forms of story as myths, folk tales, biblical narratives, rituals, and fairytales throughout the dissertation as if they were synonymous terms.[163] There are similarities among these types of stories, to be sure, but there are also tremendous differences which are immediately observable to even the casual reader, much more so to the genuine scholar of the literature. By not being careful with his categories, Wilhelm threatened his attempt to be taken seriously in the larger intellectual environment, not only as a storyteller but as a religious educator.[164]

---

161. Wilhelm's description of the format: "A three-hour presentation/participation session with parents and teachers of children on the effective use of storytelling in religious education." Ibid., p. 1.

162. For one example among many, see ibid., p. 3.

163. An example of Wilhelm's tendency to lump all story forms together was mentioned above in the overview section during the discussion on his definition of myth and its relation to "Gospel" myth.

164. Wilhelm described his normal audience for a workshop, and apparently his rationale for the lack of scholarly support, as follows: "For the most part, participants are volunteer religion teachers who feel the pressure of weekly classes. They want resources that are easily available, and they want practical advice on becoming storytellers. This workshop, however, is more of an enrichment experience, and a basic hope of mine is that the participants will 'fall in love' with storytelling during these brief sessions." Ibid., p. 4.

A third issue, curiously, was Wilhelm's inattention to the distinctives of religious storytelling, as opposed to any other kinds of storytelling. In his introductory comments, he stressed that he would be discovering some of the religious characteristics of storytelling,[165] but he never explained how the four characteristics he discussed were any different for religious storytelling than for any other form of storytelling. The argument could certainly be advanced that the four characteristics he named are essential to all forms of story, religious or not. Wilhelm did not reveal why or if he believed religious storytelling is any different than "plain" storytelling.[166]

A fourth concern was the particularity of Wilhelm's approach. As indicated by the title of the dissertation, he was specifically addressing storytelling within a Christian environment, but he often used the more generic terminology such as "religious education" and "religious educator." He told stories from the Hasidic tradition,[167] and referred often to Elie Wiesel, a Jewish storyteller.[168] Undoubtedly Christians can learn from Jewish sources, but Wilhelm never demonstrated how storytelling is an appropriate artform for adapting specifically to Christianity—if it is.[169] This fourth point is closely tied to the third. The root issue of both can probably be traced to a lack of precision in the use of language.

A fifth and final problem connected with Wilhelm's approach to storytelling is his occasional contradictory stances. For example, in his discussion of the third characteristic of storytelling, storytelling as a joyous ending, Wilhelm began this way: "Storytelling always has a happy ending . . . or does it? From our own experience, we know the stories frequently have sad endings, tragic endings, and—in the twentieth century—we have stories that have meaningless endings. Indeed, if we extend our definition of stories to include songs, movies, drama, and novels, we might have to say that most stories do not have happy endings."[170] From there, he went on to talk about how stories have a happy ending! This non sequitur is at least boldly stated, if nothing else. There are other examples of apparent contradiction as well.[171] This continual lack of precision is disturbing and damaging to Wilhelm's overall arguments for the value of stories.

Most if not all of the critical comments here point out the difficulty in using what Wilhelm called the special language of the storyteller—twilight language. What it provides in images it often lacks in clarity.[172] Without doubt, Wilhelm has advanced the cause of the storyteller and has offered some clues and some enticements for doing it better. Attention to precision and scholarly require-

---

165. Ibid., p. 7.

166. As Wilhelm noted, this kind of evaluative comment was made by some of the participants themselves after experiencing the workshop. See ibid., pp. 76 and 81.

167. This was how Wilhelm actually started the workshop. See ibid., pp. 5-6.

168. See ibid., for example.

169. Ibid., Part Four, "Synthesis," pp. 199-208, does briefly and poetically address specifically Christian elements of his storytelling.

170. Ibid., p. 19.

171. Another example came when Wilhelm discussed the second characteristic of storytelling, storytelling as escape and recreation. He talked of how stories help us escape the harshness of realities and then said that stories are not really for escapism. See ibid., pp. 11-13.

172. Ibid., pp. 11-12.

ments are easy to forget, however, when the magic of the storyteller begins to spin around the listener. May the role of the religious educator as a storyteller never be disparaged, nor allowed to become nothing more than a vehicle for entertainment.

Representative Teaching Procedure: Storytelling

To be a storyteller means being an expert in the telling of stories, so there can be no substitute teaching procedure for this role other than that of storytelling itself. The dangers here are twofold. On the one side are those who sigh resignedly and say "I don't have the gift of storytelling," excusing themselves from the responsibility and the hard work of preparation. On the other side are those who think storytelling is easy and that anyone can do it without any special forethought.[173] Both of these attitudes are erroneous. A more fitting attitude toward becoming an expert storyteller was the one expressed by Ruth Sawyer, herself a proven expert: "Storytelling is not for remedial purposes or for training. It is not a mechanical process to be made easy and pleasant. It is not a means of presenting limited material to the minds of children. It is an art demanding the utmost of your capacity and mine for living: it is dependent upon your power of creation; it asks for integrity, trust, and vision."[174]

The key to storytelling is the preparation the storyteller must undergo before the story is told. The steps of preparation for the storyteller have been advanced in a number of places with somewhat different arrangement,[175] but generally they are similar to the following ones from Edward Porter St. John, who suggested these seven steps.[176] First is determination of the purpose for which the story is to be used, clearly stated so that the storyteller can shape and mold the story to meet this end. Second is becoming thoroughly familiar with the story as a whole, getting a grasp of the flow of the story line without overemphasizing the details or performing rote memorization of the story. Third is careful analysis of the story, to determine its outline, and particularly to know what the climax of the story is so that it can be approached appropriately. Fourth is the systematic planning out of the story, either in verbal or written form, so that the story line is told and explained properly. Fifth is a critique of the story when it is structurally prepared, examining it to be sure that the message is clear and that the account has the necessary rhythm and flow. Sixth is the embellishment of the basic outline of the story with the intentional inclusion of relevant details and the exclusion of confusing information. Seventh is practice. As St. John said: "Tell the story again and again. It is not possible to carry this too far."[177]

---

173. "Some tellers of stories apparently believe that stories make themselves in the ordinary course of everyday happenings and that all the natural storyteller has to do is to recall what took place. If this were true, stories would be on everyone's lips. Yet the majority have none to tell. Why? Too many are trying to substitute talent for work and effort." Dart, *Tips for Storytellers*, p. 20.

174. Sawyer, *Way of the Storyteller*, p. 36.

175. See, for example, Chapter Two, "Five Steps in Story Building," in Dart, *Tips for Storytellers*, pp. 20-40; and Chapter Five, "Preparing to Tell the Story," in Brown, *Storyteller in Religious Education*, pp. 51-60.

176. St. John, *Stories and Story-Telling in Moral and Religious Education*, pp. 48-51.

177. Ibid., p. 51.

The procedure in *Models of Teaching* most closely related to storytelling is learning from presentations ("advance organizer model").[178] The procedure presented in the book by Joyce and Weil was designed primarily for structuring and presenting "large amounts of information as meaningfully and efficiently as possible" by way of lecture or explanation.[179] This procedure can be adapted to move from lecture and exposition to storytelling and interpretation, since the information to be transmitted is the story itself. Presentational teaching has three phases.[180] First is the "advance organizer" phase, which is the effort to come into contact with the learners and their own life situation. The religious educator discovers where learners are, and then moves them into the story. The aim of the lesson or story is identified, and the learner's experience and knowledge base is incorporated into the activity. Second is the actual presentation of the material itself—the telling of the story. The basic facts or details are given in a fashion that is both faithful to the historical realities and sensitive to the interests of the listeners. Third is the strengthening of the "cognitive organization," where the essential details and the structure of the information are discussed, clarified, and retained for further use. Joyce and Weil suggested that some critical approach to the subject matter (hermeneutic) be introduced into the discussion at this point, once the basic information has been assimilated.[181]

Experiential Simulation: Experiencing Storytelling

To become a better religious educator is to master the role of storyteller. Since the best way to gain the skills of and an appreciation for the storyteller is to be in the presence of an expert, then the best hope is to leave the pages of this book and go experience the artistry of a true storyteller.[182] Find a storyteller who will spin his or her magic around you.

In many cases, this is no easy assignment, but the goal is to fall in love with stories. Although not a substitute for a true personal encounter with a storyteller, Robert Coles' book, *The Call of Stories*,[183] is an excellent means of becom-

---

178. See Chapter 5 of Bruce Joyce and Marsha Weil, *Models of Teaching*, 3rd ed. (Englewood Cliffs, N.J.: Prentice-Hall, 1986), pp. 70-88. The basis of this procedure is the work of David Ausubel. For some background, see such resources as David P. Ausubel, *Educational Psychology: A Cognitive View* (New York: Holt, Rinehart and Winston, 1968), especially the section entitled "Discovery Learning," pp. 465-562; David P. Ausubel and Floyd G. Robinson, *School Learning: An Introduction to Educational Psychology* (New York: Holt, Rinehart and Winston, 1969), especially Part Five, "Discovery Learning," pp. 478-545; David P. Ausubel and Edmund V. Sullivan, *Theory and Problems of Child Development*, rev. ed. (New York: Grune and Stratton, 1970), especially Part Four, "Linguistic and Cognitive Aspects of Development," pp. 505-688; and David P. Ausubel, *The Psychology of Meaningful Verbal Learning* (New York: Grune and Stratton, 1963).

179. Joyce and Weil, *Models of Teaching*, p. 71.

180. Ibid., p. 80.

181. Ibid., p. 82.

182. This is the way storytellers themselves report that they improve their craft. For example: "As with all storytellers, I not only read all sorts of stories, but I listen to other storytellers. We learn much from each another." Sylvia Ziskind, *Telling Stories to Children* (New York: H.W. Wilson, 1976), p. xii.

183. Robert Coles, *The Call of Stories: Teaching and the Moral Imagination* (Boston: Houghton Mifflin, 1989).

ing sensitive to and appreciative of stories. Coles is a child psychiatrist who uses fiction as a teaching device for the preparation of psychiatric interns. *The Call of Stories* is an example of his teaching process, a rather odd but charming collection of conversations, teachings, reflections, and stories, all told by this master storyteller. Coles teaches respect for each person's individual narrative and shows the power stories have to promote health and identity.

A further suggestion is to be aware of modern storytellers in whatever garb they may appear. Storytellers are omnipresent if one will but open his or her eyes and ears. The easiest resource—and an omnipresent one—to tap is the entertainment media. Television[184] and movies obviously touch a deep need in people for the experiencing of stories, and some productions do a better job than others. One of the responsibilities of religious educators in learning about storytelling is not to dismiss out of hand the newer technological means of delivering stories but to evaluate and decide which ways are most useful and efficacious.

Another avenue to travel is to participate in a workshop or instructional activity directly related to storytelling. A number of these are available for "basic training" in the necessary orientations to storytelling.[185] Since storytelling is a skill that must be learned, honed, and practiced, intentional and focused effort is needed to get the learning process underway. The commitment to this kind of formalized educational experience would be a major step in becoming the prepared and informed storyteller.[186]

The most practical solution may be a trip to the local public library to hear stories being told. Most libraries provide a person who periodically tells stories to children in a delightful and absorbing manner.[187] Go and relive a moment of childhood. Sit on the floor at the storyteller's feet, be drawn into the story, and experience all over again the thrill of listening to an expert storyteller—and then "Go, and do thou likewise."

Summary

This chapter has been a focus upon the ancient but now somewhat overlooked role of the storyteller in religious education. The human need and demand

---

184. William White went so far as to say that "we live in a storytelling age" because of the influence of television, which he called primarily a storytelling medium. See White, *Stories for Telling*, p. 9. For more on the influence of television, see such sources as Conrad Phillip Kottack, *Prime-Time Society: An Anthropological Analysis of Television and Culture* (Belmont, Calif.: Wadsworth, 1990); John Fiske, *Television Culture* (London: Routledge, 1987); and Edward L. Palmer, *Television and America's Children: A Crisis of Neglect* (New York; Oxford: Oxford University Press, 1988).

185. For example, Jerome Berryman does these annually in Houston, Texas, through the auspices of the Children's Center Project; Robert Béla Wilhelm leads frequent workshops through the Storyfest Journeys seminars in Washington, D.C., as well as occasional other venues over the year.

186. For a literary resource, see Part IV, "The Training of Storytellers," in Pellowski, *The World of Storytelling*, pp. 157-187.

187. Anne Pellowski says this has been going on in public libraries since at least the 1880s. See Chapter Six, "Library and Institutional Storytelling," in Pellowski, *The World of Storytelling*, pp. 83-92.

for stories is as great as ever, and maybe even more pronounced in the current technical and mechanistic society. The one profession and role in society that cannot allow storytelling to become a lost art is that of the religious educator. Stories bind humans together in their faith traditions and help determine not only their individual but their corporate identities. For our own sakes, and for the sakes of those incoming generations who need our stories, the role of storyteller is one that continually demands our time, effort, and commitment. The following summary chart of the chapter points to the complexity and the importance of the role as it has been explored throughout the chapter.

Figure 10: The Religious Educator as Storyteller	
Dimensions of the Role	Evangelist
	Historian
	Mythologist
	Raconteur
Aim	Interpretation
Function	Communication
Primary Virtues	Historicity
	Contextuality
Activity	Participating
Shadow Role	Dogmatist
Faith Tradition Resource	Greek Mythology
Historical Personage	Homer
Contemporary Example	Robert Béla Wilhelm
Representative Teaching Procedure	Storytelling
Experiential Simulation	Experiencing Storytelling

Chapter Nine

The Religious Educator as Artist

From the very outset, at least two major barriers are hindrances in trying to understand the religious educator as artist. The first of these barriers has to do with the inadequacy of language. As even the least amount of investigation will soon show, a satisfactory and universally acceptable definition of art—and hence, of artists—is impossible to find.[1] To whatever extent beauty is in the eye of the beholder, then art as a whole is in the eye, ear, hand, and heart of the individual.[2] Although some basic attempt to define art is necessary, the focus and intent of this chapter is not to provide the full and final definition of art and the artist.[3] This chapter instead primarily describes what the artist does, thereby establishing an applicable metaphor for better understanding the work of the religious educator.

The second major barrier to confront is just as serious as the first, and it is similar to a problem experienced in the previous chapter on the storyteller. There,

---

1. A comforting(?) word was given by Rader and Jessup: "No all-purpose definition of art or the arts is possible." See Melvin Rader and Bertram Jessup, *Art and Human Values* (Englewood Cliffs, N.J.: Prentice-Hall, 1976), p. 124.

2. There are those who would say that no objective standards for art exist and that all value judgments related to art are totally up to each individual's subjective opinion. See this discussed, for example, in Chapter Five, "A Reply to Extreme Relativists in Criticism," Stephen C. Pepper, *The Work of Art* (Bloomington: Indiana University Press, 1955), pp. 122-150. Such an extreme form of relativism is not a position I am staking out for myself here. I am only acknowledging that there are wide differences of opinions on the definitions of art.

3. Hans Küng remarked at the first of his brief publication on meaning and art: "One difficulty must be faced. There is not a generally recognized definition of art any more than there is a generally recognized definition of religion or philosophy. But there can be no doubt about the reality of art." Hans Küng, *Art and the Question of Meaning*, trans. Edward Quinn (New York: Crossroad, 1981), p. 10.

the difficulty was describing and analyzing both story and storyteller when by all accounts the best way to understand storytelling is simply to listen to stories told by a storyteller. If this medium of linguistic scholarship is less than ideal for experiencing storytelling, the problem is even more acute in the present chapter. There is absolutely no way that words on a page can approximate or simulate the world of the artist.[4] Reading about art and the artist is very different from experiencing them, but perhaps this chapter at least opens a door onto the image of the religious educator as artist.

These words of warning and inadequacy are simply acknowledgment of the limitations of writing about something that is essentially experiential, and they serve as an important signal for the subject of this chapter. All too often religious education is approached and treated as an "it": something cognitive, verbal, rational, logical, linear, and methodological.[5] The very language used often objectifies religious education into something that appears to be isolated, independent, and separate, as if it were available for inspection, analysis, and perhaps even autopsy. One of the hopes for this chapter is that religious education—and the religious educator—can be perceived as more than an "it." Religious education and the religious educator, just as art and the artist, each resist and extend beyond the definitions, analyses, and criticisms of the observers. Artists, and religious educators, express much more than rational thought, logic, and "pure" bits of information. To capture all that they do and are in words on a page is by common agreement not possible.

A legitimate complaint at this point could be that the ambiguity already is palpable. Surely, one could say, more than enough diffusion, if not confusion, already exists in a book that deals with such notoriously illusive terms as religion and education, to say nothing of religious education. How can the introduction of another indefinable such as art possibly be of value? Although art is difficult if not impossible to define to everyone's satisfaction, the very act and process of searching for its boundaries is a helpful and clarifying effort.[6] The parallel to religious education is obvious. One of the most important activities a religious educator pursues is *searching for* the means toward

---

4. As R. G. Collingwood observed: "Art is not contemplation, it is action." R.G. Collingwood, *The Principles of Art* (New York: Oxford University Press, 1958), p. 332.

5. Unfortunately there is no shortage of books promoting such an approach. For some classic examples, see Marcel van Caster, *The Structure of Catechetics* (New York: Herder and Herder, 1965); Hubert Halbfas, *Theory of Catechetics: Language and Experience in Religious Education* (New York: Herder and Herder, 1971); and Michael Donnellan, *What to Believe: Changing Patterns of Religious Education* (Dublin: Gill and Son, 1968).

6. To get a sense of the range in definitions of art, as well as a historical perspective on art theory, see *What Is Art? Aesthetic Theory from Plato to Tolstoy*, ed. Alexander Sesonske (New York: Oxford University Press, 1965). One striking but hardly unique feature of Sesonske's selection of writers is that they are all male and Western. The contributions of women and non-Westerners to the theory of art is not addressed in the book cited. A helpful work that does some of what Sesonske's does not was edited by Suzanne Langer, *Reflections on Art: A Source Book of Writings by Artists, Critics, and Philosophers* (Baltimore: Johns Hopkins Press, 1958). To get a glimpse of the theoretical underpinnings of art, see such a volume as the one by Francis Sparshott, *The Theory of the Arts* (Princeton, N.J.: Princeton University Press, 1982). For a classic work that has had extensive influence on twentieth-century philosophy of art, see John Dewey, *Art as Experience* (New York: Minton, Bulch, 1934).

holistic nexus.[7] Art and religious education are partners in searching, attempting, and creating—which already begins to delineate the boundaries. From a functional point of view, then, the religious educator can learn from and model upon the role of the artist.

The comments of Clive Bell are still instructive. In a much-read work earlier in the twentieth century, Bell acknowledged the ambiguity and the difficulty in describing art: "It is improbable that more nonsense has been written about aesthetics than about anything else: the literature of the subject is not large enough for that. It is certain, however, that about no subject with which I am acquainted has so little been said that is at all to the purpose."[8] One reason Bell cited for the difficulty was the dominance of human emotion in evaluating art: "The starting point for all systems of aesthetics must be the personal experience of a peculiar emotion. The objects that provoke this emotion we call works of art."[9] The test, for Bell, of a great work of art was that it must evoke strong emotion. He went on in his book to examine not only the "peculiar emotions," but particular works of art that in his view were evocative. One approach to the general subject, then, is to study and experience the works of art themselves. Such study of a variety of works would presumably then lead to an understanding of art and aesthetics.[10] Although some of this kind of work will be undertaken here, the primary effort of this chapter is to concentrate on the person who creates the art: on the artist, and by analogy, on the religious educator. The attention is focused on the artist rather than on the particular works of art he or she produces.

Along the lines drawn by Bell, Otto Baensch wrote that the true significance of art is "that it elevates the emotional content of the world to universally valid consciousness."[11] This quote represents the chief emphasis of the present chapter on the religious educator as artist: that the artist is one who points toward the wholeness, beauty, and truth of humanity in a manner that is not just rational or cognitive but that is primarily achieved through touching the deepest regions of the emotions. The religious educator, then, must also learn to be sensitive to and to appeal to these fuller aspects of humanity through the exercise of religious education, since as theologian Hans Küng once asked: "You must pardon me if I raise the heretical question: Is not art too important to be left to artists?"[12]

---

7. Recall that this is the language I use to define religious education: "Systemic religious education is the search for, attempt at, and creation of holistic nexus through the existential learning-adaptive process of transforming the heritage of the past into an actualized vision of the ideal future." Timothy Arthur Lines, *Systemic Religious Education* (Birmingham, Ala.: Religious Education Press, 1987), p. 216.

8. Clive Bell, *Art*, 2nd ed. (Oxford: Oxford University Press, 1987), p. 3. First published in 1914.

9. Ibid., p. 6.

10. Edgar Carritt expressed the desire to understand aesthetics this way: "Man then has seldom been long contented to create or perceive beauty without attempting also to understand what he was doing. . . . The object of his investigation in this field plainly must be to understand what beauty is; to discover what the common quality or relation to ourselves may be in all those things which we call beautiful." Edgar F. Carritt, *The Theory of Beauty*, 6th ed. (London: Methuen, 1962), pp. 1-2.

11. Otto Baensch, "Art and Feeling," in *Reflections on Art*, p. 36. Baensch also wrote that the function of art is "to acquaint [the percipient] with something which he has not known before." Ibid., p. 10.

12. Küng, *Art and the Question of Meaning*, p. 13.

Albert Hofstadter used the language of the spirit to communicate the same fundamental dimensions of art: "Art is part of man's being. The truth of art, therefore, is more than truth-about. It is a truth of spirit. It means that beyond anything a work of art may say about this or that aspect of things, it has ultimately to be true to the being of the spirit. . . . The essence of art is the articulation of human being. . . . Its aim is to point to that essential function, the articulation of the truth of human existence."[13] Edgar Carritt said it yet another way, that "all beauty is the expression of what may be generally called emotion, and that all such expression is beautiful."[14]

One other understanding of art needs to be taken into account early on. Some choose to approach art politically, as in the following definition of art proposed by Jon Huer: "Art is a form of persuasion by which the persuader tries to change the mind of others regarding man and the world."[15] Huer focused on art as a social phenomenon, making the artist a commentator on society with a particular agenda in mind and driven by a specific point of view.[16] He contrasted art with other forms of persuasion, such as religion, politics, and romantic love. Huer found art to be the "most noble and sublime" form of persuasion, since "art springs solely from the artists' inspiration, the purest form of human thought."[17] Huer then arrived at his statement on the purpose of art: "It is the highest of life's endeavors, and all great artists are teachers of living and behaving. They teach us a new way of life, a new awareness, a new perspective about ourselves and the world around us."[18] For Huer, art is persuasion in its highest form, and the artist is the supreme persuader—the teacher—who inspires humans to see reality anew. The problem with this position, although it is one to which many ascribe, is that it tends to deny the aspect of art for art's sake.[19] While some artists do pursue their art for political reasons, a fuller understanding of the true artist is that of one who follows his or her artistic vision first and foremost, finally allowing art to speak for and of itself.[20] It is this latter, more ideal and nonpolitical form

---

13. Albert Hofstadter, *Truth and Art* (New York: Columbia University Press, 1965), p. vii.

14. Carritt, *Theory of Beauty*, p. 201.

15. Jon Huer, *Art, Beauty, and Pornography* (Buffalo: Prometheus Books, 1987), p. 22.

16. Actually, Huer identified his definition as a sociological one: "Being a sociologist by commitment and education, I tend to see artwork as social phenomena with the meaning in social behavior." Ibid.

17. Ibid., p. 23.

18. Ibid., p. 24.

19. For an overview of this concept, see Albert L. Guérard, *Art for Art's Sake* (New York: Schocken, 1936). For someone who disagrees with the whole idea, see Jacques Maritain, Chapter Two, "Art for Art's Sake," in *The Responsibility of the Artist* (New York: Scribner's, 1960), pp. 47-65.

20. The quandary dealt with in this paragraph was summarized well by Leslie Birch and Ingrid Stadler: "We are confronted, then, with a paradox: On the one side, there is the argument that art's audience, the viewer, can take steps requisite for experiencing an artwork fully and appreciatively—an argument implying that art is created to provide the viewer with an opportunity to delight in, and profit from, the experience of encountering that object. On the other hand, there is the rationale that art exists for its own sake and not for the sake of providing the viewer with a new perspective on his environment or on his world. . . . Our paradox circumambulates the point that art both has and does not have a purpose." Leslie Birch and Ingrid Stadler, "Art for Art's Sake: A Paradox," in *Contemporary Art and Its Philosophical Problems*, ed. Ingrid Stadler (Buffalo: Prometheus Books, 1987), p. 38.

of the artist that will serve the rest of this chapter as the guiding image for the religious educator.

Dimensions of the Role

To become acquainted with the artist, discussing some of the dimensions of the artist's role will prove to be helpful. The four dimensions examined here are the creator, the designer, the evocateur, and the magician. While these four help to describe the artist directly, insight into the religious educator can also result as a by-product of this survey.

Creator

In Judeo-Christian scripture, God is frequently depicted as the creator: "In the beginning God created the heaven and the earth," as Genesis 1:1 (KJV) puts it. In theological language, God performed *creatio ex nihilo*: the creation (of something) which came from out of nothing. In this image, God is the source and the producer of everything from out of nothingness.[21] Such a doctrine shows God's independence (lack of dependence) in creating the physical realm in which humans operate. This doctrine, at least as found in the first chapter of Genesis, points to no materials that God could have used to create, since before God created, there was nothing. Something to use and fashion did not exist prior to its *creatio ex nihilo* by God.[22]

Genesis 2, however, describes a slightly different situation. In this so-called "second" account of creation, God is portrayed as creating humans not *ex nihilo* but as fashioning them from the existing clay: creating something anew from that which had already been created. This kind of creating is closer to that of inventing.[23] Genesis 2:7 tells how God formed a man from the dust of the ground, and Genesis 2:21-22 relates how God made a woman from the man's rib. As humans were said to be created, so they continue to create. Humans do not speak creations into existence from out of nothing (*ex nihilo*), but humans do create by inventing something new by using and fashioning materials that are already in existence.

This second type of God-like creative activity—of inventing—is an important dimension of the role of the artist. The artist, as a creator who uses what is already available and fashions it into something new,[24] breathes the "breath of life"

---

21. "And the earth was without form, and void," as Genesis 1:2 (KJV) expressed it in the first creation account.

22. This kind of creation from nothing is also denoted as *de novo* creation.

23. Inventors create something *original* from extant materials. Leonardo da Vinci (1452-1519) had this to say about the differences between inventors and imitators: "There is but one way to judge and appraise men who are true inventors and interpreters of nature and men in contrast to those who are the trumpeters and expositors of the works of others. They are like objects placed in front of a mirror with respect to their likenesses in the mirror; one group is in itself something and the other nothing. People without close ties to nature and garbed only in the inventions of others I should class with animals." Leonardo da Vinci, *Philosophical Diary*, trans. Wade Baskin (New York: Philosophical Library, 1959), p. 20.

24. Judith Rubin wrote: "Without media and tools, there can be no art. While there is such a thing as mental imagery, and people of all ages do think in pictures, in order for such images to become

into the clay, the marble, the paper, or the canvas and brings forth a new creation. This "breath of life" is the key ingredient that the artist brings to the task. The accumulation of the artist's personality and experience is injected into the materials for the creation: The very essence of the artist's humanity gives life to the work of art. From the depths of the artist's humanity (through the artist's "breath of life") comes the artist's creation.[25]

I recall seeing a marvelous film of Pablo Picasso creating in the role of the master inventor. He was standing before a transparent surface that allowed the lens of the camera not only to catch the painting process but also the painter-creator himself. Picasso worked bare-chested, sweating, vibrant, driven, filling the "canvas" with splashes of his vision. Without much imagination at all, one could experience Picasso in the role of divine creator, breathing the breath of life into his creation. He brought his vision into reality through sheer force of will, energy, and finely-honed competence. The "canvas," brush, and paint were but stage props for a much more transcendent pageant.

It is difficult at times for the mere mortal to appreciate this dimension of creator, and Plato's concept of Forms is much more comforting and believable.[26] Those individuals who spend so much time in the mundane roles of life tend to assume that true artists simply copy some pure Form from above. Surely, they say, the artist is seeking to reproduce some kind of preexistent, true Form of art. While not denigrating the evolutionary and developmental aspects of art,[27] history and the passage of time do not adequately explain the dimension of the creator in the artist. Take, for a shining example, the Fifth Symphony of Ludwig van Beethoven, especially those four opening and unforgettable notes. For most Westerners, the term symphony and those four notes have become nearly synonymous: Ask anyone to describe a symphony, and more often than not they will respond with the familiar "da da da dum!" More than that, it is difficult to imagine a world that did not include those sounds.[28] Before Beethoven created it,

art they must be concretized in some way." Judith Aron Rubin, *The Art of Art Therapy* (New York: Brunner/Mazel, 1984), p. 7.

25. Frank Seiberling said this in his own way: "All art is representational in the sense of standing outside itself, even if this something be no more than a fancy, a whim, or an impulse of the artist. One of the most liberating awarenesses about art is to realize this, and to see that in art true presentation is impossible. After the master of ceremonies sits down, his part is over. The speaker continues on his own. But the artist always leaves the continuing mark of his presence, no matter how dispassionately he tries to present his subject. Art may have its presentational tendencies, but it can never entirely liberate the subject from the artist's vision and understanding. In the end, it is representational." Frank Seiberling, *Looking Into Art* (New York: Henry Holt, 1959), pp. 6-8.

26. George Kneller discussed this notion under the heading of "Creativity as Divine Inspiration," saying that such an explanation "doubtless arose out of the attempt to explain the extraordinary originality of great creative works. It was expressed most memorably by Plato." See the fuller discussion of this "theory" in George F. Kneller, *The Art and Science of Creativity* (New York: Holt, Rinehart and Winston, 1965), pp. 18-20; quote from pp. 18-19. See the entirety of Chapter Two, "Theories," for other views and explanations of the sources of creativity. Ibid., pp. 18-46.

27. "Every artist, great or amateur, has been inspired by the work of others." Rubin, *Art of Art Therapy*, p. 19.

28. Beethoven himself reportedly once described these opening notes of the Fifth Symphony as a representation of "fate knocking at the door." See Friedrich Kerst and Henry Edward Krehbiel, eds., *Beethoven: The Man and the Artist, as Revealed in His Own Words* (New York: Dover, 1964), p. 45.

however, the human race did not have this Fifth Symphony. Had there been no Beethoven or had he not created it, humanity would never have had it. The noncreator is left to stare at the pages of the score, wondering where this music came from and wondering how to duplicate such a feat. The noncreator is tempted to become a Platonist, discounting the difficult work the creator as inventor must put forth[29] and believing in some kind of copying or dictation theory. The artist creates, and no amount of searching for a preexistent Form will serve as a substitute for creativity.

Before Beethoven, then, there was no Fifth Symphony. Had there been no Beethoven, there would have been no Fifth Symphony. The art comes from out of the depths of the artist's humanity, which means that the artist uses and fashions common and extant materials to create—to invent—a new reality in a truly god-like way. The lesson for religious educators: They, too, are charged with the divine task of creating, not *ex nihilo*, but inventing from that which already exists all about us. They take the materials at hand and fashion them into a wholly (holy?) new invention of self-revelation and thereby take part in the divine processes of creation.

Designer

In at least some senses, artistic ability is not simply an inheritance or a birthright, but it is something that must be nurtured, trained, and educated.[30] While on the one hand it is true that some people have a seeming knack or predisposition toward some particular form of artistic expression, on the other hand it is just as true that the artist must be supremely skilled, disciplined, and trained in the process of producing a work of art.[31] Just as no one would argue that Picasso's "Guernica" is *only* smeared paint, and that Beethoven's Fifth Symphony is *only* printed notes, no one would disagree that Picasso first had to become a

---

29. Remember that it was the great inventor Thomas Edison who admitted that genius is one percent inspiration and ninety-nine percent perspiration.

30. Philip Farkas addressed this issue in terms of musicianship, but it has obvious parallels to all kinds of artists: "Is musicianship an inherited gift or a natural and unique talent?. . . . When we examine the histories of the great musicians of all times we find encouraging answers to both parts of this question. There were several generations of the great Bach family. . . . There was one great Mozart—Wolfgang Amadeus—and one not-quite-so-great, Leopold. In modern times the renowned conductor, Raphael Kubelik, is the son of the famous violinist, Jan Kubelik. There are dozens of similar examples, which should give encouragement to students whose family has proven musical talent. On the other hand, what about the backgrounds of Beethoven, Brahms, Schubert, Wagner and Stravinsky? They have done extremely well without benefit of great musical antecedents. This fact should buoy the spirits of the music students who are the first in their families to become interested in music." Philip Farkas, *The Art of Musicianship* (Bloomington, Ind.: Musical Publications, 1976), p. 6.

31. One of the better and most well-known examples of this combination was Wolfgang Amadeus Mozart (1756-1791). Certainly a child prodigy by any definition of the term, Mozart began displaying his musical talent at age three, was composing at age five, and was touring at age six. See this discussed in Chapter Two, "Child Prodigy and the Grand Tour," in *The Mozart Handbook: A Guide to the Man and His Music*, comp. and ed. Louis Biancolli (New York: World, 1954), pp. 34-51. Even with all this native ability, however, Mozart still had to do a lot of practicing, studying, and learning to put his talents to their best use, as is made clear in the chapter by Biancolli. If Mozart needed to do this much work, then without doubt all of us need to hone our own skills accordingly.

skilled painter, and that Beethoven had to become a skilled composer for such works to be created. The creativity of the artist must be communicated and transmuted through a chosen medium in which the artist is a master. Had Picasso never learned to mix paint, or had Beethoven never learned to use musical notation, humanity would not have been recipients of their masterpieces. The task of the artist is to so master the chosen medium that the artist's message can be experienced powerfully and indelibly through it.

Beyond this inextricable issue of competence, however, ranges the deeper issue of what distinguishes an artist from a craftsperson. A craftsperson may indeed have skill and competence and still not be considered an artist. One author analyzed the differences of art and craft this way: "In reply to the enquiry, What is art? an answer may be made as follows: Art is the involuntary dramatization of subjective experience. In other words, the crystallization of a state of mind in images (whether visual, auditory, or otherwise). This excludes art from the practical activity of mere illustration, which involves only the combination of empirical observation with the skill of craftsmanship. Even the setting down on paper of the signs, lines, words, musical notes, etc., that serve to communicate aesthetic experience by the indications of gesture, or audible sounds, is a practical activity to be distinguished from that of creation."[32] The chief point of distinction between the artist and the craftsperson, then, is not just the demonstration of skill, as the same author just quoted above made clear a few sentences later: "The element of skill enters only into the voluntary practical activity of externalization, the use of the language of stimulation. We cannot measure qualities of art by measuring degrees of skill."[33] The true difference is revealed in the question: "In which have we evidence of most profound vision? in which [of these] is the greater vessel?" The artist is the one who touches the deepest regions of the human, and the dimension that speaks to this ability is that of the designer.

Cecelia Davis Cunningham described the performance of art succinctly and in so doing began to explicate what the dimension of designer is about: "I am a potter, a maker of things. For my work to be good now and better in the future requires doing. [I seek] what Michelangelo called *sprezzatura*: the easy union of eye, hand, and brain that produces a worthy human work. It is only when my pot comes from my wheel that I am permitted to reflect on its form, its beauty, and its meaning. One does and then one reflects."[34] Cunningham raised several points about the artist as designer that need amplification. First, she emphasized that to be an artist, one must do something and make something. The greatest concept in the mind is not art until it has become concretized by the hand. The artist is necessarily judged, evaluated, and remembered by the work of art that is produced. Second, she observed that being an artist demands a unity and a harmony of all the artist's abilities. The "easy union of eye, hand, and brain" she mentioned refers to the total engagement of the artist with his or her work. No production-

32. Ananda K. Coomaraswamy, "Art and Craftsmanship," in *Reflections on Art*, p. 240.

33. Ibid., p. 241.

34. Cecilia Davis Cunningham, "Craft: Making and Being," in *Art, Creativity, and the Sacred: An Anthology in Religion and Art*, ed. Diane Apostolos-Cappadona (New York: Crossroad, 1985), p. 8.

line economy is in force here. The artist is personally involved in every aspect of the creative process. Third, Cunningham spoke of the reflection that follows the doing: evaluation that allows for ever deeper and better expression in future creations. The artist as designer is never satisfied that the perfect work has been created.[35] There is always more to be learned, and a better way to express the message.[36]

The dimension of designer reveals that the true artist does not just walk into the studio and start "emoting" without any preparation or prior research.[37] There is fascinating and overwhelming evidence of this kind of hard, preparatory work from Albrecht Dürer (1471-1528), for example, who made virtually innumerable sketches of humans based on direct observation and the study of anatomy.[38] Leonardo da Vinci spent time studying anatomy and physiology by dissecting cadavers to get the true sense of the human body, thereby allowing him to sculpt and paint more accurately and expressively.[39] The point here is that the artist as designer spends much time in careful planning, research and preparation in order for his or her talents to be expressed to their fullest.[40]

The dimension of designer, then, makes clear that the artist does more than just express emotion, or has a particular set of skills, but must pay close attention to both form and content.[41] As Edgar Carritt wrote: "In all that is beautiful there is form which is always the expression of feeling. Passion inexpressive and formless is the new wine of animal barbarism: polished but passionless verse is a

---

35. "The true artist is ever disappointed with what he has done, for his reach always exceeds his grasp, the ideal is ever beyond the actual." Max Schoen, *Art and Beauty* (New York: Macmillan, 1932), p. 119.

36. The task of evaluation is even mentioned in the creation accounts in Genesis. There, God the creator is first depicted as speaking the world and its inhabitants into existence. Then God considered the result of creation, and decided that "it was very good" (Genesis 1:31, NRSV). As Cunningham put it: "One does and then one reflects."

37. George Kneller discussed the four phases present in the process of artistic creation, which he identified as preparation, incubation, illumination, and verification. See Chapter Three, "The Act," in Kneller, *Art and Science of Creativity*, pp. 46-61.

38. To get the sense of Dürer's attention to detail and the amount of research he performed, examine the sketches and drawings provided in Volume Five, "Human Proportions," part of *The Complete Drawings of Albrecht Dürer*, ed. Walter Strauss (New York: Abaris Books, 1974).

39. Leonardo wrote, for example, on his investigations into the human circulatory system: "I, to get accurate and complete knowledge of the blood-vessels, have dissected more than ten human corpses, cutting up all their other members and removing with the greatest care all the flesh around them. . . . Since a single corpse did not last a sufficient time, I had to proceed from corpse to corpse and thus collect complete information; and this I repeated twice to see the differences." Leonardo da Vinci, *Philosophical Diary*, p. 53. Incidentally, Leonardo also did similar study in the comparative anatomy of animals. See, for example, his discussions in ibid., p. 52. For his drawings of human and animal anatomies, see *The Drawings of Leonardo da Vinci*, intro. and notes by A.E. Popham (New York: Reynal and Hitchcock, 1945).

40. For a fascinating discussion of this topic, see "Leonardo, Artist and Scientist," in *Paragone: A Comparison of the Arts, by Leonardo da Vinci*, trans. and intro. by Irma A. Richter (London: Oxford University Press, 1949), pp. 4-11; also see "Painting and Science," pp. 19-35.

41. "Thus, art has two interlocking aspects: that related to external description and to human moods, insights, beliefs, values—the *content* of art; and that related to visual order and effect—its *form*." Seiberling, *Looking Into Art*, p. 17. These terms of content and form have been expressed throughout this present book as substantive content and structural content. See this discussed at length in Chapter Five, "The Religious Educator as Coach."

sediment left by art in old bottles of culture."[42] In a more extended way, Paul Stern made a similar point: "There are two prevalent opinions, apparently quite opposite, on the nature of art: according to one, the ultimate function of art is to express convincingly some process or condition of the inner life; according to the other, its function is to create images which, by clarity and harmony of form, fulfill the need for vividly comprehensible appearance, which is rarely satisfied by reality. Actually, neither clear representation of external form, nor the expression of an inner life or experience, however achieved, is in itself sufficient to create art; rather, each depends on the other. . . . Form and content are unequivocally coordinated, and any change in one necessarily entails a change in the other."[43] It is the task of the artist as designer to blend content and form into the seamless work of art.

The religious educator contemplating the dimension of the designer must first of all work to be competent in the skills and practices required of the religious educator, but just the possession of these skills does not make one the artist. The designer knows how to identify and to use the flow of content and form to create the true work of art, rather than to simply practice a craft. In more familiar language, the religious educator as designer must pay as much attention to theory and evidence of the data as to the feelings and to the emotions. One without the other falls short of the artistry of religious education.

Evocateur

A third dimension of the artist is that of the evocateur. The evocateur, as distinct from the dimensions of creator and the designer, operates primarily within the realm of the affect.[44] To the degree that the artist is able to express the fullness of his or her artistic vision, the artist is then able to evoke some kind of emotional response from persons who experience[45] the expression of that art.[46] James Mursell called this effect the "aesthetic response" that is stimulated by the artist through his or her work of art, and he defined it as "response to the evocative values of organized pattern."[47] Mursell contrasted the evocative work of the artist from the referential efforts of the technician this way: "A poem differs

---

42. Carritt, *Theory of Beauty*, p. 186.

43. Paul Stern, "On the Problem of Artistic Form," in *Reflections on Art*, p. 71.

44. Virgil Aldrich had a nice way of expressing this aspect of the artist: "The aim of the artist is to rearrange contours and qualities with a view to making the world more inviting to our emotions." Virgil C. Aldrich, "Beauty as Feeling," in *Reflections on Art*, p. 8.

45. The point I am making here is that true art "comes alive" when it is encountered. Leslie Birch and Ingrid Stadler made a similar emphasis when they wrote: "We are strongly inclined to agree with the poet Wallace Stevens when he says that a poem comes alive only when it sparks the imagination of the reader. We believe that it is important to reflect on, and to articulate, the characteristic features of the (ideal) respondent's experience, or his 'aesthetic experience,' as it is sometimes called." Leslie Birch and Ingrid Stadler, "Art for Art's Sake: A Paradox," in *Contemporary Art and Its Philosophical Problems*, pp. 35-36.

46. It is not that the artist sets out to evoke something from people, but that when the artist is true and honest to his or her art, the evocation comes as a *result*. The faithfulness to that performance of art is what enables the evocation of emotion from those later experiencing it.

47. James L. Mursell, "How Children Learn Aesthetic Responses," in *The Forty-Ninth Yearbook of the National Society for the Study of Education, Part One: Learning and Instruction*, ed. Nelson B. Henry (Chicago: University of Chicago press, 1950), p. 183.

from a factual description or an argument of exposition in that, as a matter of deliberate intention, it embodies and projects evocative or emotional values in the pattern and arrangement of its language. A picture differs from a blueprint, a ballet differs from an exhibition of skilled movement such as one might see on an assembly line, and a work of architecture differs from a purely utilitarian structure in precisely the same way. On the one hand we have types of behavior explicitly directed to evocative projection. Music affords the outstanding instance of an intricate, highly articulated structure which has no referential meaning at all, or almost none, and whose significance and value is entirely evocative."[48]

Art engages a very different region of the human than does the more prosaic works of humankind, so that the true artist becomes an evocateur as one essential dimension of the role. In a choice opportunity to hear an artist speak of art for its own sake, Leo Tolstoy left behind his philosophical musings in a book entitled *What Is Art?* In the later pages of this monograph, Tolstoy spoke of this different, evocative type of communication available to the artist by contrasting science and art, resulting in a position strikingly similar to the one taken by Mursell: "Science and art are as closely bound together as the lungs and heart, so that if one is vitiated the other cannot act rightly. True science investigates and brings to human perception such truth and such knowledge as the people of a given time and society consider important. Art transmits these truths from the region of perception to the region of emotion."[49] Tolstoy was saying that while science and art are not identical, and while they do not have the same goal in mind, neither are they totally unrelated. Art is the language of the emotions, of feelings that firmly interrelates with the scientific insights of the day. Art uses a language that is able to express, in an evocative and engaging manner, the current mindset of the times. It would also be accurate to say that art can shape and profoundly influence the mindset of the times, including that of science.[50] As Frank Seiberling said: "Art thus supplies an area—a kind of testing ground—for the expression of viewpoints or insights *without penalty*. This frees it to experiment and to illumine, often to lead the way."[51]

The dimension of the artist as evocateur is often unappreciated by those comfortable and satisfied with the status quo. The artist comes and presents a work of art that offers an alternative view of reality, thereby knocking the standard manner of perception out of kilter.[52] After the introduction of the new somehow the

---

48. Ibid., p. 183-184.

49. Leo N. Tolstoy, *What Is Art?*, trans. Almyer Maude (Indianpolis: Liberal Arts Press, 1960; first published in 1896), p. 181.

50. Comments by John Dewey are interesting concerning the relationship of the scientist and the artist. He was adamant that the "odd notion that an artist does not think and a scientific inquirer does nothing else" be dispelled. He believed the two simply operate differently in terms of tempo and emphasis. Dewey insisted that the "thinker" has aesthetic moments when "ideas cease to be mere ideas," just as the artist has "problems and thinks as he works." The difference is that the artist's "thought is more immediately embodied in the object." Where the scientist deals primarily in "symbols, words, and mathematical signs," the artist thinks "in the very qualitative media he works in." See Dewey, *Art as Experience*, pp. 15-16.

51. Seiberling, *Looking Into Art.*, p. 13.

52. The key here is allowing the work of art to do its task. As Stephen Pepper wrote: "If we do not 'yield' to the masterpiece, it cannot, of course, perform its selective action upon our power of per-

old way is never quite the same any more, regardless of how much the old guard wants it to be so, and regardless of what repressive means they use to make it so. History reports that ladies' wigs were jarred out of place during the premiere performance of Beethoven's Ninth Symphony in 1824, all the more appropriate when it is realized that music was never the same again after that performance. Riots broke out in the theater during the initial performance of Stravinsky's "Rite of Spring," symbolizing Stravinsky's unveiling of a new kind of music, and introducing the new and often disturbing ways of the twentieth century. No amount of trying or protesting could ever put music back like it was either before Beethoven's ringing timpani or Stravinsky's dissonant chords.[53] When art evokes, its power can be surprising indeed.

Jon Huer spoke of the artist's palpable discontent as being one of the driving forces behind the great works of art. He wrote: "Rarely do we see a self-satisfied artist creating great artworks or art thriving in a self-satisfied society or person. Discontentment—a feeling, however vague, that there should be something better in life, a restlessness of the heart, a dissatisfaction of the status quo—is an essential part of the social or individual force that seeks the creation of art."[54] Huer perceived art as a challenge to the current perspective, as an offering designed to force a new or different view of reality to the surface. A work that does not so move society does not constitute genuine art, in his opinion: "Art that does not succeed or attempt to change human society is no art; it is merely a pleasant and beautiful thing that happens to entertain us."[55] It is this dimension of the artist—the evocateur—that for Huer distinguishes the true artist from the mere craftsperson.

Perhaps a story (probably more apocryphal than true) about Albert Einstein will further clarify this dimension of the artist as evocateur. A lady reportedly came up to Einstein at a conference and asked him to write in two or three pages what his theories of relativity were all about in plain language she could understand. Einstein stared at her a moment, blinked, and said: "Madam, that I cannot do. However, if you will visit me in my home one day, then I will play them for you on my violin." One of the greatest minds of the twentieth century was saying that in order to express the fullness of his work his musical instrument could best speak for him. Just so the entire role of the artist as evocateur, who lets the work of art communicate to the deepest regions of humanity.

Magician
One of my favorite pastimes is to watch a television show where a painter teaches the viewer how to paint. First, the artist/teacher sets up the easel, mixes the paint, and lays out the brushes. Next, we are shown what the finished picture will look like: a farm scene, a mountain range, or an ocean view. Then, step by step, the artist demonstrates how to create the painting. In minutes, before our very eyes, the

---

ception. . . . But once 'yield' to the organic structure of a masterpiece and the selective process carries us along, excluding subjective errors of irrelevancy and directing us toward the total organic whole so far as it is achieved by the artist." Pepper, *Work of Art*, p. 77.

53. Perhaps this dimension of the evocateur can then be termed the "Humpty Dumpty" syndrome.

54. Huer, *Art, Beauty, and Pornography*, p. 29.

55. Ibid., p. 24.

artist brings forth a work of art. I must confess that I never lose the child-like excitement of watching the artist create trees, or flowers, or birds with just the stroke of the brush. Regardless of how often or how well the artist shows his or her technique, when it is performed on the canvas in front of me it is still magical.

Another favorite thing for me to do is to sit in absolute silence and isolation with a symphonic score in my hands—say, the score of Johannes Brahms' First Symphony. I sit there, looking at those pages and pages of notes, reading through the different instrumental lines, and seeing the chordal structures. I study until a mental image of what the music itself looks like is committed to memory. Then I go and play a recording of the Brahms First, as loud as the neighbors will allow. Magic! The black dots come alive; the linear structures dance and intertwine; the chords explode, and then melt into one another.

The artist is a magician, who before our eyes and in our ears, transforms the mundane into the transcendent.[56] A flick of the brush, or the stroke of a pen, and what was plain and ordinary suddenly becomes new, alive, and exciting.

Speaking of the artist as magician does not imply that the artist is the possessor of some occult power.[57] Demonology, witchcraft, and black magic belong to a different discussion. For example, in all seriousness, James Frazer in *The Golden Bough* discussed the principles of magic at great length, saying: "In short, magic is a spurious system of natural law as well as a fallacious guide of conduct; it is a false science as well as an abortive art."[58] Such an approach, and such a study, of the magician is quite different from what is described here. It also takes all the fun out of the role of the artist as magician. The whole point of seeing the artist in the role of magician is to realize that the artist certainly does nothing outside of "natural law" or of normal conduct. It is the very act of transforming the simple into the glorious by purely human and natural activity that makes the artist so fascinating.

Some feel that magicians are no longer exciting when they give away their secrets.[59] This is certainly not true of the artist/magician. Why else would I sit in front of the television set watching an artist transform a blank canvas into a painting? The magnetism of the artist is much more than the technique used.[60] The mystery and the excitement does not reside in the secret of how, but in the result. The artist/magician performs the feat before my eyes, explaining how it is done, and it is still engrossing.

---

56. Frank Seiberling pointed out that in one sense the artist is only able to represent reality: "Now the artist cannot, at last, produce his subject in person nor in its natural state. He is forced to remain a *representative* of nature and the social world. He can create a certain illusion of presentation but—one of its charms—it is still a sleight of hand." Seiberling, *Looking Into Art*, pp. 5-6.

57. See Chapter Seven, "The Religious Educator as Critic," especially the dimension of debunker, for a discussion of the religious educator's responsibility in unmasking the trickster or the charlatan. The dimension being discussed here as the artist as magician is referring to another sort of "magic" entirely.

58. James George Frazer, *The Golden Bough: A Study in Magic and Religion*, abridged ed. (New York: Macmillan, 1944; first published in 1922), p. 11.

59. For a related discussion, see the dimension of debunker in Chapter Seven, "The Religious Educator as Critic."

60. The artist must certainly be competent in his or her chosen medium, but mere technical ability still does not describe or define the artist, as it may the craftsperson.

The religious educator, master of the art, is no less the magician. The religious educator takes a seemingly meaningless passage of scripture, for example, and makes it come alive and vital in our presence, showing us things we never have seen there before. He or she can be instrumental in transforming unconcerned and uninterested students into committed and lifelong members of a faith community. Is it somehow damaging or "outside natural law" that religious educators are taught to perform this "magic," and in turn teach others how?[61] If so, the entire concept of teacher education is demonic. If we cannot be taught to teach, to perform the "magic" of education, and then to train others in the art, then religious educators are back to participating in Frazer's definition of magic: "A spurious science, a fallacious guide, and an abortive art."

Summary
The dimensions of the role of artist have been described as creator, designer, evocateur, and magician. Of course, these specific dimensions of the role are not the only ones possible for examination, but these have given some basic perspective to the role. The beauty and charm of the role of artist is that each individual artist brings something fresh and unique to the role. The sections that follow will help to flesh out the role in sufficient measure to show its inestimable value to the religious educator.

Aim: Revelation/Discovery

The aim of the artist, and hence of the religious educator as artist, has the dual prongs of revelation and discovery. The key point in understanding the aim is that revelation and discovery are ways for the artist to come to know himself or herself, and by extension, to come to know the world. Revelation points to declaring what is known, discovery to finding what was previously unknown—and art goes in both of these directions. A work of art can be properly interpreted as the self-revelation and the self-discovery of the artist.[62]

But is the source of art from within the personhood of the artist, and is the essence of art simply the revelation of the artist's personality? While these may be true to a certain extent, they do not explain the depth of the aim of revelation/discovery. Martin Buber, in his classic work *I and Thou*, shed light on the more fundamental reality of art: "This is the eternal source of art: a man is faced by a form which desires to be made through him into a work. This form is no offspring of the soul, but it is an appearance which steps up to it and demands of it effective power. The man is concerned with an act of his being. If he carries it through, if he speaks the primary word out of his being to the form which

---

61. This is precisely the type of fallacious argument that James Michael Lee has labeled the "blow theory." For example, see James Michael Lee, *The Flow of Religious Instruction: A Social Science Approach* (Birmingham, Ala.: Religious Education Press, 1973), pp. 174-180.

62. "Great art is a powerful moral agent for building up a rich and healthy personality; and a great work of art is an expression of an integrated personality with deep emotional insight. By a process of cognitive intuition, a spectator responds to the emotional and perceptive insight of the artist and, insofar as these are well integrated and healthy, the spectator's dispositions are molded towards deeper insight and better adjustment." Pepper, *Work of Art*, p. 81.

appears, then the effective power streams out, and the work arises."[63]

Revelation is the unveiling of identity or the making known of a hidden truth.[64] Revelation is usually intentional, and comes as an invitation into the private world of another person.[65] Revelation is a result of the decision to make known at least a part of one's identity to another person or group of persons.[66] The major part of the activity is in the hands of the revealer: He or she is primarily in charge of the decision of what to reveal, when, and to whom. No amount of trying to peer behind the curtain will grant much success until the one who has drawn the curtain is willing for it to be opened. Revelation, then, is rooted in hiddenness.

Christians and Jews often use the term revelation in their discussions and understandings of God. The Jewish scriptures,[67] for example, are sometimes regarded as the record of God's "progressive revelation,"[68] where more and more of the nature of God was revealed as more and more of the acts of God were experienced and interpreted. The revelation of God in these scriptures came to be expressed in personal language: A God who revealed personhood to Abraham, or to Moses, or to Elijah, or to the Israelites as a whole. The God depicted in Judeo-Christian scriptures is not presented through mere ideas or philosophical information. The revelation is a self-revelation—it concerns the personhood of God.[69]

Moses and the story of the burning bush was handed down as a specific example of how the divine characteristics were communicated through the means of the personal relationship that developed between God and Moses.[70] The sacred, personal name of God, the Tetragrammaton,[71] was given to Moses

63. Martin Buber, *I and Thou*, 2nd ed., trans. Ronald Gregor Smith (New York: Scribner's, 1958), pp. 9-10.

64. "Revelation literally means an unveiling, the lifting of an obscuring veil, so as to disclose something that was formerly hidden." John Baillie, *The Idea of Revelation in Recent Thought* (New York: Columbia University Press, 1956), p. 18.

65. See this concept explored empirically by Mark H. Davis and Stephen L. Franzoni, "Private Self-Consciousness and Self-Disclosure," in *Self-Disclosure: Theory, Research, and Therapy*, ed. Valerian J. Derlega and John H. Berg (New York: Plenum Press, 1987), pp. 59-79.

66. "In ordinary social relationships, disclosure is a reciprocal phenomenon. Participants in dialogue disclose their thoughts, feelings, actions, etc., to the other and are disclosed in return." Sidney M. Jourard, *The Transparent Self*, rev. ed. (New York: Van Nostrand Reinhold, 1971), p. 66.

67. What Christians call the Old Testament. See this nomenclature discussed in Chapter Eight, "The Old Testament as Scripture," George W. Anderson, *A Critical Introduction to the Old Testament* (London: Gerald Duckworth, 1959), pp. 235-239. For Christians, the revelation of God continues on in the New Testament through the person of Jesus Christ: "Long ago God spoke to our ancestors in many and various ways by prophets, but in these last days he has spoken to us by a Son, whom he appointed heir of all things, through whom he created worlds." Hebrews 1:1-2, NRSV.

68. For example, see the discussion of progressive revelation by H. Richard Niebuhr in *The Meaning of Revelation* (New York: Macmillan, 1941), pp. 132-137.

69. As a Christian author expressed this thought: "According to the Bible, what is revealed to us is not a body of information concerning various things of which we might otherwise be ignorant. If it is information at all, it is information concerning the nature and purpose of God—that and nothing else. Yet in the last resort it is not information about God that is revealed but very God Himself incarnate in Jesus Christ our Lord." Baillie, *Idea of Revelation in Recent Thought*, p. 28.

70. Exodus 3:1-4:23.

71. For some introduction to this holy name of God, consult Gerhard von Rad, *Old Testament Theology, Vol. One: The Theology of Israel's Historical Traditions*, trans. D.M.G. Stalker (New York: Harper & Row, 1962), pp. 179-187.

as evidence of access to and knowledge of God. When Moses asked at the site of the burning bush who this God speaking to him was, the answer given was JHYH: I AM WHO I AM.[72] The only way that Moses could have gained access to this holy name was through the willful and intentional revelation of God. When a name is attached, personhood and relationship can be established, and these all became forms of revelation that Moses experienced. Another fascinating type of revelation Moses received somewhat later was the handiwork—the artwork if you will—of God. Scripture says that the decalogue was written by the fingers of God and entrusted to Moses for reading to the Israelites.[73] Not only were these "ten words" received as the revelation of the nature of God, but they were communicated through the artwork of God.

The other side of revelation is discovery.[74] As Moses received the revelation of God, Moses also revealed who and what he was: his fearfulness, his dishonesty, his craftiness, and ultimately his faithfulness. As Moses revealed himself to God in relationship, Moses also discovered a lot about who Moses was. Moses was in the cycle of self-discovery: He was allowed to see who he was as he revealed himself to another. The principle is that one learns about who he or she is (discovery) as one gives himself or herself away (revelation).[75]

An adequate understanding of revelation and discovery should sufficiently clarify the primary aim of the artist. The artist reveals himself or herself through creating the work of art. At the same time, the artist discovers more about himself or herself through this act of revelation. The "work of art," so often the focus of attention, is actually the end-product of an artist's activity of self-revelation and self-discovery. When truly experiencing the work of art, one also necessarily encounters at least something of the artist who is revealed in that work of art.

Religious educators, then, are deeply involved in the revelation/discovery process when participating in the role of artist. Religious educators need to be constantly aware that one of the primary things they communicate is self-identity: They reveal themselves every time they teach. At the same time, they are also opened to the possibility of self-discovery every time they teach. In the teaching they not only reveal themselves, but they find themselves. The religious educator can never forget that in performing the role of the artist, he or she is constantly the vessel for revelation and discovery. So much more than a mere transmitter of information, the religious educator as artist is a revealer and a discoverer

---

72. See Exodus 3:13-14, NRSV. The translation could just as easily read I AM WHAT I AM or I WILL BE WHAT I WILL BE.

73. Exodus 32:18.

74. "To disclose means to uncover, but in ordinary usage it does not mean to discover. I discover something for myself, but I disclose [reveal] it to another." Baillie, *Idea of Revelation in Recent Thought*, p. 18.

75. Hans Küng said: "Also and particularly for the work of the artist it should be of the utmost importance to know whence we came, whither we are going, who we are." Küng, *Art and the Question of Meaning*, p. 39. Sidney Jourard identified this interactive and dynamic process as a sign of a healthy personality: "Self-disclosure is a symptom of personality health and a means of ultimately achieving healthy personality. When I say that self-disclosure is a symptom of personality health, I mean a person who displays many of the other characteristics that betoken healthy personality will also display the ability to make himself fully known to at least one other significant human being." Jourard, *Transparent Self*, p. 32.

whose personality and presence can never be (and rightly so) totally factored out of the teaching/learning act.

In summary, the aim of revelation/discovery serves as a reminder that in teaching, religious educators both reveal themselves and discover themselves. The analogy comes from the role of the artist: The artist may produce a work of art that stands alone, yet the artist is never totally excised from the work of art. The artist is always to be found within the work of art. To miss the artist in the work of art is to miss the fullness of all that art has to offer.

Function: Creativity

If the aim of the religious educator as artist is revelation/discovery, with all the attendant varieties and differences each artist contributes, then the function that achieves this aim is creativity.[76] There is no one best way for the religious educator as artist to reveal and to discover. Each one must search and develop new and unique ways to mediate himself or herself, and the term "creativity" captures this need for the individuality of expression.

Viewed in this light, the genuine religious educator is by no means a drone or a pedant but fully a participant in the rich creative processes marked by the activity of the true artist. Any image of the religious educator as the disciplinarian or taskmaster of the church or synagogue school is quickly replaced by that of the artist, given the inclusion—and infusion—of the function of creativity. The religious educator as artist is not bound to denominational curricula, or to slavish record-keeping, or to repetition of the same old tired techniques. The religious educator, performing in the role of artist, and functioning with creativity, becomes *aggiornamento*, a breath of fresh air that rushes through the church or synagogue or classroom. Stimulation and excitement becomes as descriptive of the religious educator as artist as does predictability and boredom in the old dronish stereotype.

After conceding that creativity is indeed an integral function of the religious educator, one would then be justified in asking: How is creativity identified, nurtured, and performed? This simple question has no easy answer, although there have been some productive attempts to move toward an educational process that promotes creativity. Robert Weisberg, for example, took a serious and scholarly approach to creativity in the book *Creativity: Genius and Other Myths.*[77]

---

76. Paul Torrance described creative thinking (restricted here to the cognitive realm) as "taking place in the process of sensing difficulties, problems, gaps in information, missing elements; making guesses or formulating hypotheses about these deficiencies; testing these guesses and possibly revising and retesting them; and finally communicating the results." E. Paul Torrance, *Rewarding Creative Behavior: Experiments in Classroom Creativity* (Englewood Cliffs, N.J.: Prentice-Hall, 1965), p. 8. A similar definition was given by Roger Schank: "Creative thinking is a kind of game without rules, or rather the rules can be whatever you decide. Rules and facts are the playing pieces, to be moved around by the players. The moment a player tries to make serious business out of the rules and the formulas—the moment one assumes that truths are hard and fast—the Game is lost. Creativity is a game of making and testing hypotheses, taking them as far as they can be taken, then watching them crumble and wondering why." Roger Schank with Peter Childers, *The Creative Attitude: Learning to Ask and Answer the Right Questions* (New York: Macmillan, 1988), p. 5.

77. Robert Weisberg, *Creativity: Genius and Other Myths* (New York: W.H. Freeman, 1986).

Weisberg staked a position between what he described as two extremes. On the one hand was what Weisberg labeled the "genius" view of creativity, a romantic notion which he described as "the belief that creative achievements come about through great leaps of imagination which occur because creative individuals are capable of extraordinary thought processes."[78] In addition, these "geniuses" are assumed to possess "extraordinary personality characteristics" as well as great intellect which serves to set them apart from the "normal" population, and the "creative person suddenly begins to produce something complete without knowing where it came from."[79] On the other hand was what Weisberg termed the "nothing new" view, represented by the behaviorist psychologist John Broadus Watson. Watson completely dismissed the notion (myth) of genius and its accompanying mystery, claiming that nothing anyone does is truly creative.[80] This behavioristic approach saw "creativity" as either the generalization of an old behavior injected into a new environment or as a random and accidental combination of responses which produces only an apparent creative adaptation to a novel environment.[81] Weisberg himself followed neither of the extreme views, saying: "Creativity is not nearly as mysterious as the genius view leads us to believe, but neither is it as trivial as the behaviorist view claims."[82]

Acknowledging that "it is very difficult to discuss creativity because it means very different things to people,"[83] Weisberg proposed instead that the discussion should focus on "creative problem solving," which "involves a person's producing a novel response that solves the problem at hand."[84] Admittedly this approach is too dependent on cognition, and it takes much of the fun (mystery) out of the definition, but it does illumine a helpful path for the religious educator wondering how to nurture creativity.[85] From this perspective, to begin the creative process requires only that the religious educator pose issues in terms of problems to be solved and then go about the work of searching for multiple ways of solving—or at least attacking—the problem. This approach helps remove the excuse of waiting for a strike of lightning that may never come, as well as the need for marching lockstep through the same pitiful lesson plans.[86]

One of the most fruitful approaches for understanding and promoting creativity has come from the work of J.P. Guilford. Guilford constructed a com-

---

78. Ibid., p. 1.
79. Ibid.
80. Ibid., p. 2.
81. Ibid.
82. Ibid., p. 3.
83. Ibid.
84. Ibid., p. 4. For a fuller discussion of problem solving in this book, see Chapter Six, "The Religious Educator as Scientist."
85. For a good discussion that shows the necessity of providing a nurturing environment for creativity to flourish, see Torrance, *Rewarding Creative Behavior*, pp. 16-19.
86. Sharon Bailin took a similar line of attack on the "genius" myth of creativity. Her contribution to the discussion came at the point of adding continuity and effort to the formula. Bailin was convinced that rules, tradition, and hard work must not be abandoned in favor of simply waiting for the serendipitous appearance, full-blown, of a creative product. See Sharon Bailin, *Achieving Extraordinary Ends: An Essay on Creativity* (Dordrecht, The Netherlands: Kluwer Academic Publishers, 1988). For a quick summary of her position, see p. 131.

prehensive model of human intellectual processes that identified three main aspects: operations, product, and content.[87] For purposes here, Guilford's primary contribution to dispelling the aura that seems to surround creativity lies in understanding two of the five operations: convergent thinking[88] and divergent thinking.[89] In his testing of convergent thinking and divergent thinking, Guilford found that while the thinker in both cases is required to produce information, the *types* of information produced are of a very different sort. In convergent thinking, the person being tested "must arrive at one right answer. The best example of this is a mathematical problem, but an example with verbal material would be: 'What is *the* opposite of hard?'"[90] To contrast with this kind of thinking, Guilford then tested for divergent thinking, where "the thinker must do much searching around, and often a number of answers will do or are wanted. If you ask the examinee to name all the things he can think of that are hard, also edible, also white, he has a whole class of things that might do."[91] Guilford then said: "It is in the divergent-thinking category that we find the abilities that are the most significant in creative thinking and invention,"[92] which of course are precisely the abilities that are so crucial to the role of the religious educator as artist.[93] Guilford went on to make the direct application to education, and by implication to religious education: "Most of our problem solving in everyday life involves divergent thinking. Yet in our educational practices, we tend to emphasize teaching students how to find conventional answers. It is time that we give more attention to development of skills in divergent thinking and also that we show more tolerance of outcomes of divergent thinking. When the individual is later on his own and will have to depend upon his own resources, he will find that textbook answers do not solve all his problems."[94]

The suggestions of Weisberg and Guilford do not denigrate the efforts of

---

87. These three aspects allowed Guilford to discuss one hundred twenty different abilities related to creativity and intelligence. The three-dimensional model of Guilford can be found in a number of places. For example, see the primary explanation in J. P. Guilford, *The Nature of Human Intelligence* (New York: McGraw-Hill, 1967), pp. 60-68; also see J. P. Guilford, "New Frontiers of Testing in the Discovery and Development of the Human Talent," in J. P. Guilford, *Intelligence, Creativity and Their Educational Implications* (San Diego: Robert R. Knapp, 1968), pp. 3-13; J.P. Guilford, "The Three Faces of Intellect," *The American Psychologist* (1959), pp. 469-479 and reprinted in *Studies in Educational Psychology*, ed. Raymond G. Kuhlen (Waltham, Mass.: Blaisdell, 1968), pp. 59-71. A secondary source that includes an overview of Guilford's work and the model can be found in Chapter Eleven, "Creativity and Intelligence," by Guy R. LeFrancois, *Psychology for Teaching* (Belmont, Calif.: Wadsworth, 1975), pp. 231-249.

88. For a full discussion of this ability, see Chapter Seven, "Convergent-Production Abilities," Guilford, *Nature of Human Intelligence*, pp. 171-184.

89. For a full discussion of this ability, see Chapter Six, "Divergent-Production Abilities," ibid., pp. 138-170. The other three operations Guilford identified along with these two are cognition, memory, and evaluation.

90. Guilford, "New Frontiers of Testing in the Discovery and Development of the Human Talent," in Guilford, *Intelligence, Creativity and Their Educational Implications*, p. 8.

91. Ibid.

92. Ibid.

93. See evidence for this in Guilford, *Nature of Human Intelligence*, pp. 337-338.

94. Guilford, "New Frontiers of Testing in the Discovery and Development of the Human Talent," in Guilford, *Intelligence, Creativity and Their Educational Implications*, p. 8.

those we enjoy calling "creative geniuses,"[95] but they do help remove the sense of mystery and exclusivity that too often surrounds them. Creativity is a function that can definitely be nurtured in religious education *if* we are able and willing, as Guilford said, to "show more tolerance of outcomes of divergent thinking."[96] Creativity involves a lot of hard work and a lot of exploration into uncharted territories, but it is an activity open and available to the "normal" person rather than the province of an elite and chosen few.[97] In reality, then, creativity must come to be seen as endemic, inseparable, and integral to the work of the religious educator as it is to that of the musician, painter, and poet.

Primary Virtues: Expression and Disclosure

One of the great tragedies of religious education is the impersonalism it too easily assumes. Religious education without its personhood—the embodiment and enfleshment of humans—is vacuous. As mentioned earlier, religious education is not an "it," a thing to be dissected, examined, and then reassembled. Religious education is alive, dynamic, experiential, and fully human. For these reasons this book has turned as a whole to a look at the religious *educator,* in order to emphasize the flesh and blood corporeality.

The faith traditions, at their very core, are fully human systems, as opposed to disembodied ideas, theories, or philosophies. Christianity, for example, has at its very heart the incarnation: the Word which became flesh to dwell among human beings.[98] The tangibility of the Word *is* the good news, and this good news continues to be enfleshed by each person on the Way. To read the Jewish scriptures is to encounter the most human of stories, told with all the frailties and strengths of its human subjects intact. For all of its cognitive intuition and meditational techniques, Buddhism would still be virtually incomprehensible with-

---

95. For a profile of a creative person based on research evidence, see James Michael Lee, *The Content Of Religious Instruction: A Social Science Approach* (Birmingham, Ala.: Religious Education Press, 1985), pp. 174-176. Lee said at the conclusion of the profile: "This empirically supported profile of the personality characteristics of the creative performer probably is not very appealing to many Catholic or Protestant ecclesiastical officials in terms of what these officials wish to see as the fruit of their religious education programs. To be sure, institutional religion, particularly as it is enfleshed in the form of ecclesiastical officials, has always seemed ill at ease with divergent thinkers and creative performers." Ibid., p. 176.

96. This is from the earlier quote of Guilford, "New Frontiers of Testing in the Discovery and Development of the Human Talent," in Guilford, *Intelligence, Creativity and Their Educational Implications*, p. 8.

97. "Creativity is not the exclusive province of a small minority of physicists, artists, and inventors. It is really a rather common form of thinking, one that most people are hardly aware of." Schank with Childers, *Creative Attitude: Learning to Ask and Answer the Right Questions*, p. 5. These authors continued in a vein quite similar to the above comments by both Guilford and Lee: "The problem is that a great deal of effort, usually quite unintentional, goes into stopping people from being creative. Institutions such as schools, religions, governments, and businesses all effectively reduce creativity. These institutions usually don't believe that they limit creativity. But by their very nature, institutions thrive on rules and on ready answers. Creative people have the annoying habit of rejecting rules and answers and asking new, and hard, questions. Creative people make waves. Institutions abhor wave makers." Ibid., p. 5-6.

98. John 1:14.

out the Buddhas[99] who illumine the path. Separate Muhammad from Islam and the vital human link between heaven and earth ("There is no god but God, and Muhammad is the messenger") is lost.[100]

All this is to say that there is no such thing as "religious education" without the inclusion of the human element.[101] To stare into the face of religious education and miss the inherent humanity is not to see religious education at all.

The primary virtues of the religious educator as artist permit a focus on the humanity of the religious educator and on the personhood of the participants of religious education. These virtues, within this context, are expression and disclosure. These virtues have a dual focus. The religious educator as artist is involved in both expression and disclosure, but these virtues are not isolated within the person or the religious educator. At the same time that the religious educator is fulfilling these virtues, the participants he or she is leading in religious education are also actively engaged in actualizing these virtues. As the religious educator is expressing and disclosing, so each of the persons participating with the religious educator is also expressing and disclosing.

The artist teaches the religious educator about the virtue of expression. Whether through paint, notes, words, or stone, the artist works at externalizing his or her emotions and thoughts into a communicable expression.[102] Whenever one encounters the resultant work of art, he or she is able again to experience and receive the artist's original expression of himself or herself.[103] There is always something unique, personal, and idiosyncratic about art that lets the participant come to know the artist in a deeply human way. The artist is able to inject his or her self into the work of art in such a way as to provide revelation of the artist's personality, however abstractly or unconsciously it may be represented.

By implication, the religious educator as artist is not an impersonal pipeline through which substantive content flows. The religious educator as artist is truly a mediator—he or she becomes the interactive medium through which the infor-

---

99. I am referring here not only to Siddhartha Gautama, but to other past and future Buddhas who also bring enlightenment (such as the next Buddha, Maitreya), as well as to the boddhisatvas that help the people find the middle path (Maitreya is now believed to be a boddhisatva, and is a Buddha-in-the-making). See Chapter Seven, "The Religious Educator as Critic," for more discussion on the faith tradition resource of Buddhism. Also see David B. Noss and John B. Noss, *A History of the World's Religions*, 8th ed. (New York: Macmillan, 1990), pp. 187-188 and 197-201.

100. See Chapter Five, "The Religious Educator as Coach," for more on Islam as a faith tradition resource.

101. The religious educator responsible for the teaching/learning act always must acknowledge the four major cluster independent variables: the learner, the teacher, the substantive or subject matter content, and the environment. The human element is obviously inextricable from such a dynamic activity. See this discussed in Chapter Nine, "The Structure of Teaching," in Lee, *Flow of Religious Instruction*, pp. 230-268.

102. Samuel Curry wrote: "What are the fundamental elements of a work of art? Without entering into the question as to the origin of art or the philosophy of art, we can see at once that one essential characteristic of art is expression. Art is a necessity of man's nature. It is deeper than language, yet it is the highest mode the soul can secure to reveal itself. Expression is a term universally applied to all forms of art." Samuel S. Curry, *The Province of Expression: A Search for Principles* (Boston: School of Expression, 1891), pp. 100-101.

103. "Art, whether it lasts for five minutes or for a thousand years, is the unfolding of personality." Ibid., p. 110.

mation is expressed and experienced.[104] To so objectify religious education and the religious educator as to make them mere delivery systems not only depersonalizes them but profoundly misunderstands the basics of human communication. Not to see, appreciate, or even recognize the individual expression and contribution of the religious educator is to miss the vital human dimension within the entire educational enterprise. The individual and personal expression of the religious educator is seen, heard, and experienced in every religious education event.

Does the above paragraph provide an excuse for the religious educator to be brash, proud, or egocentric, and go about assuming that everyone needs to hear his or her opinions? Such a reading of the paragraph completely distorts the role of artist, to say nothing of that of the religious educator. R.G. Collingwood explained the idea clearly and plainly: "His business as an artist is to speak out, to make a clean breast. But what he has to utter is not, as the individualistic theory of art would have us think, his own secrets. As spokesman of his community, the secrets he must utter are theirs. The reason why they need him is that no community altogether knows its own heart; and by failing in this knowledge a community deceives itself on the one subject concerning which ignorance means death."[105]

Stemming directly from these comments, then, comes the realization that the artist also teaches the religious educator about disclosure. Disclosure is involved in the processes of revelation and discovery,[106] already identified as the aim of the artist. As the artist discloses who he or she is through the works of art, the artist is able to discover and experience even more of his or her true self. One of the things the artist teaches about disclosure is that there are no finite boundaries to the person, no absolute and final limits to what one is able to learn about himself or herself. The more disclosed and revealed about the self to others, the more one is allowed to discover and experience of the self.[107]

This limitless opportunity for exploration opened up by disclosure explains why the virtue of disclosure is so essential to the religious educator.[108] Not only do vistas of self-knowledge and self-discovery come into view, but an entirely different dimension of religious education now becomes a possibility. Religious

---

104. This has long been the contention and language of James Michael Lee. See *The Content of Religious Instruction*, pp. 24-26.

105. Collingwood, *Principles of Art*, p. 336.

106. Sidney Jourard stated flatly that in his opinion "no man can come to know himself except as an outcome of disclosing himself to another person." Sidney M. Jourard, *Transparent Self*, p. 6. For some research data to back up this kind of subjective statement, see Sidney M. Jourard, *Self-Disclosure: An Experimental Analysis of the Transparent Self* (Huntington, N.Y.: Krieger, 1979).

107. This concept can be seen schematically in the diagram called the Johari Window, which shows the interplay of disclosure and feedback. See this explained in detail in Chapter Three, "The Johari Window: A Graphic Model of Awareness in Interpersonal Relations," in Joseph Luft, *Group Processes: An Introduction to Group Processes*, 2nd ed. (Palo Alto, Calif.: Mayfield, 1970), pp. 11-20.

108. A helpful resource for explaining this connection is by Bede J. Healey, "Self-Disclosure in Religious Spiritual Direction: Antecedents and Parallels to Self-Disclosure in Psychotherapy," in *Self-Disclosure in the Therapeutic Relationship*, ed. George Stricker and Martin Fisher (New York: Plenum Press, 1990), pp. 17-27.

education, when touched by the artist, cannot be perceived as the transmission of cold, hard data bits of impersonal information. The very act of religious education itself becomes an opportunity for disclosure and discovery for the religious educator as well as for each participant.[109] Through the artistic religious educator, vast depths of humanity are available for exploration.

In summary, the virtues of expression and disclosure are absolutely foundational to the identity of the religious educator. These are hardly new virtues, having been at the core of the faith traditions from their very inception. It is from the brushstroke of the artist that the full realization of the broad dimensions of genuine—human—religious education comes to the attention and to the awareness.

Activity: Creating

The prime activity of the religious educator as artist is that of creating: the ceaseless, dynamic, and multifaceted quest to achieve desired objectives through new and different resources. The means of creating are as diverse and as numerous as the people doing the creating. The activity of creating is an irreducible minimum that the religious educator must perform. If this is true, then what is the proper way to go about this business of creating? This is similar to asking the question, which was the better composer, Wolfgang Amadeus Mozart (1756-1791) or Ludwig van Beethoven (1770-1827)? Dismissing for the moment those who would actually tout one or the other for such an honor, the more rational answer is surely that this is the wrong question. If both are arguably immortals in music composition, then perhaps a study of their common creative habits will unlock the door to understanding what is the "proper" way of being creative.

Wolfgang Amadeus Mozart was known for the precision and the speed at which he produced his music. His original manuscripts have the appearance of dictation, since very few additions, corrections, or revisions were apparently ever necessary. The music seemed to fairly flow from his pen, fully formed and complete. In an extant letter, derided by some to be spurious, Mozart described what it was like for him to create. He said the musical ideas came to him best when he was alone and in good humor, when riding in a carriage, perhaps, or walking after a meal. He revealed his secret to the creative process in these words: "My subject [the aforementioned musical ideas] enlarges itself, becomes methodized and defined, and the whole, though it be long, stands almost complete and finished in my mind, so that I can survey it, like a fine picture or a beautiful statue, at a glance. Nor do I hear in my imagination the parts successively,

---

109. This is one of the points of integration among the religious educator's roles as artist and therapist (see Chapter Twelve, "The Religious Educator as Therapist"). In trying to decide about the proper limits and procedures for self-disclosure, see such helps as "Criteria for Therapist Self-Disclosure," by Judith C. Simpson in *Self-Disclosure in the Therapeutic Relationship*, pp. 207-225; Marlene Christine Mills, *Adolescent Self-Disclosure: Its Facilitation through Themes, Therapeutic Techniques, and Interview Conditions* (New York: Peter Lang, 1985); and Myron F. Weiner, *Therapist Disclosure: The Use of Self in Psychotherapy* (Boston: Butterworth, 1978).

but I hear them, as it were, all at once."[110] When Mozart's imaginative hearing—creating—was complete, he then went about the business of writing it all down: "When I proceed to write down my ideas, I take out of the bag of my memory . . . what has previously collected into it. . . . The committing to paper is done quickly enough, for everything is, as I said before, already finished; and it rarely differs on paper from what was in my imagination."[111]

Is this, then, the "proper" way to compose, and by extension, to create? If so, one is put in the uncomfortable position of saying that Ludwig van Beethoven did it improperly. By all accounts and evidence, Beethoven's style of creating was poles apart from Mozart's transcribing approach. While there is no similarly revealing letter that approximates looking into the mind of Mozart, there are extant sketchbooks of Beethoven that cover over five thousand pages of musical thought. To be sure, they are not a complete set, since many were either lost in the trash or to souvenir collectors, but there is more than sufficient surviving evidence of Beethoven's method of composing. He would sometimes work and rework a musical idea over a period of years, honing it to make it just right. At other times he would completely redo an entire composition, such as his only opera "Fidelio" which went through countless revisions. The music that today sounds so inevitable and predetermined took shape slowly and painfully, so much so that even after publication Beethoven would suddenly change his mind and demand a correction. Yet today, musicologists continue to argue over the exact notation of the final wishes of Beethoven.

Perhaps these brief and well-known examples exhibit the folly of trying to isolate and prescribe precisely the "proper" or even the preferred way to compose and create. They are in reality nothing but two ways of creating. What the religious educator can learn from Mozart and Beethoven is not so much how to create as the encouragement to get busy creating. Creative religious education is not uncrating denominational materials; not studying a commentary to get the "true" interpretation of a particular passage of scripture; not assigning the memorization of a specific verse or line of poetry. The function of creating in religious education is as diverse as the ideas and persons touched by the religious educator.

What may be regarded as creative and useful religious education for one situation and one group of people may not at all be appropriate or helpful in a different setting. What is happening in other groups, environments, or faith traditions is by no means indicative of what should be happening in one's own particular situation. While it may indeed be stimulating and motivating to see and hear what others are doing, such an exercise cannot be allowed to define or prescribe the boundaries of the artistic religious educator. Let Mozart be Mozart, and let Beethoven be Beethoven. The world is much the richer for the diversity. The world awaits and cries for the creativity and the ingenuity of each individual religious educator fulfilling the role of artist in his or her unique way.

---

110. As found in Brewster Ghiselin, *The Creative Process: A Symposium* (New York: New American Library, 1952), p. 45. For more discussion of this letter and its contribution to the understanding of creativity, see also Weisberg, *Creativity*, pp. 1-2, and 128-129; and Howard Gardner, *Art, Mind, and Brain: A Cognitive Approach to Creativity* (New York: Basic Books, 1982) pp. 358-368.

111. Ghiselin, *The Creative Process*, p. 45.

Shadow Role: Pornographer

To the extent that beauty can be defined as being in the eye of the beholder, then the corruption of beauty—pornography—can be similarly defined. Such subjectivity makes judgments that are to be universally applied quite difficult, if not impossible. Pornography is not the opposite of art, in that one is ugly while the other is beautiful. Neither is pornography properly defined by that which is sexually explicit and graphic, since many great works of art are sexually explicit and graphic in their depiction. Pornography can be understood, however, as taking what is naturally beautiful and using it for degradation and exploitation.

The term "pornography" is derived from two Greek words, πόρνη (prostitute), and γράφω (writing). Pornography, taken literally, is writing about prostitutes. The pornographer is at bottom an exploiter. He or she takes the skills, abilities, and at times even the subjects, of the artist and uses them for personal profit, exploitation of the subjects, and pandering to the consumer. The pornographer is to the artist what the "mad scientist" is to the genuine scientific researcher: the tools, information, and creativity are employed for the corrupt purposes and desires of a few rather than for the edification of society as a whole.

In the midst of the optimism in this chapter on the religious educator as artist, a strong word of warning about the religious educator as pornographer is essential. If the pornographer is someone who uses his or her skills and abilities for profiteering, exploitation, and pandering, then it may be that there are as many religious education pornographers as there are any other kind. A perusal of much of the "literature" of religious education resembles, in the eye of this beholder, more pornography than art. Without doubt, some of the producers of this material are making profits, but to what end? Too much of the curriculum "panders" to what the consumer wants: a rehash of ingrained cultural habits and beliefs, or candy-coated renditions of ancient stories that have little if any application to modern societal problems. It may be that if Jesus were to bring his whip to contemporary society, he would probably bypass the churches and temples and drive out the money-changers from the "religious" bookstores and warehouses. His radical call to servanthood and sacrifice has been muted by some for the sake of profit to denominational curriculum producers and for the anesthesia they provide for the user.

The charge of exploiting the consumer falls at the feet of the religious educator. Armed with the tools and skills of the effective communicator and teacher, the pornographic religious educator refuses to use his or her abilities to stretch, challenge, or move the consumer from the comfortable status quo. Instead, the status quo is either disguised to look like the Kingdom, or the past is made to look like the proper vision of the future. The message of the religious educator is more often that of returning to the values and circumstances of the glorious past than pushing forward to confront the realities and challenges of the future. If not a return to the past, then the pornographers hold the line in the present: Work to keep the "message" pure and simple, unsullied by the flow of human events and experiences.

In reality, pornography has more to do with power and dominance than it does with sexuality. Pornography can be interpreted as one person conquering and dominating another for his or her own selfish needs. Religious educators fall prey to the same temptation. Religious education can easily become the means by which some are kept in positions of power and responsibility, while others are dominated and kept in their place with labels such as "untrained," "nonprofessional," and "layperson." It may very well be that this kind of religious educator—the pornographer—desires to keep the persons in his or her charge ignorant by keeping the truth from them. These pornographic religious educators need to be exposed as the exploiters that they are, rather than revered or respected for the profits they reap from pandering to the lower nature of humans.

Faith Tradition Resource: Shamanism

Fundamentally, shamanism refers to the ritualized activities and abilities of a person (the shaman[112]) who is "regarded as controlling spirits, exercising his mastery over them in socially recognized ways,"[113] or more pointedly as a person's "ability to enter into an altered state of consciousness *at will* in order to acquire help from spirits."[114] To appreciate shamanism as a faith tradition resource from a historical perspective requires traveling back in time to early human communal life.[115] In that more integrated, less complex, but very threatening world of the dawn of social life, the shaman was a powerful and important figure who was both revered and feared.[116] The shaman was the person in whom reli-

---

112. According to Mircea Eliade, the term "shaman" in the strict sense arose in Siberia and Central Asia. Eliade traced the etymology of the word "shaman" to show that it is of Tungusic origin. See Mircea Eliade, *Shamanism: Archaic Techniques of Ecstasy*, trans. Willard R. Trask (Princeton: Princeton University Press, 1962; first published in French in 1951), p. 4. Eliade insisted that the term "shaman" be kept as a specialized designation, as he pointed out in his classic study of shamanism: "If we take the trouble to differentiate the shaman from other magicians and medicine men of primitive societies, the identification of shamanic complexes in one or another region immediately acquires definite significance. Magic and magicians are found more or less all over the world, whereas shamanism exhibits a special magical ability. . . . Though the shaman is, among other things, a magician, not every magician can properly be termed a shaman. The same distinction must be applied in regard to shamanic healing; every medicine man is a healer, but the shaman employs a method that is his and his alone. As for the shamanic techniques of ecstasy, they do not exhaust all the varieties of ecstatic experience documented in the history of religions and religious ethnography. Hence any ecstatic cannot be regarded as a shaman; the shaman specializes in a trance during which his soul is believed to leave his body and ascend to the sky or descend to the underworld." Ibid., p. 5. Without doubt, this volume by Eliade is an excellent place to start any serious investigation of shamanism.

113. I.M. Lewis, *Religion in Context: Cults and Charisma* (Cambridge: Cambridge University Press, 1986), p. 80. See the entirety of Chapter Five, "The Shaman's Career ," ibid., pp. 78-93, for a good overview of the topic.

114. William H. Black Elk and William S. Lyon, *Black Elk: The Sacred Ways of a Lakota* (San Francisco: Harper & Row, 1990), p. xi.

115. For an excellent overview of the anthropological aspects of shamanism, see I.M. Lewis, *Ecstatic Religion: An Anthropological Study of Spirit Possession and Shamanism* (Middlesex, England: Penguin Books, 1971).

116. The role of the shaman has appeared in a wide variety of cultures. See this explained in such places as Arthur Waley, *The Nine Songs: A Study of Shamanism in Ancient China* (London: Allen and Unwin, 1955); Alan Carter Covell, *Ecstasy: Shamanism in Korea* (Elizabeth, N.J.: Hollym International Corporation, 1983); Chapter Four, "Holy Foolishness and Shamanism," in Ewa M. Thompson, *Understanding Russia: The Holy Fool in Russian Culture* (Lanham, Md.: University Press of America, 1987), pp. 97-123; and throughout *Sioux Indian Religion: Tradition and Innovation*, ed. Raymond J. Mallie and Douglas R. Parks (Norman, Okla.: University of Oklahoma Press, 1987).

gion and art were merged into what today would be more commonly called magic, but as far as early humans were concerned, the shaman was their one best hope for predicting and controlling events.[117]

Evidence of shamanistic phenomena is found as early as in the community of the Cro-Magnons.[118] For example, the key to a successful hunting party was the creation of representations of chief subjects of the hunt: the bison, or boar, or the mammoth. Representational figures of these animals were painted on cave walls, molded from clay, or carved from pieces of bone. The purpose of this "artwork," performed primarily by the shaman, was probably to gain control over the animals. To create a symbol of the animal was to capture its essence, or spirit. The power of the shaman then came to the fore. Most likely during a ritualistic ceremony, the shaman would paint arrows and darts onto the representational figures. Such magical acts were believed to foreordain success and to bring the animal spirits under human control. The shaman, performing in the role of the artist, was the tribe's principal means of magical manipulation.

John and Denise Carmody analyzed early religion by describing three functionaries: shaman, prophet, and sage. Where the prophet stressed the will and ethical imperatives, and the sage focused on the intellect and a comprehensive worldview, the shaman dealt more with the imagination and ecstatic experiences and was the central religious figure of the tribe.[119] The shaman cared for the sick, guided the spirits of the dead, and protected against the evil spirits: "The Siberian shaman goes out of himself, in what a modern Western observer might call a trance or a hallucination, and journeys in spirit to another realm, where most of the crucial battles of sickness and health, death and life, evil and good are waged."[120] This ecstatic experience was a prominent feature of the shaman's activity. The shaman left the boundaries of normality and went looking for other avenues of understanding. As the Carmodys wrote: "By discovering ways to step out of ordinary states of awareness and become more intimate with the powers of life and death, the early shamans released humanity from its first, most restrictive prisons."[121] Interestingly enough, the shaman in many ways parallels the "creative genius" that has been so successfully debunked in the twentieth century, as explained in a previous section of this chapter. A reconsideration of the shaman is a call back to the elementary mystery of life;[122] never,

---

117. In an important distinction, Lewis pointed out that "the term shaman belongs to that special category of ethnographically specific concepts used cross-culturally outside their own native contexts." Lewis, *Religion in Context*, p. 78. The terms "shaman" and "shamanism," then, are words we generally use today (informally and somewhat inaccurately) to refer to people in other cultures with such specialized designations as the medicine man or a medium.

118. See Noss and Noss, *History of the World's Religions*, pp. 7-10 for further background on the shaman in the Cro-Magnon community.

119. Denise Lardner Carmody and John Tully Carmody, *Shamans, Prophets, and Sages: An Introduction to World Religions* (Belmont, Calif.: Wadsworth, 1985), p. xv.

120. Ibid., p. 8.

121. Ibid., p. 18.

122. There is evidence of a modern resurgence of interest in the shaman and the shamanic powers. For example, Lynn Andrews wrote: "I write at a time of hope, however. Many of us are reaching out, looking for alternative ways to understand the rhythms of Mother Earth, to worship God or the Goddess, and to balance the male and female energies within ourselves and on the planet. We have come full circle in our quest, and the ancient concepts of shamanism, the sacred Dreamtime, and the

however, should contemporary persons allow themselves to be hoodwinked into returning to those "most restrictive prisons" of mind control.

The Carmodys then made a further, even more telling point about the attempt of moderns to understand and appreciate the role of the shaman: "The modern West has brought human imagination under scientific control. . . . Defining reality as what can be experienced through the senses and tested through dispassionate judgments, it has revolutionized humanity's understanding of the natural world. . . . But sometimes this scientific disciplining of our imaginations can restrict our feelings, so that reality becomes less vivid, challenging, and satisfying than it might be. Sometimes the mental world of the Westerner is arid and thin, compared to the lush poetry that ancient peoples have had in their heads. *The limits of our imaginations are the limits of our worlds.* When a shaman pictures our relation to the game on which we depend for food as decisively influenced by our relation with ultimate powers . . . he or she may be speaking a richer, more poetic truth than our scientifically disciplined minds can handle."[123]

This element of the "shamanic" role is similar to the one played by the artist in contemporary society. A world populated only by technicians, for example, would most certainly be a drab world indeed. Contemporary society has already lost many of its shamans, in any formal sense, so that now it is dependent on the artists to provide the requisite "richer, more poetic truth."

The shamanistic *artist*, then, can be regarded as one who transcends the rules, disciplines, and norms in the quest for a liberating type of experience not possible inside the safe boundaries of the familiar. The "magic" is within the technique of the artist's chosen medium, but it can still be as dazzling and as evocative as the magic of the early shaman; and while most in the modern world tend not to think that this "magic" has anything directly to do with predicting or controlling, there is the very real sense in which artists do play a part in predicting and controlling the future. True art is always avant-garde, out on the cutting edge, influencing if not creating the ways that the world will be viewed and experienced.

The religious educator needs to be willing to take on or reclaim this same kind of shamanic dimension that the role of artist allows. The future is open, waiting to be created, envisioned, predicted, influenced, and even perhaps to some extent controlled. Religious educators must become dedicated to leaving the safe and familiar boundaries of everyday life and be willing to release humanity from its restrictive prisons by venturing into new ways to experience and create truth,

---

sacred wheel of shamanic teaching are now alive and fresh again. We have been able to move around the wheel from shamanism through science and back again to the beginnings, to our origins. We can realize that we are nothing without the Great Spirit, the Creator; we are nothing without our magnificent Mother Earth, who gave us life. We are made from stars and to the stars we must return." Lynn V. Andrews, *Teachings Around the Sacred Wheel: Finding the Soul of the Dreamtime* (San Francisco: Harper & Row, 1990), p. ix. For another example of this kind of writing, see Ed McGaa, *Mother Earth Spirituality: Native American Paths to Healing Ourselves and Our World* (San Francisco: Harper San Francisco, 1990). For an interesting autobiographical account from a relatively modern shaman, see the still popular book *Black Elk Speaks: Being the Life Story of A Holy Man of the Ogala Sioux,* as told through John G. Neihhardt (Lincoln, Neb.: University of Nebraska Press, 1961).

123. Carmody and Carmody, *Shamans, Prophets, and Sages,* pp. 8-9. Emphasis added.

just as the shaman and the artist have done. For contemporary religious educators as for the ancient shaman, the same advice applies: "The limits of our imagination are the limits of our worlds."[124]

Historical Personage: Richard Wagner

Probably no personage in modern Western civilization has come as close to
personifying the artist and the shaman as the composer Richard Wagner (1813-
1883). Wagner spun his musical myths[125] with such force and power that stories
of listeners and performers alike going mad because of them still circulate.[126]
Wagner himself at times felt so under the spell of his own music that he was afraid
for his own sanity. Indeed, there are reports that Wagner came into the grip of a
near-psychotic frenzy when he finally began to put the notes to paper.[127] The
artistry of Wagner is certainly not in question; it is his "shamanic" powers that
accompanied his art which provide the fascinating link to the "medicine-man"
of the ancients to the more modern charismatic figures in contemporary art.
Wagner appears to have tapped the resources of the "collective unconscious,"[128]
and produced musical dramas of virtually unmatched power and influence.

Bryan Magee has termed the shamanic power of Wagner over his followers
as "Wagnerolatry,"[129] and described it as follows: "The devotion aroused in
some people by Wagner's music is different in kind from any other composer's. It is like being in love: a kind of madness, a kind of worship, an irrational
commitment yet abandonment that, among other things, dissolves the critical faculty."[130] Tellingly, Magee also noted that this "Wagnerolatry" has another side
as well: "The equal and opposite reaction is just as familiar: the militant advocacy is equaled by a militant dislike."[131] In trying to explain such effect, Magee
pointed to the psyche and to the unconscious as being the key: "My central contention, then, is that Wagner's music expresses, as does no other art, repressed
and highly charged contents of the psyche, and that this is the reason for its
uniquely disturbing effect. . . . The feeling is of a wholeness yet unbounded-
ness—hence, I suppose, its frequent companion with mystical or religious experience."[132] Magee went on to stress that Wagner knew precisely what he was
doing: "Wagner knew that his music had a special power to move and even dis-

---

124. Refer to the quote above from ibid., p. 9.
125. There is some cause to argue Wagner was more of the mythologist than the artist, but it is
primarily on the basis of his music that Wagner has become immortal. As Bryan Magee wrote:
"Most opera-goers . . . have never concerned themselves greatly with his ideas. . . . I think it can be
shown that Wagner would be virtually unknown today if it were not for his music." See Bryan
Magee, *Aspects of Wagner*, rev. ed. (Oxford: Oxford University Press, 1988), p. 78.
126. For illustrative stories of this type, refer to ibid., pp. 40-43.
127. See Gardner, *Art, Mind, and Brain*, p. 360.
128. For background on this topic, read Carl G. Jung, "Archetypes of the Collective Unconscious,"
in Vol. 9, *The Archetypes and the Collective Unconscious*, in *The Collected Works of C.G. Jung*, trans.
R.F.C. Hull (New York: Pantheon, 1959), pp. 3-41; and "The Concept of the Collective Unconscious,"
ibid., pp. 42-53.
129. See Chapter Three of Magee's *Aspects of Wagner*, pp. 29-44.
130. Ibid., p. 33.
131. Ibid.
132. Ibid., p. 39.

turb, and he knew that this had something to do with bringing what had been unconscious to consciousness. In addition, he regarded his true career as an artist to have dated from the time he stopped trying to lead from the head and, instead, put his trust in his intuitions even when he did not understand them."[133]

These reflections on Wagner by Magee are by no means the only current ones about Wagner. Wagner represents one of the most discussed and analyzed of all composers, and the above comments by Magee are given only as a sample of the kind of interest and controversy Wagner continues to stir. These comments of Magee's serve as a way of thematicizing the current views of Wagner: Wagner as the domineering artistic presence; the love-hate reaction to him and to his music; the virtually inexplicable but irrefutable power of Wagner's music; and Wagner's dependence on intuition, emotion, and contents of the unconscious.

Richard Wagner is a prototype for the religious educator as artist specifically because of his "larger than life" abilities and deficiencies. He serves as both model and warning to the religious educator contemplating the artist as an appropriate role to use. On the positive side, Wagner possessed an extraordinary power and ability to move and charge the emotions of his listeners. With but little effort, the personhood of Wagner is easily detectable within his operas. As Robert Gutman put it: "He fed on himself, and is to be found on every nearly every page of his operas. If nothing were known of his personality, its basic traits could be reconstructed from their evidence."[134] Wagner had every confidence that he was in the process of revealing truth: not just about himself, but about music, art, and human reality.[135] Wagner considered his music to be the very revelation of God, so much so that he spent years of his life and extreme amounts of money to construct a "temple" at Bayreuth in which people could properly experience the truth.[136]

The warning from Wagner comes when one's gaze is directed at his darker side.[137] As is possible with any shaman, Wagner fell into the trap of believing that what he did really was a magical manipulation of the spirit world: that what he said did have the authority of absolute truth. Wagner's voluminous prose works, which provide an exposition of his theories and non-musical philosophies, high-

---

133. Ibid., p. 80. Wagner believed he used this method for the first time in his fourth opera, *Der Fliegende Holländer* (The Flying Dutchman). The previous three he in effect disowned.

134. Robert W. Gutman, *Richard Wagner: The Man, His Mind, and His Music* (New York: Harcourt, Brace, and World, 1968), p. xiv.

135. Jung called Wagner "the prophet of love, whose music runs the gamut of feeling from Tristan down to incestuous passion, then up again from Tristan to the sublime spirituality of Parsifal." Carl G. Jung, "The Type Problem in Poetry," in Vol. 6, *Psychological Types,* in *The Collected Works of C.G. Jung,* trans. H.G. Baynes and rev. by R.F.C. Hull (Princeton: Princeton University Press, 1971), p. 241.

136. See this explained in Chapter Thirteen, "The Bayreuth Idea," by Earnest Newman, *The Life of Richard Wagner,* Vol. Four: 1866-1883 (New York: Knopf, 1946), pp. 269-291.

137. For a fuller treatment, see Jacob Katz, *The Darker Side of Genius: Richard Wagner's Anti-Semitism* (Hanover: University Press of New England, 1986). Carl Jung also noted these tendencies of Wagner's. See "After the Catastrophe," in Carl G. Jung, Vol. 10, *Civilization in Transition,* in *The Collected Works of C.G. Jung,* trans. R.F.C. Hull (New York: Pantheon, 1964), pp. 212, 214-215.

light the music and the operatic themes in a very different glow.[138] Wagner's anti-Semitism and passion for the Germanic people lay as a seedbed for Adolf Hitler and the fascists. As Friedrich Nietzsche prophesied[139] and as Gutman saw through the eyes of history: "That Wagner as a political and social thinker was a link between [the proto-Nazi] Jahn and Hitler cannot be denied. Hitler especially revered Wagner's prose works, emulated their turgid style, enthroned him as the artistic god of the Third Reich, and carried to the logical and appalling conclusions many of the ideas implicit in the composer's essays and dramas."[140]

Rather than accusing Wagner and his music of being responsible for Hitler and his atrocities, the point is that the power, influence, and revelation of the artist needs to be seen for what it is: truly capable of influencing if not creating world events. The word to the religious educator is to use the role of the artist with care: to use the power of revelation, but to realize that the shaman is but a fallible and potentially dangerous human who needs constant, critical, and reality-based monitoring and evaluating. Richard Wagner exemplified both the light side and the dark side of these potentialities.

Contemporary Example: Maria Harris

Choosing persons as representatives for particular categories is never easy, and never entirely successful. Real live human beings have an irritating way of slipping out of the proposed categories and being who they want to be. This is true of Maria Harris (b. 1932) and her writings. She should not be perceived as fitting the category of religious educator as artist exclusively, since this was neither her stated intention nor her personally selected category.[141] Her work and interests have ranged across the field of religious education, and especially her earlier work focused on more vocational issues, as evidenced by such publications as *The D.R.E. Book*,[142] *The D.R.E. Reader*,[143] *Parish Religious Education*,[144] and *Portrait of Youth Ministry*.[145] While these books are occasionally noted as they

138. Refer to the eleven volume set, *Richard Wagner's Prose Works*, trans. William Ashton Ellis (New York: Broude Brothers, 1966). The original works were published in English in 1897.

139. See, for example, "Nietzsche Contra Wagner," in *The Works of Friedrich Nietzsche*, ed. Alexander Tille (New York: Macmillan, 1908), pp. 59-91.

140. Gutman, *Richard Wagner*, p. xvii.

141. At the risk of becoming redundant, it must be stressed that Maria Harris' work is always "more than" what this one category will reveal. This category and all the others found throughout the book are but heuristic devices to discover more about the work of religious education. These categories are being placed after the fact over the top of the work of various religious educators—in this case, Maria Harris—to see what can be revealed. The hope is that the categories will explain not only what the theorist had to say, but also illustrate a particular role of the religious educator. It is not an effort to add to, or to subtract from, the original intent of individual theorists.

142. Maria Harris, *The D.R.E. Book: Questions and Strategies for Parish Personnel* (New York: Paulist, 1976).

143. Maria Harris, ed., *The D.R.E. Reader: A Sourcebook in Education and Ministry* (Winona, Minn.: Saint Mary's Press, 1980).

144. Maria Harris, ed., *Parish Religious Education* (New York: Paulist, 1978).

145. Maria Harris, *Portrait of Youth Ministry* (New York: Paulist, 1981). Also of general interest (unrelated to the artist's role) is a book she co-authored with Gabriel Moran. See Gabriel Moran and Maria Harris, *Experiences in Community: Should Religious Life Survive?* (New York: Herder and Herder, 1968).

relate to the role of the religious educator as artist, the following overview uses primarily those writings that link Maria Harris directly to the role of artist, as does the succeeding evaluation of her contributions to that category.

Overview

This overview looks primarily at three of Maria Harris' books that have focused mainly on teaching and curriculum development. They are the most salient to the role of the artist and demonstrate the developing images Harris used to explain her positions. The most complete and expansive treatment of her teaching philosophy and approach was stated in *Teaching and the Religious Imagination*,[146] while the book *Women and Teaching*[147] was a specialized treatment of teaching focused directly on women in the teaching role. The third work utilized in this overview, *Fashion Me a People*,[148] continued the same basic themes of the previous two books, but this time pointing toward the development of the idea of curriculum. Because of the fundamental sameness of position taken in these books, the three are treated more as a whole than analyzed separately.

In *Fashion Me a People*, Harris revealed most clearly her two foundational bases for her artistic approach to religious education, teaching, and curriculum. One was her interpretation of God as the Divine Artist. Harris explained that there are at least two alternative ways to understand this dimension of God: God as transcendent creator, who "is essentially separate from what has been made and remains outside it"; and God as "brooding, hovering, indwelling Presence, always acting from within creation."[149] Not surprisingly, Harris followed the second option in her work with curriculum: "In this book we examine the creating of curriculum as artistic educational work contribution to this fashioning of a people. . . . I propose that we begin with the assumption that curricular work is holy work, religious work, and that God dwells with us as we do it, in the midst of each of the human processes we choose."[150] She then portrayed this "alternative" understanding of God as "the source of the creative power that moves us both to will and to accomplish."[151] To further drive home her point, Harris went on to say: "At the same time, however, because we are made in the image of the Creator God, we too are fashioners. Our human vocation is to be in partnership with God to fashion even as we are being fashioned, attempting to realize our artistic capacities as this happens. For to the question, 'Who is fashioning?' the response is, 'God and ourselves.' "[152] With these words, Harris is similar in her speculating to what was said earlier in this chapter in the section on the artist as creator: Not only does the creator create, but the "created" creates as well.

146. Maria Harris, *Teaching and the Religious Imagination: An Essay in the Theology of Teaching* (San Francisco: Harper & Row, 1987).

147. Maria Harris, *Women and Teaching: Themes for a Spirituality of Pedagogy* (New York: Paulist, 1988).

148. Maria Harris, *Fashion Me a People: Curriculum in the Church* (Louisville: Westminster/John Knox, 1989).

149. Ibid., p. 15.

150. Ibid., p. 16

151. Ibid.

152. Ibid.

The second key to understanding Harris' perspective is provided by her few words in the book regarding the general topic of education.[153] While spending most of her time and effort on teaching, she did briefly speak to the larger issue of education. In the midst of a discussion on lifelong learning, Harris said: "I propose a broad and extensive understanding of education as artistic work. Education, like all other artistic endeavors, is a work of giving form. More specifically, it is a work especially concerned with the creation, re-creation, fashioning and refashioning of form."[154] She then described the molding of clay as an exercise in the discovery and understanding of form, and commented: "The molding of clay is a concrete metaphor illuminating the work of education as the fashioning and refashioning of the forms that human life offers, the forms we shape as artists at the same time we allow those forms to shape us. For as human beings we are always extending our hands into life and into experience in order to give them form."[155]

From this point, Harris then expressed the work of the educator/artist as "giving flesh to, and embodying form."[156] She was also careful to address the relationship of form and content in art and in religious education: "But form is not an arbitrary organizational element—one among many. Rather, as any artist knows, form is the actual shape of content. Form is a marshaling of materials in relation to one another. It is a setting of boundaries and limits. It is a discipline, an ordering and a fashioning according to need."[157] Connecting this fashioning of form directly to religious education, she said: "Education in the church means taking those forms which ecclesial life presents to us, places in our hands, as clay to be molded. Education is the work of lifting up and lifting out those forms through which we might refashion ourselves into a pastoral people."[158] These comments on form and embodiment are consonant in many respects with what was mentioned earlier in this present chapter on the section dealing with expression and disclosure.

Deeper insight into what Harris meant by her use of art in religious education came when she discussed its place in curriculum development.[159] She contrasted her approach to designing curriculum with the more traditional ones, align-

---

153. Also see a related discussion in Chapter Seven, "Education: The Overall Framework," in Harris, *The D.R.E. Book*, pp. 114-134.

154. Harris, *Fashion Me a People*, p. 40. Related to this point, Harris wrote on p. 42 of *Teaching and the Religious Imagination* that "teaching is the creation of form."

155. Harris, *Fashion Me a People*, p. 41.

156. Ibid.

157. Ibid.

158. Ibid. As Harris acknowledged, this is reminiscent of the views of John Dewey in both his *Art as Experience* and *Democracy and Education: An Introduction to the Philosophy of Education* (New York: Macmillan, 1916), and she cited Dewey in the very next paragraph from where this last reference was taken. Also see her comments about Dewey in *Teaching and the Religious Imagination*, pp. 140-141.

159. Harris once wrote that "one definition of a teacher is 'one who designs appropriate curriculum.' Thus, curriculum becomes a central focus and will need to be addressed in the church context by asking four questions: where, what, which, and why." Harris, *Portrait of Youth Ministry*, p. 62. See ibid., pp. 62-63 for Harris' attempt to begin answering these four questions regarding curriculum.

ing herself with a number of other religious educators[160] whom she identified as those who are trying to be more innovative: "In this book, we are attempting to join their company by looking at curriculum planning from a religious and artistic angle or vision in contrast to the one that is technical and mechanical."[161] She then briefly explained her alternative vision of what true—artistic—curriculum in the church is: "To begin with, although it includes teaching, curriculum is not equivalent to teaching or to what can be said. It includes the *entire* course of the church's life, the play and interplay of community, prayer, service, teaching, and proclamation. In addition, curriculum—as the total life and experience of the church—can never be limited to what is printed. Printed texts are at best a valuable curriculum resource."[162] In an attached footnote, Harris was even more emphatic about the need for being artistic rather than pedantic when it comes to curriculum design: "Other approaches to designing curriculum are of course needed—political, sociological, psychological, ethical, and religious. However, I would still argue that, fundamentally, to design something is to do artistic work. In addition, this approach has been slighted in the past in favor of the technical and mechanical."[163]

Harris repeated this theme concerning the need to be creative and artistic in *Teaching and the Religious Imagination*, making the point that she was offering a paradigm for teaching that was to be done "religiously and imaginatively rather than technically or psychologically."[164] She said in her introductory comments to the book: "The particular contribution I hope to make is to examine ways in which religion and imagination might be brought to bear upon teaching. More specifically, I want to bring religion and imagination together under the rubric of religious imagination."[165] Her "alternate vision of teaching" is one that "draws on the religious imagination . . . a philosophy that begins not with technique but with the majesty and mystery involved in teaching."[166] Harris specified what was necessary for such an attempt to be made: "Because imagination is the root of the following description of teaching, it must be approached with fresh eyes. Rather than address teaching as a technical skill, then, I suggest we bring to it an attitude similar to that which we bring to any work of art. Such an attitude implies a beginning readiness to see what is there and to let what is there speak, rather than an immediately active attitude that sees teachers as agents, doers, and performers. The imaginative attitude implies, initially, an attitude of receptivity."[167]

---

160. Harris, *Fashion Me a People*, p. 170. Her list included such an interesting mix of people as C. Ellis Nelson, John Westerhoff, Paulo Freire, and Mary Boys. I am not certain anyone else would see too many commonalities among such a diverse group.

161. Ibid., p. 170.

162. Ibid., pp. 170-171.

163. Ibid., note 7 of Chapter Nine, p. 195.

164. Harris, *Teaching and the Religious Imagination*, p. xiv. For other sources of Harris' views on teaching, see Chapter Three, "Didache: The Ministry of Teaching," in Harris, *Portrait of Youth Ministry*, pp. 59-84; and Chapter Eight, "Education: The Personal Framework," in Harris, *The D.R.E. Book*, pp. 135-157, especially pp. 148-152.

165. Harris, *Teaching and the Religious Imagination*, p. xiv.

166. Ibid., p. 24.

167. Ibid., p. 25.

Harris presented her ideas of how teaching comprises the work of religious imagination this way: "The process has five moments, or steps: 1) contemplation, 2) engagement, 3) formgiving, 4) emergence, and 5) release. The steps envisioned, however, are not like steps on a staircase, progressing upwards. Rather, they are like steps in a dance, where movement is both forward and backward, around and through, and where turns, returns, rhythms, and movement are essential. Indeed, it will probably be apparent that each step is present in all the others."[168] In so describing her basic paradigm for teaching, Harris used a process she believed is already familiar to "potters, sculptors, and other artistic creators."[169] Sources apparent in the formulation of her paradigm are John Dewey, Alfred North Whitehead, and Gabriel Moran.[170]

Maria Harris used the term "revelation" as a major part of her plan for teaching but with a slightly different usage than the discussion found earlier in this chapter. Harris called the kind of knowing that stems from revelation "indirect communication,"[171] saying that "the kind of knowing revelation suggests is not accomplished by handing over subject matter, by retailing information, and certainly not by telling someone who does not 'know' something that the teacher 'knows.'"[172] Instead, Harris suggested that "one who would foster revelation must take on all the roles in the house of religious imagination: contemplative (explorer of darkness and silence), ascetic (professing rigor and detachment), creator (reforming with ontological tenderness), sacrament (alert to the presence of mystery everywhere, anywhere, nowhere). One must take an approach not of direct, but of indirect communication."[173] The intention of the religion teacher, according to Harris, can then "be viewed as at least fourfold, directed toward: 1) awakening thought; 2) creating tension; 3) arousing ethical response; 4) opening a communion of subjectivity."[174] These four aspects combine to bring both religious educator and learner to fuller self-knowledge, fuller relationship, and ultimately to fuller understanding. The result of such revelation widens the horizons. Harris said of such a process: "The way of teaching offered . . . is the way of imagination—of religious imagination—where, having incarnated subject matter so that it leads to the revelation of subject matter, we discover that we (participating subjects) have received the grace of power in order to help recreate a world of communion, of justice, and of peace."[175]

168. Ibid., p. 25.

169. Ibid., p. xiv.

170. See Dewey's *Art and Experience*; Alfred North Whitehead, "Rhythms of Education," in *The Aims of Education and Other Essays* (New York: Macmillan, 1929), pp. 15-28; and Gabriel Moran, *No Ladder to the Sky: Education and Morality* (San Francisco: Harper & Row, 1987).

171. Harris, *Teaching and the Religious Imagination*, p. 66.

172. Ibid., p. 65.

173. Ibid., pp. 65-66.

174. Ibid., pp. 67-68. Harris went on to clarify a possible misunderstanding of her use of direct and indirect communication: "This analysis could be read as a brief against direct communication, where the teacher intends to deliver content in the form of facts or information. Remember, however, that such intention can always have beneath it the issue *why* the delivering of content is engaged in; namely, what the teacher *imagines* will happen as a result of his or her communication. Put another way, the relation of direct and indirect communication may be one of partners rather than of opposites." Ibid., p. 68.

175. Ibid., p. 77.

It is important to get a sense of how Maria Harris actually does this "aesthetic" type of religious education. As she herself acknowledged, she comes at the artistic dimension in a rather roundabout way: "I need to emphasize that I am not an artist by profession, but, like most of my readers, a practicing teacher."[176] She does not perceive this lack of professional identity as an artist as a hindrance, however: "One does not need long years of training in art to bring the aesthetic to educational work: One needs only the desire and the conviction that as teachers we are all artists, creating forms that enable our students to see and to live at deeper and more profound levels, levels that might accurately be called religious."[177] She described briefly the course that she teaches from the artist model,[178] saying: "The design of the course has varied somewhat through the years, but one basic assumption has held: Participation in the art form under study is essential to understanding the aesthetic. No art form has ever been chosen and then simply talked about; it has always been *done* as well. Some years this participation has been minimal and discussion has been predominant, although not exclusive. Other years, discussion has been almost nonexistent, and participation has been central."[179] Whatever the mix, Harris stressed that in theory at least both aspects are important: "The best approach, on paper, is a blend of the two—not always achievable as smoothly as I or the students would wish."[180] The "artistic forms" she has used is wide-ranging and diverse, including such activities as dance, choreography, poetry, creative dramatics, song, sculpting, silk-screening, puppetry, fairy tales, cooking, clowning, and kite-flying.[181] During the course, class members are free to take on one of four artistic roles: that of the *creator*, by designing a session; the *performer*, by demonstrating and presenting; the *audience member*, by watching the performance but also inevitably becoming an active participant; and the *critic*, by assessing the effectiveness of the class presentation.[182] All this, Harris believes, allows participation in the true vocation of teaching, which she said was "to incarnate subject matter toward revelation and power, and thus to take part in the re-creation of the universe."[183]

---

176. Ibid., p. 144.

177. Ibid.

178. Also see her comments on "an alternative framework where all of the parish activity is artistic in form, execution and criteria." For the full discussion, see Chapter Nine, "Education: Alternative Frameworks," in Harris, *The D.R.E. Book*, pp. 158-182, especially pp. 168-172; the quote is from p. 168. In this chapter, she pointed out the importance of the aesthetic program: "Lest this kind of experience be thought of as something superfluous or intended for those whose learning needed some frills, it must be insisted that what is being suggested here is an alternative framework where art is the mode for all religious education, and not a 'nice' extra which can be dispensed with as not really necessary for learning. Westerners are desperate for ways to be in touch with feeling, with loveliness, and with their own springs of creativity, and this is especially true, the less aesthetic one's surroundings." Ibid., pp. 169-170.

179. Harris, *Teaching and the Religious Imagination*, p. 148.

180. Ibid.

181. Ibid., p. 149. Harris reported: "Despite the extraordinary range of art forms and activities re-created in the course, two stand out as most memorable to the participants: the molding of clay and the experience of clowning." Ibid., p. 155.

182. Ibid., p. 149.

183. Ibid., p. 157. For the full discussion of how Harris describes her preferred teaching procedures, see Chapter Seven, "A Pedagogical Model," ibid., pp. 119-141, and Chapter Eight, "An Artistic Model," ibid., pp. 142-157.

An additional aspect of Harris' use of artistic concepts is found in the book *Women and Teaching*. There she repeated the now-familiar themes of rhythm, steps, and movement, this time as they related to a "spirituality of pedagogy." The steps she proposed moved from silence to remembering, to ritual mourning, to artistry, and to birthing. Her hope was that "in the lives of women, these themes sound a sacred musical harmony. If listened to with awareness and obedience to truth, and entered with courage and community, they hold the potential of setting the world dancing in the ways it needs to go."[184] While this image moved from molding clay to dancing to music, the process was similar to that found in Harris' other writings. Indeed, in this context she opened artistry and imagination as widely as possible: "Not only does artistry assume hearing and sound as in music and dance, it also celebrates touch, as in sculpture and pottery and molding; place and geography as in architecture; the visual powers needed for painting and the graphic arts; the powers of voice and word needed for poetry, drama and literature; and the entire range of bodily capacities which lead to the 'creation of form, expressive of human feeling' which Susanne Langer teaches is the work of art."[185] Within the chapter on artistry included in *Women and Teaching*,[186] Harris used the rhythms of embodiment, revelation, receptivity to power, and release that she had already developed at length in the 1987 book. Although she focused her comments more directly on women in the latter work, the message is fundamentally unchanged from the earlier exposition in *Teaching and Religious Imagination*.

In summary, Harris' current mission was well-stated in the introduction to *Teaching and the Religious Imagination*. The goal in that book, and in many respects the goal of the other two books under present scrutiny as well, was expressed as follows: "We need an area, a context, and an occasion to contemplate our teaching and to recover, if we have lost them, the dreams and the hopes, the vision and the grandeur, that lie at the core of teaching. We need an opportunity to rediscover the creative, artistic teachers we are and were meant to be."[187]

Evaluation

Admittedly, such a brief and highly selective overview of Maria Harris' work only gives a glimpse of what she provided in the whole. This evaluation covers only the artistic thrust of her writings and does not address whatever her larger contribution to religious education might be. In this evaluation both her strengths and her deficiencies are mentioned in terms of how she has contributed to the notion of religious educator as artist.

That Maria Harris had the idea and the élan to highlight the artistic qualities of religious education is admirable. She has endeavored to keep the field fluid enough to incorporate such neglected aspects as creativity and feelings.[188] Too

---

184. Harris, *Women and Teaching*, p. 16.
185. Ibid., p. 61.
186. Ibid., p. 60-75.
187. Harris, *Teaching and the Religious Imagination*, p. xi.
188. For a good example of her efforts to keep the definition of the field open to different metaphors, see Maria Harris, "Word, Sacrament, Prophecy," in *Tradition and Transformation in Religious Education*, ed. Padraic O'Hare (Birmingham, Ala.: Religious Education Press, 1979), pp. 35-57.

often this type of approach appears to be met with passive resistance from the more traditional religious educators[189] who plod along with their transmissive and mnemonic approaches to religious education, with the religious educator telling the learner what needs to be known. Harris gave encouragement and counsel on how to escape the deadly boredom and sameness that can sap the life from religious education. To be a champion of artistry, with its inclusion of the affect and the imagination, is by all accounts a strong factor in Harris' favor.

Harris has not come only lately to an appreciation of artistry. In the 1979 book *Aesthetic dimensions of Religious Education*,[190] she contributed a chapter that in revised form became Chapter Eight[191] of *Teaching and the Religious Imagination*, a key and autobiographical element of the 1987 book. There Harris described her long relationship with Mary Tully Anderson, an important contributor to Harris' understanding of the aesthetic aspects of religious education.[192] All of this is to say that Harris has been working with the artistic nature of religious education for years. Neither would it be fair to perceive Harris as a "one note symphony," speaking of nothing but artistry. Her three books cited in this chapter, upon examination, reveal a wide range of interests. While on the one hand much of the same material is covered in all three books, on the other hand the material was cast in different lights and given fuller meanings each time.

Harris' stubborn resistance against the religious educator being seen only as a technician is to be applauded.[193] She has insisted that the religious educator always retain his or her vitality, creativity, and individuality. In this connection, *Women and Teaching* is especially helpful. There she was addressing women, as a woman, and for all women in opposition to those who desire women to use male or authoritarian modes of education. Harris modeled the "teacher who wants to redesign a pedagogy which makes room for the multiple, creative capacities in human beings, for possibilities and processes which make for expansion, not contraction—possibilities aborted in their development before they have time to blossom."[194]

There are some aspects of Harris' work, however, that demand a more critical look. As she herself noted, Harris spoke primarily as an educator and not as

---

189. Harris began *Teaching and Religious Imagination* with these words: "One of the great sorrows in human life is the discovery, too late, of our own beauty and of the beauty of what we do. Such is often the case with teachers, as we contemplate ourselves and our vocation. At the deepest level, every teacher wants to become a better teacher, even a great teacher; in moments of insight, every teacher is aware of hidden gifts of creativity and imagination. But often the pressures, deadlines, and exigencies of dailiness keep teachers from standing back and viewing their work with the care both they and their work deserve." Harris, *Teaching and Religious Imagination*, p. xi.

190. Gloria Durka and Joanmarie Smith, eds., *Aesthetic Dimensions of Religious Education* (New York: Paulist, 1979).

191. Harris, *Teaching and Religious Imagination*, pp. 142-157.

192. For example, refer to Chapter Seven of *Teaching and the Religious Imagination*, pp. 119-141.

193. As has been observed throughout this chapter, the artist is certainly more than a mere technician, but at the same time there are skills and techniques that are essential for mastery of any art. The above comments should not be interpreted as saying that the artist, and the religious educator in the role of the artist, are ever free from the hard work of skillful practice.

194. Harris, *Women and Teaching*, p. 2.

an artist,[195] so that what inevitably results is language more educational than artistic. In an earlier section of this chapter, Richard Wagner was cited as an artist who can be helpful to the religious educator, however distantly. With Harris, the opposite situation is true. Here is a religious educator speaking to the topic of aesthetics, and the result is much closer to reformed but still fairly traditional religious education than to avant garde art. Additionally, one must question whether or not her assertion is accurate that "one does not need long years of training in art to bring the aesthetic to educational work."[196] While it is important to unite the aesthetic with religious education, as this chapter has discussed throughout, it is just as important not to take the relationship lightly or casually. It may be that the long and hard work of truly immersing oneself in the art world, exploring its theory and its practice, is precisely what is needed for the proper grounding of the religious educator. The specter of dilettantism only further threatens a field already as shallow as religious education too often allows itself to be.

In this regard, Harris never adequately explained or fully defined such central concepts as art, aesthetics, or beauty. Possibly the reason for this is an underlying conviction that it is not necessary to have in-depth training or study in the theory and practice of art and aesthetics. Harris' writings do not evince familiarity with the empirical, practical, or theoretical dimensions of art. She operates without a scholarly base and without requisite evidence. Her approach, in short, is primarily that of pop-art. She typically assumes what art is and spends time chiefly in the pop-art dimensions of the aesthetic rather than in a deeper exploration of practice, especially of theory.[197] While certainly art must be practiced if is to be art, it nonetheless seems that when dealing with art as the prime functional image for religious education, a great deal more specificity, clarity, and depth is necessary.[198]

Additionally, even if Harris has done the scholarship necessary in the field of aesthetics, she does not give her readers any help in furthering this kind of study on their own. Other than occasional references to philosophers like John Dewey[199] or Alfred North Whitehead,[200] she does not point her readers to the supporting literature or thinkers in the field. The interested religious educator is left alone to

---

195. Harris, *Teaching and Religious Imagination*, p. 144.

196. Ibid.

197. She does occasionally cite the need for theoretical work, as she did in *Portrait for Youth Ministry*: "Religious educators in the church are not well-known for an insistence on theory; indeed, we still suffer traces of anti-intellectualism." Harris, *Portrait of Youth Ministry*, p. 5. As has been a problem noted throughout this present book, a disturbing lack of precision about the nature of theory continues to cripple the current state of religious education. What Harris here calls "theory" is evidence of the slippery use of the term from any strict, formal sense.

198. Early in the chapter, the issue of a political definition of art was discussed, and the position taken was that such a definition was inadequate at best and destructive to the true meaning of art at its worst. Harris had no such qualms, saying that in effect politics and power are essential to understanding both art and religious education. While this is certainly her prerogative, it seems to do damage to true art and is more evidence of why she needed to be more explicit in her definition of art. For her discussion of power and politics in education and art, see Chapter Five, "The Grace of Power," in Harris, *Teaching and Religious Imagination*, pp. 78-96.

199. See, for example, Harris, *Teaching and Religious Imagination*, pp. 37, 119, and 140-141.

200. See, for example, ibid., pp. 163-164.

do the hunting on his or her own for help in truly researching what art is all about on a deeper level. Neither does Harris cite from the work of artists themselves. Reading Harris does not allow one to enter the world of the artist, or to get a concrete feel for art. As was mentioned earlier, the feel is more of a religious educator who has some appreciation for art but who stays safely within the traditional boundaries of religious education. The real world of the artist remains a bit foreign and separate from that of the religious educator.

This same tendency for lack of scholarly evidence or supporting documentation is obvious when the issue moves to empirically based activities such as teaching procedures or curricular innovations. Nowhere does she refer to empirical evidence that backs up her assumptions or propositions. Her primary work on teaching, *Teaching and the Religious Imagination,* has a curious lack of citations to books discussing the theory and research on effective teaching procedures, leading one to wonder whether Harris is really familiar with the evidence or whether she is winging it alone in a blissful state of ignorance. Her book *Fashion Me a People* focuses on curriculum, but she gives no evidence to indicate she is aware of the well-established field of curriculum theory, curriculum research, and curriculum practice. All of Harris' books dealt with in the overview section of this present chapter revealed her deep interest in the imagination, but she does not give any evidence that she utilizes, or is even aware of, the copious research data that exists on the nature and functioning of the imagination. In approaching the writings of Maria Harris, then, one can expect inspiration, stimulating ideas, and warm fuzzies, all unsupported by solid research evidence or theory. Thus there is no way of knowing whether Harris' ideas are lovely flights of fancy, inspirational ideas, or are workable in a wide variety of educational conditions. She is more of the speculationist type of religious educator[201] who prefers to generate creative ideas unencumbered by research evidence, requisite theory, or even a knowledge of the pertinent literature. It is important to note in this connection that virtually every great artist in history was grounded in the empirical and theoretical foundations of his or her particular zone of artistic endeavor.

One confusing issue arose in *Women and Teaching,* when Harris used artistry to describe both whole and part. First she used the term "rhythm," or the "themes" in the "choreography" of a women's pedagogy, to denote the artistic process as a whole.[202] Then, in Chapter 4, she discussed "artistry" as the fourth in the series of those themes.[203] The confusion is not fatal to the argument, by any means, but it is further evidence of the lack of precision in the use of "artistry" mentioned in an earlier paragraph of this evaluation section. The issue of repetition also became a problem here. Where in *Women and Teaching* the five steps in question were labeled silence, remembering, ritual mourning, artistry, and birth, the fuller and more comprehensive discussion of these steps in *Teaching and the Religious Imagination* used silence, political awareness, mourning, bonding,

---

201. James Michael Lee has discussed the differences between the speculative and the empirical methods in *The Shape of Religious Instruction,* pp. 120-121.

202. Harris, *Women and Teaching,* pp. 13-15.

203. Ibid., pp. 60-75.

and birth.[204] It was at the crucial (for this chapter) point of the fourth step, artistry, that the confusion or change came. By using the same or a similar paradigm for both discussions, Harris failed to clarify the paradigm itself.

Despite her critique of religious educators who would be technicians, Harris is one of the most skillful political technicians in contemporary religious education. Directly and indirectly, she has molded one or another professional religious education groups in such a way as to advance her political and ideological agenda. Her adroitness, tenacity, and resoluteness as a political technician are encased in a charming manner, thus marrying political skill and artistic style. Some are critical of such a marriage, while others applaud it.

Finally, one can get the sense that the steps of contemplation, engagement, formgiving, emergence, and release[205] are indeed *the* steps involved in artistry. Of course, there is no one best way to describe the artistic process.[206] Harris was trying to propose a process for artistry that is applicable to religious education, but she illustrated the difficulty in which all religious educators in the role of artist find themselves: trying to show and teach others how to be artistic. Such a task is by definition, as well as by effort, quite difficult and risky.

On the whole, the writings of Maria Harris should be read to see what one person suggests as a way for religious education to become more artistic. In the end, it is the task and the responsibility of each individual to become the artist, and the religious educator, that only he or she can be. The guidance and the inspiration provided by Maria Harris toward becoming the artistic religious educator is a valuable resource for exploring the possibilities.

Representative Teaching Procedure: Teaching Drawing

The first priority for the religious educator who wishes to engage in artistic religious education is to experience and to participate in being an artist himself or herself; then, and only then, is the religious educator ready to introduce others to the role of the artist. One cannot become an artist, or develop into a better one, simply by reading the words of a book. Neither can one teach others to be artists if the religious educator does not have some basic competence in art. Art is eventually concrete and experiential and must be done—practiced—in order to be genuine and owned. The teaching procedure here does not require that any religious educator become an accomplished artist, but it does require some basic competence and experience in some kind of artistic expression.

The above stance on participating in art as a prerequisite to teaching art is based on the same assumption as that expressed earlier in the chapter by Maria Harris: "Participation in the art form under study is essential to understanding the aes-

204. See Chapter Six, "Re-Creation," in Harris, *Teaching and the Religious Imagination*, pp. 97-116.

205. See ibid., pp. 24-25, for example.

206. Harris was quick to admit this: "There is no one best way to teach. Learners have different styles as do teachers; particular subject matters must be dealt with in ways integral to them; and environments, both physical and mental, can alter methods of approach." Harris, *Portrait of Youth Ministry*, p. 59.

thetic."[207] Strictly verbal, cognitive, and rational approaches are inadequate for understanding or teaching the role of the artist.[208] Although virtually any one of the arts is acceptable for initial entrance into the role of the artist,[209] the teaching procedure offered here uses drawing. For the great number of religious educators that do not consider themselves to have much, if any ability to draw, fortunately there is a book that can be of immense help in getting started: *Drawing on the Right Side of the Brain*, by Betty Edwards.[210] This is not a book simply to be read, but a teaching manual that helps the religious educator develop the ability to draw.[211] Experiencing something of what it is like to draw under the direction of an artist (even through "mentor by book") is an enriching exercise in becoming a more complete and effective religious educator. After the religious educator uses the book to gain some basic skills in drawing for himself or herself, the book can become an excellent resource for teaching others to draw as well.

Edwards' book works at overcoming some of the anxiety attached to drawing specifically,[212] and to being creative generally, by pointing to the real basis of drawing as a different way of seeing: "Drawing is a skill that can be learned by every normal person with average eyesight and average eye-hand coordination. . . . Contrary to popular opinion, manual skill is not a primary factor in drawing."[213] She explained this rather startling statement by saying: "Learning to draw is more than learning the skill itself; by studying this [Edwards'] book you will learn *how to see*. That is, you will learn how to process visual information in the special way used by artists. That way is *different* from the way you usually process visual information and seems to require that you use your brain in a different way than you ordinarily use it."[214] If nothing else about Edwards' book sounds stimulating, surely the prospect of religious educators using their brains differently is exciting enough!

The religious educator who wishes to be artistic, then, has two preconditions

---

207. Harris, *Teaching and Religious Imagination*, p. 148.

208. Two entertaining resources that help tap the creative regions are by Roger von Oech: *A Whack on the Side of the Head: How to Unlock Your Mind for Innovation* (New York: Warner Books, 1983); and *A Kick in the Seat of the Pants: Using Your Explorer, Artist, Judge, and Warrior to Be More Creative* (New York: Harper & Row, 1986).

209. Recall the long list of things Maria Harris has tried, while her suggestions emphasized two: molding of clay and clowning.

210. Betty Edwards, *Drawing on the Right Side of the Brain: A Course in Enhancing Creativity and Artistic Confidence* (Los Angeles: J.P. Tarcher, 1979).

211. Edwards stated the basic premise of her book this way: "That drawing is a teachable, learnable skill which can provide a twofold advantage. By gaining access to the part of your mind that works in a style conducive to creative, intuitive thought, you will learn a fundamental skill of the visual arts; how to put on paper what you see in front of your eyes. Second, through learning to draw with the method presented in this book you will gain in the ability to think more creatively in other areas of your life." Ibid., pp. 14-15.

212. Edwards noted this irony: "Often, in fact, people even feel that they shouldn't take a drawing course because they don't already know how to draw. This is like deciding you shouldn't take a French class because you don't already speak French, or that you shouldn't sign up for a course in carpentry because you don't know how to build a house." Ibid., p. 3.

213. Ibid., p. 3.

214. Ibid. Edwards does give some fundamental information on how the two halves of the brain function somewhat differently. This accounts for the title of the book.

to meet. One, the religious educator must learn to "see" in the "certain way" of the artist in order to be able to teach about it.[215] Two, the religious educator must indeed be prepared to try to teach others "how to see," or as Edwards said more accurately, at least to prepare the environment adequately for this kind of seeing to become possible: "The key to learning to draw, therefore, is to *set up* conditions that cause you to make a mental shift to a different mode of information-processing—the slightly altered state of consciousness that enables you to see well."[216] As one has learned and experienced, so he or she will teach.

This particular teaching procedure brings the focus of learning initially onto the religious educator. There is none of the usual preparation for a class, or for a small group, or for a religious service. Instead, the religious educator spends time alone experiencing what it is to be an artist, and in learning how to draw— at whatever level of skill and expertise seems appropriate or possible. Then, when the individual religious educator is ready, he or she can teach others to engage in artistic religious education by helping them "learn to see" and to express their vision of art through drawing. What comes out of the experience of drawing that directly and indirectly relates to religious education can be discovered afterward, in some reflection and discussion time.[217] Specific steps of this teaching procedure[218] are not conducive to summary in the present format. The best solution is for each person to work through Edwards' book (or a similar one) for himself or herself and then to facilitate the learning process for others by allowing them to experience the world of the artist.

Experiential Simulation: Experiencing Art

The suggestion for the previous chapter on storytelling was to go and experience the artistry of a true storyteller, thereby falling in love with stories. The suggestion for this chapter is the same: Go and experience the work of a true artist and fall in love with art. Do not be tempted to use an art text that reproduces famous paintings in printed plates, or even to listen to recordings of classical music. Go and experience the work of art in person.

One way to do this is to travel to an art museum. Do not just walk through, browsing casually or quickly. Select a particular painting or a sculpture and stay with it until you experience it. Stand before it, walk around it, sit in front of

---

215. "When you see in the special way in which experienced artists see, then you can draw." Edwards, *Drawing on the Right Side of the Brain*, p. 3.

216. Ibid., p. 5. Note the relevance of Edwards' comments to cognitive dissonance and to Gestalt psychology.

217. In recounting an experience where flying a kite was the "artistic activity" being employed, Maria Harris wrote: "'What does kite-flying have to do with graduate education?' one woman was asked. She replied, 'Everything.' And then went on to recount the religious depth the course had given her and to speak about how the awareness of herself, of others, of the divinity became clearer as her own gifts and talents were discovered—even needed—in the process." Harris, *Teaching and Religious Imagination*, p. 149.

218. Edwards made these suggestions to beginning art students: 1) Don't be afraid to learn to draw realistically initially and then develop into the more creative forms of representation; 2) be clear in your mind why learning to draw well is important—"to see ever more clearly, ever more deeply"; 3) draw something—anything—every day. Edwards, *Drawing on the Right Side of the Brain*, p. 199.

it, lay down beside it, but give it time to communicate. *Feel* what the artist is meaning. This time out, do not evaluate the art, or analyze it, or even classify it. Encounter it.

A second suggestion is to go to the performance of an opera. Enter into the full drama of the words, music, themes, and emotions that throb through the audience and the performers. If it is your first time, do not despair that it "makes no sense." More important than understanding every line of the libretto is to immerse yourself into the total environment of art. See it, hear it, and feel it as fully as you can. Let the opera resonate with the deeper self within.

A third suggestion is to go to a poetry reading where a poet shares his or her own work. Listen to the words, listen to his or her voice, and listen to the message—but most of all experience the poetry and the poet. Be aware of all the sensations that accompany the reading, and do not allow yourself to engage only the rational elements of your mind or you will miss the poetry, and the art. Let the poet speak to your whole being, and learn not only about the poetry and the poet—but learn and experience yourself.

Summary

This chapter has been an introduction to the role of the artist for the religious educator. The potential for what a religious educator can do with such a role is probably far beyond what anyone has yet imagined. If one could but link up his or her creativity with his or her faith, and truly create artistic religious education, what could religious education become? The answers are yet to be created, expressed, and revealed—but such are the exciting prospects ahead.

A summary chart of the role of artist as discussed in this chapter is given as Figure 11.

Figure 11: The Religious Educator as Artist	
Dimensions of the Role	Creator
	Designer
	Evocateur
	Magician
Aim	Revelation/Discovery
Function	Creativity
Primary Virtues	Expression
	Disclosure
Activity	Creating
Shadow Role	Pornographer
Faith Tradition Resource	Shamanism
Historical Personage	Richard Wagner
Contemporary Example	Maria Harris
Representative Teaching Procedure	Teaching Drawing
Experiential Simulation	Experiencing Art

Chapter Ten

The Religious Educator as Visionary

Considering the religious educator as an artist is one thing, as difficult as that might have been for some to imagine, but now as a visionary? Artists may be eccentric, and they may at times be abstract, but at least some are respectable members of society who produce artwork that can be enjoyed and experienced. Perceiving the religious educator as a visionary is something else entirely, however. In fact, the very phase "respectable visionary" sounds contradictory and misleading, since what do visionaries actually create that is of lasting or of practical value?

Unfortunately, a dominant image of the visionary seems to be the star of *The Man of La Mancha* who tilts at romanticized windmills and sings "To Dream the Impossible Dream." Such a figure may be fine for a Broadway show, and such a song may be appropriate for high-school graduations, but what about real life and real problems? Religious education is threatened enough with being "soft and fuzzy" without this kind of distraction. Why the effort to legitimize this kind of activity?

The answer to this quandary is in the proverb which says: "Where there is no vision, the people perish."[1]

The term "vision" is employed throughout the chapter, and Violet MacDermot gave a good multiple definition of it: "Today the word 'vision' can be used in three ways. It can denote the ordinary act of seeing or the faculty of eyesight. It can be used metaphorically for an imaginative conception in the mind of an artist or thinker. Finally, a vision can mean an appearance, often of a religious or prophetic character, which is seen otherwise than by ordinary sight and which

---

1. Proverbs 29:18, KJV.

313

presents during an abnormal state of mind."[2] In the present chapter, the term "vision" is used most often in MacDermot's second sense, but the third is not an entirely inappropriate understanding as long as "an abnormal state of mind" relates to an intuitive, nonlinear kind of thinking rather than to some hallucinatory state.[3]

This chapter deals specifically with the visionary, a role that needs to be distinguished still further, this time from that of the dreamer.[4] Dreams and hallucinations—the realm of the dreamer rather than the visionary—were described by Ernest Hilgard as "products of imagination in which memories or fantasies are temporarily confused with external reality. The dreams and hallucination have their own autonomy, and their courses of action are plotted independently of the usual conscious controls."[5] For purposes here, Hilgard's words stress three important points about the dreamer: the dreamer (at least temporarily) confuses external reality with the stuff of dreams (internal reality?); dreams (and hallucinations) are autonomous, in that the dreamer simply allows the dream to unfold on its own without conscious effort or imposed structure;[6] and any action—potential or real—related to dreams is beyond the control or impact of the conscious mind. The visionary, by contrast, is identified by the reverse of these same three points: the visionary is able to separate inner and outer reality, realizing that his or her vision entails the future which is "not yet" but is at least a glimpse of a grander scheme of things that can be created and constructed through deep reflection and hard work; the vision is not autonomous or separate from the visionary but is something he or she develops, revises, and enlarges volitionally and consciously; and bringing the visions to life must be accomplished through the activities of planning and organizing which are independent from the guiding vision itself.[7] In other words, the visionary as described in this chapter is neither a captive of a vision that appears unasked or unwanted, nor a recipient of a vision that comes without need of development or effort. The kind of visionary sought here does not resemble an automaton or a robot who follows directions from another world. It is someone who works to understand, refine, and

---

2. Violet MacDermot, *The Cult of the Seer in the Ancient Middle East: A Contribution to Current Research on Hallucinations Drawn from Coptic and Other Texts* (London: Wellcome Institute of the History of Medicine, 1971), p. 1. MacDermot went on to say: "In the ancient world, these distinctions which, for us, depend upon our insight into our own faculties, were less clear or nonexistent." Ibid. The rest of her book deals in depth with the ancient understandings of visions and hallucinations.

3. This is in line with MacDermot's own stated definitions, since she continued: "A hallucination, on the other hand, is defined as the apparent perception of an external object when no such object is present." Ibid.

4. Different even from this discussion of the visionary and the dreamer is understanding of the shadow role of the daydreamer, which is given its own section later in the present chapter.

5. Ernest R. Hilgard, *Divided Consciousness: Multiple Controls in Human Thought and Action*, expanded ed. (New York: Wiley, 1986), p. 87.

6. Hilgard said: "The dream is a cognitive product, and, when remembered, it qualifies as hallucination; furthermore, it has a spontaneous or nonvoluntary quality about it that distinguishes it from ordered rational thinking." Ibid., p. 89.

7. This kind of detailed work of actually bringing the vision to fruition is often left to people other than the visionary. This tendency is borne out by the example of contemporary religious educator John Westerhoff, who is discussed in a separate section below.

articulate the vision for others so that a new plane of existence can be achieved in *this* world.

Granted, there are those dreamers who live on the edges of sanity, but these few must not deter the rest from the essential life-giving task of creating visions and turning them into realities.[8] The vocation of the religious educator cannot be divorced from the continual effort to effect change and to promote progress, which is largely unattainable without the contributions of the visionaries. Visionaries live for and strain toward the future, while being forced to keep their feet anchored to the present.[9] Though at times they appear to the more practical members of society as visitors from another world, visionaries are the ones who provide the hope and the images that enable the earth-bound others to gain entrance to that "other realm" of existence. Visionaries are something like pied pipers, who play such a bewitching and enchanting tune that people follow even as they wish they could stay where they are.

What do visionaries actually produce? The future. Who needs these visionaries? Humankind. Do visionaries deal with real life and real problems? In their own—and at times, indirect—way, yes. Why bother legitimizing the role of the visionary? Without the visionaries and their ability to see, simply put, the people perish—metaphorically, and literally.

This chapter on the role of the religious educator as visionary is crucial to the continued health, not just of the profession of the religious educator, but of life on earth. This is not to say that it is always a popular role, or even an appreciated one.[10] It is to say that this role desperately needs to be given attention as humans try to survive in this mechanized, routinized, and impersonalized world. Visionaries envision and issue the call for reaching beyond the mundane to the celestial; beyond the common to the uncommon; beyond this world to the next.

Dealing with visionaries is a notoriously risky business to be sure. Since by definition the future is "not yet," visionaries can be no more certain of the future than anyone else. One person's vision conflicts with another. One version of the future threatens a particular group but appeals to the next, assuring only that the current situation must undergo change. One sees great things on the horizon,

---

8. I am certainly not suggesting here that dreams are necessarily a sign of mental illness, for as Hilgard wrote: "Dreams are the hallucination of the normal." Hilgard, *Divided Consciousness*, p. 88. Furthermore, other authors have said such things as: "A dream is any kind of mental experience during sleep." See Marino Bosinelli and Piercarla Cicogna, "Research on Dreams: Can an Introduction Be Useful?" in *Psychology of Dreaming*, ed. Marino Bosinelli and Piercarla Cicogna (Bologna: Cooperative Libraria Universitaria Editrice Bologna, 1984), p. 7. Other definitions are provided in ibid., pp. 7-8.

9. For a discussion of this type of personality, the "intuitive" type, see the primary source for these typologies by Carl G. Jung, "General Description of the Types," Vol. Six, *Psychological Types*, trans. H.G. Baynes and rev. by R.F.C. Hull, in *The Collected Works of C.G. Jung* (Princeton: Princeton University Press, 1971), pp. 330-407, especially pp. 366-373 and 398-403. Also see Isabel Briggs Myers with Peter B. Myers, *Gifts Differing* (Palo Alto, Calif.: Consulting Psychologists Press, 1980), pp. 1-7; and David Keirsey and Marilyn Bates, *Please Understand Me: Character and Temperament Types* (Del Mar, Calif.: Prometheus Nemesis, 1984), pp. 16-19.

10. As will be noted throughout the progression of the chapter, there are some fortunate few who are popular and well-liked in their role of visionary. More often than not, however, it seems that since the genuine visionary must by definition challenge the status quo and urge the comfortable majority into uncharted areas the role is easily and more often disparaged and undervalued.

another sees nothing but death and destruction. Some present believable predictions, and others give laughable ones. The thing all visionaries hold in common is their focus on what comes next; *exactly* what that will be is anyone's guess, but at least they issue the call to go forward. Visionaries keep society's eyes from being glued to the ground or fixed on the past by always running ahead, looking around the next corner, and beckoning the people forward.

The biblical story of Joseph illustrates the lot visionaries must at least occasionally expect.[11] Already despised by his brothers because of his status as a favorite son, Joseph only served to make himself even more hated by revealing dreams[12] to his brothers in which he was a ruler and they were his subjects.[13] As is frequently the case, the more practical types decided such nonsense needed to be silenced. Ultimately Joseph was sold into slavery, but over the course of the years the dreams of Joseph indeed came true: Joseph became a ruler and the brothers were his lowly subjects. The point hidden within the details of the story is that these "futurists" are by nature irritating, and normally they are neither heard nor appreciated. If visionaries are ever understood, it is only when the future "arrives." Visionaries should not be surprised by this kind of disregard, just as they must not be silenced by it. Their task is to give voice to the vision and to be faithful to its demands; otherwise, the people perish.

The other side of the coin shows that the nonvisionary must learn to take the visionary in stride, since one vision may be as likely a possibility as the next. Not every visionary needs to be followed or even heeded, but since the vast majority of people seem to spend their time being blinded by the events of the day, the special insight of the visionaries must be valued and nurtured. Especially is this true for a field so regularly mired in the pedestrian as religious education. The religious educator as visionary is sorely needed, and this chapter is an attempt to open this role to further examination and acceptance. This role, as well as all the others in this book, is not just an option to consider. It is an aspect of religious education that each religious educator must incorporate into his or her identity. Rather than looking at the visionary as an oddity to be endured, the need is to accept the visionary as an essential part of the field and as a valid element of the task as religious educators.

Dimensions of the Role

The role of religious educator as visionary is introduced through four of its dimensions: the visionary as witness, prophet, casuist, and charismatic. Each person who fulfills the role is a unique individual, so the comments that follow

---

11. See Genesis, chapters 37-50 for this ancient tale of the life of Joseph. For a whimsical but entertaining version of the same story, see "Joseph and the Amazing Technicolor Dreamcoat," a musical by Andrew Lloyd Webber and Tim Rice.

12. Technically, Joseph's dreams are an example of precognition. See Boyce M. Bennett, *An Anatomy of Revelation: Prophetic Visions in the Light of Scientific Research* (Harrisburg, Pa.: Morehouse, 1990), pp. 56-62 and p. 91.

13. Of course, the question to be asked is, was this a dream of Joseph's or a vision? How volitional was he in the process? His brothers seemed at least to hold him partially responsible because of their drastic reactions to him.

are meant to be neither comprehensive nor prescriptive, only explanatory and descriptive. Accordingly, none of these dimensions is totally separate from one another. They are elements one of another, just as the various roles are in actuality elements of a much larger whole. To expect the dimensions or the roles to be fully distinct and separate from one another is to miss the connections that make up their unity.

Witness

The visionary as witness tells what he or she has seen or experienced, regardless of the testimony or the record of anyone else. The witness does not try to harmonize his or her story with the other versions and may indeed not even be aware that other versions exist. He or she knows what has happened based upon his or her particular experience, and gives voice to it. As Urie Bender simply stated it: "One witnesses when he gives evidence based on knowledge gained from experience."[14] How it squares with others—or even if it squares—is of no fundamental concern to the witness, since what the witness expresses is his or her own experiential encounter of the phenomenon and it need not align with the way others express their experience. The witness is committed only to saying what has been and what is from his or her own unique point of view.[15]

Upon reflection, the only way a witness can be of help or of use is to be totally aware and fully convinced of his or her picture of the truth. If he or she were to try to synthesize and integrate his or her experience with that of others, the result would be a confusion of compromising and shading.[16] For this reason, in legal situations, witnesses are interviewed individually and separately. The judge and jury decide how or if all the various parts of the puzzle fit together to reveal a whole. The witness tells what he or she experienced, and leaves it at that.[17]

The visionary must treasure this element of unique and individual witness. To mold his or her image of the future into a form palatable to a majority of listeners is to abdicate the very task he or she as a witness has been called upon to perform. The visionary as witness tells his or her perceptions so as to awaken and arouse the majority from its slumber. As a result, the story he or she tells may

14. Urie A. Bender, *The Witness: Message, Method, Motivation* (Scottsdale, Pa.: Herald Press, 1965), p. 43. Bender made the definition even clearer when he stated that witnessing is founded on two essential elements: "Knowledge from personal experience and the giving of evidence based on that knowledge." Ibid., p. 42.

15. One author made the point this way: "I do not see the witness as someone who takes the initiative in speaking to others. I see the witness, rather, as a man or woman living in such a way—and looking at the world in such a way—as to make other people ask themselves, and ask those who are witnesses, what gives them their unique character." Jean-Pierre Jossua, *The Condition of the Witness*, trans. John Bowden (London: SCM Press, 1985), p. 1.

16. There are some evangelical Protestant Christians who have highly intricate and specialized ways that their followers are supposed to use in the "witnessing" of their faith. A complicated procedure of introducing leading questions is designed to get the poor victim of this premeditated assault to "make a decision" and join the particular group or cult. That kind of manipulation has nothing whatsoever to do with the present discussion of legitimate witnessing that the visionary performs. For an example of the manipulative type of programed witnessing, see D. James Kennedy, *Evangelism Explosion* (Wheaton, Ill.: Tyndale House, 1970).

17. "The strength of witnessing is its honesty and forthrightness. Any covering up or distortion is not really a witness." Bender, *The Witness*, p. 43.

sound new, different, and radical—maybe even heretical, or at least unorthodox. That new voice and different perspective are precisely what the witness has to offer. If he or she is uncomfortable in being different, or is unwilling to accept the consequences of proffering testimony to the unvarnished truth, then this role is not one to be pursued. The dimension of the witness demands faithfulness to the individual's unique perspective. If nothing unique is offered, then there is no witness.

A prime example of the courageous and faithful witness is Søren Kierkegaard (1813-1855). Known now as the father of existentialism, this Danish philosopher lived a life of frustration among those he considered to be mindlessly passive Lutheran Christians. He believed that to be a Christian—indeed, to be human—was to make radical choices, devoid of total dependence upon rationality and orthodoxy. As he wrote in his journal: "The thing is to find a truth which is true for me, to find the idea for which I can live and die."[18] To depend on an authority—be it a person, an institution, or a creed—for such a truth is to give up individual choice and hence the role of witness. Kierkegaard was unwilling and unable to give away this claim to existence—the claim to be. He continued this line of thinking in his writings: "One must know oneself before knowing anything else. It is only after a man has thus understood himself inwardly and has thus seen his way that life acquires peace and significance."[19] As one commentator on Kierkegaard said of this quest for personal truth, it is "clearly subjective, quite separate from the 'truth' of religious doctrine, for the truth of man's experience must emerge from his faithfulness to his own unique identity."[20] Kierkegaard refused to allow anyone or anything to impede his own personal witness to the truth he experienced and knew.[21]

There is often a price to pay for such individualism and faithfulness to one's own vision. As Van Cleve Morris said: "The nineteenth century paid little attention to Kierkegaard. . . . No one was interested in the prattlings of a man searching for truth within himself."[22] For decades Kierkegaard's writings lay untranslated and unattended, until the bewilderment of the twentieth century forced Kierkegaard's writings to the fore, and existentialism grew as a philosophical system.[23] Such a result is surely ironic, since the whole point of Kierkegaard's effort was to cause each individual to make his or her own decisions and certainly

---

18. Søren Kierkegaard, *The Journals of Kierkegaard*, ed. and trans. Alexander Dru (New York: Harper & Row, 1959), p. 44.

19. Ibid., p. 46.

20. S.E. Frost, Jr., *Basic Teachings of the Great Philosophers: A Survey of Their Basic Ideas*, rev. ed. (Garden City, N.Y.: Doubleday, 1962), p. 265.

21. In discussing Kierkegaard as a witness, Frederick Sontag wrote: "It is not enough to find the truth in individual search and suffering. It must be witnessed to or else it is not alive. Truth is something to be done." Frederick Sontag, *A Kierkegaard Handbook* (Atlanta: John Knox Press, 1979), p. 143.

22. Van Cleve Morris, *Existentialism in Education: What It Means* (New York: Harper & Row, 1966), p. 2.

23. I am aware that this designation for existentialism may be a bit misleading. As Walter Kaufmann said: "Existentialism is not a philosophy but a label for several different revolts against traditional philosophy." See Walter Kaufmann, *Critique of Religion and Philosophy* (Princeton, Princeton University Press, 1958), p. 26.

not to start a school of thought to be emulated or revered. He was simply trying to bear witness to his own truth and to arouse this same passion for truth in others. These factors from Kierkegaard's life tell us volumes about the witness and the visionary: They are often ignored or dismissed as eccentrics, but when their views are recognized, they are often twisted and used in ways never intended. The witness is speaking for himself or herself and not as a beacon of truth for others. The witness abhors such imitation, instead insisting that all must give their own individual and personal witness.

In summary, the witness is an essential dimension of the visionary. The witness is grounded in the present: He or she is called to tell what is, and what was, from his or her own perspective. It is not a collective view, but a unique and personal one. The witness must be faithful to his or her outlook, even in the face of being ignored, misunderstood, or misused. The witness is not charged with the responsibility of convincing others of his or her truth but rather of standing by his or her vision of it while demanding that others claim their own sources of truth.

Prophet

If the witness tells what is and what was, then the prophet declares what will be. If the witness is grounded in the present, then the prophet leans toward the future. If the witness is charged with the task of being faithful today, then the prophet is charged with the task of revealing the harvest of present deeds tomorrow. The prophet is no less frequently a lonely figure than the witness, for the prophet not only tells others what he or she observes but is driven to make those others conscious of the eventual results of their present actions.

The prophet is sometimes mistakenly identified as a soothsayer or as a fortune-teller. There is no magic connected with the prophet and nothing mysterious about his or her insights. A true prophet has no need for stage props like tarot cards, crystal balls, or astrology charts. The prophet is one who is able to see the end results of people's actions, and therefore predicts what will happen based on the activities and decisions made in the present.[24] There is a certain amount of logic that makes up the work of the prophet—if this takes place, then this will naturally result. To dismiss the words of the prophet as irrationality or fantasy is to miss the depth of thought that can be revealed. The prophet, while situated in the present, is able to project present circumstances into the future and to determine possible consequences of present action. Martin Buber discussed this relationship between the present and the future this way: "The rebelliousness of the hour, rebelling against the prophetic teaching, directs the heart of the prophet

---

24. These instructive words from Boyce Bennett help provide a clearer understanding of the biblical prophet's work: "Prophecy is not to be equated with precognition or with the prediction of future events. When applied to the phenomena found in the Bible, it has a much broader meaning than that. In recent decades, it has become fashionable in scholarly circles concerned with the study of biblical prophecy that the prophets in the Bible were 'forthtellers' as opposed to 'foretellers.' . . . The prophets were indeed primarily concerned, not with predicting what was going to happen in the future, *but with proclaiming the judgment of God upon the present*. However, the fact remains that they did, with some frequency, make predictions that were fulfilled, not in some unseen and distant future, but in their own day." Bennett, *An Anatomy of Revelation*, p. 80. Emphasis added.

to the future, which will fulfill his teaching. But the connection of the *nabi* [prophet] with the future is not that of one who predicts. To be a *nabi* means to set the audience, to whom the words are addressed, before the choice and the decision, directly or indirectly. The future is not something fixed in this present hour, it is dependent upon the real decision, that is to say the decision in which man takes part in this hour."[25]

The prophet is often depicted as a suffering and tortured individual, because he or she can see the future but do little more than warn others as to their fate. Cassandra was able to see the future, but unable to change it. Abraham Heschel described the lot of the prophet graphically: "The prophet's word is a scream in the night. While the world is at ease and asleep, the prophet feels the blast from heaven."[26] There are instances, however, where the prophet has been heard and catastrophe has been averted. The humorous if not bittersweet story of the prophet Jonah is one of the more celebrated instances of a successful prophet. After extreme effort to escape from giving his prophecy, Jonah finally did reach the town of Nineveh and proclaim his warning.[27] Much to his dismay and disappointment, the people listened to him, repented of their ways, and escaped the wrath of judgment.[28] The closing chapter of the book of Jonah has the main character so angry at his "successful" mission that he asks to die rather than to have his enemies flourish because of his heeded prophecy.[29] In this case there is a suffering and tortured individual, but the pain came because the Ninevites listened to his dire predictions and avoided the consequences. In the majority of cases, though, the prophet speaks in order to warn, to announce a frightful future, and to plead for a change of ways, but with less than the such surprising "success" of Jonah.

More typical of the prophet's fate was Hosea, who was unable to change the actions or future of his people in the face of words and acted-out behavior. Hosea was not content to let words be the vehicle for his prophecy. He involved himself in a living object lesson, which included his prostitute-wife[30] and oddly-named children.[31] Hosea suffered during the proclamation of the prophecy and during the time when the results of the actions came due. Surely the story of Hosea is enough to make anyone think twice about accepting the assignment of either the prophet or the visionary. A true prophet, however, realizes that there is no "thinking twice," since there is no alternative to seeing what is clear. In many respects, the vocation of prophet is not a voluntary one: When such a person sees the future, especially one with impending disaster, there is nothing else to do but shout out a warning.

If Søren Kierkegaard serves as a modern symbol of the dimension of the witness, then Friedrich Nietzsche (1844-1900) stands as a symbol of the dimension of the prophet. Nietzsche not only understood his present situation but looked into the future and saw its frightful countenance. As Walter Kaufmann

25. Martin Buber, *The Prophetic Faith* (New York: Harper & Row, 1949), pp. 2-3.
26. Abraham J. Heschel, *The Prophets* (New York: Harper & Row, 1962), p. 16.
27. See the biblical book of Jonah, Chapters 1 and 2.
28. Ibid., Chapter 3.
29. Ibid., Chapter 4.
30. Hosea 1:2 called Hosea's wife Gomer a "wife of whoredom."
31. See Hosea 1:2-8.

put it: "Nietzsche was 'prophetic' in the sense that he divined what the mass of his generation was blind to: he anticipated problems that today stare us in the face."[32] This is not a reference just to the most well-known prophecy of Nietzsche—that God is dead and we have killed him[33]—but to the whole realm of twentieth century difficulties of trying to be human in a nonhuman age.

Calling Nietzsche a prophet and encouraging further study of him in that role is academically tenuous. Karl Jaspers confronted this problem years ago and gave this rationale: "Since Nietzsche's thoughts are to be considered as neither vindicated by authority nor as absolutely valid truths, it would be wrong to become his 'disciple.' It is inherent in the very nature of this kind of truth that it is communicated only insofar as it awakens an appropriate personal response. Hence, from the beginning to end, Nietzsche is the 'prophet' who, unlike all prophets, *refers everyone to himself.*"[34] This quote shows the close connection between the discussion earlier concerning Kierkegaard with the present one on Nietzsche. Neither man was looking to start a personality cult or a philosophical school. Both were pointing to the need for individual choice and independent direction.

Walter Kaufmann gave a helpful word in understanding and summarizing the concept of portraying Nietzsche as a prophet: "Sometimes prophecy seems to consist in man's ability to experience his own wretched fate so deeply that it becomes a symbol of something larger. It is in this sense that one can compare Nietzsche with the ancient prophets."[35] Nietzsche astutely perceived the circumstances in which he lived and carried them to their logical conclusion. His own "wretched fate" has indeed become a symbol to successive generations. He spent his life trying to make others conscious of the eventual results of their actions, and his prophecy continues to be heard today.

Casuist

The witness says what is and what has been, the prophet says what will be. The dimension that speaks of what should be—of right and wrong, of good and bad, of ought and ought not[36]—is that of the visionary as the voice of conscience,[37] or

---

32. Walter Kaufmann, *Nietzsche: Philosopher, Psychologist, Antichrist*, 3rd ed. (New York: Random House, 1968), p. 115.

33. See the parable of the Madman in Friedrich Nietzsche, *The Joyful Wisdom* (*La Gaya Scienza*), trans. Thomas Conn, Vol. 10, in *The Complete Works of Friedrich Nietzsche*, ed. Oscar Levy (New York: Russell and Russell, 1964), pp. 167-169.

34. Karl Jaspers, *Nietzsche: An Introduction to the Understanding of His Philosophical Activity*, trans. Charles F. Wallraff and Frederick J. Schmitz (Tucson, Ariz.: The University of Arizona Press, 1965), p. 21; first published in German in 1935.

35. Kaufmann, *Nietzsche*, p. 98.

36. "Moral judgments, or the judgments of conscience, are judgments which employ such words as 'right' and 'wrong,' 'ought' and 'ought not,' 'virtue' and 'vice,' 'duty' and 'sin'; judgments such as 'It is right, or my duty, to do so-and-so'; 'I have behaved wrongly or left undone what I ought to have done.'" Kenneth E. Kirk, *Conscience and Its Problems: An Introduction to Casuistry*, 3rd ed. (London: Longmans, Green, 1948), p. 4.

37. This elusive term "conscience" can be explored in its multiple meanings in such representative overviews as the compilation of essays published under the title of *Conscience*, ed. by The Curatorium of the C.G. Jung Institute in Zurich (Evanston, Ill.: Northwestern University Press, 1970); and *Conscience: Theological and Psychological Perspectives*, ed. C. Ellis Nelson (New York: Paulist, 1973).

the casuist (moral reasoner). The term and the role of the casuist has something of a negative cast for many, primarily because of its past abuse as what one author called "a fixed and legalistic process" which made "big moral points of little contingent factors."[38] As evidence of the current confusion over the word, a casuist can be defined in two radically different ways: as one skilled in reasoning about rights and wrongs based on underlying religious or ethical principles,[39] or as one who engages in specious or sophistical types of arguments.[40] Defining casuistry as "a deliberative process of relating general principles to specific cases"[41] properly identifies this activity of the genuine religious educator, hopefully rescuing a useful term from an ignominious misuse in the past.[42] Choice is still the right and the privilege of each individual, but the person acting as a social conscience (the casuist) is not content simply to ask for everyone to choose a position, and be satisfied that some choice has been made. The issue is for the choices to be the best choices, what the visionary sees as the moral choice in both short and long-term consequences. This dimension of the visionary as casuist moves from observing and pursuing decisions to calling out and demanding the best decisions *based on the guiding vision*, and as such is a significant addition to the dimensions of witness and prophet.

The divisions here are for clarity only and should not be mistaken for an absolute separation of the dimensions. The voice of conscience is but another facet of the whole of the visionary. In a sense, the aspect of casuist has a direct connection to the previous dimension of prophet, as Boyce Bennett made clear when he contrasted the prophetic visionary with "ordinary" people: "Our dreams [visions] are more personal, whereas their visions seem to deal in religious terms with the broad social, political, and moral issues. No doubt personal matters disturbed the prophets, too, and they had dreams of a private nature that were not relevant to society at large. One never hears of those dreams. But they seem to have been concerned enough over *the moral and religious plight of their people* to make their visions psychologically understandable."[43] The vision-

---

38. Edward LeRoy Long Jr., *A Survey of Christian Ethics* (New York: Oxford University Press, 1967), pp. 104-105.

39. "Casuistry, as we have defined it, is no more than the attempt to extend the principles of morality to unforeseen cases and new problems." Ibid., p. 125.

40. "Few intellectual activities have been more reviled than casuistry; yet few practical activities are more indispensable." Albert R. Jonsen and Stephen Toulmin, *The Abuse of Casuistry: A History of Moral Reasoning* (Berkeley: University of California Press, 1988), p. 11. As Kirk noted: "The bad odour into which 'casuistry' has fallen belongs, therefore, to its abuse rather than to its real nature; and that abuse itself has its rise not so much in hypocrisy or lax immoralism as in the aberrations of a high-minded moral rigidity." Kirk, *Conscience and Its Problems*, p. 126.

41. Long, *Survey of Christian Ethics*, p. 104.

42. As Long explained: "The fundamental meaning of the word 'casuistry' refers to the process of relating the high demands of faith to the perplexing moral dilemmas that appear in daily life. . . . In the history of the church, however, the word 'casuistry' has been applied not only to the process of guiding conscience . . . but to the confessional process by which penitents have been assessed penalties through the performance of which they could earn their pardon." Edward LeRoy Long Jr., *Conscience and Compromise: An Approach to Protestant Casuistry* (Philadelphia: Westminster, 1954), p. 9. For an example of what the term is not meant to represent in the present discussion (as identified in Long's second definition) see the three volume work *The Casuist: A Collection of Cases in Moral and Pastoral Theology*, no editor given (New York: Joseph F. Wagner, 1906).

43. Bennett, *An Anatomy of Revelation*, p. 99. Emphasis added.

ary as casuist is not being highlighted so that he or she can promote his or her own personal point of view, although in matters of conscience an individualized focus is most often employed.[44] The effort instead is for "the moral and religious plight of the people" to be addressed and developed—through the power of the vision. It is the vision of better ways and better days that provides the magnetism of the visionary's call.[45]

Casuistry is closely related to the study of ethics. Jacques Thiroux[46] divided ethics into the scientific approach (an empirical description of human behavior) and the philosophical approach. The philosophical category he further subdivided into the normative (prescriptive) type of ethics and metaethics (analytic ethics). While the scientific approach relates more to the role of scientist (already considered in Chapter Six of this book), the philosophical approach includes normative or prescriptive ethics, and this is a helpful distinction for understanding the role of the visionary. Here the religious educator proclaims not "merely descriptions but *prescriptions*; that is ... *prescribing* how humans *should* behave, not merely describing how they *do* in fact behave."[47] To further clarify these differences, Raziel Abelson and Marie-Louise Friquegnon wrote: "The experimental scientist discovers new facts, and the theoretical scientist constructs a theory that explains them and predicts further discoveries. In contrast, an ethical theory reasons from commonsense facts known to everyone, and it formulates principles whose function is not to predict new events but to guide our choices and actions. This difference is often summed up by saying that science is 'descriptive' while ethics is 'normative,' meaning that science tells us what was, is, or will be the case, whether we like it or not, while ethics tells us what ought to be and what we ought to do."[48] The casuist upholds the standard for moral action, pressing for what is right and what should be done. This distinction may or not be the case for either the witness or the prophet but is absolutely incumbent upon the casuist.[49]

---

44. "Normally we use the word 'conscience' for individual moral judgment. . . . In the majority of cases, the words seem to be used in a more individualistic sense; that is, of a private person's judgment of his own actions." Henry Chadwick, *Some Reflections on Conscience: Greek, Jewish, and Christian* (London: The Council of Christians and Jews, 1968). p. 5.

45. Geoffrey Peterson addressed a related attribute of the conscience, saying that "it is socially responsible. Caring in its broadest sense includes responsibility. If we are genuinely concerned about other human beings, we will also be concerned about the social and political structures that affect their lives so profoundly." Geoffrey Peterson, *Conscience and Caring* (Philadelphia: Fortress, 1982), pp. 73-74.

46. Jacques P. Thiroux, *Ethics: Theory and Practice*, 3rd ed. (New York: Macmillian, 1986), pp. 5-7.

47. Ibid., p. 6. The second part of the philosophical approach, metaethics, is not unimportant here, but it is more universal and analytic than the pointed message of the visionary tends to be.

48. Raziel Abelson and Marie-Louise Friquegnon, eds., *Ethics for Modern Life*, 3rd ed. (New York: St. Martin's Press, 1987), p. 3. This quote is from the introduction written by the editors.

49. Another author said that an ethicist is primarily interested in the theory of ethics, while a moralist is primarily interested in the practical issues of how to make people better. In this schema, the term used for the section would indeed be more properly moralist. Such a division, though, seems to separate theory and practice too sharply. See Oliver A. Johnson, *Ethics: Selections from Classical and Contemporary Writers*, 5th ed. (New York: Holt, Rinehart and Winston, 1984), p. 3.

An example of the contemporary casuist at work is found in Jonathan Schell's *The Fate of the Earth*.[50] Evidence of both the witness and the prophet can be found in the book, where Schell described the then-current situation in regard to the use and production of nuclear weapons by way of being a witness, and by being a prophet he portrayed what the future would hold if and when those weapons were ever used. A closer reading of the book, however, reveals the deeper purpose of the author—to show that (in Schell's opinion) the nuclear weapons contest ever-growing among the nations was immoral and intolerable. He was not naive in his judgment, but his values of right and wrong are unmistakably etched throughout the book. He was in fact calling for a change in behavior that would fit his moral stance.

Of course, the big question is whether or not the casuist does indeed call for the proper action. Here is the major difficulty in dealing with the visionary: Is he or she right, deserving to be taken seriously, or just another oddity or eccentric? The answer to this question depends in large part upon the ability of the visionary to make his or her case and to demonstrate that what is being declared is indeed the proper course of action. This leads us directly to the fourth and final dimension of the visionary—the charismatic.

Charismatic

The witness, the prophet, and the societal conscience (casuist) are all essential dimensions of the visionary, but the problem with these three dimensions is that their advice may never be heard or followed. The fourth dimension, that of the charismatic, ensures that the message will be heard and, even more importantly, will be acted upon, because the charismatic has the ability to draw people to the vision and to lead them to a new and different place. This dimension contributes movement and action, which fulfills the proclamations of the previous elements. The fullness of the image is not only dreaming of the promised land but also of leading people toward it.[51] Such is the task and the ability of the charismatic.

The term "charismatic" is a transliteration of a form of the Greek word for grace or kindness, (χάρις). The "charismatic" is one who possesses a special outpouring of the gifts of grace which results in loyal and devoted followership.[52] People seem to be attracted to this kind of person, expecting that this person will be able to lead them out of difficulty into a better life. When a charismatic says "we go this way," there are usually those people who will follow.[53] The com-

---

50. Jonathan Schell, *The Fate of the Earth* (New York: Knopf, 1982).

51. For an overview of some of the theories that have developed around the concept of the charismatic leader, see Jay A. Conger, "Theoretical Foundations of Charismatic Leadership," in *Charismatic Leadership: The Elusive Factor in Organizational Effectiveness*, ed. Jay A. Conger, Rabindra N. Kanungo, and Associates (San Francisco: Jossey-Bass, 1988), pp. 12-39.

52. "Etymologically, charisma means a gift of grace, being favored by the gods." Manfred F.R. Kets de Vries, "Origins of Charisma: Ties That Bind the Leader to the Led," in ibid., p. 237. Max Weber had this to say of the charismatic: "The natural leaders in distress have been holders of specific gifts of the body and spirit; and these gifts have been believed to be supernatural, not accessible to everybody." Max Weber, *From Max Weber: Essays in Sociology*, trans. and ed. H.H. Gerth and C. Wright Mills (New York: Oxford University Press, 1946), p. 245.

plete visionary includes the witness, the prophet, and the casuist, all bound together into a charismatic individual who leads the people wherever the vision takes them.

While the image of the charismatic as portrayed here is one who leads people toward a better life and a more promising future, there is another side to the issue. Just because someone displays charisma and the ability to motivate people does not qualify him or her as a legitimate visionary who is to be obeyed. The vision that is offered must be examined and evaluated, since it is the vision that is the prime focus rather than the individual. The personalities of Charles Manson[54] and Jim Jones[55] included charisma, but they could not be counted as valid role-models for the religious educator.[56] One person who has done extensive research into cult leaders describes the processes apparently at work there: "The strength of commitment to the charismatic leader is expressed through affective ties that closely parallel the bonds between parent and child. These bonds, unlike social ties to the community, are formed at deeper levels of the unconscious and therefore have a greater impact on the individual than the adoption of the social identity associated with group affiliation. The charismatic authority attributed to the leader derives from a process of internalization through which the leader is identified with three representations in the unconscious: the symbol of the divine; the idealized parent; and the idealized self. Each of these unconscious associations contribute to a form of contemporary idolatry wherein the charismatic leader is both loved and revered by his followers."[57] Described thus far is a leader who has built loyalty and followship on a personal basis, and the vision is used only as an instrument to gain power. Unfortunate, and sometimes tragic, results follow: "As love becomes the defining emotion experienced during conversion, the notions of surrender and submission become dominant themes in the charismatic relationship."[58] This kind of charismatic

---

53. "Charisma knows only inner determination and inner restraint. The holder of charisma seizes the task that is adequate for him and demands obedience and a following by virtue of his mission. His success determines whether he finds them. His charismatic claim breaks down if his mission is not recognized by those to whom he feels he has been sent. If they recognize him, he is their master—so long as he knows how to maintain recognition through 'proving' himself. But he does not derive his 'right' from their will, in the manner of an election. Rather, the reverse holds: it is the duty of those whom he addresses his mission to recognize him as their charismatically qualified leader." Weber, *From Max Weber*, pp. 246-247.

54. See the comments about Manson throughout the book by R.C. Zaehner, *Our Savage God* (London: Collins, 1974).

55. See the following resources on Jim Jones and Jonestown: David Chidester, *Salvation and Suicide: An Interpretation of Jim Jones, the Peoples Temple, and Jonestown* (Bloomington: Indiana University Press, 1988); John R. Hall, *Gone From the Promised Land: Jonestown in American Cultural History* (New Brunswick: Transaction Books, 1987); and *The Need for a Second Look at Jonestown*, ed. Rebecca Moore and Fielding M. McGehee III (Lewiston, N.Y.: Edwin Mellen Press, 1989).

56. See this issue of modeling and the charismatic leader discussed by Bernard M. Bass, "Evolving Perspectives on Charismatic Leadership," in *Charismatic Leadership*, pp. 49-55.

57. Janet Liebman Jacobs, *Divine Disenchantment: Disconverting from New Religions* (Bloomington: Indiana University Press, 1989), p. 73.

58. Ibid. Bernard M. Bass said in a similar vein: "Charismatic leaders often emerge in times of crisis as prospective saviors who by their magical endowments will fulfill the unmet emotional needs of their completely trusting, overly dependent, submissive followers." Bass, "Evolving Perspectives on Charismatic Leadership," in *Charismatic Leadership*, pp. 40-41.

leader is certainly not the intention of the dimension presently under discussion. Any "surrender and submission" should relate only to the attainment and actualization of the *vision* and not some kind of misplaced loyalty to the personality of the visionary.

One of the most known and revered charismatics in a legitimate sense was Moses.[59] He gave witness to the present situation in Egypt, he provided a vision of the future, he gave guidance on the right course of action. When the time came, however, talk was finished. Moses stood, held out his staff, and ordered the people across the Red Sea.[60] He went, and the Hebrews followed, off to find the promised land. The Pentateuch is full of stories of this charismatic leader who led by a pillar of a cloud by day and a pillar of fire by night.[61] One remarkable thing about this visionary, as about most of them: He never made it to the promised land, but only brought the people closer to it.[62] There is something about visionaries that never quite lets them complete their task. The visions are always grander than that which is really attainable, which may of course explain in part—if not in whole—why people follow them.

Summary

The primary dimensions of the visionary have been described as the witness, the prophet, the casuist, and the charismatic. No one of these elements need be separate and distinct from the other; indeed, the true visionary combines all of these elements into a unified whole. The key to all of the dimensions, however, is the vision. Excise the unique and particular perspective of the future that the visionary offers and no power remains. The vision of the future pulls people toward it as a pillar of a cloud by day and a pillar of fire by night. The visionary gives it a voice and a plan of action. The rest of this chapter fills in more of the role of the visionary, especially as to how it can be developed in the religious educator. This role is an essential one that the complete religious educator must include in his or her full identity, since this role is responsible for inspiration—a subject taken up more directly in a later section.

Aim: Animation

The aim of the visionary is animation: to breathe the breath of new life into the people by showing them a different and a better future than the one they see presently.[63] The effective visionary stimulates people to leave their familiar

---

59. Interestingly enough, however, not all of Moses' recorded actions should be taken as exemplary. Remember that he fled from Egypt because he was a murderer. See Exodus 2:11-15.

60. See Exodus 14:26-31.

61. As described in Exodus 13:21.

62. See Deuteronomy 34:1-7. It is important to note that although Moses did not get to the promised land, this did not mean that the Israelites gave up and returned to Egypt. They did eventually get there, which should point out the predominance of the vision over any one personality.

63. The etymological roots of "animation" are from the Latin *anima*, breath or soul. The image is like that recorded in Genesis 2:7 (NRSV), where God is portrayed as forming a man from dust, after which God "breathed into his nostrils the breath of life," thereby giving the man life—or, animating him. The same basic image is repeated in Ezekiel 37, where the prophet had a vision of bones that

location to seek someplace unfamiliar—someplace new, exciting, and more promising than the present. Exactly how or where is usually an unknown, but faith in the vision is sufficient to get the process started.[64] The details will follow soon enough, as long as the vision inspires movement and action. For the visionary, the call is to the future, so the less time spent wallowing in the misery of either the past or the present, the better.

A visionary is one who shows people possibilities where they may think none exist and helps them to envision change in some of the most fundamental structures of life—which is the essence of the process of animation. It is not enough for the visionary simply to experience a personal vision. That vision must be universalized and eventually translated into action, to whatever degree possible, so that the world which appears after a visionary's reframing of the situation is forever a different world. The entire vision will probably never approach fulfillment, and in virtually every case the original vision itself will necessarily be transformed and transcended as it moves closer to reality through time. The purpose of the visionary is not so much to force people to conform precisely to a specific vision[65] but to inspire and motivate them to begin the process of movement toward a better future.

The visionary enables people to lift up their eyes, to see the broader horizons, and to begin moving ahead. The visionary provides the overall vision which stimulates others to see new possibilities and animates them into bringing these possibilities into reality. The visionary introduces the hope born of purpose but is open—and often unconcerned—about precise methodology of actually bringing it to fruition. A variety of means is available for achieving the ends as long as the people see ends that are worthy of their time and effort. The visionary hovers at the leading fringe of the movement like the pillars of cloud and fire, pointing out the direction but not the method.[66] The visionary is not bound to the world and its mundane details. He or she is off scouting ahead, leaving it to others to figure out exactly how to get from one point to the next. The visionary keeps his or her eyes on the future and is unwilling or unable to be held up by present difficulties or barriers.[67]

---

gathered flesh onto themselves and then lived: "I prophesied as he commanded me, and the breath came into them, and they lived, and stood on their feet, a vast multitude." Ezekiel 37:10, NRSV.

64. The call and the travels of Abram (later Abraham) recounted in the book of Genesis are an example behind this language. The Jewish scripture puts it this way: "Now the Lord said to Abram, 'Go from your country and your kindred and your father's house to the land that I will show you. I will make you a great nation, and I will bless you and make your name great, so that you will be a blessing.'" Genesis 12:1-2, NRSV.

65. One of the accompanying characteristics of the visionary is that he or she provides the vision but not the details of how to bring it about. Visionaries tend not to have the patience to work out exactly how it is done—that can be left to others. Their interests are more related to the big picture, what the future holds, and to animating people toward possibilities for change.

66. Again recalling the image of Moses in Exodus 13:21.

67. Elise Boulding spoke of this as the eschatological dimension that the visionary employs, saying it is "the element which enables the visionary to breach the bonds of the cultural present and mentally encompass the possibility of a totally other type of society, not dependent on what humans are capable of realizing." Elise Boulding, "Learning to Image the Future," in *The Planning of Change*, ed. Warren G. Bennis, Kenneth D. Bene, Robert Chin, and Kenneth Corey, 3rd ed. (New York: Holt, Rinehart and Winston, 1976), p. 432.

This discussion raises the issue of progress.[68] The visionary is not normally interested in movement just for the sake of movement, but movement toward a better future. This is the difference between change and progress. Change can denote any kind of movement, regardless of direction or purpose.[69] Progress is movement toward the ideal, the goal. Without the vision, which reveals the goal, "leadership" will either result in inaction or random change. The visionary is not seeking turmoil or chaos—at least not for their own sake. The visionary is providing a vision of the future which will bring progress—movement toward an ideal future.

Crucial to the visionary is that the vision be regarded by the people as progress. If not, they will not follow. The future described must be one they want and will strive for, or the visionary will become one more of history's innumerable dreamers. The visionary has only as much power and as much strength to animate as the vision will engender.

The religious educator as visionary must be able to see an idealized future,[70] and to describe it in such a way that people are drawn to it. The person in this role is not bound by the limits, barriers, or inherent problems of the earth-bound religious educator. The visionary religious educator wanders into the future, initially free of worry about means and looks for what is ideal and desirable and needed. He or she knows that if the vision is powerful enough, and presented clearly enough, people will be animated enough to follow and devise the means to achieve the ideal future. The present and its resources do not dictate the vision of the future. For the visionary religious educator, the situation is entirely the opposite.

Function: Insight

The visionary leads, moves, and animates people through the power of the vision. This vision supplies the visionary with energy, drive, and power—but most of all it provides the necessary insight to recognize the deeper realities and needs of the future. The true visionary is no dictator, who forces followers to submit through intimidation, and no monarch, who requires subjects to obey through divine right. The visionary is heeded because of the insight that results in nourishing the guiding vision, which the visionary incarnates through both personal affirmation[71] and inspiration. Similar was Alfred North Whitehead's descrip-

---

68. For an introduction to the topic of progress, see two different perspectives: Raymond Aron, *Progress and Disillusion: The Dialectics of Modern Society* (New York: New American Library, 1968); and Russell L. Ackoff, *Redesigning the Future: A Systems Approach to Societal Problems* (New York: Wiley, 1974). A good philosophical and historical treatment of the topic can be found in Charles Van Doren, *The Idea of Progress* (New York: Praeger, 1967).

69. See the discussion on purpose in Timothy Arthur Lines, *Systemic Religious Education* (Birmingham, Ala.: Religious Education Press, 1987), pp. 46-54.

70. Recall that this phrase "idealized future" is integral to the definition of systemic religious education. See Lines, *Systemic Religious Education*, p. 216. In explaining the definition in that book, these words related to a visionary perspective were used: "Systemic religious education is process, dynamically, interactively, and holistically creating a more desirable future." Ibid., pp. 217-218.

71. This is a way of stating the obvious truth that the visionary must be totally committed to the vision, and that this unshakable confidence in the vision and in the future it reveals is infectious to those who would follow.

tion of God, whose *modus operandi* was distinguished from more violent images of leadership: "God's role is not the combat of productive force with productive force, of destructive force with destructive force. . . . He is the poet of the world, with tender patience leading it by his vision of truth, beauty, and goodness."[72]

The visionary's function of insight helps people to consider new possibilities, and these stimulating views of the future can be communicated when the visionary takes at least one of two positions: above or ahead. These positions are similar in that they require the visionary (at least initially) to see reality from a bit different angle than do most others because of the insight gained from the vision, but the two stances are also rather distinctive in character. Insight shared from above means that the leader is perceiving the action from a standpoint that gives a good overall view of what is happening, but still is detached from the details and the logistics. This notion is symbolized by the figure of Moses standing on the mountaintop overlooking the valley and raising his staff for all the people to see as the signal of encouragement and support.[73] He observed their movement and the general flow of the activity and also served as an inspirational symbol for the people to see.[74]

Insight gained from being out ahead of the group takes more advance effort[75] because of the preparatory work which must be performed in order to convince the people that the envisioned future is worth traveling toward and that the leader has a clear enough vision of what is ahead to guide them there successfully. Again turning to the example of Moses, this kind of insight into what lay ahead was demonstrated extensively. The early years of Moses were spent in the wilderness tending sheep,[76] so that he knew intimately the terrain and the landmarks necessary to guide the people. Moses' primary power, however, came from traveling ahead of the people symbolically by means of his vision. The pull of a home ahead "filled with milk and honey" was irresistible. Moses was personally convinced of the eventuality of their destination and was able to inspire the entire people of Israel to follow him for forty years through the wilderness to fulfill the journey.

The religious educator as visionary needs to demonstrate insight into the future that stems from being both above and ahead of the present conditions. Oversight of the mission—making sure that the general direction is clearly identified—is insight provided from above, which still allows each individual the free-

---

72. Alfred North Whitehead, *Process and Reality: An Essay in Cosmology*, ed. David Ray Griffin and Donald W. Sherburne, corrected ed. (New York: Free Press, 1978), p. 346. The editors report Whitehead wrote "persuading" and "swaying" in the margins of his copy of the original book in place of "leading." These are helpful additional terms in understanding how a visionary leads.

73. See Exodus 17:8-12.

74. This relates to the discussion of the strategist in Chapter Five, "The Religious Educator as Coach."

75. "What is important here is that always a high level of passionate interest and energetic concentration is required—the old saw that insight comes only to the prepared mind seems confirmed by every account—and that the insight is first given as an immediate whole, a new image or order of reason." Douglas Sloan, *Insight—Imagination: The Emancipation of Thought and the Modern World* (Westport, Conn.: Greenwood Press, 1983), p. 144.

76. Exodus 3:1 says that Moses was keeping the flock of his father-in-law when he experienced the encounter with the burning bush.

dom to be faithful to the vision's fulfillment in his or her own fashion or style. The primary resource of the visionary remains the power of the vision, since without it, the people, and the visionary, perish. The visionary who is ahead of the crowd, waving them on to a better and more exciting future, is providing a different kind of insight into the depths of the vision. This understanding of and commitment to the vision is not artificial, phony, or manufactured. It is a grasp of the vision for which the visionary is prepared to sacrifice his or her life— not only figuratively, but literally. Until the religious educator has this level of commitment, and this depth of insight, he or she is well-advised to follow the example of Moses: to wander for a bit in the wilderness, tending sheep, until a better future is envisioned. When the vision becomes sufficiently compelling, the visionary will then begin to inspire the people, to help them catch the vision, to develop insights for themselves,[77] and to move forward together in quest of the desired future.

Primary Virtues: Inspiration and Hope

One of the requirements for grasping the role of the visionary is understanding that not only does the visionary draw his or her own sources of energy from inspiration and hope but that these virtues must be in such evidence that the visionary embodies them and instills them into the followers. Those who join with the visionary in the quest of fulfilling the vision must also be filled with the inspiration and the hope that flows from seeing the vision and believing that it promises a better future. The religious educator as visionary, then, must be totally committed to the vision, wherever it leads and whatever its cost. Part of the trauma of being a visionary is not knowing in any exact detail either the final destination or cost but realizing and accepting the consequences in the present for the creation of a better future. The visionary is obedient and subservient to the demands of the vision, both in its proclamation and its actualization, so that these virtues of inspiration and hope are lived out and modeled by the religious educator as visionary.

The term "inspiration" is virtually self-explanatory when its etymology is unfolded. The term has its origin in the Latin verb *inspirare*—to breathe into. The same root provides the English word "spirit"—breath, as in "breath of life."[78] To be inspired is to draw the very breath of life into oneself, or as it could be said, to receive the spirit. Inspiration is the act or state of being infused with the very energy of life. This is what the visionary gains from catching the vision—the breath of new life concerning a glimpse of a better future. This same gentle breeze flows from the vision through the visionary, filling those who are sensitive and open to this kind of reception of the spirit. When understood in this way, the role of the visionary is no longer viewed as an appendage to modern life

---

77. As is always true with the religious educator, the emphasis is not just on sharing what insight or information the religious educator has. Just as importantly the religious educator is constantly helping others to deepen their own insights and to explore their own visions into what the future can be made to be.

78. The concept here is the same as that described in the earlier section on animation, where in Genesis 2:7 humans are formed by the breath of God and they became living beings.

or suitable only for eccentrics. It is the visionary who allows the fresh wind of a better tomorrow to inspire the people so that "they shall renew their strength, they shall mount up with wings like eagles, they shall run and not be weary, they shall walk and not faint."[79] The visionary brings inspiration—the breath of life.

Genuine inspiration both requires and produces courage,[80] which is facing the challenges and difficulties of today with resoluteness and determination so that challenges and difficulties do not stand in the way of a better future. Inspiration is not found in the future but in the present; it enables one to reach for the future with both hands, fearless of what it may hold, because of the confidence that the future is not fixed but malleable to the contours of the vision. The kind of courage involved in inspiration is neither recklessness nor foolhardiness and is not blind to the realities of the present. Indeed, it is just the opposite. Inspirational courage demands a complete awareness of the situation, with a full understanding of the resources available—or the lack thereof. True courage is knowing as much as possible about the cost and then having the willingness to pay it. This kind of reasoned and prepared approach to the future was precisely the point of Jesus' injunction to his disciples: "No one who puts a hand to the plow and looks back is fit for the kingdom of God."[81] The time for consideration and decision making is before putting the "hand to the plow," and this caution is proper. No one should begin without surveying the field and its demands. Once embarked upon the task, however, inspirational courage sustains and never turns back. The vision of the future rivets the eyes on the goal ahead, and the plower embodies the inspiration and engenders it in the others who work alongside.

One of the great exemplars of inspiration, and incidentally of courage, is the "Maid of France," Joan of Arc (1412-1430). Whatever the realities behind the legends and stories that have grown up around her memory,[82] at least she remains a study of the visionary who inspired great throngs of people—both in her lifetime and beyond.[83] One can read of her visions and hear the descriptions of the voices she heard,[84] but it is very difficult to explain her power over people without acknowledging that she was (to say the least) inspirational. Leading people

---

79. Isaiah 41:31, NRSV.

80. This is to acknowledge that one does not necessarily have to be courageous to be either visionary or inspirational, but to be true to the entirety of the vision does require courage. It is to this ideal that this paragraph points, even though many visionaries fail at the point of courage when the fullness of the vision is revealed.

81. Luke 9:62, NRSV.

82. "A story lives in relation to its tellers and its receivers; it continues because people want to hear it again, and it changes according to their tastes and needs. Joan of Arc is the center of a story so famous that it transcends the media or the forms that have transmitted it; she is a heroine of history. Unlike a fictional character, she does not belong to the mind of a writer or the imagination of a painter. She has objective reality." Maria Warner, *Joan of Arc: The Image of Female Heroism* (London: Weidenfeld and Nicolson, 1981), p. 3.

83. By this I refer to the fact that although Joan was burned as a criminal and a heretic on May 30, 1431, she was canonized by Pope Benedict XV on May 16, 1920. See what has been called "the rehabilitation" of Joan described by Henri Guillemin, *The True History of Joan 'of Arc,'* trans. William Oxferry (London: Allen and Unwin, 1972), pp. 172-215.

84. For example, see V. Sackville-West, *Saint Joan of Arc* (New York: Literary Guild, 1936), pp. 53-56.

into battle, and being victorious, requires no little inspirational ability, but it is her lasting memory in the collective human consciousness that demonstrates the fascination, the need, and the discomfort that remains concerning the figures with inspirational visions. It was appropriate that George Bernard Shaw ended his play *Saint Joan* with Joan herself crying plaintively: "O God that madest this beautiful earth, when will it be ready to receive Thy saints? How long, O Lord, how long?"[85] Those contemplating the role of the religious educator as visionary should not be unaware of the range of emotions that can be aroused by the virtue of inspiration—with not all of those emotions being positive ones.

Inspiration leads to and develops hope, and hope provides the reasons to go on living. Hope is the belief that the future will be better and that something done today will have a positive impact on the future. Hope, regardless of the present circumstances, sees a new day and longs for it—longs for it so much, in fact, that anything and everything will be sacrificed for it today so that tomorrow will be different. The vision is the seed of hope, a glimpse of what the future can be. The vision pulls its followers toward itself and thereby creates the future. Hope is the substance of an as yet unformed and uncreated future[86] but one seen in the eye and mind of the visionary.

The virtue of hope found expression in one of the outstanding visionaries of the twentieth century, Pierre Teilhard de Chardin (1881-1955). Teilhard was a Jesuit priest by calling and a paleontologist by profession, but a visionary by his very nature. All of these elements in one person made for a threatening situation to the Catholic hierarchy. Whenever he tried to synthesize his calling, profession, and nature through his writings the result always sounded too much like common, ordinary heresy for the authorities. Teilhard was not permitted to publish his "visions," and only after his death have his insights made their way into world discussions. In spite of the persecutions and isolation he had to endure, never did Teilhard lose his hope. He continued to write, primarily to and for himself, revealing his vision of the integration of science and religion and of the movement toward what he called the Omega Point, the climax of evolution.[87] He never gave up his vision because he was convinced of the hope that the future would be better.

In the Foreword (which he revealingly entitled "Seeing") to what may be his most known work, *The Phenomenon of Man*,[88] Teilhard tried to explain what would follow in the bulk of the book—as well, in a sense, to explain all of his attempts to publish. He pleaded poignantly: "To try to see more and better is not

---

85. George Bernard Shaw, *Saint Joan: A Chronicle Play in Six Scenes and an Epilogue* (New York: Dodd, Mead, 1924), p. 163.

86. Not unrelated is the definition of faith that is given in Hebrews 11:1, NRSV: "Now faith is the evidence of things hoped for, the conviction of things not seen."

87. Doran McCarty defined Teilhard's concept of the Omega Point as "the climax of evolution where there is the convergence of the material and spiritual." Doran McCarty, *Teilhard de Chardin* (Waco, Tex.: Word, 1976), p. 146. See Teilhard's own discussion of Omega Point in Pierre Teilhard de Chardin, Chapter Two of Book Four, "Beyond the Collective: The Hyper-Personal," *The Phenomenon of Man* (New York: Harper & Row, 1959), pp. 254-272.

88. Teilhard de Chardin, "Preface," *Phenomenon of Man*, pp. 29-36.

a matter of whim or curiosity or self-indulgence. *To see or to perish* is the very condition laid upon everything that makes up the universe, by reason of the mysterious gift of existence."[89] The plea was in vain, however, since publication had to await his death. His hope eventually won out over his detractors, however, and the world now revels in Teilhard's posthumously published visions. The mystical visions of Teilhard were recorded voluminously, and any attempt to summarize them here would ultimately come to grief. One representative sentence that symbolizes his hope of a better day tomorrow is contained in an essay written very early in his career (probably in 1918). It epitomizes his thirst for life and his confidence in the future: "For the love of our Creator and of the universe, we must fling ourselves boldly into the crucible of the world to come."[90] Such a statement, and such an author, provides a model for any religious educator who wishes to pursue the role of visionary.

The virtues of inspiration and hope must be embodied by the religious educator and infused within the lives of the learners. Perhaps the historical figures of Joan and of Teilhard will continue to provide inspiration and hope of sufficient quantity and quality that the tasks of religious education can be tackled with even greater enthusiasm and energy so that indeed tomorrow will be better than today. There could be no greater legacy for either of them than that.

Activity: Imagining

Oddly enough, the primary activity required of the mature and effective visionary is one which children perform so naturally: imagining.[91] Just as oddly, but more sadly, it is one activity that too often adults do their best to eradicate. It is as if one of the marks of becoming an adult is to lose the imagination, irrevocably entering the harsh (cruel?) world of reality, truth, and facts.[92] The visionary retains one of the genuine but fragile gifts of childhood—the gift of the imagination. Facts and figures are relatively easy for many adults to manipulate; it is the "other world" of fantasy and fiction that is difficult for many adults to

---

89. Ibid., p. 31.

90. Pierre Teilhard de Chardin, "Operative Faith," in *Writings in the Time of War*, trans. René Hague (New York: Harper & Row, 1968), p. 243.

91. See this general topic addressed throughout the book by Robert S. Siegler and Erick Jenkins, *How Children Discover New Strategies* (Hillsdale, N.J.: Lawrence Erlbaum Associates, 1989). For some interesting and still useful research on children and imagination, see these two older volumes: Ruth Griffiths, *A Study of Imagination in Early Childhood and Its Function in Mental Development* (Westport, Conn.: Greenwood Press, 1970; first published in 1935); and Frances V. Markey, *Imaginative Behavior of Preschool Children* (New York: Arno Press, 1970; first published in 1935).

92. Brian Vandenberg said: "To be human, and to live in a meaningful way in a culture, requires that we live in and through a very sophisticated, abstract, and symbolic system that is largely imaginary. To be incapable of fantasy is to be barred from human culture. Thus, the importance of play and fantasy is not to be found in indirect stimulation of cognitive, social, educational, and problem-solving skills. Rather, play and fantasy are central features of what it means to be human, and these other skills are spinoffs of the ability to imagine." Brian Vandenberg, "Play Theory," in *The Young Child at Play: Reviews of Research*, Vol. 4, ed. Greta Fein and Mary Rivkin (Washington, D.C.: National Association for the Education of Young Children, 1986), p. 25.

appreciate.[93] The world of the "not yet" is the one the visionary inhabits. Is it any wonder that visionaries are seen as oddities and misfits? In a world of "adults," they are!

Joseph Chilton Pearce gave this simple definition of imagination: "When we close our eyes and produce images of things not present out there, this is imagination."[94] He meant, of course, the closing of the physical eyes and use of the "third" eye to imagine.[95] The whole point of having a vision is to see what is not yet and to imagine what can and will be.[96] It is the responsibility of the imagination to conjure up a make-believe world that can serve as a guide or model for its eventual actualization.[97] Humans landing on the moon would never have happened if some active imaginations had not only thought of doing such a thing, but had also dreamed up notions of how it could be done. Science fiction for one generation becomes reality for another, and history for the next—all

---

93. To help overcome this denigration of the imagination, see—and use—Chapter One, "Developing the Adult's Imagination," in Dorothy G. Singer and Jerome L. Singer, *Partners in Play: A Step-by-Step Guide to Imaginative Play in Children* (New York: Harper & Row, 1977), pp. 16-29.

94. Joseph Chilton Pearce, *Magical Child Matures* (New York: Dutton, 1985), p. 14. For a more scholarly overview of the definitions of imagination, see Chapter One, "Imagination: Definitions and Problems," in Margaret B. Sutherland, *Everyday Imagining and Education* (London: Routledge and Kegan Paul, 1971), pp. 1-23. As Sutherland said at the beginning of her chapter: "Imagination is a word which we keep using without thinking very much about it. . . . It is in fact one of those useful but misleading words which can fit without any perceptible jarring into a good many contexts." Ibid., p. 1. See also Chapter One, "Theories of Play and the Origins of Imagination," in Jerome L. Singer, *The Child's World of Make-Believe: Experimental Studies of Imaginative Play* (New York: Academic Press, 1973), pp. 1-26. For some closely related discussions, see Chapter One, "Imagery: Definition and Types," by Alan Richardson, in *Imagery: Current Theory, Research, and Application*, ed. Anees A. Sheikh (New York: Wiley, 1983), pp. 3-42; and Part One, "Phenomenology of Image Formation," in Mardi Jon Horowitz, *Image Formation and Psychotherapy* (New York: Jason Aronson, 1983), pp. 1-55.

95. "We find that in the imaginal existence we are able to *see* with a vision not limited by the ordinary time-space parameters of concrete reality. This seeing allows us to 'get outside' of the personal self and thus see our existence from a different, nonhabitual point. What is seen brings with it knowledge about the individual's relationship to the concrete world and to his own biological being, a knowledge that is unshakable and that can be used in everyday life." Gerald Epstein, *Waking Dream Therapy: Dream Process as Imagination* (New York: Human Sciences Press, 1981), p. 18.

96. "We have evidence that make believe play is preparation for the adult ability to plan ahead and to anticipate practical consequences. A childhood rich in fantasy also lays the foundation for an adult life with well-developed imaginative and playful capacities, and with adaptive skills useful and necessary in dealing with complex society. We are in fact suggesting that pretending and making believe, activities that start so early in childhood and continue into adult life, are basic characteristics of a rounded, fulfilled human being." Singer and Singer, *Partners in Play*, p. 4. See ibid., pp. 4-9, for an overview of some of the benefits of the make-believe activity for children.

97. "Because linear thought does not contain the potential for action it cannot help us fulfill our possibilities. Linear thought by its very nature can only reflect the past. The future on the other hand is by definition potential and nonexistent. By trying to apply linear thought to the future, we can become only more and more fragmented, since we are always applying the past to our experience, and removing ourselves from the present moment at the same time. The future, from my perspective, is transformed into the present by its fulfillment through our physical presence and physical action in the world of concrete reality. It is cyclical because the newly transformed present simultaneously generates a new potential, a new future. Here we see how the nonmaterial world influences the material." Epstein, *Waking Dream Therapy*, p. 22.

freed and stimulated by the healthy functioning of the imagination.

What kinds of futures can religious educators imagine? Is a future with no more war too ridiculous to imagine? Maybe no more so than humans playing golf on the surface of the moon was to people a generation ago. Is a future where every human has sufficient food and decent shelter too silly to imagine? Maybe no more so than when people a few decades ago dreamed of a cure for polio. Is a future where religious educators work to integrate—"bind together"—the human race toward holistic nexus rather than to nurture dissension and strife too unreal to imagine? Well, maybe so.[98]

It would be a tragic mistake to assume that imagining is "making things up" that are unreal or unimportant.[99] As Robert Johnson observed: "Our culture of the twentieth century has a tremendous collective prejudice against the imagination. It is reflected in the things people say: 'You are only imagining things,' or, 'That is only your fantasy, not reality.'"[100] Johnson went on to say that the imagination uses material which originates in the unconscious and that the imagination is actually a "transformer that converts the invisible material [in the unconscious] into images the conscious mind can perceive."[101] The imagination and its products are not, therefore, "unreal" or from "out there." The imagination makes visible the unconscious within ourselves. To imagine is to know ourselves more intimately.[102] To imagine is to "dialogue with genuine interior parts of ourselves. We confront the powerful personalities who live inside us at the unconscious level and who are so often in conflict with our conscious ideas and behavior."[103]

To so perceive the imagination—as an extension of our conscious self—puts the visionary in a new and revealing light.[104] This oft-regarded eccentric may not be so much traveling to a world beyond as to a world within. A description such as the one the prophet and visionary Jeremiah gave of his inner experience makes sense when seen from this perspective: "If I say, 'I will not mention him, or speak any more in his name,' then within me there is something like a burning fire shut up in my bones; I am weary with holding it in, and I cannot."[105] Jeremiah was saying that for a visionary not to speak of the vision within is to deny who he or she is, to the point that one's very bones are on fire. Can there

---

98. With tongue securely placed in cheek, this is a reference to the visionary message of my earlier book, *Systemic Religious Education*.

99. On this point, Douglas Sloan wrote: "But in many cases the imagination is still confused with the fictive and the 'imaginary' in the sense of being basically unreal. As a result, in both science and education, the imagination is pushed into the background, and the main focus remains upon the content of knowledge that the imagination, it is conceded, has produced." Sloan, *Insight—Imagination*, pp. 139-140.

100. Robert A. Johnson, *Inner Work: Using Dreams and Active Imagination for Personal Growth* (San Francisco: Harper & Row, 1986), p. 22.

101. Ibid.

102. See this discussed thoroughly by Sheryl C. Wilson and Theodore X. Barber in Chapter Twelve, "The Fantasy-Prone Personality: Implications for Understanding Imagery, Hypnosis, and Parapsychological Phenomena," in *Imagery*, pp. 340-387.

103. Johnson, *Inner Work*, p. 25.

104. For a helpful theoretical discussion here, see Chapter Eight, "Some Theoretical Implications," in Singer, *The Child's World of Make-Believe*, pp. 183-230.

105. Jeremiah 20:9, NRSV.

be a more graphic description of the revelatory power of the imagination?

Religious educators must "learn" (actually, to be freed) to imagine, which is to learn who they are. As Pearce said, the religious educator must "close [the] eyes and produce images of things not present out there," since the images are present within. One speaks because one cannot be silent—because of the "burning fire within the bones." To be silent would be to ignore or to deny the very self. As an adult, one should not give up his or her imaginings, retaining and treasuring that gift of childhood in the face of being perceived as an oddity and a misfit. The future depends upon the depth and the articulation of those guiding inner visions.

Shadow Role: Daydreamer

In the midst of this affirming talk about the visionary, it is time to turn to the ever-present danger of the shadow role.[106] The genuine role of the visionary, whose activity was described in the previous section, deals in active imagination: purposeful and intentional explorations into the possibilities of the future so that the future will be better. The shadow role results in the daydreamer, who engages in passive imagination: uninvolved and useless wonderings about the future, wholly without intent to influence for good (or for ill) the course of the future.[107] The daydreamer, so to speak, could predict a train wreck but sit idly by and do nothing to present it. The visionary would die trying to see that it did not happen.

There are many ways to indulge in passive imagination. One is to spend time worrying. Worry is imagining the worst that could happen but doing nothing actively to remove the threat or even to warn others of it. It is simply stewing over what could be and being no more responsive to the situation than spending the effort to wring one's hands. The productive—and healthy—form of "worry" is planning. Planning also takes into account "worst-case scenarios" but is the development of action plans either to design out such eventualities or to develop contingency plans to follow that remedy the situation should it occur anyway.[108]

Another way to daydream—engage in passive imagination—is to play "what

---

106. Daydreams are to be differentiated from dreams and visions, as mentioned early in the chapter. Recall that Ernest Hilgard defined dreams as "products of imagination in which memories or fantasies are temporarily confused with external reality." Hilgard, *Divided Consciousness*, p. 87. Another useful definition here is the one provided by James Michael Lee: "A dream is a series of cognitive, affective, or lifestyle behaviors which occur in the form of imagery during sleep." James Michael Lee, *The Content of Religious Instruction: A Social Science Approach* (Birmingham, Ala.: Religious Education Press, 1985), p. 569. A daydream, in contrast, is a fantasy experienced while awake that deals with wish fulfillment in a frivolous and superficial way. Additionally, daydreams are not backed up with any effort or force of convictions, as a true vision must be.

107. Alex Osborn called this "noncreative imagination," writing: "Daydreaming is the most common use of noncreative imagination. Sometimes called reverie, this is for some of us the usual form of our so-called thinking. It takes less than effort. We merely let our imaginations join hands with our memories and run here and there and everywhere—without design and without direction, except as set by our prejudices, our desires, or our fears." Alex Osborn, *Applied Imagination: Principles and Procedures of Creative Problem-Solving*, rev. ed. (New York: Scribner's, 1957), p. 101.

108. For a good discussion of the use of scenarios in planning, see G.K. Jayaram, "Open Systems Planning," in *The Planning of Change*, pp. 275-283.

if." This is the game people play who have no intention of taking responsibility for either the past or the present, much less the future: If only I had gone to another seminary; if only our denomination had decided differently; if only God had answered my prayer. Excuses are easy and plentiful. Visions of the future and work to make them into reality are not as easy to accomplish and create.

Passive imagination can also be such a preoccupation that no concrete action is ever attempted.[109] This is the procrastinator, who is so concerned about grand designs, perfect preparation, and proper insight that nothing ever happens.[110] This person always intends to do good things but never quite seems to get them under way, which of course is of no use to anyone. The adage of the native Americans is appropriate here: A journey of a thousand steps is started by taking the first one.

The religious educator who daydreams without action is no visionary but is simply a lazy and ultimately an uncaring person. Daydreamers do not build the future, but true visionaries do. Daydreamers are content to dream while true visionaries are compelled to act.[111] The daydreamer is dangerous, and a shadow role of the true visionary, for he or she wastes what little time is available to each individual for making a real difference in the world. It was in this vein that the poet wrote what appropriately could be an epitaph for the daydreamer:

> Of all sad words of tongue or pen,
> The saddest are these: "It might have been!"[112]

Faith Tradition Resource: Mysticism

The faith tradition resource selected for the visionary—mysticism—cuts across traditional boundaries of religions and specific categories of faith traditions.[113] No one religion or group has a monopoly on mysticism. Its ways and

---

109. "There is a great deal of difference between Active Imagination and idle fantasy. Fantasy, because it does not lead into actions in the world of objective reality, can actually lead an individual away from reality, for such fantasies can be more fascinating and less demanding than the outer world." Rix Weaver, *The Wise Old Woman: A Study of Active Imagination* (New York: Putnam's, 1973), p. 3.

110. This topic is discussed also in Chapter Five, "The Religious Educator as Coach."

111. "Everyone knows that it is possible to fantasize in a passive way, and one recognizes these fantasies which seem to happen of their own accord. Now when one steps in and consciously takes part in the fantasy or theme of the unconscious, maintaining awareness of the ego, one has stepped into Active Imagination. Consequently, the ego has effect on what happens, bringing its own characteristics to bear upon the material." Weaver, *The Wise Old Woman*, p. 15.

112. John Greenleaf Whittier, "The Saddest Words," from "Maude Muller," in *Immortal Poems of the English Language: An Anthology*, ed. Oscar Williams (New York: Washington Square Press, 1952), p. 349.

113. "Mysticism is a human experience which is not limited to any one religion; it is found in all major world religions." Lee, *Content of Religious Instruction*, p. 663. In regard to the apparent need for stating a definition, Lee went on to admit: "While many scholars more or less concur on the spirit of mysticism, there seems to be no single definition of mystical experience upon which all or even most scholars can agree." Ibid., p. 663. Lee did, however, provide "eight fundamental characteristics of mystical experience on which most scholars of spiritual living agree" in ibid., pp. 664-665.

means are found scattered throughout all the various faith traditions,[114] and the visions provided by its practitioners, while individual and unique, have a certain universal quality that binds them together.[115] It is as if all these mystic visionaries are gazing at the same reality from an amazing and dizzying array of perspectives. It seems appropriate that these visionaries are not segregated into a specific or single faith tradition, but that a few representatives from each of the faith traditions peer into the future toward some kind of possible collective vision.

F.C. Happold underlined the point made above when he wrote that mysticism "has its fount in what is the raw material of all religion."[116] He was referring to "a consciousness of a *beyond*, of something which, though it is interwoven with it, is not of the external world of material phenomenon, of an unseen over and above the seen."[117] He went on to say: "In the true mystic there is an extension of normal consciousness, a release of latent powers and a widening of vision, so that aspects of truth unplumbed by the rational intellect are revealed to him."[118] The mystic is full of assurance and confidence in the vision, since "he has been 'there,' he has 'seen,' he 'knows.' "[119] What the mystic has "seen" is the vision of the unity: "It has been the eternal quest of mankind to find the one ultimate Truth, that final synthesis in which all partial truths are resolved. It may be that the mystic has glimpsed this synthesis."[120]

Such talk is not commonly encountered in the Western world during the twentieth century. If visionaries are regarded as oddities and misfits by the rationalists in our world, then so much more are the mystics. In discussing the term mysticism, Walter Stace said at the beginning of his classic work that to some it "suggests mist, and therefore foggy, confused, or vague thinking. It also suggests mystery and miraclemongering, and therefore hocus-pocus."[121] This is not to say that mysticism is dead in present culture. It is to say that it is normally explained away psychologically or academically, thereby denying the reality of the experience with the "other," or as Happold said, with a "beyond" and an "unseen." This caused Morton Kelsey to write: "Therefore many theologians who write about these things [mystical experiences] are like geologists who have

---

114. For some scholarly sources that deal with this aspect of mysticism, see Rudolph Otto, *Mysticism East and West: A Comparative Analysis of the Nature of Mysticism*, trans. Bertha L. Bracey and Richenda C. Payne (New York: Macmillan, 1932); Sidney Spencer, *Mysticism in World Religion* (New York: A.S. Barnes, 1963); and Walter T. Stace, *The Teachings of the Mystics* (New York: New American Library, 1960).

115. Walter Stace wrote: "The most important, the central characteristic in which all *fully developed* mystical experiences agree, and which in the last analysis is definitive of them and serves to mark them off from other kinds of experiences, is that they involve the apprehension of *an ultimate nonsenuous unity in all things*, a oneness or a One to which neither the senses nor the reason can penetrate. In other words, it entirely transcends our sensory-intellectual consciousness." Stace, *Teachings of the Mystics*, pp. 14-15.

116. F.C. Happold, *Mysticism: A Study and an Anthology*, rev. ed. (Middlesex, England: Penguin Books, 1970), p. 18.

117. Ibid., pp. 18-19.

118. Ibid.

119. Ibid.

120. Ibid., p. 21.

121. Walter T. Stace, *Mysticism and Philosophy* (London: Macmillan, 1961), p. 15. Also see Stace, *Teachings of the Mystics*, pp. 10-12, for a discussion of what mysticism is *not*.

never been in the field. Since they have no taste of their own inner experience, seeking out their opinion is about like consulting a wine expert who is a teetotaler or a cheese fancier who has tasted only one kind."[122]

In this vein, it is useful to note what Richard Woods said: "As an established institution in society, religion seems to have functioned historically as a largely conservative force, whereas the mystical element in religion has been a reforming drive."[123] In the true nature of the visionary, the mystic has visions most often when the present needs reformation. It is natural for the mystic to be at odds with traditional institutionalism in calling for a different and better future. The nature of institutions—and their caretakers—is to remain as they are. The nature of the mystic/visionary is to envision something new, or at least something beyond the status quo.

Mysticism has much to offer the religious educator who desires to fulfill the role of the visionary.[124] It is not enough to study mysticism, however. It is that which must be experienced, received, or absorbed. It is more a matter of accepting and of letting go than grasping and clutching. A final word from Teilhard will clarify. He wrote: "The mystic only gradually becomes aware of the faculty he has been given of perceiving the indefinite fringe of reality surrounding the totality of all created things, with more intensity than the precise, individual core of their being. . . . Happy the man who fails to stifle his vision."[125]

Historical Personage: Martin Luther King Jr.

One of the persons in modern history who has performed the role of visionary admirably was Martin Luther King Jr. (1929-1968). If ever a man lived by a vision of a better world, died for it, and changed the world through the force of it, King was the man. As seems to be descriptive of many (although admittedly not all) visionaries, King was reviled and hated by some and revered and loved by others during his life—and the divisions remain to this day, years after his death. It is safe to say, though, that more people tend to appreciate a visionary after he or she is gone, and this also seems to be accurate in the case of Martin Luther King Jr. In most quarters, he is now honored as a true prophet by a vast range of peoples.[126] Such a

---

122. Morton T. Kelsey, *The Other Side of Silence: A Guide to Christian Meditation* (New York: Paulist, 1976), p. 129.

123. Richard Woods, "Introduction," in *Understanding Mysticism*, ed. Richard Woods (Garden City, N.Y.: Image Books, 1980), p. 7.

124. James Michael Lee wrote: "What can the religious educator do in order to directly facilitate intense religious experience, including mysticism, in learners? In general, the religious educator should structure the pedagogical situation in such a manner as to exclude as far as possible those activities known to inhibit mystical experience and to include those activities known to facilitate mystical experience." Lee, *Content of Religious Instruction*, p. 670.

125. Pierre Teilhard de Chardin, *Hymn of the Universe* (New York: Harper & Row, 1965), pp. 85-86.

126. As Frederick Downing said: "He was not a prophet without honor! Few Americans have ever won so many awards and tributes as Martin Luther King Jr." Downing continued: "For many Americans King remains the most important religious personality of this part of the twentieth century, and for others he continues to be the symbol of a most significant historical movement." Frederick L. Downing, *To See the Promised Land: The Faith Pilgrimage of Martin Luther King Jr.* (Macon, Ga.: Mercer University Press, 1986), pp. 3-4.

legacy is testimony to his faithfulness to the vision.

As complex a man as King was, and as convoluted the period of history in which he participated, the irony is that portions of only two speeches by King are sufficient to reveal the power and the nature of his vision. Both still inhabit the societal consciousness of the twentieth century. The first one was delivered on August 28, 1963, in Washington, D.C. at the March on Washington for Civil Rights. One speech in a long day of speeches, this is the one still quoted and remembered as *the* speech of the day. In it, King articulated his vision of equality, and galvanized a nation if not the world. It was a grand vision that King revealed, not a daydream or a fantasy spun on the spur of the moment and forgotten minutes later, but a true vision that aroused not only emotion but action. After opening words of encouragement and description of the current conditions, he began the now-famous litany of his vision of the future:

> So I say to you, my friends, that even though we must face the difficulties of today and tomorrow, I still have a dream. It is a dream deeply rooted in the American dream that one day this nation will rise up and live out the true meaning of its creed—we hold these truths to be self-evident, that all men are created equal.
>
> I have a dream that one day on the red hills of Georgia, sons of former slaves and sons of former slave owners will be able to sit down together at the table of brotherhood. . . .
>
> I have a dream my four little girls will one day live in a nation where they will not be judged by the color of their skin but by the content of their character. . . .
>
> I have a dream that one day every valley shall be exalted, every hill and mountain shall be made low, the rough places shall be made plain, and the crooked places shall be made straight and the glory of the Lord will be revealed and all flesh shall see it together.
>
> This is our hope. This is the faith that I go back to the South with.
>
> With this faith we will be able to hew out of the mountain of despair a stone of hope. With this faith we will be able to transform the jangling discords of our nation into a beautiful symphony of brotherhood.
>
> With this faith we will be able to work together, to pray together, to struggle together, to go to jail together, to stand up for freedom together, knowing that we will be free one day.[127]

King's "dream" speech[128] has been quoted extensively because these excerpts contain virtually all the elements of the visionary discussed throughout this

127. Martin Luther King Jr., "I Have a Dream," in *A Testament of Hope: The Essential Writings of Martin Luther King Jr.*, ed. James Melvin Washington (San Francisco: Harper & San Francisco, 1986), pp. 217-220.

128. This speech is popularly referred to as the "dream" speech, but in light of the distinctions made early in the chapter between dreams and visions it is clear that King was not just "dreaming." He was articulating a vision in a way that truly exemplifies virtually all of the points of this chapter on the visionary. See this topic discussed by Mary R. Sawyer, "Legacy of a Dream," in *Martin Luther King Jr.: A Profile*, ed. C. Eric Lincoln, rev. ed. (New York: Hill and Wang, 1984), pp.

chapter. Here King personified the dimensions of witness, prophet, casuist, and charismatic. Clearly, his aim was animation, his function was insight, and the virtues he instilled and exemplified were inspiration and hope. Without doubt, he was able to imagine, and to enable others to imagine with him. The full realization of the vision has not yet come true, but it remains a vision worthy of sacrifice and continued effort to make it come true.[129] He was able in these few paragraphs to highlight the role of visionary in gripping and dynamic fashion.[130]

Yet another facet of the visionary requires highlighting, and again a speech by King does the job nobly. That facet is seeing the "promised land" but not being able to make the final journey into it personally. The image is taken from the life of the Hebrew visionary Moses, and King was something of a modern-day version of this figure.[131] King's haunting words of April 3, 1968, the night before he was assassinated, tell the lot of the visionary and of the ultimate cost some are required to pay. For some, the dream and the vision are worth life itself:

> Well, I don't know what will happen now. We've got some difficult days ahead. But it doesn't matter to me now. Because I've been to the mountaintop. And I don't mind. Like anybody, I would like to live a long life. Longevity has its place. But I'm not concerned about that now. I just want to do God's will. And He's allowed me to go up to the mountain. And I've looked over. And I've seen the promised land. I may not get there with you. But I want you to know tonight, that we, as a people will get to the promised land. And I'm happy tonight. I'm not worried about anything. I'm not fearing any man. Mine eyes have seen the glory of the coming of the Lord.[132]

Let the religious educator who wishes to enter the world of the visionary hear and heed the words of one who paid the ultimate cost of following the vision to its end. All who follow carry the same responsibility and must be prepared to pay the same price. May few ever be called upon to pay such a price, but may few ever refuse if the vision is truly worthy of such a cost.

Contemporary Example: John H. Westerhoff III

The contemporary religious educator chosen to illustrate the visionary is John Westerhoff (b. 1933). A prolific writer, editor and journalist, and sought-after speaker and teacher, Westerhoff envisions better days ahead for religious

---

260-270; and by Ira G. Zep Jr., "The Dream Theme in King's Thought," in *The Social Vision of Martin Luther King Jr.* (New York: Carlson Publishing, 1989), pp. 215-222.

129. "All prophets suffer the burden of being ahead of their time and not living to see their ideas realized." Zep, *The Social Vision of Martin Luther King Jr.*, p. 45.

130. As one author put it: "King possessed a remarkable capacity to communicate his dream, indeed the nation's dream and destiny, to all rational people." Robert Michael Franklin, *Liberating Visions: Human Fulfillment and Social Justice in African-American Thought* (Minneapolis: Fortress, 1990), p. 139.

131. See this image of King developed fully by Downing in *To See the Promised Land.*

132. Martin Luther King Jr., "I See the Promised Land," in *Testament of Hope*, p. 286.

education than currently exist and cannot keep his eyes off the future. Even when he deals with history, it is for the purpose of trying to make the future better.[133] Westerhoff is the inveterate and incurable visionary.

Westerhoff is fully aware of his futuristic approach to life, and he told about it in an autobiographical article. He wrote: "More innovative than practical, I am a dreamer, most at home in the world of mystery and imagination. I enjoy solving problems, but I'm uncomfortable in dealing with details or following through on a new idea. The future is of more interest to me than either the past or the present. Indeed, the present is of little interest. The life of fantasy is appealing and the world of visions and dreams quite real. Typically I am happiest when speculating about possibilities; I experience dissatisfaction when life is not changing."[134] In light of what has already been seen in this chapter about the visionary, this one quote leaves little doubt that Westerhoff represents the role in both its inherent strengths and weaknesses.

Although it is clear that Westerhoff is by all accounts a visionary in approach and attitude, it seems necessary to note that some aspects of the visionary as described here do not correlate precisely with Westerhoff. Much of the previous discussion in this chapter has described the visionary as something of an "outsider," as one who goes against popular opinion. In this regard, Westerhoff is an anomaly. He is popular and well-liked, as evidenced by his mass readership and following. The image of a lonely eccentric who hopes others will listen, but they do not, does not fit Westerhoff. For some, this popularity may disqualify Westerhoff from being considered as the exemplar of the role. For others, he is one of the "lucky" visionaries who articulates a vision and gets rewarded for it. The reader must make up his or her own mind as to which stance is appropriate.

As an author, Westerhoff has dealt with the future but in a very different way than, say, James Michael Lee has done. Lee has written long and intricately wrought scholarly volumes that he expects to survive the tests of time and to be useful for decades to come. Westerhoff, in contrast, has written about the future he envisions but not in a scholarly or academic manner. He has called the church to action and offered an alternate view of the future. Westerhoff does not expect his writings to last but instead is providing an educated guess about what he hopes lies ahead. For example, at the first of *Values for Tomorrow's Children*, he wrote to the reader: "This is a personal statement. . . . I have penned my present opinions. They are neither meant to be a lecture nor an academic thesis to be debated by scholars. I want my opinion to be the basis for a conversation."[135]

133. See his introductory comments to *Who Are We?: The Quest for a Religious Education*, ed. John H. Westerhoff III (Birmingham, Ala.: Religious Education Press, 1978), pp. 1-13. Also see John H. Westerhoff III, *McGuffey and His Readers: Piety, Morality, and Education in Nineteenth-Century America* (Nashville: Abingdon, 1978) for Westerhoff's most historical treatment of a subject to date.

134. John H. Westerhoff III, "A Journey into Self-Understanding," in *Modern Masters of Religious Education*, ed. Marlene Mayr (Birmingham, Ala.: Religious Education Press, 1983), p. 118.

135. John H. Westerhoff III, *Values for Tomorrow's Children: An Alternative Future for Education in the Church* (Philadelphia: Pilgrim Press, 1970), p. xi. Similarly, Westerhoff introduced *Will Our Children Have Faith?* as a tract whose "purpose is to stimulate reflection, conversation, and perhaps debate." See John H. Westerhoff III, *Will Our Children Have Faith?* (New York: Seabury, 1976), p. ix.

In a similar vein, Westerhoff identified one of his books as a "short tract" written in three weeks for lay persons and ministers in the local churches and should therefore not be taken as a "definitive work."[136] Since Westerhoff used the term "tract," it needs the clarity of definition so that Westerhoff's work can be properly identified and evaluated. James Michael Lee gave this definition: "A tract is a popular short book or pamphlet written in zealous and tittupping manner for the purpose of rousing persons to action. The adequacy and validity of a tract stem from the degree to which it echoes its author's personal passionate persuasion; hence a tract may be adequate and valid even though it contains empty slogans, fallacious reasoning, gross imprecisions, factual errors, and internal contradictions."[137] Westerhoff, as a tractarian, is not particularly interested in scholarship and cannot be evaluated in the same way as is someone who purports to produce scholarly writings.[138] Such statements and purposes put the present writing at some risk, because the intent in this book has been to examine and evaluate religious education scholarship. Since Westerhoff has characterized his own work as that of a tractarian and not as a scholar, the brief overview and evaluation sections which follow must deal directly with the audience and aim that Westerhoff had in mind, rather than an artificial mode of evaluation that is unfair to Westerhoff's intent and product.

Overview

Because Westerhoff has written so many tracts on such a wide variety of topics, any kind of systematic overview of his themes and message is difficult if not impossible. Instead, a select few of his writings are examined that overview the range of his interests and that explain his living out the role of visionary. These works are typical and give the flavor of Westerhoff's approach, as well as describe the functioning of a visionary.

One of Westerhoff's first books was mentioned above, *Values for Tomorrow's Children*. In an introduction to that book, Robert Lynn captured the essence and the fervor of Westerhoff's writing style: "In this book John Westerhoff renews an honorable tradition in American religious literature. He has written a 'tract for the times' at a moment in history when it is sometimes difficult to know where one stands and even more hazardous to assess what is needed 'for the times.'"[139] At the end of that Introduction, Lynn concluded: "John Westerhoff is a 'tractarian' suited to the present era. In an interim time between certainties,

---

136. John H. Westerhoff III, *Tomorrow's Church: A Community of Change* (Waco, Tex.: Word, 1976), p. 10.

137. James Michael Lee, "The Authentic Source of Religious Instruction," in *Religious Education and Theology*, ed. Norma H. Thompson (Birmingham, Ala.: Religious Education Press, 1982), p. 119; see the entire discussion in pp. 119-121.

138. In a footnote disagreeing with Westerhoff's understanding of the term "catechesis," Lee expressed this view about how to evaluate Westerhoff's work: "One can, I suppose, forgive Westerhoff for his fundamentally erroneous understanding of catechesis since he is basically a tractarian and a religious journalist and therefore is not subject to the same rules of evidence and accuracy as is the case with a scholar." See James Michael Lee, "Catechesis Sometimes, Religious Instruction Always," in *Does the Church Really Want Religious Education?*, ed. Marlene Mayr (Birmingham, Ala.: Religious Education Press, 1988), p. 41, n.36.

139. Robert W. Lynn, "Introduction," in *Values for Tomorrow's Children*, p. viii.

he has declared himself."[140] What did Lynn mean about Westerhoff as a tractarian? Westerhoff's own purpose statement of the book began to explain, which was phrased this way: "This book intends to provide the basis on which together we might build an alternative future for church education. The notion of an alternative future suggests a style for dealing with the present. Too often we conceive of futuristic thinking as making predictions. I do not intend to predict the future. Rather, I hope to introduce a way of talking about the present which will make alternatives to our present condition possible in the future."[141] Illustrative of Westerhoff's approach is the overarching concern for the future, appropriate for someone performing the role of the visionary.

Westerhoff's impatience with details and scholarly apparatus while trying to "arouse the troops" was also born out a few paragraphs later when he identified his chief audience: "This is primarily a book for those who are interested in acting in the present on behalf of the future; its purpose, to incite discussion; its form, a personal proposal for the church's educational mission. I did not choose to write a carefully reasoned and precise scholarly statement. There are others who have done or will do that job. This book is written with an audience of anxious, searching laymen in mind. I assume that they are interested in the future of the church's educational ministry."[142] Throughout the book, in conversational style, Westerhoff explored a number of these "alternative futures" and did take his own stand, however temporarily.[143]

The book that continued the journey started by Westerhoff in *Values for Tomorrow's Children* began with these words: "*Will Our Children Have Faith?* marks an end and a beginning in my pilgrimage, a journey which began in 1970 when I penned my first tract, *Values for Tomorrow's Children*, as a challenge to dream of an alternative future for the church's educational mission and ministry."[144] He explained further: "Now I am ready to take a stand: to propose an alternative framework for evaluating, planning, and engaging in religious education."[145] These important and revealing words followed: "However, like my first book, this is also a tract. Its purpose is to stimulate reflection, conversation, and perhaps debate."[146] Westerhoff, the "tractarian visionary," never claimed to contribute a scholarly work supporting the positions he was taking. He was still trying to arouse rather than to convince.

The proposal in *Will Our Children Have Faith?* grew out of Westerhoff's analysis of the current educational ministry of the church. He found it to be based upon the "schooling-instructional paradigm" provided by public schools, where "our image of education has been founded upon some sort of a 'school' as the context

---

140. Ibid., p. x.
141. Westerhoff, *Values for Tomorrow's Children*, p. 4.
142. Ibid., p. 5. Did this last sentence imply that the scholars are too busy researching to be truly interested in the future? Westerhoff went on to say that the book was "a tract—nothing more, nothing less," and that it represented his "thought at the moment. I expect that my mind will change as I talk with my readers." Ibid. This is a novel way to write a book, to say the least—to make up your mind as you write, and to warn your readers of changes that may come at any moment.
143. For specifics, see ibid., Chapter IX, "Alternatives."
144. Westerhoff, *Will Our Children Have Faith?*, p. ix.
145. Ibid.
146. Ibid.

and some form of instruction as the means."[147] Westerhoff's solution to the problem: "My contention is that the context or place of religious education needs to be changed from an emphasis on schooling to a community of faith. No longer is it helpful or wise to emphasize schools, teachers, pupils, curricula, classrooms, equipment, and supplies. Instead we need to focus our attention on the radical nature and character of the church as a faith community."[148] The name he attached to this proposal was the "community of faith-enculturation paradigm."[149] In this context, he turned to the socialization processes of the church[150] and to faith development[151] as the more natural means of education in the faith community.

This interest in socialization, culture, and the power of community had been partially explored earlier by Westerhoff and a co-author in *Generation to Generation*.[152] Published in 1974, it fell chronologically between *Values for Tomorrow's Child* and *Will Our Children Have Faith?* and hence provided a clue to where Westerhoff was headed in the later book. Westerhoff as the impatient visionary (along with his partner) identified this work as aiming not at "the church or seminary" but at "providing a resource that attempts to bridge the gap between professional and lay persons involved in religious education."[153] By this they meant: "We chose large issues and handled them in an introductory fashion. Deciding that it was important for these issues and questions to be raised and discussed now, we chose not to wait until we had formulated fully defensible and footnoted positions or a single thesis."[154] The resultant book was a collection of essays by Westerhoff (as religious educator) and Neville (as anthropologist) occasionally in dialogue concerning "the almost unexplored union of anthropology and religious education."[155] It was this initial foray into anthropology that evidently propelled Westerhoff into "taking a stand" in the 1976 book on the faith enculturation issue.

Another effort from Westerhoff's earlier writings is a chapter in a book he edited entitled *A Colloquy on Christian Education*.[156] The article in question was the final one in the book, and he called the article (appropriately enough for purposes here) "The Visionary: Planning for the Future."[157] He began it this way: "Most of us are concerned about the future, but few of us feel confident that we can do very much to shape it. Many of us have dreams about a future we

---

147. Ibid., p. 6.

148. Ibid., p. 51.

149. Ibid., p. 50.

150. See especially Chapter Three, "In Search of Community," ibid., pp. 51-78.

151. See his discussion of "styles of faith" (as differentiated from stages of faith) in ibid., pp. 89-99. These "styles" are not empirically based or tested out as were James Fowler's stages, but represent Westerhoff's speculation. See Fowler's work examined in more detail in Chapter Six, "The Religious Educator as Scientist." For Westerhoff's fuller statement on faith development issues, see John H. Westerhoff III, *Bringing Up Children in the Christian Faith* (Minneapolis: Winston, 1980).

152. John H. Westerhoff III and Gwen Kennedy Neville, *Generation to Generation: Conversations on Religious Education and Culture* (Philadelphia: Pilgrim, 1974).

153. Ibid., p. 11.

154. Ibid., p. 12.

155. Ibid., p. 11.

156. *A Colloquy on Christian Education*, ed. John H. Westerhoff III (New York: Pilgrim Press, 1972).

157. Ibid., pp. 236-245.

would like to see, but few of us believe we have the power to turn those dreams into reality."[158] In the article, Westerhoff proceeded to tell his readers of a procedure he had found called "futures planning" which would enable them to influence the future. In describing such planning, Westerhoff (inadvertently?) ended up describing the role of the visionary: "Futures planning begins with a vision of the future we hope for and only looks at the present and its problems much later. Unlike other styles of planning which begin with the present and attempt to get from that present to the future, futures planning begins with the future we desire and then looks at the present to see what has to happen in the interim so that it might be realized. . . . It rather asks what I want it to be, that is the future that I hope for."[159]

In typical fashion, Westerhoff closed the article with words of confidence and a personal vision of the future: "Obviously, my assumption is that we need to frame an alternative future. I am hopeful it can be done, and I believe futures planning provides the means to bring it about. There is hope."[160] This article, although written early in Westerhoff's career, is representative of his style. He is upbeat, hopeful, and looking for a way to transfer to the layperson what is being developed in the academic community—in this case, "futures planning" developed at Syracuse University—for use in the church.

The next work referenced is *Tomorrow's Church*. Again, the title focused on the future, not the past or present. Of particular interest is Chapter Two, entitled "Visions: The Future from God's Perspective."[161] Earlier in the book, Westerhoff had already said that "our sin is . . . a lost vision, a lost hope, a lost will to act."[162] In this second chapter, he gave the remedy: "One of the central tasks of church education today is to help us regain a vision of God's kingdom. That vision is not unreal. It is a motivating force, a hope by which to live and a direction to travel."[163] Of this vision, Westerhoff said: "It is a vision worthy of our lives and our deaths,"[164] and then he gave this charge to the church and its educators: "Church education must once again be focused upon the development of visionaries who have committed their lives to Jesus' vision of God's kingdom as *the* future for the world and all humanity."[165] In Chapter Three, "Hope: History Is Going Somewhere,"[166] Westerhoff addressed the need for making the dreams real: "It is one thing to dream dreams and long for visions. It is another to face reality. If we are to have hope, it must make sense of the dissonance between dreams and reality."[167] The reality of hope, however, is what Westerhoff believed keeps us alive: "Without hope we are dead. With hope all things are possible. . . . With hope, living for visions makes sense."[168] All of this evidence from

158. Westerhoff, "The Visionary: Planning for the Future," ibid., p. 236.
159. Ibid., p. 241.
160. Ibid., p. 245.
161. Westerhoff, *Tomorrow's Church*, pp. 37-60.
162. Ibid., p. 17.
163. Ibid., p. 37.
164. Ibid., p. 38.
165. Ibid., p. 29.
166. Ibid., pp. 61-77.
167. Ibid., p. 61.
168. Ibid., p. 76.

Tomorrow's Church is surely convincing that Westerhoff has been fulfilling the role of visionary for the religious education world. His writings have touched virtually every theme mentioned in this chapter on the role of the visionary.

Another resource for further evidence of Westerhoff the visionary is *On the Threshold of God's Future*, co-written with Caroline Hughes.[169] This book, again with its forward-looking title, was conceived after watching the television movie *The Day After* (shown in 1983) that described the horrors of nuclear war. The authors stated that it was written in an attempt "to wrestle with this mix of despair and innocence and hope that is the day-to-day reality of all who inhabit 'this fragile earth, our island home,' in these days of extraordinary uncertainty and danger."[170] The book was meant to be a "breathing, moving statement of our personal faith in the God who always has been acting in the sweep of history and who always will act, in spite of everything we can do to block and hinder and impede and kill."[171] Most tellingly, the book was an effort to embrace the future as seen through the eyes of Christians, as when they said: "It is so easy to forget and so important to remember that we Christians are a people who believe in fact that we have seen 'the day after.' . . . The day after has come and gone, and all life has been made new. . . . The old world has passed away; a new world has been born. Our continuing sin is that we do not see it, acknowledge it, and act accordingly. Our sin is our denial of the truth about life."[172]

In the first two chapters of *On the Threshold of God's Future*, Westerhoff and Hughes provided the classic descriptions one would expect from visionaries: "The Christian vision of the future is of all creation's being one; all creatures living in community, prosperity, and security and seeking the well-being of the whole."[173] Then they set the context for the remainder of the book: "We Christians live on the threshold of God's future. . . . By witnessing to an alternative way of life, we become God's agents of transformation in history. Our faith makes real for us what is true."[174] The book goes on to detail the "life, mission, and ministry" of the church as it faces a new millennium with its vision firmly in place.[175]

In this book, as in all his books, Westerhoff was consumed with rendering a vision of the future; with making that future fully "Christian," in the best ecumenical sense of the term; and with finding ways of sketching some basic outlines of procedures and methodologies to accomplish all this. The obvious attendant problem, however, is the lack of any solid research or serious scholarship—at least as far as a scholarly audience is concerned. He is, true to his words, "uncomfortable in dealing with details or following through on a new idea."[176]

This overview has been an attempt to see if Westerhoff could be accurately portrayed as a visionary religious educator. The evidence, as selective as it has

---

169. John H. Westerhoff III and Caroline A. Hughes, *On the Threshold of God's Future* (San Francisco: Harper & Row, 1986).

170. Ibid., p. xii.

171. Ibid., pp. xii-xiii.

172. Ibid., p. 23.

173. Ibid., p. 31.

174. Ibid., p. 32.

175. Ibid., p. 33.

176. This was quoted earlier. See Westerhoff, "A Journey into Self-Understanding," in *Modern Masters of Religious Education*, p. 118.

been, seems overwhelming that this is so.

Although Westerhoff displays his own individual style, fulfilling the role of visionary without the trauma or the angst that many visionaries experience, on the whole he fits the category quite well. No attempt has been made to give an overview of all of Westerhoff's themes or emphases throughout his career but only to describe one way of viewing his approach to the work of religious education.[177]

Evaluation

Evaluation of John Westerhoff comes rather easily, because Westerhoff has already done much of the work for us. He has been self-critical and self-aware of his strengths and weaknesses and has never been hesitant to acknowledge them. Virtually every work by him gives the basis for its own evaluation and if followed makes the task quite simple.

Westerhoff's proclivity to write short, quickly-written tracts[178] makes for short, quickly-read books. They are generally written for the professionally untrained or lightly trained layperson or clergyperson serving in the field, and so while his books lack scholarly apparatus and style, they speak to their target audience. It is not accurate that such a casual approach is typical of all visionaries, since to say this would denigrate the role. With their impatience for present detail, however, there is at least a grain of truth hidden in the thought. One of the temptations of the visionary is to cut corners and to rush ahead without doing either the necessary foundational or follow-up work, especially when such work is rigorous, exacting, time-consuming, and demanding of a comprehensive, well-thought-out perspective.

Related to the lack of detail is Westerhoff's self-identified manner of skipping from one topic or idea to the next in his writings, without warning. This is further evidence of his transitory style and of his personality type. Westerhoff is widely known for his frequent change and even contradiction of position, sometimes even within the same book. Far from seeing this as a weakness, Westerhoff regards his frequent shifts and contradictions as appropriate to his identity as a journalist and tractarian. In *Tomorrow's Church* he made note of his own style: "As a professor, I have done what professors do; I have professed what I believe at this moment in order to stimulate you to think and act for yourselves."[179] Of course what Westerhoff says professors do is precisely the opposite of what professors do. Professors are supposed to base their utterances and writing not on what they believe at the moment, but on what serious solid research and the-

---

177. For example, if this were to be a comprehensive analysis, I would need to show that the term Westerhoff preferred was catechesis rather than religious education. This is just further evidence of the selectivity of this overview for a narrow purpose.

178. Recall that this is the term Westerhoff used to describe his work. See, for example, *Tomorrow's Church*, p. 10.

179. Ibid., p. 130. See a similar statement in *Will Our Children Have Faith?* p. x. The truth, however, is that while John Westerhoff may do this as a professor, it is hardly descriptive of what the great majority of professors would feel comfortable doing. True professors spend the requisite time studying, researching, and thinking out positions in order to provide learners an adequate informational base upon which to pursue individual opinions.

ory show is true or false or probable. In an autobiographical article, Westerhoff wrote: "Most content when skipping from one activity to another, I am like a farmer who plants a field and then goes off before the crop begins to break ground. Instead of staying around to see my vision come to fruition, I am off looking for new fields to plow."[180] It is difficult to criticize someone harshly when they have simply followed their own vision and personality type.[181] It may be enough to say that religious education needs its planters and sowers, as well as some reapers and harvesters.

John Westerhoff is without doubt an example of the visionary within religious education—with all that may imply. He has continually looked to the future and what it can hold if the proper effort is expended. He has made good use of his imagination and has encouraged others to use theirs. He has tried at times to give the people in the churches a sense of what those in academic circles are doing, but Westerhoff is convinced that it is the relatively untrained or lightly trained practitioner who can bring about the necessary changes in religious education. He spoke directly to practitioners of this type, with the result that he is probably the most recognizable religious educator to those outside the circle of academic religious educators.

Westerhoff is to be commended for his desire to find new territory to scout. The best example of this kind of effort is found in *Generation to Generation*, where he and his co-author explored the "middle ground" between religious education and anthropology. The difficulty is that the hard work of synthesizing the deeper research, after these initial conversations, was left to unnamed others to pursue. It is difficult if not impossible to build any kind of lasting and effective program of religious education if positions and stances are to be changed at any given moment. This is further evidence of Westerhoff continuing to plant fields and then going off before the crops begin to break ground, to use his own image again. The obvious question arises: Is anyone tending the plowed-up fields, or are they being left to go to seed?

Another interesting issue related to Westerhoff is his journalistic style and its broad effect on the field of religious education. He has done so much popular writing, and has been read so widely, that many now think the kind of writing he has done is indicative, representative, and normative of all religious education — that short books, with virtually no research or evidence of accompanying scholarship, and that follow the latest fads, are what religious educators are supposed to produce. There is a familiar joke in academic religious education circles that if one wishes to know what Westerhoff will say in his next book, just find out the person(s) with whom Westerhoff spoke last. It should be underscored that Westerhoff undertook the challenge of speaking to the uninitiated and bears responsibility

---

180. Westerhoff, "A Journey into Self-Understanding," in *Modern Masters of Religious Education*, p. 118.

181. It is important to realize that most of the time Westerhoff is providing his own personal view of things and that he is not attempting to give an objective portrayal of an issue or topic based on research data or hard evidence. One must take his comments with this in mind and carefully scrutinize his statements for any factual findings. This is to say that one should be confident that Westerhoff is expressing what he thinks at the moment but that these fleeting opinions should not be accepted as his hard and fast positions.

for showing them the best that is available. Whatever serious scholarship is going on with religious education has not always shown through in his popularizing attempts.

One of the biggest problems Westerhoff presents to the religious educator in the role of visionary is precisely this role modeling. Granted, Westerhoff has the right if not the responsibility to write in his own personal style and to his own particular audience. He has performed in his chosen style admirably. The role of the visionary, however, above and beyond the way that Westerhoff fulfilled it, does not have to be so whimsical, transitory, and nonscholarly based as characterized by the work of Westerhoff. For example, Westerhoff's desire to be popular takes away from his ability to be truly prophetic and to call out the bad as well as the good that he sees in religious education.[182] Just so, there is nothing inherent in the role which rules out solid research and scholarship, and because the one contemporary example cited here has chosen not to fulfill the role in a scholarly manner does not mean that such could not or should not be the case. Westerhoff is but one illustration of the role, and the role is not limited to the way in which he or any other lone individual has gone about fulfilling it.

Following up on the theme of the previous paragraph, Westerhoff's self-acknowledged strong need to be loved and to be well-received blunts, and even possibly destroys the prophetic edge of Westerhoff's visionary stance in that it leads him first to ascertain intuitively or through conversation whether or not a particular visionary idea he seeks to advance will be accepted or rejected by others, especially by persons whom he regards as important for one reason or another. Thus, ironically, Westerhoff is controlled by the very persons whom he seeks to influence. Another unfortunate (and previously mentioned) fallout from Westerhoff's need to be loved and popular is that it often is trendy and faddish rather than solid and well-grounded.

The weaknesses of Westerhoff's visionary work, then, are just as obvious as his strengths. He leaves to others the filling in of the details of his visions, such as how to implement the creative ideas and suggestions, while he is off ahead imagining new thoughts. If the hard work of actually creating a better world is simultaneously being carried out by someone, then the process works well enough. If the religious educator is seen only as a dreamer who does not have the ability or the strength to turn those dreams into reality, then not only the individual but the field and the world at large are so much the poorer. The possibilities inherent in the role of the visionary are quite real, as are the dangers within the role of the dreamer, and both are apparent throughout the work of John Westerhoff.

Representative Teaching Procedure: Brainstorming

There is no way to teach an individual or a group to have a vision. Either the vision is seen—experienced—or it is not. What can be influenced is the

---

182. Granted, Westerhoff does rail against the "schooling-instructional paradigm," but he does not explain what this entails or who is behind such an approach. The reader is left with a vague sense of indictment but not against anyone or anything in particular. See, for example, Westerhoff, *Will Our Children Have Faith?*, p. 9.

preparation of the environment for this kind of "seeing" to take place and the conditioning of awareness to make people sensitive to the need for seeing the future. It will come as no surprise that visionaries are not created by means of following a teaching procedure, only that the preconditions and the environment can be set up in ways so as to allow and encourage the development of the true visionary.

A teaching procedure that keeps faith with the inspirational qualities of the visionary and yet does give some elementary structure to the facilitative process is formally known as "organized ideation," but more popularly and descriptively called "brainstorming."[183] Alex Osborn is credited with introducing this procedure, which now seems so widespread that it is difficult to imagine when it was not being used. As he phrased it: "Brainstorming has since evolved as a principle—the principle of suspended judgment. And two types of brainstorming are now recognized—group ideation and individual ideation, with the brainstorming principle applying to each type of effort."[184] The group process is the focus of the present section.

Brainstorming, as prescribed by Osborn, has four basic rules that need to be followed scrupulously. He presented them this way:

(1) *Criticism is ruled out.* Adverse judgment of ideas must be withheld until later.

(2) *"Free-wheeling" is welcomed.* The wilder the idea, the better; it is easier to tame down than to think up.

(3) *Quantity is wanted.* The greater the number of ideas, the more the likelihood of winners.

(4) *Combination and improvement is sought.* In addition to contributing ideas of their own, participants should suggest how ideas of others can be turned into better ideas; or how two or more ideas can be joined into still another idea.[185]

Little other direction or structure is necessary. Osborn did make two additional suggestions. One was that there "should be a written record of all ideas suggested. This list should be reportorial rather than stenographic. At times, the ideas will tumble out so fast that even a shorthand expert could hardly record them verbatim."[186] The second aspect Osborn stressed was: "The spirit of the brainstorm is important. Self-encouragement is needed almost as much as mutual encouragement. A perfectionism complex will throttle effort and abort ideas."[187]

The task here is for learners to be freed from the perceived—or real—boundaries of mundane thinking and envisioning that too often encircle religious education so that they can stir up some new ideas and produce some new visions. In

---

183. "It was in 1938 when I first employed organized ideation in the company I then headed. The early participants dubbed our efforts 'Brainstorming Sessions': and quite properly so because, in this case, 'brainstorm' means using the *brain* to *storm* a problem." Alex Osborn, *Applied Imagination: Principles and Procedures of Creative Problem-Solving*, rev. ed. (New York: Scribner's, 1957), p. 80.

184. Ibid.

185. Ibid., p. 84.

186. Ibid., pp. 84-85.

187. Ibid., p. 85. For more directions on the group ideation process, see Chapter Nineteen, "Detailed Procedure of Group Brainstorming," ibid., pp. 227-247.

following Osborn's procedure,[188] the religious educator has responsibility for getting the process started and then for "getting out of the way" of the learners as the ideas begin to flow.

Experiential Simulation: Expanding Awareness

Just as it is impossible to teach an individual or a group to have a vision, it is useless to try to simulate the experiencing of a vision. Those who have visions have no need for simulations, and those who do not have visions cannot artificially feel the full impact of what it is like. As in the previous section, the best that can happen is to produce the conditions and the environment conducive to receiving visions, and then to hope for the best. The appearance of visions is not at the visionaries' beck and call, but their appearance can be encouraged and nurtured. Two suggestions are offered below that may help facilitate the process of expanding awareness, but be assured there are actually innumerable ways of achieving this goal. The attempt here is to provide some guidelines for initially opening up the boundaries of consciousness, and then seeing what develops.

One suggestion for stimulating the appearance of visions is to engage in guided imagery. Although designed originally for children, an excellent resource for this activity is *Spinning Inward* by Maureen Murdock.[189] In this book, Murdock described guided imagery as a tool to unlock creativity and provided the following metaphor: "Using imagery is like eating an artichoke. When we peel off the tough outer petals of the artichoke, we find the softer, more subtle inner petals and tasty core of the fruit. Imagery works in a similar way. The thick outer petals are like the high-level tensions that exist in our everyday environment. As we shut out the distractions of our hectic daily lives, we begin to find a wealth of creativity and wisdom within ourselves."[190] This type of experience is nothing new to the visionary, but it may seem somewhat mysterious to the uninitiated who have not tapped the inner resources as fully.

Murdock provided numerous exercises for educators to use for unlocking children's creativity through guided imagery and gave instructions as to how to facilitate the process. There is certainly no reason that these same exercises would not be useful and appropriate for use by adults. In fact, a large part of guided imagery is to reenter the world of children, where fantasy and fiction are normal and expected. This indeed is the world which the visionary naturally inhabits.

One way to utilize Murdock's book, or any other similar resource, is to read it in isolation—by yourself—as most other books are read. The result is a simulation of her suggested simulations. This is obviously not the most productive way, however. The best way to encounter guided imagery is to have someone

---

188. There does not seem to be a teaching procedure in Bruce Joyce and Marsha Weil, *Models of Teaching*, 3rd ed. (Englewood Cliffs, N.J.: Prentice-Hall, 1986) that relates directly to this concept.

189. Maureen Murdock, *Spinning Inward: Using Guided Imagery with Children for Learning, Creativity and Relaxation*, rev. ed. (Boston: Shambhala, 1987).

190. Ibid., p. 10.

actually guide you through it, so that the preferred manner is to have someone else read the book aloud, leaving you free to experience the imagery. Incidentally, the easiest—and most fun—way to enter this "other world" is with a group of children. They have fewer of the inhibitions and prejudices that plague the "grown-ups" of *this* world and make the journey inward—and outward—a trip full of excitement and enjoyment.

Another suggestion for a simulation is to experience an encounter group[191] whose primary purpose is the expansion of awareness.[192] This kind of activity is fully consonant with the theme of this chapter on the visionary, in that the visionary must know himself or herself in order to understand the visions.[193] The first two dimensions of the visionary mentioned in this chapter, the witness and the prophet, are the ones most directly affected by this process: The witness gives an account of what he or she sees and hears in the present, and the prophet predicts the outcome of the future based on the observation of the current direction of events. These dimensions are both based upon the awareness of the individual. This awareness the religious educator can help attend to, and then the visions themselves can begin to arise of their own accord.

William Schutz described the fundamentals of an encounter group: "An encounter group has no pre-set agenda. Instead, it uses the attention and interaction of group members as the focus of attention. The process of achieving personal growth begins with the exploration of feelings within the group and proceeds to wherever the group members take it. A strong effort is made to create an atmosphere of openness and honesty in communicating with each other. Ordinarily, a strong group solidarity develops and group members are able to use each other very profitably."[194] The essence of the groups, however, revolves around increased awareness, as Schutz pointed out: "And so it appears that these are methods to help us experience ourselves anew; to be able to cope more effectively with our feelings of unworthiness, ineptitude, coldness; and to

---

191. Carl Rogers defined an encounter group as tending "to emphasize personal growth and development and improvement of interpersonal communication and relationships through an experiential process." Carl R. Rogers, *Carl Rogers on Encounter Groups* (New York: Harper & Row, 1970), pp. 4-5. Other terms are also frequently employed to refer to the same basic activity, such as T-groups, sensitivity training, and creativity workshops. See these different labels defined and differentiated in ibid., pp. 4-5.

192. See this discussed as a teaching procedure in Chapter 11, "Increasing Awareness," in Joyce and Weil, *Models of Teaching*, pp. 184-202. They said of what they called awareness training: "The purpose of awareness training is to increase self-understanding and awareness of one's own behavior and that of others and also to help students develop alternative patterns for their social development." Ibid., p. 185.

193. William Schutz was one of the people responsible for the popularity of encounter groups, and he identified the primary features of them as "openness and honesty. A man must be willing to let himself be known to himself and others. He must express and explore his feelings and open up areas long dormant and possibly painful, with the faith that in the long run the pain will give way to a release of vast potential for creativity and joy. This is an exhilarating and frightening prospect, one which is often accompanied by agony, but which usually leads to ecstasy." William C. Schutz, *Joy: Expanding Human Awareness* (New York: Grove Press, 1967), pp. 16-17.

194. Ibid., p. 21; refer as well to pp. 187-189 for more description of the encounter group. Also see Chapter Two, "The Process of the Encounter Group," in Rogers, *Carl Rogers on Encounter Groups*, pp. 14-42.

come to accept, respect, and love ourselves more."[195]

The effects and results of the encounter session are ultimately left to each participant to determine and utilize. Those wishing to enact the role of visionary can use this increased personal and social awareness to feed and nurture the development of visions. The visionary must always start the process of "seeing" from within himself or herself and from within the environmental context in which he or she exists. The way to the future has its origin in the existential present.

What can be too easily missed in a description of this kind of experience is the intentional inclusion of the affective domain. However sterile or bland encounter groups may appear to be on paper, they are everything but that in real life.[196] This is important to understanding the groups themselves, certainly, but even more important to note about the role of the visionary. The visionary does not argue the people into movement toward the vision. The visionary moves people through animating the emotions and by allowing the vision to draw the people forward. The hope of the "promised land" has tremendous power, and the visionary uses this magnetic power to its full extent. This suggestion to increase awareness exemplifies this means of energizing and empowering those that catch the vision.

Summary

This chapter has attempted to give a taste of what it is like to be a visionary and to stress the importance of this role for religious education. The visionary is not a role easily entered, since it requires such an intensely personal and concentrated effort at seeing and perceiving, and since it makes the individual so publicly vulnerable. The life of the visionary can be a tortured and exhausting one, but as these lines from a song explain, it is at the same time a vivid, exciting, and restless lifestyle:

> The light is long,
> The sun is low,
> I'm riding fast across this dusty road—
> But I don't want to be,
> No, I don't want to be.
> Above the ridge an eagle flies
> In lazy circles in the western skies.
> I want to fly with him—
> I want to walk the spirit trail.[197]

---

195. Schutz, *Joy: Expanding Human Awareness*, p. 222.

196. As Rogers noted: "There are times when the term feedback is far too mild to describe the interactions that take place—when it is better said that one individual *confronts* another, directly 'leveling' with him. Such confrontations can be positive, but frequently they are decidedly negative." Rogers, *Carl Rogers on Encounter Groups*, p. 31. For those that prefer a more playful approach to self awareness, see Claus-Jürgen Höper, Ulrike Kutzleb, Alke Stobbe, and Bertam Weber, *Awareness Games: Personal Growth through Group Interaction*, trans. Hilary Davies (New York: St. Martin's Press, 1975).

197. Dan Fogelberg, "The Spirit Trail," *The Wild Places* (C.B.S. Records, 1990).

Without the ones who "walk the spirit trail," despite the costs, all would be left to endure walking the dusty roads. The call of the religious educator as visionary is never to lose sight of the eagle's flight.

Figure 12 summarizes the characteristics of the religious educator as visionary discussed throughout the chapter.

Figure 12: The Religious Educator as Visionary	
Dimensions of the Role	Witness
	Prophet
	Casuist
	Charismatic
Aim	Animation
Function	Insight
Primary Virtues	Inspiration
	Hope
Activity	Imagining
Shadow Role	Daydreamer
Faith Tradition Resource	Mysticism
Historical Personage	Martin Luther King Jr.
Contemporary Example	John H. Westerhoff III
Representative Teaching Procedure	Brainstorming
Experiential Simulation	Expanding Awareness

Chapter Eleven

The Religious Educator
as Revolutionary

Every role in this book addresses change in one form or another, but this particular one has its own distinctive and unmistakable attitude toward it. The religious educator as revolutionary approaches change head on, without benefit of subtlety or mystery. Absolutely no doubt is left as to whether or not change is going to take place when a revolutionary is in charge; all that is left to be determined is when, what kind, and how much change will result.[1] Even these uncertainties are not left unattended for long. The revolutionary does not wait passively for an opportunity for change eventually to develop but takes intentional steps to see that the situation does indeed develop in a way amenable to his or her intentions—and sooner is usually preferable to later for the revolutionary.

Such directness and intentionality toward constructive but fundamental change is often both unusual and unexpected coming from a religious educator. To some minds, the whole concept of the religious educator as revolutionary sounds like an oxymoron. Surely these are two terms that do not logically go together! If, for example, the religious educator is perceived *only* (or even primarily) as an individual responsible for transmitting religious culture, as the "keeper of the flame," and as the guardian of the heritage of the inviolate past, then indeed there is no common ground between the revolutionary and the religious educator. The true revolutionary is out to upset the status quo, and for some the expressed mission of the religious educator seems to be just the oppo-

---

1. One of the ways to define and understand revolution is to view it as "simply the most radical form of social change." Anthony D. Smith, *The Concept of Social Change: A Critique of the Functionalist Theory of Social Change* (London: Routledge and Kegan Paul, 1973), p. 96. While Smith himself did not agree with this view of revolution, he gave a good overview and evaluation of it in Chapter Five, "Revolution," ibid., pp. 96-129.

site—to guard *against* such an attack on traditional values at all costs. As acknowledged elsewhere in this book, the religious educator does at times have the task of being the conservator of the past,[2] but by no means should this be construed as the entire or as the primary purpose of the religious educator.

One of the ways to introduce the image of the religious educator as revolutionary is to distinguish early on what the image is *not*, or at least what it is not in its entirety. First and foremost the revolutionary in this chapter should not be understood as the political revolutionary—the person who uses power and force to gain control of people, institutions, or of ideology.[3] Such an image is indeed incongruent and inconsistent with the genuine role of the religious educator; in even stronger language, it is in opposition to the way the religious educator is being imaged in this chapter and throughout the book. John Pottenger noted this dangerous and threatening combination: "Whether for destructive or constructive ends, the mixture of ideas and power has always been volatile."[4] For example, true political revolution is what Malcolm Little (1925-1965), better known as Malcolm X, experienced and advocated. He described this kind of revolution from first-hand experience: "Revolution is bloody, revolution is hostile, revolution knows no compromise, revolution overturns and destroys everything that gets in its way. And you, sitting around here like knots on a wall, saying, 'I'm going to love these folks no matter how much they hate me.' No, you need a revolution. Whoever heard of a revolution where they lock arms . . . singing 'We Shall Overcome'? You don't do that in a revolution. You don't do any singing, you're too busy swinging."[5] Here is the revolution of might, power, and politics, stripped bare of fantasy, and it is surely what very few religious educators actually desire to experience or advocate. The image here needs to be quite different from this commonly associated definition.

A second role distinct from that of the revolutionary is the image of the visionary. The role of the revolutionary comes at this point in the book, following the visionary, because it is both continuous and discontinuous with the role of the visionary. The revolutionary may and probably does have a vision and is prepared to exert all possible energies and resources to achieve its reality. The continuity relates to the magnetism of that vision which draws people into its future—as articulated and crystallized by the visionary. The discontinuity is that a visionary generally is not ready or equipped to take the radical step of actually starting and leading a revolution. The visionary allows the vision to do the pulling into the future. The revolutionary wants to bring that future in now and is willing to go about the task of filling in the details and the strategies that the visionary often eschews in favor of more visions. Most revolutionaries are

2. For one example, see Chapter Eight, "The Religious Educator as Storyteller." Of course, even there the storyteller is not content only to pass on information but to interpret and apply stories to the present.

3. A good study of these forces is *Power and Control: Social Structures and Their Transformation*, ed. Tom R. Burns and Walter Buckley (London: Sage Publications, 1976).

4. John R. Pottenger, *The Political Theory of Liberation Theology: Toward a Reconvergence of Social Values and Social Science* (Albany: State University of New York Press, 1989), p. 34.

5. Malcolm X, "Message to the Grass Roots," in *Malcolm X Speaks: Selected Speeches and Statements*, ed. George Breitman (London: Secker and Warburg, 1965), p. 9.

visionaries, but few visionaries are revolutionaries. The difference is devising and implementing the means to make the vision real, whatever the ultimate costs.[6]

The revolutionary must also be differentiated from the mere reformer. The reformer is content to work *within* the structures and rules of the particular organization and society to achieve the desired ends peaceably and in orderly fashion. The revolutionary may also initially try these same means but is neither hesitant nor afraid to step *outside* the boundaries when the present structures and rules are not sufficiently responsive.[7] Indeed, revolution is aimed at fundamental change, which virtually requires strong and sometimes discomforting short-term actions for the achievement of longer-term purposes. The issue may very well be that the revolutionary may have to change the system itself—while the reformer is content to stay within prescribed rules and boundaries.

These few images of what does not describe the fullness of the revolutionary prepares the way for the positive statements about the role of the revolutionary that make up the rest of the chapter. The role, properly understood and interpreted, is not one to be feared or denied, but honored and valued. The revolutionary spends his or her life seeing that tomorrow will be better today. How this kind of constructive change is facilitated and accomplished is the subject of the sections that follow.

Dimensions of the Role

For a more complete picture concerning the nature of the revolutionary, four dimensions of the role are examined: the dimensions of innovator, planner, agitator, and change agent. Taken separately, these dimensions may appear to be rather mundane and nonthreatening. Taken together, they become a synergism of vitality, drive—and potential threat, at least to the serenity of the status quo. The four dimensions offered here are not meant to be comprehensive or exclusive but are mere descriptors that serve to flesh out the role. Only enough information to introduce these dimensions follows, and then the discussion continues regarding specifics of the role. The role of the revolutionary is complex, and these dimensions serve to demonstrate the range of possible components.

Innovator

An innovation has been defined as "an idea, practice, or object perceived as new by an individual," with the "newness" of the innovation being expressed "in knowledge, in attitude, or regarding a decision to use it."[8] Although many characteristics of innovations could be cited, at least five are instructive for grasping their nature and value. First is *relative advantage*, which is how much "an inno-

---

6. Further clarification of this point is found in the following dimension of planner.

7. See Russell L. Ackoff, *Redesigning the Future: A Systems Approach to Societal Problems* (New York: Wiley, 1974), pp. 26-31.

8. Everett M. Rogers with F. Floyd Shoemaker, *Communication of Innovations: A Cross-Cultural Approach*, 2nd ed. (New York: Free Press, 1971), p. 19. Another, similar definition of an innovation is "any thought, behavior, or thing that is new because it is qualitatively different from existing forms." H.G. Barnett, *Innovation: The Basis of Cultural Change* (New York: McGraw-Hill, 1953), p. 7.

vation is perceived as better than the idea it supersedes."[9] Second is *compatibility*, or how "an innovation is perceived as being consistent with the existing values, past experiences, and needs of the receivers."[10] Third is *complexity*, where the issue is "the degree to which an innovation is perceived as difficult to understand and use."[11] Fourth is *trialability*, "the degree to which an innovation may be experimented with on a limited basis."[12] Fifth is *observability*, where "the results of an innovation are visible to others."[13]

In like manner, then, innovators themselves are the persons who devise and bring into existence these new ideas, practices, or objects. Many terms can be used to describe the qualities of innovators, such as insatiable curiosity, bulldog tenacity, and incurable optimism. The essence of the innovator, though, was best captured this way: "The salient value of the innovator is venturesomeness. He desires the hazardous, the rash, the daring, and the risky. The innovator also must be willing to accept an occasional setback when one of the new ideas he adopts proves unsuccessful."[14]

While certainly "venturesomeness" must be the distinctive quality of the innovator, as well as of the revolutionary, the aspects of "the hazards, the rash, the daring, and the risky" should not be presumed to refer necessarily to physical or political kinds of feats or derring-do. In religious education, especially, the risks that need to be taken for innovation's sake deal much more with the areas of cognition, affectivity, and spirituality, but the demand for innovation is just as real, and just as threatening, as in any other field. One of the great historical examples of this kind of innovator is John Amos Comenius (1592-1670).

Comenius stands as one of the monumental figures in educational revolution, but he went about it for the most part in a quite nonpolitical fashion.[15] To be sure, he was deeply and involuntarily enmeshed in politics because of the turbulent times in which he lived, and his entire life was marked by the raging political violence that seemed to follow him wherever he traveled.[16] He is remembered and revered, though, for his magnificent and distinctly revolutionary plan for education. Just by reading the "Greeting to the Reader" at the opening of his masterpiece, *The Great Didactic* (*Didactica Magna*, written 1633-1638), one quickly grasps the innovative scope of Comenius' educational scheme: "We venture to promise a Great Didactic, that is to say, the whole art of teaching all things to all men, and indeed of teaching them with certainty; . . . further, of teaching

---

9. Rogers with Shoemaker, *Communication of Innovations*, p. 22. Also see ibid., pp. 138-145.

10. Ibid. Also see ibid., pp. 145-154.

11. Ibid. Also see ibid., pp. 154-155.

12. Ibid., p. 23. Also see ibid., p. 155.

13. Ibid. Also see ibid., pp. 155-157.

14. Ibid., p. 183.

15. For an examination of Comenius and his relationship with politics, see Chapter Eight, "Reform," in John Edward Sadler, *J. A. Comenius and the Concept of Universal Education* (London: Allen and Unwin, 1966), pp. 164-186.

16. For one of the better biographical treatments of Comenius, see Matthew Spinka, *John Amos Comenius: That Incomparable Moravian*, 2nd ed. (New York: Russell and Russell, 1967). In regard to Comenius' constant travels, see especially Chapter Six, "The Wandering Scholar: The Swedish Interlude," ibid., pp. 90-120, and Chapter Seven, "The Wandering Scholar: The Hungarian Period," ibid., pp. 121-133.

them pleasantly, that is to say, without annoyance or aversion on the part of the teacher or pupil, but rather with the greatest enjoyment for both; . . . further, of teaching them thoroughly, not superficially and showily; . . . Lastly, we wish to prove all this *a priori*, that is to say, from the unalterable nature of the matter itself . . . that we may lay the foundations of the universal art of founding universal schools."[17] Just within this one brief passage by Comenius these educational innovations for his time period are apparent: the teaching of all people of both sexes, regardless of social class or parentage;[18] the education provided should be comprehensive;[19] the education should be done humanely and without harsh discipline;[20] the teaching act should be performed skillfully;[21] the educational process should follow the direction of nature;[22] and schooling should be provided from infancy to maturity through different types of institutions in each community.[23] Many other similarly innovative suggestions for his day can be found throughout Comenius' writings—and many of them continue to be used, developed, or debated today.

Innovators like Comenius are people initially out ahead of the pack, introducing new ideas and procedures that are revolutionary for their time, but often these same innovative ideas, once incorporated into practice, are soon accepted as normal routine.[24] The ironic nature of being an innovator, and a revolutionary, is that one can sometimes measure success by the rapidity with which innovative and revolutionary ideas or suggestions are regarded as commonplace! This was certainly true of Comenius, and he set a worthy example for all religious educators in the effort to become both innovative and revolutionary—at least temporarily.

Planner

Describing the revolutionary as planner may initially strike one as the antithesis of the true revolutionary rather than as a helpful or identifying characteristic.

---

17. John Amos Comenius, *The Great Didactic*, trans. and ed. M.W. Keatinge (New York: Russell and Russell, 1967; reissue of the 2nd ed. of 1919), Part II, p. 5.

18. See Chapter Nine, "All the Young of Both Sexes Should be Sent to School," ibid., pp. 66-69.

19. "For we must take strong and vigorous measures that no man, in his journey through life, may encounter anything so unknown to him that he cannot pass sound judgment upon it and turn it to its proper use without serious error." Ibid., p. 70.

20. See Chapter Twenty-Four, "Of School Discipline," ibid., pp. 249-254.

21. See Chapter Eighteen, "The Principles of Thoroughness in Teaching and Learning," ibid., pp. 142-159.

22. See Chapter Fourteen, "The Exact Order of Instruction Must be Borrowed from Nature," ibid., pp. 98-103.

23. Comenius proposed a "School of the Mother's Knee" for infants; the Vernacular School for childhood; the Latin-School or Gymnasium for "boyhood"; and the University for youth. Comenius wrote: "A Mother-School should exist in every house, a Vernacular School in every hamlet and village, a Gymnasium in every city, and a University in every kingdom or in every province." See ibid., p. 256.

24. "Adopter categories" help clarify this concept, as they provide "classifications of members of a social system on the basis of innovativeness." Rogers with Shoemaker, *Communication of Innovations*, p. 27. The movement is from innovators to early adopters, to early majority, to late majority, and finally to laggards. Individuals can be regarded as innovators only so long as few others have as yet adopted their suggestions. Also see ibid., pp. 183-185, for further discussion. See Chapter Ten, "The Advocates of Change," in Barnett, *Innovation*, pp. 291-312, for a parallel discussion.

Depending on the definition and attitude one has toward planning, this presumption of it as an antithesis to the revolutionary may very be accurate. Russell Ackoff, in a fascinating book *Redesigning the Future*,[25] described four types of planners, and indeed three of them are quite divergent from the role of the revolutionary. A brief summary of the four types of planners as outlined by Ackoff will not only explain the potentially revolutionary dimension of a planner but will significantly help in explicating the fuller identity of the genuine revolutionary.

One of these types is the *inactivists*: "Inactivists are satisfied with the way things are and the way things are going. Hence they believe that any intervention in the course of events is unlikely to improve them and is very likely to make them worse. Inactivists take a do-nothing posture."[26] Obviously, this approach to planning has little to do with the revolutionary, other than to describe what he or she is not like. A second type of planner is the *reactivists*: "Reactivists prefer a previous state to the one they are in and they believe things are going from bad to worse. Hence they do not only resist change but they try to unmake previous changes and return to where they once were. They are generally nostalgic about the 'good old days.'"[27] This is the kind of attitude and direction of movement the revolutionary is trying to overcome, not emulate. The third type of planner that Ackoff described is the *preactivists*: "They believe the future is essentially uncontrollable but that they can accelerate its coming and control its effects on them. Therefore, they plan for the future; they do not plan the future itself."[28] Even more tellingly Ackoff said of this type: "Preactivists seek change *within* the system but not change *of* the system or its environment. They are reformers, not revolutionaries. They seek neither to ride with the tide nor to buck it but to ride in front of it and get to where it is going before it does."[29] While not as abusive of true planning as the previous two types, preactivists are still not revolutionaries. Preactivists simply predict and prepare.[30]

The fourth type of planner is the one that characterizes the true revolutionary— the *interactivists*. Ackoff wrote of this fourth type: "Interactivists are not willing to settle for the current state of their affairs or the way they are going, and they will not return to the past. They want to design a desirable future and invent ways of bringing it about. They believe we are capable of controlling a significant part of the future as well as its effect on us. They try to *prevent*, not merely prepare for, threats, and to *create*, not merely exploit, opportunities."[31] Further distinguishing the revolutionary type of planner from the ones previously identified, Ackoff wrote: "Interactivists are not willing to settle for survival or growth. They seek self-development, self-realization, and self-control: an

---

25. Russell L. Ackoff, *Redesigning the Future: A Systems Approach to Societal Problems* (New York: Wiley, 1974). A good contrast to the approach Ackoff advocated can be found in the more conventional and orthodox text on planning theory by Melville C. Branch, *Planning: Aspects and Applications* (New York: Wiley, 1966).

26. Ackoff, *Redesigning the Future*, p. 22.

27. Ibid., p. 24.

28. Ibid., p. 25.

29. Ibid., p. 26.

30. Ibid., p. 25.

31. Ibid., p. 26.

increased ability to design and control their own destinies."[32] Perhaps the most revelatory characteristics of this kind of planner are these: "Interactivists are radicals; they try to change the foundations as well as the superstructure of society and its institutions and organizations. They desire neither to resist, ride with, nor ride ahead of the tide; they try to redirect it."[33]

When planning is viewed from the perspective of the interactivist, then it is clear why the revolutionary must be interested in and committed to planning. As Ackoff said: "Planning provides us with a way of acting now that can make the kind of future we want more likely."[34] This kind of planning allows the revolutionary to pull in and to create the future that he or she desires, because the future to the interactivist—and to the revolutionary—is malleable rather than fixed and predetermined. Ackoff said of this stance in another context: "Planning is predicated on the belief that the future can be improved by active intervention now."[35] If the revolutionary were not convinced that his or her action would make a difference, then there would be no reason to be involved in any revolutionary activity. Even more, the revolutionary is aware that the sort of fundamental change they are imagining[36] will not happen without careful and detailed planning.[37] The revolutionary is not like the visionary in this respect, where the visionary is content to dispense the vision but remains relatively uninterested in attending to the specifics. The genuine revolutionary is actually consumed with planning the details, because this is the way to "reinvent the system,"[38] or as Ackoff also expressed it, of designing the idealized future.[39]

Agitator

Turning to the dimension of agitator within the role of the revolutionary begins to make the role even more identifiable, and possibly more threatening, because the stated purpose of the agitator is to cause comfortable people to become uncomfortable.[40] Such an element or intent is not usually appreciated by the status quo, for obvious reasons. The agitator is like the "troubler of Israel,"[41] and he or she is quite often seen as nothing more than a troublemaker.[42] There is

---

32. Ibid.

33. Ibid., p. 27.

34. Ibid., p. 33.

35. Russell L. Ackoff, *A Concept of Corporate Planning* (New York: Wiley, 1970), p. 23.

36. The term Ackoff used here was "idealizing"—planning "to do better in the future than the best that presently appears possible." Ackoff, *Redesigning the Future*, p. 26.

37. Guidance on the particulars of going about this kind of planning can be found in ibid., pp. 28-30, as well as throughout Ackoff, *Concept of Corporate Planning*.

38. See this concept discussed in Ackoff, *Concept of Corporate Planning*, pp. 59-63.

39. Ackoff, *Redesigning the Future*, p. 30.

40. The more technical term for the activity of the agitator is that he or she creates *disequilibrium*, which "occurs when the rate of change is too rapid to permit the social system to adjust." Rogers with Shoemaker, *Communication of Innovations*, p. 339. Disequilibrium upsets *equilibrium* or "the tendency of a system to achieve a balance among the various forces operating within and upon it." Ibid.

41. What Ahab called Elijah in Kings 18:37, NRSV.

42. For an interesting and somewhat parallel discussion, see Chapter Seven, "Diakonia: The Ministry of Troublemaking," in Maria Harris, *Portrait of Youth Ministry* (New York: Paulist, 1981), pp. 173-203.

a ring of truth to this accusation. The agitator is indeed a troublemaker, but for a reason and toward a goal. Unlike the common misconception, then, the agitator is much more than a societal "pain in the neck."

In his discussion of planning theory, Russell Ackoff said that one of the requirements of the planner is to create an amount of "disquiet," a sense of dissatisfaction and unrest in those participating in the planning activity so that something new can be envisioned and created.[43] The Brazilian educator Paulo Freire has suggested that educators carry responsibility for *conscientização*, the "making aware" of the cultural circumstances, so that those in the culture can change it in ways that will liberate them.[44] Neil Postman and Charles Weingartner described teaching as a subversive activity, with its main goal to cultivate learners who are "experts at 'crap detecting.'"[45] All of these are various examples of people exemplifying the dimension of agitator. All, incidentally, are also much-loved and deeply appreciated by the powers that be!

Leon Festinger has shed light on the dimension of agitator through his study of cognitive dissonance. He defined dissonance as "the existence of nonfitting relations among cognitions," affirming that dissonance in and of itself is indeed a "motivating factor in its own right."[46] Festinger defined cognition as "any knowledge, opinion, or belief about the environment, about oneself, or about one's behavior."[47] Therefore, he stated that "cognitive dissonance can be seen as an antecedent condition which leads to activity oriented toward dissonance reduction."[48] In other words, what the religious educator can do as the agitator is to introduce cognitive dissonance intentionally into an otherwise calm and satisfied environment, thus creating the conditions conducive to and providing the necessary motivation for constructive change—an eventual (if temporary) reduction of the dissonance, since as Festinger noted, "as soon as dissonance occurs there will be pressures to reduce it."[49]

The agitator, then, is one who stirs up trouble so that problems can be recognized and dealt with in a constructive manner, rather than ignored or accepted as a given. In this sense the dimension of agitator is indispensable to the rev-

---

43. See, for example, Ackoff, *Redesigning the Future*, pp. 26-32.

44. See Paulo Freire, *The Pedagogy of the Oppressed*, trans. Myra Bergman Ramos (New York: Seabury, 1968).

45. Neil Postman and Charles Weingartner, *Teaching as a Subversive Activity* (New York: Delacorte, 1969), p. 3. The authors noted that this idea arose from Ernest Hemingway, who described the one essential ingredient for a great writer is that "a person must have a built-in, shockproof crap detector." Quoted in ibid, p. 3.

46. Leon Festinger, *A Theory of Cognitive Dissonance* (Stanford: Stanford University Press, 1957), p. 3. In another place, Festinger explained that "two elements are dissonant if, for one reason or another, they do not fit together." Ibid., p. 12.

47. Ibid., p. 3.

48. Ibid. One of Festinger's basic hypotheses for the study was this: "The existence of dissonance, being psychologically uncomfortable, will motivate the person to try to reduce the dissonance and achieve consonance." Ibid.

49. Ibid., p. 5. The premise was more formally stated this way: "The presence of dissonance gives rise to pressures to reduce or eliminate the dissonance. The strength of the pressures to reduce the dissonance is a function of the magnitude of the dissonance." Ibid., p. 18. For further studies on this topic, see also Leon Festinger (with collaborators), *Conflict, Decision, and Dissonance* (Stanford: Stanford University Press, 1964).

olutionary. The revolutionary does not sit awaiting passively for a cause to arise and an invitation for action to be delivered. The revolutionary identifies the problem, and develops it into a cause that demands attention.[50] The revolutionaries of the American colonies in the 1770s knew this. Taxation without representation was the issue, but without some agitation it engendered little public excitement. A masqueraded night raid on a British ship, termed the "Boston tea party," sufficiently aroused the people, galvanized wide-spread interest, and sparked an eventual call to arms. It was not until the idea was turned into what today would be called a "media event" that it spurred the colonists to action.

Revolution requires that someone light the fuse that sets off the explosion. It is the agitator who obliges by striking the match. In the present context, the religious educator holds the matchbook, and the problems are waiting to be ignited. The means to produce a reaction are many and varied—from drastic measures to quiet, considered conversation. The goal is to create at least some measure of disquiet—to agitate.

Change Agent

The revolutionary is not content only to strike the match, however. The revolutionary is fully committed to some kind of process of "fanning the flame," guaranteeing that the fire of revolutionary and fundamental change burns long enough and hot enough to destroy sufficient amounts of the old structure so that a new one can, and will have to be, erected. This introduces the dimension of the revolutionary as change agent—the one who ensures that the revolution will have lasting and permanent effect.[51] Gerald Zaltman and Robert Duncan followed this line of thinking when they defined the change agent as "any individual or group operating to change the status quo in the client's system such that the individuals involved must relearn how to perform their roles."[52] This kind of activity was the subject of the famous quote by Karl Marx: "The philosophers have only interpreted the world in various ways; the point is to change it."[53] As was true in the previous dimension of the agitator, however, the change agent does not have to be a flamboyant personality[54] or engage in outrageous acts that attract attention.[55] Writing scholarly books or articles, teaching a Sunday school class,

---

50. The agitator, however, does not necessarily have to be militant to be true to his or her calling. One can go about the activity of agitation quietly, using such ordinary means as writing letters to concerned parties or using the telephone to rally support, as surely as the more raucous style of being on the front lines of a protest march—and often the results of the subtle approach are much more effective. In other words, there are a great many ways of fulfilling the dimension of agitator.

51. A more formal definition of change agent is "a professional who influences innovation-decisions in a direction deemed desirable by a change agency," Rogers with Shoemaker, *Communication of Innovations*, p. 227.

52. Gerald Zaltman and Robert Duncan, *Strategies for Planned Change* (New York: Wiley, 1977), p. 186.

53. Karl Marx, "Theses on Feuerbach," in *Selected Writings*, ed. David McLellan (Oxford: Oxford University Press, 1977), p. 158.

54. See Zaltman and Duncan, *Strategies for Planned Change*, pp. 187-190 for characteristics of successful change agents; and pp. 190-197 for basic qualifications of change agents.

55. See Donald R. Fessler, *Facilitating Community Change: A Basic Guide* (La Jolla, Calif.: University Associates, 1976), pp. 32-34 for a discussion of nine basic attitudes of the change agent.

or ladling soup in an innercity kitchen may all be proper spheres of the change agent—as long as some kind of concrete action is performed that promotes positive, revolutionary change.[56]

The change agent, then, is one who becomes personally engaged in the process and the workings of the revolution. Where at this point the visionary may be ready to depart and have yet another enticing (and safe) vision, the true revolutionary draws upon all of his or her powers and energies and puts them into play.[57] This is no time for empty talk or symbolic posturing. Now is the time for whole-hearted commitment and dedication to the task. The revolutionary must be one who has thought out the future and his or her own commitment level deeply enough that there is no wavering or turning back.[58] A revolutionary without the dimension of the change agent is projecting only the hollow shell of the role.

A price must be paid for being a change agent and a revolutionary. Saul Alinsky (1909-1972), a controversial, much-hated, and much-loved activist of another era, told how graduates of a Catholic seminary would come to meet with him the day before their ordination. Alinsky recounted the meetings as follows:

> Once, at the end of such a day, one of the seminarians said, "Mr. Alinsky, before we came here we met and agreed that there was one question we particularly wanted to put to you. We're going to be ordained, and then we'll be assigned to different parishes, as assistants to—frankly—stuffy, reactionary, old pastors. They will disapprove of a lot of what you and we believe in, and we will be put in a killing routine. Our question is: how do we keep our faith in true Christian values, everything we hope to do to change the system?"
>
> That was easy. I answered, "When you go out that door, just make your own personal decision about whether you want to be a bishop or a priest, and everything else will follow."[59]

Alinsky was advising the students to decide whether or not they really wanted to be change agents and to make the decision with both eyes open. Staying with the images Alinsky used, real change agents are not often appointed bishops. More often than not, bishops are appointed to take care of and to silence those who see

---

56. See Rogers with Shoemaker, *Communication of Innovations*, pp. 229-230 for a description of the seven roles of the change agent. The list includes: 1) Develops need for change; 2) Establishes a change relationship; 3) Diagnoses the problem; 4) Creates intention to change in the client; 5) Translates intent into action; 6) Stabilizes change and prevents discontinuances; 7) Achieves a terminal relationship.

57. For a resource on the preparation of change agents, see Ronald G. Havelock and Mary C. Havelock, *Training for Change Agents: A Guide to the Design of Training Programs in Education and Other Fields* (Ann Arbor, Mich.: Institute for Social Research, University of Michigan, 1973).

58. This issue receives a thorough review in Chapter Two, "Models and the Process of Change," in Gordon L. Lippitt, *Visualizing Change: Model Building and the Change Process* (Fairfax, Va.: NTL Learning Resources Corporation, 1973), pp. 37-69.

59. Saul D. Alinsky, *Rules for Radicals: A Practical Primer for Realistic Radicals* (New York: Random House, 1971), p. 13. A minister friend who read this story said a third option should be added: "Unemployed."

themselves as the agents of fundamental change.

The religious educator who accepts the role of change agent—integral to the role of the revolutionary—makes a choice that may have long-ranging and far-reaching consequences. Of course, the genuine and the complete religious educator has no real choice in the matter. Either one does the full work of the religious educator, including the inseparable dimension of change agentry, or one pursues another vocation entirely. Genuine religious education and unquestioning acceptance of the status quo are incompatible partners. One will have to subsume the other.

Have you chosen between becoming (symbolically, at least) a priest or a bishop? The choice is one that must be made, and the alternatives with their consequences are clearly marked.

Summary

A revolutionary can be described as one who fulfills four interlocking dimensions: the innovator, the planner, the agitator, and the change agent. While these are not the only dimensions of the entire role, they sufficiently sketch the role's general contours. Already a sense of the potential, both positively and negatively, that the role carries within it should be apparent. With these introductory dimensions in mind, other aspects of the role can be examined, starting with the aim of the religious educator as revolutionary.

Aim: Transformation

The genuine religious educator as revolutionary, out to change the world[60] for constructive and healthy reasons, realizes that transformation is his or her true aim for action. This means that the revolutionary has an over-arching purpose for the actions undertaken—that the actions will eventually result in radical, but positive, change[61]—rather than random and unplanned activity. Furthermore, the revolutionary is able to motivate and rally others to the call for fundamental transformation because the attraction is toward creating a better tomorrow, while accepting the present difficulties and the dangers in achieving such a future. In fact, the true revolutionary is intimately aware that change is ever-present,[62] and that while change is not introduced simply for the sake of change, the management and control of it can be directed toward intentional goals and objectives. Such a process of transformation is ultimately without end, because the revolu-

---

60. Describing transformation as changing the world, as contrasted to handing on tradition, is the way several authors addressed the topic in *Tradition and Transformation in Religious Education*, ed. Padraic O'Hare (Birmingham, Ala.: Religious Education Press, 1979). For an overview of the use of these terms in that book, see the introduction by O'Hare in ibid., pp. 1-7.

61. Transformation can either be viewed as a continual and evolutionary process, or as an instantaneous conversion. James Loder used the term in the previous sense, defining it as "a change in form from lower to higher orders of life along a continuous line of intention or development." James E. Loder, *The Transforming Moment: Understanding Convictional Experiences* (San Francisco: Harper & Row, 1981), p. 38. The conversion of Saul of the road to Damascus was also a transforming moment, but the change in him was sudden and shocking (see Acts 9:1-9). The issue here is change, whatever the time it takes. A revolutionary does not have to insist on violent change to be genuine.

tionary is always able to find areas that need further reconfiguration.

One of the great religious educators from early in the twentieth century was George Albert Coe (1862-1951), and his approach to religious education could legitimately be labeled transformational. His well-known question to Christian religious educators posed this stance quite clearly: "Shall the primary purpose of Christian education be to hand on a religion, or to create a new world?"[63] Even a brief perusal of Coe's work will show that his efforts were directed toward the transformational activities of creating a new world, and certainly not in handing on tradition. His own definition of Christian education pointed out the need for experiential transformation, which in part said: "It is the systematic, critical examination and reconstruction of relations between persons."[64] The emphasis was not to be on doctrine, or dogma, or authority,[65] but on relationships—which cannot by definition be "handed on." Coe thus stands as an admirable example of the religious educator as revolutionary because of his tireless efforts toward the aim of transformation.[66]

Coe probably remains an important and symbolic figure of transformation in religious education at least in part because of his strong emphasis on the sociological aspects of education.[67] He began his 1917 book *A Social Theory of Religious Education* with these words: "What consequences for religious education follow from the now widely accepted social interpretation of the Christian message?"[68] He was convinced that this kind of emphasis, rather than the extreme

---

62. In using the term as descriptive of adult development, Roger Gould said that adult transformation is "not a plateau; rather it is a dynamic and changing time for all of us." Roger L. Gould, *Transformations: Growth and Change in Adult Life* (New York: Simon and Schuster, 1978), p. 14.

63. George Albert Coe, *What Is Christian Education?* (New York: Scribner's, 1929), p. 28.

64. Ibid., p. 296. The rest of the definition said: "Guided by Jesus' assumption that persons are of infinite worth, and by the hypothesis of the existence of God, the great valuer of persons."

65. As Mary Boys said in her discussion of Coe: "In 1917 he had argued that the aim of Christian education was *not* the instruction of children in things Christians ought to know, *not* to prepare them for church membership, *not* to save their souls, *not* to impose truth." Mary C. Boys, "Access to Traditions and Transformations," in *Tradition and Transformation in Religious Education*, p. 11. She then quoted from the 1917 work, where Coe proposed that Christian education was to promote "growth of the young toward and into mature and efficient devotion to the democracy of God, and happy self-realization therein." George Albert Coe, *A Social Theory of Religious Education* (New York: Scribner's, 1917), p. 55.

66. Boys went on to say that she believed Coe's approach to be inadequate in and of itself: "Using scripture as my principal exemplar, I maintain that religious education must necessarily be concerned with both traditions and transformation. I find Coe's polarity between transmission and reconstruction ultimately to be a false dichotomy and argue that a deepened understanding of tradition is the key in holding both in tension." Mary C. Boys, "Access to Traditions and Transformations," in *Tradition and Transformation in Religious Education*, p. 30. For a similar discomfort with these dichotomies, but with a different kind of suggestion as to their resolution, see Letty M. Russell, "Handing on Traditions and Changing the World," ibid., pp. 73-86.

67. "George Albert Coe is not only thought of as the father of modern religious education but he is the first to attempt a social theory from the discipline. Religious education for him was greatly informed by appropriating the insights from sociology." Allen J. Moore, "A Social Theory of Religious Education," in *Religious Education as Social Transformation*, ed. Allen J. Moore (Birmingham, Ala.: Religious Education Press, 1989), p. 33.

68. Coe, *Social Theory of Religious Education*, p. vii.

individualism preached by the revivalists,[69] was of utmost importance: "The future of society depends upon the sort of social education that we think it worthwhile to provide."[70] Coe was unwilling to allow religious education to be concerned only with individuals, and thereby to miss engaging in the needed transformations of the larger structures of society. Indeed, as Allen Moore noted: "Coe was preoccupied in his professional career and in his retirement with social reform and a better society for all persons."[71] Coe insisted that religious education be highly attuned to the social interactions, because, in his words, "society is not merely one educator among many; it is the prime educator within all educational enterprises."[72] His efforts (and those of other progressivists) early in the twentieth century have succeeded in keeping at least some of the attention of religious education focused on transformation as it relates to the sociological aspects, and interest in these vital relational issues continues to the present day.[73]

This ultimate aim of transformation—of ceaseless and continuous progress toward productive goals—is important to keep clearly in mind, since revolution and change can easily shift to become their own ends. Revolution and change should not be allowed to become purposes in and of themselves but means to a larger end.[74] The genuine revolutionary not only seeks the removal of obstacles in the way of progress, but he or she also seeks the creation of something positive in its place. At least in terms of specifics, the revolutionary is looking to put himself or herself out of a cause; when the process of transformation is underway in one arena, the revolutionary is already seeking what else needs to be changed as a result of the previous transformation. In other words, there is no such thing as a self-satisfied and comfortable revolutionary because the needs for transformation are to be found continually in every sphere of human society.

Transformation can be linked to liberation from oppression, but it is impor-

---

69. See Chapter Four, "The Place of the Individual in a Socialized Education," in ibid., pp. 38-50.

70. Ibid., p. ix.

71. Allen J. Moore, "A Social Theory of Religious Education," in *Religious Education as Social Transformation*, p. 11.

72. Coe, *Social Theory of Religious Education*, p. 14.

73. Good evidence of this interest is the chapter written and the book edited by Allen Moore. The thesis statement of the chapter was made clear when Moore said: "Our concern here is to give renewed attention to the sociological and ethical roots of religious education with the recognition that the social order continues to serve as an important focus for religious education." Moore, "A Social Theory of Religious Education," in *Religious Education as Social Transformation*, pp. 10-11. Moore also acknowledged: "A revised social theory of religious education must be grounded in the works of George Albert Coe and the other progressive theorists who provided the first systematic theory of religious education written from a sociological point of view." Ibid., p. 11.

74. A useful cautionary word was offered by Mary Elizabeth Moore on this point: "We cannot simply work at transforming society so as to reduce injustice and poverty while we perpetuate uncritically our own community's tradition. Our community's beliefs and actions may, in fact, be part of our problems. We must be open to transforming our own community as well." Mary Elizabeth Moore, *Education for Continuity and Change: A New Model for Christian Religious Education* (Nashville: Abingdon, 1983), p. 132.

tant not to romanticize or to politicize[75] this notion of liberation. So-called "liberation" can become just as destructive as overt oppression if not handled carefully. Alistair Kee clarified the pitfalls of liberation: "Liberation is largely defined by the domination which it opposes, and it would appear that those who suffer under one form of domination may themselves be responsible for imposing another form of domination on some other group."[76] The revolutionary can become so identified or preoccupied with beating or overcoming the opposition that he or she may lose sight of the larger goal of transformation and actually become instead part of the cycle of dominance and repression. The process of attaining liberation from the oppressors may slip into seeing that the current oppressors become the oppressed, with the result that the revolutionary then evolves into the role of an oppressor—who in turn must be overthrown.[77] The grievous cycle of hate and rancor is only made worse and more endemic. True transformation for constructive purposes, as opposed to revenge or control, is impossible in such an adversarial environment.

Religious educators in the role of revolutionary must handle this aim of facilitating transformation[78] very carefully so that it does not become just another avenue for a different kind of domination. The revolutionary, for example, may help individuals reject a particular set of dogma that is stifling and stunting. The revolutionary may then help the people to see that there is another way to interpret scripture, or other means of finding information than relying on a specific authority. If, on the other hand, the revolutionary simply substitutes another set of dogma, or another authorized and correct way of interpretation, or becomes the new source of authority himself or herself, then nothing has been accomplished but an exchange of bondage. One form of domination is as bad as the other, regardless of the good intentions that may be behind either one. No real transformation, growth, or development can be said to have taken place. Only the type of oppression or the source of it has changed. True transformation permits new growth and development to arise in an environment amenable to the flourishing of new identities and the nurture of creative ideas, and their appearance must be the rewards of the revolutionary—even if he or she does not personal-

---

75. One of the problems with turning to liberation theology, for example, is the dependence there on political means for the achievement of transformation. While admittedly there are times when it is difficult to separate politics from the process of liberation, the two do not have to be indistinguishable. For a view of religious education that is overtly linked to the political realm and to the exercise of power, see Thomas H. Groome, *Christian Religious Education: Sharing Our Story and Vision* (San Francisco: Harper & Row, 1980), especially pp. 15-17. Groome started this section by noting: "Educational activity with pilgrims in time is a political activity." Ibid., p. 15. He also wrote: "Integral to recognizing the political nature of what educators do is to see educational activity as an exercise of power." Ibid., p. 16.

76. Alistair Kee, *Domination or Liberation: The Place of Religion in Social Conflict* (London: SCM Press, 1986), p. x.

77. This danger was addressed by Paulo Freire in *Pedagogy of the Oppressed*, pp. 37-56. Freire's work is examined in the section below on the contemporary example.

78. This rendering of the aim was echoed by Mary Boys to include all of education: "How, then, might it be possible to think about the goal of education? It seems to me that all education must necessarily have a transformative purpose." Mary C. Boys, *Educating in Faith: Maps and Visions* (San Francisco: Harper & Row, 1989), p. 210. Interestingly, Boys then went on to discuss the role of politics in education in the next paragraph.

ly agree with the specifics themselves.[79] The role of the religious educator as revolutionary in one form or another will always be necessary: The types and targets of revolutionary change will change, but the need will always be present for the clear-eyed and genuine revolutionary who facilitates the aim of transformation.

Function: Reconstruction

If the aim of the revolutionary is transformation, then the function that the revolutionary must effectively perform to accomplish this objective is reconstruction. This aspect of the revolutionary is central to the entire role, since it reveals the complexity of the tasks that must be performed and the depth of the issues that need to be addressed in order for real transformation to be actualized. In turning to reconstruction, the efforts cannot be half-hearted or mildly reformational. Reconstruction in general means changing for the better whatever outdated and outmoded fundamental structures and processes are involved, so that in this discussion of the religious educator as revolutionary, the focus of the reconstruction is of the entire educational process. The primary person that anchors this discussion about reconstruction is Theodore Brameld (1904-1987), educator and philosopher who labeled his own philosophy of education "reconstructionist."[80] While his specific designs for educational reconstruction were naturally and necessarily attuned to the time and conditions in which he worked,[81] the general approach and attitude he espoused as a reconstructionist educator are still quite relevant and applicable to present educational thought.[82]

The general approach and attitude of Brameld's work is apparent in this overall goal statement: "The goal of reconstructionism is, then, the enunciation of beliefs demanded of the revolutionary age in which we live—beliefs that are concretely grounded in experience, and that imply practicable measures for the betterment of the human condition."[83] One can easily catch the fire burning in the eyes and in the soul of Brameld—the sure marks of any revolutionary. These characteristics continued to be expressed throughout his writings. When Brameld wrote to those who thought his reach and his vision exceeded his grasp by much

79. Mary Boys also wrote: "A religious educator serves as a catalyst of transformation." Ibid., p. 203. See her develop this idea more fully throughout ibid., pp. 203-214.

80. The two primary sources to consult for understanding Brameld are companion volumes. One is Theodore Brameld, *Philosophies of Education in Cultural Perspective* (New York: Dryden, 1955). In this first volume Brameld discussed the other philosophies of education, such as progressivism, essentialism, and perennialism. The second work is Theodore Brameld, *Toward a Reconstructed Philosophy of Education* (New York: Dryden, 1956). This second volume is devoted to Brameld's exposition of his reconstructionist philosophy.

81. For an example of the specific proposals, see Chapters Eight and Nine, "Curricular Designs for Schools of the People," in Brameld, *Toward a Reconstructed Philosophy of Education*, pp. 211-260.

82. The extent of Brameld's plans for educational revolution can be glimpsed in the following comment: "The reconstructionist wishes to transform education into a powerful means for social change toward world civilization." Theodore Brameld, *Education as Power* (New York: Holt, Rinehart and Winston, 1965), p. 39.

83. Brameld, *Toward a Reconstructed Philosophy of Education*, p. 24.

too far, he made no apology or reductions of his proposals: "However gigantic these undertakings are, the reconstructionist is convinced that Western civilization is at an end if we fail in them."[84] In fact, rather than backing down, Brameld proceeded to state his case even more boldly: "Instead of being satisfied with gradual transition, with cultural conservation, or with a kind of intellectualized regression, the reconstructionist throws in his lot with those who believe (as some have always come to believe in critical times) that only a thorough refashioning of principles and institutions will make them serviceable in the future."[85] Here one gets the true sense of the function of reconstruction. The future is too important to allow it to come without preparation, and it is too valuable to let the old ways be carried forward without evaluation. Brameld stated: "For this philosophy seeks, above all, to develop a kind of education that can contribute powerfully to rebuilding, not merely to perpetuating, hitherto dominant cultural structures, habits, and attitudes."[86] This type of fundamental reconstruction does not just happen because of wishes or pipedreams, but it is accomplished by nothing other than hard work—brick by brick and thought by thought: "It rests squarely upon the contributions of the social and psychological sciences, the pure and applied arts, and education. For this reason reconstructionists would defend themselves as ultimately more practical than those who, in the name of common sense or caution, delimit their theories to the point of ineffectiveness."[87]

The future is an irresistible and powerful force in reconstruction.[88] In Brameld's words: "Reconstructionism is a philosophy of magnetic foresight—a philosophy of ends attainable through the development of powerful means possessed latently by the people."[89] The future is not fixed and predetermined—far from it, in Brameld's view. He wrote: "The reconstructionist does not hold that analyzing future trends makes it possible to know whither mankind is inevitably bound; he does not believe that the groove of the future is already mysteriously cut. He does hold that to know what the future *should* be like is essential to knowing what it *could* be like and that, if we implement our choices with sufficient determination, we can determine what it *will* be like."[90] If such words and desires for the future sound radical, then there is good reason, for Brameld said: "The reconstructionist is the radical; he would face our problems, not by conserving, not merely by modifying, nor by retreating; but by future-looking, by building a new order of civilization under genuinely *public* control, and dedicated to the fulfillment of the human values for which most men have been struggling, con-

---

84. Ibid., p. 39.
85. Ibid.
86. Ibid., p. 167.
87. Ibid., p. 39.
88. "[Reconstructionism] insists . . . that where as the past and present condition the future, the future also conditions the past and present. The view of the future held by the present observer thus helps to determine what is to be interpreted and reinterpreted according to the cultural purposes he embraces." Ibid., p. 70.
89. Theodore Brameld, *Ends and Means in Education: A Midcentury Appraisal* (New York: Harper & Brothers, 1950), p. 16.
90. Brameld, *Toward a Reconstructed Philosophy of Education*, p. 71.

sciously or unconsciously, for many centuries."[91]

One of the things reconstruction means, then, is bringing decision making and self-determination to those who are affected by the decisions. Peter Berger and Richard Neuhaus spoke of institutional reconstruction as one illustration of the overall topic: "One of the most debilitating results of modernization is a feeling of powerlessness in the face of institutions controlled by those who we do not know and whose values we often do not share. . . . Our belief is that human beings, whoever they are, understand their own needs better than anyone else."[92] This attitude and approach can be expanded to include all of public policy: that the persons involved know their needs, and that these persons have the right and the responsibility to determine the ways in which those needs are met. Genuine revolution is the process of seeing that the people speak with their own voices and act on their own decisions. A revolutionary with another type of function or end in view is suspect at best and dangerous by any account.

Demagogues and despots who collect power to dominate and to prop themselves up are rather easy to spot. The more subtle forms of oppression are the difficult ones to uncover. Paternalism/maternalism, for example, often shows itself outwardly as concern for those who apparently cannot care for themselves, when the issue is that authority wants to keep the group in submission and under control: Whites make the proper decisions for blacks; men see that women are protected; religious and church officials determine doctrine and behavior to keep their charges out of hell—or so the arguments are posed by the authorities in power. Reconstruction unmasks such dishonest manipulation and reveals it for the domination that it is. The genuine religious educator as revolutionary rejects the philosophies and the procedures of the oppressor and returns to the learners the responsibility for finding their own way and for making up their own minds— all of which is reflective of true education, rather than indoctrination.[93]

The effective religious educator as revolutionary works to reconstruct society and its structures through educational empowerment, accomplished at least in part by allowing learners to begin making their own decisions. The nature and result of these decisions are left to the people. The task of the revolutionary is only to enable the people make up their own decisions. This translates into the religious educator becoming one who facilitates a process of choosing rather than determining; of searching rather than telling; of liberating rather than dominating.

---

91. Brameld, *Ends and Means in Education*, p. 16.

92. Peter L. Berger and Richard John Neuhaus, *To Empower People: The Role of Mediating Structures in Public Policy* (Washington, D.C.: American Enterprise Institute for Public Policy Research, 1977), p. 7.

93. See Chapter Ten, "Shall the Schools Indoctrinate?," in Brameld, *Ends and Means in Education*, pp. 86-94. At the first of this chapter, Brameld wrote: "The kind of education here being discussed encourages students, teachers, and all members of the community not merely to *study* knowledge and problems considered crucial to our period of culture, but *to make up their minds* about promising solutions, and then to act concertedly. Its emphasis on *commitment* to agreed-upon, future-looking goals thus raises once more the old problem of bias and indoctrination." Ibid., p. 86. Brameld's stand was clear: that of "unequivocal opposition to indoctrination; and equally unequivocal support of academic freedom, in the sense of impartial and thorough study of all kinds of evidence and alternatives." Ibid., p. 87.

Primary Virtues: Equality and Autonomy

The virtues that guide the religious educator are nowhere more important than in this particular role. The religious educator in the role of the revolutionary abides by and believes in equality for and autonomy among all persons, and he or she works both to instill them and to embody them. These virtues protect the learners and the innocents from continued harm—even from the revolutionary—and direct the revolutionary along the proper path of transformation and reconstruction. When one of these primary virtues is violated, the revolution has gotten untracked and must be righted immediately; otherwise the revolution turns into just another force for oppression.

Equality is a somewhat difficult virtue to pin down because it may sound like a belief that all people are identical and uniform, and any glance around renders such a notion ridiculous.[94] A truly adequate definition of equality must include within itself proper room for diversity. Bryan Turner identified four types of equality which get at the fullness of the term: "The first [type of equality] is ontological equality or the fundamental equality of persons. Second, there is equality of opportunity to achieve desirable ends. Third, there is equality of condition where there is an attempt to make the conditions of life equal for relevant social groups. Fourth, there is equality of outcome or equality of result."[95] These distinctions by Turner are helpful since they all are valid aspects of equality and all are legitimate for the revolutionary to keep in view. Indeed, each of the four meanings of equality interlock and need to be taken together into one larger whole. The idea of equality as the "fundamental equality of persons" (Turner's first point) is the starting place, but the other dimensions grow out of the first and are essential to the nurture of true equality in long-term commitment.

Charles Hurst went at the issue from the opposite direction, preferring to discuss the types of inequality found in modern society and thereby giving the revolutionary causes and needs to address, rather than an ideal to imagine. He analyzed such issues as the stratification of races, socioeconomic groups, and geographic areas which work together to cause inequality. Hurst highlighted inequality to show that what one sees depends upon what one looks for: "The manner in which a term is defined and measured has clear implications for what we see and choose to focus on. The concepts we use organize our world and determine what we see."[96] Hurst wanted to draw attention to the glaring inequalities within society, with all of their dangers and effects, so that they are not glossed over. He was suggesting that the problems and their roots need to have a place in defining and shaping our plans alongside the more positive images of an ideal world.

---

94. Of course, the Declaration of Independence uses the phrase "all men are created equal." This idea apparently stems from the environmentalist philosophy of John Locke, who said that indeed all persons are created equal—just as *tabula rasas* (blank slates). In other words, all persons start as equals in the sense that all start as blanks. This concept countered the belief in innate ideas. See more about this discussed in Nathan Tarcov, Chapter Three, "The Lockean Virtues," Locke's *Education for Liberty* (Chicago: University of Chicago Press, 1984), pp. 129-183.

95. Bryan S. Turner, *Equality* (London: Tavistock Publications, 1986), p. 34.

96. Charles E. Hurst, *The Anatomy of Social Inequality* (St. Louis: Mosby, 1979), pp. 6-7.

Amid all the talk and concern for the broader social entities, a word for the individual must be sounded.[97] Although the revolutionary often tends to be more interested in the group than in the individuals that make up those groups, it is dangerous and harmful to let the focus slip too far from personhood. The cautionary words of David Thompson are still important, although they originally spoke to a different time and to a different situation. In his discussion of democracy and egalitarianism following the Second World War, he wrote: "However much collective action and cooperative planning may be desirable as means toward these ends, the ideals of equality and liberty can be reconciled only if both are firmly rooted in reverence for the individual personality."[98] The revolutionary religious educator must keep the person as well as the group in mind throughout the revolution. The end still includes the transformation of individuals, and no amount of effort to free groups will have any meaning without this abiding and pervasive "reverence for the individual personality."

Autonomy is a companion virtue to that of equality for the religious educator performing the role of the revolutionary. Foundational to this virtue is independence,[99] since independence is found at the very heart of revolution. Revolution is breaking away, a tearing from the past, a struggling to be free from the tyranny that was oppressive and repressive. Independence is affirmation and confidence that freedom is possible and that the future can be different from the past.

Upon closer analysis, however, independence stretched to its logical conclusion is not the best term for what the revolutionary really is seeking. Absolute independence means total isolation, separation, and detachment. Even if such a state of being were possible, no rational human would desire it. All humans to some degree or another are continually dependent on each other for physical, psychological, and spiritual support.[100] The true issue, then, is independence from domination in order to allow for free choice and decision making—which is autonomy.[101] As Robert Young put it: "The fundamental idea in autonomy is that of authoring one's own world without being subject to the will of oth-

---

97. "Either an environmental approach or a person approach is able to explain considerable variance in behavior, for the two parts of the interaction are like two sides of the same coin. Yet a fuller account of behavior necessitates attending to the person, the environment, and their interactive effects. Both the person approach and the environment approach have their advantages and disadvantages." Edward L. Deci, *The Psychology of Self-Determination* (Lexington, Mass.: Heath, 1980), p. 15.

98. David Thompson, *Equality* (Cambridge: At the University Press, 1949), p. 149.

99. See a helpful introduction to how this applies to the individual in Chapter One, "Free Will in Psychology and Human Affairs," in James A. Easterbrook, *The Determinants of Free Will: A Psychological Analysis of Responsible, Adjustive Behavior* (New York: Academic Press, 1978), pp. 3-15.

100. "The separate individual is an abstraction; we all grow up in social environments and become human through our associations with other persons. Without these social relations we would not have developed our specifically human capacities and skills, and without any relations with nature we would all cease to be living human beings, assuming that these relations once existed, otherwise we would never have endured in the first place." William L. Ewens, *Becoming Free: The Struggle for Human Development* (Wilmington, Del.: Scholarly Resources, 1984), p. 19.

101. For a good overview of the meanings of autonomy, see Joel Feinberg, "Autonomy," pp. 27-53, and Gerald Dworkin, "The Concept of Autonomy," pp. 54-62, in *The Inner Citadel: Essays on Individual Autonomy*, ed. John Christman (Oxford: Oxford University Press, 1989).

ers."[102] What the revolutionary genuinely seeks is not solitary confinement but enough freedom for self-determination;[103] not complete removal from others but a safe level of interaction and co-existence; not independence but interdependence.[104]

The difficulty that presents itself immediately with the more accurate term "autonomy" substituted for the term "independence" is the *amount of dependency* that is healthy and tolerable. Too much dependence and the situation repeats itself: identity and personhood are compromised to such a measure that another revolution must be instigated to gain freedom once again.[105] Too much independence, however, and the resultant isolation strangles any hope of meaningful existence.[106] The effort to balance the poles of independence and dependence describes the constantly dynamic virtue of autonomy.

The religious educator is forever caught in the effort to nurture persons into a healthy balanced kind of autonomy—not too much dependence, while not too much independence. The key word here is *health*. Health exists somewhere in the flow of dependence and independence, where the boundaries and the rules are never sure and fixed. The religious educator at times must allow the person to "lean" on him or her—to help "bear one another's burdens" (Galatians 6:2, NRSV). At other times, the religious educator must send the person off alone— to let "each one bear his or her own burdens" (Galatians 6:5, NRSV). This seemingly paradoxical advice eventually results in "healthy autonomy," a product of the sensitivity and the diagnostic skills representative of the virtues of the revolutionary religious educator.

The combined virtues of equality and autonomy make up an inseparable pair. Equals can become partners in the effort toward establishing autonomy. The strengths in one party aid the weaknesses in the other party. Equality does not imply sameness, but complementarity. Autonomy does not imply isolation, but identity. These two virtues mature and work together to serve the religious educator as he or she spreads the "good news" of revolution in a healthy and developmental fashion. The end result of true revolution is thus always healthier persons who operate in their shared environment freely and confidently.

---

102. Robert Young, *Personal Autonomy: Beyond Negative and Positive Liberty* (New York: St. Martin's Press, 1986), p. 19.

103. "Instead of thinking of individual autonomy as 'freedom from' the governance of others, it is more appropriate to understand it in a positive way as self-government or self-determination." Ibid., p. 8.

104. "The full formula for autonomy, then, is authenticity plus procedural independence. A person is autonomous if he identifies with his desires, goals, and values, and such identification is not in some way alien to the individual. Spelling out procedural independence involves distinguishing those ways of influencing people's reflective and critical faculties which subvert them from those who promote and improve them." Gerald Dworkin, "The Concept of Autonomy," in *The Inner Citadel*, p. 55.

105. In a nice crystallization of the problem, Edward Deci said: "The key question is, 'Who will be in charge of my life?'" Deci, *The Psychology of Self-Determination*, p. 138.

106. "Thus every person's life could be portrayed by a graph of differentiation—how far has he freed himself from automatic dependencies, become an individual, able then to relate to his fellows on the new level of self-chosen love, responsibility and creative work?" Rollo May, *Man's Search for Himself* (New York: Norton, 1953), pp. 120-121.

Activity: Individuating

The primary activity which distinguishes the religious educator in the role of the revolutionary is individuating, which means breaking away from the limitations of dependence and establishing a fresher, firmer identity in its place.[107] As one author put it: "Individuation is a life process of 'centering' or becoming whole."[108] This kind of focus does not represent dependency as necessarily bad or evil, but rather as a temporary crutch to be used until fuller individuality can be developed. Of course no one exists totally independent from their environment, but each one is required to create boundaries that define who and what he or she is—as well as who and what he or she is *not*. These identifying boundaries are forged through the process of individuation.[109]

Much attention has been drawn to individuation through the work of Carl Jung,[110] and one of the ways Jung defined individuation is as follows: "In general, it is the process by which individual beings are being formed and differentiated; in particular, it is the development of the psychological *individual* as being distinct from the general, collective psychology. Individuation, therefore, is a process of *differentiation*, having for its goal the development of the individual personality."[111] This quote and definition helps to clarify why the activity of individuation is central to the religious educator as revolutionary: The revolutionary as discussed here is one who is in the "process of differentiation," developing his or her individual personality in such a way that new paths and new means to the future are visible. It is not a matter of rebelliousness per se, or of trying to be different just to be different. It is following one's own journey to selfhood,[112] which is bound to be different than others.'[113] As Jung said in another con-

---

107. Gerhard Adler described individuation as a "gradually emerging pattern of inner order, of a continuous process of integration, of a sense-giving factor in the psyche; in short, of the creative function of the unconscious, the 'objective psyche.'" Gerhard Adler, *The Living Symbol: A Case Study in the Process of Individuation* (New York: Pantheon Books, 1961), p. 4. For an in-depth study of individuation, see Chapter One, "The Problem of Individuation," in Jorge J.E. Gracia, *Introduction to the Problem of Individuation in the Early Middle Ages* (Washington, D.C.: Catholic University of America Press, 1984), pp. 17-63.

108. Jeanette Pruyn Reed, *Emergence: Essays on the Process of Individuation Through Sand Therapy, Art Forms, and Dreams* (Albuquerque, N.M.: JPR Publishers, 1980), p. 22.

109. "The self is at first a preconscious image of potential wholeness, of which increasing awareness can be gained by the ego. This process of increasing awareness is synonymous with the process of individuation." Adler, *The Living Symbol*, p. 9.

110. One of the better ways for gaining a basic understanding of Jung's meaning of individuation is to consult Josef Goldbrunner, *Individuation: A Study of the Depth Psychology of Carl Gustav Jung*, trans. Stanley Goodman (New York: Pantheon, 1956). Especially relevant and helpful is Chapter Twelve, "Individuation," ibid., pp. 119-145.

111. Carl G. Jung, Vol. 6, *Psychological Types*, trans. H.G. Baynes, rev. R.F.C. Hull, in *The Collected Works of C.G. Jung* (Princeton: Princeton University Press, 1971), p. 448, paragraph 757.

112. See a helpful discussion by Mark C. Taylor, *Journeys to Selfhood: Hegel and Kierkegaard* (Berkeley: University of California Press, 1980). Taylor's book is an attempt to address this well-phrased question: "In the confusing theater of modernity whose strange scenery obscures the way and where innovative playrights constantly revise the script, how *is* one to journey to selfhood?" Ibid., p. 13.

113. "Individuation is a spiritual process by which the personality is built up. It takes as many different forms as there are individuals." Goldbrunner, *Individuation*, p. 119.

text: "In the last analysis every life is the realization of a whole, that is, of a self, for which reason this realization can also be called 'individuation.' All life is bound to individual carriers who realize it, and it is simply inconceivable without them. But every carrier is charged with an individual destiny and destination, and the realization of these alone makes sense of life."[114]

Gregory Hamilton gave a helpful analogy of the individuation process in general when he described the process as undergone by infants. He spoke of the infant, who lives a symbiotic existence with the mother-figure for approximately the first five months after birth, when some new dynamic begins to transpire: "Symbiosis blends into the beginnings of the separation-individuation phase when the child is about 5-6 months old. The first sub-phase of separation-individuation is appropriately called hatching, or more technically, differentiation."[115] "Hatching" catches the sense of breaking out of the old, confining environment into a new and risky one, but one that allows for proper growth and development. Hamilton was careful not to overstate the case, in that differentiation does not imply that suddenly the child is responsible for himself or herself and forever free from continued care. Instead, separating is a gradual process that goes on to some extent throughout life: "A to-and-fro movement of closeness and distance—the dance of separation-individuation—has begun."[116] This effort is the one described earlier, of balancing dependence and independence into a workable form of interdependence.

Infants moving from symbiosis toward differentiation provide a way of understanding revolution. Revolution is a term that denotes separation from ways or procedures of the past and movement into the future. It is a normal and natural process of rejecting the old that has been surpassed, and creating the new—as logical as knowing that old wineskins will not hold the new wine.[117] The methods and the degree of difficulty for the revolution may vary from evolutionary change to desperate violence, but the new must always emerge from the old while the "dance" of closeness and distance is an eternal one.[118]

Individuation becomes even clearer when contrasted to the related process of socialization.[119] William Damon defined socialization as "all of one's tendencies to establish and maintain relations with others, to become an accepted member of society-at-large, to regulate one's behavior according to society's codes and

---

114. Carl G. Jung, Vol. 12, *Psychology and Alchemy*, in *The Collected Works of C.G. Jung* (1971), p. 222, paragraph 330.

115. N. Gregory Hamilton, *Self and Others: Object Relations Theory in Practice* (Northvale, N.J.: Jason Aronson, 1988), p. 41.

116. Ibid., p. 43.

117. Matthew 9:17.

118. For an interesting and revelatory way of studying scripture along these same lines, see Edward F. Edinger, *The Bible and the Psyche: Individuation Symbolism in the Old Testament* (Toronto: Inter City Books, 1986). Edinger wrote: "The events of the Bible, although presented as history, psychologically understood are archtypal images, that is, pleromatic events that repeatedly erupt into spatio-temporal manifestation and require an individual ego to live them out." Ibid., p. 13.

119. For a related discussion that distinguishes between individuation and narcissism, see Mario Jacoby, *Individuation and Narcissism: The Psychology of the Self in Jung and Kohut*, trans. Myron Gubitz and Françoise O'Kane (London, Routledge, 1990).

standards, and generally to get along well with other people."[120] He called it the "*integrating* function of social development, since it ensures the integration of the individual into society as a respected participant."[121] By contrast, Damon called individuation the "*differentiating* function of social development."[122] He then explained that "socialization and individuation are quite distinct processes, even at times operating in opposition to one another. Establishing one's individuality very often requires a different sort of activity than that required for 'socialized' behavior in the traditional use of the term. Defining one's distinctness from others and staking out one's unique social position sometimes place one in an antagonistic relation to others."[123] This reality of separating and being "distinct from others" describes the task and the challenge of the true revolutionary. Sometimes (oftentimes) the revolutionary's stance is not the most socially acceptable one—but it is the necessary one for progress and development, and taking the route of individuality is the price for being a genuine revolutionary.

At least two complaints could be lodged regarding the identification of "differentiating" as the activity of the revolutionary. The first is a charge of male bias, following the lead of Carol Gilligan who has addressed the entire concept of development from a female point of view.[124] Gilligan's general comment was that male theorists cannot and should not speak for females, and that as more females contribute to developmental theory the inherent male bias will become ever more apparent. The specific complaint, however, would relate to saying that individuation happens as a result of differentiation, or separation. Gilligan proposed that females make decisions and develop by way of a "network of relationships" in which connection is the key (often mistakenly associated with dependency and immaturity), while males tend to make decisions and develop by way of logic and separation (often mistakenly associated with growth and maturity).[125] The potential result is that female patterns of development are seen as inferior. Whether or not Gilligan is correct in her observations does not affect the process of individuation itself, which is still a matter of determining a separate identity. It may be carried out in a relational web or by individual logic, but the point here is only that the process of individuation must indeed take place.

---

120. William Damon, *Social and Personality Development: Infancy through Adolescence* (New York: Norton, 1983). p. 2.

121. Ibid.

122. Ibid.

123. Ibid., p. 3. It is important to note the other part of Damon's discussion as well: "Yet there is a sense in which there are profound connections between socialization and individuation. Developmentally, the two often go hand in hand for important psychological reasons: as one learns more about others, one learns more about the self, and vice versa." Ibid., p. 4. In summary, Damon wrote: "In short, socialization and individuation are to a certain extent distinct from one another, and there is always the possibility that actions which will further one may not be in the service of another. But in the normal course of development, they go hand in hand, supporting each other's growth. There is a creative tension between the two, a dialectical interplay between the needs of the individual to maintain relations with others and the needs of the individual to construct a separate self." Ibid., p. 5.

124. See Carol Gilligan, *In a Different Voice: Psychological Theory and Women's Development* (Cambridge: Harvard University Press, 1982).

125. See the related and helpful comments of Robert Kegan in *The Evolving Self: Problem and Process in Human Development* (Cambridge: Harvard University Press, 1982), pp. 108-109.

If it comes to pass that it is found that males and females go about this in different manners, the activity will continue to remain constant although the understanding and conceptualizing of it will change.[126]

The second objection one could raise against the identification of individuation as the primary activity of the religious educator as revolutionary is its incompleteness. The only possible and rational response is that of course it is incomplete.[127] Separating is only one activity among the huge panoply of activities necessary for genuine religious education.[128] It just happens that this particular one can so easily be a force unto itself and run out of control. In some sense, this is the essence of revolution—to break the old controls and to start anew, but as Robert Kegan noted: "Development is not a matter of differentiation alone, but of differentiating and reintegration."[129] Revolution and separation are not ends in and of themselves. They are, in the longer term, means to further ends.

The religious educator as revolutionary nurtures and facilitates the process of individuation. It is the birth of the process eventuating in wholeness and fuller identity.[130] Once that process is underway, then there is the need for follow-up activities. It remains the primary responsibility of the revolutionary, though, to help initiate the difficult and often painful differentiation process that permits the appearance of new growth.

Shadow Role: Ideologue

For many, the role of revolutionary itself may already sound like a shadow role[131]—a dangerous and frightening specter that threatens the true nature of religious education. To these people, there seems to be no need for creating an even worse monster. Obviously, the contention of this chapter has been that the role of the revolutionary is nothing to be feared but encouraged as long as the aim (transformation), function (reconstruction), and virtues (equality and autonomy) described are upheld. When the revolutionary deviates from these guidelines and hardens into the real shadow role of the ideologue, though, the nightmare comes true. The aim of genuine transformation fades into license for imposition of the truth, and virtually any method is accepted and employed as long as the objective of proper thinking is achieved. Virtues are no longer sought jointly but dictated by a powerful authority. Such a journey from freedom to slavery is

---

126. "The primacy of separation or connection leads to different images of self and relationships." Gilligan, *In a Different Voice*, p. 39.

127. Recall that the discussion above of individuation and socialization not only showed how these two processes were different, but also how they are complementary for full development.

128. Specifically, see a companion activity of participating as discussed in Chapter Eight, "The Religious Educator as Storyteller."

129. Kegan, *Evolving Self*, p. 67.

130. "Individuation leads step by step and deeper and deeper into the core of the personality." Goldbrunner, *Individuation*, pp. 119-120. Gerhard Adler called this process one in which "the true and integrated individuality of a person emerges out of its unconscious prefiguration." Adler, *The Living Symbol*, p. 25.

131. A good example of this attitude is captured in the title of a book edited by Lonnie D. Kliever, *The Terrible Meek: Essays on Religion and Revolution* (New York: Paragon House, 1987).

startlingly easy and quick to make.[132] More than one revolutionary movement has raged out of control and changed into the very definition of repression itself. Such, however, is the contribution and handiwork of the ideologue rather than the true revolutionary—and indeed the ideologue is someone to fear. In this discussion, the ideologue is someone who makes all ideas, behaviors, and data conform to a strict set of predetermined beliefs and postulates that must be accepted without question.

One of the classic works on ideology was written by Karl Mannheim, who documented how the meaning of the term changed from positive to threatening during the days of Napoleon. Until that time, "ideology" in its pure form simply meant the study or referencing of ideas. Mannheim wrote: "The modern conception of Ideology was born when Napoleon, finding that this group of philosophers was opposing his imperial ambitions, contemptuously labeled them as 'ideologists.' Thereby the word took on a derogatory meaning which, like the word 'doctrinaire,' it has retained to the present day."[133] The label of ideologists, or ideologues, was then taken as a negative one. Interestingly enough, Napoleon himself today would be more likely described as an ideologue for his "imperial ambitions" rather than those who were initially opposing him.[134] The definition of an ideologue, as the term is employed today, is one who uses and manipulates ideas, and resultant plans for action, for his or her own good and to the disadvantage of others.

Another dimension of the term appears when the ideologue revises and creates history from the present backwards to rationalize the activity and the nature of the ideology. Such a process is called "presentism," which is the misuse and corruption of history by making it conform to a theory created in the present. In his discussion of presentism, Gerald Gutek gave this helpful comment: "If necessary, past events may be shaped to fit a preconceived thesis that justifies a present or future program."[135] For the ideologue, the ends dictate the means, and if that requires a rewriting of history, so be it.

The employment of Marxist ideology[136] to understand and interpret history provides a vivid example of how reality can be represented in different ways, depending on one's initial viewpoint and set of presuppositions. Simply reading through the brief *Communist Manifesto* is sufficient to grasp how this radical polit-

---

132. Douglas Elwood noted that "it is not surprising if the ideological movements sometimes try to make use of persons and institutions for the sake of achieving their own goals. Herein lies the ambiguous nature of all ideologies." Douglas J. Elwood, *Faith Encounters Ideology: Christian Discernment and Social Change* (Quezon City, Philippines: New Day Publishers, 1985), p. 10.

133. Karl Mannheim, *Ideology and Utopia: An Introduction to the Sociology of Knowledge* (London: Routledge and Kegan Paul, 1954), p. 64.

134. Illustrative of the sudden switch in public opinion of Napoleon the liberator to Napoleon the oppressor is the evidence we have from the works of Ludwig van Beethoven. Initially his third symphony—Symphony No. 3 ("Eroica") in E Flat (Op. 55)—was to have been dedicated to Napoleon. Upon hearing of Napoleon taking the title of Emperor, Beethoven violently scratched Napoleon's name from the title page of the symphony. This page and its markings are extant. See, for example, the discussion in George Groves, *Beethoven and His Nine Symphonies*, 3rd ed. (New York: Dover Publications, 1962; first published in 1898), pp. 51-56.

135. Gerald L. Gutek, *Philosophical and Ideological Perspectives on Education* (Englewood Cliffs, N.J.: Prentice-Hall, 1988), p. 153.

136. Marxism is discussed in more detail in the following section on the faith tradition resource.

ical philosophy reinterprets all of history from the point of view of class struggle and economics.[137] Early in the *Manifesto*, its authors began to paint history with their own pre-selected tints, stating: "Freeman and slave, patrician and plebian, lord and serf, guild-master and journeyman, in a word, oppressor and oppressed, stood in constant opposition to one another, carried on an uninterrupted, now hidden, now open fight, a fight that each time ended, either in a revolutionary re-constitution of society at large, or in the common ruin of the contending class."[138] Extending throughout the work, Karl Marx and Friedrich Engels viewed history through their own selective lenses, until they reached their conclusions about the inevitable future: "In place of the old bourgeois society, with its classes and class antagonisms, we shall have an association in which the free development of each is the condition for the free development of all."[139] These men, and the following they produced, illustrate that the use of ideology to interpret and reinterpret reality should never be underestimated, just as it may in the final analysis may be unavoidable *in toto*.[140]

Another practice of the ideologue is the use of authority to explain activity and justify group goals. Gerald Gutek made the following observation: "Ideology serves to give theoretical legitimacy to a group's outlook, aspirations, program, and action. Rather than appearing to be based on personal or group special interests, ideological justification or legitimacy appeals to a higher and seemingly more generalizable, hence more applicable, authority. Often the appeal to myth or history is used to legitimize policies and actions."[141] This authority, real or imagined, allows the ideologue to push for political and educational action in a concentrated, nearly fanatical, way. To top off the threat, the ideologue tends to use history and authority in such a manner as to give to the adherents some measure of validity and sense of "rightness." The twisted view of history allows the followers of the ideologue to believe that they are at the pinnacle of history and that their just and foreordained actions will usher in a new age. Such boundless energy and blind commitment to being unmistakenly right—infallible and inerrant—creates a powerful force to be reckoned with.

Ideologues are virtually always a threat to human freedom, in whatever guise they appear,[142] since they try to impose their oppressive view of reality onto everyone and assume that they alone know what is right. Religion and education are natural targets for ideologists to manipulate, so certainly religious educa-

137. "The history of all hitherto existing society is the history of class struggles." Karl Marx and Friedrich Engels, *Manifesto of the Communist Party*, in *The Marx-Engels Reader*, ed. Robert C. Tucker (New York: Norton, 1972), p. 335.

138. Ibid., pp. 335-336.

139. Ibid., p. 353.

140. Meaning that any effort to interpret and reinterpret history may be said by someone to reveal some underlying ideology. This points out the difficulty of absolute objectivity in regard to history—or any other social science. See this concept of the historian discussed in more detail in Chapter Eight, "The Religious Educator as Storyteller." The issue of objectivity also receives extended discussion in Chapter Six, "The Religious Educator as Scientist."

141. Ibid., p. 147.

142. Ideologues of either the political right or the political left are just as deep a threat to freedom. Now is the day of being "politically correct," the type of "correctness" depending on one's prejudged political stance.

tion is in omnipresent danger of being taken over by fanatics. Presently one of the greatest threats to genuine religious education is the rising tide of right-wing fundamentalism, exposing itself most obviously in numerous Protestant denominations.[143] These fundamentalists have little interest in human freedom or the quest for truth, insisting instead upon the imposition of their brand of "Truth," acquiescence to their heavy-handed authority, and acceptance of the party line. The fundamentalist holds tightly to his or her idea of what the "Truth" is, and is willing to rewrite all history to make it conform to that conception of "Truth." Since he or she is serving this "Truth," any activity or device to further the cause is legitimate. The end justifies the means. All this is supposedly based on their ultimate authority, the Bible, which is "Truth," infallible and inerrant—as long as the fundamentalist (read, correct) method of interpretation is followed. Any who disagree are to be silenced and purged, since these "heretics" are nonbelievers, either standing in the way of the "moral majority" (actually the immoral minority) and its new age of purity, or even worse, leading others further astray by asking questions. Such deviants cannot be tolerated by those who already have their own version of the "Truth" prepackaged and ready for distribution.

These fundamentalist ideologues have no time or place for true religious education. They have their "Truth," and their goal is nothing short of extinguishing the quest for truth which in any way may differ from theirs. Their plan is to keep their adherents ignorant, powerless, and obedient. In short, these ideologues want indoctrination, not education.[144] Such ideologues cannot be permitted to continue deluding the people with their lies. Genuine religious *educators*, accepting the role of revolutionary, must work to help educate[145] those imprisoned by the ideology of others and to help each individual search for his or her own source of truth.

Faith Tradition Resource: Marxism

While certainly not declaring itself to be a formal, organized religion, there is sufficient cause and reason to turn to Marxism as the faith tradition resource

---

143. One of the better and most evident examples is the takeover by the right-wing fundamentalists of the Southern Baptist Convention beginning in earnest in 1979, but there are signs that extremists are not content to stop with the destruction of any one denomination. The mainline denominations and Catholicism are under attack as well from extremists of both the right and the left, and will surely be feeling the effects for decades to come. One need only to watch the fanaticism of Islamic fundamentalists to appreciate the power and the destruction such dedication to "God's Truth" can generate. For an inside account of the demise of the Southern Baptists, see Bill J. Leonard, *God's Last and Only Hope: The Fragmentation of the Southern Baptist Convention* (Grand Rapids, Mich.: Eerdmans, 1990).

144. See indoctrination and education contrasted by Timothy Arthur Lines, "A Plea for Authentic Religious Education," in *Does the Church Really Want Religious Education?* ed. Marlene Mayr (Birmingham, Ala.: Religious Education Press, 1988), pp. 148-149.

145. The Latin root of the term education (*educo*) means "to lead out." Education "leads out" from ignorance and blind obedience to freedom and individuality. See this discussed in more detail in Timothy Arthur Lines, *Systemic Religious Education* (Birmingham, Ala.: Religious Education Press, 1987), pp. 185-187. An interesting word of warning was sounded by Brameld: "A favorite dogma of educational conservatives is that schools seldom if ever lead and create; they always follow and

for the religious educator as revolutionary. While Marxism is not actually a faith tradition in any commonly accepted sense, it is for some a strongly held faith in a way of thinking, as well as a worldview and a philosophy followed by millions of people for more than a century, and as such it has produced vast changes in the world geopolitical landscape. Since it is probably best considered as post-Christian, or even post-religious,[146] this becomes one of its teaching strengths: Marxism permits the observation of the functions and dynamics of a faith tradition resource that is itself devoid of a deity.[147] Over the years it has evolved and developed differently in the various regions of the world, with a variety of interpreters taking the essential ideas and adapting them to specific needs and situations. Marxism has been assumed to be such a threat to democratic and capitalistic societies[148] that it has not gotten the kind of scrutiny that allows for insight, but rather for defeat and demolition. For all these reasons, and more to follow, Marxism is a fertile field for the religious educator to encounter in depth.

What follows is but the barest of introductions to this odd type of a faith tradition resource, in the hope that each religious educator then will proceed on his or her own for a fuller investigation. The struggle for many will be to approach Marxism with an open and receptive attitude, in contradiction to how most Western societies have indoctrinated their people to approach it. In light of this anticipated difficulty, this introduction will be a recitation of some essential and foundational characteristics that may provide the basis for studying Marxism more thoroughly. Hopefully, enough positive information can be uncovered to convince others that Marxism can serve as a valuable paradigm as a faith tradition resource that remains largely unexplored by too many religious educators who see it only as a negative or threatening enemy.[149]

reflect. This dogma is challenged by educational liberals and radicals." Brameld, *Ends and Means in Education*, p. 118.

146. "Marx was likewise [following a discussion of anti-semitism in Marx's writings] hostile to Christianity, in both practice and philosophy. His antipathy applied to church, clergy, and governments that called themselves Christian." Saul K. Padover, "Notes," in *The Essential Marx: The Non-Economic Writings—A Selection*, ed. Saul K. Padover (New York: New American Library, 1988), p. 282.

147. This is a risky statement. Marx and Lenin, among others of the communist movement, have something of the aura of deity about them for some adherents. For evidence of how this process evolves, see the early work by Sergei Bulgakov, *Karl Marx as a Religious Type: His Relation to the Religion of Anthropotheism of L. Feuerbach*, trans. Luba Barna (Belmont, Mass.: Nordland, 1979; first published in 1907).

148. See the best evidence of this by Marx in his life work, *Capital (Das Kapital)*, on which he worked for nearly thirty years, with the first volume being published in 1867. The other two volumes were incomplete and in raw form, so that the fuller three volume work is the result of editing by Friedrich Engels following Marx's death.

149. One interesting door of entrance into a study of Marxism is its founder and articulator, Karl Marx (1818-1883). Here is a founding figure of a "faith tradition" not completely shrouded in the mists and myths of history, but one close enough in time for us to possess his original writings and to understand his personal life. While hero-worship can and does surround him, it is still possible to get a reasonably accurate accounting of him and his thought without being dependent on and sorting through years—even centuries—of stories and legends about him, real and imagined. It is even possible to read his writings and compare them with what disciples after him wrote and did. Accessibility to the writings, produced in a familiar and modern language, is relatively quickly and easily acquired. The "quest for the historical Marx" is not as much of an issue as it is in some other faith tradition resources.

The first characteristic of Marxism to be mentioned is an obvious one for the subject of this chapter: Marx was undoubtedly a revolutionary.[150] His friend and collaborator Friedrich Engels said at Marx's graveside service: "For Marx was before all else a revolutionist. His real mission in life was to contribute, in one way or another, to the overthrow of capitalist society and of the state institutions which it had brought into being, to contribute to the liberation of the modern proletariat, which he was the first to make conscious of the conditions of its emancipation. Fighting was his element. And he fought with a passion, a tenacity and a success few could rival."[151] Though indeed the revolutionary as described in this chapter has rejected the politics and the violence often associated with the role, Marx nevertheless is an example of a "quiet" but still powerful figure who effected deep and fundamental change. Though he himself did not take up arms, he provided the thought and the reasoning for the revolutionary movement. His contribution to the revolution was the *call* to arms, the awakening of the slumberers. René Coste gave a good description of this aspect of Marx: "All his life he wanted to be a revolutionary, and was it not a revolutionary's goal above all to confound the exploiting classes and to open the eyes of the exploited classes? He surely knew well that revolution normally involved recourse to violence and he accepted this eventuality without hesitation. But he thought that the principal weapon of the revolution was the manifestation of truth. That was the great undertaking of his life. Few individuals in history have believed as strongly as he did in the power of thought or, even more precisely, the power of truth."[152] What better person to exemplify the role of the revolutionary than an icon of revolution itself?

A second characteristic is a close corollary of the first. Marx was primarily a philosopher and educator who worked to establish the proper conditions and to spread his version of revolution through his writings, rather than through direct leadership.[153] In collaboration with Friedrich Engels (1820-1895), he wrote the classic revolutionary tract, *The Communist Manifesto*, which closed with these rousing words: "The Communists disdain to conceal their views and aims. They openly declare that their ends can be attained only by the forcible overthrow of all existing social conditions. Let the ruling classes tremble at a Communist revolution. The proletarians have nothing to lose but their chains. They have a world to win."[154] Then came the ringing call to action: "Workingmen of all countries, unite![155] Such is an example of the power of the written word—and of the potential virtually all persons have for promoting some degree of revolutionary change through exploitation of their individual skills and personality traits. Marx and his followers never left any doubt that their goal was anything less than

150. See Chapter Three, "Biography of a Revolutionary," in Gary North, *Marx's Religion of Revolution: The Doctrine of Creative Destruction* (Nutley, N.J.: Craig Press, 1968), pp. 21-31.
151. Friedrich Engels, "Speech at the Graveside of Karl Marx," in *The Marx-Engels Reader*, p. 603.
152. René Coste, *Marxist Analysis and Christian Faith*, trans. Roger A. Couture and John C. Cort (Maryknoll, N.Y.: Orbis, 1985), p. 2.
153. For a quite negative view of this kind of revolution, see Chapter Five, "The Economics of Revolution," in North, *Marx's Religion of Revolution*, pp. 121-172.
154. Karl Marx and Friedrich Engels, *Manifesto of the Communist Party* (New York: International Publishers, 1948; reprint of 1848 edition), p. 44.
155. Ibid.

total revolution.[156] The old order had to go, and the new would emerge from it.[157] Marx viewed this process as inevitable and that the day of the proletariat had arrived. Capitalism had to be defeated for the new order to take its rightful place,[158] and this end was worth whatever means it took to achieve.[159]

The third characteristic derives from the previous one. Marx used social science for his analytic purposes, especially economics, rather than religion or education. He thus saw history unfolding through economic terms, which allowed him to have a fresh viewpoint and perspective to the flow of events.[160] For example, Marx and Engels wrote: "History is nothing but the succession of the separate generations, each of which exploits the materials, the capital funds, the productive forces handed down to it by all preceding generations, and thus, on the one hand, continues the traditional activity in completely changed circumstances and, on the other, modifies the old circumstances with a completely changed activity."[161] Such a relatively new and different angle on history and development revealed another set of problems and issues to address. Such a procedure and process of looking for a new perspective from which to analyze and develop religious education is of tremendous importance. Although it may not be that economics is the issue that reveals new insights about religious education, some other topic that may be as apparently foreign to the traditional perception of religious education could prove to be just the necessary impetus to reimage the field and help in its revitalization.

The fourth characteristic is the challenge Marxism gives to the assumptions of traditional Christianity. Marxism has been described as post-theistic, in that it places itself beyond the need for a God on whom humans need to be dependent.[162] Marxism thus expects humans to bring about their own revolutions and their own improvements, since there is no one else—some supernatural power—to do it for them. To wait on God or for God's leaders to do it is a part of what Marx addressed as religion in one of his better known passages: "Religious suffering is at the same time the expression of real suffering and the protest against

---

156. "Total revolution" is a phrase Marx himself often used. For example: "The antagonism between the proletariat and the bourgeoisie is a struggle between class and class, a struggle that carried to its highest expression, signifies a total revolution." Karl Marx, *The Poverty of Philosophy*, in *The Essential Marx*, p. 74.

157. One of the clearest examples of this is found in Karl Marx, "General Rules and Administrative Regulations of the International Working Men's Association," ibid., pp. 89-90.

158. Marx and Engels put their primary goal of destroying capitalism succinctly: "In this sense, the theory of the Communists may be summed up in the single sentence: Abolition of private property." Marx and Engels, *Manifesto of the Communist Party*, in *The Marx-Engels Reader*, ed. Robert C. Tucker, p. 346.

159. "In short, the Communists everywhere support every revolutionary movement against the existing social and political order of things." Ibid., p. 362.

160. "Marx was not a historian in the conventional sense and did not write history as such, but his writings are imbued with a sense of history. . . . Marx's philosophy of history is based on dialectical materialism, or what is known as the 'materialist interpretation of history.' This involves the fundamental idea that the determining factors in the development, relations, and institutions of mankind are not mystical or ideological, but economic." Padover, "Notes," in *The Essential Marx*, p. 227.

161. Marx and Engels, *The German Ideology*, in *The Marx-Engels Reader*, p. 136.

162. See, for example, Thomas Dean, *Post-Theistic Thinking: The Marxist-Christian Dialogue in Radical Perspective* (Philadelphia: Temple University Press, 1975). Other designations include post-Christian and post-modern.

real suffering. Religion is a sigh of the oppressed creature, the heart of a heartless world, as it is the spirit of spiritless conditions. It is the opium of the people."[163] These brief and normally misinterpreted words have great meaning for any serious religious educator. Marx was saying that religion can be, and usually is, used as a silencer of the deep inner voice of the human. It was not the "sigh of the oppressed creature" that Marx wanted to still, but the false covering[164] and manipulation of it.[165] Surely any true religious educator has awareness of the ever-present potential for misuse of religion as a manipulator of the people, and is ready to fight any such abuse. The struggle, of course, is to create a healthy religion that is not an opiate.[166] It was this possibility that Marx was unwilling to accept, and Marx's point of view cannot be dismissed out of hand.

A fifth, and final, characteristic to be offered here is that world events have shown a tremendous shaking of the foundations of Marxism and the communist forms of government. How will this "faith tradition" react and change in the face of the counterrevolutionary challenges of democracy? Will it simply become a relic of the past and a "dead religion"—only of interest to future historians— or will it recover and become new like a phoenix in some different form? Is the fate of violent and political movements naturally to be treated violently and politically? If so, this is even more evidence for eschewing such tactics, and for viewing the religious educator as revolutionary in very different terms than as political. The opportunity to watch the evolution and transformation of a faith tradition before one's very eyes is instructive and invigorating.

These five briefly stated characteristics of Marxism may provide some motivation for taking a closer and a more serious look at Marxism as a faith tradition resource. Many more characteristics will be discovered upon further investigation, and the only purpose for listing these introductory ones was to encourage exploration. If nothing else, Marxism may provide an example of what the religious educator as revolutionary does not want to emulate—the political revolutionary. If so, the opportunity to broaden horizons and to consider the religious educator from a differing perspective is always enriching and valuable, whatever the final results.

Historical Personage: Huldrych Zwingli

The choice of Huldrych Zwingli (1484-1531) as a historical personage to represent the revolutionary may strike a surprising if not confusing note for

---

163. Karl Marx, "Towards a Critique of Hegel's *Philosophy of Right: Introduction*," in *Selected Writings*, ed. David McLellan (Oxford: Oxford University Press, 1977), p. 64.

164. Marx was saying that the opium of religion can so anesthetize the adherents that they do not feel the very real and necessary pain that can lead to productive change. The result is that they remain in a dazed state, doing as they are told by the same authorities who are dispensing the anesthesia. This, of course, works to the advantage of the oppressors, and to the continued subjugation of the oppressed.

165. For a fascinating discussion of Marx as a "secular theologian," see Catherine Riegger Harris, *Karl Marx: Socialism as Secular Theology: A Philosophic Study* (St. Louis: Warren H. Green, 1988).

166. This topic is addressed in more detail in Chapter Four, "Religion," in Lines, *Systemic Religious Education*, pp. 127-181.

some. The point of confusion may come because Zwingli is remembered primarily as a figure in the Protestant Reformation, and reform has already been distinguished from revolution. In this particular use of the term, however, it seems appropriate to classify the events of the Reformation more accurately as revolutionary and the participants as revolutionaries. Both in effect—a new movement that was born of the old—and in intent—transformation and reconstruction—the Reformation had the qualities of a revolution, and the changes and realignments spawned by this conflict have yet to die down completely.

If the Reformation is fertile ground for discovering revolutionaries, then why choose Zwingli? The obvious choice would appear to be Martin Luther (1483-1546), the man who by nailing the ninety-five theses to the church door in Wittenberg symbolically marked the beginning of the Protestant Reformation. Certainly a good case could be made for Luther, but two hindrances present themselves. First, Luther's initial intentions really were only to spark reform in the church. He was hesitant to advocate a clear break with the old regime, and he distanced himself from the more radical—revolutionary—elements. Second, and in close connection, Luther's memory is stained with the blood of the peasants, against whom he turned in favor of the nobility.[167] Whatever the reasons for his decisions—and there were some—Luther seems inappropriate to champion the role of the religious educator as a nonpolitical revolutionary in light of his overtly political actions. In retrospect, Luther was at best a reluctant and relatively modest model of a revolutionary.

A true revolutionary of the Reformation was Huldrych Zwingli. He did not turn on the peasants, but instead went with them and led them into battle against the opponents of fundamental change. The result was that he died on the battlefield, and the body of the "heretic" was quartered and burned. It is easy to see why Luther was not anxious to join the "rabble"! Thus Zwingli was not only pastor and theologian who taught the people how to improve their lot, but he was willing to pay the supreme sacrifice to help them in their struggle for transformation and reconstruction. It is important to note, however, that Zwingli was not chosen here for this political and violent type of revolutionary involvement, especially since the results for him were so disastrous. The role-modeling of Zwingli comes at points other than his military actions.

Zwingli, historically, occupies the middle ground between the true reformers like Luther and his companion Philip Melanchthon (1497-1560), on the one hand, and the extremists like Thomas Müntzer (ca. 1490-1525) and Melchior Hoffman (ca. 1495-1543) on the other hand. Indeed, Zwingli was rejected by Luther for his radical views on the sacraments,[168] but Zwingli in turn broke with

---

167. See Martin Luther, *Against the Robbing and Murderous Hordes of Peasants*, trans. Charles M. Jacobs, in *Luther's Works: American Edition*, Vol. 46: The Christian in Society III, ed. Robert C. Schultz (Philadelphia: Fortress, 1967; written ca. 1525), pp. 49-55. For the negativist position against Luther and his decision, see the classic by Friedrich Engels, *The Peasant War in Germany* (New York: International Publishers, 1926; first published in 1850).

168. See this described in G.R. Potter, *Zwingli* (Cambridge: Cambridge University Press, 1976), Chapter 12, "Zwingli and Luther," pp. 287-315.

the far-left wing of the reformers.[169] This positioning reveals that Zwingli was not the most radical of the movement by any means, and he did his best to provide a moderating influence as long as possible.

An example of why Zwingli's writings and his approach are useful to understanding the religious educator as revolutionary is found in his *Commentary on True and False Religion*,[170] which has been called "the earliest truly comprehensive treatise on Protestant theology."[171] Here Zwingli made his case for reliance on the "true religion of the Bible" as opposed to tradition and church authority. In the book, the seeds of true and effective revolution are quickly discernible. Zwingli promoted the power of the individual to interpret and apply scripture, without benefit of approval or direction. In this theological way, Zwingli was opening the door to the liberation and empowerment of the people and closing the door on repression and paternalism. Zwingli gave evidence that there are all kinds of ways to enable people to break their bonds and begin the process of revolution—even through the channel of theology!

Contemporary Example: Paulo Freire

While normally religious educators do not actually stoke the fires of political revolutions, the person chosen for the contemporary example of the role of the revolutionary—Paulo Freire—has advocated just this kind of activity. In addition, however, Freire has proposed a revolutionary educational scheme that can, at least in part, be separated from the politics. In keeping with the overall position of the chapter, the focus in this overview section is upon Freire's *educational* revolution rather than the overtly political aspects of his work. For Freire, this separation is not necessary or useful; to him, it would be more natural to be so deeply involved with transformation, reconstruction, and learners that the educator himself or herself should be swept along in the inevitable struggles that describe both political and educational revolution.

Paulo Freire (b. 1921) is a native Brazilian, and he began his life as an educational revolutionary under inauspicious conditions. He started his work as a teacher of adult literacy, which hardly sounds like a platform for subversive activity, but in Freire's hands it resulted in becoming precisely that. He believed that the peasants, the "wretched of the earth,"[172] should learn to read and write— not just for the possession of the skills, but for the purpose of becoming participating and determining Subjects[173] in their own countries and destinies. Education, as Freire proposed it, is a process of becoming aware of the individual's world

---

169. See a discussion of this in Robert C. Walton, *Zwingli's Theocracy* (Toronto: University of Toronto Press, 1967), Chapter 11, "The Open Split between Zwingli and the Radicals," pp. 176-208.

170. Huldrych Zwingli, *Commentary on True and False Religion*, ed. Samuel Macauley Jackson and Clarence Nevin Heller (Durham, N.C.: Labyrinth Press, 1981; reprint of 1929 edition; first published in 1525).

171. William Walker Rockwell, "Preface," ibid., p. iii.

172. The phrase of Richard Schaull in "Foreword," in Paulo Freire, *Pedagogy of the Oppressed*, trans. Myra Bergman Ramos (New York: Seabury, 1968), p. 10.

173. This was the way the translator, Myra Bergman Ramos, represented Freire's idea. She wrote in a translators note: "The term 'Subjects' denotes those who know and act, in contrast to 'objects,' which are known and acted upon." See Freire, *Pedagogy of the Oppressed*, p. 20, n.2.

in such a way that the individual acts upon it and transforms it for the good of the people, rather than for the comfort and the pleasure of the ruling class. This kind of education soon becomes subversive, indeed!

There are sacrifices for such activity, and Freire has often been *persona non grata* in a number of so-called "Third World" countries in South America because his export of educational revolution has not always been well received by the ruling governments. He has spent recent years living in Geneva, Switzerland, working with the World Council of Churches in religious educational planning.[174] In fact, Freire himself has admitted that his experience with the details of actual political revolution has been so scant that he may be an inappropriate spokesperson for it: "It is possible some may question my right to discuss revolutionary cultural action, a subject of which I have no concrete experience. However, the fact that I have not personally participated in revolutionary action does not negate the possibility of my reflecting on this theme."[175] These comments show that Freire is not an example of an activist sort of revolutionary, leading the people from the front lines of danger. He has actually led a rather quiet life for most of the time, studying and writing in the relative security of Switzerland. This is but further evidence that the revolutionary does not have to be a rabble-rouser in the streets to be effective or genuine. There are a great number of ways to lead and nurture a revolution.

What follows is the barest of introductions to Paulo Freire's work in the role of an educational revolutionary. It must be repeated that his work is by no means devoid of the political dimensions of the revolutionary, and that because of this perspective his comments and procedures are deeply affected by his political and ideological stance as a Marxist. Still, with some careful attention and interpretation, enough of the nonpolitical educational revolutionary can be extracted to be of great use. In the overview section, his writings on the topic of the "pedagogy of the oppressed," are briefly sketched, and then later his efforts are given some brief evaluation. As has been true throughout the book, these introductions should be taken as samplings and not as anything approaching completeness. They serve as but an invitation to more serious study and consideration.

Overview

As mentioned above, Paulo Freire the educational revolutionary has been primarily interested in promoting adult literacy[176]—a rather mild-sounding way to start a revolution, but an effective one.[177] The way he went about such a pro-

---

174. For a fuller biographical treatment, see Denis E. Collins, *Paulo Freire: His Life, Works, and Thought* (New York: Paulist, 1977), or "Introduction," by Robert Mackie, in *Literacy and Revolution: The Pedagogy of Paulo Freire*, ed. Robert Mackie (London: Pluto Press, 1980), pp. 3-8.

175. Freire, *Pedagogy of the Oppressed*, p. 24.

176. For an introduction to this specific interest of Freire's, see Paulo Freire and Donaldo Macedo, *Literacy: Reading the Word and the World* (South Hadley, Mass.: Bergin and Garvey, 1987).

177. "In *Pedagogy of the Oppressed* Freire explicitly turned his attention to education as a necessary means for bringing about a revolution." John L. Elias, *Conscientization and Deschooling: Freire's and Illich's Proposals for Reshaping Society* (Philadelphia: Westminster, 1976), p. 75. Elias refers to some criticisms of Freire's noninvolvement in political revolutionary action in ibid., pp. 73-80.

gram, however, was different than the regular means of learning the alphabet and then memorizing words. Freire recognized that reading and writing were political activities as well as purely educational ones, and he used the political aspects to spur interest and awareness of the illiterates in their specific situation. Freire wrote: "We have never understood literary education of adults as a thing in itself, as simply learning the mechanics of reading and writing, but, rather, as a political act, directly related to production, to health, to the regular system of instruction, to the overall plan for the society still to be realized."[178] Freire made sure that the adult education had immediate application and relevance, so that literacy could be seen as a means working directly toward larger and more revolutionary and reconstructive ends.

The centerpiece of Freire's plan was to make the peasants aware of their situation and to give them hope that it would improve. Freire called this entire effort "humanization," showing that humanization brings awareness of dehumanization. He began the ground-breaking *Pedagogy of the Oppressed* with this emphasis: "While the problem of humanization has always, from an axiological point of view, been man's central problem, it now takes on the character of an inescapable concern. Concern for humanization leads at once to recognition of dehumanization, not only as an ontological possibility but as a historical possibility. And as man perceives the extent of dehumanization, he asks himself if humanization is a viable possibility. Within history, in concrete, objective contexts, both humanization and dehumanization are possibilities for man *as an uncompleted being conscious of his incompletion.*"[179]

This process of humanization—and the companion awareness of dehumanization—is essential for the oppressed to experience, or they can never be truly free, according to Freire. It is only when the oppressed are able to see themselves as other than parts of the oppressors that the oppressed can be liberated. The central focus of this kind of freedom was made explicit by Freire in the following quote: "The oppressed, having internalized the image of the oppressor and adopted his guidelines, are fearful of freedom. Freedom would require them to eject this image and replace it with autonomy and responsibility. Freedom is acquired by conquest, not by gift. It must be pursued constantly and responsibly. Freedom is not an ideal located outside of man; nor is it an idea which becomes a myth. It is rather *the indispensable condition for the quest for human completion.*"[180]

Here, then, was the key to unlocking Freire's thought: Freedom as the "indispensable condition for the quest for human completion," and the dual awareness of humanization/dehumanization reveals the human as "an uncompleted being conscious of incompletion." Literacy was Freire's way of bringing awareness and of beginning the struggle for freedom—his means for revolution.

Another important sentence was contained in the words from Freire quoted above: "Freedom is acquired by conquest, not by gift." Freire's pedagogy did not

---

178. Paulo Freire, *Pedagogy in Process: The Letters to Guinea-Bissau*, trans. Carman St. John Hunter (New York: Seabury, 1978), p. 13.
179. Freire, *Pedagogy of the Oppressed*, p. 27. Emphasis added.
180. Ibid., p. 31. Emphasis added.

depend upon the oppressor giving the education or the freedom. Liberation pedagogy, as espoused by Freire, makes it the necessary responsibility of the oppressed to acquire their own freedom. Freire noted that this is a very real problem for the uneducated and the poor, as when he wrote: "The central problem is this: How can the oppressed, as divided, unauthentic beings, participate in developing the pedagogy of their liberation? Only as they discover themselves to be 'hosts' of the oppressor can they contribute to the midwifery of their liberating pedagogy. As long as they live in the duality in which *to be* is *to be like*, and *to be like* is *to be like the oppressor*, this contribution is impossible. The pedagogy of the oppressed is an instrument for their critical discovery that both they and their oppressors are manifestations of dehumanization."[181] Freire was stating the hard truth that until the oppressed realize that they are part and parcel of the cycle of oppression, no true transformation or reconstruction is possible. The oppressed must take up their own cause, and find their own solutions. In the process, the oppressed then not only liberate themselves but *also the oppressor*.[182] In oppression, all parties—the oppressed as well as the oppressor—are dehumanized, and for real freedom to flourish all parties must become humanized. Freire placed the hope for humanization on the oppressed, and it begins with the dawning of their own awareness—achieved in Freire's schema through adult literacy.

To understand Freire, one must be conversant with two words: *Conscientização* and "praxis," and the two are intimately related. *Conscientização* is a Portuguese word which in Freire's writings means "learning to perceive social, political, and economic contradictions, and to take action against the oppressive elements of reality."[183] All of this has been referred to in the above text as "becoming aware," an awkward and not fully revelatory designation to be sure, but a close translation of the term. "Praxis" is a well-known and well-worn Marxist word,[184] and in Freire's usage it means "reflection and action upon the world in order to transform it."[185] By this, Freire refused to endorse the dichotomies of thinking and action but instead was saying that critical thinking (reflection) and purposeful activity (action) must be done together and must inform each other. One does not think and then act, or act and then think. The two are parts of the whole, and are done simultaneously. It is similar to saying that theory and practice are not separate and distinct, but are elements of a larger whole. Praxis is both theory and practice performed interactively, and focused toward transformation.[186] *Conscientização* is achieved through praxis.

A summary of Freire's plan for educational revolution was provided by Freire himself: "The pedagogy of the oppressed, as humanist and libertarian peda-

---

181. Ibid., p. 33. Emphasis from Freire.
182. "This, then, is the great humanistic and historical task of the oppressed: To liberate themselves and their oppressors as well." Ibid., p. 28.
183. Ibid., p. 19, translator's note.
184. It is well to remember that Freire is a Marxist and that his particular field of expertise is educational philosophy, so it is natural for him to pick up and employ these terms.
185. Freire, *Pedagogy of the Oppressed*, p. 36.
186. "Animal activity, which occurs without a praxis, is not creative; man's transforming activity is." Ibid., p. 91.

gogy, has two distinct stages. In the first, the oppressed unveil the world of oppression and through the praxis commit themselves to its transformation. In the second stage, in which the reality of oppression has already been transformed, this pedagogy ceases to belong to the oppressed and becomes a pedagogy of all men in the process of permanent liberation."[187] Freire did not teach dependency or paternalism. He taught personal responsibility to the peasants. The oppression was their problem, and the solution to it was theirs to find. In the search, all the people would eventually become free.

A word about the role of the educator in Freire's pedagogy is essential. As one would imagine from the previous discussions, the educator is not a transmitter of information but a facilitator of a self-directed process. Freire described it this way: "Thus the educator's role is fundamentally to enter into dialogue with the illiterate about concrete situations and simply offer him the instruments with which he can teach himself to read and write. This teaching cannot be done from the top down, but only from the inside out, by the illiterate himself, with the collaboration of the educator."[188] It is not the educator who teaches, but the subject/student who learns. As Freire said in this quote and elsewhere, the task of the educator is to engage the illiterate in dialogue with what is already known and understood and then to express it in formal language.[189] Freire made the point even more pronounced: "I wish to emphasize that in educating adults, to avoid a rote, mechanical process one must make it possible for them to achieve critical consciousness so that they can teach themselves to read and write."[190] To advocate any other method would, to Freire, violate the principles of freedom and *conscientização*.

In this regard, Freire contrasted the traditional way of teaching with his newer dialogical manner. The old way he called the "banking" concept of education: "Education thus becomes an act of depositing, in which the students are the depositories and the teacher is the depositor. Instead of communicating, the teacher issues communiques and makes deposits which the students patiently receive, memorize, and repeat."[191] Pressing the point even further, Freire said: "In the banking concept of education, knowledge is a gift bestowed by those who consider themselves knowledgeable upon those whom they consider to know nothing."[192] In its place, Freire proposed what he called "problem-posing education," which he described this way: "Through dialogue, the teacher-of-the students and the students-of-the-teacher cease to exist and a new term emerges: teacher-student with students-teachers. The teacher is no longer merely one-who-teaches, but one who is himself taught in dialogue with the students, who in turn while being taught also teach. They become jointly responsible for a process in which all grow."[193] Later, Freire summed up this difference of the change in

---

187. Ibid., p. 40.
188. Paulo Freire, *Education for Critical Consciousness*, trans. Myra Bergman Ramos (New York: Seabury, 1973), p. 48.
189. See ibid., p. 43, and *Pedagogy of the Oppressed*, p. 54.
190. Freire, *Education for Critical Consciousness*, p. 56.
191. Freire, *Pedagogy of the Oppressed*, p. 58.
192. Ibid.
193. Ibid., p. 67.

perspective: "The students—no longer docile listeners—are now critical coin-vestigators in dialogue with the teacher."[194]

One final issue remains for this overview to include as a way of introducing Freire's teaching, and this is his use of the base[195] community idea for his own educational and transformational purposes. Base communities have developed among the poor throughout Latin America in order to continue the local traditions threatened by rapid societal change and to recapture the sense of togetherness and community that too easily cuts them off from other people in similar circumstances.[196] These informal, relational, small, but very vital communities[197] were the target areas that Freire used for his adult literacy programs. He taught the poor to read in their base communities, which not only provided them with the abilities to read and write, but gave them the foundation for self-determination and removal of oppression.[198] Rather than teaching literacy by some mechanical or "banking" process, Freire used the "problem-posing" approach where the problems the people worked on were ones they faced each and every day together.[199] This made their education relate directly to their communities and to the solution of common difficulties.[200]

In his own unique and forthright manner, Freire captured what he was trying to help the oppressed achieve through their revolution in this simply way: "We need, then, an education which would lead men to take a new stance toward their problems—that of intimacy with those problems, one oriented toward

---

194. Ibid., p. 68.

195. The term "base" was defined by Daniel Schipani as referring "to the 'popular classes'—the poor, oppressed, believing Christians and their ties of class, race, and culture." Daniel S. Schipani, *Religious Education Encounters Liberation Theology* (Birmingham, Ala.: Religious Education Press, 1988), p. 218. See the extended discussion in Chapter Five, "The Oppressed and the Base Community," ibid., pp. 210-260.

196. An introduction to the concept of base communities can be found in Chapter Eleven, "Latin American Theology and Education," by Robert T. O'Gorman in *Theological Approaches to Christian Education*, ed. Jack L. Seymour and Donald E. Miller (Nashville: Abingdon, 1990), pp. 195-215.

197. Robert O'Gorman explained the Christian forms of these base communities: "Basic Ecclesial Communities are an attempt to restore community to the Christian religion—the personal relationships as preached by Jesus—to live together less anonymously, more personally." Ibid., pp. 198-199.

198. In describing these base communities, Freire explained some of his deeper reasons for using the group approach: "One of the basic themes (and one which I consider central and indispensable) is the anthropological concept of culture. Whether men are peasants or urban workers, learning to read or enrolled in a post-literacy program, the starting point of their search to know more (in the instrumental meaning of the term) is the debate of the concept. As they discuss the world of culture, they express their level of awareness of reality, in which various themes are implicit. Their discussion touches upon other aspects of reality, which comes to be perceived in an increasingly critical manner. These aspects in turn involve many other themes." Freire, *Pedagogy of the Oppressed*, p. 117.

199. Freire noted: "Problem-posing education is revolutionary futurity." Ibid., p. 72.

200. "Problem-posing education, as a humanist and liberating praxis, posits as fundamental that men subjected to domination must fight for their emancipation. To that end, it enables teachers and students to become Subjects of the educational process by overcoming authoritarianism and an alienating intellectualism; it also enables men to overcome their false perception of reality. The world—no longer something to be described with deceptive words—becomes the object of that transforming action by men which results in their humanization." Ibid., p. 74.

research instead of repeating irrelevant principles. An education of 'I wonder,' instead of merely, 'I do.'"[201]

Evaluation

The first thing to come to mind in evaluating Paulo Freire as he relates to this chapter's role is that he does address religious education from the perspective of a revolutionary. The difficulty this poses is that he is both an educational revolutionary, which is what this examination of Freire has principally discussed, and a political revolutionary. His moral support of political revolution is well known, and so his pedagogical procedures are inherently and inevitably radical and disruptive to the old order as well as intimately tied to his political agenda. In a time, though, when education is so often seen as a tool of continuing the status quo and as an instrument of authority, Freire turns oppressive education on its head and shows it as the dynamic force it truly is. Rather than revolutionizing a country and then trying to educate the liberated people for managing their freedom, Freire taught and demonstrated that liberation can begin with education. As people gain their "humanization," they will take care of the revolution themselves.

The second issue is to recognize Freire's role modeling of the revolutionary religious educator—both in the political and educational sense. Freire has had a great influence recently on the formulation of many types and proposals in religious education, especially through the work of theorists Thomas Groome[202] and Daniel Schipani,[203] but also at least indirectly with a group of writers represented by Allen Moore[204] and Robert O'Gorman.[205] For example, Thomas Groome paid Freire tribute a number of times in *Christian Religious Education* for his help in providing the philosophical background to Groome's neo-Marxist understanding of praxis,[206] which of course is foundational to Groome's entire proposal of "shared Christian praxis."[207] Groome also was quite similar to Freire in

---

201. Ibid., p. 36.

202. See Thomas H. Groome, *Christian Religious Education: Sharing Our Story and Vision* (San Francisco: Harper & Row, 1980). The use of praxis, for example, is pervasive in Groome's work.

203. See Daniel S. Schipani in *Religious Education Encounters Liberation Theology*. Schipani noted in the preface of his book that "the work and thought of Paulo Freire serves as the centerpiece of the book," (p. 4.) and indeed the book was dedicated to Freire. Although Schipani's book had a broader scope than just Freire's contribution, it is an excellent resource for seeing the Freireian influence on liberation theology and on the whole of religious education. Also see Daniel S. Schipani, *Conscientization and Creativity: Paulo Freire and Christian Education* (Lanham, Md.: University Press of America, 1984), which is a revision of Schipani's dissertation produced at Princeton Theological Seminary in 1981.

204. See Allen J. Moore, "A Social Theory of Religious Education," in *Religious Education as Social Transformation*, pp. 9-36; and Allen J. Moore, "Liberation and the Future of Christian Education," in Seymour and Miller, with others, *Contemporary Approaches to Christian Education*, pp. 103-122.

205. See Robert T. O'Gorman discuss Latin American types of religious educational models in *Theological Approaches to Christian Education*, ed. Jack L. Seymour and Donald E. Miller (Nashville: Abingdon, 1990), pp. 195-215.

206. See, for example, Groome, *Christian Religious Education*, pp. 175-177. Actually, references to Freire can be found throughout Groome's work. The term "praxis" was introduced into modern philosophy by Karl Marx, and has been used by Marxist and neo-Marxist philosophers ever since.

207. See this proposal detailed in Chapter Nine, "Shared Christian Praxis," ibid., pp. 184-232.

accepting the fundamental role of politics in religious education, which he stated plainly: "Educational activity with pilgrims in time is a political activity."[208] As Groome further noted, Freire was not the only influence toward this position,[209] but Freire has been one of the primary figures recently to propound this idea. Politics appears to be firmly rooted in the religious education ideas of many recent writers,[210] and it is now an issue—thanks in large measure to Freire—that must be consciously addressed as to its appropriateness in the field.[211]

A third evaluative comment about Freire's educational philosophy relates to its emphasis on the cognitive dimension of the human to the exclusion of the affective dimension. His position seems to be that cognition—right thinking—leads to right action and to right lifestyles. For example, his support of praxis is in contradistinction to his attack on the "banking" idea of education. The "banking" education is described as "an act of depositing, in which the students are depositories and the teacher is the depositor."[212] This assumes a hyper-cognitive approach where telling people what to think ensures that people will act accordingly. Freire's praxis approach, though, is also based on cognition: "Liberation is a praxis: the action and reflection of men upon their world in order to transform it."[213] Praxis is thus a process of intertwined thinking and doing. The even larger dimensions of the human, most obviously the affective, are left untapped and unrecognized. It is as if Freire assumes that to think is to do, and surely this is too much of an oversimplification. The irony here is that Freire began *Pedagogy of the Oppressed* by addressing the "problem of humanization,"[214] but left the examination of the problem incomplete.

A fourth reflection on the work of Freire is that as a revolutionary who has built his life around a dialogical process of education, it is hardly fair or possibly even relevant to discuss his methods in such a cut-and-dried manner as this literary review is forced to do. Freire's educational procedures are better understood and experienced in the relational environment of a base community rather than in the rarified air of academia, and the majority of his books are collections of papers, essays, letters, or interviews given in the midst of such activity.[215] The

---

208. Ibid., p. 15.
209. Groome mentions Plato, Aristotle, and John Dewey as philosophers who discussed the political nature of education. Notwithstanding, Groome grounds his own educational ideas primarily on two contemporary neo-Marxist philosophers, namely Paulo Freire and Jürgen Habermas.
210. In addition to Groome, see such contemporary examples as Mary C. Boys, *Educating in Faith: Maps and Visions* (San Francisco: Harper & Row, 1989), p. 7-8, where she asks each of the "classic expressions" of religious education: "In what way is education a political activity?"; and Chapter Five, "The Grace of Power," in Maria Harris, *Teaching and Religious Imagination: An Essay in the Theology of Teaching* (San Francisco: Harper & Row, 1987), pp. 78-96. Other examples abound in the literature.
211. For an example of a religious educator who is opposed to this kind of emphasis, see James Michael Lee, *The Content of Religious Instruction: A Social Science Approach* (Birmingham, Ala.: Religious Education Press, 1985), pp. 671-672; 685-689; and 757-758.
212. Freire, *Pedagogy of the Oppressed*, p. 58.
213. Ibid., p. 66.
214. Ibid., p. 27.
215. For a representative example of this kind of collection, see Paulo Freire: *The Politics of Education: Culture, Power, and Liberation*, trans. Donaldo Macedo (Branby, Mass.: Bergin and Garvey, 1985).

prime exception is *Pedagogy of the Oppressed*, which is his most formal and reasoned exposition of his thought.[216] Freire was not specifically addressing the academics, or even the educated of the "developed" countries in his writings. He was working with the illiterate and the poor of the so-called Third World, so to pull him into the context of academic scrutiny puts him in an alien and distorted environment.

The fifth evaluative comment, implied in the one above, relates to the target audience for Freire's pedagogy. He was not writing to the oppressors or for the "haves." He was writing to and for the oppressed and the "have-nots." Ironically, virtually anyone reading this present book, or for that matter any of Freire's books, are more likely to be oppressors and "haves." It is as if the "haves" are stealing his revolutionary pedagogy and using it either to work against his hopes for liberation or to so domesticate it that it no longer sounds or functions in a true revolutionary manner. It seems that most of Freire's readers are part of the problem more than elements of the solution and that such persons should not properly be reading someone else's strategy for overthrowing their own tyranny.[217]

The above issue raises a sixth critical question: What exactly are the criteria for determining who is an oppressor and who is the liberator? Does the fact that someone resides in a non-Third World country automatically exclude him or her from having any positive influence on the lives of the oppressed?[218] One of the difficulties of dealing with political power is deciding who gets it and who does not. An example of the dilemma can be drawn easily from Freire's own writings. Freire made any number of times contradictory statements like the following: "The correct method lies in dialogue."[219] Then he said directly after, in the next sentence: "The conviction of the oppressed that they must fight for their liberation is not a gift bestowed by the revolutionary leadership, but a results of their own *conscientização*."[220] How do dialogue and fighting go together? In dialogue, the effort is to find some kind of agreement or some common ground for at least co-existence. Fighting means that some win, and others lose. This potential for exclusivity and "party-line" adherence seems to be in direct con-

---

216. Of this relatively expository work, Freire said that "this admittedly tentative work is for radicals." Freire, *Pedagogy of the Oppressed*, p. 21.

217. Of course, there are those who criticize Freire for doing this himself. John Elias, for example, wrote: "Freire's theory and strategy of revolution appear to be rather naive. . . . He discusses revolution without discussing any particular social and historical contexts. He appears to be generalizing from his reflections upon the Brazilian situations in which he was involved. He is like the crusader who, after the brave and good fight, stands ready to generalize his theories and strategies to the situation of all oppressed peoples. *Pedagogy of the Oppressed* was written by Freire to tell himself what he and his fellow reformists should have done to bring about real change in Brazil in the early 1960s. But the simplistic analysis of Brazilian society into oppressed and oppressors does not do justice even to that historical situation. Its application as a universal theory of social analysis is even more unacceptable." Elias, *Conscientization and Deschooling*, p. 88. See ibid., pp. 88-93 for more critical comments about Freire's revolutionary strategy.

218. Freire addresses this, somewhat incompletely it seems, in *Pedagogy of the Oppressed*, pp. 46-48. One could address this to Freire himself, since he has spent most of his life in the more economically developed countries.

219. Ibid., p. 55.

220. Ibid.

tradiction to Freire's intent for praxis and dialogical activity,[221] but it remains a problem when a set of dichotomies such as oppressed and oppressor are continually emphasized.

A seventh question relates to the future viability of Freire's views. Freire bases his educational principles and practices on the philosophy of Karl Marx. Yet the political enactment of Marxism throughout the world has been an abject failure wherever and whenever it has been tried. The collapse of the Marxist-based Soviet Union, and the hatred for Marxism which the peasants, workers, and intellectuals had for Marxism in that former country, is just one illustration of the complete failure of Marxism in the concrete. If the political and practical enfleshment of Marxism has failed so consistently and so miserably, and was typically put into place only by force and oppression, then what may be said about the future of Paulo Freire's view of education is that of freeing learners from oppression, yet Marxist-based governments in the twentieth century were among the most oppressive regimes the world has ever experienced.

A final word about Freire's contributions is that whatever role one plays in the oppressor/oppressed drama, each individual can experience the sense of *conscientização* to oppression and the need for transformation in our individualized forms of the "base community," albeit in differing degrees. Freire's pedagogy has special fertility for religious education, both in warning and in utilization. Freire has been effective in sensitizing many in religious education to the fact that either one plays the part of oppressor, or that one becomes committed to being a liberator. There is no middle ground, at least in Freire's rendering of the situation. Such a message is vital to the health of religious education and provides a refreshing perspective for the complacent religious educator. Paulo Freire has brought both educational and political revolution to the borders—if not to the halls—of religious education. What exactly should be done with such a mixture of revolutionary proposals is still being debated.

Representative Teaching Procedure: Consciousness Raising

The first task of an educational revolutionary is to make the learner conscious of the true situation in which he or she is immersed. Any other starting place leaves the learner in the dark as to why he or she is supposed to be learning something and leaves him or her unconcerned with the process. The basic idea is encapsulated by the old saying, "If it ain't broke, don't fix it." The religious educator who wants to start a revolution must begin by helping the learners perceive the brokenness, and only then can remedying the situation get underway with fervor and passion. This introduction to reality is what the teaching procedure in this section is designed to do—to raise the consciousness of the learner concerning the present state of circumstances, thereby revealing the need if not the necessity for fundamental and constructive change.

Although there are obviously a number of ways to raise the consciousness level

---

221. "In *Pedagogy of the Oppressed* Freire valiantly attempts to make his theory of the dialogical character of the revolution hold up against the stated views of revolutionaries. The effort must be pronounced a failure." Elias, *Conscientization and Deschooling*, pp. 91-92.

of persons, the one explored here is based on the work of William Glasser, which he termed "reality therapy."[222] Glasser came to the task as a psychiatrist, and hence the use of the term "therapy,"[223] but he and others have made adaptations to a variety of other fields, including education.[224] The foundational process of consciousness raising—reality therapy—remains the same in whatever garb it may appear.[225] Glasser's starting point was that a person's basic problem is, simply stated, inadequacy: "He is unable to fulfill his essential needs."[226] Second, he said: "In their unsuccessful effort to fulfill their needs, no matter what behavior they choose, all patients have a common characteristic: they all deny the reality of the world around them." His goal with persons who sought his help was just as succinctly stated: "Therapy will be successful when they are able to give up denying the world and recognize that reality not only exists but that they must fulfill their needs within its framework."[227] This goal is achieved through the teaching of responsibility, which Glasser defined as "the ability to fulfill one's needs, and to do so in a way that does not deprive others of the ability to fulfill their needs."[228] The educator's[229] primary task, then, is consciousness raising, where the educator helps the learner to "face a truth that he has spent his life trying to avoid: he is responsible for his behavior."[230]

These same goals and tasks of reality therapy have been adapted specifically to educational activities by Glasser through a process similar to what Freire called "problem-posing education,"[231] but which Glasser termed "social problem-solving meetings."[232] The intent of this kind of educational procedure is to "attempt to solve the individual and group educational problems of the class and the school,"[233] where the learners "discover that each class is a working, problem-solving unit and that each student has both individual and group responsibilities."[234] Glasser explained how this process was intimately connected to consciousness raising, to reality, and to the need for taking personal responsibility: "Under ordinary conditions, because there is no systematic effort to teach them

222. The clearest description is found in William Glasser, *Reality Therapy: A New Approach to Psychiatry* (New York: Harper & Row, 1965).

223. Glasser defined therapy as "a special kind of teaching or training which attempts to accomplish in a relatively short, intense period what should have been established during normal growing up." Ibid., p. 20.

224. As Glasser noted in the introduction to *Reality Therapy*: "This book will describe Reality Therapy, explain in detail how it differs from conventional psychiatry, and show its successful application to the treatment of juvenile delinquents, chronic mental hospital patients, private psychiatric patients, and disturbed children in the school classroom." Ibid., p. 3.

225. Glasser's primary effort to relate reality therapy to education is *Schools Without Failure* (New York: Harper & Row, 1969).

226. Glasser, *Reality Therapy*, p. 5.

227. Ibid., p. 6.

228. Ibid., p. 13.

229. Glasser uses the term "therapist," but for purposes here the term educator is more relevant and appropriate.

230. Ibid., p. 27.

231. See Freire, *Pedagogy of the Oppressed*, pp. 99-118, as well as the discussion in the previous section of the chapter.

232. Glasser, *Schools Without Failure*, p. 122.

233. Ibid., p. 122.

234. Ibid., p. 123.

social problem solving, school children find that problems that arise in getting along with each other in school are difficult to solve. Given little help, children tend to evade problems, to lie their way out of situations, to depend upon others to solve their problems, or just to give up. The social problem-solving meeting can help children learn better ways."[235]

Bruce Joyce and Marsha Weil developed the classroom meeting proposed by Glasser into a teaching procedure that has six phases.[236] First is the establishment of a safe climate for involvement, where each learner "speaks for himself or herself, and all persons are encouraged to participate. It is clear that everyone's views are equally valued and respected."[237] Second is the discovery or exposing of the particular problem for discussion, surfaced by either the religious educator or the learners. When the specific problem has been outlined, then the learners "identify (1) the consequences if the situation continues and (2) the social norm that usually governs the situation."[238] Third, the learners make individual value judgments about their behavior in regard to the problem under discussion and to explain why they act as they do. Fourth is an effort to create alternative behaviors and to agree on which ones are to be normative. Fifth is the public commitment to perform the agreed-upon alternative behavior. Sixth, after some time has passed, and at another meeting, the effectiveness of the new behavior implementation is examined and evaluated by the class.

This teaching procedure reinforces the virtues stressed earlier in the chapter, equality and autonomy, as well as the aim and function of transformation and reconstruction. Each class and each individual takes responsibility for a problem that becomes apparent to them when their consciousness is raised to the level that the realities of the situation have become clear—and unacceptable. The way is thus opened for some truly revolutionary religious education, where the religious educator does not mandate a particular kind of change but facilitates the group in making its own decisions.

Experiential Simulation: Designing the Future

Maybe one of the least understood but one of the most important aspects of the religious educator in the role of the revolutionary relates to designing the future—not just preparing for it, or trying to predict it, but creating it to be what is desired. The revolutionary as presented in this chapter is not some wild-eyed extremist who advocates burning the system down with no plan or purpose other than chaos and disruption. If there is any deconstruction, it is purposeful and ultimately constructive and positive because the removal is done to make way for a better structure or procedure. This means that the religious educator must be skilled in the business of designing the future.

There are at least two good ways to simulate this designing of the ideal future. One suggestion is to play a game where that is exactly the purpose: to experience

235. Ibid., pp. 123-124.
236. Bruce Joyce and Marsh Weil, *Models of Teaching*, 3rd ed. (Englewood Cliffs, N.J.: Prentice-Hall, 1986), pp. 209-214.
237. Ibid., p. 211.
238. Ibid.

imagining and planning what the future could be like. As Charles Plummer put it: "Future-oriented simulations/games move us away from the-die-is-cast past and present viewpoints toward the fluid shape of things to come. Out of the awareness of the possibility of change we develop a desire to create preferred events."[239] Why is gaming and simulating the future important to the revolutionary? The point is that planning can indeed design the future, since as Plummer also pointed out: "Concrete experience with hypothetical events become reality."[240] One good game among the great number of possibilities is *Futuribles*, developed by George Koehler.[241] It has been described this way: "*Futuribles* is an informal gaming situation for people who want to learn about the future, for people who want to plan for the future, and for people who want to focus on particular futures."[242] Its result on the players is explained as follows: "The game provides an interesting way of gaining insight into one's ideas about the future and into the need for interplay and discussion in developing the policies for the future."[243]

A second, more individualized suggestion is to simulate an interactivist's attempt to design or redesign an organization according to the process of idealization. The five interdependent phases have been outlined by Russell Ackoff as follows:[244]

1. *Ends planning.* Determining what is wanted: the design of a desired future. This requires specifying goals, objectives, and ideals; short-run, intermediate, and ultimate ends.
2. *Means planning.* Determining how to get there. This requires selecting or inventing courses of action, practices, programs, and policies.
3. *Resource planning.* Determining what types of resources—for example, men, machines, materials, and money—and how much of each will be required, how they are to be acquired or generated, and how they are to be allocated to activities once they are available.
4. *Organizational planning.* Determining organizational requirements and designing organizational arrangements and the management system that will make it possible to follow prescribed means effectively.
5. *Implementation and control.* Determining how to implement decisions and control them: maintaining and improving the plan under changing internal and external conditions.

Probably the first and foremost impression one has in beginning to work through this kind of revolutionary activity—whether by gaming or by simulat-

---

239. Charles M. Plummer, "Futures Games and Simulations: An Evaluation," in *The Guide to Simulations/Games for Education and Training*, eds. Robert E. Horn and Anne Cleaves, 4th ed. (Beverly Hills, Calif.: Sage Publications, 1980), p. 108.

240. Ibid.

241. *Futuribles*, created by George E. Koehler, and copyrighted in 1973, is produced by the Book Service division of World Future Society in Washington, D.C.

242. Horn and Cleaves, eds., *The Guide to Simulations/Games for Education and Training*, p. 405.

243. Ibid.

244. Ackoff, *Redesigning the Future*, pp. 29-30.

ed interactive planning—is being overwhelmed by the amount of work and the attention to detail that is necessary—which is precisely the point of the simulation. The work required of the revolutionary is intense, and so the concept of a shoot-from-the-hip type of character in the role should be easily dispelled; in addition, the work is complex and involved, so the companion notion of the revolutionary as a lone ranger is just as quickly jettisoned. The work of the religious educator as a revolutionary is to bring about fundamental and positive change and to make the necessary effort do so is not to be considered or undertaken lightly. The level of commitment demanded of the revolutionary is enormous, matching the desperate need to design the ideal future.

Summary

The role of the revolutionary is exceedingly important to religious education, but it is also one rarely exhibited or experienced by the religious educator. For most, it is not one adopted easily or quickly because of the extremes of energy output and emotional investment required. The aim of transformation and the function of reconstruction, though, are so fundamental to genuine religious education that each individual needs to find a way that is appropriate to the perceived task and congruent with his or her personality to be a revolutionary— not a political, or violent, or manipulative type of revolutionary, but a constructive, positive, courageous, and innovative one. The future of better tomorrows depends upon the call to commitment and to action that is sounded and actualized by the true religious education revolutionary.

Figure 13 summarizes the discussion of the revolutionary religious educator's role as it has been developed throughout the chapter.

Figure 13: The Religious Educator as Revolutionary	
Dimensions of the Role	Innovator
	Planner
	Agitator
	Change Agent
Aim	Transformation
Function	Reconstruction
Primary Virtues	Equality
	Autonomy
Activity	Individuating
Shadow Role	Ideologue
Faith Tradition Resource	Marxism
Historical Personage	Huldrych Zwingli
Contemporary Example	Paulo Freire
Representative Teaching Procedure	Consciousness Raising
Experiential Simulation	Designing the Future

Chapter Twelve

The Religious Educator as Therapist

The role of the therapist, and ultimately the role of the religious educator as therapist, is a complex activity and one difficult to master. This may be surprising, because probably most people associate the role of therapist with relational activity[1]—which may initially sound like a relatively natural and uncomplicated process that virtually anyone should be able to perform. Although high levels of innate ability for developing interpersonal relationships and for showing deep care and concern are indeed preferable if not requisite for the therapist, fundamentally the role demands the performance of specific skills and the exercise of discipline in a finely-honed manner. The therapist is a professional who is thoroughly prepared, educated, and experienced through a rigorous curriculum of formal learning as well as through involvement in continued supervised learning opportunities.[2] The therapist does not arrive casually or cavalierly at functioning as an interventionist in other's lives but through years of focused atten-

---

1. There is a kernel of truth here, which Carl Rogers gave some support to: "I have long had the strong conviction—some might say it was an obsession—that the therapeutic relationship is only a special instance of interpersonal relationships in general, and that the same lawfulness governs all such relationships." Carl R. Rogers, *On Becoming a Person: A Therapist's View of Psychotherapy* (Boston: Houghton Mifflin, 1961), p. 39. Rogers then went on to spell out how the special case of the psychotherapist's relationship was both similar and dissimilar to other more general kinds of relationships.

2. This is not meant to imply that the therapist is programed to say the right answers or to ask the proper questions, as Reuben Fine made clear: "Unless the therapist has the inner conviction and the theoretical background to back up his belief that the procedure he is using makes very good sense, it is more apt to fail than to succeed. A mechanical approach will never go far in therapy; the human situations involved are too varied, the emotions too powerful, the need for sincerity too great. The beginning therapist should be encouraged to question the value of every procedure until its underlying rationale really becomes second nature to him." Reuben Fine, *The Healing of the Mind: The Technique of Psychoanalytic Psychotherapy* (New York: David McKay, 1971), p. 7.

tion and evaluation. A glance at the books for beginning therapists shows that the primary concern of the beginning therapist should be the mastery of technique and that the breadth of issues necessary for continued development then increases when these basic skills have been put in place.[3]

This is to say that the therapist is primarily involved in dealing skillfully with human relationships and in being specially attuned to understanding the affective dimension[4] of the human. It is not to say that the therapist is the only person in society concerned with these human interactions or qualities but that the therapist is the one who attends to them in a professional and considered way. Carl Rogers termed this an expertise in providing a *helping relationship*, which he described as "a relationship in which at least one of the parties has the intent of promoting the growth, development, maturity, improved functioning, improved coping with life of the other. The other, in this sense, may be one individual or a group. To put it another way, a helping relationship might be defined as one in which one of the participants intends that there should come about, in one or both parties, more appreciation of, more expression of, more functional use of the latent inner resources of the individual."[5] Abraham Maslow came at this issue in a similar way, saying that "psychotherapy is not at its base a unique relationship, for some of its fundamental qualities are found in *all* 'good' human relationships" and suggesting that "this aspect of psychotherapy must be subjected to a more thoroughgoing critique than it has ordinarily received, from the viewpoint of its nature as a good or bad human interpersonal relation."[6]

An important caveat must be injected here. While the therapist does deal in human relationships that in many ways parallel what all humans experience in one way or another, still the helping relationship of the therapist is a very specialized type of relationship and procedure distinctively offered by the professional therapist. Abraham Maslow came back around to make this aspect of the therapist clear: "The differences between technical and lay therapy are vast and important. Psychological developments in this century, starting with the revolutionary discoveries of Freud, Adler, and others, have been transforming psychotherapy from an unconscious art into a consciously applied science. There are now available psychotherapeutic tools that are not automatically available to

---

3. One disturbing example is by Amy Lamson, *Guide for the Beginning Therapist: Relationship Between Diagnosis and Treatment*, 2nd ed. (New York: Human Sciences Press, 1986). In this book of thirteen chapters introducing the role and responsibility of the therapist, fully one paragraph was devoted to the topic of the characteristics of an effective therapist (p. 33). Fortunately, not all authors are this brief in this kind of exposure, as the following paragraphs of the introduction will show. One nice example is this quote about the education of a Jungian analyst: "The education of the analyst extends beyond anything that can be verbally expressed. It is, more than anything, an experience of transformation in which one comes to know one's own soul and to befriend it. In the process, it is hoped that one may become what one really is." June Singer, "The Education of the Analyst," in *Jungian Analysis*, ed. Murray Stein (La Salle, Ill.: Open Court, 1982), p. 367.

4. There is some danger in making this a general statement that applies to all kinds of psychotherapy because of the different emphases that are possible. A Skinnerian, for example, would not want to be identified with exploring the affective dimension but rather with the behavioral or lifestyle dimension.

5. Rogers, *On Becoming a Person*, pp. 39-40.

6. Abraham H. Maslow, *Motivation and Personality*, 3rd ed., rev. Robert Frager, James Fadiman, Cynthia McReynolds, and Ruth Cox (New York: Harper & Row, 1987), p. 98.

the good human being, but are available only to people of sufficient intellect who have in addition been rigorously trained to use these new techniques. They are artificial techniques, not spontaneous or unconscious ones. They can be taught in a way that is to some extent independent of the character of the psychotherapist."[7] It is critical to note that the religious educator learns from studying the image and practice of the therapist but that the religious educator is not a psychotherapist just because the religious educator offers a kind of helping relationship.[8] A little knowledge can be a dangerous thing, and the religious educator should not be tempted to become the dilettante who dabbles with another's psyche without proper credentials or background.

Carl Rogers once set down what he called some "significant learnings" regarding the role of the therapist, and a select few of these are mentioned here to provide a basic introduction to the therapist's approach.[9] As even Rogers noted about his own "findings": "They are not fixed. They keep changing. Some seem to be acquiring a stronger emphasis, others are perhaps less important to me than at one time, but they are all, to me, significant."[10] Rogers' list included the following statements, which serve here to give a sense of the attitude of the therapist, rather than any specific or strict guidelines of performance that each individual therapist must strictly adhere to.

1. In my relationships with persons I have found that it does not help, in the long run, to act as though I were something that I am not. . . . What I am saying here, put another way, is that I have not found it to be helpful or effective in my relationships with other people to try to maintain a façade; to act in one way on the surface when I am experiencing something quite different underneath.[11]
2. I find I am more effective when I can listen acceptantly to myself, and can be myself. . . . One way of putting this is that I feel I have become more adequate at letting myself *be* what I *am*.[12]
3. I have found it of enormous value when I can permit myself to *understand* another person. . . . Very rarely do we permit ourselves to understand precisely what the meaning of his statement is to him [the client]. I believe this is because understanding is risky. If I let myself really understand another person, I might be changed by that understanding.[13]
4. I have found it enriching to open channels whereby others can communicate their feelings, their private perceptual worlds to me. Because understanding is rewarding, I would like to reduce the barriers between me and others, so that they can, if they wish, reveal themselves more fully.[14]

---

7. Ibid., p. 108. For a more extended discussion of this point, see ibid. pp. 108-109.

8. It may be true that a religious educator could also be a psychotherapist. The statement here is that religious educators are not automatically psychotherapists just because they are in a helping relationship and are modeling the role of the therapist.

9. For the full listing and discussion by Rogers, see Rogers, *On Becoming a Person*, pp. 16-27.

10. Ibid., p. 16.

11. Ibid., pp. 16-17.

12. Ibid., p. 17.

13. Ibid., p. 18.

14. Ibid., p. 19.

5. I have found it highly rewarding when I can accept another person. . . . I find that when I can accept another person, which means specifically accepting the feelings and attitudes and beliefs that he has as a real and vital part of him, then I am assisting him to become a person: and there seems to me great value in this.[15]

6. The more I am open to the realities in me and in the other person, the less do I find myself wishing to rush in and "fix things." As I try to listen to myself and the experiencing going on in me, and the more I try to extend that same listening attitude to another person, the more respect I feel for the complex processes of life. So I become less and less inclined to hurry in and fix things, to set goals, to mold people, to manipulate and push them in the way that I would like them to go. I am much more content simply to be myself and to let the other person be himself.[16]

This sixth point of Rogers' brings out an issue that needs even further highlighting. One of the most demanding of the skills and disciplines associated with this role is that of purging oneself of as much bias and prejudice toward another person as humanly possible. To be a therapist requires first and foremost the ability to be totally "present" with the person seeking therapy,[17] thereby removing the personal agendas and considerations of the therapist as much as humanly possible so that the other individual—the client[18]—can be seen and heard clearly. This skill requires constant monitoring and effort to accomplish to any worthwhile degree. The irony is that often the most valuable thing the therapist has to offer is a blank screen[19] upon which the individual can project him-

---

15. Ibid., pp. 20-21.
16. Ibid., p. 21.
17. Carl Rogers said he asked himself these questions in regard to "being present": "Can I let myself enter fully into the world of his [the client's] feelings and personal meanings and see these as he does? Can I step into his private world so completely that I lose all desire to evaluate or judge it?" Rogers, *On Becoming a Person*, p. 53.
18. For the religious educator, the preferable term is "learner." For the professional therapist, the term "client" is the one more often used. "Client" refers to the person receiving the attention of the therapist in the therapeutic relationship. The therapist's difficulty in finding the proper designation is to not make one of the people in the relationship to appear as sick and the other person as healthy, as the terms "patient" and "physician" tend to do. The use of "client" follows the lead of Carl Rogers (among others) in trying to solve this semantic problem. See, for example, an early discussion of this issue in Carl R. Rogers, *Client-Centered Therapy: Its Current Practice, Implications, and Theory* (Boston: Houghton Mifflin, 1951), especially pp. 11-18. In addition, the term "client" is used in this chapter primarily as a singular noun, but only for convenience. Therapists, and religious educators, deal with groups just as often and hopefully just as effectively. Either groups or individuals can be the focus of attention whenever the term "client" is employed throughout the chapter.
19. This notion of being able to offer a totally blank screen is certainly an arguable one. Can anyone really be alive and be free of agendas or values? Some therapists even deny the need to offer such a blank screen—such an attempt, to them, would wipe away their humanity, which is precisely what they feel they have to offer. Maslow summed up the issues this way: "A therapist can consider himself the active, deciding, managing boss of his patient, or she can relate herself to the patient as a partner in a common task, or finally, he can transform himself into a calm emotionless mirror to the patient, never becoming involved, never coming humanly close, but always remaining detached. This last is the type that Freud recommended, but the other two types of relationships are the ones that actually prevail most often, although officially the only label available for any

self or herself. At bottom, then, it may be that the most valuable resource the therapist has to offer is the *fullness* of the therapist's personality and attention—or, possibly even more accurately, the therapist's *emptiness*.

This paradox of fullness and emptiness is well-known to Christians, who revere the "kenosis" (emptying) of Christ through the incarnation. Philippians 2:7 said that Christ "emptied himself,"[20] expressed by the use of a form of the Greek root word κενόω—"to evacuate," or "to empty." The idea in this passage was that Christ "emptied" himself of his divine identity and took on the form of a human to fulfill the task assigned him. Christians generally believe that this "emptying" did not negate Christ's divinity but subordinated it to the larger task at hand. By way of analogy, the therapist is called upon to be kenotic: to subordinate his or her own needs so that those of the client can become known and dealt with therapeutically.[21]

This process of emptying comprises one of the chief contributions the role of therapist has to make to the religious educator, and this theme runs through the chapter: The religious educator as therapist comes to the learners (or as the therapist would say, clients) primarily with an open heart and an open mind, ready to accept and listen to their needs and hopes, for the purpose of facilitating their continued growth, health, and integration. The role of the therapist keeps the focus on the one receiving the therapy, or at least on the development of the relationship between the therapist and client, rather than upon the one providing the therapy.[22] The intent is to show that the therapist teaches how to diagnose and meet the needs of the client, instead of the client merely providing a forum of performance for the therapist.

As this chapter develops, the role of therapist will not be taken in any one direction or follow any one particular school, in that the therapist must be understood exclusively as a Freudian, a Jungian, or a Rogerian.[23] Admittedly, each type of therapist has particular techniques and practices, but there is sufficient common ground for the overall role of the therapist to be identified. An attempt is

---

normal human feelings for the analysand is countertransference, that is irrational, sick." Maslow, *Motivation and Personality*, p. 99.

20. NRSV. The KJV has the misleading translation of "made himself of no reputation."

21. This is not to say that the therapist has no growth or true interaction in the therapeutic relationship. For a more in-depth examination of this complex issue, see it discussed in terms of transference and countertransference in Chapter Nine, "Self-Awareness and Personal Growth of the Psychotherapist," in Albert Ellis, *Humanistic Psychotherapy: The Rational-Emotive Approach*, ed. Edward Sagarin (New York: McGraw-Hill, 1973), pp. 129-145. Ellis took the position that the therapist must grow in order to be of any real use to the client: "*Real* personal growth and maturity on the part of the therapist, it would appear, is almost always beneficial to the client, because it involves the acceptance by the therapist of the unvarnished reality that doing therapy is not invariably a thing of beauty and joy; that some clients are obnoxious and distressing, but that's the way they are; and that, believe it or not, the main function of therapy is to *try* (though not necessarily to succeed) to help the client to get better." Ibid., p. 142.

22. Sheldon Kopp had a characteristically unorthodox view of his work as a psychotherapist, which provides yet another way to view the role: "I practice psychotherapy not to rescue others from their craziness, but to preserve what is left of my own sanity: not to cure others, but to heal myself." Sheldon Kopp, *Even a Stone Can Be a Teacher: Learning and Growing from the Experiences of Everyday Life* (Los Angeles: Jeremy P. Tarcher, 1985), p. 12.

23. Both the historical personage and the contemporary example sections of this chapter do focus on the Jungian perspective, however.

made to identify the structure and practice of the therapist without addressing specifically the content of the therapy, as much as this is possible, with full realization the limits this approach imposes.

Alongside the limits of the above paragraph, this chapter primarily employs the term "therapist" in the sense of "psychotherapist."[24] A wide variety of other kinds of therapists exists, such as physical therapists and vocational therapists. The exclusion of them is not for lack of relevance but for clarity and simplicity. The greatest danger in excluding other types of therapists is that it may seem as if valid therapy only deals with the mind or the emotions, thereby devaluing the myriad other aspects of the human. Such tunnel vision is certainly not the intent of the chapter, as will be specified later. The boundary of psychotherapist is only for ease of explanation not for lack of respect or appreciation for the other types of therapy required in various circumstances.

The dimensions of the role that follow further explicate the nature of the therapist's task. Once the role is more firmly established, the discussion ranges to the broader scope of topics such as aim, function, and virtues. The plan is to see only enough of the role to glimpse the potential it holds for the continued development of the religious educator. A more detailed exploration of the role beyond this introductory glance must be left for the individual to pursue.

Dimensions of the Role

The role of the therapist as presented in this chapter is explored by looking at four dimensions: healer, catalyst, facilitator, and fellow traveler. Of course, these are not the only dimensions of the therapist, since the role is much more diverse and complex than any four descriptions could capture. Neither are these specific dimensions the exclusive property of the therapist, since, for example, some aspects of the healer dimension can be detected in the role of minister as well.[25] The hope for combining this particular set of dimensions is to provide a gestalt of the role, allowing the identity of the therapist to emerge when perceived in its totality and thereby revealing its relevance to the religious educator.

Healer

The dimension of the therapist as healer is fundamental to and deeply rooted in the role, however it is performed. Jack Walters expressed the efforts of the heal-

---

24. This follows the pattern of one author who used the term "therapist" as "the generic term for counselor, social worker, psychologist, psychiatrist, mental health worker, [and] psychiatric nurse." See Jeffrey A. Kottler, *On Being a Therapist* (San Francisco: Jossey-Bass, 1986), p. 2. There is no suggestion that a religious educator who studies the role of the therapist, however, is equipped to perform psychotherapy. Such activity is specialized and needs the sanctioning of the appropriate licensing agencies. A good resource for nonprofessional counselors who need basic help in giving care is Eugene Kennedy, *On Becoming a Counselor: A Basic Guide for Non-Professional Counselors* (New York: Seabury, 1977). Kennedy introduced his book this way: "This book is written for all those people who, without extensive psychological training, must deal with troubled people in the course of their work." Ibid., p. vii.

25. For example, the image of the wounded healer is taken up in the following chapter, "The Religious Educator as Minister," in the discussion of compassion.

er this way: "The objective, then, in the healing process is to bring into unity and harmony what existed in disunity and disharmony."[26] Different approaches to therapy have different ways of pursuing this healing process. In trying to characterize the Jungian approach to psychotherapy, Jolan Jacobi gave strong evidence that the healing aspect is central: "Jungian psychotherapy is no analytical procedure in the usual meaning of this term, although it holds strictly to the medically, scientifically, and empirically confirmed premises of research in all relevant fields. It is a *Heilsweg*, a 'way of healing' in both meanings of the German term which signifies at the same time 'healing' and 'salvation.' It has all the requisites for 'healing' a person from his psychic and therewith connected psychogenic sufferings. It has all the instruments for . . . combating successfully the most complicated and threatening developments of mental disease. But besides this it knows the way and has the means to lead the individual to his own 'healing' (*Heil*), to that knowledge and perfection of his own personality which has ever been the aim and goal of all spiritual striving."[27]

The therapist as healer, whether or not a Jungian perspective is employed, focuses on the individual and seeks ways for that person to find his or her *own* healing. Frederick Perls, in pursuing a Gestalt psychology, used the image of the healer as well, stressing that the healing process itself was accomplished by the individual, not by the therapist doing it *for* the person.[28] Perls explained: "Energy and attention have gone into forcing yourself, because of a mistaken feeling of 'oughtness,' along lines that run counter to your healthy interests. To the extent that you regain and redirect this energy, the area of restored vitality will progressively increase. It is nature that cures—*natura sanat*. A wound heals or a bone knits by itself. There is nothing the physician can do but to clean the wound or set the bone. It is the same with the personality."[29] A similar perspective was stated by Reuben Fine, when he noted that the health of the person was always kept in focus by the therapist but that health was not a commodity which the therapist could simply dispense. It is something the person must develop—with the aid of the therapist. Fine wrote: "The goal of psychotherapy for the patient is growth rather than cure. But what of the therapist? If he is not curing the patient, what is he doing? He is contributing to the growth of another human being."[30]

Erich Fromm took up the subject of the healer and the "curing" process from a psychoanalytic viewpoint. Fromm, following Freud's lead, spoke of the therapist as the "physician of the soul."[31] Fromm's perspective was: "The analyst is not a theologian or a philosopher and does not claim competence in those fields, but as a physician of the soul he is concerned with the very same problems as phi-

26. Jack Walters, *Healing the Fractured Self* (Minneapolis: Seabury, 1985), p. 159.

27. Jolan Jacobi, *The Psychology of Jung: An Introduction,* trans. K.W. Bash (New Haven: Yale University Press, 1943), p. 58.

28. "One of the elements which appears to stand out prominently in the initial reaction of the client is the discovery that he is responsible for himself." Rogers, *Client-Centered Therapy,* p. 71.

29. Frederick Perls with Ralph E. Hefferline and Paul Goodman, *Gestalt Therapy: Excitement and Growth in the Human Personality* (New York: Dell, 1951), p. 112.

30. Fine, *Healing of the Mind,* p. 140.

31. See Chapter Four, "The Psychoanalyst as 'Physician of the Soul,'" Erich Fromm, *Psychoanalysis and Religion* (New Haven: Yale University Press, 1950), pp. 65-98.

losophy and theology: the soul of man and its cure."[32] Although Fromm seems to be disagreeing with the earlier responses to the physician as the one "curing" the patient, he clarified and resolved the conflict by noting that "cure has not the single connotation of remedial treatment which modern usage commonly implies, but is used in its larger sense of 'caring for.'"[33]

The dimension of healer requires the therapist occasionally to be confrontive with the client.[34] The therapist, however, does not really confront the client as much as the client faces the truth—which the therapist provides by offering a mirror and letting the client see the reality for himself or herself.[35] Because the client must become aware of the glaring realities that he or she has been assiduously avoiding, often for very good reasons, the confrontational work of the therapist is designed to remove the blinders from the client, allowing him or her to see what the therapist sees in the bright light of clear vision.[36] The one affirming fact the therapist has on his or her side is that the client must want this kind of honest feedback or the client would not initiate this kind of therapeutic relationship, for as George Weinberg noted: "The essence of psychotherapy is to enable the patient to appreciate how he has been keeping himself the same—and how he can change."[37] This does little to ease the pain, however, at the moment when a harsh truth is uncovered for the client to examine.[38]

Confrontational healing is an art that includes what the New Testament admonition called "speaking the truth in love."[39] Howard Clinebell put confrontation in the context of growth: "Growth occurs in the tension and interplay between caring and confrontation, between love and justice, between playfulness and decision."[40] Confrontation is honest feedback given at the appropriate time when the client is ready, willing and able to face an unvarnished version of the truth.

---

32. Ibid., p. 7.

33. Ibid., p. 65.

34. Reuben Fine wrote: "From the vantage point of the therapist, the whole process of learning in psychotherapy can be divided into four stages: confrontation, clarification, interpretation, and working-through. The definition of the problem proceeds by a series of confrontations; usually one confrontation is not sufficient for the purpose." Fine, *Healing of the Mind*, pp. 176-177.

35. From a Jungian perspective, what is usually confronted is the shadow self, of which Jacobi said: "Confronting one's shadow means becoming unsparingly critically conscious of one's own nature." Jacobi, *Psychology of Jung*, p. 58. Carl Jung wrote: "The shadow personifies everything that the subject refuses to acknowledge about himself and yet is always thrusting itself upon him directly or indirectly—for instance, inferior traits of character and other incompatible tendencies." Carl G. Jung, "Conscious, Unconscious, and Individuation," in Vol. 9, Part One, *The Archetypes and the Collective Unconscious*, trans. R.F.C. Hull, in *The Collected Works of C.G. Jung* (New York: Pantheon, 1959), pp. 284-285.

36. For a good discussion of effective ways for the therapist to confront the client, see Gerard Egan, *The Skilled Helper: Model, Skills, and Methods for Effective Helping*, 2nd ed. (Monterey: Brooks/Cole, 1982), pp. 186-197. Egan's summary statement about helpful confrontation: "Confrontation . . . is an invitation to examine some form of behavior that seems to be self-defeating or harmful to others and to change the behavior if it is found to be so." Ibid., p. 186.

37. George Weinberg, *The Heart of Psychotherapy: A Journey into the Mind and Office of the Therapist at Work* (New York: St. Martin's Press, 1984), p. 81.

38. For more on types of therapeutic confrontation, see B.G. Berenson and K.M. Mitchell, *Confrontation: For Better or Worse* (Amherst: Human Resource Development Press, 1974).

39. Ephesians 4:15, NRSV.

40. Howard Clinebell, *Growth Counseling: Hope-Centered Methods of Actualizing Human Wholeness* (Nashville: Abingdon, 1979), p. 55.

It is always provided as one possible alternative for the client to use as he or she constructs a picture of the larger whole."[41] The truly competent therapist keeps in mind that his or her task is to reflect what he or she sees, but to leave the final decision making to the client. It is always within the purview of the client to reject the feedback, and to deflect the confrontation.[42]

The religious educator should be no stranger to confrontational healing, although he or she may struggle with the timing and the appropriateness of how to go about the confrontation. Many would not expect or appreciate confrontation in a religious context, but the assignment of the religious educator—with emphasis on the educator—cannot be completed adequately without some degree of allowing learners to confront the truth. Such an encounter may be experienced by the presentation of new information, a differing method of interpretation, or the suggestion of a moral or ethical obligation, yet the moments of confrontation can never be excluded from the religious educator's task. The truth, from the perspective of the individual religious educator, spoken in love, for the further development of the learner, must be expressed clearly and honestly for the religious educator to have any integrity.[43] In this regard, the religious educator is also obligated to accept such feedback from others when it is offered. Feedback has to travel at least two directions to be complete.

The entire dimension of healer should be a natural and inseparable part of the work of the religious educator. If, as Jack Walters said, healing is bringing unity and harmony to disunity and disharmony,[44] there can surely be no doubt that true religious education relates to such a description. The religious educator, modeling the role of the therapist, allows learners to confront the truth, from their own perception and experience of it, thereby having learners take responsibility for their own particular forms of healing. Just as the therapist or physician does not actually heal but prepares the conditions to be more conducive for it, neither does the religious educator heal—but prepares the conditions to be more conducive for it. More on precisely how this can be accomplished is the topic of the following dimension of the therapist.

Catalyst

The term "catalyst" is often misused as an analogy, but in the case of the therapist it can be used appropriately. The catalyst, in the hard sciences, is a substance used to precipitate or accelerate a chemical reaction wherein the elements are transformed but the catalyst itself is left unchanged. With care and within limitations, this image of the catalyst is analogous to one of the dimensions of the therapist. Frederick Perls made the connection and the application between

---

41. "If confrontation is actually an attack, then it seems to help the confronter get a load off his or her chest rather than help the other person live more effectively." Egan, *The Skilled Helper*, p. 186. He went on to note: "There is such a thing as responsible and caring confrontation." Ibid.

42. See Chapter 4, "The 'Nice' Psychotherapist," in George Bach and Herb Goldberg, *Creative Aggression: The Art of Assertive Living* (Garden City, N.Y.: Anchor Press, 1983), pp. 91-111. This chapter was written to the client on how to be assertive with the therapist.

43. "Confrontation needs to focus on both negative, growth-limiting attitudes, beliefs, and behavior in persons and on the positive potential for change of which they are unaware." Clinebell, *Growth Counseling*, p. 55.

44. Walters, *Healing the Fractured Self*, p. 159.

the catalyst and the therapist to be quite understandable: "Our view of the therapist is that he is similar to what the chemist calls a catalyst, an ingredient which precipitates a reaction which might not otherwise occur. It does not prescribe the form of the reaction, which depends upon the intrinsic reactive properties of the materials present, nor does it enter as a part into whatever compound it helps to form. What it does is to start a process, and there are some processes which, when once started, are self-maintaining or autocatalytic. This we hold to be the case in therapy. What the doctor [therapist] sets in motion the patient continues on his own."[45]

One of the inevitable results and goals of successful therapy is some kind of fundamental change—change which is focused primarily on the client, since this is surely why he or she has come for help.[46] As the previous discussion of the healer pointed out, at least a part of the role of the therapist is to facilitate the client's awareness of the actual situation and to allow the person to decide where and how the options for change should be introduced. The focus and the reason for therapy, then, is to enable the *client* to change and develop in healthy ways that are appropriate to the individual. The client deserves and expects this personal and individualized attention.

The notion of the catalyst arises at this point. The client does not expect the therapist to change as a result of their relationship. As far as the client is concerned, change and the reason for therapy resides within himself or herself. As a catalyst, the therapist works to precipitate and accelerate change—in the client. Whether the therapist changes as a result of the therapeutic relationship is of no consequence to or responsibility of the client.[47]

The qualifications for using "catalyst" with care and within limitations become clearer now. In reality, if indeed a therapeutic relationship is established, the therapist must be so engaged as to experience at least some degree of change as a result of it. Albert Ellis put it in a rather unforgettable way: "Asking a modern psychologist whether he thinks it advisable for therapy to lead to the continuing self-awareness of the psychotherapist is like asking a good Christian whether he

---

45. Perls with Hefferline and Goodman, *Gestalt Therapy*, p. 15.

46. Perls continued his comments from the above quote on the catalyst: "The 'successful case,' upon discharge, is not a 'cure' in the sense of a finished product, but a person who now has tools and equipment to deal with problems as they may arise. He has gained elbow-room in which to work, unencumbered by the cluttered odds and ends of transactions started but unfinished." Ibid.

47. The issue of the relationship between the therapist and the client is a difficult one that has received extensive discussion over the years. The more technical terms are transference and countertransference. Lawrence Rockland defined transference as "the distorting influence of past relationships upon present relationships," and reports that Sigmund Freud first used the term in 1895 in *Studies on Hysteria*. Lawrence H. Rockland, *Supportive Therapy: A Psychodynamic Approach* (New York: Basic Books, 1989), p. 100. Rockland then defined countertransference as "the emotional responses of the therapist to the patient," and noted that the term was introduced by Freud in 1910. Ibid., p. 113. Rockland said of countertransference: "It can be used in two very different ways. One focuses on the therapist's irrational responses to the patient; the other concentrates on the impact of the patient's irrationality on the therapist. Neither model views countertransference negatively; it is an inevitable phenomenon, and an opportunity for the therapist to learn more about the patient and about him- or herself." Ibid. Virtually every author in the field deals with these crucial topics in one way or another. For some examples, see Weinberg, *Heart of Psychotherapy*, pp. 129-163; and Fine, *Healing of the Mind*, pp. 24-168.

is against sin. Few recent authorities have failed to emphasize that one of the main goals of psychological treatment is to help the therapist as well as the patient to develop into a more creative and self-fulfilled individual."[48] The very nature of human relationships requires that both parties change and adapt in order for an effective relationship to develop. In the therapeutic relationship, however, the therapist is aware of his or her own needs and keeps them under control so that the client receives the focus and the attention. The therapist has means outside of this relationship to resolve his or her particular issues. The discussion should never degenerate to the point where the client surrenders center stage and the therapist's needs are then met to the exclusion of the client's.

Again, the lessons for the religious educator are obvious. No one can be an effective educator without being affected by the teaching process and the relationships involved in it. The direction and the intent of the educational process, however, is for the instructional act to meet the needs and interests of the learners, rather than those solely of the religious educator.[49] In this restricted sense, the religious educator, like the therapist, serves as a catalyst to facilitate change in learners. Change in the educator is desired, expected, and even necessary, but is it not the *reason* for the activity. Such a situation where the educational process is designed to meet the needs of the educator rather than the learners describes the worst kind of misuse and manipulation of learners,[50] out of bounds for the proper role of either the effective therapist or the effective religious educator.

Facilitator

Another dimension of the therapist that is often misunderstood and mishandled is that of facilitator. The therapist has responsibility for helping the client find his or her way through the thicket of broken dreams, unrealistic fantasies, impossible expectations, and invalid hopes, and the previous dimensions of healer and catalyst are valuable instruments in this regard. The therapist does *not* have the right to take over the decision-making activity for the client, however. The dimension of facilitator points to the effort of the therapist to help the client sort out for himself or herself the options and the possibilities but stops short of telling the client what to do. What the client finally does is up to the client. Carl Rogers made this point when he said that "it is the *client* who knows what hurts, what directions to go, what problems are crucial, what experiences have been deeply buried. It began to occur to me that unless I had a need to demonstrate my own cleverness and learning, I would do better to rely upon the client for the direction of movement in the process."[51] There is a very real boundary related to the client's own responsibility and personal integrity which the effective therapist does not violate. The therapist can facilitate the deci-

---

48. Ellis, *Humanistic Psychotherapy*, p. 129.

49. For a fuller examination of this topic, see Chapter Nine, "Student-Centered Teaching," in Rogers, *Client-Centered Therapy*, pp. 384-428.

50. See an example of the misuse of education described by Carl R. Rogers, *Freedom to Learn for the 80's* (Columbus: Charles E. Merrill, 1983), pp. 12-15. See him contrast the facilitation and the abuse of students in ibid, pp. 199-307.

51. Rogers, *On Becoming a Person*, pp. 11-12.

sion-making process *of* the client, but cannot perform it *for* the client.[52]

The client often seems to want the therapist to do something for him or her, or to take over the decision-making process for him or her, which is very different than understanding the dimension of the therapist as facilitator. As Frederick Perls put it: "The job is not, in line with widespread misconception, for the doctor to 'find out' what is wrong with the patient and then 'tell him.' People have been 'telling him' all his life and, to the extent that he has accepted what they say, he has been 'telling' himself. More of this, even if it comes from the doctor's authority, is not going to turn the trick. What is essential is not that the therapist learn something about the patient and then teach it to him, but that the therapist teach the patient *how* to learn about himself. This involves his becoming aware of how, as a living organism, he indeed does function. This comes about on the basis of experiences which are in themselves nonverbal."[53] The absolute core of the facilitator is contained in these further words of Perls: "We undertake to do nothing *to* you. Instead, we state some instructions by means of which, if you so desire, you may launch yourself on a personal adventure wherein, by your own active efforts, you may do something for your self—namely, discover it, organize it, and put it to constructive use in the living of your life."[54]

Admittedly the issues are clearer in an antiseptic discussion like this one than in actual practice. The very act of exploring options and evaluating them puts the therapist in an unusually influential position. The fact that a client comes to a therapist often denotes that the client is experiencing some difficulty in making decisions or in coping with life situations. The client is by every estimation a vulnerable human being, open to abuse and manipulation by the therapist as well as others in society.[55] It is the genuine therapist's commitment to realize and respect this vulnerability and to work with the client to shore up that person's boundaries, enabling thoughtful and reflective decisions that work for the good of the client. This model of the therapist was one advocated by Abraham Maslow: "His conscious effort is not to impose his will on the patient, but rather to help the patient—inarticulate, unconscious, semiconscious—to discover what is inside *him*, the patient. The psychotherapist helps him to discover what he himself wants and desires, what is good for him, the patient, rather than what is good for the therapist. This is opposite of controlling, propagandizing, molding, teaching in the old sense."[56]

---

52. See an overview of the various "facilitative conditions" from which the therapist can choose in James C. Hansen, Richard R. Stevic, and Richard W. Warner, Jr., *Counseling: Theory and Process* (Boston: Allyn and Bacon, 1972), pp. 229-238.

53. Perls with Hefferline and Goodman, *Gestalt Therapy*, pp. 15-16.

54. Ibid., p. 4.

55. This is precisely the place where the issues of transference and countertransference mentioned earlier take on such great importance. If the therapist is not conscious of these processes, and thus is not in some control of them, he or she can easily be swept away in the emotions of the moment and take advantage of this vulnerability of the client. This, of course, says nothing of the unscrupulous therapist—the manipulator—who is discussed more thoroughly in the later section on the shadow role.

56. Abraham H. Maslow, *The Farther Reaches of Human Nature* (New York: Viking, 1971), p. 15.

The image, then, is of the therapist who facilitates the client's ability to make decisions with insight and awareness, based on his or her own bank of experiences, rather than the therapist who makes the decisions for the client. The enabling therapist does not program the client as if the client were some kind of automaton, depriving the client of the learning and the preparation needed for future difficulties, but teaches the client how to *be* themselves, and to take care of himself or herself.[57] This was what Rogers meant when he wrote: "Psychotherapy does not supply the motivation for such development or growth. This seems to be inherent in the organism. . . . But therapy does play an extremely important part in releasing and facilitating the tendency of the organism toward psychological development or maturity, when this tendency has been blocked."[58]

The religious educator has much to learn from the dimension of facilitator. The religious educator does *not* carry responsibility for deciding what paths are the proper ones, where they should lead, and when they should be followed. The religious educator facilitates the learner to know and to feel who he or she really is, and then to act on that self-understanding. It is to help with what Rogers identified as one of the fundamental issues of human development: "It seems to me that at bottom each person is asking, "Who am I, *really*? How can I get in touch with this real self, underlying all my surface behavior? How can I become myself?"[59] There is no greater task or responsibility than for the religious educator to be available for facilitating the learner on such a personal and meaningful quest for self-understanding.

Fellow Traveler

The role of therapist necessarily includes the dimension of fellow-traveler— one who walks alongside in a caring, open, and compassionate manner.[60] The client is by common consent doing his or her own walking, but the therapist is also on the journey, and the two walk together as far as is necessary and appropriate. When the time for individual and independent path making comes, as it will, the therapist bids the pilgrim adieu. Until that time, the therapist is a comforting and supportive presence. The key here, though, is that each traveler is responsible for himself or herself, and no one else can determine the way or the truth other than the individual. As Sheldon Kopp said: "The Zen master warns: 'If you meet the Buddha on the road, kill him!' This admonition points up that no meaning that comes from outside of ourselves is real. . . . Killing the Buddha on the road means destroying the hope that anything outside of ourselves can be our master. No one is bigger than anyone else. There are no

---

57. Egan, in describing client self-responsibility, said: "The function of helpers [therapists] is not to remake their client's lives but to help them handle problems in living and refashion their lives according to their own values." Egan, *Skilled Helper*, p. 12.

58. Rogers, *Client-Centered Therapy*, p. 60.

59. Ibid., p. 108.

60. This image is similar to what Morton T. Kelsey described as the companion, but companion can be misconstrued to sound too friendly and social to describe the fuller aspects of the role. See Morton T. Kelsey, *Companions on the Inner Way: The Art of Spiritual Guidance* (New York: Crossroad, 1986). This book is explored in more detail in the section on the contemporary example later in the present chapter.

mothers or fathers for grown-ups, only sisters and brothers."[61]

Many people perceive therapy as a frightening and threatening activity. The prospect of seeing yourself with clarity and without a mask is not one too many people want or desire, especially if you are used to hiding behind fantasies or disguises.[62] Entering therapy, therefore, requires courage, while completing it requires even more. Knowing there is someone who is also on the journey of self-discovery is encouraging and motivating. The fellow traveler brings no magic map or flying carpet that avoids the pain, but this companion is committed to being there, continuing to be present during the darkness to come and willing to stand by and wait while the unique and personal burdens of the individual are being processed.

Sheldon Kopp used the image of the guru to express his understanding of the therapist as a fellow traveler. Kopp described this person as a "special sort of teacher [who] helps others through the rites of initiation and transition by seeming to introduce his disciples to the new experiences of higher levels of spiritual understanding. In reality, what he offers them is guidance toward accepting their imperfect, finite existence in an ambiguous and ultimately unmanageable world."[63] One important aspect of the guru that Kopp pointed out is this: "Even the contemporary Western guru, the psychotherapist, can only be of help to that extent to which he is a fellow-pilgrim."[64] Teaching is a prime responsibility of the guru, but it is certainly not the instructional style of the classroom authoritarian: "The guru teaches indirectly, not by way of dogma or lecture, but by means of parable and metaphor."[65] Kopp went on to explain what this kind of indirect teaching—or therapy—entails: "Instruction by metaphor does not depend primarily on rationally determined logical thinking nor on empirically objective checking of perceptual data. Instead, knowing metaphorically implies grasping a situation intuitively, in its many interplays of multiple meanings, from the concrete to the symbolic."[66] Perhaps the most important point about the guru that Kopp stressed was the end result of the relationship: "The teaching mis-

---

61. Sheldon B. Kopp, *If You Meet the Buddha on the Road, Kill Him! The Pilgrimage of Psychotherapy Patients* (New York: Bantam Books, 1972), p. 188.

62. This is called hiding behind a "persona," which too often "stiffens, becomes automatic and, in the real meaning of the word, a grown-on mask, behind which the individual shrivels and runs the risk of becoming ever more empty." Jacobi, *Psychology of Jung*, p. 19. Jung defined the "persona" this way: "The mask, i.e., the *ad hoc* adopted attitude, I have called *persona*, which was the name for the masks worn by actors in antiquity." Then Jung defined what he meant by persona: "The persona is thus a functional complex that comes into existence for reasons of adaptation or personal convenience, but is by no means identical with individuality. The persona is exclusively concerned with the relation to objects. The relation of the individual to the object must be sharply distinguished from the relation to the subject." Carl G. Jung, Vol. 6, *Psychological Types*, in *The Collected Works of C.G. Jung* (1971), p. 465.

63. Kopp, *If You Meet the Buddha on the Road, Kill Him!* p. 11. Elsewhere, Kopp gave this definition of a guru: "A spiritual guide who helps others move from one phase of their lives to another is sometimes called a 'guru.' He is a special sort of teacher, a master of the rites of initiation. The guru appears to introduce his disciples to new experiences, to high levels of spiritual understanding, to greater truths. Perhaps, in reality, he gives them the freedom that comes with accepting their imperfect, finite human situation." Kopp, *Even a Stone Can Be a Teacher*, p. 7. For more on Kopp's view of the guru, see ibid., pp. 7-10.

64. Kopp, *If You Meet the Buddha on the Road, Kill Him!* p. 11.

65. Ibid., p. 12.

66. Ibid.

sion of the guru is an attempt to free his followers from him. His metaphors and parables make it necessary for the pilgrims who would be disciples to turn to their own imaginations in the search for meaning in their lives. The guru instructs the pilgrims in the tradition of breaking with tradition, in losing themselves so that they may find themselves."[67] The ultimate truth that the guru has to share is often something of a shock to the person receiving therapy: "*The secret is that there is no secret*. Everything is just what it seems to be. This is it! There are no hidden meanings."[68]

The dimension of fellow traveler collects the other three dimensions of the therapist and gives them cohesion. The caring and involved therapist acts as a healer, allowing the client to become his or her own person. The therapist as catalyst is not primarily the one seeking change, although in the normal course of relationships some degree of change in all parties is inevitable. The catalyst evokes reactions rather than causing them or being an element in the process. The therapist as facilitator helps the client sort out feelings and interactions, allowing the client to experience himself or herself more fully, and allowing him or her to decide where he or she desires to go. The fellow traveler cares deeply about the other, and knows intimately the struggles, fears, and hopes of the one walking alongside. He or she is a pilgrim who listens, who understands, who lends a hand when the going gets rough. In the end, however, it is always the responsibility of each individual traveler to find his or her own self and to reach his or her own final destinations: "Search we must. Each man must set out to cross his bridge. The important thing is to begin."[69]

Summary

The outline of the therapist's role can now be faintly recognized through the dimensions of healer, catalyst, facilitator, and fellow traveler. These dimensions are not intended to be comprehensive of the role, and are not meant as the exclusive property of the role. When combined in the pattern of the preceding discussion, however, the general contours of the therapist's role begin to emerge. The sections that follow will fill in more of the details of the role of therapist, and of what that role has to teach the religious educator. The role of therapist, with the modern sound to its title and dimensions, is found to be an ancient and time-honored role. It has appeared in many guises and actions. The rest of the chapter will point to some of ways the role of the therapist has long been an essential part of genuine religious education.

Aim: Wholeness

The actual aim of the therapist is the wholeness of the client.[70] It is ultimately an unachievable aim, however, because wholeness is never attained in any kind

---

67. Ibid., p. 19.
68. Ibid., p. 187.
69. Ibid., p. 10.
70. The aim of the therapist is to help the client achieve wholeness. This does not imply that the therapist in his or her own personal life is not also striving to achieve wholeness, but in keeping with the role the primary attention stays on the client's needs.

of totality. Wholeness is a process, a dynamic reality that is never static or fixed.[71] In fact, what defines wholeness for one does not necessarily describe wholeness for another. While such an aim seems impossible and therefore useless, the quest is not hopeless. The reality is that wholeness does not come canned or prepackaged. It is an individual and personal quality that each must develop and create. The therapist does not give it or prescribe it. The therapist accompanies the individual in the search for what wholeness means to the individual, and participates in the creation of that wholeness.[72]

Although the reality of wholeness may be elusive, its meaning can be rather easily described. The etymology of the word is instructive and illuminating. It derives from the Old English word "hale," which translates into healthy, unhurt, and entire. The derivation from the word "entire" is related to our word "integrate," which literally in the Latin meant "untouched." The point is that to be whole is to be integrated: healthy ("hale"), unspoiled ("untouched"), and complete ("entire"). Wholeness is related etymologically and functionally to health and integration, and none of these are states or static entities but processes. To be in the process of wholeness is to be in the process of health and integration.[73] Wholeness is a journey where there is no final destination but rather increasing manifestations of completeness and fullness—a process of *becoming*. As Carl Rogers said: "The goal the individual most wishes to achieve, the end which he knowingly and unknowingly pursues, is to become himself."[74]

Carl Rogers described the movement toward wholeness, without specifically using the word, when he sketched "the flow of a process of change which occurs when a client experiences himself as being received, welcomed, understood as he is. This process includes several threads, separable at first, becoming more of a unity as the process continues."[75] A brief summary of this process[76] reveals seven stages along a continuum of wholeness and becoming: 1) a freeing up of feelings; 2) a change in the manner of experiencing; 3) a shift from incongruence to congruence; 4) a change in the manner in which, and the extent

---

71. In describing his approach to therapy, for example, Rogers noted: "There has been a tendency to regard the nondirective or client-centered approach as something static—a method, a technique, a rather rigid system. Nothing could be further from the truth. The group of professional workers in this field are working with dynamic concepts which they are constantly revising in the light of continuing clinical experience and in the light of research findings. The picture is one of fluid changes in a general approach to problems of human relationships, rather than a situation in which some relatively rigid technique is more or less mechanically applied." Rogers, *Client-Centered Therapy*, pp. 5-6. Rogers' comments hold true for the larger process of psychotherapy in general.

72. Howard Clinebell went so far as to say that "the fundamental goal of all counseling and of all psychotherapy (as well as of all creative education) is to maximize human wholeness!" Howard Clinebell, *Contemporary Growth Therapies: Resources for Actualizing Human Wholeness* (Nashville: Abingdon, 1981), p. 15. He went on to state: "The central task of counselors, therapists, and growth-oriented teachers is to awaken realizable hopes for creative change in persons and then to help them actualize these hopes." Ibid.

73. The concept and the derivation of the term "wholeness" receives more extensive treatment in Timothy Arthur Lines, *Systemic Religious Education* (Birmingham, Ala.: Religious Education Press, 1987), especially pp. 143-146.

74. Rogers, *On Becoming a Person*, p. 108.

75. Ibid., p. 156.

76. The fuller statement of Rogers' stages can be found in ibid., pp. 132-156.

to which the individual is able and willing to communicate himself in a receptive atmosphere; 5) a loosening of the cognitive maps of experience; 6) a change in the individual's relationship to his problems; 7) a change in the individual's manner of relating.[77] Rogers' concluding words: "In general, the process moves from a point of fixity, where all the elements and threads described above are separately discernible and separately understandable, to the flowing peak of moments of therapy in which all these threads become inseparably woven together. . . . Thus, as the process reaches this point the person becomes a unity of flow, of motion. He has changed, but what seems most significant, he has become an integrated process of changingness."[78] This is a fine illustration of the *process* of becoming a whole, which in whatever manner it is achieved is the aim of the religious educator as therapist.

The process of wholeness is found, not in a collection of parts, but in an organism that is integrated and alive. An aggregate, by contrast, is simply a collection of parts with no true relation or connection to one another other than proximate geographic vicinity.[79] A bag filled with trash is an aggregate—the contents of the bag have no inherent relationships among themselves and no purpose to perform other than to be discarded as refuse and waste. The trash never becomes "complete" or "whole." It just fills the bag. The living human body is an organism which has a large degree of integration among its integral elements and a purpose that orders its activity and progress.[80] It can and does develop toward completeness and wholeness. While each individual moves toward completeness and wholeness in different ways, at different times, and to different degrees, it can still be said that wholeness is the aim of the therapist as he or she works with the client. Frederick Perls gave illustration of this in his statement of advocacy for the Gestalt type of therapy: "The greatest value in the Gestalt approach perhaps lies in the insight that the *whole determines the parts*, which contrasts with the previous assumption that the whole is merely the sum of its elements. The therapeutic situation, for instance, is more than just a statistical event of a doctor plus a patient. It is a *meeting* of the doctor and patient. If the doctor is rigid and insensitive to the specific requirements of the ever-changing situation, he will not be a good therapist. He might be a bully or a businessman or a dogmatist; but he is not a therapist if he refuses to be a part of the ongoing process of the psychiatric situation."[81]

The close connection of health and wholeness with religious education has been noted in the past. For example, a religious educator of a previous generation, Lewis Joseph Sherrill, was attuned to the association between these ideas and coined the term "wholth" to denote the presence of wholeness and health in

---

77. This summary is given in ibid., pp. 156-157.

78. Ibid., p. 158.

79. For a good discussion of the nature of aggregates and how they differ from integrated systems, see Andras Angyal, "A Logic of Systems," in *Systems Thinking*, ed. Fred E. Emery (New York: Penguin Books, 1969), pp. 17-29.

80. For an overview of this concept, see Gerald M. Weinberg, *An Introduction to General Systems Thinking* (New York: Wiley, 1975), and Ludwig von Bertalanffy, *General System Theory: Foundations, Development, Applications*, rev. ed. (New York: Braziller, 1968).

81. Perls with Hefferline and Goodman, *Gestalt Therapy*, pp. xi-xii.

the individual.[82] In his effort to define wholeness, Sherrill wrote: "It is difficult to describe wholeness without referring to its opposites. Thus, to be whole is *not* to be divided, split up, and the like."[83] He went on to discuss the individual in relation to wholeness, saying that an individual is "an entity which cannot be further divided; it cannot be further broken down into its component parts without destroying it. It must be taken as a whole, a unity."[84] His conclusion was: "To be whole, then, is to be one. To be made whole is to be integrated."[85] From this basis, Sherrill went on to prescribe a form of religious education that ministered to the whole person, not some "part" of the individual such as the "religious" part or the "spiritual" part. The individual is so much a unity that these concepts are inseparable from the whole and meaningless when isolated by themselves.

The therapist is one who works for the wholeness of the individual, unbound by artificial divisions such a body, mind, and spirit. To identify these "parts" immediately breaks the human into an aggregate, with no inherent unity or binding purpose, destroying the basic identity of the human.[86] The therapist has the responsibility to recognize, know, and care for the entirety of the individual, and to encourage that individual toward a greater degree of wholeness. The religious educator functioning in the role of the therapist, then, has no less of an aim than wholeness.

Function: Integration

If the aim of the therapist is to bring the client into wholeness, then the means or function the therapist employs to achieve it is integration. Integration binds the brokenness or weaves together the elements of an organism to form an inseparable whole. The "parts" cease to be discrete elements, and become integrated into one ontic entity. No longer can the mechanistic image of interchangeable parts be an appropriate description for an organism, particularly of the human organism. Hearts, lungs, and appendages, for example, are not bolted together to create a human on an assembly line but rather the human body results from an astounding process of fertilization, growth, and development. The "parts" arise and form according to a very intricate, programed, and coordinated plan of maturation before birth and continue to develop and change throughout life.[87] The human is

---

82. See Lewis Joseph Sherrill, *The Gift of Power* (New York: Macmillan, 1955), p. 22.
83. Ibid.
84. Ibid.
85. Ibid.
86. This move away from separation and toward wholeness is referred to by Jungians as a process of individuation. Josef Goldbrunner defined individuation as "a spiritual process by which the personality is built up. It takes as many forms as there are individuals." Josef Goldbrunner, *Individuation: A Study of the Depth Psychology of Carl Gustav Jung*, trans. Stanley Godman (New York: Pantheon, 1956), p. 119. Goldbrunner noted: "Individuation leads step by step and deeper and deeper into the core of the personality. It begins with personal acceptance." Ibid., pp. 199-220. See more about individuation in the section below and in Chapter Ten, "The Religious Educator as Revolutionary."
87. This image is reminiscent of one used by Erik Erikson. See especially Erik H. Erikson, *Childhood and Society*, 2nd ed. (New York: Norton, 1963), pp. 269-273.

more of an integrated whole than the machine analogy can ever capture.

If the machine analogy is inappropriate for the human body, how much more for the entirety of the human—including concepts such as the personality, the mind, and the emotions. The therapist is not able to search and find one simple problem in the human psyche and repair it as the mechanic does. The problems are as tightly integrated and interrelated as the constituents of the human are.[88] Can the psychotherapist ignore or claim disinterest in a client's physical ailments or complaints? Can the physical therapist treat only the body and overlook the emotions and the motivations of the client? The human is an integrated whole, and therapists are obliged to appreciate and deal with the totality of this highly complex and fascinating creature.

To push integration even farther is to understand the issue of social relationships. The aim of wholeness and the function of integration do not stop with the individual, but extend to include the individual in community.[89] The therapist works to facilitate the person as an able social being, who moves in and out of innumerable social identities each day. The therapist and the client work on being a part of family, of neighborhood, of faith community, and so on, through the various social interactions. There is no such thing as wholeness and integration in isolation, so the relatively simple examination of the relationship between the therapist and client must eventually be expanded to include a multitude of other relationships.[90]

Carl Rogers addressed the topic of integration when he proposed the characteristics of the fully functioning person—the result of successful therapy. His list of three characteristics started with the person exhibiting an "increasing openness to experience."[91] By this he meant that there was a "movement away from the pole of defensiveness toward the pole of openness to experience. The individual is becoming more able to listen to himself, to experience what is going on within himself."[92] A second characteristic was "an increasing tendency to live fully in each moment."[93] Rogers described it this way: "Such living in the moment means an absence of rigidity, of tight organization, of the imposition of structure on experience. It means instead a maximum of adaptability, a discovery of structure *in* experience, a flowing, changing organization of self and personality."[94] The third was "an increasing trust in his organism as a means of arriving at the most satisfying behavior in each existential situation."[95] Rogers

---

88. Maslow described facilitating the process of integration this way: "What the good clinical therapist does is to help his particular client to unfold, to break through the defenses against his own self-knowledge, to recover himself, and to get to know himself." Maslow, *Farther Reaches of Human Nature*, p. 52.

89. Perls stated his goal for his book was "to assist you to discover yourself and to mobilize it for greater effectiveness in satisfying your requirements both as a biological organism and as a social human being." Perls with Hefferline and Goodman, *Gestalt Therapy*, p. 3.

90. "The isolated organism and its abstractions—mind, soul and body—and the isolated environment . . . are not the concern of psychology." Ibid., p. xii.

91. Rogers, *On Becoming a Person*, p. 187.

92. Ibid., p. 188.

93. Ibid.

94. Ibid., p. 189.

95. Ibid.

went on to say of these people: "Yet as I observe the clients whose experiences in living have taught me so much, I find that increasingly such individuals are able to trust their total organismic reaction to a new situation because they discover to an ever-increasing degree that if they are open to their experience, doing what 'feels right' proves to be a competent and trustworthy guide to behavior which is truly satisfying."[96] Summarizing these characteristics, Rogers said: "It appears that the person who is psychologically free moves in the direction of becoming a more fully functioning person."[97] As these characteristics are woven together into this more fully functioning person, the process revealed is truly that of integration.

When depth psychologists deal with integration, they have in mind the integration of the whole person—which means linking up the conscious self and the unconscious aspects of the self into a fully functioning whole.[98] The effort is to contact and to make known the inner forces and then to integrate them into a more complete and healthier unity. Carl Jung, for example, stressed this process of integration in his writings, as Peter O'Conner made clear: "Indeed, I think it is fair that over and above all the things that Jungian psychology is, it is, in the final analysis, about the reconciliation of the opposites within us and the psychic energy that springs from its source in the tension between these opposites."[99] O'Conner explained why and how this is such a fundamental process in Jungian psychology: "For Jung, in the simplest possible terms, this reconciliation of opposites and their resulting in transcendence is fundamentally achieved by bringing into consciousness the unconscious aspects of our being. This process is called *individuation* and the agent and the goal of this process is termed 'Self.' The process of individuation, as Jung said himself, is the central concept of his psychology."[100]

The religious educator considering the role of the therapist may be sorely tempted to short circuit the full meaning of integration. With the limitations of time, expertise, and knowledge many carry to the task of religious education, the thought of dealing with integration on a scale anywhere near what has been described above is nearly unthinkable. It is as if the best one could hope for is the memorization of a Bible verse or the acceptance of a particular doctrine. What religious educator has the resources to deal with the implications of religion for the life and health of the human in the broad terms of the above discussion?

96. Ibid.
97. Ibid., p. 191.
98. An excellent resource that provides four typologies for "identifying, distinguishing, and relating characteristic types of approaches regarding the construct of the unconscious" is Natalino Caputi, *Guide to the Unconscious* (Birmingham, Ala.: Religious Education Press, 1984); quote is from p. 20. The four types are: the Bio-Physical approach; the Psycho-Personal approach; the Socio-Cultural approach; and the Transpersonal-Spiritual approach.
99. Peter O'Conner, *Understanding Jung, Understanding Yourself* (New York: Paulist, 1985), p. 67.
100. Ibid., p. 68. Although this was discussed in some detail in the previous chapter, Jung's definition of individuation is important to keep in mind: "In general, it is the process by which individual beings are formed and differentiated, in particular, it is the development of the psychological *individual . . .* as being distinct from the general, collective psychology. Individuation, therefore, is a process of differentiation . . . having for its goal the development of the individual personality." Carl G. Jung, Vol. 6, *Psychological Types,* in *The Collected Works of C.G. Jung* (1971), p. 448.

What religious educator is willing to struggle not only with individual issues but with communal ones as well? Only the genuine religious educator!

To accept the call of the religious educator from the perspective of the therapist is first to accept the commitment to seek personal integration. The religious educator must be willing to do the hard work of bringing himself or herself into full view and finding at least some degree of integration personally before bringing others under his or her tutelage. A struggle with recasting the old divisions of body, mind, and soul into an integrated whole is essential for the individual therapist/religious educator in advance of facilitating others in the quest. In other words, the religious educator as therapist—seeking to use integration to gain the wholeness of others—must be on the quest of integration and wholeness personally, or as the biblical proverb put it: "Doctor, cure yourself!"[101] Religious educators cannot show others the path if they themselves are not walking it. The issue is not that each therapist/religious educator must "be" integrated, since such a final state of perfection is unattainable and even undesirable, but the requirement is that each one be on the path toward it.

The mystical reality is that once the journey has begun, the vision of wholeness and the sense of integration continues to expand. What wholeness is, and what needs to be integrated into that wholeness, increases exponentially to the time devoted to the exercise of seeking. The good news: The quest for integration is exciting and life-giving. The bad news: The quest is equally as demanding and ever more confusing. The more one sees and understands, the more there is to integrate and accept. The religious educator as therapist is engaged in a lifelong journey of exploration on which he or she invites others to join.

Primary Virtues: Affectivity and Actualization

Although any individual therapist may exhibit a great number of virtues, these two particular virtues of affectivity and actualization provide significant insight into the fundamental nature and process of the therapist's activity. This discussion on virtues directs its attention toward two foci: what the therapist develops and nurtures in the client, as well as what should guide the therapist in his or her work as an integral part of the therapist's personality. The same two virtues apply to both necessary directions. These virtues are not of such a nature—if any of the virtues are—that they can be willed or given to the learner, but they can be modeled, encouraged, and facilitated by the actions, attitudes, and lifestyle of the therapist.

The first virtue, affectivity, is defined simply as the ability to feel, recognize, and express appropriately the emotions of the individual.[102] This area of dis-

---

101. Attributed to Jesus in Luke 4:23, NRSV.

102. There is no one way to go about the discussion of the affective dimension of the human, as these comments by Willard Gaylin make clear: "Despite its importance, there is an incredible amount of confusion about feelings and emotions in both the minds of the public and the attention of the 'experts.' Even the nomenclature presents a problem. Generally speaking, the field of psychology has settled down to the use of three terms: 'emotion' is the general term which encompasses the feeling tone, the biophysiological state, and even the chemical changes we are beginning to understand underlie the sensations we experience; 'affect,' introduced from psychoanalysis, is used

cussion is certainly full of possible disagreement or at least amenable to a lack of precision.[103] Willard Gaylin said it this way: "Feelings are mushy, difficult, non-palpable, slippery things even by definition. In that sense they are immune to the kind of analysis to which most behavior is typically exposed. They are difficult to quantify, to communicate, difficult even to distinguish within ourselves one from another."[104] In spite of the difficulties, the religious educator as therapist must have some basic grasp of the dimensions of affectivity, so below is a brief introduction to four basic qualities necessary for understanding and for demonstrating this particular virtue.

One fundamental aspect of affectivity that the therapist needs to display, and to nurture in the learner, is *sensitivity* to the emotions. One must work to become aware of the feelings that are present, bringing them to the surface by acknowledging them and giving them permission to "be." There are no right or wrong emotions, only real, denied, or rejected emotions. Emotions in and of themselves are value-free in the sense that they simply *are*—it is what one does with them that brings in the moral and ethical dimensions. One author underscored this point, encouraging the need to be sensitive to the emotions this way: "There are no good or bad types of emotion. Both 'positive' and 'negative' can be misused or not used when they should be. In order to increase the probability of correct emotional choice it would seem desirable to increase a person's access to his or her emotions, so that the person may allow whatever emotion is called for by the circumstances. Theoretically, this should increase responsiveness and sensitivity and should decrease the chance of getting stuck in one emotion because of the unavailability of another emotion that is required by the situation."[105] The first step toward wholeness in affectivity, in other words, is becoming aware of and accepting—being sensitive to—the emotions that individuals possess, and *are*.[106]

A second quality for the therapist to emphasize is *intentionality*. This means

---

to describe the dominant emotional tone of an individual, and is particularly used in relationship to our recognition of the feelings of others; 'feeling' is our subjective awareness of our own emotional state. It is that which we experience; that which we know about our current emotional condition." Willard Gaylin, *Feelings: Our Vital Signs* (New York: Ballantine, 1979), p. 1. In this discussion, I am following the lead of Francis Dunlop, who used the affective as the more general term, and the terms emotions and feelings are elements of the affective sphere. See Francis Dunlop, *The Education of Feeling and Emotion* (London: Allen and Unwin, 1984), p. 31.

103. For a good overview of the quest for a theory of emotions, see *Feelings and Emotions: The Loyola Symposium*, ed. Magda B. Arnold (New York: Academic Press, 1970). For a sampling of the variety of ways that the study of the emotions can be described and categorized, see *The Nature of Emotion: Selected Readings*, ed. Magda B. Arnold (Middlesex, England: Penguin Press, 1968). For a sense of the historical and philosophical attempts to explain emotion, see *What Is an Emotion?: Classic Readings in Philosophical Psychology*, eds. Chesire Calhoun and Robert C. Solomon (New York: Oxford University Press, 1984).

104. Gaylin, *Feelings*, p. 10.

105. Joseph De Rivera, "Development and the Full Range of Emotional Experience," in *Emotion in Adult Development*, ed. Carol Zander Malatesta and Carroll E. Izard (Beverly Hills: Sage Publications, 1984), pp. 57-58.

106. Sheldon Kopp said in this regard: "By reducing the demands of what we should be, we can live more comfortably with what we *are*. Paradoxically, it is this acceptance of what is that increases our chances of becoming all that we might yet be." Sheldon Kopp, *Mirror, Mask, and Shadow: The Risk and Rewards of Self-Acceptance* (New York: Macmillan, 1980), p. 183.

that one is not forced just to "have" emotions, or to be controlled by them.[107] The task is first to be aware of the emotion that arises and then to make considered decisions about what to do *with* the emotion.[108] This approach does not divorce rationality from the affective domain or make one superior over the other,[109] but seeks to find some sense of integration between them. Willard Gaylin helped to make this clear: "Feelings are the instruments of rationality, not—as some would have it—alternatives to it. Because we are intelligent creatures—meaning that we are freed from instinctive and patterned behavior to a degree unparalleled in the animal kingdom—we are capable of, and dependent on, using rational choice to determine our futures. Feelings become guides to that choice."[110] Rochelle Albin expressed a similar thought a bit more fully: "The capacity to think about our emotions also improves our ability to control them. We still feel them, but we develop some choices about what to do with them. We understand better what has caused a particular feeling, and we can decide whether we want to keep the feeling inside us, express it in some way . . . or act on it in a way that usually affects other people."[111]

Third is *congruence*, a word normally associated with the work of Carl Rogers.[112] Rogers was convinced that without congruence no true therapeutic or learning relationship could occur, saying: "If therapy is to occur, it seems necessary that the therapist be, in the relationship, a unified, or integrated, or congruent person. What I mean is that within the relationship he is exactly what he is—not a façade, or a role, or a pretense. I have used the term 'congruence' to refer to this accurate matching of experience with awareness. It is when the therapist is fully and accurately aware of what he is experiencing at this moment in the relationship, that he is fully congruent."[113] Rogers summarized the image of the congruent person as being one who "is freely, deeply, and acceptantly himself, with his actual experience of his feelings and reactions matched by an accurate awareness of these feelings and reactions as they occur and as they change."[114] In the simplest of language, then, to be congruent is to be your feelings.

107. "Emotions themselves—love, joy, hate, and anger—do not make us act in certain ways. Rather, it is the meaning we give to our emotions that may lead to certain behaviors." Rochelle Semmel Albin, *Emotions* (Philadelphia: Westminster, 1983), p. 20.

108. For an interesting discussion on this issue, see Chapter Five, "Educating the Emotions," Dunlop, *Education of Feeling and Emotion*, pp. 87-115.

109. "We live in a society that has a long tradition of valuing the rational and intellectual aspects of our lives over the emotional. Not only is thinking considered more valuable and more important than feeling, but it is viewed as more controllable and thus less dangerous. We have come to believe that we can control our thoughts better than we can control our emotions, and that, because of this, emotions represent the weaker side of human nature." Ibid., p. 11.

110. Gaylin, *Feelings*, p. 7.

111. Albin, *Emotions*, p. 14.

112. Rogers has said he coined this meaning of the term "congruence." See Rogers, *On Becoming a Person*, p. 61.

113. Ibid., p. 282. Rogers also said of congruence: "No one fully achieves this condition, yet the more the therapist is able to listen acceptantly to what is going on within himself, and the more he is able to be the complexity of his feelings, without fear, the higher the degree of his congruence." Ibid., p. 61.

114. Ibid., p. 283.

The fourth quality of affectivity crucial to the effective functioning of the therapist is *empathy*, defined as "the sharing of the perceived emotion of another. Specifically, empathy is an affective state that stems from the apprehension of another's emotional state or condition and that is congruent and quite similar to the perceived state of another."[115] The issue here is that the therapist must be able not only to recognize and express his or her own emotions but must also be able to work with the client's affect and to resonate with the emotional state of the client.[116] The need is not so much for sympathy, which is defined as "a vicarious emotional reaction based on the apprehension of another's emotional state or situation, which consists of feeling sorrow or concern for another,"[117] although this may be appropriate and necessary occasionally. Empathy is the ability to *respond* to the other person's affective state in such a way as to communicate understanding and concern of that other's situation and to provide the client some help in sorting out those feelings. This is the ability to connect with other people, to "get inside their shoes," and to make yourself available to them in a therapeutic way. Without genuine empathy, therapy becomes hollow, sterile, impersonal, and ultimately ineffectual.

Though these few paragraphs have given but the barest of introductions to the virtue of affectivity, it is now possible to turn to a second virtue that has links to affectivity—actualization. The companion virtue of actualization addresses a slightly different and a broader avenue of therapy—the facilitation of fulfilling the personal needs and dreams of the *client*. If the therapist cannot accept responsibility for the feelings of the client, then neither can the therapist perform the feat of actualizing a client. This is indeed an activity achievable only by each individual for himself or herself. The therapist can, however, enflesh such a virtue and provide a healthy model for such a process to be fostered.

The mere mention of self-actualization probably brings the name of Abraham Maslow (1908-1970) immediately to mind. Maslow was the great advocate of this concept,[118] which he perceived to sit atop the "needs" hierarchy and to be a part of the natural developmental tendencies of the human.[119] Maslow explained self-actualization this way: "Musicians must make music, artists must paint, poets must write if they are to be ultimately at peace with themselves. What humans *can* be,

115. Nancy Eisenberg, "Editor's Notes," in *Empathy and Related Emotional Responses*, ed. Nancy Eisenberg (San Francisco: Jossey-Bass, 1989), p. 1.

116. This is what Carl Rogers called "empathic understanding," which he described as "when the therapist is sensing the feelings and personal meanings which the client is experiencing in each moment, when he can perceive these from 'inside,' as they seem to the client, and when he can successfully communicate something of that understanding to his client." Rogers, *On Becoming a Person*, p. 62.

117. Nancy Eisenberg et al., "Sympathy and Personal Distress: Development, Gender Differences, and Interrelations of Indexes," in *Empathy and Related Emotional Responses*, p. 108.

118. Although Maslow gave credit to Kurt Goldstein for coining the term "self-actualization" in Goldstein's book *The Organism* (New York: American Book, 1939), Maslow is the person more often directly associated with the term. See Maslow, *Motivation and Personality*, p. 22, for Maslow's comments about Goldstein.

119. See these described in Chapter Two, "A Theory of Human Motivation," in Maslow, *Motivation and Personality*, pp. 15-31. The list includes physiological needs, safety needs, belongingness and love needs, esteem needs, and self-actualization.

they *must* be. They must be true to their own nature."[120] Maslow said of self-actualization: "It refers to people's desire for self-fulfillment, namely, the tendency for them to become actualized in what they are potentially. This tendency might be phrased as the desire to become more and more what one idiosyncratically is, to become everything that one is capable of becoming."[121] Where the "lower" needs are driven by deficiencies, this higher process is not—at least in the same sense.[122] As Maslow noted, while the lower elements of the hierarchy of needs may be properly identified, "self-actualization" is not truly a need: "Self-actualization is not a lack or deficiency. . . . It is not something extrinsic the organism needs for health."[123] At this point of development the "needs" of the individual are fulfilled, and he or she moves to another kind of motivation. Maslow explained: "Self-actualization is intrinsic growth of what is already in the organism, or more accurately of what *is* the organism itself. . . . Or, to say it another way, self-actualization is growth-motivated rather than deficiency motivated."[124]

Self-actualization could easily be misunderstood or misinterpreted to mean selfish or egocentric types of behavior. Maslow effectively quashed such a notion: "Self-actualizing people are, without a single exception, involved in a cause outside their own skin, in something outside of themselves. They are devoted, working at something which is very precious to them—some calling or devotion in the old sense, the priestly sense."[125] Maslow went on to identify eight characteristics which reveal what it means to self-actualize.[126] First, he wrote, "self-actualization means experiencing fully, vividly, selflessly, with full concentration and total absorption . . . At this moment of experiencing, the person is wholly and fully human. This is a self-actualizing moment. This is a moment when the self is actualizing itself."[127] Second, "self actualization is an ongoing process; it means making each of the many single choices about whether to lie or be honest, whether to steal or not to steal at a particular point, and it means to make each of these choices as a growth choice."[128] Third, self-actualization "implies that there is a self to be actualized,"[129] by which Maslow meant that each individual must learn to listen to his or her own voice and let the true self emerge.[130] Fourth, "when in doubt, be honest rather than not. . . . Each time one takes responsibility, this is an actu-

---

120. Ibid., p. 22.
121. Ibid.
122. Where the lower needs are deficiency driven, self-actualization is growth driven. See Abraham H. Maslow, *Toward a Psychology of Being*, 2nd ed. (New York: Van Nostrand Reinhold, 1968), pp. 21-27.
123. Maslow, *Motivation and Personality*, p. 66. It is true, however, that Maslow did continue to speak of self-actualization as a need. For example, in his introduction of the term in *Motivation and Personality*, he said: "This *need* we may call self-actualization." Ibid., p. 23. Emphasis added.
124. Ibid., p. 66.
125. Maslow, *Farther Reaches of Human Nature*, p. 43.
126. There are a number of other places where Maslow expressed his views on self-actualization. See, for example, the topic discussed throughout Maslow, *Toward a Psychology of Being*, but especially in Chapter Three, "Deficiency Motivation and Growth Motivation," pp. 21-43.
127. Maslow, *Farther Reaches of Human Nature*, p. 45.
128. Ibid.
129. Ibid.
130. Ibid., p. 46.

alizing of the self."[131] Fifth, "one cannot choose wisely for a life unless he dares to listen to himself, *his own self*, at each moment in life, and to say calmly, 'No, I don't like such and such.' . . . To be courageous rather than afraid is another version of the same thing."[132] Sixth, "self-actualizing is not only an end state but also the process of actualizing one's potentialities at any time, in any moment."[133] Seventh, "peak experiences are transient moments of self-actualization. They are moments of ecstasy which cannot be bought, cannot be guaranteed, cannot even be sought."[134] Eighth, "finding out who one is, what he is, what he likes, what he doesn't like, what is good for him and what is bad, where he is going and what his mission is—opening oneself up to himself—means the exposure to psychopathology. It means identifying defenses, and after defenses have been identified, it means finding the courage to give them up."[135] If this description of a person who is in the process of self-actualization sounds familiar, the reason may be that Maslow indicated it was a parallel process to what Carl Rogers meant when Rogers used the term "fully functioning person,"[136] which was discussed in the section above.

In an ideal situation, the therapist himself or herself is in the process of becoming self-actualized. The "need" to do therapy is not a need driven by some deficiency, whether emotional, financial, or professional. The therapist has gotten to the point where the deficiencies have been or are being fulfilled sufficiently so that he or she is able to make himself or herself available to others. He or she has something to offer, rather than the need to take. Maslow described this phenomena in a discussion of how the self-actualized person loves: "Self-actualizers have no serious deficiencies to make up and must now be looked upon as freed for growth, maturation, development, in a word, for the fulfillment and actualization of their highest individual and species nature. What such people do emanates from growth and expresses it without striving. They love because they are loving persons. . . . Such epiphenomena are as little motivated as is physical growth or psychological maturation."[137]

In a therapeutic relationship, the client is hopefully the only one with deficient needs, while the therapist is the one already in the process of being self-actualized—as the one without the deficiency of needs but with something to give. The client comes into such a relationship precisely because he or she is driven by needs and is as yet not self-actualized. The purpose of the therapist is to help the *client* identify his or her needs, facilitate healthy ways to fulfill them, and continue the journey toward self-actualization.[138]

---

131. Ibid.

132. Ibid., p. 47.

133. Ibid.

134. Ibid., p. 48. For more on this important topic, see Abraham H. Maslow, *Religions, Values, and Peak-Experiences* (New York: Penguin Books, 1970).

135. Maslow, *Farther Reaches of Human Nature*, pp. 48-49.

136. For example, see ibid., p. 73; Maslow, *Motivation and Personality*, p. 160; and Maslow, *Toward a Psychology of Being*, p. 105.

137. Maslow, *Motivation and Personality*, p. 156.

138. Maslow was fully in support of therapists continuing to receive therapy, however: "It follows from the theory presented here that any force that will make therapists into better personalities will thereby make them better therapists. Psychoanalysis or other profound therapy of therapists *can*

This kind of therapy and education has implicit within it the understanding that there will come a time when the therapy and the therapist are no longer necessary, because the process of becoming self-actualized is adequately underway.[139] The effective therapist does not create clients who need him or her if indeed he or she is self-actualized. The virtue of actualization leads the therapist to facilitate wholeness and integration within the client, so that eventually the client moves sufficiently toward being self-actualized that he or she can go on alone. Indeed, successful and effective therapy has exactly this as its end and as its evaluation criteria. A therapy that does not strengthen the individual so that over time the individual is able to function without the therapist is deeply flawed, and likely evidence that the therapist is using the client to serve his or her needs, rather than the other way around.[140]

The virtues of affectivity and actualization are fundamental and foundational to any religious educator who wishes to function effectively in the role of the therapist. The religious educator should first be a person who exhibits the healthy virtues of affectivity and self-actualization (or at least "on the journey" toward them) before undertaking the role. This is supremely important, because otherwise the learner will be used for the needs satisfaction of the religious educator (probably unknowingly) and hindered from pursuing his or her own understanding of the affective realm and of moving toward personal self-actualization. Such a position puts rather severe demands and qualifications upon the religious educator. Is he or she willing to teach others to face their own feelings and emotions without judging them, or to teach them to ignore or reject the unpleasant or threatening emotions? Is he or she willing for learners to go their own way, to believe their own way, and eventually to leave the religious educator behind in their quest for self-actualization, or is the religious educator convinced there are boundaries outside which they should not wander? These are just a few examples of the challenges and the demands confronting the genuine religious educator as therapist, a role which requires the virtues of affectivity and actualization to be exhibited by the religious educator before he or she can be of help facilitating their growth and development in the learner.

Activity: Being Present

Of all the activities expected and required of the human, the one it seems would be the most natural and universal is that of feeling, which is the act of truly "being present" in the here and now. Is it not ludicrous, then, to say that the role of the therapist helps people explore, allow, and experience their feelings, since that is something which happens automatically? As nice as it may be to think

---

help to do this. If it fails to cure altogether, at least it can make therapists aware of what is likely to threaten them, of the major areas of conflict and frustration within them. Consequently, when they deal with their patients, they can discount these forces within themselves and correct for them. Being always conscious of them, they can make them subject to their intelligence." Ibid., p. 109.

139. Maslow then suggested self-therapy. Ibid., p. 103. For some suggestions on this topic, see the section in the present chapter regarding the experiential simulation.

140. Maslow struggled with the concept of a proper model or image for the therapist's role. See Maslow, *Farther Reaches of Human Nature*, pp. 51-53.

that all people are in touch with their feelings and that they have no difficulty in expressing them, such an assumption would be dead wrong. In reality, many people have become unconnected from the full range of their emotions,[141] and are not fully present. They have long since cut themselves off from this most vital and natural part of being human.[142] For this reason therapists are needed to help individuals become "human" once again.[143]

The activity of the therapist in helping people be present in their totality is much like the subject of Paul Tillich's classic work *The Courage to Be*.[144] The therapist is indeed the one who is present and allows the client to find the courage to "be." Whatever the client feels, or experiences, or thinks, is acceptable to the therapist, and the therapist creates a safe and protective environment where those individual reactions can be expressed.[145] Tillich wrote about this courage to be: "Courage is the self-affirmation of being in spite of the fact of nonbeing. It is the act of the individual self in taking the anxiety of nonbeing upon itself by affirming itself either as part of an embracing whole or in its individual self-hood. Courage always includes a risk, it is always threatened by nonbeing, whether the risk of losing oneself and becoming a thing within the whole of things or of losing one's world in an empty self-relatedness."[146] While of course Tillich was not addressing specifically the experiencing of emotions, the above description of the need for courage and individuation does parallel what happens in the relationship of the therapist and the client. The client finds within the therapeutic relationship the safety to experience human "being," or as one author said of psychotherapy: "Patients do not learn a subject; they learn about themselves."[147]

---

141. Joseph De Rivera discussed three factors that distort our emotion choices: "First, most persons learn to deny certain emotions. . . . Second, most persons like to encourage and hold on to pleasant emotions. . . . Third, most persons like to avoid the unpleasantness that may accompany 'negative' emotions and the vulnerability required by their acknowledgement and expression." Joseph De Rivera, "Development and the Full Range of Emotional Experience," in *Emotion in Adult Development*, p. 57.

142. Sheldon Kopp wrote: "Remaining unconscious of these disowned parts of ourselves is both costly and dangerous. No matter how much we limit our experience in the service of protecting their inner constraints, we can never eliminate the risk of episodic outbreak of the forbidden impulses. In any case, demands that are not faced within ourselves will be confronted unexpectedly in the world about us." Kopp, *Mirror, Mask, and Shadow*, p. 17.

143. "Accepting our emotions and choosing constructive ways to use them is not easy. None of us does it perfectly, and most of us struggle constantly with how best to handle our feelings. In the end, struggling with them and using them can be most pleasant and rewarding. It can also be the most human." Albin, *Emotions*, p. 36.

144. Paul Tillich, *The Courage to Be* (New Haven: Yale University Press, 1952).

145. "In our daily lives there are a thousand and one reasons for not letting ourselves experience our attitudes fully, reasons from our past and from the present, reasons that reside within the social situation. It seems too dangerous, too potentially damaging, to experience them freely and fully. But in the safety and freedom of the therapeutic relationship, they can be experienced fully, clear to the limit of what they are." Rogers, *On Becoming a Person*, p. 111.

146. Tillich, *The Courage to Be*, p. 155. For more on this, see the entirety of Chapter Twelve, "Love in Self-Actualizing People," ibid, pp. 150-157.

147. Reuven Bar-Levav, *Thinking in the Shadow of Feelings: A New Understanding of the Hidden Forces That Shape Individuals and Societies* (New York: Simon & Schuster, 1988), p. 246.

Turning from the philosopher/theologian Tillich to a therapist proper, Alvin Mahrer, the role of the therapist in helping clients deal with feelings becomes more focused. Mahrer described it this way: "The therapist allows, encourages, and instructs the patient on how to let bodily experiencing occur. The patient is to allow heightened sensations and feelings to occur anywhere and everywhere in the body. The key is letting at least moderate bodily experiencing occur. Some of these bodily sensations may be pleasant and some may be unpleasant. . . . In effect, the therapist tells the patient how to let bodily sensations and feelings carry forward until they are at least moderate."[148] In other words, what Tillich talked about in philosophical and theological terms, Mahrer explained in functional and physiological terms. The therapist, in helping the client to experience emotions, is encouraging the client to have the courage to "be."[149]

The previous juxtaposition of Tillich and Mahrer illustrates the enormously important task of the therapist. The therapist works to take the individual client just as he or she is, without qualification or judgment.[150] The therapist teaches the client, not just to think about having the courage to be, but facilitates the *expression* and the *feeling* of it.[151] The therapist works to bring the client into wholeness, where the negative as well as the positive aspects of the person are accepted as one.[152] One might add that the spiritual aspect is also to be found here, although not in traditionally observable ways. The human as an integrated whole is not divided up into the compartments that have somehow been devised to make ourselves "inhuman."

The key to the process is the therapist: He or she must be one who is fully present[153] in order to teach others to be so. The therapist must be constantly work-

---

148. Alvin R. Mahrer, *Experiential Psychotherapy: Basic Practices* (New York: Brunner/Mazel, 1983), pp. 49-50.

149. Carl Rogers' term for this was "unconditional positive regard": "When the therapist is experiencing a warm, positive, and acceptant attitude toward what is in the client, this facilitates change. It involves the therapist's genuine willingness for the client to be whatever feeling is going on in him at that moment—fear, confusion, pain, pride, anger, hatred, love, courage, or awe. It means that the therapist cares for the client, in a nonpossessive way. It means that he prizes the client in a total rather than a conditional way. . . . It means an outgoing positive feeling without reservations, without evaluations." Rogers, *On Becoming a Person*, p. 62.

150. "It has seemed clear, from our clinical experience as well as our research, that when the counselor perceives and accepts the client as he is, when he lays aside all evaluation and enters into the perceptual frame of reference of the client, he frees the client to explore his life and experience anew, frees him to perceive in that experience new meanings and goals. But is the therapist willing to give the client full freedom as to outcomes? Is he genuinely willing for the client to organize and direct his life? Is he willing for him to choose goals that are social or antisocial, moral or immoral? If not, it seems doubtful that therapy will be a profound experience for the client." Rogers, *Client-Centered Therapy*, p. 48.

151. "A basic tenet for rational living is that people not rate themselves in terms of any of their performances but instead fully accept themselves in terms of their being, their existence." Ellis, *Humanistic Psychotherapy*, p. 17.

152. "It appears that one of the characteristics of deep or significant therapy is that the client discovers that it is not devastating to admit fully into his own experience the positive feeling which another, the therapist, holds toward him. Perhaps one of the reasons why this is so difficult is that essentially it involves the feeling that 'I am worthy of being liked.'" Rogers, *On Becoming a Person*, p. 86.

153. This brings to mind the instructions of a guru to Richard Alpert, who was soon to become known as Baba Ram Dass: "Don't think about the past. Just be here now." Baba Ram Dass,

ing to be whole and integrated so as to be able to instruct others in this most human of activities.[154] Those religious educators seeking to fulfill the role of the therapist have serious work to do, the most foundational and fundamental of which is to learn what it is to be human—to learn to embody the courage to be, by being fully present with others and with the self.

Shadow Role: Manipulator

The image of the genuine therapist has been described in terms of promoting wholeness and integration in the client while keeping the primary attention off the personal needs and the desires of the therapist. In the opening paragraphs of the chapter, the notion of the therapist as a kenotic (self-emptied) figure was introduced. The shadow role of the therapist makes it necessary to demonstrate more clearly the importance of keeping the focus on the client's needs rather than those of the therapist's within the therapeutic relationship.

The role of the therapist "gone wrong" is depicted in the shadow role of the therapist as manipulator. In a book on this subject by Everett Shostrom and Dan Montgomery, the manipulator was defined in psychological terms as "one who exploits, uses, and/or controls himself or herself and others, *as things*, in certain self-defeating ways."[155] Shostrom and Montgomery did not deal with the manipulator as someone "out there" but brought the issue directly to each individual: "The manipulator is legion. The manipulator is all of us, consciously or unconsciously enjoying all the phony tricks learned between cradle and grave. In the process, we reduce ourselves and those around us into things to be controlled."[156] These authors identified a manipulator as possessing four fundamental characteristics: deception, unawareness, control, and cynicism.[157] They contrasted the manipulator with the actualizer:[158] "An actualizer, by contrast, may be defined as a person who appreciates and trusts himself or herself and others, learns from the past and plans for the future but lives *in the present*."[159] An actualizer possesses four counterbalancing characteristics to those of the manipulator: honesty, awareness, freedom, and trust.[160] To explain the purpose of their writing, they said: "The paradox is that each of us is partly a manipulator and partly an actualizer.

Remember: Be Here Now, Now Be Here (San Cristobal, N.M.: Lama Foundation, 1971), first part (no pages given).

154. "One way of putting this which may seem strange to you is that if I can form a helping relationship to myself—if I can be sensitively aware of and acceptant toward my own feelings—then the likelihood is great that I can form a helping relationship to another." Rogers, *On Becoming a Person*, p. 51.

155. Everett L. Shostrom and Dan Montgomery, *The Manipulators* (Nashville: Abingdon, 1990), p. 28.

156. Ibid., pp. 24-25.

157. See these characteristics developed more fully in ibid., pp. 59-60.

158. Shostrom and Montgomery acknowledged their debt here to Maslow, saying the roots of the notion of actualization are from Maslow's work and that the term "actualizer" is a synonym for "authentic, real, genuine, as opposed to such words as phony, manipulative, and deceitful." Ibid., pp. 16-17.

159. Ibid., p. 29.

160. These characteristics are developed more fully in ibid., pp. 59-60.

The goal, of course, is to tip the scale to the side of the actualizer."[161]

One of the ways the shadow role of the manipulator enters religious education is through the guise of the moralizer. The moralizer is someone concerned with determining, regulating, and policing the morals of others, which is to say that this kind of manipulator wants to impose his or her brand of morals onto others. This kind of person is unable to turn loose of the decision-making process and allow others to make their own determinations, believing that he or she knows what is right and wrong behavior and that all others should follow this prescribed moral code scrupulously.[162] Often, but not always, the moralizer has some kind of rigid set of external guides or rules he or she believes should be followed universally. This source may be his or her interpretation of scriptures, the teachings of some ancient and revered father figure, or possibly only an individually designed procedure for action, but the emphasis is not actually on true decision making. The moralist insists on absolute rights and wrongs, and one either accepts and follows the rules or the person is immoral.[163] For those who do not follow the particular set of rules the moralist advocates, there is literally (according to the moralist) hell to pay.[164]

There have always been these kinds moralizing bullies and "emissaries from

---

161. Ibid., p. 29.

162. Contrast this with Carl Rogers' view of the therapeutic relationship: "It seems to me that the individual moves toward *being*, knowingly and acceptingly, the process which he inwardly and actually *is*. He moves away from being what he is not, from being a façade. He is not trying to be more than he is, with the attendant feelings of insecurity of bombastic defensiveness. He is not trying to be less than he is, with the attendant feelings of guilt or self-deprecation. He is increasingly listening to the deepest recesses of his physiological and emotional being and finds himself increasingly willing to be, with greater accuracy and depth, that self which he most truly is." Rogers, *On Becoming a Person*, pp. 175-176.

163. Albert Ellis wrote that he teaches people "to accept themselves and others as inevitably fallible *humans*, and not to expect, in any way whatever, that they or any other person will be perfect, nonerrant, and *super*human. When I expect myself to be superhuman, I become anxious and depressed; when I expect you to be, I become hostile; when I expect the world to be superperfect, I become self-pitying and rebelliously inert. If I am to be truly human, and expect nothing but humanness from others, I shall practically never upset myself about anything." Ellis, *Humanistic Psychotherapy*, p. 39.

164. One of the most blatant of this type of moralizers is Jay E. Adams, a figure in the Christian Evangelical/Fundamentalist movement. His most widely dispensed book has been *Competent to Counsel* (Grand Rapids, Mich.: Baker, 1970). He argued in that book that the primary qualifications for being "competent to counsel" were first that one be a Christian filled with the "goodness and knowledge" gained as a result of his or her becoming a Christian, and second to be willing to confront (assault?) those who are not of the "born-again" ilk. Ibid., p. 59. His goal was to put "counseling" on a purely "biblical basis," as he stated in the introduction to his book: "All concepts, terms, and methods used in counseling need to be re-examined biblically. Not one thing can be accepted from the past (or the present) without biblical warrant. . . . In other words, there is no standard apart from God's divinely imposed objective Standard, the Bible." Ibid., pp. xviii-xix. The nature of Adams' book is even more clearly marked with the following disclosure: "The conclusions in this book are not based upon scientific findings. My method is presuppositional. I avowedly accept the inerrant Bible as the Standard of all faith and practice. The Scriptures, therefore, are the basis, and contain the criteria by which I have sought to make every judgment." Ibid., p. xxi. Other examples of his books in this vein are *The Christian Counselor's Manual* (Grand Rapids, Mich.: Baker, 1973); *How to Help People Change: The Four-Step Biblical Process* (Grand Rapids, Mich.: Ministry Resource Library, 1986); *The Biblical View of Self-Esteem, Self-Love, Self-Image* (Eugene, Oreg.: Harvest House, 1986); and *The Call to Discernment* (Eugene, Oreg.: Harvest House, 1987).

God" who are more than happy to tell people exactly what to do with their lives.[165] They prey upon those weak and insecure individuals who are only too willing to let others make decisions for them and lock them into the bondage of dependency and subservience. None of this sick process has anything to do with true therapy, however. The words of religious educator James Smart ring out across the years when he labeled such a perspective the "suffocating fog of moralism,"[166] declaring it to be the eventual death of religious education. He was correct for his day, and his words still apply today.[167] It is a portrait of the therapist gone desperately wrong, lapsing into the ever-present danger of fulfilling one of the apparitions of the manipulator's shadow role which contributes to the disease of clients rather than toward their health, wholeness, and integration.[168]

The warning to religious educators fairly shouts from the page. What is the motivation of religious educators performing in the role of therapist? Is the goal to seek disciples who obey the whims of the religious educator or to be kenotic and allow the needs of the learner to dictate the course of therapeutic religious education? Is there an external moral code to which all must conform, and if so, which one is it and from whence does it come? Is anyone in the relationship being manipulated—either the religious educator or the learner?[169] Whose needs are being met, and how? It appears that this shadow role of the manipulator lays bare some of the most foundational and basic issues that run through all of religious education.

Faith Tradition Resource: Taoism

> There is a thing confusedly formed,
> Born before heaven and earth.
> Silent and void
> It stands alone and does not change,
> Goes round and does not weary.
> It is capable of being the mother of the world.
> I know not its name
> so I style it 'the way.'[170]

---

165. See these discussed in more detail in Everrett L. Shostrom and Dan Montgomery, *God in Your Personality* (Nashville: Abingdon, 1986), and Maxie Dunham and Gary Herbertson, *The Manipulator in the Church* (Nashville: Abingdon, 1986).

166. James D. Smart, *The Teaching Ministry of the Church: An Examination of the Basic Principles of Christian Education* (Philadelphia: Westminster, 1954), pp. 77-80.

167. I will confess that though I share Smart's contempt for moralizing in place of effective religious education, I would not want to imply that his suggestions for its replacement and mine are in any way identical!

168. For some help in escaping from the manipulator's role, refer to Chapter Sixteen, "Experiential Exercises to Overcome Manipulation," in Shostrom and Montgomery, *The Manipulators*, pp. 169-174.

169. See Chapter Twelve, "Teachers and Students," in Everett L. Shostrom, *Man, the Manipulator: The Inner Journey from Manipulation to Actualization* (New York: Bantam Books, 1967), pp. 110-119. This is the earlier edition of *The Manipulators*, but this particular chapter was removed in the 1990 edition. Shostrom discussed in this chapter how both the teacher and the student can be manipulators.

170. Lao Tzu, *Tao Te Ching*, trans. D.C. Lau (New York: Penguin Books, 1963), p. 82.

This description and explanation of the Tao—the way—was taken from the primary literary resource of Taoism, the *Tao Te Ching*. At first reading such words may appear to be nonsense, and for some it remains so after many readings. For others it is a set of paradoxes approximating but hiding truth. For still others, the above lines are directions to the heart and soul of the universe, the Tao. Whatever the individual's ultimate decision, this description serves to open Taoism as a faith tradition resource for the religious educator functioning in the role of therapist.

As is obvious from the start, Taoism is not an easy or simple faith resource to encounter. At least for Westerners, it is often a confusing interplay of apparent nonsense and paradox[171] that frustrates the logical thinking processes—which of course is exactly the point. The Tao is not something discovered purely through the intellect or through scientific inquiry, which are ways many Westerners prefer.[172] It is the unseen and the unfelt, even the nameless, yet it is what one commentator on Taoism, Diesetz Suzuki, called "the great principle regulating the course of Nature."[173] He explained: *"Tao* literally means 'a path' or 'a way' or 'a course,' but it is more than a map for orientation schematically drawn up for the traveler to follow. The Tao is actually our walking on this 'way' or coursing through it. No, it is more than that. It is the walking itself, or the coursing itself, which is Tao. The Tao is not where we follow the way as indicated in the map. We are the Tao, the walker and the Tao are the same."[174] The *Tao Te Ching* expressed the indescribable Tao this way:

> Its upper part is not dazzling;
> Its lower part is not obscure.
> Dimly visible, it cannot be named
> And returns to that which is without substance.
> This is called the shape that has no shape,
> The image that is without substance.

---

171. "Everything to do with Taoism is paradoxical." John Blofeld, *Taoism: The Road to Immortality* (Boulder, Colo.: Shambala, 1978), p. 90.

172. Taoism has had something of a resurgence of interest in the West in recent years, primarily because of the connections some see between Taoism (and other Eastern religions) and modern physics. Two widely read books that are examples of this kind of interest in the larger, unitary vision are Fritjof Capra, *The Tao of Physics: An Exploration of the Parallels Between Modern Physics and Eastern Mysticism* (New York: Bantam Books, 1975), especially Chapter Eight, "Taoism," pp. 101-106; and Gary Zukav, *The Dancing Wu Li Masters: An Overview of the New Physics* (New York: Bantam Books, 1979). Zukav said: "The Wu Li Master does not teach, but the student learns. The Wu Li Master always begins at the center, at the heart of the matter." Ibid., p. 8. This is not an inappropriate analogy of a good therapist, to say nothing of a physicist.

173. Diesetz T. Suzuki, "Introduction," in *The Texts of Taoism*, trans. James Legge (New York: Julian Press, 1959), p. 13.

174. Ibid. The mention of Suzuki brings to mind the story comparative mythologist Joseph Campbell told about him: "I once heard a lecture by a wonderful old Zen philosopher, Dr. D.T. Suzuki. He stood up with his hands slowly rubbing his sides and said [about Christianity], 'God against man. Man against God. Man against nature. Nature against man. Nature against God. God against nature—very funny religion!'" See Joseph Campbell with Bill Moyers, *The Power of Myth*, ed. Betty Sue Flowers (New York: Doubleday, 1988), p. 56. These dualities of Western though patterns are not found in the more Eastern religions such as Taoism and Zen Buddhism.

This is called indistinct and shadowy.
Go up to it and you will not see its head;
Follow behind it and you will not see its rear.[175]

Taoism is an ancient Chinese religion that took a recognizable form sometime during the fifth century B.C.E.,[176] roughly during the time when Confucius was alive. Taoism and Confucianism were formulated at approximately the same time and were often at odds,[177] and before Buddhism entered China they were the dominant options of the Chinese for religious activity.[178] The normally assumed author of the *Tao Te Ching* is Lao Tzu, about whom virtually nothing is known for certain. This is only fitting for a follower of the Tao. It would be too contradictory for a strong and well-known leader to be identified with Taoism, since the focus must be directed toward the Tao and never on the "teacher" of it.[179]

Other texts of Taoism are extant, but for present purposes the *Tao Te Ching* is sufficient to introduce Taoism. Those particularly interested in the teachings of Taoism and what it has to offer the role of the therapist will want to explore others of the Taoist writings.[180] In addition, the discussion here is on the philosophical dimensions of Taoism. Popular Taoism is another study unto itself, and there are a number of resources helpful in understanding what this form of Taoism meant, and means, to a large majority of practicing Taoists.[181]

The relevance of Taoism to the role of the therapist is that in Taoism the individual never looks externally for direction or authority. The Tao is within and without, but it is not "supplied" by someone else. The Tao is the great principle that regulates the course of nature,[182] leaving each individual to find his or her own way. The "teacher" only helps each person to understand the principle and to facilitate the "way" in each.[183] The therapist, as discussed throughout this chapter, is not the one with the answers, the morals, or the truth, but the one who gives the freedom for the individual to search and find his or her path (the Tao?). The

---

175. Lao Tzu, *Tao Te Ching*, p. 70.

176. See the historical discussion in Henri Maspero, *Taoism and Chinese Religion*, trans. Frank A. Kierman Jr. (Amherst: University of Massachusetts Press, 1981), especially pp. 25-37.

177. "Lao-tzu and Confucius were but two of some hundreds of wandering sages eager to instruct the feudal princes of those days." Blofeld, *Taoism*, p. 23.

178. Ibid., pp. 53-74.

179. For an overview of the discussion of authorship of the *Tao Te Ching*, see Holmes Welch, *Taoism: The Parting of the Way*, rev. ed. (Boston: Beacon Press, 1965), pp. 179-182.

180. For example, the *Chuang Tzu* and the *Thai Shang*.

181. For example, see Matthias Eder, *Chinese Religion* (Tokyo: Asian Folklore Studies, Monograph No. 6, 1973), pp. 141-149; Chapter Six, "The Jade Emperor's Court (Taoism as a Popular Religion)," in Blofeld, *Taoism*, pp. 90-112; and John Lagerwey, *Taoist Ritual in Chinese Society and History* (New York: Macmillan, 1987).

182. "The Tao is unknowable, vast, eternal. As undifferentiated void, pure spirit, it is the mother of the cosmos; as non-void, it is the container, the sustainer and, in a sense, the being of the myriad objects, permeating all. As the goal of existence, it is the Way of Heaven, of Earth, of Man. No-being, it is the source of Being. It is not conscious of activity, has no purpose, seeks no rewards or praise, yet performs all things to perfection. Like water, it wins its way by softness. Like a deep ravine, it is shadowy rather than brilliant." Blofeld, *Taoism*, pp. 2-3.

183. See, for fuller background and understanding of the practice of Taoism, Book Nine, "Methods of Nourishing the Vital Principle in the Ancient Taoist Religion," in Maspero, *Taoism and Chinese Religion*, pp. 445-554.

therapist does not use force to convince. The therapist does not perform great feats for the client to watch and admire. The therapist fades into the background, giving the space and the attention to the client as the client makes his or her decisions.

Taoism focuses on the way rather than on the teacher of the way, and such is the role of the therapist. The religious educator who wishes to be a therapist must be a person on the way, and be one who allows others to search for their expression of the way. This quote from the *Tao Te Ching* gives a description of the follower of the Tao as well as a summary statement of the religious educator fulfilling the role of the therapist:

> He who knows others is clever;
> He who knows himself has discernment.
> He who overcomes others has force;
> He who overcomes himself is strong.
> He who knows contentment is rich;
> He who perseveres is a man of purpose;
> He who does not lose his station will endure;
> He who lives out his days has had a long life.[184]

Historical Personage: Carl Jung

A person from the recent past who epitomizes the image of the therapist for many people, especially those in religion, has been Carl Gustav Jung (1875-1961). Starting as a friend and confidant of Sigmund Freud, Jung destroyed the relationship when he disagreed with the basic psychosexual stance that Freud espoused.[185] Jung remained in the psychodynamic camp, but took his theories in different directions than Freud approved of—especially when it came to the meaning and role of religion in healthy psychic life.

Jung has become a favorite of many religious folk because he saw at least some kinds of religion as a healthy manifestation rather than as a disease or a neurosis, as Freud had analyzed it.[186] Jung noted: "Freudian analysis would brush all them [religious questions and concerns] aside as irrelevant, for in its view, it is basically a question of repressed sexuality, which the philosophical or religious doubts only serve to mask."[187] Some of the most quoted and appreciated words written by Jung were ones that opened the door to another approach in psychodynamic theory toward religion: "Among all my patients in the second half of life—that is to say, over thirty-five—there has not been one whose problem in

---

184. Lao Tzu, *Tao Te Ching*, p. 92.

185. For Jung's description of the break, see Carl G. Jung, *Memories, Dreams, Reflections*, recorded and edited by Aniela Jaffé, trans. Richard and Clara Winston (New York: Pantheon, 1963), pp. 155-169; for an example of a secondary account, see Vincent Brome, *Jung* (New York: Atheneum, 1978), pp. 145-154.

186. The classic source for experiencing Sigmund Freud's withering attack on religion is his *The Future of an Illusion*, trans. W.D. Robinson Scott, rev. and ed. James Strachey (Garden City, N.Y.: Doubleday Anchor, 1961).

187. Carl G. Jung, "Psychotherapists or the Clergy," in Vol. 11, *Psychology and Religion*, in *The Collected Works of C.G. Jung* (1958), p. 337.

the last resort was not that of finding a religious outlook on life. It is safe to say that every one of them fell ill because he had lost what the living religions of every age have given to their followers, and none of them has been really healed who did not regain his religious outlook."[188] Curiously, those that quote this passage from Jung too often delete the concluding sentence to that paragraph: "This of course has nothing whatever to do with a particular creed or membership of a church."[189]

Pointing to Jung as one who allowed a place for religion within the boundaries of a healthy psyche, then, may not be as safe as it sounds. As his biographer and collaborator, Aniela Jaffé, wrote: "Jung's concept of religion differed in many respects from traditional Christianity—above all in his answer to the problem of evil and his conception of a God who is not entirely good or kind. From the viewpoint of dogmatic Christianity, Jung was distinctly an 'outsider.' "[190] What Jaffé meant is immediately clear in the following words which Jung wrote very late in life: "Therefore the individual who wishes to have an answer to the problem of evil, as it is posed today, has need, first and foremost, of *self-knowledge*, that is, the utmost possible knowledge of his own wholeness. He must know relentlessly how much good he can do, and what crimes he is capable of, and must be aware of regarding the one real and the other as illusion. Both are elements within his nature, and both are bound to come to light in him, should he wish—as he ought—to live without self-deception or self-delusion."[191] Jung, then, did not point his patients to an external source—to God or to the approved answers—but inward. His solution was self-knowledge, not theology or dogma, which to Jung were nothing but self-knowledge externalized and objectified.[192]

One of the more fascinating but controversial aspects of Jung's work related to his investigations into such areas of psychic phenomena as parapsychology and extrasensory perceptions, and his chief interest here was the study of acausality, or more specifically, of synchronicity.[193] The primary source for his investigations is the essay "Synchronicity: An Acausal Connecting Principle," in which he gave this definition of synchronicity: "Synchronicity therefore means the simultaneous occurrence of a certain psychic state with one or more external events which appear as meaningful parallels to the momentary subjective state—and, in certain cases, vice versa."[194] Jung refused to take the easy way out and to label the source of synchronnicity as either God or mere chance: "Here, for

---

188. Ibid., p. 334.

189. Ibid.

190. "Introduction," by Aniela Jaffé, in Jung, *Memories, Dreams, Reflections*, p. x.

191. Jung, *Memories, Dreams, Reflections*, p. 330.

192. For example, Jung wrote: "Creeds are codified and dogmatized forms of original religious experience. The contents of the experience have become sanctified and usually congealed in a rigid, often elaborate, structure. The practice and the reproduction of the original experience have become a ritual and an unchangeable institution." Carl G. Jung, *Psychology and Religion* (New Haven: Yale University Press, 1938), p. 6.

193. For a good overview of this entire topic, see Chapter One, "Parapsychology: Experience and Theory," in Aniela Jaffé, *From the Life and Work of C.G. Jung*, trans. R.F.C. Hull (New York: Harper & Row, 1971), pp. 1-45.

194. Carl G. Jung, "Synchronicity: An Acausal Connecting Principle," in Vol. 8, *The Structure and Dynamics of the Psyche*, in *The Collected Works of C.G. Jung* (1969), p. 441.

want of a demonstrable cause, we are all too likely to fall into the temptation of positing a *transcendental* one. But a 'cause' can only be a demonstrable quantity. A 'transcendent cause' is a contradiction in terms, because anything transcendental cannot by definition be demonstrated."[195] Jung concluded: "However incomprehensible it may appear, we are finally compelled to assume that there is in the unconscious something like an *a priori* knowledge or an 'immediacy' of events which lacks any causal basis. At any rate our conception of causality is incapable of explaining the facts."[196] Jung, through his investigations of the unconscious, was not afraid to challenge the rationalistic biases of Western thought so well defined by causality and to see what could be revealed by altering the perspectives from a more Eastern point of view.[197]

The juxtaposition of Jung and Taoism in the present chapter is not accidental or contrived. His understanding of the Eastern religions, including Taoism, was deep and influential in his work.[198] As has all ready been noted, Jung relied upon paradox and the juxtaposition of opposites to reveal the larger truth. Jung's discussions of the animus and the anima, for example, are ways to sense the wholeness of the human.[199] Commentator Joseph Campbell said in this regard: "Jung's concept is that the aim of one's life, psychologically speaking, should not be to suppress or repress, but to come to know one's other side, and so both to enjoy and to control the whole range of one's capacities; i.e., in the full sense, to 'know oneself.' "[200] In fact, Jung identified himself with Lao Tzu at the conclusion of *Memories, Dreams, Reflections* with the predictable list of paradoxes and incongruities: "When Lao-tzu says: 'All are clear, I alone am clouded,' he

---

195. Ibid., p. 446.

196. Ibid., p. 447.

197. This notion of acausality was stimulated by Jung's association with physicists like Niels Bohr, Wolfgang Pauli, and Albert Einstein as they were fashioning the basis of the "new physics," as well as Jung's fascination with Eastern philosophy. These relationships are given detailed account by Ira Progoff in *Jung, Synchronicity, and Human Destiny: Noncausal Dimensions of Human Experience* (New York: Julian Press, 1973), especially in Chapter Four, "The Foundations of Synchronicity," pp. 46-59, and Chapter Ten, "Einstein and the Larger View," pp. 147-158. This influence of modern physics and Eastern philosophy has found its way into the public awareness through such writings as the aforementioned books of Capra's *The Tao of Physics* and Zukav's *The Dancing Wu Li Masters*.

198. See this discussed, for example, by June Singer, "The Education of the Analyst," in *Jungian Analysis*, pp. 374-383; and Chapter Six, "Leibniz and Tao," in Progoff, *Jung, Synchronicity, and Human Destiny*, pp. 67-76; and throughout Harold Coward, *Jung and Eastern Thought* (Albany: State University of New York Press, 1985).

199. See Carl G. Jung, "Animus and Anima," in Vol. 7, *Two Essays on Analytic Psychology*, in *The Collected Works of C.G. Jung* (1969), pp. 188-211. Jung wrote: "The feelings of a man are so to speak as a woman's and appear as such in dreams. I designate this figure by the term *anima*, because she is the personification of the inferior functions which relate a man to the collective unconscious. The collective unconscious as a whole presents itself to a man in feminine form. To a woman it appears in masculine form, and then I call it the *animus*. I chose the term anima because it has always been used for that very same psychological fact. The anima [and animus] as a personification of the collective unconscious occurs in dreams over and over again. I have made long statistics about the anima figure in dreams. In this way one establishes these figures empirically." Carl G. Jung, "The Tavistock Lectures," Lecture Three, in Vol. 18, *The Symbolic Life: Miscellaneous Writings*, in *The Collected Works of C.G. Jung* (1976), p. 89.

200. Joseph Campbell, "Editor's Introduction," in *The Portable Jung*, ed. Joseph Campbell (New York: Viking, 1971), p. xxvii.

is expressing what I now feel in advanced old age. Lao-tzu is the example of a man with superior insight who has seen and experienced worth and worthlessness, and who at the end of his life desires to return to his own being, into the eternal unknowable meaning. The archetype of the old man who has seen enough is eternally true. . . . Yet there is so much that fills me: plants, animals, clouds day and night, and the eternal in man. The more uncertain I have felt about myself, the more there has grown up in me a feeling of kinship with all things."[201]

The work of Jung is too voluminous, complex, and important for these few paragraphs to do anything more than introduce it. The attempt here is only to suggest that a study of Jung would be a fruitful one for those seeking a historical figure related to the role of the religious educator as therapist. A concluding word from Jung expresses his stance as a therapist, displays again his effort to integrate seeming opposites, and shows how he relates to the themes of this chapter: "The psychotherapist who takes his work seriously . . . must decide in every single case whether or not he is willing to stand by a human being with counsel and help upon what may be a daring misadventure. He must have no fixed ideas as to what is right, nor must he pretend to know what is right and what is not—otherwise he takes something from the richness of the experience. He must keep in view what actually happens—and only that which acts is actual. If something which seems to me an error shows itself to be more effective than a truth, then I must first follow up the error, for in it lie power and life which I lose if I hold to what seems to me true. Light has need of darkness—otherwise how could it appear as light?"[202]

Contemporary Example: Morton Kelsey

Morton Trippe Kelsey (b. 1917) has a number of defining identities. Although now retired, he has functioned as an Episcopal priest, a college professor, a marriage and family counselor, an encounter group leader, and a prolific author. His most singularly descriptive identity, however, is the one under scrutiny here: He is a religious educator in the sense of being a spiritual director or guide, which brings together and uses all the other pieces of his identity. Exploring what being this kind of religious educator means—with all its ambiguity and misunderstanding—will explain how Morton Kelsey serves as the contemporary example of one who links together the role of the therapist with that of the religious educator. The following discussion, then, should be read with the understanding that Kelsey could legitimately be classified under a number of labels, such as spiritual director,[203] therapist,[204] or religious educator. Perhaps the most

---

201. Jung, *Memories, Dreams, Reflections*, p. 359.

202. Jung, "Psychotherapists or the Clergy," in Vol. 11, *The Collected Works of C.G. Jung*, p. 343.

203. Although this is not a term that strictly applies to Kelsey's approach in the classical sense, he does use it of himself occasionally. See Chapter One, "The Spiritual Journey," Morton T. Kelsey, *Companions on the Inner Way: The Art of Spiritual Guidance* (New York: Crossroad, 1986), pp. 1-9.

204. Kelsey is not a licensed psychotherapist and makes this clear so as not to be misleading. For example, see his comments in Morton T. Kelsey, *Psychology, Medicine, and Christian Healing* (San Francisco: Harper & Row, 1988), pp. 67-70. He does hold memberships and licenses from a variety of counseling organizations, however. See Kelsey, *Caring*, p. vii.

descriptive term is religious therapist, since Kelsey conducts religious education therapeutically. This section shows how Kelsey's approach illuminates the connections between the therapist and the religious educator but acknowledges that his approach differs from what many expect from either a therapist or a religious educator.

Further, Kelsey writes with passion and fervor but without with the precision and nuancing of the scholar. His writing is full of anecdotes and stories of his life experience and that of others' experience because he has been a participant in so many therapeutic relationships. This type of writing style is hardly surprising for such a person as Kelsey, noting his identities and his audience, but it does present some difficulties in this context. Hard empirical data and explicit references are hard to come by in Kelsey's writings. What he produces is not the same sort of material or evidence as, say, that of James Fowler,[205] who has attempted to use a scientific framework and process to whatever degree of success. Indeed, as shall be shown, Kelsey is quite obviously discomfited by the limitations of the Western materialistic and scientific worldview and not in the least concerned with making his writing conform to its standards.[206] Such a difference in intent, style, and point of view by Kelsey should not be used against him unfairly, but it does make for interesting comparisons with other contemporary examples of the religious educator examined throughout this book.

The final caveat before overviewing Kelsey's contribution to the role of the therapist in relation to the religious educator is that such a focus demands severe limitations on what will be examined among Kelsey's work. As mentioned above, he has written many books and articles, although in virtually every one of them he approaches the specific topic from a therapeutic point of view. After reading several of Kelsey's writings, one begins to get a real sense of familiarity. He often says the same thing in different books. Both the scope and space do set limits on what can be discussed here, however. The small slices that follow are portions cut for the specific purpose of demonstrating the religious educator as therapist, but they hopefully will not be unfair or misrepresentative of Kelsey's primary message.

Overview

To overview and illustrate Morton Kelsey's contribution to the subject, then, is to concentrate on only a small portion of his writings.[207] The books that sufficiently introduce the reader to pursue further investigations and explo-

205. Fowler's work was addressed in Chapter Six, "The Religious Educator as Scientist."

206. In virtually every book, Kelsey has a chapter that explains the limitations of the Western worldview (the "illusory world") and the need for openness to the nonphysical or "psychoid" world. This follows from Kelsey being strongly influenced by the work of Carl Jung. Jung's own discomfort with the strictly rational approach of the West was discussed briefly in the previous section of the chapter related to synchronicity and acausality.

207. Other books to be consulted for a broader view of Kelsey's message include *Myth, History and Faith: The Remythologizing of Christianity* (New York: Paulist, 1974); *Afterlife: The Other Side of Dying* (New York: Paulist, 1980); *Caring: How Can We Love One Another?* (New York: Paulist, 1981); *Transcend: A Guide to the Spiritual Quest* (New York: Crossroad, 1981); *Prophetic Ministry: The Psychology and Spirituality of Pastoral Care* (New York: Crossroad, 1982); and *Reaching: The Journey to Fulfillment* (San Francisco: Harper & Row, 1989).

ration of Kelsey's work include *Can Christians Be Educated?*,[208] *Encounter with God*,[209] *Dreams*,[210] *Psychology, Medicine, and Christian Healing, Companions on the Inner Way*, and *Christo-Psychology*.[211] Here Kelsey presented the foundation of the "art of spiritual guidance" that to Kelsey at least provides the link between the role of the therapist and the religious educator and makes them one.

An initial effort to understand Morton Kelsey as therapist and religious educator draws from a book that gathered together some of Kelsey's essays directly addressing his version of religious education, entitled *Can Christians Be Educated?* One of those essays was "A Parish Model for Educating Christians," a rather rare opportunity to hear a theorist propose a model for implementing his or her ideas. In this essay, the essence of Kelsey's entire approach to religion and to religious education was encapsulated. It is an excellent place for a person new to Kelsey's work to begin reading. The underlying issue he questioned was whether or not Christians can be educated, meaning is Christianity something that can be taught or must it be gained independently by each individual.[212] In his characteristically blunt way, he said one must "admit that educating Christians is important and to take it as seriously as preaching or financing church buildings or conducting rummage sales."[213] Kelsey then went on to detail his successful teaching experiment in the parish where he and others taught in seminars, led in small group experiences, and even accomplished some resultant personal counseling activity.[214] His conclusion: "Can Christians be educated? The answer we found was an unqualified yes."[215]

He started precisely where one would expect a depth psychologist and a follower of Jung to begin: with the inner resources of the person, with the spirit, or the unconscious, albeit linked with good educational preparation: "Trying to communicate religion today without some knowledge of depth psychology and educational methods is just as foolish as it would be for a missionary to go to some underdeveloped, poverty-stricken country without a knowledge of medicine, hygiene, and agriculture. If Christians want to share their religion with others, they must know the nature of the persons they are teaching, their uniqueness, their hang-ups, their backgrounds, and how they can be taught."[216] Then Kelsey brought in one of the issues that is repeated in virtually every one of his books

---

208. Morton T. Kelsey, *Can Christians Be Educated?: A Proposal for Effective Communication of our Christian Religion*, comp. and ed. Harold William Burgess (Birmingham, Ala.: Religious Education Press, 1977).

209. Morton T. Kelsey, *Encounter with God: A Theology of Christian Experience* (Minneapolis: Bethany Fellowship, 1972).

210. Morton T. Kelsey, *Dreams: A Way to Listen to God* (New York: Paulist, 1978).

211. Morton T. Kelsey, *Christo-Psychology* (New York: Crossroad, 1982).

212. Hence, the title of the edited work. The obvious implication is, can religion be taught? This is a place where Kelsey's particularism of Christianity can be universalized into religion and religious education without doing damage to his message.

213. Morton T. Kelsey, "A Parish Model for Educating Christians," in *Can Christians Be Educated?* p. 9.

214. See Kelsey discuss his method in ibid., pp. 10-12.

215. Ibid., p. 20.

216. Ibid., p. 12.

or articles: a basic worldview which allows for the breaking in of the spirit world.[217]

This basic worldview is not only essential to grasping Kelsey's perspective but is fundamental to why he is about the business of religious education. He did not see himself as one who was primarily a lecturer, or formal teacher, but a "companion on the inner way," and he was concerned that too many who pass as religious educators miss the mark entirely because they take the wrong world-view: "I came to believe that religious educators with little or no understanding of the process of spiritual growth into mature religion were indeed blind guides for the blind."[218] The "wrong" or distorted worldview is the closed, rationalistic, and cause-and-effect type of thinking that pervades and infects the West and its religion.[219] The result of this worldview, with its emphasis only on the empirical, the scientific, the conscious, and the subsequent shutting out of the unconscious,[220] was a disregard for religion: "It is difficult, if not impossible, for most people to keep a vital interest in religion without some conviction that a real religious reality exists."[221] Kelsey then made his recommendation for improvement of the situation: "There is, however, another view of the world. It is widespread and has been accepted in many times and places. This view proposes that both the physical world and the spiritual world are real. Human beings need to participate in both of these worlds if they are to be fully alive. It took me ten years of work with some of the friends of Dr. Jung to realize that Jung was suggesting this very point of view."[222] It is this view of reality, and the paths into it, that make up the real responsibility of the true religious educator—these truths are found on the inner journey and not by disregarding or ignoring the larger and deeper realities of existence. It should now be obvious why Kelsey can be regarded as such a stellar example of the role of the religious educator as therapist.

Kelsey, then, took many of his cues to spiritual guidance from the works of Carl Jung and of other Jungians, not only studying the works of Jung but himself undergoing Jungian analysis.[223] Much of what was said about Jung's approach to reality in the previous section of this chapter relates directly to understanding Kelsey. Kelsey is also concerned with the deeper aspects of the human: the unconscious, both the individual and the collective; the dreams which reveal

---

217. This was the place Kelsey started his classes in Christian education. See ibid., p. 13.

218. Kelsey, *Companions on the Inner Way*, p. ix.

219. Probably the best source for grasping the dimensions of Kelsey's dissatisfaction with this worldview, and his reasons for it, are found throughout *Encounter with God*. In this book he deals with both the psychological and the theological problems of the classical Western science perspective.

220. See the various charts Kelsey provides to schematize this closed world view as contrasted to the spiritual view. They are provided in virtually every book. See, for example, Chapter Two, "Spiritual Guidance and the Western World," *Companions on the Inner Way*, pp. 10-29; Chapter Thirteen, "A Place for Religious Healing in the Modern World," in *Psychology, Medicine, and Christian Healing*, pp. 263-296; and Chapter Nine, "Communicating Religion," *Encounter with God*, pp. 213-240.

221. Kelsey, *Encounter with God*, p. 26.

222. Ibid., p. 19.

223. See in particular the first two chapters of *Christo-Psychology*, where Kelsey described Jung's influence in some detail.

the deeper world;[224] and healing the brokenness that exists between the two realms of reality.[225] However, Kelsey was not willing to be too closely identified as a disciple of Jung, as he said: "Because of my extensive involvement with analytical psychology, I am sometimes asked if I am a Jungian. I usually answer, 'No, I am a Christian who has found the thinking of Jung helpful in communicating the worldview and message of Jesus to seeking, educated, modern men and women.'"[226] With that self-proclaimed distance, Kelsey's work is still deeply imprinted and filled with Jungian quotes and stories. It is perhaps not too misleading to say that Kelsey took the more universal and generic religious views of Jung and directed them specifically toward a Christian interpretation.

The above paragraph leads to another foundational aspect of Kelsey: He is undeniably and inextricably Christian. He has some knowledge and appreciation for other world religions, particularly Eastern ones, although principally through the influence of Jung's own interest in them.[227] Since Kelsey uses and teaches the meditational disciplines, he often draws on these resources. In no instance, though, does he ever display any interest in being other than his own (meaning self-styled) type of Christian. Admittedly his understanding of Christianity is interpretive, such as his insistence that "God is like Jesus"[228] (instead of the more usual reverse), and that his preferred term for God is "Divine Lover" (as distinct from some appellation as "Heavenly Father"); yet it is impossible to interpret Kelsey as anything other than as a Christian and his solutions as anything other than as Christian ones.

This combination of Jungian psychology and Christian spirituality into the therapeutic approach that Kelsey forged is illustrated in the following excerpt from *Christo-Psychology*. Here he emphasized that religious educators, however defined or labeled, are charged with helping to heal brokenness. Kelsey began by saying: "The most important problem for personal growth is this: How can we bring all of ourselves into the fullness of divine love and how do we keep ourselves from falling into the disunity propagated by the dark destructive forces?"[229] This question of Kelsey's is important because it shows his therapist's quest for the unity and integration of the whole person, while also showing his Jungian understanding of the opposing forces within the human that need to be harmonized. He answered his question by using Jung's four steps of individuation, which Kelsey saw as "comparable to the steps on the traditional Christian path."[230] He explained: "The first step is abreaction, in psychological terms, or con-

---

224. See Kelsey's rather popular-style book *Dreams*, where he developed this theme: "If, however, humankind is open to another dimension of reality, then the dream may be one of the most common avenues through which God reaches out to us." Kelsey, *Dreams*, p. 1. Also see Kelsey's more in-depth book *God, Dreams, and Revelation: A Christian Interpretation of Dreams* (Minneapolis: Augsburg, 1974).

225. See Kelsey's *Psychology, Medicine, and Christian Healing.*

226. Kelsey, *Christo-Psychology*, p. 1.

227. For a good discussion of this, see Morton T. Kelsey, *The Other Side of Silence: A Guide to Christian Meditation* (New York: Paulist, 1976), pp. 1-2. Also see *Companions on the Inner Way*, pp. 16-18.

228. Kelsey, *Companions on the Inner Way*, p. 58.

229. Kelsey, *Christo-Psychology*, p. 92.

230. Ibid.

fession, in the Christian idiom. It means knowing one's faults and owning them, usually in the presence of another person. . . . The second step is transference or love. We grow as we develop relationships and understand them. . . . The third step is integration. It involves knowing the outer world and the people in it along with the inner depths and trying to function as a unity inspired by love. It requires a great deal of reflection, education, and hard work. The goal of wholeness is seldom reached by our own efforts alone. It is given in the last stage, resolution, that brings us together into harmony with the divine. Christianity knows this experience as the beatific vision."[231] Then Kelsey made his summative point, revealing the task of the religious educator in the role of therapist: "The work of the spiritual counselor is to guide others through these four stages so that they can eventually walk on this path by themselves."[232] Kelsey as the therapist/religious educator was describing the maturing process that is essential for the guide as well as for the traveler.

Kelsey was careful to set boundaries on the therapeutic relationship. He stated explicitly that a therapeutic relationship existed primarily for the needs of the client and not those of the therapist, yet he warned against ignoring the needs of the therapist. Kelsey wrote: "The counselee must never be used to meet the counselor's needs. And it is likely that the counselor will have needs; the important thing is to be aware of them."[233] Kelsey used the following standard to keep the boundaries and the responsibilities of the spiritual director (therapist) clear: "The most important criterion for the spiritual director is to do nothing that does not express genuine concern and caring, to stay in the orbit of love."[234]

Kelsey defined his understanding of religious education as "the deliberate attempt to accompany other people on their journeys into God and, in the process, to share what we have learned as we have made our own journeys."[235] He acknowledged that such a term and activity are often misunderstood as being authoritarian, but that in his mind it is offering direction, never forcing it.[236] He made the further point that there is one prime consideration for those who wish to be involved in this kind of work. Kelsey said that "it is most unwise for people to be charged with spiritual formation who are not on their own spiritual journeys and who are unable to be spiritual companions."[237]

Religious education (or, as Kelsey would often say, spiritual direction) was prescribed by Kelsey neither as a lockstep process nor, as was mentioned above, an authoritarian issue. Individuality and personal choice are paramount. He was careful to keep these realities clearly in view: "There is much written on the *from what* and the *to what*, but not so much is found . . . on the *how*. The task of spiritual guidance, spiritual formation, or spiritual direction (as well as that of genuine Christian education) is to provide ways, methods, and practices that will help

---

231. Ibid.
232. Ibid.
233. Ibid., pp. 104-105.
234. Ibid., p. 63.
235. Kelsey, *Companions on the Inner Way*, p. 7. Actually, he labeled this the definition of spiritual guidance.
236. Ibid.
237. Ibid.

us move from our alienation to our consummation. It is not easy to travel from one to another, and since each of us is unique, each of us will have a unique way of coming to the right path and staying on it. General prescriptions can be helpful, but each of us has his or her particular pit to escape and his or her specific journey to achieve the goal."[238] In case someone missed the point, Kelsey said later: "Telling people . . . to buck up and take the dogmas and dictates of an authoritarian church or book on faith simply doesn't work."[239]

Earlier in the chapter was a discussion of the shadow role of the therapist, that of the manipulator and moralizer. His comments on such a role are informative and summative: "Does a moralistic condemnation of sin as such really help anybody? What, in fact, is sin? It is anything which keeps us from coming into our unique destiny, into total relationship with love and the risen Christ. This may be different for each person each day. To say one is against sin helps no one. If we can listen to what is troubling another, and bear the burden of that person, then we can help our client or friend to pass through that problem. It is difficult to get over a psychic or spiritual problem, a sin or a fear that is hard to face. Usually we cannot do this on our own and we need another to share with us by listening to our pain and confusion."[240] The question that needs to be asked is this: If you had a problem, would you go to someone like Morton Kelsey for help? If so, then he provides an example of the role of the religious educator as therapist worthy of study and reproduction.

Evaluation

Evaluating Morton Kelsey is difficult because it makes so much difference whether or not one basically agrees with his initial philosophical and psychological positions. Although this is true in large measure with virtually any author, it is particularly true of Kelsey because of his Jungian handling of the concept of worldview, where the spirit world and the unconscious have the highest importance and priority. He left little room for doubting where he stood, and if you agree with him, then his work would naturally be considered exceedingly strong. If one disagrees, which probably means not accepting his worldview, then much of what he had to say was rather weak. In fact, if one disagrees, then one probably needs Jungian therapy to get in contact with both the true self and with the spirit world![241] Indeed, how *does* one "prove" the existence of the spirit world and the power of the unconscious? The most objective and useful way to evaluate Kelsey here is simply to comment on his illumination of the role of therapist and to let each individual make the final decision about the specific content of his contributions.

The rebuttal to the above paragraph would involve Kelsey's close identification with Carl Jung. Kelsey, and Jung, put such stock in the nonphysical world that

---

238. Ibid., p. 31.

239. Ibid., p. 62.

240. Kelsey, *Christo-Psychology*, p. 94.

241. "According to the model we have suggested, man is not only in touch with the space-time or material world, the world of sociology and research methods and behaviorism; he is also in touch with non-spacetime or spiritual world of images and intuitions, dreams, and phantasies, myths and numinous contents which are autonomous and of more than individual significance." Kelsey, *Encounter with God*, p. 144.

to ignore that part of his writings would render them to be virtually incomprehensible. Kelsey repeatedly made such statements as this one: "Both the physical and spiritual realms are real and valuable. They are interrelated. Human beings are caught in the tension between the two. Unless human beings are in touch with both realms, they are likely to fall into neurosis or psychosis."[242] Such statements, so grounded in Jungian thought, are difficult to classify as right or wrong, good or bad. One's evaluation of the position, though, is fundamentally dependent on the strength of such a worldview. An understanding of the therapist from a behaviorist perspective, for example, would find such talk nonsense. One key difference between Jung and Kelsey, however, is that while Jung was careful to gather and report empirical data and reports,[243] Kelsey had little time or patience for such. Other than anecdotal evidence, Kelsey did not back up his statements with findings.

An important evaluative question to be asked of Kelsey is why he was so enamored of Jungian approaches? Why was he so convinced of their rightness? It is as though he somewhat arbitrarily starts with the Jungian categories and then fits virtually everything into them. Is Jung above criticism? Kelsey does not cite his reasons for following Jung, as opposed to following some other psychologist or philosopher, other than to say he thinks Jung was correct.[244] What are the criteria, and why should others follow Kelsey in their adherence to Jungian approaches? These questions Kelsey left unasked and unanswered—at least publicly.

The above issues raise a related point of evaluation connected to Kelsey's work. Beyond his dependence upon Jungian ideas, Kelsey does not give any real scholarly depth to his writings. Most of the time he addresses his readers as if he were speaking at a retreat or informal lecture,[245] and rarely if ever does he deal with the deeper philosophical or theological issues that are raised. This results in Kelsey's writings and positions appearing to be rather simplistic, since they are not grounded in larger theoretical perspectives, and reductionistic, by making his own positions look strong by characterizing the opposing positions as weak and indefensible but without the solid evidence to demonstrate it. He did not deal in any depth, for example, with behavioristic psychology and with its objections to the assumptions of depth psychology, although this would seem to have been a natural and necessary point of emphasis.[246]

Another related point of discomfort that Kelsey's work raises is its apparent

242. Kelsey, *Companions on the Inner Way*, p. 22.

243. An excellent example is found in Jung's essay "Synchronicity." As unusual and as seemingly nonempirical as this subject was, Jung gave statistics and studies to document his text. See Carl G. Jung, "Synchronicity," in Vol. 8, *The Structure and Dynamics of the Psyche*, in *The Collected Works of C.G. Jung*, pp. 461-484.

244. One interesting passage from Kelsey is the following: "Before one can go very far spiritually, he must accept at least tentatively that there is a realm of the spirit, that there is something to explore. . . . This is something on which a person stakes his life and his action simply because it might be true." Kelsey, *Encounter with God*, p. 175.

245. This is indeed how many of his books are produced—a result of lecture transcriptions from tapes. For example, see his explanation in Kelsey, *Caring*, p. vi.

246. At most he would mention it to disregard it, but did not actually refute the arguments. Note how he mentioned but never really engaged B.F. Skinner in *Companions on the Inner Way*, p. 165, and in *Psychology, Medicine, and Healing*, pp. 204 and 270.

disvaluing of the cognitive and the lifestyle dimensions of the human in favor of the affective.[247] Kelsey put so much emphasis on the affective realm that the entire perspective is in danger of getting out of balance.[248] Kelsey aptly argued with the notion of the adequacy of reason alone,[249] for instance, but the same dangers appear when the affect is given attention exclusively as well. The human must be approached from a holistic perspective (a view which Kelsey would surely condone), and this is not accomplished by overemphasizing any one aspect or dimension, regardless of how neglected it may have been culturally or historically.[250]

For those seeking a strictly conventional view of Christianity, Kelsey was not concerned with staying inside any restrictive or traditional boundaries. He drew deeply from other religious traditions and did not shrink from seeing value in them. His favorite term for God was "Divine Lover," for as he said: "The motivating and creative core of the universe is often seen as Divine Love or the Divine Lover. This is true of mystical Christianity, Sufism, and Hasidism."[251] Kelsey sought truth where he could find it, but he did not find it in authoritarian or dogmatic doctrine.[252] Kelsey did acknowledge the similarities and the differences of the Western and the Eastern religions related to spirituality, as when he wrote: "Both East and West offer the same disciplines for the beginning of the spiritual life. Both emphasize detachment, quiet, stilling the emotions, withdrawal, receptivity, listening, and ceasing ego activity and striving."[253] He then launched immediately into a discussion of how the two diverge. He thus showed openness to other faith tradition resources, but his preference was for decidedly Western (more accurately, Christian) practices. Whether or not this is a strength or a weakness depends upon individual judgment, but it has great impact upon how one views and goes about the role of the religious educator as therapist.

Turning more directly to the religious educator as therapist, Kelsey was somewhat careless with his terminology. To describe his and others' vocation, he would occasionally use the term spiritual guide or director, other times psychotherapist, and still others a wide range of words like minister, psychologist, and companion.[254] From his perspective, all of these terms fit his experience

---

247. For a good statement of his position on the affective dimension, see Morton T. Kelsey, "The Place of the Affect in Religious Education: Psychodynamics of Affectivity and Emotion," *Lumen Vitae* 26:1 (March, 1971), pp. 68-80.

248. For example, Kelsey wrote: "Genuine belief in the spirit, as expressed in behavior, is a rarity in our modern world. It is doubtful whether a change of the magnitude required to know and deal with this spiritual dimension can be brought about other than through affect." Ibid., p. 79.

249. See a representative passage in Kelsey, *Companions on the Inner Way*, pp. 68-72.

250. See Kelsey try to address this need for holism in Chapter Eleven, "Body, Emotions, and Healing," in *Psychology, Medicine, and Christian Healing*, pp. 202-233. The result is still quite tilted toward the affective.

251. Kelsey, *Companions on the Inner Way*, pp. 22-23. See ibid., pp. 55-58 for Kelsey's discussion of "God as Daddy."

252. Kelsey's book *Encounter with God* was an effort to ground his Jungian point of view in a Christian light, however, and one he regarded as a book of theological exploration. Hence the subtitle of the book: "A Theology of Christian Experience."

253. Kelsey, *Companions on the Inner Way*, p. 23.

254. In fact, but only as one example, all of these can be found throughout Kelsey's book *Companions on the Inner Way* without any real discrimination of use.

and caused no substantial problems. In an attempt such as this to find some clarity and definition, Kelsey may have provided more confusing terminology than any that was distinctive or helpful. Of course, a counter-argument says that the role of therapist is indeed diverse and wide-ranging and that such a multiplicity of terms is necessary to cover the role adequately.

The final issue to evaluate is whether or not one can legitimately call Kelsey a religious educator. This was not really much of an issue for Kelsey, since in a number of places Kelsey himself directly equated religious education with his own kind of activity and with his vocational identity.[255] The more traditional boundaries of the role of religious educator may indeed need be expanded to include such activity, if the example of Kelsey and the discussion of this chapter are to have had any relevance; and if Morton Kelsey did have anything to say to religious educators—as this section has struggled to reveal—then just perhaps the identity of the religious educator can be widened sufficiently to include the role of the therapist.

Representative Teaching Procedure: Nondirective Teaching

A teaching procedure representative of the role of therapist and helpful to the religious educator is found in an adaptation of Carl Rogers' approach to therapy, one which he originally referred to as Student-Centered Teaching.[256] In making the application, Rogers asked: "If, in therapy, it is possible to rely upon the capacity of the client to deal constructively with his life situation and if the therapist's aim is best directed toward releasing that capacity, then why not apply this hypothesis and this method to teaching? If the creation of an atmosphere of acceptance, understanding, and respect is the most effective basis for facilitating the learning called therapy, then might it not be the basis for the learning which is called education?"[257] Indeed, in these two formative questions Rogers gave the foundation not only for his view of therapy but for what came to be called the nondirective teaching procedure. First, Rogers stressed that the client (in this case, the learner) must be trusted to know what he or she needs to know and that he or she has the capacity to find it. Second, the most important task of the educator is to create, in Rogers' words, "an atmosphere of acceptance, understanding, and respect."[258]

In a later writing, Rogers gave additional attention to what he then called "significant learning," saying that it takes place when these five conditions are met: "When the client perceives himself as faced by a serious and meaningful problem; when the therapist is a congruent person in the relationship, able to *be* the person he *is*; when the therapist feels an unconditional positive regard for the client; when the therapist experiences an accurate empathic understanding of the client's private world, and communicates this; [and w]hen the client to some

255. See, for example, the first page of the Preface to *Companions on the Inner Way*, p. ix.

256. Chapter Nine, "Student-Centered Teaching," in Rogers, *Client-Centered Therapy*, pp. 384-428.

257. Ibid., p. 384.

258. Ibid.

degree experiences the therapist's congruence, acceptance, and empathy."[259] Change the terminology of therapist to religious educator, and client to learner, and one has what Rogers considered to be an environment for significant learning to take place.[260]

The nondirective teaching procedure described by Bruce Joyce and Marsha Weil builds upon this Rogerian therapeutic posture.[261] Even though this procedure may initially appear to have no structure, actually it can be outlined as having five phases.[262] First, the religious educator as facilitator develops enough of a relationship that the learner is free to express his or her feelings and to trust the leader. Second, the learner in discussion with the facilitator identifies a problem or situation that seems to be blocking or inhibiting growth and development. Third, through conversation and relationship with the leader, the learner develops insight into the problem and his or her inappropriate responses to it currently. Fourth, the learner and the leader explore options for overcoming the difficulties. The religious educator limits his or her role to helping identify alternatives and to facilitating the evaluation of the alternatives. It remains the responsibility of the learner to make the final decisions and to carry them through. Fifth, the learner moves out of the protective and nurturing relationship into the reality of the problem area and tries out the new behavior or approach. The facilitator-learner relationship is still in place for support, but the learner moves on to become increasingly interdependent.

The above brief description of a learning situation is normally a process developed over a long period of time and need not be performed quite so formally. In many ways, this teaching procedure is but a concretizing of natural mentor relationships.[263] It can be accomplished one-on-one, or in a group.[264] The aim of the therapist or religious educator is to nurture and support the individual to the point where he or she can make personal decisions and be responsible for his or her own life. The person then becomes interdependent, which guards against both isolation and dependency.

Experiential Simulation: Inner Journey

Certainly there is no one way to become a therapist and not even one best way. The only thing that seems to be universally true is that the therapist, to use an image of Morton Kelsey's, must be on the path of the "inner way" in order to be a companion along it. This translates into the therapist personally traveling

---

259. Rogers, *On Becoming a Person*, p. 285.

260. See ibid., pp. 286-290, where Rogers spelled out the "implications for education" of these five conditions.

261. Consult Rogers, *Freedom to Learn for the 80's* for the fullest exposition of Rogers' educational philosophy and reports of its success and failures.

262. This procedure is overviewed formally in Bruce Joyce and Marsha Weil, *Models of Teaching*, 3rd ed. (Englewood Cliffs, N.J.: Prentice-Hall, 1986), pp. 141-158. These phases are outlined on p. 151.

263. A good resource here is Laurent A. Daloz, *Effective Teaching and Mentoring* (San Francisco: Jossey-Bass, 1986).

264. For Rogers' views on group efforts related to the above teaching procedure, see Carl R. Rogers, *Carl Rogers on Encounter Groups* (New York: Harper & Row, 1970).

toward increased maturity and health while engaging in therapeutic relation-ships with others. Since the therapist has only the tool of himself or herself to "use" on others, it is essential for that one tool to be as prepared as possible. In parallel fashion, the same type of commitment to the inner journey is proper preparation and experience for the religious educator wanting to understand more fully the role of the therapist.

The primary suggestion of an experiential simulation for a person seeking to explore the role of the therapist is to become engaged in therapy. There really is no substitute for a personal relationship, so if possible that is the avenue to trav-el—to engage in a therapeutic relationship with a professional therapist. The particular type of therapist one chooses is not so important as the therapist him-self or herself, for as Carl Rogers noted: "It is the attitudes and feelings of the ther-apist, rather than this theoretical orientation, which is important. His procedures and techniques are less important than his attitudes."[265] What is the expected result of being in such a relationship? Again, Rogers put it succinctly: "It seems that gradually, painfully, the individual explores what is behind the masks with which he has been deceiving himself. Deeply and often vividly he experiences the various elements of himself which have been hidden within. Thus to an increasing degree he becomes himself—not a façade of conformity to others, not a cynical denial of all feeling, nor a front of intellectual rationality, but a living, breathing, feeling, fluctuating process—in short, he becomes a person."[266]

This type of exercise is important to the budding therapist because it allows the therapist to receive the therapy. This guards against the therapist using the client to resolve his or her own personal issues, allowing an appropriate time and place for the therapist to work out some initial conflicts. This was identified at the head of the chapter as "kenosis": the need to "empty out" the therapist in order for the client to be seen and helped honestly and with integrity. Until this jour-ney has begun, the role of the therapist is closed.

If such a therapeutic relationship is impossible, or initially too threatening, then two other ways are offered. First, a book by psychiatrist Eileen Walkenstein, enti-tled *Your Inner Therapist*,[267] undertook the task of "teaching readers the steps they can take to contact their Inner Therapist."[268] This book (or another like it) may serve as a means of knowing more about yourself and of experiencing something of what it is like to be in therapy. Most importantly, it will put the spotlight on you. Walkenstein's book is not one that can be read through without some degree of personal reflection and evaluation.

In the prologue to the book, Walkenstein stated that hers was a different kind of "self-help" book from most others. Rather than teaching the reader to listen and follow some outside authority, the book was designed to teach the reader to turn inward to the "inner therapist": "The saving grace of *Your Inner Therapist* is that it is truly a guide to that self within the reader, that Inner Therapist who is the ultimate authority for the good life."[269] She went on to say: "Although we

---

265. Rogers, *On Becoming a Person*, p. 44.
266. Ibid., p. 114.
267. Eileen Walkenstein, *Your Inner Therapist* (Philadelphia: Westminster, 1983).
268. Ibid., p. 12.
269. Ibid., p. 13.

want to be led by an external authority, what we *need* is to discover and follow our own *internal* authority. Our needs, not our wants, are our lifeline and should therefore be our top priority."[270]

Second is a closely related suggestion of experiencing intensive journaling. One of the best ways for this to be accomplished is to use the resources of Ira Progoff—either by attending one of the workshops[271] that teach one how to go about the process of this specialized type of journaling (using his *Intensive Journal*) or by utilizing his basic text on the subject, *At a Journal Workshop.*[272] In this text, Progoff explained at least some of what he hoped journaling would accomplish: "A primary purpose of the *Intensive Journal* is to provide an instrument and method by which the qualitative evolution of life can take place within us as individuals. It seeks to maintain for the elusive subjectivities of our inner life an open space in which the processes of life-integration can proceed objectively in the context of each person's experience. The *Intensive Journal* becomes the outer embodiment of our inner life. It also serves as the sanctuary to which we go for our most intimate and private, our most profound and universal experiences. But most fundamentally, the *Intensive Journal* is our inner workshop, the place where we do the creative shaping of the artwork of our life."[273]

In the place of a therapeutic relationship with a therapist, this process substitutes dealing with the inner thoughts and experiences of the individual in a private journal. The basic processes, however, remain much the same as in a more conventional therapy experience: "The *Intensive Journal* plays an active role in reconstructing a life, but it does so without imposing any external categories or interpretations or theories on the individual's experience. It remains neutral and open-ended so as to maintain the integrity of each person's development, while drawing him further along the road of his own life process."[274] This kind of journaling[275] is a useful activity for those who are unable for whatever reason to be in a therapeutic relationship, as well as for those who wish to pursue another avenue that is personal and private but also relatively structured and orderly.

Summary

The role of the religious educator as therapist requires an unusual degree of personal discipline and preparation. It demands the kenosis, or the "emptying out," of the therapist as much as humanly possible so that the needs of the client are served, rather than the therapist using the client to meet his or her own needs. This does not mean that the therapist is any less human as a result of this kenotic process—ironically, he or she is even *more* human because of it. The therapist is on the path to wholeness and maturity, and so is a "companion on the inner

---

270. Ibid.
271. Progoff instituted The Dialogue House specifically for holding these workshops.
272. Ira Progoff, *At a Journal Workshop: The Basic Text and Guide for Using the Intensive Journal* (New York: Dialogue House, 1975).
273. Ibid., p. 297.
274. Ibid., p. 9.
275. Progoff made clear that what he was describing was very different from just keeping a diary. See ibid., p. 31.

way," but the boundaries are clear: The therapist never does the work for the client and never becomes the controller of the client. The therapist helps the client to activate his or her own "inner therapist," and the therapeutic relationship leaves both therapist and client with a greater degree of integration and health. Let there be no mistake: The role of the therapist for the religious educator is difficult, disciplined, but essential for the continued health and maturity of the field.

Figure 14 summarizes the role of the religious educator as therapist as it was developed throughout the chapter.

Figure 14: The Religious Educator as Therapist	
Dimensions of the Role	Healer
	Catalyst
	Facilitator
	Fellow-Traveler
Aim	Wholeness
Function	Integration
Primary Virtues	Affectivity
	Actualization
Activity	Being Present
Shadow Role	Manipulator
Faith Tradition Resource	Taoism
Historical Personage	Carl Jung
Contemporary Example	Morton Kelsey
Representative Teaching Procedure	Nondirective Teaching
Experiential Simulation	Inner Journey

Chapter Thirteen

The Religious Educator as Minister

To be a minister is to be a person for others: to make one's self available to those others in as many ways possible so that each individual may search, attempt, and possibly even create what for them is holistic nexus—his or her center and core of reality—but without each one having to do it in total isolation. The minister cannot do this work *for* anyone else, but he or she can facilitate the process, lend a helping hand in times of difficulty, and give of himself or herself to whatever degree one has the strength and the courage. Using his own phrasing, Henri Nouwen similarly defined the work of the minister: "Ministry means the ongoing attempt to put one's own search for God, with all the moments of pain and joy, despair and hope, at the disposal of those who want to join in this search but do not know how."[1] This kind of functional ministry gets at the very heart of actualizing true religious education, since religious education can be defined as "the search for, attempt at, and creation of holistic nexus through the existential learning-adaptive process of transforming the heritage of the past into an idealized vision of the ideal future."[2]

An examination of the role of the religious educator as minister reveals that the role of minister is not locked within the grasp of the vocational ministry—the clergy. The ministerial vocation is a proud and worthy profession, and is often truly involved in the activity of providing ministry, but just because someone is given—or takes—the official *title* of minister in no way signifies or guarantees that he or she is truly engaged in providing ministry.[3] Conversely, just because someone does not possess the professional title of minister by no means eliminates a person

---

1. Henri J.M. Nouwen, *Creative Ministry* (Garden City, N.Y.: Doubleday, 1971), p. 111.
2. Timothy Arthur Lines, *Systemic Religious Education* (Birmingham, Ala.: Religious Education Press, 1987), p. 216.
3. Lest this sound like a knock at a locked door, I am writing as an ordained minister.

from providing genuine ministry. In many cases, the lack of a title or official sanctioning may even enhance the opportunities for ministry.

The subject of this chapter, then, does not rest simply upon investigating the vocation of the career minister.[4] Neither does it set the boundary of ministry within the limits of the clergy—those ordained to the "ministry"—and exclude the so-called laypersons.[5] To so restrict and compartmentalize ministry is to miss and misrepresent its meaning. The minister is one who works actively and intentionally to provide care to those who need it—in whatever form that care may need to take. Such concern for others knows no boundaries of ordination, profession, or vocation. It is one human reaching out to another in the midst of the pains and trials of life that are common to all humanity. However precious or rare the performance of genuine ministry may be, it never excludes anyone who is willing to render aid because of race, gender, creed, nationality, sexual preference, political stance, or vocation. One need only to be a member of the human race to offer another the gift of ministry.

In the same vein, there is no particular environment that is best suited for the performance of ministry. While it may take place in the pastor's study, the confessional booth, or the hospital chapel, it just as easily, and more naturally, can happen in the living room of a home, in the factory lunchroom, on the street corner of downtown, over the telephone, or though the mail. The only requirement is that at least two people have the opportunity to be in contact with one another to help bear the burden. It need not be formal, planned, or even a conscious activity. It may be that the best ministry, and hence the best minister, is the result of simply being a caring and loving human being. Carmen Caltagirone summarized the issue this way: "A person is not a minister because he is ordained or because he goes to India to work with the poor. *A person is a minister because he serves.*"[6]

Depending upon one's own particular faith tradition, one may immediately object that the minister needs to have more than this: the right belief, or the right preparation, or the right authority bestowed upon him or her. Some Christians, for example, would even go so far as to insist that to be a minister one must first be a Christian.[7] It seems that for some, it is not enough to be a genuine human, but something else must be added—as in saying the right answers to the right questions. In this chapter, those kinds of limits are no limits. Ministry is not the property of any one sectarian group, and the key to it does not lie in holding the orthodox view of some sect's doctrine. To suggest that it does cor-

---

4. Noting the shifts in the use of the term minister and ministry, one author said of the recent past: "Ministry belonged to hierarchy, hierarchy lent some of it out on occasion. Now it's all up for grabs." William J. Bausch, *Ministry: Traditions, Tensions, Transitions* (Mystic, Conn.: Twenty-Third Publications, 1982), p. 12.

5. One layperson said succinctly: "Ministry is too important and demanding a task to leave entirely to ministers." Recorded in Milo L. Brekke, Merton P. Strommen, and Dorothy L. Williams, *Ten Faces of Ministry* (Minneapolis: Augsburg, 1979), p. 19.

6. Carmen L. Caltagirone, *The Catechist as Minister* (New York: Alba House, 1982), p. 6.

7. This seemed to be the point of H. Richard Niebuhr when he said that the first element of a call to ministry is the call to be a Christian. See H. Richard Niebuhr, *The Purpose of the Church and Its Ministry: Reflections on the Aims of Theological Education* (New York: Harper & Row, 1956), p. 64.

rupts if not destroys the very meaning of ministry. Indeed, a Christian, a Buddhist, and an atheist may each minister differently, but the difference is in style and content, not in function or purpose. Ministry is still provided. The religious educator seeking to understand and model the role of minister must learn to recognize the role wherever and whenever it manifests its true identity.

The above paragraph is important because this chapter may take on the character of "Christian" ministry, but this is only by way of illustration. The examples used are more often taken from Christian models than from any other source, not because of intentional exclusivism, but because of my own personal experience and data base. With but little effort, the "Christian" tint can be washed out and the structure of true ministry would still remain. This cleansing, in fact, will be essential for each person, depending upon the individual faith tradition one holds.

The generic quality of the minister can be detected in the well-loved, and hence well-worn story of the Good Samaritan.[8] Here Jesus told the story of a "certain man" who was robbed, beaten, and left for dead on the road. Both a priest and a Levite—career or official "ministers"—passed him by. It was the Samaritan, not one of the most loved nationalities in Jesus' audience, who performed the ministry needed. The Samaritan bound the wounds, provided transportation, and paid for the victim's care—in short, he "had compassion on him." There is no mention of what the Samaritan believed, what he professed to the wounded man, or even his "relationship to Jesus." The point was that the minister (the Samaritan) cared for the person who needed help. To explicate further the point of the previous paragraph, there is nothing in this story that makes it Christian—or Jewish, or even Samaritan—other than that Jesus told it. It is simply a story of ministry and of humanity—one human helping another. It illustrates the one distinguishable criteria of the true minister: "No one has greater love than this, to lay down one's life for one's friends."[9]

It is this "Good Samaritan" model of being willing to lay down one's life that guides the following discussion of the religious educator in the role of the minister. It is neither a Christian discussion nor a non-Christian discussion, and at the same time it is not limited to a clerical or "professional"[10] discussion in the

---

8. Luke 10:30-37.

9. John 15:13, NRSV. Of this verse, Henri Nouwen said: "For me these words summarize the meaning of all Christian ministry." Nouwen, *Creative Ministry*, p. 110.

10. Although not limited to such a clerical definition of the minister, the chapter *does* discuss the minister as a professional. As noted in the Preface of this book, Charles Stewart has defined "profession" as "a type of work performed in a social setting which requires particular education, entrance, and relationship to one's peers and to the public. Commitment to the education, entrance rights, one's peers, and public one serves gives the profession its unique character." Charles William Stewart, *Person and Profession: Career Development in the Ministry* (Nashville: Abingdon, 1974), p. 24. On the topic of the minister as a professional, Seward Hiltner wrote: "The real meaning of professional is 'responsibility.' It is not privilege, not impersonality, and not money, but basically the exercise of responsibility—in certain ways." Seward Hiltner, *Ferment in the Ministry* (Nashville: Abingdon, 1969), p. 178. Hiltner's definition of professional is an appropriate one for anyone who takes responsibility for giving care to others, but he went on to discuss more about the vocational aspects of ministry. See ibid., pp. 178-180. For more on the concept of the minister as a professional in terms of vocation, see Chapter Two, "The Ministry as a Profession," in David C. Jacobsen, *The Positive Use of the Minister's Role* (Philadelphia: Westminster, 1967), pp. 17-28.

sense of a career choice. Ministry is a much broader topic than any one faith tradition, or any one vocation, can fulfill. What follows is a human discussion,
meaning it is open and applicable to any who choose to reach out to others.

Dimensions of the Role

The chapter begins in similar manner to all the previous discussions of the
roles—by overviewing some dimensions of the role of minister. The dimensions selected are not meant to be comprehensive or definitive, but only basic
enough to sketch the outlines of the role as used in this chapter.[11] The additional information of the chapter will serve to fill in the gaps, allowing for a sufficient
grasp of the total role. The four dimensions of the role of minister discussed
below are priest, celebrant, defender, and servant.

Priest

In spite of the warnings and introductory words at the head of this chapter,
there are probably some who will read the heading of priest and automatically
associate the hierarchical order and the authority granted to a priest by ordination in many Christian traditions.[12] Although the bestowal of ordination can
allow one to perform the functions of ministry to some individuals or groups in
a more meaningful way, its abuse is just as easily found. Emile Pin spoke of
the model of the priesthood in the past where ordination was understood "to
bestow on the individual an essentially different character; by virtue of this
character, the individual acquired a certain 'power' and the right to demand
obedience from others."[13] Pin also noted that some priests are seen as "inter-
mediaries between God and the faithful in obtaining favors," making these
priests "feel that it makes sorcerers or medicine men out of them."[14] Such hierarchical ecclesiastical structures[15] or magical gifts of power are not the focus

---

11. An examination of the vocational definitions and understandings would lead only to further
frustration and ambiguity. For example, Niebuhr called ministry the "perplexed profession." Niebuhr,
Purpose of the Church and Its Ministry, pp. 48-58. In a monumental study of ministers, Samuel
Blizzard noted: "There is much confusion in contemporary usage in American society with respect
to the nomenclature used to designate clergymen and to describe their professional behavior."
Samuel W. Blizzard, with assistance of Harriet B. Blizzard, *The Protestant Parish Minister: A
Behavioral Science Interpretation* (Storrs, Conn.: Society for the Scientific Study of Religion,
1985), p. 31. Joseph Blomjous discussed the "general feeling of uneasiness, doubt, and irrelevance"
related to the Catholic priesthood. Joseph J. Blomjous, *Priesthood in Crisis* (Milwaukee: Bruce,
1969), p. 3. This chapter, then, does not try to address or resolve all of the identity issues of the
vocational minister's role but attempts to show how the role can be identified in such a way as to
expand and explain the activity of the religious educator.

12. One author noted that a faulty view of ordination "translates to mean that only ordination gives
competence, authority, and the right of professional governance. It goes further astray when eventually all jurisdictional and administrative powers of the church come to be seen as an extension of
the sacramental powers conferred at ordination." Bausch, *Ministry*, p. 30.

13. Emile Pin, "The Priestly Function in Crisis," in *The Identity of the Priest: Pastoral Theology*,
ed. Karl Rahner (New York: Paulist, 1969), p. 52.

14. Ibid., p. 54.

15. William Bausch appropriately described the structuring of some clergy positions as a "caste
system." See Bausch, *Ministry*, p. 49.

of the use of the term here and have little if anything positive to add to understanding the minister in the role of religious educator. Hierarchism, authoritarianism, and power-grabbing are more descriptive of what the religious educator is trying to defeat, rather than impose.[16] What does the dimension of priest have to offer if the magic is removed?

The priest that remains is the one who mediates, the one who "bridges the gap."[17] The priest puts himself or herself between the known and the unknown, between the learner and the information, between the future and the present, bringing them together into a new relationship and fusing them into a new ontic reality. There is nothing "magical" about the activity of the priest, in that the priest does not change or transform either side to make them compatible. The priest allows the two to become one through his or her mediatorship. It is a function, a facilitation that the priest performs through his or her personhood of uniting two or more parties or issues. The results of the union are not up to the priest to determine. His or her only responsibility is to bring the parties together.

One of the major contributions of the radical Reformers (such as Baptists) to the history of the Christian church has been to uphold the concept of the priesthood of all believers. Roughly translated, the idea is that no one person or group of persons is somehow granted the authority or right to forgive sin or to hear confession.[18] Such activity is the work of the entire people of God.[19] Each one helps the other bear his or her burden, and each one listens to the confessions of the other.[20] In this view, the priesthood is no longer an exclusive club that only a select few who are duly approved can enter, but is instead a role to which all members

---

16. "The mission of the church is service, not authoritarianism." Ralph J. Bastain, *Priesthood and Ministry* (Glen Rock, N.J.: Paulist, 1969), p. 3.

17. "His [the priest's] mediating role sets the priest to bridge the divisions between men. There is neither Jew nor Greek nor any other people as he stands with his community before God." James O'Connell, "The Priest and Revolution," in *Identity of the Priest*, p. 128. Richard Hanson said that "the priesthood consists of a ministry of men or women who stand for God to their fellow-men and represent their fellow-men to God." Richard Hanson, *Christian Priesthood Examined* (Guildford: Lutterworth Press, 1979), p. 100.

18. Catholic author Richard McBrien indicated the lessening of distance between the radical Reformers' use of the concept of priesthood of believers and that of Catholicism when he wrote: "From the time of the Council of Trent, and largely in reaction to Protestantism's stress on the 'priesthood of all believers,' the Catholic Church has tended to restrict the notion of ministry to the ordained (bishops, priests, and deacons) and to those steps taken in preparation for ordination (lector, acolyte, exorcist). Today the opposite extreme has shown itself: Everyone is regarded as called to ministry by Baptism." Richard P. McBrien, *Catholicism*, Vol. Two (Minneapolis: Winston, 1980), p. 842. Another example of this is from Dennis Geaney: "Ministry is an old church word that has been given a new reprieve. Today, Roman Catholics are talking more about ministry and less about priesthood. It may sound as if we are opening and cauterizing old Reformation wounds when the Protestants replaced the priest with a new category of professional church workers called ministers." Dennis J. Geaney, "What Must I Do to Minister?" in *Ministering in a Servant Church*, ed. Francis A. Eigo (Villanova, Pa.: Villanova University Press, 1978), p. 155.

19. Catholic theologian Hans Küng has written in this same vein: "The Christian needs no priest as mediator at the innermost part of the temple, with God himself. Rather, he is granted an ultimate immediacy to God which no ecclesiastical authority can destroy or even take away from him. No one has the power to judge, control, or command decisions which fall within this innermost realm." Hans Küng, *Why Priests?: A Proposal for a New Church Ministry*, trans. Robert C. Collins (Garden City, N.Y.: Doubleday, 1972), p. 28.

20. This is what Exodus 19:6 referred to as a "nation of priests." See also 1 Peter 2:5, 9.

of the body are invited to perform for one another.[21] Such a corporate and joint access to each other and to God made for a radical reform indeed, and there are still vast majorities who dislike such a reading of the role of priest—oddly enough, even those who now (unconscionably) trace their historical heritage back to the ranks of radical reformers.[22]

To see the connection of the priest/mediator with the task of religious education, one need only remember the earlier discussion of James Michael Lee,[23] where he distinguished the mediator stage of the religious instructional act from the messenger boy stage and the translation stage.[24] He stated that in the mediator stage religious instruction is a "fundamentally new entity" and a "radically new ontic reality," because "it is the religious instruction act itself which is the mediator."[25] In the same sense, the religious educator is also a new entity and a new reality by becoming the mediator of the religious instructional act. The religious educator is indeed the one who "stands in the gap," first to bridge the two sides and second to fuse them into a new whole. This is the religious educator in the dimension of the priest.

The dimension of priest for the minister is not a bestowal of power, not an authorization to use force, and not an invitation to expect obedience from learners, but it is an acceptance of a responsibility and a duty.[26] It is the willingness to come alongside and help shoulder the cause and the pain of another who is unable to bear the load alone. The minister as priest has solidarity with the other, mediating a new reality into existence. The image is not that of one who comes from on high to deliver a message and who then reascends—untainted, though unaffected and essentially irrelevant[27]—but rather one who emerges from the shadows to kneel and to stay for as long as aid is needed.

---

21. Richard McBrien stressed this same issue from his particularistic and Catholic perspective: "In principle, every baptized Christian is empowered to administer every sacrament. Ordination does not confer a kind of magical power. It is a public act concerned with order." McBrien, *Catholicism*, Vol. Two, pp. 846-847.

22. I am referring to certain right-wing Protestant fundamentalists that have taken over some of the Christian denominations, such as the Southern Baptists. Baptists, of all people, were historically known as the champions of individual access to God and of the freedom of each person to read and interpret the Bible for himself or herself. The efforts of the fundamentalists in squelching such historic practice—and the parallel squelching of practitioners of such freedom—is an amazing and frightening reminder of the ever-present resurgence of fascism.

23. See the discussion of Lee in Chapter Five, "The Religious Educator as Coach."

24. Although Lee's position was discussed in Chapter Five of this book, for further study also see James Michael Lee, *The Content of Religious Instruction: A Social Science Approach* (Birmingham, Ala.: Religious Education Press, 1985), pp. 25-26, and James Michael Lee, *The Flow of Religious Instruction: A Social Science Approach* (Birmingham, Ala.: Religious Education Press, 1973), pp. 17-19.

25. Lee, *The Content of Religious Instruction*, p. 25.

26. Similarly, Ralph Bastain described "a concept of priesthood which does not depend on power or prestige but rests on the basis of self-denial and service." Bastain, *Priesthood and Ministry*, p. 1.

27. "When a minister discovers that he really can give life to people by enabling them to face their real life-condition without fear, he will at the same time cease looking at himself as a man on the periphery of reality. He is then right in the center." Nouwen, *Creative Ministry*, p. 47.

Celebrant

A second dimension of the true minister, and one intimately related to that of the priest, is the minister as celebrant. The unfortunate stereotype of the minister may be that of utter somberness and soberness, as Richard Foster noted with some personal chagrin: "It is an occupational hazard of devout folk to become stuffy bores. That should not be. Of all people we should be the most free, alive, interesting."[28] The minister is one who is charged with helping people know how and when to *celebrate* life—in the midst of all the harsh reality that human life has to offer. Henri Nouwen explained that the genuine minister "challenges us to celebrate life; that is, to turn away from fatalism and despair and to make our discovery that we have but one life to live into an ongoing recognition of God's work with man."[29] The effective minister does not disguise reality, or evil, or suffering; neither does he or she ignore it or explain it away. The task of the minister is "to make it possible for man not only to fully face his human situation but also to celebrate it in all its awesome reality."[30]

Richard Foster went on to speak of some benefits of being celebrative: "Celebration adds a note of gaiety, festivity, hilarity to our lives. After all, Jesus rejoiced so fully that He was accused of being a wine-bibber and a glutton. Many of us lead such sour lives that we couldn't possibly be accused of such things."[31] Celebration should not be taken to refer only to merry-making, however. Nouwen anticipated this misrepresentation, and had this response: "Celebration is only possible through the deep realization that life and death are never found completely separate. Celebration can only really come about where fear and love, joy, and sorrow, tears and smiles can exist together. Celebration is the acceptance of life in a constantly increasing awareness of its preciousness."[32] The minister helps people see life in all its richness and teaches them how to redeem each moment and each experience to make them fully human.[33]

The minister has opportunity to act as a celebrant throughout the lives of people, marking the special occasions or rites of passage as each moves through the life cycle. Donald Capps addressed this aspect of the parish minister through use of the term "ritual coordinator": "The ritual coordinator is one who assumes responsibility for integrating the various ritual processes in the total life of the parish community, assisting it in shaping its ritual elements into a coherent and meaningful whole."[34] Capps utilized the work of Erik Erikson on the "stages of ritualization"[35] to make specific applications for the pastoral

---

28. Richard J. Foster, *Celebration of Discipline: The Path to Spiritual Growth*, rev. ed. (San Francisco: Harper & Row, 1988), p. 196.
29. Nouwen, *Creative Ministry*, p. 90.
30. Ibid., p. 91.
31. Foster, *Celebration of Discipline*, p. 196.
32. Nouwen, *Creative Ministry*, pp. 91-92.
33. Richard Foster said: "Celebration comes when the common ventures of life are redeemed." Foster, *Celebration of Discipline*, p. 193.
34. Donald Capps, *Life Cycle Theory and Pastoral Care* (Philadelphia: Fortress, 1983), p. 56.
35. See this discussed throughout Erik Erikson, *Toys and Reasons: Stages in the Ritualization of Experience* (New York: Norton, 1977).

care ministry.[36] Actually, although Capps does provide an orderly schema for such care, he was simply describing what most ministers have always been expected to do: to pay attention to people at crisis points of life, such as birth, marriage, and death. The minister is a leader and facilitator of these celebrations[37] and is allowed if not expected to care for persons literally from the first moments of life to the last—as well as to help deal with the multitude of transitional and developmental issues in between. Of course, celebrations are not only to be carried on because of special events or days but can be weekly or daily responsibilities. The priest may *celebrate* the Eucharist daily, or even several times daily,[38] and the minister may lead in worship celebrations several times each week.[39]

The life-span perspective of celebrations brings the issue of faith development back into view once again.[40] To bring these topics all together, Daniel Aleshire has used the neologism "faithcare": "For me, 'faithcare' is the task of attending to and caring for people who experience faith in the moments and movements of their lives. . . . It is the sensitive process of attending to and ministering with individuals who are struggling—sometimes in the most ordinary of ways—to let faith emerge and grow in them."[41] Gary Chamberlain has used the phrase "fostering faith" as the way to express the need to match human developmental issues with faith and religion.[42] However it is denoted, the minister has a prime responsibility and a unique opportunity for celebrating and thereby promoting the individual's development and growth in faith.[43]

The religious educator as minister and celebrant is spending his or her effort in attending to the needs and celebrations of others, rather than drawing the attention and the focus into the religious educator. This is what Aleshire referred to when he spoke of this ministry of "attending": "Paying attention is not so

---

36. See Capps, *Life Cycle Theory and Pastoral Care*, pp. 58-76. Also see Matthew Linn, Sheila Fabricant, and Dennis Lynn, *Healing the Eight Stages of Life* (New York: Paulist, 1988).

37. The term "celebration" fits even for funerals if the aspects of the previous paragraph are taken seriously.

38. For some of the inherent difficulties of this issue, see *Can We Always Celebrate the Eucharist?*, eds. Mary Collins and David Power (New York: Seabury, 1982), and Karl Rahner and Angelus Häussling, *The Celebration of the Eucharist*, trans. W.J. O'Hara (New York: Herder and Herder, 1968), especially Chapter One, "The Principle Regarding the Frequency of Mass," pp. 1-9.

39. For a good orientation to the relationship of religious activity and the life cycle, see Chapter Six, "Religion and the Art of Life Cycle Maintenance," in Robert C. Fuller, *Religion and the Life Cycle* (Philadelphia: Fortress, 1988), pp. 116-135. In this chapter, Fuller used "developmental concepts to assess the nature and meaning of such religious activities as worship, prayer, ritual, and the ministry." Ibid., p. 116.

40. The discussion of faith development and James Fowler's *Stages of Faith* was conducted in Chapter Six, "The Religious Educator as Scientist." Also refer to Fowler's other book that is highly relevant here, James W. Fowler, *Faith Development and Pastoral Care* (Philadelphia: Fortress, 1987).

41. Daniel O. Aleshire, *Faithcare: Ministering to All God's People Through the Ages of Life* (Philadelphia: Westminster, 1988), p. 13.

42. See Gary L. Chamberlain, *Fostering Faith: A Minister's Guide to Faith Development* (New York: Paulist, 1988). See especially Chapter Three, "Religious Education and the Growth of Faith," pp. 42-62, and Chapter Four, "Religious Education for Maturing Faith," pp. 63-81.

43. For a helpful resource in connecting the family into the life cycle, see Edwin H. Friedman, "Systems and Ceremonies: A Family View of Rites of Passage," in *The Family Life Cycle: A Framework for Family Therapy*, eds. Elizabeth A. Carter and Monica McGoldrick (New York: Gardner Press, 1980), pp. 429-460.

much complicated work as it is hard work. It requires a minister to spend more emotional energy noticing than getting noticed, and that is not always done."[44] The criterion for the minister is to serve rather than to be served, and this applies to the often public duties of the celebrant. The celebrant cannot disregard his or her public persona and actions, since they require careful and intentional scrutiny, but neither can he or she allow them to overshadow the reasons for their appearance. As Aleshire noted with appropriate honesty: "Ministers have needs to be affirmed, but a commitment to the ministry of attending focuses energy on other people and their needs."[45]

Defender
Lest the minister appear passive, feeble, or ineffectual, the protective and defensive dimension of the minister needs recognition. The beatitude "Blessed are the meek"[46] is sometimes applied to the minister more than to others, but falsely interpreted "weak" instead of "meek." Being meek has less to do with possessing strength or power and more to do with attitude and motivation, but all of these aspects are involved to a certain extent. The issue of power relates to the ability to support the needy and the afflicted while not abusing those powers in the process.[47] One of the fundamental assignments of the minister is to defend the weak and to protect the helpless while remaining caring and compassionate to all the people, regardless of circumstance. Early Christian church theologian Ambrose put the task this way: "The duty of the priest or minister is to help all, if it is possible, and to harm no one."[48] This assignment is not an easy one, since it requires such a delicate balance between providing needed "first aid" and promoting unhealthy dependence.[49]

A common designation for ministers of congregations is the term "pastor." This term refers to the analogy[50] of the minister as a shepherd, who feeds and guides the sheep while being sure that the environment is safe. When danger comes, the "good shepherd" actively defends the sheep. If one is lost, the shepherd goes and finds it.[51] Although most congregations of today are far removed from an agrarian setting and hence have little awareness of the function of a

44. Aleshire, *Faithcare*, pp. 22-23.
45. Ibid., p. 23. This topic got additional discussion in Mary José Hobday, "To Serve and Not To Be Served: The Church as Servant in Our Time," in *Ministering in a Servant Church*, pp. 1-17.
46. Matthew 5:5, NRSV.
47. The issue of power and how it relates to authority and ministry have gotten good discussion in such resources as Don Kimball, *Power and Presence: A Theology of Relationships* (San Francisco: Harper & Row, 1987), and Karen Lebacqz, *Professional Ethics: Power and Paradox* (Nashville: Abingdon, 1985).
48. Ambrose, "Duties of Ministers," quoted in Bastain, *Priesthood and Ministry*, p. 16. The passage continued with these words: "It belongs to the priestly office to do harm to no one and to be desirous of helping everyone; but the accomplishment of this can come only from God." Ibid.
49. This topic received more extensive treatment under the heading of "individuation" in Chapter Eleven, "The Religious Educator as Revolutionary."
50. Actually, the term is something more than an analogy, since the term "pastor" derives from the Latin word for feeding or grazing. It is more of a philosophical position that identifies the roles of ministers, educators, and learners.
51. These images arise from John 10:1-17, where Jesus is described as the "Good Shepherd."

shepherd, this notion of the minister is still a popular one.[52] It has a cozy and warm feeling to it.

The image of pastor/shepherd may give cozy and warm feelings, but it is fraught with the perils of paternalism and maternalism.[53] The minister can easily assume he or she carries responsibility for persons to the extent that it is his or her task to decide what is appropriate for people to think and do—that without the minister the people are lost sheep, unable to find their way. To extend the analogy is to assume that the people are as stupid as sheep and need someone of superior intellect and spirituality to guide them, keeping them out of mischief. Obviously, this facet of the minister is not one being promoted here, but such a view does have its adherents.[54]

In place of the title of pastor for this dimension, the term defender is proposed. The mission of the minister as defender is to find those who are helpless and unprotected and to give them sanctuary until they are ready to face the world on their own again.[55] The minister is not to be the perpetual custodian of everyone's thoughts and lives, but the temporary guardian while the wounds heal and adequate defenses are rebuilt.[56] This does not make the minister into a fortress, but rather as a temporary safe harbor. Such a conception of the minister demands genuine creativity and, paradoxically, for a certain kind of weakness. Henri Nouwen explained: "It calls for ministers in the true sense, who lay down their lives for their friends, helping them to distinguish between the constructive and the destructive spirits and making them free for the discovery of God's life-giving Spirit in the midst of this maddening world. It calls for creative weakness."[57]

The difficulty for ministers is discerning who needs help and protection,

---

52. An example of this kind of popular and devotional type of writing is Jerram Barrs, *Shepherds and Sheep: A Biblical View of Leading and Following* (Downers Grove, Ill.: InterVarsity Press, 1983).

53. For one example among many, see these difficulties explored in John Reumann, "Ecclesial Recognition of the Ministry of Women: New Testament Perspectives and Contemporary Applications," in *Ministering in a Servant Church*, pp. 99-149.

54. See such philosophy promoted by Jay E. Adams in *Shepherding God's Flock: A Preacher's Handbook on Pastoral Ministry, Counseling, and Leadership* (Grand Rapids, Mich.: Baker, 1979).

55. Documents from Vatican II expressed this concern: "Although priests owe service to everyone, the poor and the weaker ones have been committed to their care in a special way. It was with these that the Lord himself associated, and the preaching of the Gospel to them is given as a sign of his messianic mission." "Decree on the Ministry and the Life of Priests," in *Decree on Priestly Training of Vatican Council II and Decree on the Ministry and Life of Priests of Vatican Council II*, commentary by Frank B. Norris (Glen Rock, N.J.: Paulist, 1966), p. 115.

56. Some would say that an additional responsibility to the dimension of defender is to be deeply involved in the societal and political processes that tend to exclude the poor and the oppressed, so that the minister is a defender and champion of their rights. The minister then works to allow those who are traditionally and habitually denied access to power to gain a hearing and to have a part in the determination of their own lives. Margaret Farley identified this as "political ministry": "There has been a significant shift from traditional understandings of ministry as works of charity to understandings of it as a sharing of the burdens of the poor and oppressed in order to bring about a sharing of resources and power which will eventually meet the rightful claims of persons to what they essentially need. This has sometimes meant a corresponding shift from traditional charitable works to what has come to be called 'political ministry.'" Margaret A. Farley, "The Church as Christ Living in the World: What Needs Must Be Ministered to Today?" in *Ministering in a Servant Church*, p. 83.

what kind of help is appropriate, and for how long it should be supplied. It is just as important for the minister to know when to step back and let the person try it on his or her own as it is to know when to come alongside. The calling is to be available for carrying another's burden when it is too heavy to handle alone, and then to know when and how to give the burden back.[58] This image is quite different from pastoring stupid sheep who can never learn to be on their own—who always need a shepherd around to steer them clear of thinking and living for themselves.

Servant

To suggest that the minister should take on the dimension of a servant certainly does not sound very inviting. Ronald Sutherland addressed this understandably prevalent attitude toward servanthood by saying: "Indeed, servanthood has been debased to such a degree that it is usually deemed antithetical to those ideals customarily associated with 'success.' The term is more likely to be perceived in a pejorative manner, in the sense of servitude."[59] Small wonder that the title or function of servant is not a particularly exciting or popular one.[60] The truth is, however, that the root term for ministry is διάκονος, which when translated means service.[61] The most fundamental meaning of being a minister is being a servant—serving others in their need rather than one's own.[62] To be called a min-

---

57. Nouwen, *Creative Ministry*, p. 116.

58. The task is to work with the tension to "bear one anothers burdens" while also remembering that "all must carry their own loads." See these oddly juxtaposed ideas in Galatians 5:2 and 5:5, NRSV.

59. Ronald H. Sutherland, "The Character of Servanthood," in *The Pastor as Servant*, ed. Earl E. Shelp and Ronald H. Sutherland (New York: Pilgrim Press, 1986), p. 20.

60. This issue was given some good rationale by Avery Dulles: "The term 'servant,' indeed, contains certain ambiguities. It connotes three things: work done not freely but under orders; work directed to the good of others rather than to the worker's own advantage; and work that is humble and demeaning ('servile')." Avery Dulles, *Models of the Church* (Garden City, N.Y.: Doubleday, 1974), pp. 92-93. In trying to stress what the concept of ministry involves, Carmen Caltagirone said: "It means becoming a servant, giving up status and prestige in order to serve. The cost of the Kingdom ultimately requires a spirit of self-renunciation. Many believe that self-renunciation is a way of life reserved for sisters and priests, when in reality, all must renounce the world in favor of Jesus. It does not mean living in a private world, unaware and unresponsive to its problems. Self-renunciation means having a unique set of priorities." Caltagirone, *Catechist as Minister*, p. 48.

61. "The word *ministry* means 'service.' " McBrien, *Catholicism*, p. 843. Michael Green pointed out that there are actually three of these terms in the New Testament: δοῦλος, or bondslave; λει-τουργία, service or ritual, now transliterated into the term liturgy; and διόκονος, slave or servant—now usually translated deacon. See the fuller discussion in Michael Green, *Freed to Serve* (London: Hodder and Stoughton, 1983), pp. 24-27. Avery Dulles noted: "The term diakonia is certainly one of the most important New Testament terms applied to the Church. The term applies to all types of ministry—including the ministry of the word, of sacraments, and of temporal help. All offices in the Church are forms of diakonia." Dulles, *Models of the Church*. p. 93.

62. Avery Dulles made a useful point about the direction of the service when he was explaining the church as servant: "The beneficiaries of the church's action . . . are not exclusively, or even primarily, the members of the church itself. Rather, they are all those brothers and sisters the world over, who hear from the church a word of comfort or encouragement, or who obtain from the church a respectful hearing, or who receive from it some material help in their hour of need." Dulles, *Models of the Church*, p. 91. Dulles made clear that service is to be directed *outside* the church, not back toward itself. As Dulles noted, the church is tempted to be "too much turned in upon itself." Ibid.

ister means the acceptance of the servant's role. If one has no honest desire to serve, then one must not accept the title or designation of servant—or of minister.

Christians take their cue for accepting the servant role of ministry from the model of Jesus,[63] and have commemorated that model in the remnants of the hymn recorded in the second chapter of Philippians, which begins with the words: "Let the same mind be in you that was in Christ Jesus," and goes on to say that Jesus "emptied himself and took the form of a slave, being born in human likeness."[64] The obvious message was that a follower of Christ—a "Christian"— must also "empty" oneself[65] and become a servant ("slave"). In Christianity, the concepts of ministry and servanthood are synonymous,[66] taken from the example of Jesus' own humanity and humility.[67]

To follow the concept of ministry and servanthood through to the teachings of Jesus, one would turn to the story he told of the judgment criteria at the last day. Some were welcomed in to the kingdom, and others were banished. The decision was made on the basis of actions taken: "Just as much as you did it to one of the least of these who are members of my family, you did it to me,"[68] and "just as you did not do it to one of the least of these, you did not do it to me.[69] Jesus' point was that to identify as a servant with the hungry, the thirsty, the naked, and the imprisoned was to identify with him. Anything less was to deny or reject Jesus himself.

As Tom Driver put it, the call to servanthood is more generic and more pressing than merely getting wrapped up in particularistic doctrines or dogmas. Servanthood is "identification with the poor, and out of such identification, the raising of one's voice in solidarity with society's victims. A good servant of justice will teach others to listen for those cries and will build a company of human beings who are willing to speak and act on behalf of those who need help from heaven because the social structure is unjust to them."[70] A servant— a minister—identifies with the poor, the sick, the abused, and the oppressed, and gives up his or her life on their behalf.[71] One need not be a Christian to so

---

63. "If there is one word to sum up the ministry of Jesus, it is this: service. His whole ministry was one of service." Green, *Freed to Serve*, p. 17.

64. Philippians 2:5-7, NRSV.

65. The concept of emptying one's self—"kenosis"—was discussed in Chapter Twelve, "The Religious Educator as Therapist."

66. "The New Testament gives no suggestion that one could possibly be a Christian without at the same time being called to some ministry within the church. . . . It is hardly surprising, therefore, that the sole point of [Paul's] argument in Romans 12 and Corinthians 12 is that every member of the church has his or her part to play in the service of God. All without exception have a ministry." Green, *Freed to Serve*, p. 24.

67. As Reginald Fuller explained: "Jesus did not teach *expressis verbis* that he was the servant, but he did understand his role in servant terms, in contradistinction to the zealot-political conception of Messiahship." Reginald H. Fuller, "The Son of Man Came to Serve, Not to Be Served," in *Ministering in a Servant Church*, p. 67.

68. Matthew 25:40, NRSV.

69. Matthew 25:45, NRSV.

70. Tom F. Driver, "Justice and the Servant Task of Pastoral Ministry," in Shelp and Sutherland, *Pastor as Servant*, p. 52.

71. As William Bausch put it: "A profound sense of service . . . is the only way to keep ourselves humble, and, literally and figuratively, 'in touch' with all people." Bausch, *Ministry*, p. 115.

uphold those who need care, or limit the concept to the province of Christianity. Identifying with the poor and the victimized has boundaries that far outdistance those of any one faith tradition. There is more than enough room for anyone to hear and respond to the call of servanthood.

Summary

The dimensions of the role of minister have been presented as priest, celebrant, defender, and servant. While these dimensions are not meant to be comprehensive of the role, they are adequate to provide a background and a context. The role of minister as discussed in this chapter, again, is not limited to the cleric hired by a congregation to lead them; in fact, it may not even necessarily include him or her. The focus is on the role, not the specific vocation. The sections that follow begin to fill in some of the details of the role of minister that have only been sketched thus far.

Aim: Altruism

One of the most distinguishing characteristics of the religious educator in the role of the minister appears in the aim of altruism. The term "altruism" is of rather recent invention, being popularized by Auguste Comte in the nineteenth century,[72] but the behavior it describes is as ancient as humankind.[73] The Latin base of the term, *alter*, means simply "other."[74] The term, then, naturally refers to someone or something other than the individual. Nicholas Rescher defined altruism as being counter to pure egoism: "A person is *altruistic* (rather than *egoistic*) if he gives such weight to the welfare of others that he is prepared in principle to subordinate his own welfare to that of others, setting his own welfare aside in the interest of theirs in certain circumstances."[75] Rescher termed altruism one of the "vicarious affects" that are more "acquired reactions" than instinctive and inborn.[76] The umbrella word he used to cover all the "vicarious affects" was the common word "unselfishness."

Daniel Bar-Tal employed the term "prosocial behavior" to denote "acts [that] can be seen to have positive social consequences," such as helping, aiding, sharing, donating, and assisting.[77] One of those prosocial behaviors is altruism, which he defined as "voluntary behavior that is carried out to benefit another without

---

72. For example, see Auguste Comte, *A General View of Positivism*, trans. J.H. Bridges (London: Trubner, 1865; Dubuque, Iowa: Brown Reprints, 1971; first published in 1848), pp. 340-341.

73. As one author noted: "Life would be nasty, brutish, and poverty-stricken indeed, if there were no mutual trust and voluntary compliance at all." Rolan N. McKean, "Economics of Trust, Altruism, and Corporate Responsibility," in *Altruism, Morality, and Economic Theory*, ed. Edmund Phelps (New York: Russell Sage Foundation, 1975), p. 30.

74. For an excellent overview of different definitions and schools of thought on the topic of altruism, see Samuel P. Oliner and Pearl M. Oliner, *The Altruistic Personality: Rescuers of Jews in Nazi Europe* (New York: Free Press, 1988), pp. 4-12.

75. Nicholas Rescher, *Unselfishness: The Role of the Vicarious Effects in Moral Philosophy and Social Theory* (Pittsburgh: University of Pittsburgh Press, 1975), p. 9.

76. Ibid., p. 6.

77. Daniel Bar-Tal, *Prosocial Behavior: Theory and Research* (New York: Wiley, 1976), p. 4.

anticipation of external rewards [which] is performed . . . [for] its own end."[78] Bar-Tal's discussion reinforced the idea that altruism is activity done for the good of others rather than for self-aggrandizement.

Is altruism more natural and more wide-spread than, say, aggression? Such a question and its answer depends primarily upon one's view of human nature. Should one take a psychoanalytic view, with the dominance of the id, then altruistic behavior must be learned by identification and through constraints imposed by society to mute innate aggressiveness.[79] A cognitive development theory perspective would see altruism come about as a result of "progressing through stages of moral reasoning as a result of mental maturational process interacting with experience."[80] A follower of Pitirim Sorokin would see the potential of goodness as inborn and natural, and altruism would be as much if not more expected than aggression.[81] The explanations of the origin of altruism are as varied as its acts. Exactly *why* someone would choose to lay down his or her life for friends is quite possibly unanswerable.[82]

The ancient question recorded in Genesis can be used as the measure of the depth of genuine altruism: "Am I my brother's keeper?"[83] For the religious educator aiming at the role of minister, the answer is at least a qualified yes. The minister is altruistic, which means he or she is concerned for the welfare of another rather than only for that of oneself. The qualification is that no one ever takes on total responsibility for another, which would lead to an unhealthy type of dependence or submission.

The mark of the functional minister, whatever the title or occupation of the individual, is the presence of altruism. Rescher referred to the "conscientious professionals," such as the physician, lawyer, or cleric, as deliberately not allowing himself or herself to become personally involved: "The conscientious professional does not connect his own welfare-interests with those of his clients."[84] He said that it is important for these persons to keep a "professional detachment" that does not force them to put themselves on the line every moment. Such a view of the true professional,[85] however, is fundamentally flawed—not only of the physician or lawyer, but most assuredly of the genuine minister.[86] Such a person may be

---

78. Ibid.

79. Oliner and Oliner, *Altruistic Personality*, p. 4.

80. Ibid.

81. Sorokin was a great champion of social-science research on altruistic behavior earlier in the twentieth century. For a sample of his work, see Pitirim A. Sorokin, *Altruistic Love: A Study of American "Good Neighbors" and Christian Saints* (Boston: Beacon Press, 1950).

82. However, the question of "Why Risk One's Life?" formed the first chapter and the direction of the research for the study by Samuel P. Oliner and Pearl M. Oliner, *The Altruistic Personality*. See pp. 1-12.

83. Genesis 4:9, NRSV.

84. Rescher, *Unselfishness*, p. 8.

85. A good resource for properly perceiving the professional is Chapter Four, "Being Professional," in Lebacqz, *Professional Ethics*, pp. 63-76.

86. The issue here is that one does not attempt to do what one is not equipped or able to do. Such an act would also be nonprofessional. A professional knows his or her limits and does not put others in jeopardy because of them. Seward Hiltner said that the true professional "is explicit to himself and others about the principle of limitation of function and responsibility. When someone in his own or another profession is prepared better than he to perform a service, he refers as soon as he can—

employed in the particular role, but he or she is not fulfilling it. The functional and truly professional minister has the aim of altruism: subordinating his or her own welfare—on occasion—for the good of others. The minister (or any other true professional) worthy of the role does not keep his or her personhood hidden behind any protection of "professional detachment," but rather plunges totally into the situation—prepared to give his or her life for others.[87]

The religious educator is pursuing altruism when the focus and the intent of religious education is for the good of those in need of it, rather for the fulfillment of those providing it. The forms and structures of religious education change and adapt as the needs of the recipients warrant, rather than as the interests and desires of the religious educator dictate. It is not that the religious educator is unable to find fulfillment in the work but that the goal and the criteria for evaluating the work does not center on the person of the religious educator. The religious educator as minister strives to give himself or herself away for the benefit of the others. This is attempted through the means of sacrifice.

Function: Sacrifice

The aim of the minister is altruism, which is thereby achieved through the function of sacrifice. If altruism is working for the welfare of others at the expense of one's own welfare, then the function of sacrifice is knowingly giving up one's welfare for the sake of others.[88] To be a true professional, of any sort, is to be prepared to give of one's self and of one's resources sacrificially. To be a minister means that sacrifice of some sort—time, energy, emotion, information,

---

and does not wait until he has tried everything and is at the end of his rope." Hiltner, *Ferment in the Ministry*, p. 178.

87. Gaylord Noyce, however, argued for what he called "professional distance": "Effective pastoral ministry demands a nuanced balance of intimacy and professional distance. The right professional distance—a balance of empathy and objectivity—is a subtle concept for any conscientious helping professional. It is an especially difficult assignment for the pastor. We want to identify with people; we speak of unconditional love and caring; we strive for a deep rapport. But we must also remain separate enough from people's own profound inner turmoil that we can sustain objective judgment." Gaylord Noyce, *Pastoral Ethics: Professional Responsibilities of the Clergy* (Nashville: Abingdon, 1988), p. 83; also see p. 192. This troublesome issue will rise again when both the historical and contemporary examples of the minister are examined later in this chapter. The primary reason for their being chosen, and for their being held in such high esteem, can be traced at least partially to the fact that they apparently intentionally *rejected* such professional distance. This is a key dilemma for anyone considering the role of the minister—what are the proper and healthy boundaries?

88. A more specifically Christian view of sacrifice was the focus of Norman Pittenger when he described the ritual type of sacrifice: "Etymologically, it appears to signify 'the making holy' that is brought about by some ritual action. In religious practice, sacrifice has come to mean the offering of some valuable object or objects to a divine being, so that blessing and benefits may be secured." W. Norman Pittenger, *The Christian Sacrifice: A Study of the Eucharist in the Life of the Christian Church* (New York: Oxford University Press, 1951), p. 101. Pittenger then went on to speak of the Eucharist as the focus of this kind of sacrifice. The discussion of the present chapter obviously goes in a somewhat different although related direction. Sacrifice here is better defined as the offering of the life of the individual to other *human* beings, so that *their* blessing and benefits may be secured. The function of sacrifice here focuses on the action of the giver—the minister—rather than on some object given to receive favor of a divine being.

finances, or the total self—is the norm, and not the exception. How such sacrifice is offered depends on each situation and each circumstance the minister faces.[89]

In the story of the Good Samaritan the sacrifice provided by the Samaritan (the minister image in the story) was fairly tolerable. The Samaritan took the time and the effort to give emergency care to the wounded person, transported him to safety, and paid for his care, but then went on with his business. In the example of the Good Shepherd, also referred to above, the situation was more demanding. Although there were a number of requirements for the shepherd, such as leadership, feeding, and protection, the outstanding characteristic of the Good Shepherd, however, was that of the ultimate sacrifice: "I am the good shepherd. The good shepherd lays down his life for the sheep."[90] The thing to remember about true sacrifice is its exorbitant cost. While the good shepherd is ready to give his or her life for the sheep, there is only one chance to provide that kind of sacrifice. There is no changing the mind about it once the sacrifice is underway, so the decision needs to be made beforehand carefully and thoughtfully, free of any bravado or machismo. Sacrifice on the part of the genuine minister has nothing to do with securing professional advancement[91] or fulfilling personal interests. Indeed, true sacrifice normally works *against* getting the minister these things.[92]

One of the great examples of someone who certainly understood the meaning of true sacrifice and its extreme cost is found in the life and death[93] of theologian, pastor, and martyr[94] Dietrich Bonhoeffer (1906-1945). Early in his career[95] Bonhoeffer explained with startling and seemingly prescient clarity the cognitive aspects of the cost of discipleship and sacrifice.[96] One of the most memorable and foreshadowing of Bonhoeffer's contributions to Christian the-

---

89. This is at least in part what Nouwen meant when he said: "Every professional is responsible for his own definition." Nouwen, *Creative Ministry*, p. 61.

90. John 10:11, NRSV.

91. See the highly relevant discussion by Hans Küng on the differences between the functions of ministry and the office of ministry in *Why Priests?*, pp. 39-41.

92. Of course, the other side of the issue is the great existential question of Jesus: "For what is a man profited, if he shall gain the whole world and lose his own soul? or what shall a man give in exchange for his soul?" Matthew 16:26 (KJV). Since a variety of answers to this are possible, more about this is explored in the section below on the shadow role of the minister—the profiteer.

93. A good introductory biography of Bonhoeffer is by Mary Bosanquet, *The Life and Death of Dietrich Bonhoeffer* (New York: Harper & Row, 1986).

94. This was how his friend and correspondent Eberhard Bethge identified Bonhoeffer. See Eberhard Bethge, *Bonhoeffer: Exile and Martyr*, ed. John W. De Grunchy (London: Collins, 1975). Bethge was the primary person with whom Bonhoeffer corresponded while in prison, and the corpus of that writing provided the basis for the invaluable collection we have today known as Dietrich Bonhoeffer's *Letters and Papers from Prison*, enlarged ed., ed. Eberhard Bethge (New York: Macmillan, 1971; first published in 1953).

95. Bonhoeffer's development has been categorized into three formative periods: 1927-1933, when he was a student teacher; 1933-1940, when he served as a pastor and protester to the Nazi movement; and 1940-1945, when he was active in the underground resistance and while he was imprisoned. He wrote *The Cost of Discipleship* during the second formative period. See "Introduction," by E.J. Tinsley, *Dietrich Bonhoeffer*, ed E.J. Tinsley (London: Epworth Press, 1973), pp. 37-40.

96. This was detailed in Dietrich Bonhoeffer, *The Cost Of Discipleship*, rev. ed., trans. R.H. Fuller and Irmgard Booth (New York: Macmillan, 1959; first published in German in 1937).

ology was the contrast between cheap grace and costly grace. Cheap grace he termed this way: "Cheap grace means grace sold on the market like cheapjack's wares. The sacraments, the forgiveness of sin, and the consolations of religion are thrown away at cut prices. Grace is represented as the church's inexhaustible treasury, from which she showers blessings with generous hands, without asking questions or fixing limits. Grace without price; grace without cost!"[97] Then Bonhoeffer revealed the other side of grace: "Costly grace is the treasure hidden in the field; for the sake of it a man will gladly go and sell all that he has. It is the pearl of great price to buy which the merchant will sell all his goods."[98] Then Bonhoeffer wrote the words which haunt his memory to this day: "Such grace is costly because it calls us to follow, and it is *grace* because it calls us to follow *Jesus Christ*. It is costly because it costs a man his life, and it is grace because it gives a man the only true life."[99]

The deeper reason we hold the evidence and the man in such esteem today is not only because of this type of theologizing, but because of his personal act of sacrifice in laying down his life for his friends. In July, 1944, he was part of a political plot to remove Adolf Hitler from power and to topple the Nazi regime. The effort was unsuccessful and Bonhoeffer was imprisoned. On April 9, 1949, days before the Allied liberation, Bonhoeffer paid the ultimate price for what he considered to be his own effort at altruism.[100] He obviously knew the risk going into the coup attempt and was willing to make the sacrifice for the good of others (which, oddly enough, involved trying to take the life of another).

As Bonhoeffer showed, real sacrifice is nothing to be taken lightly. There is no room or opportunity for "professional detachment" here. Indeed, sacrifice is the act of giving up personal or career identity, or any other barrier, for the welfare of others. The call to minister is the call to sacrifice oneself on behalf of others. The cost must be carefully considered in advance, since by definition there is no looking back and no retreat from an act of sacrifice.

Primary Virtues: Humility and Compassion

The primary virtues of the minister, humility and compassion, are easy to discuss but difficult to perform. They are foundational to the aim of altruism and its avenue of sacrifice. Focusing briefly on these two virtues themselves helps to make the overall role of the minister clearer and more readily accessible by being explicit about the attitudinal and behavioral expectations of the true minister.

Humility can be taken as a negative aspect of personality, or as an aberration, much like the misuse of the term "meek" referred to earlier in the chapter. This disdainful view was reflected in the aphorism of Nietzsche: "The trodden worm curls up. This testifies to its caution. It thus reduces its chances of being trodden

97. Ibid., p. 35.
98. Ibid., p. 36.
99. Ibid., p. 37.
100. See this portrayed in all its grim detail in Donald Goddard, *The Last Days of Dietrich Bonhoeffer* (New York: Harper & Row, 1976).

again. In the language of morality: Humility."[101] This kind of distorted humility is an appropriate identification only of the defeated and the fearful. As per usual with Nietzsche, however, there is a kernel of truth within the aphorism, since a feigned humility may very well be a cover for a damaged personality. This need not be the universal understanding of humility, though.

The writer of the book of Romans referred to humility obliquely and obversely as "not to think of yourself more highly than you ought to think, but to think with sober judgment."[102] To state the same thought positively: Think of yourself realistically and honestly. Humility is having a realistic view of oneself and functioning accordingly.[103] A distinctively theistic cast[104] was given to humility in the following definition by Roberta Bondi: "This basic attitude of humility recognizes that no person loves or does any good without the help of God, so that whatever acts of kindness or virtue a person performs, whatever strength or happiness one has, one's ability to work well and to love well—all these are possible because God gives them to the creatures as God's good gifts. No one is in a position to look down on another from a superior height because of his or her hard work or piety or mental superiority. We are all vulnerable, all limited, and we each have a different struggle only God is in a position to judge."[105] Here the idea is to view all people as equals, with only God as superior, so that no one can then "think more of yourself than you ought to think."

A classic treatment of humility was written by Bernard of Clairvaux (1090/1-1153 C.E.) in *The Steps of Humility*.[106] Bernard described one of the difficulties with humility in the preface of the book. Having been asked to set forth in written form the steps to humility, Bernard was caught in a dilemma: "I hesitated a long time, wondering which path was safe to follow, and fearing that a useful discourse would violate what humility I have, while humble silence would nullify what utility I have."[107] Bernard was feeling the pinch of answering the question—who is worthy to speak about humility? To believe that one is worthy seems to be a disqualification![108] He decided: "Since I saw neither as safe, yet one

---

101. Friedrich Nietzsche, *The Twilight of the Idols and The Anti-Christ*, trans. R.J. Hollingdale (Baltimore: Penguin Books, 1968), p. 26, Aphorism #31. First published in 1889.

102. Romans 12:3, NRSV.

103. "Part of the realism of humility is its conviction that every one of us, being human, is prone to sin. We suffer congenitally from a weakness in the face of temptation, and a lack of purity of motives. This means we must watch ourselves and our motives. We must not allow ourselves to feel we have 'risen above' temptation, nor allow ourselves to be shocked when we meet sin in ourselves or others. Humility does not abandon its commitments; it does not indulge itself in the luxury of disillusionment. In short, it is humility that goes hand in hand with love, that makes love finally possible in such a jagged world as ours." Roberta C. Bondi, *To Love as God Loves: Conversations with the Early Church* (Philadelphia: Fortress, 1987), pp. 55-56.

104. For a broader view of humility than from only the Christian perspective, see Klaus Wengst, *Humility: Solidarity of the Humiliated*, trans. John Bowden (Philadelphia: Fortress, 1988). Wengst presented humility from Graeco-Roman, Jewish, as well as from early Christian perspectives.

105. Bondi, *To Love as God Loves*, p. 43.

106. Bernard, Abbott of Clairvaux, *The Steps of Humility*, trans. George Bosworth Burch (Cambridge: Harvard University Press, 1942).

107. Ibid., p. 121.

108. "A most distasteful though common trait of humankind is the certainty that one is kind, or good, or pious. . . . May a good man *say* that he is good man?" Samuel H. Dressner, *Prayer, Humility, and Compassion* (Philadelphia: Jewish Publication Society of America, 1957). p. 120.

or the other must be chosen, I have decided to share . . . with you . . . rather than seek my own safety in the haven of silence."[109]

Bernard defined humility as "that thorough self-examination which makes a man contemptible in his own sight."[110] For Bernard, humility was the way to truth,[111] and there were three steps to it: Knowing yourself, knowing your neighbor, and knowing God.[112] The path away from truth was the path of pride, and elsewhere he also discussed the steps of pride which must be descended to attain truth.[113] Without humility, no accurate vision or relationship with others was possible according to the teachings of Bernard.

Thomas Aquinas (1225-1274) also gave commentary on the virtue of humility, as found in *Summa Theologica*,[114] and in the course of the discussion he referred to the work of Bernard. Aquinas constructed his writings as an interplay of objections and replies to the objections, thus giving a full airing of the topic. One of the objections was related to "the twelve degrees of humility that are set down in the Rule of blessed Benedict"[115] because they were understood to "proceed from within to externals, as do other virtues." Aquinas successfully refuted the objection (or rather resolved the seeming contradiction), providing a balanced view on the attainment of humility in the process: "Man arrives at humility in two ways. First and chiefly by a gift of grace, and in this way the inner man precedes the outward man. The other way is by human effort, whereby the first of all restrains the outward man, and afterwards succeeds in plucking out the inward root."[116]

Nivard Kinsella referred back to the wisdom of Bernard when she summarized humility as the most foundational of virtues: "Humility then is fundamental, not only because it is the necessary preparation for charity, but also because it is the unifying principle of all the other virtues. To quote St. Bernard once more: 'Humility receives, fosters and perfects all the other virtues.' It is the unifying principle binding them together, the mould which shapes them. It is the fundamental virtue."[117] To be able to see oneself clearly is the first and most important task.[118] It is the appropriate starting point for anyone wishing to fulfill the role of minister.

---

109. Bernard, Abbott of Clairvaux, *Steps of Humility*, p. 121.

110. Ibid., p. 125.

111. Ibid., p. 123.

112. Ibid., pp. 147-159.

113. Ibid., pp. 181-225. These twelve steps were parallels to the twelve steps in *The Holy Rule of Saint Benedict*. As one descended the steps of pride, one ascended the twelve steps of St. Benedict. See Ibid, pp. 177-179.

114. Thomas Aquinas, "Treatise on Temperance: Question CLXI, Of Humility," in *Summa Theologica*, Second Part of the Second Part, Vol. 13, trans. Fathers of the English Dominican Province (London: Burns, Oates and Washbourne, 1921), pp. 215-231.

115. Ibid., pp. 225-226.

116. Ibid., pp. 230-231.

117. Nivard Kinsella, *Unprofitable Servants: Conferences on Humility* (Westminster, Md.: Newman, 1961), p. 10. In regard to the last sentence quoted, Thomas Aquinas wrote: "Therefore after the theological virtues, after the intellectual virtues which regard reason itself, and after justice, especially legal justice, humility stands before all others." Thomas Aquinas, "Treatise on Temperance," in *Summa Theologica*, Second Part of the Second Part, Vol.13, p. 226.

118. In referring to the difficulty of achieving humility and overcoming pride, Dressner wrote: "Our own hand, held before the eyes, can shut out even the light of the sun." Samuel H. Dressner, *Three Paths to God and Man* (New York: Harper and Brothers, 1960), p. 66.

The companion virtue to humility is compassion. This word "compassion" itself is a compound of the preposition *cum*—together (with)—and the Latin verb root *passio*—to bear, to tolerate, to experience. Compassion literally means suffering together[119] with another.[120] To be compassionate is to be totally with another while also being full of passion.[121] Carmen Caltagirone saw compassion as central to the task of the religious educator, because "compassion means to enter the world of [the] students and to suffer with them and rejoice with them."[122] In like manner, Samuel Dressner truly understood compassion and gave this insight into its depths: "This then is the deepest meaning of compassion. To know the needs of men and to bear the burdens of their sorrow is the most profound way in which we love our neighbor. By knowing his needs, by feeling his pain, by sharing his anguish, by bearing the burden of his sorrow, we pour forth from the heart the love which God extends to us."[123] Compassion is a companion virtue to humility, because those who see themselves realistically and honestly are then able to see the true condition and needs of others and to stand alongside them in solidarity and support.[124]

Unfortunately, the minister is sometimes falsely stereotyped as being a colorless and dull type of public figure. The genuine minister sketched in this chapter is just the opposite. He or she is full of passion, linking oneself with the poor, the sick, and the abused, and working to improve their lot. A tepid and passionless "minister" may hold an office with the title but cannot be a truly functional minister. A passionate and compassionate minister is full of surprises, more likely to take a whip and clear out the charlatans from a house of prayer than to kneel and pray piously at the altar.[125] One is never quite sure what will attract the sensitivity of the minister and where or with whom he or she will engage in ministry, since it is the needs of others that set the agenda for genuine and effective minister.[126]

---

119. "Compassion involves suffering. There is no way around the blunt fact that compassion will increase our experience of suffering. To suffer with another is still to suffer, even if we do not suffer another's suffering as he or she does." Andrew Purves, *The Search for Compassion: Spirituality and Ministry* (Louisville: Westminster/John Knox Press, 1989), p. 83.

120. "Compassion is not pure feeling or sentiment. It involves the relief of the pain of others." Matthew Fox, *A Spirituality Named Compassion and the Healing of the Global Village, Humpty Dumpty and Us* (San Francisco: Harper & Row, 1979), p. 4.

121. "Passion" does not carry a good connotation for everyone. For example: "Our monastic forebears are using the word 'passion' in a different way. They would not speak of a passion for life. As a word, 'passion' carries a negative meaning most of the time because for them a passion has as its chief characteristics the perversion of vision and the destruction of love." Bondi, *To Love as God Loves*, p. 58. For the broader discussion, see Chapter Four, ibid., pp. 57-77.

122. Caltagirone, *Catechist as Minister*, p. 67. For a good overview of this entire topic in relation to the religious educator, see Chapter Eight, "Compassionate Ministry," ibid., pp. 67-79.

123. Dressner, *Prayer, Humility, and Compassion*, pp. 196-197.

124. "It is important for those who are not numbered among the humiliated to learn and practice humility as solidarity with the humiliated. That would be an ecumenical virtue fundamentally different from patronizing condescension." Wengst, *Humility*, p. 60.

125. This is an allusion to the passionate and compassionate figure described in Matthew 21:12-14.

126. "The truth of all truths is that every man is our brother, that we are all children of one Father, all sheep of one Shepherd, all creations of one Creator, all parts of one infinite, gracious Spirit that pervades and sustains all of mankind. When we are aware of that . . . then we are no longer encased

To tie the virtues of humility and compassion together, Henri Nouwen recounted a Talmudic story of the search for the Messiah. The legend identified the Messiah this way: "He is sitting among the poor covered with wounds. The others unbind all their wounds at the same time and then bind them up again. But he unbinds one at a time and binds it up again, saying to himself, 'Perhaps I shall be needed: If so I must always be ready so as not to delay for a moment.' "[127] Nouwen then made the application: "The Messiah, the story tells us, is sitting among the poor, binding his wounds one at a time, waiting for the moment when he will be needed. So it is too with the minister. Since it is his task to make visible the first vestiges of liberation for others, he must bind his own wounds carefully in anticipation of the moment when he will be needed. He is called to be the wounded healer, the one who must look after his own wounds but at the same time be prepared to heal the wounds of others."[128]

The minister, in humility, knowing his or her true place in life, is sitting among the poor, the sick, and the downtrodden. The minister, in compassion, is suffering with his or her fellow-sufferers, ready to offer whatever healing may be possible.[129] The true minister, incarnating the virtues of humility and compassion, is typified by the image of the wounded healer.[130]

Activity: Self-Giving

The hallmark of the minister is the giving of self. A minister is one who gives freely of whatever he or she has to give with no thought or expectation of receiving anything in return. An image of the minister is that of the profligate sower of seed[131] who tosses the seeds on the ground without regard for the terrain. If it roots and grows, so be it. If not, the minister still continues to throw the seeds into the wind. Who is to say where they will land and prosper?

The act of giving whatever the minister has (primarily the self) was illustrated by Peter in the book of Acts. Peter was confronted by a beggar who wanted money. Peter's response was: "I have no silver or gold, but what I have I give you."[132] It is not the responsibility of the minister to give out any one particular thing, or to meet any one specific need. Each minister is unique and indi-

---

in the armour of our own ego, utterly consumed by our own cares, utterly unaware of the concerns of others, utterly unbound by the bond which joins each man to his neighbor and all men to God." Dressner, *Three Paths to God and Man*, p. 107.

127. Henri J.M. Nouwen, *The Wounded Healer: Ministry in Contemporary Society* (Garden City, N.Y.: Doubleday, 1972), p. 82.

128. Ibid.

129. "The spirituality for compassion is a spirituality that must pay special attention to our woundedness. It is sheer illusion to imagine that we can walk intimately with others in their woundedness if we have not been first of all intimately acquainted with our own woundedness. Education for compassion becomes education in our own woundedness." Purves, *The Search for Compassion*, p. 117.

130. "It is precisely our woundedness, when it has been uncovered and accepted for what it is, which allows us to be ministers, and which in particular makes compassion possible for us. If we are separated from our own woundedness, for whatever reason, compassion will in all likelihood become an impossibility for us." Ibid., p. 119.

131. See Matthew 13:3-9, 18-23; Mark 4:3-20; and Luke 8:4-15.

132. Acts 3:6, NRSV.

vidual, as is each ministry circumstance. The minister is called upon only to give what he or she has to give.

There are limits to what each person will give, but those limits must be decided by each individual. Cicero (106-43 B.C.E.) told the story of Damon and Phintas as an example of what one could offer another.[133] Phintas was condemned to death for plotting to overthrow the tyrant Dionysius. Damon took Phintas' place as bail while Phintas went home to put his affairs in order, and Damon was nearly executed when his friend was delayed in returning. The limits of what Damon would give extended to his very life. The story is reminiscent of the words of Jesus which are thematic for this chapter: "No one has greater love than this, to lay down one's life for one's friends."[134] The limit of what one person can give to another appears to be reached here.

The call to ministry is not necessarily to die for others. The call is to be willing to live for others and to give whatever one has—up to and including one's life. Of course, the challenge most ministers face is in the smaller tasks of life, and the religious educator must be sensitive to what "giving" entails in everyday life as well as in ultimate situations. Stopping to ask questions, showing concern in the midst of crisis, and being available to listen are examples of the simple things religious educators can give in the absence of "silver and gold," but they are even more precious and rare.[135]

Shadow Role: Profiteer

The genuine minister is an altruist—one who acts on behalf of others solely for the good of others. No strings are attached, and no gain is accrued to the one giving the ministry. The shadow role of the minister is the profiteer—one who makes a personal profit from the sale or misuse of essentials items or products. In the broader terms of ministry, the profiteer is anyone who performs the role of minister in order to make money or to achieve personal gain rather than to give care and concern freely. As Nolan Harmon wrote: "Using the ministerial, or priestly, position to get financial gain for oneself has long been known as simony. Technically, simony is 'the buying or selling of a church office or ecclesiastical preferment.' "[136] In other words, in the case of the ministerial profiteer, there are definitely some strings attached to the apparent act of mercy, regardless of how well camouflaged those strings may be. The activity of the shadow is notable not by giving but by taking. Sometimes the taking may be obvious, sometimes it may be subtle and hidden, but the profiteer's agenda is always reducible to the profiteer ending up ahead—at least in the profiteer's eyes. Ministry is seen as just one more easy way to take advantage of the weak and the vulnerable.

---

133. Marcus Tullius Cicero, *Tusculan Disputations*, trans. J.E. King, rev. ed. (Cambridge: Harvard University Press, 1945), pp. 488-489.

134. John 15:13, NRSV.

135. "What is decisive is not whether someone has an 'office' in the church or what office he has, but whether and to what extent he is purely and simply a 'believer': that is, one who believes, obeys, serves, loves, hopes." Küng, *Why Priests?*, p. 28.

136. Nolan B. Harmon, *Ministerial Ethics and Etiquette*, 2nd rev. ed. (Nashville: Abingdon, 1987), p. 26.

The specter of the profiteer is one reason why someone who simply holds the title of minister cannot be automatically accepted as an authentically functional minister. A hired minister is paid to provide ministry, and only time and experience can prove whether this individual is interested in providing ministry or merely earning a paycheck.[137] The motives of the particular minister are quickly discernible, and the avaricious profiteer is usually soon unmasked. Agendas have a way of asserting themselves and becoming obvious over time.

The presence of profiteering in religious circles is as common and as old as religious circles themselves. Indeed, the two seem to go hand in hand. The New Testament, for example, is full of examples of profiteers, some out for monetary profit but others looking for more subtle but just as deceitful kinds of personal advantage. Acts 8:9-25 tells the story of Simon the sorcerer (whom we remember by calling his offense "simony") who offered Peter money for the power that Peter displayed, and Peter's reported response is instructive: "May your silver perish with you, because you thought you could obtain God's gift with money!"[138] Two forms of profiteering were advanced by Jesus' disciples James and John. One form was a misuse of power and force. They were ready to send fire down on those who did not offer them welcome.[139] Once again, a rebuke was given, this time by Jesus himself.[140] The second form was a case of naked ambition. The "sons of Zebedee," in collaboration with their mother, wanted a place of prestige and importance in Jesus' retinue.[141] This prompted Jesus to teach them that to be a minister is not a matter of honor but of lowly service: "Whoever wishes to be first among you must be your slave."[142] In each of these cases, profiteering was denounced as antithetical and destructive to the functioning of the true minister.

One of the more interesting and convoluted modern examples of this intertwining of motives is the history of the spread of Sunday schools across the western parts of the United States in the latter 1800s. Evangelists or Sunday school "starters" would travel across great stretches of farmland and come to tiny towns or villages that had no library or school. These "missionaries" would spend a few days organizing a Bible study group and providing basic literature for the initial consumption. Many present-day church libraries, and even public school systems, have their roots in these frontier study groups.[143] The catch was that these traveling agents were employed and paid by the various Sunday school unions, and when the study groups were performing at a certain level, the trav-

---

137. This second figure is certainly no true professional, but rather a pretender or an impostor. For a discussion of the meaning of the term "professional" and how it relates positively to the minister, see Chapter Two, "Profession and Vocation," in Alastair V. Campbell, *Professionals and Pastoral Care* (Philadelphia: Fortress, 1985), pp. 25-41.

138. Acts 9:20, NRSV.

139. See Luke 9:51-56.

140. Some of the manuscripts report Jesus telling James and John: "You do not know what spirit you are of, for the Son of Man has not come to destroy the lives of human beings but to save them." Luke 9:55-56 (NRSV note).

141. See the story as recorded in Matthew 20:20-33.

142. Matthew 21:27, NSRV.

143. See Robert W. Lynn and Elliott Wright, *The Big Little School: 200 Years of the Sunday School*, rev. ed. (Birmingham, Ala.: Religious Education Press, 1980).

eling salesperson sold the group a library of books to sustain it and moved on to start another group in another town—to sell more libraries.[144] The goal was to create a demand, and then to supply that demand. Is it not fascinating to realize that many of our Sunday schools were started with profit in mind? Could it be that profit is still a possible motive in many of the so-called "church growth" activities popular today?[145]

Religious profiteers are no strangers to anyone today who owns a television set, for example. Any time of the day or night, profiteers masquerading behind the title minister can be found begging or otherwise scheming for money over the airwaves. Some are obvious, and some are more subtle. Do you want a prayer offered for you? It is available for a price. Do you want a Bible study booklet? Call in now and you will be on a fund-raising list for the rest of your life. Listen carefully and virtually every "minister" seen on television has an agenda that works for his or her profit.[146] Otherwise, why would he or she be appearing on the screen? Can a "minister" provide care and comfort to anyone from the safety and separation of a television studio? It may be that such an intention is a possibility, but it is more likely to be only a cruel hoax perpetrated upon the gullible.[147]

The religious educator in the role of minister must be exceedingly careful in choosing models to use as a pattern of emulation. Just because the title of minister is present, or because a particular face is recognizable, does not at all mean that ministry is being performed or offered. In fact, the whole concept of success has a different cast to it than a profiteer can ever comprehend. The religious educator in the role of minister has as an agenda only for giving care without consideration of personal gain or receipt of anything in return.[148] Any attempt to use others for personal, political, or financial gain points away from ministry to some other role entirely. As Nolan Harmon admonished: "The minister must never forget that he or she is one who serves and must be on guard against any temptation the profession presents."[149] The recast words of the Apostle Peter are still appropriate, this time aimed at the contemporary profiteers: "May your silver perish with you, because you thought you could retail God's gift with money!"[150]

---

144. "Missionaries were under strict instructions not to leave a struggling new Sunday school without first selling it a library." Ibid., p. 57.

145. Such a possibility does come to mind when reviewing the literature of modern church growth gimmicks. Is it not ironic that greater numbers of people often result in larger offerings? Is the lust after church "growth" altruism or profiteering?

146. I do not wish to imply that every media "minister" is out just for a monetary profit. Profiteering can be accomplished in other avenues than money. Power, fame, and political clout come to mind as other types of profit sought by these salespeople.

147. Variations on these tricksters and swindlers are also discussed in Chapter Seven, "The Religious Educator as Critic."

148. Wayne Oates gave a helpful caveat on this seemingly innocuous issue of helping: "The need to help, then, is not a pure unadulterated need to serve others. It is the crude ore (or oil) that needs refining through soul-searching and spiritual discipline. It is generously contaminated with the fantasy of our all-powerfulness, the desire to control even the smallest details of other's lives, the desire to take God's place in other people's lives." Wayne E. Oates, *Temptation: A Biblical and Psychological Approach* (Louisville: Westminster/John Knox, 1991), p. 33. For more on this, see the entirety of Chapter Two, "The Most Subtle Temptation," ibid., pp. 28-39.

149. Harmon, *Ministerial Ethics and Etiquette*, p. 22.

150. This is a paraphrase of the verse quoted earlier in this section, Acts 9:20, NRSV.

Faith Tradition Resource: Apostolic Christianity

Turning to the origins of the faith tradition resource of Christianity is not as easy or as uncomplicated as it may first appear. As has been true in trying to encounter the true identities of the founders of other faith traditions such as Siddhartha Gautama in Buddhism and Lao Tzu in Taoism, finding the "historical Jesus" is virtually an impossible task. Whatever is used as a source has already come through so many filters and interpretations that all of them must be handled with at least a degree of suspicion. Referring to "Apostolic Christianity"[151] and to the figure of Jesus of Nazareth (c. 6 B.C.E.-30 C.E.),[152] then, is done in full awareness of the tentativeness with which a scholar must examine the stories and traditions possessed today.

Three compounding factors in citing Apostolic Christianity need to be acknowledged.[153] First, a clear and fresh beginning point for Apostolic Christianity is impossible to find. Jesus was a Jew, and he is unfathomable without reference to the Jewish scriptures and to the Judaism of his day.[154] One could even argue that Jesus himself should not be regarded so much a founder of a new faith tradition as a questioning if not somewhat heretical Jew.[155] Second, the portraits and documents concerning Jesus are primarily from the New Testament, and more specifically from the gospels. This literature is the work of the early church, which means that what one may think he

---

151. The term "Apostolic Christianity" is an attempt to separate the beginnings of Christianity and the person of Jesus from the ecclesiological trappings that rapidly grew up around his memory. "Apostolic Christianity," then, refers to the general time period from the life of Jesus through the reign of Hadrian (117-138). This is the period when the earliest documents that were to form the corpus of the New Testament were being written and circulated, but as Williston Walker said: "To this obscure period is due the composition of the Gospels. No subject in church history is more difficult." Williston Walker, *A History of the Christian Church*, 3rd ed., rev. Robert T. Handy (New York: Scribner's, 1979), p. 31.

152. There is ambiguity and controversy concerning the exact dates of Jesus' life. For an introduction to this complex issue, see James L. Price, *Interpreting the New Testament*, 2nd ed. (New York: Holt, Rinehart and Winston, 1971), pp. 21-26, where the year of Jesus' death was placed at 30 C.E. Williston Walker placed Jesus' death in 29 C.E. Walker, *History of the Christian Church*, p. 19. Also see the discussion in David S. Noss and John B. Noss, *A History of the World's Religions*, 8th ed. (New York: Macmillan, 1990), p. 448.

153. If left to themselves, these three issues would take up more than the rest of this book. Suffice it to say that these issues have generated enough scholarship to leave one researching a lifetime. I am not making light of the problems, but in light of the scope here I can only refer to the enormous difficulties and plow ahead.

154. See Chapter Two, "The Jewish Background," in Walker, *History of the Christian Church*, pp. 12-17; W.D. Davies, Section One, "Judaica," in *Jewish and Pauline Studies* (Philadelphia: Fortress, 1984), pp. 3-88; John and Kathleen Court, *The New Testament World* (Cambridge: Cambridge University Press, 1990); Edwin D. Freed, "Introduction: The Settings of the New Testament," in *The New Testament: A Critical Interpretation* (Belmont, Calif.: Wadsworth, 1986), pp. 1-34; and Charles B. Pukas, Chapter Two, "The Jewish Background of the New Testament," in *An Introduction to the New Testament* (Peabody, Mass.: Hendrickson, 1989), pp. 30-59.

155. A classic treatment of this issue is by Gustav Dalman in *Jesus-Jeshua: Studies in the Gospels*, trans. Paul P. Levertoff (London: Society for the Promoting of Christian Knowledge, 1929). Also see Michael Hilton with Gordian Marshal, *The Gospels and Rabbinic Judaism: A Study Guide* (London: SCM Press, 1988); and James H. Charlesworth, *Jesus Within Judaism: New Light from Exciting Archaeological Discoveries* (Garden City, N.Y.: Doubleday, 1988).

or she is seeing of the "real Jesus" in the gospels is instead what the early church believed about Jesus.[156] The gospel accounts are much less historical documents than they are faith or belief statements.[157] The differences between these two types of information are vast. Third, the "quest for the historical Jesus" has been going on in some form for two millennia, and with full academic fervor for well over a century.[158] The effect, however, is that whatever Christians have believed for all these years about Jesus virtually eliminates any need for historical evidence. The image of Jesus is so firmly implanted in the Western mind that historical reality may be past its value. It may be that whatever historical evidence is discovered or manufactured about the actual Jesus of Nazareth will never change the Christ of Christianity. It is with these caveats and acknowledgements that Apostolic Christianity as a resource for the role of minister is explored.

In Luke 4:16-21, Jesus was portrayed as defining his ministry in his hometown of Nazareth. He was asked to read the scripture for the Sabbath, and the passage was from Isaiah 61:1-2:

> The Spirit of the Lord is upon me,
> because he has anointed me to bring good news to the poor.
> He has sent me to proclaim release to the captives,
> and recovery of sight to the blind,
> to let the oppressed go free,
> to proclaim the year of the Lord's favor.[159]

---

156. For an overview and an introduction, see Robert A. Spivey and D. Moody Smith, Chapter Twelve, "Literature and Community: The New Testament and Early Christianity," in *Anatomy of the New Testament: A Guide to Its Structure and Meaning* (New York: Macmillan, 1989), pp. 426-451; Price, Chapter Two, "Methodological Considerations," *Interpreting the New Testament*, pp. 17-30; George A. Wells, Chapter One, "The Reliability of the Gospels," in *Who Was Jesus?: A Critique of the New Testament Record* (La Salle, Ill.: Open Court, 1989), pp. 5-24; Hans Conzelmann and Andreas Lindemann, Part One, "Methodology," in *Interpreting the New Testament: An Introduction to the Principles and Methods of New Testament Exegesis*, 8th ed., trans. Siegfried S. Schatzmann (Peabody, Mass.: Hendrickson, 1988), pp. 1-104.

157. "The gospel record is primarily a witness to the divine event of Jesus, the Christ; and its details have doubtless been colored by the experiences and situations of the early church. Scholars are sharply divided concerning the historical accuracy of many incidents narrated in the gospels." Walker, *History of the Christian Church*, p. 18.

158. The source of the modern debate is normally attributed to Friedrich Schleiermacher in *Das Leben Jesu* (Berlin: G. Reimer, 1864). The classic resource for this activity is Albert Schweitzer, *The Quest of the Historical Jesus: A Critical Study of Its Progress from Reimarus to Wrede* (New York: Macmillan, 1968); first published in 1906. Schweitzer by no means ended the discussion, and in fact only exacerbated the discussion. The arguments are still going full force. For some later versions of this type of study, see George A. Wells, *The Historical Evidence for Jesus* (Buffalo: Prometheus Books, 1982); Leander E. Keck, *A Future for the Historical Jesus: The Place of Jesus in Preaching and Theology* (Philadelphia: Fortress, 1981); Michael L. Cook, *The Historical Jesus* (Chicago: Thomas More Press, 1986); James D.G. Dunn, *The Evidence for Jesus* (Philadelphia: Westminster, 1984); *In Search of the Historical Jesus*, ed. Harvey K. McArthur (New York: Scribner's, 1969); and Ernst Kasemann, Chapter One, "The Problem of the Historical Jesus," in *Essays in New Testament Themes* (Philadelphia: Fortress, 1982), pp. 15-47.

159. This quote is from the New Testament (Luke 4:18-19, NRSV) rendering of Isaiah 61:1-2, which reads a bit differently from the Jewish scripture (Old Testament) version.

His application and interpretation of these scriptures was personal: "Today this scripture has been fulfilled in your hearing."[160] Everything related to genuine ministry in this chapter is captured in the mission Jesus accepted for himself from these words in the book of Isaiah, and those wanting to minister have their own mandate to fulfill as it stems from those words.

Drawing on the Servant Songs of Isaiah,[161] Jesus identified himself repeatedly with the Suffering Servant and taught his disciples to adopt that image of servanthood. In Mark 9:35 (NRSV), he said: "Whoever wants to be first must be last of all and servant of all." Asking ministers to be last and to be servants first still goes down rather hard even today. In a parallel passage in Matthew 20:26-28 (NRSV), Jesus expanded on this concept of servant ministry: "Whoever wishes to be great among you must be your servant, and whoever wishes to be first among you must be your slave; just as the Son of Man came not to be served but to serve, and to give his life a ransom for many."[162] In this passage Jesus was even more explicit: If you are going to follow me, you must do what I do.

In another closely related passage, Jesus linked up this servant image with the virtue of humility: "The greatest among you will be your servant. All who exalt themselves will be humbled, and all who humble themselves will be exalted."[163] In other places Jesus phrased the idea memorably: "But many who are first will be last, and the last will be first."[164]

Jesus never seemed to have missed an opportunity to excoriate the religious authorities of his day, and he called them the equivalent (among other things) of profiteers. For example, in a list of indictments, he said: "Woe to you, scribes and Pharisees, hypocrites! For you clean the outside of the cup and of the plate, but inside they are full of greed and self-indulgence."[165] He especially despised the appearance but not the actual performance of good: "So you also on the outside look righteous to others, but inside you are full of hypocrisy and lawlessness."[166]

One example of the many in the gospels that reflects Jesus' sense of altruism, and hence is a picture of his expectations of true ministry to those that need it, is this one: "When you give a luncheon or a dinner, do not invite your friends or your brothers or your relatives or rich neighbors, in case they may invite you in return, and you would be repaid. But when you give a banquet, invite the poor, the crippled, the lame, and the blind. And you will be blessed, because they cannot repay you, for you will be repaid at the resurrection of the righteous."[167] This is the task and life of the minister, which Jesus described elsewhere in these startling but unmistakable terms: "But I say to you that listen, love your ene-

---

160. Luke 4:21.

161. For example, see Isaiah 40.

162. The designation "Son of Man" was a term Jesus used to describe himself and to identify with the Jewish scripture's term. See, for example, the use in Ezekiel 2:1 and thereafter throughout the book of Ezekiel. A good introduction to this topic can be found in Douglas R.A. Hare, *The Son of Man Tradition* (Minneapolis: Fortress, 1990).

163. Matthew 23:11-12, NRSV. See parallel passages in Luke 14:11 and Luke 18:14.

164. Matthew 19:30, NRSV; see also Matthew 20:16; Mark 10:31; and Luke 13:30.

165. Matthew 23:25, NRSV.

166. Matthew 23:28, NRSV.

167. Luke 14:12-14, NRSV.

mies, do good to those who hate you, bless those who curse you, pray for those who abuse you. If anyone strikes you on the cheek, offer the other also; and from anyone who takes away your coat do not withhold even your shirt. Give to everyone who begs from you; and if anyone takes away your goods, do not ask for them again. Do to others as you would have them do to you."[168] In the face of the call to this kind of ministry, each potential minister today, like the disciples, must decide how to answer the question posed by Jesus: "Are *you* able to drink the cup that I am about to drink?"[169]

Historical Personage: Damien of Molokai

One who indeed was able to drink of the cup, and who paid the ultimate price for it, was Damien of Molokai (1840-1889). Born in Tremeloo, Belgium as Joseph De Veuster, he became Brother Damien (soon to be Father) by taking the religious habit in 1859 as a member of the Congregation of the Sacred Hearts.[170] Even before his ordination he was sent[171] in 1863 to the place that would later claim his life—the Hawaiian Islands. He served as a priest and helper in various capacities on the Islands until May 10, 1873 when he went to the settlement of Kalawao on Molokai—the lepers camp.[172] He served there as "the leper priest" until April 15, 1889, when he died of leprosy.[173]

Damien was fully aware of the dangers of ministering in the contagious environment of Kalawao but made the conscious decision to stay, for as he said when he wrote to his superiors asking to be assigned there permanently: "You know my disposition. I want to sacrifice myself for the poor lepers."[174] Over time, as Damien himself contracted the disease himself, the quality of his relationships with the lepers changed. Upon his arrival he often would begin his sermons with the phrase "We lepers . . . " but this artificial perception soon changed dramatically. One biographer made this observation after it was known that Damien too was truly one of the lepers: "Now, when he would use the

---

168. Luke 6:27-30, NRSV.

169. Matthew 20:22, NRSV.

170. This congregation is overviewed in Appendix One of Vital Jourdain, *The Heart of Father Damien*, trans. Francis Larkin and Charles Davenport (Milwaukee: Bruce, 1955), pp. 398-402.

171. Actually he volunteered. His older brother was scheduled to go, but contracted typhus and was unable to take the trip. Upon receiving permission from his superiors, Damien, at age twenty-three, is reported to have told his brother with delight: "I am going in your place." See this recounted in Gavan Daws, *Holy Man: Father Damien of Molokai* (New York: Harper & Row, 1973), p. 30-32.

172. To get a sense of the size of the settlement, and the high incidence of death that took place there, see the tabulations of entrants and deaths to Kalawao during the lifetime of Damien in Steven Debroey, *Father Damien: The Priest of the Lepers*, trans. Staf Gebruers (Dublin: Clonmore and Reynolds, 1966), p. 175.

173. The actual name of the disease that Damien had was *Mycobacterium leprae*, the "worst of all categories" of leprosy. See more of this in ibid., pp. 236-240. One author described the disease this way: "Leprosy gnaws and devours with continual activity the projecting parts of the head, hands, feet, elbows, and knees." Debroey, *Father Damien*, p. 84. The description of leprosy by these authors gets more graphic and detailed regarding the progress of the disease, so read further in these passages (if you are able to endure it) to get a sense of what Damien experienced.

174. Quoted in Daws, *Holy Man*, p. 63.

words 'we lepers . . . ' in his sermons, they sounded quite differently to the ears of his friends."[175] Gavan Daws described the evolution this way: "Somewhere along the way—in the confines of the confessional, in the touch of the hand on body during the administering of extreme unction, or perhaps in the sharing of a meal, or in an embrace of greeting or farewell—leprosy passed from parishioner to priest. If it went unremarked at first, an imperceptible transformation of Damien's flesh and blood, still it made him what he, from the beginning, said out of priestly charity that he was: one of his congregation, 'we lepers.' "[176]

Damien was totally committed to his ministry and never regretted his decision to go, since his presence there was a result of his own volition. When he finally got the news confirming his leprosy, he seemed somewhat relieved that the waiting was over and was able to write: "There is no more doubt about me, *I am a leper*. Blessed be the Good God!"[177] Damien himself, in fact, was unsurprised by his lot, and with good reason: "Father Damien told his English friend and visitor, Edward Clifford, that he had always expected to become a leper sooner or later, though exactly how he had caught it he did not know. How could he miss it, when all day long he took care of them, heard their confessions, gave them the Sacraments, lived and worked with them? He breathed the same air, touched their wounds, handled their tools and they handled his."[178] Damien did not pray for a miracle cure, but accepted his sickness as a natural consequence of his decisions. He once told a friend: "I would not be cured if the price of my cure was that I must leave the island and give up my work."[179] In a widely read open letter concerning the character of Father Damien,[180] Robert Louis Stevenson contrasted Damien's situation with that of other professional helpers: "No doctor or nurse is called upon to enter once for all the doors of that gehenna [Kalawao]: they do not say farewell, they need not abandon hope, on its sad threshold; they but go for a time to their high calling and can look forward as they go to relief, to recreation, to rest. But Damien shut to with his own hand the doors of his own sepulchre."[181]

Could there be a better or more accurate depiction of the minister than Damien, the servant, the person for others, the wounded healer? The following description of Damien's work epitomizes the role of the religious educator as minister:

---

175. Debroey, *Father Damien*, p. 113.

176. Daws, *Holy Man*, p. 153.

177. Jourdain, *The Heart of Father Damien*, p. 253. Damien probably suspicioned that he had leprosy as early as 1884. In the midst of it all, he "professed himself to be happy and content and said he would go on working in the hope of being useful for many years." Daws, *Holy Man*, p. 153.

178. Jourdain, *The Heart of Father Damien*, pp. 255-256.

179. Ibid., p. 253. Gavan Daws added: "So, although he could not ask his friends to pray for the miracle of a complete cure, something of which he held himself to be unworthy, those who remembered him in prayer might properly ask for at least 'a stay of the progress of the malady.'" Daws, *Holy Man*, p. 200.

180. Stevenson wrote the letter in 1890 to refute charges against Damien leveled by Charles M. Hyde, a resident of Honolulu who had repeated unsubstantiated gossip about Damien. The charges against Damien are contained in a letter written by Hyde reprinted in Jourdain, *The Heart of Father Damien*, p. 346. For a more complete account of the controversy, see Chapter Twenty One, "Stevenson's Letter," ibid., pp. 345-362.

181. Robert Louis Stevenson, *Father Damien: An Open Letter to the Reverend Doctor Hyde of Honolulu* (New York: Cobble Hill Press, 1968), p. 39.

"To be a priest, and especially the priest of Kalawao, was to live and move, physically and spiritually, in the territory between life and death, trying by teaching and example to show others the way to make the passage."[182] To be a true minister, then, is to do for the persons that surround him or her just as Father Damien did: all day long, to take care of them, hear their confessions, give them the Sacraments, live and work with them; to breathe the same air, touch their wounds, and handle their tools as they handle the minister's. The next, and ultimate step, is to be privileged to address the people in the same way that Damien did, as equals: "We lepers."

Contemporary Example: Teresa of Calcutta

Another "hero of suffering and renunciation" that typifies the role of minister is Teresa of Calcutta (b. 1910), more popularly known as Mother Teresa. Like Damien of Molokai, she too left the comforts of home and family to become a servant of the needy, but her efforts have had somewhat happier results, since she has been honored with such acclaim as receiving the Nobel Peace Prize in 1979.[183] Also like Damien, Teresa leaves behind no great legacy of scholarship or writings. She is too busy with her mission, serving the "poorest of the poor."[184] As one author put it: "Mother Teresa speaks little, publishes even less."[185] All the written information that is available from her at this point—and likely all that will ever be available—is collections of her speeches, correspondence, and interviews.

The immediate concern here, then, is how and why should she be considered a contemporary example of a religious educator? Surely the small sum of devotional materials with her name attached are insufficient to qualify her for inclusion. Such would be true—except for the consideration of the role of minister. The role demands being one with the people, and virtually no one else in view exemplifies the role so fully as does Mother Teresa. The following examines what she has done, rather than any formally expressed educational theory. It seems highly appropriate that a religious educator in the role of minister would be known more through her works than through her words. Teresa has a larger mission than simply gaining converts, and she is much too busy to spend unnecessary energy crafting words. As one of her foremost biographers, Malcolm Muggeridge, said: "Mother Teresa has no need to be an evangelist in the old propagandist sense. She preaches Christ every moment of every day by living for and in him."[186]

---

182. Daws, *Holy Man*, p. 118.

183. This was just one of a number of awards she has received. One author noted: "Perhaps no living person has received as many world-famous awards as Mother has." Edward Le Joly, *Mother Teresa of Calcutta: A Biography* (San Francisco: Harper & Row, 1983), p. 287. See Chapter Nineteen, "The Awards," ibid., pp. 287-297.

184. "Our mission is to labor at the salvation and sanctification of the poorest of the poor not only in the slums but all over the world, wherever they may be." Mother Teresa, *Total Surrender*, rev. ed., ed. Angelo Devananda (Ann Arbor, Mich.: Servant Publications, 1985), pp. 16-17.

185. Georges Gorrée and Jean Barbier, eds., *The Love of Christ: Spiritual Counsels, by Mother Teresa* (San Francisco: Harper & Row, 1982), p. vii.

186. Malcolm Muggeridge, *Something Beautiful for God: Mother Teresa of Calcutta* (New York: Harper & Row, 1971), p. 59.

Born Agnes Gonxha Bejaxhiu in Skopje, Albania, she took the name Teresa ("Little Flower") from Teresa of Lisieux.[187] Teresa felt the call to missionary work at age twelve, and at age eighteen joined the Sisters of Our Lady of Loreto. For some years she taught high school in Calcutta but finally got permission to leave the Loreto Sisters to work directly with the poor in 1948. She has been with the poor, literally with, ever since. There is good cause to say that Teresa never left her initial vocation of religious education but only modified the context in which she performed it. She simply moved her work from the school and the classroom into the streets and into the hospitals, still carrying on her ever-expanding ministry of compassion[188] and education.

Teresa described leaving the Sisters to live with the poor as "a call within my vocation—a second vocation. It meant leaving the Loreto convent, where I was very happy, to go to the streets and serve the poor."[189] Elsewhere she said: "But my vocation, within the vocation, was for the poorest of the poor."[190] Teresa (again like Damien) is one who has found a way to serve and to be a functional minister while staying within the vocation, where someone like Albert Schweitzer, for example, felt compelled to leave the vocational ministry in order to pursue what he perceived as his own more genuine form of ministry.[191]

Teresa soon founded her own order called the Missionaries of Charity (approved October 7, 1952), which is now worldwide in its efforts to care for the poor, the sick, and the dying. One story illustrates the work and the character of Teresa and her order. In December of 1968, Pope Paul VI was in Bombay for the International Eucharistic Congress. Mother Teresa was also in Bombay at the time, visiting the sisters and helping the poor. When the Pope left, he donated the limousine he had used while in Bombay as a gift to Mother Teresa for use in her "universal mission of love." (She was not there to receive it, incidentally. She was at the bedside of a dying man.) Neither Teresa nor the sisters ever used the car, but instead raffled it off for funds to help the poor. A widow won the raffle, but the car was too expensive to operate, so she sold it. The widow kept half of the

---

187. "Saint Teresa of Avila? Oh, no! I haven't called myself after the big Teresa, but after the little one, Teresa of Lisieux." Mother Teresa, *My Life for the Poor*, ed. Jose Luis González-Balado and Janet N. Playfoot (San Francisco: Harper & Row, 1985), p. 105.

188. "'We should experience toward the poor not pity,' says Mother, 'but compassion. Pity implies superiority; but we are fundamentally equal as God's creatures. Compassion arises between people on the same level, on the human level, all members of humanity knowing themselves as such.'" Le Joly, *Mother Teresa of Calcutta*, p. 223.

189. Mother Teresa, *The Love of Christ*, p. 62. She dated this understanding from September 10, 1946 ("Inspiration Day"), and she called it her "call within a call": "In a train taking her to a hill station in the Himalayas she heard what she identified as a second call from God. She had already been called to the religious life and to her there was never any question of abandoning it, but the second call was to another form of service within that life. She was to leave the convent and help the poor while living among them." Kathryn Spink, *I Need Souls Like You: Sharing in the Work of Mother Teresa through Prayer and Suffering* (San Francisco: Harper & Row, 1984), p. 3.

190. Mother Teresa, *The Love of Christ*, p. 65.

191. Albert Schweitzer (1875-1964) left his life as musician, educator, and pastor in France to become a medical doctor, spending the greater part of his later life as a medical missionary in equatorial Africa. See him explain this in Albert Schweitzer, *Out of My Life and Thought: An Autobiography*, trans. C.T. Campion (New York: Henry Holt, 1949).

money—and donated the other half to Mother Teresa to help the poor.[192]

A further word about Teresa as a religious educator is in order. Although she does not teach in any formal setting, and is not known for her theoretical treatises, there is every reason to identify her a religious educator. Yet another story describes her style of educational ministry: "Mother Teresa was teaching her young sisters to wash the bodies of those in need, to clean their sores and bandage their wounds. They were to do this not a few times, but thousands of times. Their service of love was not to last a few days, not even a year or two, but a whole life, as long as the Lord God wanted them to serve him in their sisters and brothers."[193] Was Mother Teresa then free of her responsibilities to the poor? The end of the story reveals the true religious educator as minister. Teresa said: "'At times . . . they arrive in a terrible state, filthy, covered with sores, eaten up with syphilis. We wash them all. Of course when a case is really too bad, I do it myself.'"[194]

As with the other contemporary examples of religious educators, Mother Teresa's work is overviewed and then evaluated. The type of examination will of necessity be different because the references are of a very different type. The role of the minister is well-represented in the person of Teresa, however, in spite of what the following discussion lacks in terms of formal academic resources.

Overview

Mother Teresa stated that the purpose of her order (the Missionaries of Charity) was "to take God and his love to the poorest of the poor, irrespective of their ethical origin or the faith that they profess."[195] These "poorest of the poor" she identified as "the hungry, the thirsty, the naked, the homeless, the ignorant, the captives, the crippled, the leprosy sufferers, the alcoholics and drug addicts, the dying destitutes and the bereaved, the unloved, the abandoned, the outcasts and all those who have lost all hope and faith."[196] Such a list certainly covers a lot of human tragedy and suffering but most revealingly correlates with the list with Matthew 25:31-46, where at the Last Judgment the acts done to these "least" of society (the hungry, the thirsty, the stranger, the naked, the sick, and the imprisoned) were actually done to the "Son of man." Here is the key to understanding the activity of Mother Teresa and her workers: "The Missionaries of Charity do firmly believe that they are touching the body of Christ in his distressing disguise whenever they are touching and helping the poor."[197] They see themselves as "feeding the hungry Christ, clothing the naked Christ, taking care of the sick Christ, and giving a home to the homeless Christ."[198]

---

192. This story is recounted in José Luis González-Balado, *Always the Poor: Mother Teresa, Her Life and Message* (Liguori, Mo.: Liguori Publications, 1980), pp. 67-68.

193. Le Joly, *Mother Teresa of Calcutta*, pp. 25-26.

194. Ibid., p. 26.

195. Mother Teresa, *Life in the Spirit: Reflections, Meditations, Prayers*, ed. Kathryn Spink (San Francisco: Harper & Row, 1983), p. 81.

196. "The Co-Worker's Way of Life," in González-Balado, *Always the Poor*, pp. 97-98.

197. Mother Teresa, *My Life for the Poor*, p. 15.

198. Ibid.

Mother Teresa understood and experienced the lot of the poor early in her ministry, and it set the tone for all that was to follow. She described her initiation this way:

> Soon after leaving Loreto, I was on the street, with no shelter, no company, no helper, no money, no employment, no promise, no guarantee, no security.
> Then I prayed, "My God, you, only you. I trust in your call, your inspiration. You will not let me down."
> I needed a roof to shelter the abandoned, so I started to search.
> I walked and walked all the time, until I couldn't walk any more.
> Then, I understood better the exhaustion of the really poor, always in search of a little food, of medicines, of everything.[199]

This slice from Teresa's life helps distinguish the difference between the office of the minister and the function of the minister. Teresa, as a true functional minister, identified her very being with the poor, living and experiencing exactly what and where they were.[200] There is no distance or separation, save one exception. Teresa made this clear when she spoke of the "safeguard" of poverty accepted by herself and her order: "Our strict poverty is our safeguard. We do not want to begin by serving the poor and little by little end up serving the rich, like other religious orders in history. In order to understand and help those who lack everything, we must live like them. The difference is that our destitute ones are poor by force of circumstance, whereas we are by choice."[201] The difference between Teresa and her order from the truly poor is that Teresa and her order live in poverty by choice.

One author said the Mother Teresa's first love was that of teaching,[202] and indeed that was her initial training and vocation. In her role of minister, teaching is never far from the surface. In fact, religious education is central and essential to understanding what she is about in her unique type of ministry. To her, ministry and religious education are inseparable. This becomes especially obvious when someone comes to her who wants to make a donation but does not want to get too personally involved. Then Mother Teresa the experiential teacher gets to work. She explained: "I want people to get involved in the actual work we do, for their own sakes and for ours. I never ask them for money, nothing like that. I only ask them to bring their love, to bring their hands to help. Then, when they meet those in need, their first reaction is to do something for them. And when they come the second time, they are already committed. After a while, they feel they belong to the poor; they understand their need for love, who they are, and what they themselves can do for them."[203]

To illustrate the kind of involvement which Teresa fosters, she told the following story: "For example, an Australian came the other day to make a large

---

199. Ibid., p. 10.
200. This was what she called her "call within a call."
201. Mother Teresa, *The Love of Christ*, pp. 47-48.
202. González-Balado, *Always the Poor*, p. 17.
203. Mother Teresa, *The Love of Christ*, p. 33.

donation. But after making the donation he said: 'This is something outside of myself; now I want to give something of myself.' Since then, he comes regularly to the Home for the Dying to shave the sick and talk with them. He gives not only his money but also his time. He could have spent both his money and his time on himself, but he wanted to spend himself instead."[204] Such is the essence of the role of the minister—he or she spends himself or herself. Also vital to the role of the minister as religious educator is inviting others to experience and to share the work. Mother Teresa in this story demonstrated that her kind of religious education demands much more than thinking right thoughts, or answering questions properly. It demands self-giving and compassionate caring.

The kind of teaching she and her co-workers do is the "silent" type. They act rather than talk. Teresa put it this way: "We preach Christ without preaching. Not by words but by putting his love and our love into a living action of serving the people in their needs; by loving and serving the dying, the homeless, the abandoned destitute, the lepers."[205] She made the same point elsewhere a bit more bluntly: "There should be less talk; a preaching point is not a meeting point. What do you do then? Take a broom and clean someone's house. That says enough."[206]

It would be misguided to perceive Mother Teresa and the Missionaries of Charity as figures of mercy who do not give proper respect to the poor. They have avoided this trap of superiority and of paternalism/maternalism, since as Teresa has said: "The poor are great people. They don't need our sympathy. They don't need our pity. They are great people! They are very lovable people!"[207] She carried the thought a bit further: "The poor do us the honor of allowing us to serve them."[208] Her only mission is to care for those that get no care, and to tend to the wounds of the outcasts. In fact, she went so far as to say: "The poor are our 'hope.' By their courage they truly represent the hope of the world. They have taught us a different way of loving God by making us do our utmost to help them."[209] Her perspective becomes clearer, and helps readers perceive their own poverty better, when they hear her say: "I have come to realize that the greatest disease and the greatest suffering is to be unwanted, unloved, uncared for, to be shunned by everybody, to be just nobody to no one."[210]

One quickly gets a sense of the strength of Mother Teresa, and there is no room for false humility in her. She addressed this directly when she said: "Often, under the pretext of humility, of trust, of abandonment, we can forget to use the strength of our will. Everything depends upon these words: 'I will' or 'I will not.' And into the expression 'I will' I must put all my energy."[211] In a positive way, she said of humility: "It is a great virtue to practice humility without

204. Ibid., p. 42.
205. Mother Teresa, *My Life for the Poor*, p. 88.
206. Mother Teresa, *A Gift for God: Prayers and Meditations* (San Francisco: Harper & Row: 1975), pp. 44-45.
207. Mother Teresa, *My Life for the Poor*, p. 82.
208. Ibid., p. 96.
209. Mother Teresa, *The Love of Christ*, p. 23.
210. Mother Teresa, *My Life for the Poor*, p. 96.
211. Mother Teresa, *The Love of Christ*, p. 20.

our knowing we are humble."[212] But in a letter to her order she was once again blunt and to the point: "Do not think that hiding your gifts of God is the sign of humility. No, do and use whatever gifts God has given you."[213]

Perhaps these few paragraphs have introduced enough of Mother Teresa to illuminate her as a contemporary example of the religious educator in the role of minister. These words were meant only to give a brief overview and not to provide a comprehensive treatment of her work. One final statement from her will end this overview section, and in it Teresa places the blame for suffering squarely where she thinks it belongs. In the process, she identified her understanding of the essential tasks of the minister. Who can deny its truth, or avoid its indictment? "If sometimes the poor people have had to die of starvation, it is not because God didn't care for them, but because you and I didn't give, were not instruments of love in the hands of God, to give them that bread, to give them that clothing; because we did not recognize him, when once more Christ came in distressing disguise—in the hungry man, in the lonely man, in the homeless child, and seeking shelter."[214]

Evaluation

The task of evaluating a person such as Teresa of Calcutta—who is probably as close to the embodiment of a saint as anyone in contemporary society—is no easy assignment. Rather than trying to find points of weakness or inconsistency in her work, the plan is to describe some of the more outstanding characteristics of her personality and of her ministry and then to give alternative views of them. One of the fascinating things about Teresa is that she has a convincing response or a defense about virtually every criticism, so little will be provided here that tarnishes her halo.

The undeniably positive attributes of Teresa can be stated quickly and simply. Mother Teresa is without doubt the enfleshment of what this chapter has promoted as the genuine role of the minister. She is altruistic, she is sacrificial, she is full of humility and compassion, and she has spent her life in giving of herself. Perhaps her own self-description makes the point well enough: "By blood and origin . . . I am all Albanian. My citizenship is Indian. I am a Catholic nun. As to my calling, I belong to the whole world. As to my heart, I belong entirely to the heart of Jesus."[215] Even though she may be an enfleshment of the genuine minister, however, this does not mean she is perfect. Indeed, because she is an enfleshment—a human—she has flaws and blind spots like the rest of humanity. It would do her an injustice to make her into a modern icon to be worshiped. A few of her more human characteristics are considered below.

First, one could complain that her writings are not academically credible for holding up as a model of a contemporary religious educator. Teresa cannot be legitimately criticized for not being a scholar or an academic, and such a criticism would be sadly misplaced. She has never made any claim to be an aca-

---

212. Ibid., p. 78.
213. Ibid., p. 79.
214. Mother Teresa, *A Gift of God*, p. 24.
215. Quoted in Eileen Egan, *Such a Vision of the Street: Mother Teresa—The Spirit and the Work* (Garden City, N.Y.: Doubleday, 1985), p. 357.

demic. She has been included here because she is an example of the functional minister, a practitioner, and not because of her academic achievements or scholarly writing. Indeed, she made no claim that her ministry was based on any theoretical type of basis: "'In the choice of the works of the apostolate,' said Mother, 'there was neither planning nor preconceived ideas. We started work as needs and opportunities arose. God showed us what he wanted us to do.'"[216] It may be that it is unfair or inappropriate to include her and her writings in such a comparative context as this, but this cannot be laid at her feet. The example she gives and the contrast she provides seems to be well worth the risk for our purposes here.

Second, Mother Teresa can be described as an ascetic and that her life with the poor goes to an extreme. She would probably agree with both observations and see them as no criticism at all. Her argument is that she and her workers should participate in the life and the conditions of the poor they serve as fully as possible. There is no room or cause for "professional distance" in her understanding of ministry with the poor. One brief example illustrates: "Some people would advise me to change certain things. For instance, they tell me that the sisters should have fans in the common room or in the chapel. I do not want them to have fans. The poor whom they are to serve have no fans."[217] One can see Teresa's point, but there are limits of endurance, it would appear.[218] One also gets a hint of Teresa's strength of will, which some would interpret as stubbornness. Of course, how someone could perform the ministry she performs and not be "stubborn" would be a mystery indeed.

Third, Mother Teresa is an orthodox Catholic with little time for liberal intrusions, being more concerned with keeping and conserving the ancient traditions and beliefs. While this is certainly not the basis of a valid criticism, another way to view her is as inflexible[219] and authoritarian.[220] Again, a brief story will illustrate.[221] She told of the time a newly ordained priest came to instruct the Sisters and, in her words, "laughed at a number of our traditional beliefs." She

---

216. Quoted in Le Joly, *Mother Teresa of Calcutta*, p. 42.

217. Mother Teresa, *My Life for the Poor*, pp. 30-31.

218. She explained the reason for her insistence on the simplest of lifestyles: "Poverty is necessary because we are working with the poor. When they complain about the food, we can say: we eat the same. They say: 'It was so hot last night, we could not sleep.' We can reply, 'We also felt very hot.' The poor have to wash themselves, go barefoot; we do the same. We have to go down and lift them up. It opens the heart of the poor when we can say we live the same way they do. Sometimes they only have one bucket of water. It is the same with us. The poor have to stand in line; we do too. Food, clothing, everything must be like that of the poor." Mother Teresa, *Total Surrender*, p. 57.

219. To the charge that she is inflexible comes this passage from one of the compiled editions of her sayings: "Mother Teresa's vocabulary is very much that of Roman Catholicism, but her message is also one of supreme tolerance. 'God has his own ways to work in the hearts of men and we do not know how close they are to him, but by their actions we will always know whether they are at his disposal or not.' Thus if the individual chooses what may be called the 'Christian way' of living—and of dying, whether he is Catholic, Protestant, Hindu, or Muslim he will draw nearer to God." Spink, *I Need Souls Like You*, pp. 12-13. Malcolm Muggeridge made a similar point: "It would be absurd to suggest that Mother Teresa is neutral as between Christianity and Hinduism. Her preference is clear for all to see and understand. Yet she manages nonetheless to induce high-caste Indian ladies to participate in ever increasing numbers in her work." Muggeridge, *Something Beautiful for God*, p. 59.

220. Malcolm Muggeridge put it nicely: "Controversy . . . does not arise in the case of those who, like Mother Teresa, are blessed with certainties." Muggeridge, *Something Beautiful for God*, p. 25.

related that he dismissed the notions of genuflecting before the Sacrament, of religious devotion, and of traditional worship practices. When he finished, Teresa "led him to the door, thanked him, and told him he need not come here any more." She went back to where the Sisters were assembled "and for one hour refuted all that he had said." In this story one gets a sense, not only of Teresa's conservative stance, but of her bluntness and directness. She leaves no doubt about her opinions and apparently expects her charges to follow her in them.

The fourth area is closely related to the third and has brought her the most criticism. It is her absolute condemnation of abortion and the use of any birth control practice other than abstinence.[222] The logic of her position is clear. Children are God's gift, and abortion is destroying God's gift.[223] She and her order are trying to save the resultant unwanted children by providing adoption services. To hear this logic proclaimed in places like India and Bangladesh, with thousands of unwanted children dying of neglect and starvation, seems to many to beg the question. Malcolm Muggeridge, for example, asked her: "Some people say that there are too many people in India, and yet you're saving children many of whom otherwise would die."[224] Teresa responded: "Yes, many would die, especially those children that are unwanted. Quite possibly they would have been either thrown away or killed. But that way is not for us; our way is to preserve life, the life of Christ in the life of a child."[225] To tell people, in terms of birth control, to rely on self-control[226] may indeed sound hopelessly archaic and unrealistic to some, but this issue is included here because it points to the difficulty of fulfilling the role of minister. The ethics, the theology, and the logic of a person's position on the nature of the human dictates in large measure the nature of ministry. For Mother Teresa, her ministry must include caring for the unborn as well as the born.

Fifth, also closely related to the above, is the simplistic perspective Teresa often displays. One example is this comment: "If we have today so many unhappy and broken families, and if we have in the world so much unhappiness and so much suffering, I think it is because the mother is not in the home!"[227] Part of the problem here is that Mother Teresa in her pronouncements is not trying to be academically acceptable and so makes these kind of broad, sweeping comments that she makes no effort to back up with studies or empirical data. Another is that she is indeed very simple in her views and in her analysis. Of course, whether this is a weakness or a strength is a debatable issue. Whatever one may think of her stands, however, it is obvious that she is sincere and honest in trying to improve the lot of the poor in her own humble way. She has little patience with complex and time-wasting sophistries.

Sixth, Teresa has been criticized for using inadequate methods and procedures

---

221. See Mother Teresa, *My Life for the Poor*, p. 35.
222. This has been one of the chief points of contention between Teresa and the Indian government. See Egan, *Such a Vision of the Street*, pp. 356-357.
223. Mother Teresa discussed this in many places. For example, see ibid., pp. 61-69.
224. Muggeridge, *Something Beautiful for God*, p. 100.
225. Ibid.
226. For example, see the comments in Mother Teresa, *The Love of Christ*, p. 41.
227. Mother Teresa, *My Life for the Poor*, p. 61.

in her work. In the face of the vast numbers of people that need care, Malcolm Muggeridge asked her about the need for larger, more collective solutions.[228] She responded: "I do not agree with the big way of doing things. To us what matters is an individual. To get to love the person we must come in close contact with him. If we wait till we get the numbers, then we will be lost in the numbers. And we will never be able to show love and respect for the person. I believe in person to person; every person is Christ for me, and since there is only one Jesus, that person is only one person in the world for me at that moment."[229] As she told Muggeridge later, she and her community are well aware of the overwhelming needs: "We ourselves feel that what we are doing is just a drop in the ocean. But if that drop was not in the ocean I think the ocean will be less because of that missing drop."[230] Teresa is also clear that, as far as she is concerned, she and her community are providing ministry and not social work: "The difference between our work and social work is that we give wholeheartedly, free service for the love of God."[231]

Seventh, as the above comments would lead one to expect, Mother Teresa demands not just effort but perfection. One biographer wrote in this connection: "To all Mother preaches perfection, saying, 'Holiness is not just for the few only. All are invited to it.' "[232] Once again, this can be taken as a problem, or as evidence of her genius. She expects so much, one is left wondering who can measure up, as when she wrote: "With you, my sisters, I will not be satisfied with your just being a good religious. I want you to be able to offer to God a perfect sacrifice."[233] She demands much of herself and expects nothing less of anyone else who says they are called to perform ministry. With this we are left imagining her asking each individual that considers working with her the same question encountered earlier: "Are *you* able to drink the cup that I am about to drink?"

Representative Teaching Procedure: Laboratory Training

No teaching procedure can ever prepare one to be a minister like Mother Teresa is a minister. A life of sacrificing and giving cannot be programed or

---

228. Muggeridge, *Something Beautiful for God*, p. 118.
229. Ibid.
230. Ibid., p. 119. Another example of this kind of response gives even a fuller understanding of Teresa's stance: "On several occasions, those interviewing her have objected, 'You merely distribute food to the hungry; what you should do is to give them means to support themselves. You should provide them with instruments, say with a fishing rod and tackle with which they might earn their living.' Mother answered, 'The people picked up on the street or brought back to our houses are too weak to even hold a fishing rod; we try to give them back enough strength so that they can hold a fishing rod." Le Joly, *Mother Teresa of Calcutta*, p. 226.
231. Mother Teresa, *Total Surrender*, p. 83. The rest of the quote shows that no one stands in Teresa's way when it comes to her ministry: "In the beginning, when the work started, I got a fever and had a dream about St. Peter. He said to me, 'No, there is no place for you here. No slums in heaven.' 'Alright,' I answered him, 'then I shall go on working. I'll bring the slums to heaven." Ibid.
232. Le Joly, *Mother Teresa of Calcutta*, p. 189.
233. Mother Teresa, *The Love of Christ*, p. 69.

packaged. At first glance, the laboratory teaching procedure may appear to be the least likely candidate even to approximate such an enterprise. Granted the impossibility of producing a Mother Teresa through merely conducting any teaching activity, nevertheless this teaching procedure can provide a basic introduction to the practice of ministry within a controlled and relatively safe environment—the laboratory.[234]

This chapter has emphasized that the minister simply gives as the other has need to receive. The minister employs no pre-set pattern to be followed slavishly and produces no particular product but enters into an experience or relationship determined to try and meet whatever needs present themselves in as creative and helpful way as possible. The teaching procedure proposed here is an opportunity to go into an experience without foreknowledge of what will happen—since what will go on is primarily determined by the group's processes and dynamics—and react as humanely and as helpfully as possible under the circumstances that present themselves.

Laboratory training can promote growth in one or more of four areas: intrapersonal, interpersonal, group dynamics, and self-direction.[235] Intrapersonal experience focuses on self-knowledge, primarily gained from feedback given by others in the group. Interpersonal learning comes from the interaction and relationships with the other persons in the group. Group dynamics is learned by understanding the functioning of the group and watching the development of patterns and structures among persons. Self-direction is learned by the individuals and by the group as a whole as they determine that the structure and the purpose of the experience is up to the group members themselves and not to any kind of authority or leader.

The example of a teaching procedure for a one-day or weekend type of experience is simple. First a site is selected—the "laboratory"—which is a different and unfamiliar environment for the participants, "removed from their day-to-day work and familiar context."[236] Second, there is a person called a "trainer," who is neither an authority nor even a leader but simply a monitor who sets the process in motion, and who gives occasional feedback—but no direction.[237] Third, the group, ideally numbered from ten to twelve persons, is assembled in the laboratory area. Fourth, a time limit for the laboratory experience is determined, ranging anywhere from eight to forty-eight hours in length. Then the group members are given "the vague task of constructing a group which will meet the requirements of all its members for growth"[238] and left to its own devices under the watchful eye of the monitor. What happens next is unplanned, unknown, and evolutionary. It depends upon the group and its

---

234. The term "laboratory" here should not be confused with the antiseptic environment of the scientist, but refers to the "nitty-gritty" atmosphere of reality that is simulated or created with special attention given to supervision and intervention. It is a term best taken literally—a "place to do labor," so that the learners' labor can be observed and evaluated.

235. See Bruce Joyce and Marsha Weil, *Models of Teaching*, 3rd ed. (Englewood Cliffs, N.J.: Prentice-Hall, 1986), pp. 279-281.

236. Ibid., p. 279.

237. The monitor is not the religious educator. The religious educator experiencing the role of minister is a participating member of the group, *not* a detached observer.

238. Joyce and Weil, *Models of Teaching*, p. 278.

decisions as to what transpires—if anything.[239]

A more lifestyle-centered approach, and one that involves much more time and expense, is the undergoing of an internship program, where the "laboratory" is not some artificially isolated environment but is the actual field where service and ministry are conducted. In this approach, people are not removed from the place of work for a retreat type of experience but are placed in the *midst* of the work to experience the "real world" of ministry.[240] For teachers being prepared for a career in the public school, there is the "student-teacher" semester, where the prospective teacher goes into a school and teaches in a real-life setting under the supervision of an experienced teacher.[241] For ministers and social workers, part of the educational process is field work, or supervised ministry experience.[242] The principle there is basically the same as that involved in student teaching. The minister or social worker is placed in an environment where actual ministry or social service is rendered, and the work is evaluated by an experienced person on site.[243] Such activities are still "laboratory" exercises, because the activity is being conducted in a structured and at least somewhat protective (supervised) environment, but the experiences themselves are quite real and highly educational if sufficient time is provided for the learner to reflect on both successes and mistakes in conversation with the supervisor and other participants.[244]

---

239. A cognitive approach would reveal this four-phase pattern that often takes shape. First is the Dilemma, when group members grapple with what they are supposed to be doing and what the purpose of the experience is to be. This phase may very well be quite lengthy, and possibly even interminable if the group members do not take responsibility for themselves. Second is Invention, when members invent ideas, goals, solutions, and directions for the time together. Third is Feedback, when some kind of solidarity and agreement is worked out among the members as to what the purpose will be and how to achieve it. Fourth is Generalization, where group members reflect on what processes they used during the experience, and theorize about what learning took place as a result of the experience. See this described in more detail in ibid., pp. 282-283.

240. This is what James Michael Lee was advocating for seminarians when he suggested that they should not just gain knowledge in seminary, but understanding, which can be gained only from experience: "Knowledge, then, can be gained vicariously, while understanding can be gained only by a direct encounter, a total plunging into 'the other.'" James Michael Lee, "Overview of Educational Problems in Seminaries: I—Objectives and Administration," in *Seminary Education in a Time of Change*, ed. James Michael Lee and Louis J. Putz (Notre Dame, Ind.: Fides Publishers, 1965), p. 94.

241. "In their educational programs many of the professions provide an opportunity for the neophyte to try his hand—to see how it feels to do the work of the professional practitioner. In the preparation of a teacher, student teaching has long been that initial experience; when the college student directs the learning of a group of pupils under the immediate observation of an experienced teacher." L.O. Andrews, *Student Teaching* (New York: Center for Applied Research in Education, 1964), p. 1.

242. An especially helpful overview of the variety of approaches to such supervisory experiences is contained in Chapter Three, "Approaches to Field Instructions," in Marion Bogo and Elaine Vayda, *The Practice of Field Instruction in Social Work: Theory and Process* (Toronto: University of Toronto Press, 1987), pp. 20-28. Also see *Field Work in Social Work: Contemporary Issues and Trends*, ed. Dean Schneck, Bart Grossman, and Urania Glassman (Dubuque: Kendall/Hunt, 1991), especially Part Two, "Field Instruction Models," pp. 81-184.

243. For further development on the phases involved, see Chapter Two, "Guidelines for Understanding the Phases of Learning," in Martha L. Urbanowski and Margaret M. Dwyer, *Learning through Field Instruction: A Guide for Teachers and Students* (Milwaukee: Family Service America, 1988), pp. 17-27. The phases were listed as Stage I: Acute consciousness of self; Stage II: Sink-or-swim adaptation; Stage III: Understanding the situation with little power to control one's activity in it; State IV: Relative mastery; and Stage V: Teaching what one has mastered.

These exercises can prove to be highly relevant to the religious educator experiencing the role of the minister, possibly for the first time. Depending upon the type of ministry involved, the only predetermined goals or agendas may be caring for the needs of the people being served. These particular needs, and people, must first be understood and accepted before any "ministry" can be provided. Going into a group without a set of directions is often frightening, threatening, and frustrating. To experience some of this in the controlled learning environment of the laboratory is instructive for the minister and protective of the ones who will eventually be the recipients of ministry.

The obvious challenge to the religious educator is to be sensitive to the needs of the group, rather than to deliver some canned answers to unasked questions, or to provide help when none is needed or desired. The needs must arise out of the group experience, and the ways of meeting the needs must also be generated from within the group environment. The additional experiential aspect of the laboratory training is that the religious educator as minister is an integral part of the group. He or she is not "other than" the group members but is just one element of the much larger whole. No special reverence need be attached to the religious educator/minister, and no special status need be given. Whatever help or service is rendered must come in reaction to the needs of the group, or no ministry is provided. Something of this kind of experience is suggested for trial in the next section.

Experiential Simulation: Observant Participation

The theme of this chapter has been that the role of minister is constantly attuned to the needs of people. There is no chance for detached analysis or professional distance, because the minister has to be a part of the people, sharing in their grief, pain, and misery, as well as their joy, happiness, and exaltation. The preceding examples of Father Damien and Mother Teresa pointed out that when their day was over and they went to bed, they did not leave the people and go to a distant hotel or resort to sleep. They lived among the people to whom and with whom they ministered and were actually a part of the people with whom they ministered. That participatory goal is the aim of this particular experiential simulation.

For those who want a taste of what it is like to be at one with those who will be served in the role of the minister, the suggestion is to experience a variation on the process of participant observation.[245] Participant observation is a method

---

244. "Field instruction is an important educational experience through which students can be guided and supported in integrating theory with practice and in achieving a better balance among thinking, feeling, and doing. Through the process, self-awareness is stimulated and professional values are clarified and integrated. The evaluation process sums up achievements and identifies ongoing learning goals." Urbanowski and Dwyer, *Learning through Field Instruction*, p. 41.

245. For an introduction to participant observation techniques, see Dan Rose, *Living the Ethnographic Life*, Quantitative Research Methods, Vol. 23 (Newbury Park: California: Sage Publications, 1990); Chapter One, "Participant Observation, Field Research, and Objectivity in Sociology," in John M. Johnson, *Doing Field Research* (New York: Free Press, 1975), pp. 1-29; and Chapter Two, "Participant Observation: Rationale and Roles," in William Foote Whyte with Kathleen King Whyte, *Learning from the Field: A Guide from Experience* (Beverly Hills: Sage Publications, 1984), pp. 23-33.

of getting into the everyday world of a particular group of people to see and experience what life is like from their perspective.[246] Danny Jorgensen explained the methodology of participant observation as a focus "on the meanings of human existence as seen from the standpoint of insiders."[247] Elsewhere Jorgensen said participant observation "seeks to uncover, make accessible, and reveal the meanings (realities) people use to make sense out of their everyday lives."[248] In a way like no other, "through participation, the researcher is able to observe and experience the meanings and interactions of people from the role of an insider."[249] The suggested variation is to perceive one's self as an observant *participator*, however. The difference is truly becoming a part of the people being studied—observing them carefully and respectfully, [250] but from the inside by becoming one of them.[251]

Crucial here is recognizing that observant participation is still one step from actually fulfilling the role of minister but is instead simulating the role of minister. The observant participator undertakes the research to understand a particular group and then after a period of time leaves to return to his or her own world. The actual minister has no such option of leaving since he or she *is* at home.

One of the more sensational accounts of participant observation and of observant participation was the 1960 book by John Griffin, *Black Like Me*.[252] In that book, Griffin explored this question: "What is it like to experience discrimination based on skin color, something over which one has no control?"[253] Griffin, a white man, found a way to pigment his skin color to pass for a black man and recorded his experience as a black in the deep South of the United States. This example of participant observation was effective enough to be one of many

---

246. One respected and experienced researcher in this method gave this warning: "The participation of the researcher in the activities of the people being studied will be shaped in part by the degrees of difference in cultural background, race, or ethnic identification between the field worker and the study subjects. Where these differences are minimal, the researcher may be accepted almost as a native. Where the differences are large, participation opportunities will be more limited, but we can hope to be accepted as friendly and sympathetic observers." Whyte with Whyte, *Learning from the Field*, p. 28.

247. Danny L. Jorgensen, *Participant Observation: A Methodology for Human Studies* (Newbury Park, Calif.: Sage Publications, 1989), p. 14.

248. Ibid., p. 15.

249. Ibid., p. 21.

250. For a sense of the ethical issues involved, see Part III, "Down in the Trenches: Quandaries in Participant Research," in Robert D. Reece and Harvey A. Siegal, *Studying People: A Primer in the Ethics of Social Research* (Macon, Ga.: Mercer University Press, 1986), pp. 71-132.

251. This suggestion is a way of overcoming the criticism offered of participant observation as it is normally practiced: "To be a good and successful fieldworker, it is often felt and stated, one must learn to be detached and objective and to suppress human feelings and concerns that can only interfere with the task at hand. This view, which can be termed the tabula rasa approach to fieldwork, is rooted in good intentions. . . . But the tabula rasa approach to fieldwork distorts reality by implying that one can forget or temporarily blank out what one knows and has experienced, and that, during the period of encounter with subjects, one can operate *in vacuo*." Robert A. Georges and Michael O. Jones, *People Studying People: The Human Element in Fieldwork* (Berkeley: University of California Press, 1980), p. 153.

252. John Howard Griffin, *Black Like Me* (Boston: Houghton Mifflin, 1960).

253. Ibid., p. 1.

influences during the 1960s that shocked the nation into demanding that changes be made.

A simulation common to many sociology students is the "plunge," an event that requires courage and involves a degree of danger but is a means of identifying with the lot of the destitute. The beginner sociologist dresses in old and ragged clothing, takes nothing but fifty cents for an emergency phone call, and is "plunged" into the innercity culture for a period of twenty-four to forty-eight hours. The student as observant participant must find someplace to eat, sleep, and use the bathroom just as does anyone who lives on the street. No contact with anyone else from the "outside" world is permitted, so that the person can truly experience what it is like to be a streetperson.

Observant participation is one way, then, to get the basic sense of what it is like to live among the people in a particular environment and set of circumstances. It is temporary, and when sufficient research has been gathered the observer goes back home. Even more important, however, is to realize that for the functional minister, there is no "going home." The minister casts his or her lot with the people for whom ministry is being provided and becomes one with them.

Summary

The role of the minister is not one to be taken up lightly or easily. It is a role that demands one's very life. When Jesus asked his disciples: "Are *you* able to drink the cup that I am about to drink?" they answered without full knowledge of what their answer meant: "We are able." Jesus replied: "You will indeed drink my cup."[254] The religious educator as minister leaves behind the safety and security of books, of curriculum, of theory, and enters into the world of the people. The religious educator now teaches with his or her life—and at the cost of it. Who indeed is able to drink of this cup?

The message of this book is that the true religious educator integrates all of the ten roles into a single identity. This role of the minister, as demanding and as sacrificial as it is, is really not an option. It is an inseparable and integral part of the life and experience of the genuine religious educator—to whatever each one is able to fulfill the role. Figure 15 below summarizes the role of minister as it has been viewed from the perspective of this chapter. The following chapter in Part Three, however, attempts to put all of the roles together, stressing that no picking and choosing is possible. Indeed, the question must be considered again, this time even more deeply: Who is able?

---

254. Refer to Matthew 20:22-23, NRSV.

Figure 15: The Religious Educator as Minister	
Dimensions of the Role	Priest
	Celebrant
	Defender
	Servant
Aim	Altruism
Function	Sacrifice
Primary Virtues	Humility
	Compassion
Activity	Self-Giving
Shadow Role	Profiteer
Faith Tradition Resource	Apostolic Christianity
Historical Personage	Damien of Molokai
Contemporary Example	Teresa of Calcutta
Representative Teaching Procedure	Laboratory Training
Experiential Simulation	Observant Participation

Part Three

Holistic Perspectives
of the Religious Educator

Chapter Fourteen

Systemic Integration
of the Religious Educator

Part One of this book introduced some possible taxonomies of the religious educator, looking at the environmental context (Chapter One), some differentiative typologies (Chapter Two), and diagnostic categories (Chapter Three) of the religious educator. Part Two examined and explored the multiple roles of the religious educator, each taken separately and analyzed in similar fashion (Chapters Four through Thirteen). Part Three completes the effort to identify the religious educator. Here the goal is to gain some holistic perspectives of the religious educator, approached from two different directions: an effort to show some of the ways the multiple roles can be systemically integrated (Chapter Fourteen), and a fictional conversation that responds to some of the remaining overarching questions related to the identity of the religious educator (Chapter Fifteen).

Thus far in the book, then, the primary attention has been given to analyzing and diagnosing the diverse aspects of the religious educator, as illustrated by the disparate chapters of Part Two on the roles of the religious educator. Left to itself, such a process could produce the impression of a diffused and disorganized religious educator—an aggregative view of the religious educator rather than a systemic one.[1] The requirement now, and the goal of this chapter, is to understand that *all of the ten roles are vital and interdependent elements within the overall identity of the genuine religious educator. Every effective religious educator partakes of all ten roles.*

---

1. An aggregate is a collection of unrelated and unconnected parts, while a system is an integrated and unified whole.

The integration of the religious educator is portrayed graphically in Figure 16. The ten roles, with all of their various characteristics and categories, are combined to reveal the totality of the religious educator. No one role or characteristic is more important than any other, and any deletion or subtraction from the whole affects the entire entity. *The full identity of the religious educator is not found in any of the individual parts or in any of the different roles in and of themselves but is instead revealed through the integration and synthesis of the whole.* The aims make no sense without the functions, the values have no meaning separate from the activities, and so on down the list. In fact, even one of the roles without the others is itself incomplete and provides a distorted picture of the genuine religious educator. All of the elements contribute to the total harmony like notes to a musical chord: A chord is more than the sum of the individual notes, but the

Figure 16: The Integration of the Religious Educator					
The Religious Educator as:	Parent	Coach	Scientist	Critic	Storyteller
Dimensions of the Role	Provider	Supervisor	Discoverer	Analyst	Evangelist
	Protector	Trainer	Theoretician	Philosopher	Historian
	Model	Motivator	Experimenter	Debunker	Mythologist
	Theologian	Strategist	Cybemeticist	Infidel	Raconteur
Aim	Maturity	Performance	Problem Solving	Awareness	Interpretation
Function	Nurture	Instruction	Experimentation	Investigation	Communication
Primary Virtues	Morality	Competence	Curiosity	Skepticism	Historicity
	Faith	Discipline	Analysis	Evaluation	Contextuality
Activity	Trusting	Playing/ Working	Exploring	Reflecting	Participating
Shadow Role	Child Abuser	Procrastinator	Scientist-King	Cynic	Dogmatist
Faith Tradition Resource	Judaism	Islam	The Enlightenment	Classical Buddhism	Greek Mythology
Historical Personage	Horace Bushnell	Ignatius Loyola	Galileo	Socrates	Homer
Contemporary Example	C. Ellis Nelson	James Michael Lee	James Fowler	Gabriel Moran	Robert Béla Wilhelm
Representative Teaching Procedure	Observational Learning	The Project	Inquiry Training	Maieutic Teaching	Storytelling
Experiential Simulation	Parent Training	Coaching Styles	Scientific Experimentation	Socratic Dialogue	Experiencing Storytelling

Figure 16: The Integration of the Religious Educator (con't)					
The Religious Educator as:	Artist	Visionary	Revolutionary	Therapist	Minister
Dimensions of the Role	Creator	Witness	Innovator	Healer	Priest
	Designer	Prophet	Planner	Catalyst	Celebrant
	Evocateur	Casuist	Agitator	Facilitator	Defender
	Magician	Charismatic	Change Agent	Fellow-Traveler	Servant
Aim	Revelation/ Discovery	Animation	Transformation	Wholeness	Altruism
Function	Creativity	Insight	Reconstruction	Integration	Sacrifice
Primary Virtues	Expression	Inspiration	Equality	Affectivity	Humility
	Disclosure	Hope	Autonomy	Actualization	Compassion
Activity	Creating	Imagining	Individuating	Being Present	Self-Giving
Shadow Role	Pornographer	Daydreamer	Ideologue	Manipulator	Profiteer
Faith Tradition Resource	Shamanism	Mysticism	Marxism	Taoism	Apostolic Christianity
Historical Personage	Richard Wagner	Martin Luther King Jr.	Huldrych Zwingli	Carl Jung	Damien of Molokai
Contemporary Example	Maria Harris	John H. Westerhoff III	Paulo Freire	Morton Kelsey	Teresa of Calcutta
Representative Teaching Procedure	Teaching Drawing	Brainstorming	Consciousness Raising	Nondirective Teaching	Laboratory Training
Experiential Simulation	Experiencing Art	Expanding Awareness	Designing the Future	Inner Journey	Observant Participation

individual notes determine the quality of the chord—and it all comes together to make wonderful, magical music.

When seen in its entirety, the identity of the religious educator appears to be so massive and complex that it is difficult to comprehend. The sight of the whole bears out the fact that identifying the religious educator is indeed a complex and difficult task and that becoming a religious educator demands committing to a lifetime of dedication. Beyond that, the full identity of the religious educator is more than any one individual, profession, or faith tradition can encompass. Just as no one role can describe the whole of the religious educator, so no one individual is the "complete" religious educator. All religious educators work together to bring the potential into wholeness—which illustrates the reason for using the designation *religious* educator.

Just as the ten roles themselves are heuristic devices, so the attempts in this chapter to provide integrative images of them are heuristic.[2] Any number of ways could be pursued in integrating the roles of the religious educator, and all that will be undertaken in this chapter is to provide some examples of the process. Three perspectives on the integration of the religious educator are offered below: *process* integration, which focuses on how the roles coalesce in terms of their overall enterprise; *dynamic* integration, which examines the two primary forces that energize the performance of the roles; and *personal* integration, which demonstrates how an individual religious educator can forge his or her own unique identity by emphasizing various combinations of the roles while still making the effort to be holistic.

Process Integration

One way to view the integration of the religious educator is to focus on the overall purpose of each of the roles, and to see that they divide into five analogous enterprises. These five pairs provide yet another view of the responsibilities of the religious educator: training, evaluating, telling, leading, and serving. The five pairs are not mutually exclusive—elements of each can be found throughout the other pairs. This but illustrates again the holistic and interdependent nature of the roles. The pairs of images are also dynamic—totally engaged with the activities of the learners, which is characteristic of all that the religious educator does.

Training Roles

The first two roles of the religious educator discussed in this book, the parent and the coach, can be generalized as training roles. Both roles spend their energies equipping and preparing the learner for accepting the responsibilities of maturity and individuality, while giving attention to the need for socialization as well. The parent works to make the learner a trusting person—one who trusts himself or herself, as well as one who experiences the community as supportive and trustworthy rather than as frightening or threatening. The parent works toward the time when the learner no longer needs to be dependent, but who in turn goes on to parent those of the next generation. The coach simulates real-life experiences so that the learner is prepared to perform as needed when the time is right. The coach instills discipline, so that when the coach is not present the same dedication to the task is still at work. These training roles keep clearly in mind that the learner is "theirs" only for a short period of time, and that the training provided must suffice in place of their continued presence. The need for further training goes on throughout life, so that what the parent and coach have taught should provide an adequate basis for this continual educational process—whether the particular parent or coach is actually present or not.

---

2. By "heuristic" I mean that the images and their synthesis should provoke and stimulate new and creative ways to perceive and perform the role of the religious educator. Heuristics is not the study of what *is* so much as the exploration of possibilities about what *could* and *should* be.

Evaluating Roles

Evaluation is the key process in performing the next pair of roles—the scientist and the critic. These two roles focus on the ability to see clearly and to make the best decisions possible based on the evidence available. The scientist goes about the task of evaluation deliberately and carefully by way of scientific experimentation. Attention to such painstaking work as developing hypotheses, testing theories, and collecting data allows the scientist to provide more reliable information than is possible from guessing, hoping, or assuming. The evidence assembled forms the basis for the decisions of the scientist, and the evaluations he or she makes must be supported by the data. The critic also evaluates and uses sound criteria for judgments but is not confined to the strict boundaries of scientifically collected data. The critic always looks for what was not accomplished, for what else could have been done, or for why something was attempted. The critic does not normally create but rather steps back and assesses what has already happened. These evaluative roles help signal what needs to be changed, and what needs to be constructed, through their provision of honest and constructive feedback.

Telling Roles

The next pair of roles takes responsibility for performing one of the most predictable activities of the religious educator—telling.[3] These roles are the storyteller and the artist. The storyteller passes on information by way of a narrative, which involves two different kinds of effort. One is telling the story in a relevant, interesting, and memorable fashion. The other is facilitating the interpretation of the meaning of the story, and then applying that meaning to present circumstances. The storyteller does not so much communicate facts that are to be memorized word for word as ideas and metaphors that are to be stretched and pulled to meet the needs of the moment. The artist is also a "teller" but uses different types of media than the spoken narrative: paint and canvas, stone and chisel, notes and instruments. The artist creates in order to reveal or to discover the deeper realities. The artist is less dependent on the more logical knowing processes, and draws upon the intuitive and the emotive processes of communication. The artist "tells" truth that words alone cannot express. These telling roles of the storyteller and the artist convey truthful information which lives in the metaphors and the analogies rather than lying encased in mummified form.

Leading Roles

Both the visionary and the revolutionary are concerned with leading forward into the desired future, but one leads by providing and articulating a vision that attracts the people toward it, while the other leads by careful planning and creating means for permanent and extensive change. The visionary allows the vision to do the pulling and the drawing, letting sight of the potentiality and the

---

3. "Telling" should not be understood in some kind of pedantic or authoritarian light. The focus is on communication—assimilation and accommodation—rather than on rote memorization or passive acceptance. Neither should "telling" be understood as one-way impartation, but as true interactive communication. A good synonym here could be disseminating—spreading the good news freely and widely.

promise provide the motivation and the power. The vision may come into reality today, tomorrow, or next year—but the visionary is absolutely certain that it will eventually come to fruition. The revolutionary too has hope of a better day but is unwilling just to wait for it to happen. The revolutionary works for transformation by reconstructing the very structures of the system, thereby creating the means of entering the promised land—today. The visionary and the revolutionary are never satisfied with what is, continually concerned if not obsessed with what could be. Their means of achieving the future, however, are very different. What they hold in common is their ability to lead—to move people ahead of where they are at present.

Service Roles

The final pair of roles is composed of the therapist and the minister, and the binding element between them is their service to others. The closer one looks for either of these, the more they recede into the face of the crowd, because they are known by what they give and do for others. The therapist is the healer, opening people's eyes to their wounds while nursing them into wholeness and health. The therapist is present with individuals while they grow into their fuller, truer selves, encouraging, confronting, and comforting them whenever the path gets rough. The service that the therapist provides is often that of simply being present, acting as a fellow traveler who is walking along similar paths as others are. The minister simply does whatever is necessary to help others, with no regard for personal consequences. The minister gives himself or herself away—freely, spontaneously, with no questions asked, and with no strings attached. The minister has counted the cost and found fellow humans to be worth it—whatever the price. The therapist and the minister come not to be served, but to serve.

Summary

One of the ways to identify the religious educator is through these five processes: training, evaluating, telling, leading, and serving. Each process is important, and each one must be combined with the others to form the whole. At any one time, a religious educator may be more heavily involved in one particular process, but over time all of the processes must be expressed. An individual religious educator may have one of the areas as a particular strength, but the complete religious educator struggles to incorporate all of the facets into his or her identity. The composite of the five types of process integration is displayed in Figure 17 below. Yet another way of grasping this larger identity of the religious educator is discussed in the following section.

Dynamic Integration

In a very real sense, all integration is by definition dynamic, so the heading of this section sounds tautological. Actually the focus here is on the *direction* the dynamism takes—toward the center or away from it. The first is descriptive of centripetal force, which is movement toward unification and integration. The second is centrifugal force, which is movement toward decen-

Figure 17: Process Integration of the Religious Educator	
Training Roles	Parent
	Coach
Evaluating Roles	Scientist
	Critic
Telling Roles	Storyteller
	Artist
Leading Roles	Visionary
	Revolutionary
Service Roles	Therapist
	Minister

tralization and separateness. The roles of the religious educator involve both of these dynamic forces, allowing the religious educator to value simultaneously the forces of holism and differentiation. Another way to integrate the roles of the religious educator is to see how these dynamic forces energize the various roles.

Centripetal Roles

Five roles of the religious educator contribute to centripetal dynamism—the movement toward the center and toward unification and holism. The parent role helps to bind together the generations, linking old and young, tradition and innovation. The coach builds a team competence and spirit, forging an identifiable unit out of previously isolated and independent players. The critic cuts through the extraneous involvements and reveals the heart of the matter with a singleness of mind that demands coherence. The storyteller uses the stories themselves to bind people together and to establish identity. The therapist works to bring the individual and the community into wholeness, healing the rifts and integrating the entities. The religious educator in all of these roles promotes the necessary movement toward holism.

Centrifugal Roles

Five roles of the religious educator contribute to centrifugal dynamism—

the movement away from the center and toward individuality and differentiation. The role of the scientist dispenses with the dependence on tradition and reaches out for new explanations and different understandings supported by empirical evidence. The artist creates new perceptions of truth through personal expression and disclosure, opening up areas of exploration undetected in the past. The visionary sees the future and beckons the people toward it, never allowing them to become complacent and self-satisfied. The revolutionary facilitates the arrival of positive change and brings in the future with all its exciting (or frightening?) new structures and expectations. The minister is one who gives himself or herself away, never retreating to the comforts of the past but welcoming the sacrifices which change the present. The religious educator in these five roles promotes the necessary movement toward differentiation.

Summary

The religious educator is responsible for attending to both centripetal and centrifugal forces. Too much of the centripetal brings sameness and uniformity. Too much of the centrifugal allows diffusion and chaos. The task is to integrate both into harmonic homeostasis, accomplished by mastering and performing appropriately the ten roles of the genuine religious educator. The two types of dynamic integration are pictured in Figure 18 below.

Figure 18: Dynamic Integration of the Religious Educator

Centripetal Roles 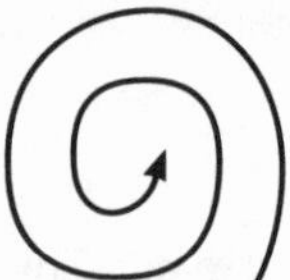	Parent
	Coach
	Critic
	Storyteller
	Therapist
Centrifugal Roles 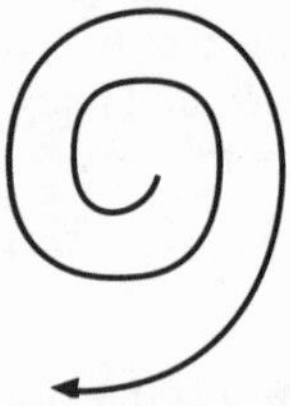	Scientist
	Artist
	Visionary
	Revolutionary
	Minister

Personal Integration

Just because there are ten roles which mark out the boundaries of the religious educator does not imply that all religious educators are the same—far from it. Each religious educator is unique, with individual strengths and weaknesses, insights and abilities, interests and concerns. There is as much variety in the ways that different religious educators fulfill the roles as there is in religious education itself. This section illustrates how personal—unique and individual—integration is accomplished within the performance of the ten roles.

In Part Two of this book, ten different religious educators were examined under the headings of "contemporary examples." Only that part of their writings which gave evidence of the particular role was discussed. While helpful in illustrating the applicability of the various roles to religious educators, unfortunately such a methodology used exclusively tends to deemphasize the integration of the roles. It may imply that each individual religious educator only employs one primary role while ignoring the other vital ones. In reality, while each religious educator does indeed have individual tendencies toward the performance of a dominant role or roles, he or she must also be prepared to employ the other roles to whatever extent is necessary and appropriate.

Another way to deal with the roles in a manner that emphasizes the integration of the roles is to take one individual religious educator and trace how he or she creates a unique identity by weaving several of the roles together in a particular fashion. It would have been possible, for example, to have used only one religious educator as the contemporary example for the entire book and to have shown how he or she fulfilled each of the ten roles in some fashion or another through the examination of his or her writings. Because of the diversity and comprehensiveness of the images, however, it is highly improbable that any one individual could be used to demonstrate all of the ten roles adequately. The result of such a process would likely have been a stretching of the person's work beyond any semblance of what it actually was intended to mean.

Instead of forcing one ideal example upon the reader and showing how he or she is the complete religious educator—if one could indeed be found—the suggestion is for each reader to do his or her own evaluative search. Take the writings of any one of the contemporary examples of religious educators in the book, or any other religious educator that has produced an adequate corpus of writing to support such a project, and see what evidence of the various images can be detected. In all probability, several particular emphases will be found, as will some areas of virtual absence.

Another suggestion for personalizing the integration process is for each reader to evaluate himself or herself against the ideal categories represented in the chart (Figure 16). Where are your areas of natural strength or tendencies? Where are your weaknesses? Where are your skills or past experiences totally absent in the range of foundational images? It may be helpful to get the feedback of colleagues and fellow-learners about the matter of strengths and weaknesses. What may be obvious to you may not be borne out in discussion with others, and others may realize aspects of your abilities that for you are currently unrecognized.

A final suggestion is for various groups of religious educators that work together on the tasks of religious education to evaluate their collective strengths and weaknesses. A religious education department in an educational institution, the teaching personnel of a church or synagogue, or the collection of religious educators in a community across denominational or institutional boundaries may give the broader view of the resources available. If it is virtually impossible for one individual to become the complete religious educator, then perhaps the larger corporate body of religious educators can join forces and provide more comprehensive fulfillment of the foundational images. It may still be that a community is lacking in some of the multiple roles because of the homogeneity of the group, and such an analysis would reveal the need for diversity and signal the need for the inclusion of others who could bring additional images of the religious educator into view.

Summary

The subject of this chapter has been to discuss the systemic integration of the religious educator. First a view of all the ten roles and all of the categories connected to the roles was provided. Then brief discussions on various types of integration were undertaken: process integration, dynamic integration, and personal integration. These are but illustrations of the myriad ways that the integration of the religious educator is accomplished.

The next, and final, chapter is another attempt at integration. The intent there is to revisit the wider issues that have undergirded this book, and to engage in a dialogue about them. The "concluding conversation" is one last effort to respond to questions raised by the efforts in this book to identify the religious educator.

Chapter Fifteen

A Concluding Personal Conversation

Question: What is the purpose of this chapter? Haven't you said everything there is to say yet?

Response: This final brief chapter is an attempt to clarify some issues and to answer some questions in a different format than the one used throughout the rest of the book. The other chapters have necessarily been in narrative form, with little opportunity to demonstrate how interactive actual religious education must be. In this chapter, the process takes the form of questions and responses.

Question: Where did these questions come from?

Response: The questions posed are those still in my mind, or ones I think should be asked by readers. They take two different directions. One direction points toward a need for further clarification on a few of the specifics. The other direction is not about lack of clarity but simply disagreement. It is possible to understand the message of the book but to differ with it. Some of the questions may belie a certain tentativeness about where all this leads.

Question: Will this chapter solve all the problems and answer all the questions left over from the discussion in the book?

Response: No more so than that the book itself has solved all the problems and answered all the questions related to the identity of the religious educator. The questions here are all valid, but the responses given may not be so universally acceptable. Since questions tend to pinpoint problem areas rather than areas of strength, the responses may indicate where work still needs to be done. There is no claim that these questions are the only ones left, or that the responses to them are full and final. All of the problems are not solved, and solid questions remain. The questions must continue—as well as the search for answers.

Question: One of the most surprising things about this book is the virtual lack of discussion on systems theory. In your previous book,[1] that was all you talked about. Have you given up on systems theory?

Response: Surely you are joking. No, I have not abandoned systems theory in the least. The earlier book, *Systemic Religious Education*, was indeed devoted to showing how systems theory could help redefine and recreate religious education. This book takes that theory and applies it to the religious educator, which is why all the ten roles are important and need to be integrated into a systemic whole. It is not necessary to understand all about systems theory to read this book, or even to have read the previous one, but this book could be seen as an illustration of the systemic theory presented in the earlier work.

Question: You mentioned the ten roles, which raises issues that still puzzle me. Are the ten roles in Part Two the only images of the religious educator, and why the number ten? Are they absolutes, or are there other ways to view the religious educator?

Response: The images explored in Part Two are certainly not absolutes. They provide an alternative way of viewing the religious educator, and untold numbers of other ways are yet possible. There is nothing special about the number ten—the number could have been eight or fifty. The way I perceive the comprehensive religious educator was fulfilled by using these ten roles. The ten roles presented are only metaphors that sketch the basic profile of the religious educator and should not be taken in programatic or literalistic terms. This kind of translation into concrete activity is what each individual religious educator must do for himself or herself, which is to say that this book was not meant to be a training manual for the religious educator. It only outlines the broad contours and allows each person to fill in the details as appropriate. No book could or should attempt to do the kind of personalized work which is appropriate only for the individual religious educator.

Question: Of the ten roles you proposed, is any one more important than the others? Are the roles developmental, or hierarchical in arrangement?

Response: In a word, no. All of the images are important, and the issue is to bring all of them into some kind of synthesis. All of the roles can be developed, but they are not developmental in the sense that they build one upon the other in any certain order or in any sort of hierarchy. They all have their own identities, which allows for the separate discussions, but they cannot be seen as independent of one another. All are parts of the whole and are hence interdependent with one another.

---

1. Timothy Arthur Lines, *Systemic Religious Education* (Birmingham, Ala.: Religious Education Press, 1987).

Question: So, the boundaries between the roles are not distinct? Isn't this a cover for imprecision?

Response: A valid concern, and arguable. To recall some systems language, the boundaries of open systems are permeable. This means there is a flow or movement through the boundaries, which makes for coherence and interdependence. At the same time, permeability necessarily blurs the lines of demarcation (more accurately, the interface) between roles. The discussion of Chapter Fourteen was an attempt to elucidate the need for integration of the roles, balancing the discussion of Part Two which tended to emphasize the individuality of the roles. The true identity of the religious educator, then, is found in the dynamism of the whole, rather than in the sum of parts.

Question: This "permeability" seems to cause problems, especially in the category of contemporary example of religious educators. Did the religious educators cited for each role perform in that one role exclusively?

Response: Permeability is not a problem if the concept of the whole is kept in mind. No religious educator functions in any one of the roles exclusively. The religious educators cited as contemporary examples gave evidence of fulfilling the particular role in specific portions of their work, but this is not to say that evidence of other roles could not be found in their work. As I said repeatedly, I was not trying to encapsulate every single thing any one religious educator wrote, but to give a representative consideration of the main thrusts of the writings. The focus was instead on exploring the roles, and various religious educators were used to illustrate those roles by providing selections from their writings. Participation in one role does not prohibit a religious educator from employing other roles; otherwise, one of the main points of the book—that the genuine and complete religious educator must spend a lifetime mastering all ten roles— would be lost. Further, just because a particular religious educator was chosen to illustrate a certain role does not imply that he or she fulfilled it perfectly or completely, just as the way that he or she went about performing the role is *the* way to do it. The persons cited should be understood as examples, but nothing more.

Question: Gloria Durka years ago wrote: "Religious education can no longer be perceived as that which transpires between a student and a teacher."[2] Aren't you disagreeing with her? Are you that far behind the times to see religious education as such a simple transaction?

Response: I do not disagree in the least with Durka's comment, and this book on the religious educator should not be perceived as a manual for classroom teaching alone. Such a notion of the religious educator completely misses what this book is trying to promote. The term "religious educator" has most often been used here to refer to an individual, and there is no reason to denigrate such a usage. The concept of the religious educator, though, cannot be removed from

---

2. Gloria Durka, "Preparing for the Profession," in *Parish Religious Education*, ed. Maria Harris (New York: Paulist, 1978), p.180.

the community, the society, and the environment.[3] Families, churches and synagogues, denominations—all of these are "religious educators" as well and are exceedingly powerful. There is no sense in which the roles used in this book must be taken only individualistically. The roles are just as applicable corporately.[4]

Question: Thinking of the roles corporately leads back to the faith traditions. I get the impression you do not want people to be a part of any one faith tradition, but to be eclectic—picking and choosing from all of them and forming some kind of new quasi-religion. Is that true?

Response: To be eclectic—picking and choosing parts at random—is nonsystemic, so I am certainly not proposing that. I am suggesting that members of faith traditions need to have the permeable boundaries of an open system. A member of a faith tradition finds his or her identity and community in that specific faith tradition, so such a relationship is exceedingly important.[5] The danger appears when any one group believes it has all the answers, all the truth, and anyone not a part of that group is either stupid or satanic. An open system interacts with other open systems, becoming stronger, healthier, but different, as a result of the process.

Question: So one faith tradition is the same as the next—it really doesn't matter which one you choose as long as you are somehow "religious"?

Response: No, one religion or faith tradition is not just as "good" as another. That is why people choose to be adherents of various faith traditions. Please remember Figure 4 in Chapter One. The faith traditions discussed in this book may be examples of those that potentially can move toward health and integration, but there are just as many, if not more, avenues toward disease and disintegration. In truth, any one of those mentioned are also just as potentially dangerous as they are potentially healthy. The prime reason for spending time on virtues in this book was to develop a way to appraise the faith traditions and to show what a vital responsibility religious educators have in facilitating this evaluative activity. Religious educators are neither salespersons nor cheerleaders for their particular faith tradition; instead, they are constant monitors of it, determining its progress toward health and integration and exploring ways to improve it.

---

3. Most careful writers in religious education will always include the environment as an important variable. For example, James Michael Lee discussed the four molar variables related to teaching that must always be given consideration as the teacher, the learner, the environment, and the subject matter content. See James Michael Lee, *The Flow Of Religious Instruction: A Social Science Approach* (Birmingham: Ala.: Religious Education Press, 1973), p.234. For a fuller development, see the entirety of Chapter Nine, "The Structure of Teaching," ibid., pp.230-268. In the categories of analysis developed by Harold William Burgess, the environment was one of six key variables. See Harold William Burgess, *An Invitation to Religious Education* (Birmingham, Ala.: Religious Education Press, 1975), p.11.

4. Incidentally, later in the same paragraph quoted above, Durka wrote: "What is needed is a new type of religious education that incorporates a wide variety of ideas and covers a broad scope of concerns." I could not agree more, and that is a good description of the religious education this present book advocates. See ibid., p.181.

5. For a helpful discussion here, see C.J. Arthur, *In the Hall of Mirrors: Some Problems of Commitment in a Religiously Plural World* (London: A.R. Mowbray, 1986).

Question: Why all the attention on the *religious* educator? Are you opposed to people being faith tradition educators?

Response: The issue is understanding our multiple identities. Religion is much broader than what any one faith tradition can contain or communicate, but the specific faith traditions are participants of this larger sphere of religion (refer to Figure 2 in Chapter One). An analogy is the connection between being a citizen of the United States and being a citizen of the world. Someone who thinks only about the interests of the United States ("America") and of its citizens ("Americans") is dangerous not only to the country but to the world at large.[6] Jingoism ("my country, right or wrong") leads directly to prejudice, oppression, aggression, and imperialism—all of which is easily found in any cursory study of "American" history. Being a citizen of the United States does not preclude one from being a part of the human race! In fact, such grounding radically affects how one lives out being a citizen of the United States.

The relationship between religious education and faith tradition education is similar. The same dangers of thinking "my tradition, right or wrong" can (and have) led to the specter of prejudice, oppression, aggression, and imperialism fueled and supported by an isolated faith tradition. Religious education helps to ground faith tradition education in the deeper family of humanity and allows us to see ourselves as integral parts of the larger global community. The religious educator helps to break down the egocentrism that comes by assuming only your viewpoint—and faith tradition—is the valid one.

Question: Are you saying that we become better members of our own faith tradition as we connect more with others?

Response: Yes. The more we learn about others, the more we learn about ourselves. The first task of the religious educator is to develop a healthy sense of identity, and this is never accomplished in isolation. The true religious educator is always on the quest of holistic nexus—following wherever it may lead, and creating whatever it demands. This means building bridges to reach others rather than erecting walls to keep them away.

Question: That sounds difficult enough, but you are asking us to reach out farther than just to other faith traditions, correct?

Response: Correct. The ten roles include a study of various faith traditions, but the larger task is to draw from even wider resources of humanity—parenting, coaching, science, and so on. If religious education is truly to participate in creating holistic nexus, then religious educators must be constantly working at the task of integration and synthesis. Religious education must break out of its isolation, and interact with the larger spheres of the global community. Staying inside the walls of the church buildings or institutions is not going to bring about holistic nexus. In fact, that will only ensure that such integration does not

---

6. For a discussion on the misuse of the term "America" and the ideology it raises, see Gabriel Moran, *Religious Education as a Second Language* (Birmingham, Ala.: Religious Education Press, 1989), pp.15-18.

happen. Religious education must find ways to connect directly with the larger spheres of reality.

Question: Overwhelming! Isn't this vision of the religious educator too idealistic to be of any real consequence?

Response: The concept may be overwhelming and idealistic, but the pursuit of such a goal surely will produce some "real consequences." If religious education is important, then it can only demand our best—which means becoming more than what we are now. This vision of the religious educator may be beyond what any one religious educator can fulfill, but is that any reason to reduce the vision? The vision serves as a challenge, a goal to be reached for, a pull into the future. If such an effort to improve and expand our abilities has no true consequences, then we are all in trouble.

Question: So you are at heart Utopian?

Response: If not Utopian, at least a romantic. If I thought we could not create better religious education than what has already been accomplished, then I would quit. Does acknowledging that we religious educators are not perfect, and that we have so much more to do, make me Utopian? If so, then I plead guilty with no apologies.

Question: In the final analysis, how do you regard this book?

Response: I suspect that it may be in some ways an autobiography. I have probably told as much about myself as I have about religious education, since every book, every lecture, every act can be understood as self-revelation to at least some degree. From a more objective position, I regard this book as a helpful and scholarly effort to provide a perspective on the professional identity of the religious educator through the means of ten foundational images. The book is an attempt to expand the horizons of the religious educator, demonstrating that the religious educator's tasks are not simple or inconsequential but complex, multifaceted, and highly important. In the final analysis, the book is but the most modest of introductions to the images of the religious educator, since certainly all of the ten images and most of the subdivisions within each of the images are deserving of a book of their own for fuller development. The hope is that each reader will take the discussions in the chapters only as places to start reading, thereby researching and experiencing the broader dimensions of what the profession has to offer. May the images and their brief descriptions provide the impetus toward a genuine search for, attempt at, and creation of holistic nexus for each religious educator.

Index of Names

Abbott, Lawrence F., 207
Abélard, Peter, 201-203, 204
Abelson, Raziel, 323
Abraham, 282, 327
Abram, 327
Ackoff, Russell L., 108, 153, 158, 328, 358, 361-362, 363, 400
Adam, 243-245, 249
Adams, Jay E., 433, 464
Adamson, William R., 82, 83, 84, 85
Adler, Alfred, 404
Adler, Gerhard, 376, 379, 439
Adorno, T.W., 250
Ahab, 362
Aicken, Frederick, 143
Aklya, Einosuke, 207
A'La Maududi, S. Abdul, 120, 121, 122
Albin, Rochele Semmel, 425, 430
Aldrick, Virgil C., 277
Aleshire, Daniel O., 86, 172, 462-463
Alinsky, Saul, 365
Almy, Millie, 198
Alpert, Richard, 61, 431
Ambrose, 463
Amirthan, Sam, 246
Ananias, 192
Andersen, Hans Christian, 187
Anderson, George W., 282
Anderson, James D., 171
Anderson, Mary Tulley, 305
Andrews, L.O., 494
Andrews, Lynn, V., 294-295
Angyal, Andras, 419
Ansoff, H. Igor, 144
Apostolos-Cappadona, Diane, 275

Applegate, Kenneth W., 206
Aquinas, Thomas, 130, 202, 473
Aristophanes, 210
Aristotle, 162, 210, 395
Arkin, Robert M., 105
Arnold, Magda B., 424
Aron, Betty, 250
Aron, Raymond, 328
Arthur, C.J., 514
Ashby, W. Ross, 151
Astley, Jeff, 133
Atkinson, G.B.J., 156, 182
Ausubel, David P., 264

Babbie, Earl, 173
Bach, George, 411
Baensch, Otto, 270
Bailey, Kenneth, D., 159
Bailie, John, 282-283
Bailin, Sharon, 285
Bainton, Roland, 192
Baker, A.E., 222, 223
Baldwin, Alfred L., 61
Bamberger, Bernard J., 79
Bandura, Albert, 60-61, 92-94
Barber, Theodore X., 335
Barberini, Maffeo, 167
Barbier, Jean, 484
Barbour, Ian G., 156, 167, 169
Bardige, Betty, 72
Bar-Levav, Reuven, 430
Barna, Luba, 383
Barnett, H.G., 358, 360
Barraclough, Geoffrey, 233
Barrett, Eric C., 141

517

Index of Subjects